SAN FRANCISCO PUBLIC LIBRARY

3 1223 90077 3517

Y0-BWC-237

THE ROYAL HOUSE OF STUART

Isaac Oliver   *Photo Tom Scott*

King James VI & I

By kind permission of the Buchanan Society and
the Scottish National Portrait Gallery

The
ROYAL HOUSE
of
STUART

The Descendants of King James VI of Scotland
James I of England

VOLUME ONE

—

A.C. ADDINGTON

LONDON: CHARLES SKILTON LTD

© A. C. ADDINGTON, 1969

PRINTED IN GREAT BRITAIN
BY COMPTON PRINTING LTD, AYLESBURY
AND PUBLISHED BY CHARLES SKILTON LIMITED
50 ALEXANDRA ROAD, LONDON S.W.19

REF
f929.7
St91A
v.1

79 79

S. F. PUBLIC LIBRARY

90077-3517

CONTENTS
Volume One

ILLUSTRATIONS
Volume One

INTRODUCTION

IN THE NIGHT of the 23rd/24th March, 1603, there lay dying at Richmond an old lady of 69, the last of her line, whose zest for life had passed. "She grew worse because she would be so" said her cousin, Sir Robert Carey, and as her life ebbed away word was sent to Scotland summoning her cousin the King to London. At three o'clock in the morning Elizabeth I, the last Tudor Queen of England, died, and England and Scotland were united. The news reached Holyrood House on Saturday night the 26th March: James VI, King of Scotland since he was one year old, was now King of England.

This work is an attempt to trace out his descendants.

The Stuarts were a gifted family and are believed to have originated in Normandy. Alan, son of Flaald, a Norman knight, obtained a grant of lands in Shropshire and it was his son Walter who went to Scotland, where he quickly made his mark. Appointed Steward of Scotland, the office became vested in the family and in 1315 his namesake, Walter 6th High Steward of Scotland married Marjorie, daughter of King Robert the Bruce, and when in 1371 King Robert the Bruce's son David II died, it was his nephew Robert the Steward who succeeded him as King of Scotland.

Two hundred and thirty-two years later James VI became King of England, but like the history of Scotland the story of the Stuarts is a long and turbulent one. King James I was murdered at Perth, by his uncle the Earl of Atholl; James II was killed by a piece of exploding cannon at Roxburgh Castle; James III was assassinated at Sauchieburn, whilst his son James IV fell at Flodden Field fighting the English; James V died of a broken heart following the defeat of his troops at Solway Moss, and his daughter Mary, the ill-fated Queen of Scots, was beheaded at Fotheringay Castle after nineteen years in captivity.

It is not the purpose of this work, however, to tell their story. When Henry Benedict, Cardinal York, died at Frascati in 1807 the male line of the Royal House of Stuart came to an end; but there are still many descendants of this famous House to be found all over the world, and this work is an attempt to trace out all the descendants of King James VI & I in both the male and female lines. It lists more than 15,000 descendants, and includes more than 25,000 names spanning fifteen generations and four centuries. To find a legitimate descent from an earlier English King it is necessary to go back to King Henry VII, 1455–1509: to find a legitimate descent from a Scottish King it is necessary to go back even further to James II, 1430–1460.

At the turn of the last century the famous Jacobite genealogist the Marquis of Ruvigny and Raineval completed a similar work entitled *The Blood Royal of Britain*, and first of all I must acknowledge the debt I owe to this work. Inevitably however, because it was a first work, many important lines were omitted. In the present work it is believed that all of the omissions have been repaired and that this work is as complete and exhaustive as possible.

Like Ruvigny however, I have been obliged to confine myself to the legitimate descendants only, to keep the work within bounds. All of the descendants of King Charles II and his brother James II by Arabella Churchill have therefore had to be omitted, although I hope to treat them in a later work; but one or two small exceptions have been made to this rule where children have been legitimized by the subsequent marriage of their parents. Thus for instance Sophie Gräfin v. Stepperg is included as are the descendants of the Elector Wilhelm II of Hesse-Kassel and Emilie Ortlöpp Gräfin v. Reichenbach-Lessonitz.

Not only are the exact dates and places of birth, marriage and death given for each descendant, but also their full Christian names and each descendant is shown in heavy type. People not descended from King James are shown in lighter type, and an additional index appears at the end of Volume II to facilitate the cross-referencing of the many inter-marriages between descendants. Also shown is the name of the father of each lady who married a descendant. Unfortunately for reasons of space it has not been possible to include the names of their mothers as well, or to give details of the previous or subsequent marriages of those people marrying a descendant. Likewise dates of divorces are not given (although they are indicated) or naval or military ranks, orders of knighthood or subsidiary titles.

The plan has been to divide the work up as conveniently as possible into Chapters. Volume I deals with the British Royal Family, and the descendants of King Charles I, the Elector Karl Ludwig of Palatine, and Prince Edward of Palatine with the exception of the descendants of his daughters Princess Anne, wife of Henri Jules Prince de Condé, and Princess Benedikta, wife of Johann Friedrich Duke of Brunswick-Lüneburg. They are included in Volume II with the descendants of the Electress Sophia. The information in the body of the work is complete up to the end of 1966, the 400th anniversary of the birth of King James, and subsequent changes will be found in the Addenda to Volume II.

Because of the size of the work it has also been necessary to list each descendant only once under his or her first descent in the male line, and the need for this will be clear when it is remembered that for example the Prince of Wales is descended from King James 22 times, and King Constantine II of Greece 32 times. Indeed Prince François d'Orleans, elder son of Mgr. le Comte de Clermont and grandson of the French Pretender, is descended from King James 114 times! King Constantine therefore appears in Chapter XVIII despite his descent from Queen Victoria, because in the male line his first link with the Royal House of Stuart is through the marriage of Wilhelm Duke of Schleswig-Holstein-Sonderburg-Glücksburg with Princess Louise of Hesse-Kassel, granddaughter of Princess Mary, fourth daughter of King George II, and it is for this reason that H.R.H. Duke Albrecht of Bavaria, senior descendant of King James and lineal heir of the Royal House of Stuart, appears in Chapter IV.

Only two exceptions have been made to this rule. Prince Christian of Schleswig-Holstein-Sonderburg-Augustenburg and Prince Franz Duke of Teck both married English Princesses, and their children, including the late Princess Marie Louise and Queen Mary, became very much a part of the British Royal Family, and are therefore included in Chapter I.

In this work I have tried to give the Christian names of each descendant as they would appear in his or her native land, and I have tried to treat titles in the same way, but in some cases it has been necessary to modify this principle a little since many people might for instance have difficulty in recognising the Polish "Hrabia" as meaning "Count". In such cases I have therefore used the English version. Titles of members of the reigning and former reigning families are given in English. Place names like Vienna and Rome are given in their original form, i.e. Wien and Roma.

Another problem which has occupied a great deal of my attention is the discrepancies which are often found in dates, but I have not sought to burden the reader with endless footnotes regarding them. In all cases I have tried to satisfy myself that the dates I have used are correct, and those readers interested in apparent anomalies will doubtless pursue this matter for themselves from the many sources available. Almost inevitably however with more than 50,000 dates some errors may occur, and if any readers should detect any mistakes or omissions, I should be grateful if they would let me know, so that the necessary corrections can be made to any future editions.

This work embraces every European Royal House, and in it will be found the names of all the descendants of, amongst others: Victor Amadeus II, King of Sardinia 1666–1732; Louis XV, King of France 1710–1774; Philip I, Duke of Parma 1720–1765; Ferdinand I, King of Naples and Sicily 1751–1825; Rinaldo III, Duke of Modena 1655-1737; the Emperors Joseph I, 1678–1711, and Charles VII, 1697–1745; Frederick Augustus II, Elector of Saxony and King of Poland 1696–

1763; Adolphus Frederick King of Sweden 1710–1771; Jerome Bonaparte, King of Westphalia 1784–1860; Frederick Eugen, Duke of Württemberg 1732–1797; and Tsar Paul I of Russia 1754–1801.

A descent from the Royal House of Stuart is also interesting because as Ruvigny remarked, from King James can also be traced descents from William the Conqueror, King of England 1027–1087, and his adversary King Harold II 1022–1066; Egbert King of England –839; St Louis IX, King of France 1215–1270; Sancho III King of Castille –1035; the Byzantine Emperors Alexius I Commenus 1048–1118, and Isaac II Angelos—1204; Rudolf Habsburg 1218–1291; Friedrich Barbarossa 1123–1190; Arpad Prince of Hungary –907; Wsewolod Grand Duke of Kiev 1030–1093; and the Emperor Charlemagne 742–814.

To enumerate my thanks to everyone who has so kindly contributed to the completion of this work would be impossible. It is largely the product of the help of the people who comprise it, and I hope that having expressed my thanks personally to everyone they will not interpret it a lack of gratitude that their name is not listed here. However among the many contributors I would like to acknowledge the special debt of gratitude that I owe to Alfons Fürst v. Clary u. Aldringen, who for many years has patiently and unfailingly answered all my questions and allowed me to rely so heavily on his work on the descendants of his great-great-grandparents; to Laszlo Edler v. Erdeös for all his help with the Hungarian sections of the work; to Jacques dell'Acquo-Bascourt whose knowledge of French genealogy has been invaluable; to Comte Antonin de Mun; to the Duque de Vistahermosa and Doña Maria Guillamas de Muguiro; to Prince Pio de Saboya for his help with information about Spanish and Italian families; to the Marquise de Maupeou for help with some of the illustrations; to Comtesse Louis de Mailly Nesle and Signora Giulia Castellani; to Duke Constantine of Leuchtenberg; to the late Hans Friedrich v. Ehrenkrook; and to Franz Josef Fürst zu Hohenlohe-Schillingsfürst without whose sustained help and painstaking enquiries on my behalf this work would be sadly incomplete.

Finally I would also like to thank Mrs Sybil Grose for so patiently typing out the manuscript of this work; Miss Pamela Seward for her care in setting the work; Mr Leonard Ellis and Miss Hildi Gunnell for their help with translations; Miss Joy Mooring for so carefully checking the proofs; and my family and friends for all their patience and encouragement.

Kimpton, Hertfordshire   ARTHUR ADDINGTON
1969

METHOD OF WORKING

Apart from Chapter 1, which deals with the British Royal Family, and which has been divided up into convenient sections, the material assembled in these volumes has been arranged in continuous form. Each descendant is shown in order of his or her date of birth, and the plan has been to list each person's descendants before passing on to deal with their brothers and/or sisters and their issue.

The Roman numerals in the left hand margin denote the generation in descent from King James, and each generation is further identified by use of different prefixes viz:- a. a) (a) 1a. 1b. 1c. which are successively indented.

Thus for example in the extract seen below, it will be observed that H.R.H. The Duke of Bavaria is descended from King James in the twelfth generation. His elder brother and sister are shown as 1a. and 2a. whilst his younger brother and half-brother and half-sisters are listed elsewhere as 4a. 5a. etc. The prefix 1b. 2b. etc. is used to distinguish his children whilst his grandchildren are preceded by the prefix 1c. 2c. etc.

XII
    1a. **Luitpold Maximilian Ludwig Karl Prince of Bavaria** * Bamberg 8.5.1901 + Berchtesgarden 27.8.1914

    2a. **Irmingard Maria Therese José Cäcilia Adelheid Michaela Antonia Adelgunde Princess of Bavaria** * Kreuth 21.9.1902 + Tegernsee 21.4.1903

    3a. **Albrecht Luitpold Ferdinand Michael Duke of Bavaria** * München 3.5.1905 = Berchtesgarden 3.9.1930 **Marita Gräfin Draskovich v. Trakostjan** * Wien 8.3.1904 dau. of Dionys Graf Draskovich v. Trakostjan, and has issue:

XIII
    1b. **Marie Gabriele Princess of Bavaria** * München 30.5.1931 = Nymphenburg 23.10.1957 Georg 7 Fürst v. Waldburg zu Zeil u. Trauchburg * Würzburg 5.6.1928, and has issue:

XIV
    1c. **Maria Walburga Monika Charlotte Mathäa Gräfin v. Waldburg zu Zeil u. Trauchburg** * Ravensburg 21.9.1958

KEY

*	date of birth	x	killed
=	date of marriage	dau.	daughter
+	date of death	s.p.	sine prole (without issue)
	s.p.l.	sine prole legitima (without legitimate issue)	

VOLUME ONE

1 The Royal Houses of Stuart, Hannover, Saxe-Coburg and Windsor.

JAMES VI and I, King of England, Scotland, France and Ireland[1] * Edinburgh Castle 19.6.1566
+ Theobalds Park, Hertfordshire 27.3.1625 = Oslo 24.11.1589 Anne Princess of Denmark * Skanderborg 12.10.1574
+ Hampton Court Palace, London 12.3.1618 daughter of Frederik II King of Denmark, and had issue:

1. **Henry Frederick Prince of Wales, Prince of England, Scotland, and Ireland** * Stirling Castle 19.2.1594
   + St. James's Palace London 6.11.1612

2. **Elizabeth Princess of England, Scotland, and Ireland** * Falkland Castle 19.8.1596 + Leicester House,
   London 14.2.1662 = Palace of Whitehall, London 14.2.1613 Friedrich V Elector Palatine of the Rhine,
   King of Bohemia, Duke of Bavaria * Arnberg 26.8.1596 + Mainz 29.11.1632, and had issue see later

3. **Margaret Princess of Scotland** * Dalkeith Castle 24.12.1598 + Linlithgow, March 1600

4. **Charles Duke of York and Albany afterwards Prince of Wales & Charles I**

5. **Robert Duke of Kyntyre, Prince of Scotland** * Dunfermline 18.2.1602 + Dunfermline 27.5.1602

6. **Mary Princess of England, Scotland, and Ireland** * Greenwich 8.4.1605 + Stanwell Park 16.9.1607

7. **Sophia Princess of England, Scotland, and Ireland** * Greenwich 22.6.1606 + Greenwich 23.6.1606

---

1 A stillborn son was also born to Queen Anne in May 1603

I   **Charles I King of England Scotland and Ireland** * Dunfermline 19.11.1600 + Whitehall, London 30.1.1649
= by Proxy Paris 11.5.1625 and in Person Canterbury 13/23.6.1626 Henrietta Maria Princess of France * The Louvre,
Paris 25.11.1609 + Château de Colombes, Paris 10.9.1669 daughter of Henri IV King of France, and had issue:

II   1.   **Charles James Duke of Cornwall, Prince of England Scotland and Ireland** * & + Greenwich 13.5.1629

      2.   **Charles II King of England Scotland and Ireland** * St. James's Palace 29.5.1630 + Palace of Whitehall
6.2.1685 = Winchester 21.5.1662 Catherine Princess of Bragança Infanta of Portugal * Villa Vicosa 25.11.1638
+ Palace of Bemposta, Lisbon 30.11.1705 daughter of João IV King of Portugal s.p.l.

      3.   **Mary Princess of England Scotland and Ireland** * St. James's Palace 4.11.1631 + Palace of Whitehall, London
24.12.1660 = Palace of Whitehall, London 2.5.1641 William II Prince of Orange, Prince of Nassau * The Hague
27.5.1626 + The Hague 6.11.1650 and had issue:

III   1)   **William III Prince of Orange, King of England Scotland and Ireland** * The Hague 14.11.1650
+ Kensington Palace 8.3.1702 = St. James's Palace 4.11.1677 **Mary Princess of England Scotland and
Ireland** * St. James's Palace 30.4.1662 + Kensington Palace 28.12.1694 daughter of James II King of
England s.p.

II   4.   **James Duke of York afterwards James II**

      5.   **Elizabeth Princess of England Scotland and Ireland** * St. James's Palace 29.12.1635 + Carisbrooke Castle
8.9.1650

      6.   **Anne Princess of England Scotland and Ireland** * St. James's Palace 17.3.1637 + Richmond Palace 5.11.1640

      7.   **Katherine Princess of England Scotland and Ireland** * & + Palace of Whitehall 29.1.1639

      8.   **Henry Duke of Gloucester, Prince of England Scotland and Ireland** * Oatlands Park 8.7.1640 + Palace of
Whitehall 13.9.1660

      9.   **Henriette Anne Princess of England Scotland and Ireland** * Bedford House, Exeter 16.6.1644 + St.-Cloud
30.6.1670 = Palais-Royal, Paris 31.3.1661 Philippe Duc d'Orleans * St. Germain-en-Laye 21.9.1640 + St.-Cloud
9.6.1701 and had issue see Chapter 2.

4

Anthony van Dyck   *By gracious permission of H.M. The Queen*

1   Charles I with his wife, Queen Henrietta Maria
and two of their children, Prince Charles,
later Charles II, and Princess Mary

II **James II King of England Scotland and Ireland** * St. James's Palace 14.10.1633 + St. Germain-en-Laye 16.9.1701
= (1) Breda 24.11.1659 Anne Hyde * Cranborne Lodge, Windsor 22.3.1638 + St. James's Palace 31.3.1671 daughter
of Edward Hyde 1 Earl of Clarendon; = (2) Modena 30.9.1673 Marie Beatrix Princess of Modena * Modena
5.10.1658 + St. Germain-en-Laye 8.5.1718 daughter of Alphonse III Duke of Modena, and had issue:

by 1st marriage:

III 1. **Charles Duke of Cambridge, Prince of England Scotland and Ireland** * Worcester House, London 22.10.1660
+ Palace of Whitehall 5.5.1661

2. **Mary II Queen of England Scotland and Ireland** * St. James's Palace 30.4.1662 + Kensington Palace 28.12.1694
= St. James's Palace 4.11.1677 **William III Prince of Orange, King of England Scotland France and Ireland**
* The Hague 14.11.1650 + Kensington Palace 8.3.1702 s.p.

3. **James Duke of Cambridge, Prince of England Scotland and Ireland** * St. James's Palace 11.7.1663 + Richmond
Palace 20.6.1667

4. **Anne Queen of England Scotland and Ireland** see later

5. **Charles Duke of Kendal, Prince of England Scotland and Ireland** * St. James's Palace 4.7.1666 + St. James's
Palace 22.5.1667

6. **Edgar Duke of Cambridge, Prince of England Scotland and Ireland** * St. James's Palace 14.9.1667 + Richmond
Palace 8.6.1671

7. **Henriette Princess of England Scotland and Ireland** * Palace of Whitehall 13.1.1669 + St. James's Palace
15.11.1669

8. **Catherine Princess of England Scotland and Ireland** * Palace of Whitehall 9.2.1671 + St. James's Palace
5.12.1671

by 2nd marriage:

9. **Catherine Laura Princess of England Scotland and Ireland** * St. James's Palace 10.1.1675 + St. James's Palace
3.10.1675

10. **Isabel Princess of England Scotland and Ireland** * St. James's Palace 28.8.1676 + St. James's Palace 2.3.1681

11. **Charles Duke of Cambridge, Prince of England Scotland and Ireland** * St. James's Palace 7.11.1677 + St. James's
Palace 12.12.1677

12. **Elizabeth Princess of England Scotland and Ireland** * in 1678 and died young

13. **Charlotte Maria Princess of England Scotland and Ireland** * St. James's Palace 16.8.1682 + 6.10.1682

14. **James Francis Edward Prince of Wales**, titular King James III, known as The Chevalier St-George, and The Old
Pretender * St. James's Palace 10.6.1688 + Rome 1.1.1766 = Monte Fiasone 3.9.1719 Maria Clementina
Princess Sobieska * 17.7.1702 + Rome 18.1.1735 daughter of Prince James Sobieski, son of King John
Sobieski of Poland

IV 1) **Charles Edward Louis Philip Casimir Prince of England Scotland and Ireland**, titular King Charles III, known
as "The Young Pretender" * Rome 31.12.1720 + Rome 31.1.1788 = Macerata 17.4.1772 Louisa
Princess of Stolberg-Gedern * Mons 21.9.1752 + Florence 29.1.1824 daughter of Gustav Adolf Prince of
Stolberg-Gedern s.p.l.

2) **Henry Benedict Prince of England Scotland and Ireland**, titular King Henry IX, known as "Cardinal York"
* Muti Palace, Rome 6.3.1725 + Frascati 13.7.1807

III 15. **Louisa Maria Theresa Princess of England Scotland France and Ireland** * St. Germain-en-Laye 18.6.1692
+ St. Germain-en-Laye 18.4.1712

III   **Anne Queen of England Scotland and Ireland** * St. James's Palace 6.2.1665 + Kensington Palace 1.8.1714 = St. James's Palace 28.7.1683 George Prince of Denmark, Duke of Cumberland * Kopenhagen 21.4.1653 + Kensington Palace 28.10.1708 and had issue:

IV

1.   **Lady Mary** * Palace of Whitehall 2.6.1685 + 8.2.1686

2.   **Lady Anne Sophie** * Windsor Castle 12.5.1686 + 2.2.1687

3.   **Lady Mary** * & + St. James's Palace 14.10.1690

4.   **William Duke of Gloucester, Prince of England Scotland and Ireland** * Hampton Court Palace 24.7.1689 + Windsor Castle 30.7.1700

5.   **Lord George** * & + Syon House 17.4.1692

I   **Elisabeth Princess of England Scotland and Ireland** * Falkland Castle 19.8.1596 + Leicester House, London 14.2.1662 = Palace of Whitehall, London 14.2.1613 Friedrich V Elector Palatine of the Rhine, King of Bohemia, Duke of Bavaria * Arnberg 16.8.1596 + Mainz 29.11.1632 and had issue:

II   1.   **Heinrich Friedrich Count Palatine of the Rhine** * Heidelberg 1.1.1614 + drowned, Haarlem Meer 17.1.1629

    2.   **Karl Ludwig[1] Elector Palatine of the Rhine, Duke of Bavaria** * Heidelberg 22.12.1617 + bei Dorf Edingen 28.8.1680 = Kassel 22.2.1650 Charlotte Landgräfin of Hesse-Kassel * Kassel 20.11.1627 + Heidelberg 26.3.1686 daughter of Wilhelm V Landgraf of Hesse-Kassel, and had issue:

III   1)   **Karl II Elector Palatine of the Rhine, Duke of Bavaria** * Heidelberg 31.3.1651 + Heidelberg 26.5.1685 = Heidelberg 20.9.1671 Wilhelmine Princess of Denmark * Kopenhagen 20.6.1650 + Lichtenberg 22.4.1706 daughter of Frederik III King of Denmark s.p.

      2)   **Elisabeth Charlotte Countess Palatine of the Rhine** * Heidelberg 27.5.1652 + St-Cloud 8.12.1722 = Metz 21.11.1671 Philippe I Duc d'Orleans * St. Germain-en-Laye 21.9.1640 + St-Cloud 9.6.1701 and had issue see Chapter 3

      3)   **Friedrich Count Palatine of the Rhine** * Augsburg 12 + 13.5.1653

II   3.   **Elisabeth Countess Palatine of the Rhine** * Heidelberg 26.12.1618 + Hervorden 21.2.1680

    4.   **Rupert Count Palatine of the Rhine, Duke of Cumberland,** the celebrated Prince Rupert of the Civil War * Prag 27.12.1619 + London 29.11.1682

    5.   **Maurice Count Palatine of the Rhine,** known as Prince Maurice * Küstrin 16.1.1621 lost at sea 1654 (it is also thought he may have died in captivity in Algiers)

    6.   **Luise Hollandine Countess Palatine of the Rhine** * The Hague 18.4.1662 + Maubisson 11.2.1709

    7.   **Ludwig Count Palatine of the Rhine** * The Hague 21.8.1623 + The Hague 24.12.1625

    8.   **Eduard Count Palatine of the Rhine** * The Hague 5.10.1625 + Paris 13.3.1663 = Paris 24.4.1645 Donna Anna de Gonzaga * Mantua 1616 + Paris 6.7.1684 daughter of Charles I Duke of Nevers and Mantua, and had issue:

III   1)   **Luise Marie Countess Palatine of the Rhine** * Paris 23.7.1647 + Aachen 11.3.1679 = Paris 20.3.1671 Carl Theodor Otto Fürst zu Salm * Anholt 27.7.1645 + Aachen 10.11.1710, and had issue see Chapter 5

      2)   **Anna Henriette Julie Countess Palatine of the Rhine** * Paris 23.7.1648 + Paris 23.2.1723 = Paris 11.12.1663 Henri Julius de Bourbon Prince de Condé * Paris 29.7.1643 + Paris 1.4.1709, and had issue see Chapter 12

      3)   a son * 27.12.1650 + 30.7.1651

      4)   **Benedikta Henriette Countess Palatine of the Rhine** * Paris 14.3.1652 + Hannover 12.8.1730 = Paris 30.11.1668 Johann Friedrich Duke of Brunswick-Lüneburg * Herzberg 25.4.1625 + Augsburg 28.12.1679, and had issue see Chapter 13

II   9.   **Henriette Marie Countess Palatine of the Rhine** * The Hague 7.7.1626 + Fogaras 18.9.1651 = Patak 26.6.1651 Sigismund Rákóczy * circa 1623 + Fogaras 11.2.1652 son of Georg Rákóczy Prince of Transylvania s.p.

   10.   **Philipp Count Palatine of the Rhine** * The Hague 26.9.1627 X Rethel, 15.12.1650

   11.   **Charlotte Countess Palatine of the Rhine** * The Hague 19.12.1628 + The Hague 24.1.163i

   12.   **Sofie Countess Palatine of the Rhine** * The Hague 13.10.1630 + Herrenhausen 8.6.1714 = Heidelberg 30.9.1658 Ernst August I Duke of Brunswick-Lüneburg, Elector of Hannover * Herzberg 20.11.1629 + Herrenhausen 23.1.1698, and had issue:

---

[1] The Elector Karl Ludwig divorced his first wife, and married 2ndly at Schwetzingen 6.1.1658 Marie Louise v. Degenfeld * Strassburg 28.11.1634 + Mannhein 18.3.1677 daughter of Christoph Frhr. v. Degenfeld. The legality of this divorce however is frequently questioned, and it is hoped to treat the descendants of this marriage in a subsequent volume.

III   1)   **Georg Ludwig Elector of Hannover, Duke of Brunswick-Lüneburg,** later George I King of Great Britain

        2)   **Friedrich August Prince of Hannover** * Hannover 3.10.1661 ✕ St. Georgen, in Transylvania 10.1.1691

        3)   **Maximilian Wilhelm Prince of Hannover** * Schloss Iburg 14.12.1666 + Vienna 27.7.1726

        4)   a son * & + Schloss Iburg 14.12.1666

        5)   **Sophie Charlotte Princess of Hannover** * Schloss Iburg 20.10.1668 + Hannover 1.2.1705 = Herrenhausen 8.10.1684 Friedrich I King of Prussia * Königsberg 11.7.1657 + Berlin 25.2.1713, and had issue see Chapter 16

        6)   **Carl Philipp Prince of Hannover** * Schloss Iburg 13.10.1669 ✕ Pristina, Albania, fighting the Turks 1.1.1690

        7)   **Christian Prince of Hannover** * Schloss Iburg 29.9.1671 + drowned in the Danube near Ulm, fighting the French 31.7.1703

        8)   **Ernst August Prince of Hannover, Duke of York and Albany** * Osnabrück 18.9.1674 + Osnabrück 14.8.1728

II   13.   **Gustav Count Palatine of the Rhine** * The Hague 14.1.1632 + The Hague 9.1.1641

Daniel Mytens   *By gracious permission of H.M. The Queen*

2   Elizabeth, Queen of Bohemia, 1596–1662

George I King of Great Britain and Ireland, Elector of Hannover, Duke of Brunswick-Lüneburg
* Hannover 28.5./7.6.1660 + Osnabrück 11/22.6.1727 = Celle 21.11.1682 Sophie Dorothea
Princess of Brunswick-Celle * Celle 15.9.1666 + Schloss Ahlden 13.11.1726 daughter of Georg Wilhelm,
Duke of Brunswick-Celle, and had issue:

IV

1. **George Augustus, Prince of Wales, later George II**

2. **Sophie Dorothea Princess of Hannover** * Hannover 16.3.1685 + Monbijou Palais, Berlin 29.6.1757
   = Berlin 28.11.1706 **Friedrich Wilhelm I, King of Prussia** * Berlin 15.8.1688 + Berlin 31.5.1740,
   and had issue see elsewhere

IV   **George II King of Great Britain and Ireland, Elector of Hannover, Duke of Brunswick-Lüneburg** * Hannover 30.10.1683 + Kensington Palace 25.10.1760 = Herrenhausen 22.8.1705 Wilhelmine Charlotte Caroline Margräfin of Brandenburg-Ansbach * Ansbach 1.3.1683 + St. James's Palace, London 20.11.1737 daughter of Johann Friedrich Margraf of Brandenburg-Ansbach, and had issue:

V   1.   **Frederick Lewis Prince of Wales** see later

      2.   **Anne Princess of Great Britain and Ireland, Princess of Hannover** * Herrenhausen 2.11.1709 + The Hague 12.1.1759 = St. James's Palace, London 25.3.1734 William IV Prince of Orange * Leeuwarden 1.9.1711 + The Hague 22.10.1751, and had issue see Chapter 17

      3.   **Amelia Sophia Eleonore Princess of Great Britain and Ireland, Princess of Hannover** * Herrenhausen 10.6.1711 + at her house in Cavendish Square, London 31.10.1786

      4.   **Caroline Elizabeth Princess of Great Britain and Ireland, Princess of Hannover** * Herrenhausen 10.6.1713 + St. James's Palace, London 28.12.1757

      5.   **George William Prince of Great Britain and Ireland** * St. James's Palace, London 2.11.1717 + Kensington Palace, London 6.2.1718

      6.   **William Augustus Duke of Cumberland, Prince of Great Britain and Ireland** * St. James's Palace, London 15.4.1721 + at his house in Upper Grosvenor Street, London 31.10.1765

      7.   **Mary Princess of Great Britain and Ireland** * Leicester House, London 22.2.1723 + Hanau 14.1.1772 = St. James's Palace, London 8.5.1740 Friedrich II Landgraf of Hesse-Kassel * Kassel 14.8.1720 + Schloss Weissenstein 31.10.1785, and had issue see Chapter 18

      8.   **Louise Princess of Great Britain and Ireland** * Leicester House, London 7.12.1724 + Schloss Christiansborg 19.12.1751 = Hannover 30.10.1743 Frederik V King of Denmark * Kopenhagen 31.3.1723 + Schloss Christiansborg 14.1.1766, and had issue see Chapter 19

V   **Frederick Lewis Prince of Wales, Prince of Great Britain and Ireland, Prince of Hannover** * Hannover 20.1.1707 + Leicester House, London 20.3.1751 = St. James's Palace, London 27.4.1736 Augusta Princess of Saxe-Gotha * Gotha 30.11.1719 + Carlton House, London 8.2.1772 daughter of Friedrich II, Duke of Saxe-Gotha, and had issue:

VI   1.   **Augusta Princess of Great Britain and Ireland** * St. James's Palace, London 31.7.1737 + London 23.3.1813 = St. James's Palace 17.1.1764 **Charles William Duke of Brunswick-Wolfenbüttel** * Wolfenbüttel 9.10.1753 + at Altona from wounds received at the Battle of Auerstadt 10.11.1806, and had issue see elsewhere

     2.   **George William Frederick Prince of Wales, later George III**

     3.   **Edward Augustus Duke of York and Albany, Prince of Great Britain and Ireland** * Norfolk House, London 14.3.1739 + Monaco 17.9.1767

     4   **Elizabeth Caroline Princess of Great Britain and Ireland** * Norfolk House 30.12.1740 + Kew Palace 4.9.1759

     5.   **William Henry Duke of Gloucester and Edinburgh, Prince of Great Britain and Ireland** * Leicester House 14.11.1743 + Gloucester House, London 25.8.1805 = London 6.9.1766 Maria Walpole * 10.7.1736 + Brompton 22.8.1807 widow of James 2nd Earl Waldegrave, and illegitimate daughter of Hon. Sir Edward Walpole, and had issue:

VII   1)   **Sophia Matilda Princess of Gloucester, Princess of Great Britain and Ireland** * Gloucester House 29.5.1773 + at her house at Blackheath, London 29.11.1844

         2)   **Caroline Augusta Maria Princess of Gloucester, Princess of Great Britain and Ireland** * Gloucester House 24.6.1774 + Gloucester House 14.3.1775

         3)   **William Frederick 2nd Duke of Gloucester and Edinburgh, Prince of Great Britain and Ireland** * Palazzo Theodoli, Rome 15.1.1776 + Bagshot Park 30.11.1834 = Buckingham House 22.7.1816 **Mary Princess of Great Britain and Ireland** * Buckingham House 25.4.1776 + Gloucester House 30.4.1857 daughter of George III, King of Great Britain, s.p.

VI   6.   **Henry Frederick Duke of Cumberland and Strathern, Prince of Great Britain and Ireland** * Leicester House 27.10.1745 + Cumberland House 18.9.1790 = London 2.10.1771 Lady Anne Lutterel * 24.1.1743 + Trieste 28.12.1808 widow of Christopher Horton, and daughter of Simon Lutterel 1st Earl of Carhampton, s.p.

     7.   **Louise Anne Princess of Great Britain and Ireland** * Leicester House 8.3.1749 + Carlton House 13.5.1768

     8.   **Frederick William Prince of Great Britain and Ireland** * Leicester House 13.5.1750 + Leicester House 29.12.1765

     9.   **Caroline Matilda Princess of Great Britain and Ireland** * Leicester House 11.7.1751 + Zelle 10.5.1775 = Schloss Frederiksborg 8.11.1766 **Christian VII King of Denmark** * Kopenhagen 20.1.1749 + Rendsborg 13.3.1808, and had issue see elsewhere

VI   **George III King of Great Britain and Ireland, King of Hannover** * Norfolk House 4.6.1738 + Windsor Castle 29.1.1820 = St. James's Palace 8.9.1761 Charlotte Sophie Duchess of Mecklenburg-Strelitz * Mirow 19.5.1744 + Kew Palace 17.11.1818 daughter of Karl Ludwig Duke of Mecklenburg-Strelitz, and had issue:

VII   1.   **George IV Augustus Frederick, King of Great Britain and Ireland, King of Hannover** * St. James's Palace 12.8.1762 + Windsor Castle 26.6.1830 = St. James's Palace 8.4.1795 **Caroline Princess of Brunswick-Wolfenbüttel** * Wolfenbüttel 17.5.1768 + Brandenburg House, London 7.8.1821 daughter of Karl II Duke of Brunswick-Wolfenbüttel, and had issue:

VIII   1)   **Charlotte Augusta Princess of Wales, Princess of Great Britain and Ireland** * Carlton House 7.1.1796 + Claremont 6.11.1817 = Carlton House 2.5.1816 Leopold Prince of Saxe-Coburg * Coburg 16.12.1790 + Laeken 10.12.1865, and had issue:

IX   (1)   a stillborn son 5.11.1817

VII   2.   **Frederick Augustus Duke of York and Albany, Prince of Great Britain and Ireland** * St. James's Palace 16.8.1763 + at his house in Arlington St., London 5.1.1827 = Charlottenburg 29.9.1791 **Friederike Princess of Prussia** * Charlottenburg 7.5.1767 + Oatlands Park 6.8.1820 daughter of Friedrich Wilhelm II King of Prussia, s.p.

      3.   **William IV Henry King of Great Britain and Ireland, King of Hannover** * Buckingham House 21.8.1765 + Windsor Castle 20.6.1837 = Kew 11.7.1818 Adelaide Princess of Saxe-Meiningen * Meiningen 13.8.1792 + Bentley Priory, Stanmore 2.12.1849 daughter of Georg Duke of Saxe-Meiningen, and had issue:

VIII   1)   **Charlotte Augusta Louisa Princess of Great Britain and Ireland** * & + Hannover 21.3.1819

         2)   **Elizabeth Georgina Adelaide Princess of Great Britain and Ireland** * St. James's Palace, London 10.12.1820 + St. James's Palace 4.3.1821

VII   4.   **Charlotte Augusta Matilda Princess of Great Britain and Ireland** * Buckingham House 29.9.1766 + Ludwigsburg 6.10.1828 = Chapel Royal St. James's Palace 18.5.1797 **Friedrich I King of Württemberg** * Treptow 6.11.1754 + Stuttgart 30.10.1816, and had issue see elsewhere

      5.   **Edward Augustus Duke of Kent and Strathern, Prince of Great Britain and Ireland** * Buckingham House 2.11.1767 + Sidmouth 23.1.1820 = Kew 11.7.1818 Victoria Princess of Saxe-Coburg * Coburg 17.8.1786 + Frogmore House, Windsor 16.3.1861 daughter of Franz Duke of Saxe-Coburg, and had issue:

VIII   1)   **Victoria Alexandrina Queen of Great Britain and Ireland**

VII   6.   **Augusta Sophia Princess of Great Britain and Ireland** * Buckingham House 8.11.1768 + Clarence House, London 22.9.1840

      7.   **Elizabeth Princess of Great Britain and Ireland** * Buckingham House 22.5.1770 + Frankfurt-am-Main 10.1.1840 = Buckingham House 7.4.1818 Friedrich VI Landgraf of Hesse-Homburg * Homburg 30.7.1769 + Homburg 2.4.1829 s.p.

      8.   **Ernest August, King of Hannover, Duke of Cumberland, Prince of Great Britain and Ireland** * Buckingham House 5.6.1771 + Schloss Herrenhausen 18.11.1851 = Neustrelitz 29.5.1815 Friederike Duchess of Mecklenburg-Strelitz * Hannover 2.3.1778 + Hannover 29.6.1841 dau. of Karl II Duke of Mecklenburg-Strelitz, and had issue see later

      9.   **Augustus Frederick Duke of Sussex, Prince of Great Britain and Ireland** * Buckingham House 27.1.1773 + Kensington Palace 21.4.1843 = (1) Roma 4.4.1793 Lady Augusta Murray * London 27.1.1768 + Ramsgate 5.3.1830 dau. of John Murray 4th Earl of Dunmore, = (2) circa 2.5.1831 Lady Cecilia Saunders * circa 1785 + Kensington Palace 1.8.1873 Duchess of Inverness, dau. of Arthur Saunders, 2nd Earl of Arran, and widow of Sir George Buggin, and had issue:

        by 1st marriage:

VIII   1)   **Sir Augustus Frederick d'Este** * 13.1.1794 + 28.12.1848

VIII   2)   **Augusta Emma d'Este** * London 11.8.1801 + London 21.5.1866 = 13.8.1845 Thomas Wild 1st Baron Truro * London 7.7.1782 + London 11.11.1855 s.p.

VII 10.   **Adolphus Frederick Duke of Cambridge, Prince of Great Britain and Ireland** * Buckingham House 24.2.1774 + Cambridge House 8.7.1850 = Kassel 7.5.1818 and in London 1.6.1818 **Augusta Princess of Hesse-Kassel** * Schloss Rumpenheim 25.7.1797 + St. James's Palace 6.4.1889 dau. of Friedrich Landgraf of Hesse-Kassel, and had issue see later

    11.   **Mary Princess of Great Britain and Ireland** * Buckingham House 25.4.1776 + Gloucester House 30.4.1857 = Buckingham House 22.7.1816 **William Frederick 2nd Duke of Gloucester and Edinburgh, Prince of Great Britain and Ireland** * Palazzo Theodoli, Roma 15.1.1776 + Bagshot Park 30.11.1834, s.p.

    12.   **Sophia Princess of Great Britain and Ireland** * Buckingham House 3.11.1777 + Vicarage Place, Kensington 27.5.1848

    13.   **Octavius Prince of Great Britain and Ireland** * Buckingham House 23.2.1779 + Kew 3.5.1783

    14.   **Alfred Prince of Great Britain and Ireland** * Windsor Castle 22.9.1780 + Windsor Castle 20.8.1782

    15.   **Amelia Princess of Great Britain and Ireland** * Windsor Lodge 7.8.1783 + Augusta Lodge, Windsor 2.11.1810

VIII **Victoria Alexandrina Queen of Great Britain and Ireland, Emperess of India** * Kensington Palace 24.5.1819 + Osborne
House 22.1.1901 = Chapel Royal, St. James's Palace 10.2.1840 **Albert Prince of Saxe-Coburg and Gotha** * Schloss
Rosenau b. Coburg 26.8.1819 + Windsor Castle 14.12.1861, and had issue:

IX 1. **Victoria Adelaide Mary Louise Princess of Great Britain and Ireland** * Buckingham Palace 21.11.1840
+ Friedrichshof 5.8.1901 = Chapel Royal, St. James's Palace 25.1.1858 **Friedrich III Emperor of Germany,
King of Prussia** * Neues Palais b. Potsdam 18.10.1831 + Neues Palais 15.6.1888, and had issue see elsewhere

2. **Albert Edward VII King of Great Britain and Ireland, Emperor of India** * Buckingham Palace 9.11.1841
+ Buckingham Palace 6.5.1910 = Windsor Castle 10.3.1863 **Alexandra Princess of Denmark** * Amalienborg
Palace, Copenhagen 1.12.1844 + Sandringham House 20.11.1925, daughter of Christian IX King of Denmark,
and had issue:

X 1) **Albert Victor Christian Edward, Duke of Clarence and Avondale, Prince of Great Britain and Ireland**
* Frogmore Lodge, Windsor 8.1.1864 + Sandringham House 14.1.1892

2) **George V Frederick Ernest Albert King of Great Britain and Ireland, Emperor of India** * Marlborough
House, London 3.6.1865 + Sandringham House 20.1.1936 = Chapel Royal, St. James's Palace 6.7.1893
Mary Princess of Teck * Kensington Palace 26.5.1867 + Marlborough House 24.3.1953 daughter of
Francis Duke of Teck, and had issue:

XI (1) **Edward VIII Albert Christian George Andrew Patrick David, King of Great Britain and Ireland,
Emperor of India,** now Duke of Windsor * White Lodge, Richmond 23.6.1894 = Château de Cande
3.6.1937 Wallis Warfield * Monterey, Virginia, U.S.A. 19.6.1896 daughter of Teakle Wallis Warfield

(2) **Albert Frederick Arthur George VI, King of Great Britain and Ireland, Emperor of India** * York
Cottage, Sandringham 14.12.1895 + Sandringham House 6.2.1952 = Westminster Abbey, London
26.4.1923 Lady Elizabeth Bowes-Lyon * St. Paul's Waldenbury, Hertfordshire 4.8.1900 daughter of
Claude 14th Earl of Strathmore and Kinghorne, and had issue:

XII a. **Elizabeth II Alexandra Mary Queen of Great Britain and Northern Ireland** * Bruton Street,
London 21.4.1926 = Westminster Abbey 20.11.1947 **Philip Prince of Greece and Denmark,
Duke of Edinburgh** * Corfu 10.6.1921, and has issue:

XIII a) **Charles Philip Arthur George Prince of Great Britain and Northern Ireland, Prince of
Wales** * Buckingham Palace 14.11.1948

b) **Anne Elizabeth Alice Louise Princess of Great Britain and Northern Ireland** * Clarence
House, London 15.8.1950

c) **Andrew Albert Edward Christian Prince of Great Britain and Northern Ireland**
* Buckingham Palace 19.2.1960

d) **Edward Antony Richard Louis Prince of Great Britain and Northern Ireland** * Buckingham
Palace 10.3.1964

XII b. **Margaret Rose, Princess of Great Britain and Ireland** * Glamis Castle, Scotland 21.8.1930
= Westminster Abbey 6.5.1960 Antony Armstrong-Jones, 1st Earl of Snowdon * London
7.3.1930, and has issue:

XIII a) **David Albert Charles Armstrong-Jones, Viscount Linley** * Clarence House 3.11.1961

b) **Lady Sarah Frances Elizabeth Armstrong-Jones** * Kensington Palace 1.5.1964

XI (3) **Victoria Alexandra Alice Mary Princess of Great Britain and Ireland** * Sandringham House 25.4.1897
+ Harewood House 28.3.1965 = Westminster Abbey 28.2.1922 Henry Lascelles 6th Earl of Harewood
* London 9.9.1882 + Harewood House 24.5.1947, and had issue:

XII a. **George Henry Hubert Lascelles 7th Earl of Harewood** * Chesterfield House, London 7.2.1923
= London 29.9.1949 Marion Stein * Vienna 18.10.1927 daughter of Erwin Stein, and has issue:

14

Camera Press   *Photo Patrick Lichfield*

3   The Royal Family at Buckingham Palace

Left to right: Prince Charles, Prince Andrew, Princess Anne, Prince
Edward, H.M. The Queen, The Duke of Edinburgh

XIII   a)   **David Henry George Viscount Lascelles** * London 21.10.1950

                      b)   **Hon. James Edward Lascelles** * London 5.10.1953

                      c)   **Hon. Robert Jeremy Hugh Lascelles** * London 14.2.1955

XII   b.   **Hon. Gerald David Lascelles** * Goldsborough Hall 21.8.1924 = London 15.7.1952 Angela Dowding * Hanwell 20.4.1919 daughter of Charles Dowding, and has issue:

XIII   a)   **Henry Ulick Lascelles** * London 19.5.1953

XI   (4)   **Henry William Frederick Albert Duke of Gloucester, Prince of Great Britain and Ireland** * Sandringham House 31.3.1900 = Buckingham Palace 6.11.1935 Lady Alice Montague-Douglas-Scott * London 25.12.1901 daughter of John Montague-Douglas-Scott 7th Duke of Buccleuch, 10th Duke of Queensberry and has issue:

XII   a.   **William Henry Andrew Frederick Prince of Gloucester, Prince of Great Britain and Ireland** * Barnet 18.12.1941

                 b.   **Richard Alexander Walter George Prince of Gloucester, Prince of Great Britain and Ireland** * Northampton 26.8.1944

XI   (5)   **George Edward Alexander Edmund Duke of Kent, Prince of Great Britain and Ireland** * Sandringham House 20.12.1902, ✗ on active service, Morven 25.8.1942 = Westminster Abbey 29.11.1934 **Marina Princess of Greece and Denmark** * Athens 13.12.1906 daughter of Nicholas Prince of Greece and Denmark, and has issue:

XII   a.   **Edward George Nicholas Paul Patrick 2nd Duke of Kent, Prince of Great Britain and Ireland** * Belgrave Square, London 9.10.1935 = York 8.6.1961 Katherine Worsley * Hovingham Hall, York 22.3.1933 daughter of Sir William Worsley 3rd Bart., and has issue:

XIII   a)   **George Philip Nicholas, Earl of St. Andrews** * Coppins, Iver 26.6.1962

                     b)   **Lady Helen Marina Lucy Windsor** * Coppins, Iver 28.4.1964

XII   b.   **Alexandra Helen Elisabeth Olga Christabel Princess of Kent, Princess of Great Britain and Ireland** * Belgrave Square, London 25.12.1936 = Westminster Abbey 24.4.1963 Hon. Angus Ogilvy * London 14.9.1928, and has issue:

XIII   a)   **James Robert Bruce Ogilvy** * Thatched House Lodge, Richmond 29.2.1964

                     b)   **Marina Victoria Alexandra Ogilvy** * Thatched House Lodge, Richmond 31.7.1966

XII   c.   **Michael George Charles Franklin Prince of Kent, Prince of Great Britain and Ireland** * Coppins, Iver 4.7.1942

XI   (6)   **John Charles Francis Prince of Great Britain and Ireland** * York Cottage, Sandringham 12.7.1905 + Wood Farm, Wolferton 18.1.1919

X   3)   **Louise Victoria Alexandra Dagmar Princess of Great Britain and Ireland** * Marlborough House 20.2.1867 + Portman Square, London 4.1.1931 = Buckingham Palace 27.7.1889 Alexander Duff 1st Duke of Fife, 6th Earl of Fife * Edinburgh 10.11.1849 + Assuan, Egypt 29.1.1912, and had issue:

XI   (1)   **Alexandra Victoria Alberta Edwina Louise Princess of Fife, 2nd Duchess of Fife** * East Sheen Lodge 17.5.1891 + London 26.2.1959 = Chapel Royal, St. James's Palace 15.10.1913 **Arthur Prince of Connaught, Prince of Great Britain and Ireland** * Windsor Castle 13.1.1883 + Belgrave Square 12.9.1938, and had issue see elsewhere

15

XI		(2) **Maud Alexandra Victoria Georgina Bertha Princess of Fife** * East Sheen Lodge 3.4.1893 + London 14.12.1945 = London 12.11.1923 Charles Carnegie 11th Earl of Southesk * Edinburgh 23.9.1893, and has issue:

XII — a. **James George Alexander Bannerman Carnegie 3rd Duke of Fife, Lord Carnegie** * London 23.9.1929 = Perth 11.9.1956 Hon. Caroline Dewar * Bardowie Castle, Milngavie 12.2.1934 daughter of Henry Dewar 3rd Baron Forteviot — div. and has issue:

XIII — a) **Lady Alexandra Clare Carnegie** * Edinburgh 20.6.1959

b) **David Charles Carnegie, Earl of Macduff** * Edinburgh 3.3.1961

X — 4) **Victoria Alexandra Olga Mary Princess of Great Britain and Ireland** * Marlborough House 6.7.1868 + Coppins, Iver 3.12.1935

5) **Maud Charlotte Mary Victoria Princess of Great Britain and Ireland** * Marlborough House 26.11.1869 + London 20.11.1938 = Buckingham Palace 22.7.1896 **Haakon VII King of Norway**, then Prince Charles of Denmark * Charlottenlund 3.8.1872 + Oslo 21.9.1957, and had issue see elsewhere

6) **Alexander John Charles Albert Prince of Great Britain and Ireland** * Sandringham House 6.4.1871 + Sandringham House 7.4.1871

IX — 4.3. **Alice Maud Mary Princess of Great Britain and Ireland** * Buckingham Palace 25.4.1843 + Darmstadt 14.12.1878 = Osborne House 1.7.1862 **Ludwig IV Grand Duke of Hesse-Darmstadt** * Bessungen 12.9.1837 + Darmstadt 13.3.1892, and had issue see elsewhere

5.4. **Alfred Ernest Albert Duke of Saxe-Coburg and Gotha, Duke of Edinburgh, Prince of Great Britain and Ireland** * Windsor Castle 6.8.1844 * Rosenau b. Coburg 30.7.1900 = St. Petersburg 23.1.1874 **Marie Alexandrovna Grand Duchess of Russia** * Tsarskoie, Selo 5.10.1853 + Zurich 24.10.1920 daughter of Alexander II Emperor of Russia, and had issue:

X — 1) **Alfred Alexander William Ernest Albert Hereditary Prince of Saxe-Coburg and Gotha, Prince of Great Britain and Ireland** * Buckingham Palace 15.10.1874 + Meran 6.2.1899

2) **Marie Alexandra Victoria Princess of Saxe-Coburg and Gotha, Princess of Great Britain and Ireland** * Eastwell Park 29.10.1875 + Sinaia 18.7.1938 = Sigmaringen 10.1.1893 **Ferdinand I King of Roumania, Prince of Hohenzollern-Sigmaringen** * Sigmaringen 24.8.1865 + Sinaia 20.7.1927, and had issue see elsewhere

3) **Victoria Melita Princess of Saxe-Coburg and Gotha, Princess of Great Britain and Ireland** * Malta 25.11.1876 + Amorbach 2.3.1936 = (1) Coburg 19.4.1894 **Ernst Ludwig Grand Duke of Hesse-Darmstadt** * Darmstadt 25.11.1868 + Wolfsgarten 9.10.1937 — div., = (2) Tegernsee 8.10.1905 **Cyrill Vladimirovitch Grand Duke of Russia** * Tsarskoie-Selo 30.9.1876 + Neuilly-sur-Seine 13.10.1938, and had issue by both marriages, see elsewhere

4) **Alexandra Louise Olga Victoria Princess of Saxe-Coburg and Gotha, Princess of Great Britain and Ireland** * Coburg 1.9.1878 + Schwabisch Hall 16.4.1942 = Coburg 20.4.1896 **Ernst Fürst zu Hohenlohe-Langenburg** * Langenburg 13.9.1863 + Langenburg 11.12.1950, and had issue see elsewhere

5) a daughter * & + Eastwell Park 13.10.1879

6) **Beatrice Leopoldine Victoria Princess of Saxe-Coburg and Gotha, Princess of Great Britain and Ireland** * Eastwell Park 20.4.1884 + Sanlucar de Barrameda 13.7.1966 = Rosenau b. Coburg 15.7.1909 **Alfonso Prince of Orleans, Infant of Spain, 3rd Duke of Galliera** * Madrid 12.11.1886, and has issue see elsewhere

IX — 6.5. **Helena Augusta Victoria Princess of Great Britain and Ireland** * Buckingham Palace 25.5.1846 + Schomberg House, London 9.6.1923 = Windsor Castle 5.7.1866 **Christian Prince of Schleswig-Holstein-Sonderburg-Augustenburg** * Augustenburg 22.1.1831 + Schomburg House, London 28.10.1917, and had issue:

X 1) **Christian Victor Albert Ludwig Ernest Anton Prince of Schleswig-Holstein-Sonderburg-Augustenburg**
* Windsor Castle 14.4.1867 + Pretoria 29.10.1900

2) **Albert John Charles Frederick Alfred Georg Duke of Schleswig-Holstein-Sonderburg-Augustenburg**
* Frogmore House, Windsor 26.2.1869 + Berlin 27.4.1931

3) **Victoria Louise Sophia Augusta Amelia Helena Princess of Schleswig-Holstein-Sonderburg-Augustenburg**
* Frogmore House 3.5.1870 + London 13.3.1948

4) **Franziska Josepha Louise Augusta Marie Christina Helena Princess of Schleswig-Holstein-Sonderburg-Augustenburg** * Cumberland Lodge, Windsor 12.8.1872 + London 8.12.1956 = Windsor Castle
6.7.1891 **Aribert Prince of Anhalt-Dessau** * Wörlitz 18.6.1864 + München 24.12.1933 — div. s.p.

5) **Frederick Christian Augustus Leopold Edward Harold Prince of Schleswig-Holstein-Sonderburg-Augustenburg** * Cumberland Lodge 12.5.1876 + Cumberland Lodge 20.5.1876

6) a son * & + 7.5.1877

IX 6. **Louise Caroline Alberta Princess of Great Britain and Ireland** * Buckingham Palace 18.3.1848 + Kensington Palace 3.12.1939 = Windsor Castle 21.3.1871 John Campbell 9th Duke of Argyll * London 6.8.1845 + Kent House, Cowes 2.5.1914 s.p.

7. **Arthur William Patrick Albert Duke of Connaught and Strathern, Prince of Great Britain and Ireland**
* Buckingham Palace 1.5.1850 + Bagshot Park 16.1.1942 = Windsor Castle 13.3.1879 **Luise Margarete Princess of Prussia** * Marmorpalais, Potsdam 25.6.1860 + Clarence House, London 14.3.1917, daughter of Friedrich Carl Prince of Prussia, and had issue:

X 1) **Margaret Victoria Augusta Charlotte Norah Princess of Connaught, Princess of Great Britain and Ireland**
* Bagshot Park 15.1.1882 + Stockholm 1.5.1920 = Windsor Castle 15.6.1905 **Gustaf VI Adolf King of Sweden,** then Crown Prince of Sweden * Stockholm 11.11.1882, and had issue see elsewhere

2) **Arthur Frederick Patrick Albert Prince of Connaught, Prince of Great Britain and Ireland** * Windsor Castle 13.1.1883 + Belgrave Square, London 12.9.1938 = Chapel Royal, St. James's Palace 15.10.1913 **Alexandra Princess of Fife** * East Sheen Lodge 17.5.1891 + London 26.2.1959, and had issue:

XI (1) **Alastair Arthur 2nd Duke of Connaught and Strathern** * Mount Street, London 9.8.1914 + Ottawa 26.4.1943

X 3) **Victoria Patricia Helena Elizabeth Princess of Connaught, Princess of Great Britain and Ireland**
* Buckingham Palace 17.3.1886 = Westminster Abbey 27.2.1919 Sir Alexander Ramsey * London 29.5.1881, and has issue:

XI (1) **Alexander Arthur Alfonso David Maule Ramsey** * London 21.12.1919 = Fraserburgh 6.10.1956 Hon. Flora Fraser * Edinburgh 18.10.1930 daughter of Alexander Fraser 19th Baron Saltoun, and has issue:

XII a. **Katherine Ingrid Mary Isabel Ramsey** * Edinburgh 11.10.1957

b. **Alice Elizabeth Margaret Ramsey** * Edinburgh 8.7.1961

c. **Elizabeth Alexandra Mary Ramsey** * Inverness 15.4.1963

IX 8. **Leopold George Duncan Albert Duke of Albany, Prince of Great Britain and Ireland** * Buckingham Palace 7.4.1853 + Cannes 28.3.1884 = Windsor Castle 27.4.1882 **Helena Princess of Waldeck and Pyrmont** * Arolsen 17.2.1861 + Hinterriss, Tirol 1.9.1922 daughter of Georg Viktor Fürst v. Waldeck u. Pyrmont, and had issue:

X 1) **Alice Mary Victoria Augusta Pauline Princess of Albany, Princess of Great Britain and Ireland** * Windsor Castle 25.2.1883 = Windsor Castle 10.2.1904 **Alexander Prince of Teck, later Earl of Athlone** * Kensington Palace 14.4.1874 + Kensington Palace 16.1.1957, and had issue see elsewhere

X	2)		**Leopold Charles Edward George Albert Duke of Saxe-Coburg and Gotha, Duke of Albany, Prince of Great Britain and Ireland** * Claremont House 19.7.1884 + Coburg 6.3.1954 = Glücksburg 11.10.1905 **Victoria Adelheid Princess of Schleswig-Holstein-Sonderburg-Glücksburg** * Grunholz 31.12.1885 daughter of Friedrich Ferdinand Duke of Schleswig-Holstein-Sonderburg-Glücksburg, and had issue:

XI   (1)   **Johann Leopold Wilhelm Albert Ferdinand Viktor Hereditary Prince of Saxe-Coburg and Gotha** * Schloss Callenberg b. Coburg 2.8.1906 = (1) Dresden 14.3.1932 Feodora Freiin. v. der Horst * Wolka 7.7.1905 daughter of Bernhard Frhr. v. der Horst — div. = (2) Bad Reichenhall 3.5.1962 Theresia Reindl * Reichenhall 13.3.1908 daughter of Max Reindl, and has issue:

XII   a.   **Caroline Mathilde Adelheid Sibylla Marianne Erika Princess of Saxe-Coburg and Gotha** * Hirschberg 5.4.1933 = Mühlacker 5.12.1953 Michael Nielsen * Frankfurt-am-Main 12.8.1923, and has issue:

XIII   a)   **Margarete Brigitte Nielsen** * Mühlacker 31.8.1954

          b)   **Renate Christine Nielsen** * Leverkusen-Wiesdorf 1.4.1957

XII   b.   **Ernst Leopold Eduard Wilhelm Josias Prince of Saxe-Coburg and Gotha** * Hirschberg 14.1.1935 = Herrenberg 4.2.1961 Ingeborg Henig * Nordhausen 16.8.1937 daughter of Richard Henig — div. = (2) Regensburg 29.5.1963 Gertraude Pfeiffer * Strobitz 1.7.1938, and has issue:

by 1st marriage:

XIII   a)   **Hubertus Richard Ernst Eduard Prince of Saxe-Coburg and Gotha** * Herrenberg 8.12.1961

XII   c.   **Peter Albert Friedrich Josias Prince of Saxe-Coburg and Gotha** * Dresden 12.6.1939 = Tegernsee 11.5.1964 Roswitha Breuer * Wolznach 1.9.1945

XI   (2)   **Sibylla Calma Marie Alice Bathildis Feodora Princess of Saxe-Coburg and Gotha** * Gotha 18.1.1908 = Coburg 20.10.1932 **Gustaf Adolf Crown Prince of Sweden** * Stockholm 22.4.1906 + Kastrup b. Kopenhagen 26.1.1947, and has issue see elsewhere

        (3)   **Caroline Mathilde Helene Ludwiga Auguste Beatrice Princess of Saxe-Coburg and Gotha** * Schloss Callenberg 22.6.1912 = (1) Coburg 14.12.1931 Friedrich Wolfgang Graf zu Castell-Rüdenhausen * Berlin 27.6.1906 ✗ over Portland Bill 11.6.1940 — div. = (2) Berlin 22.6.1938 Max Schnirring * Stuttgart-Untertürkheim 20.5.1896 + Stralsund 7.7.1944, = (3) Coburg 21.12.1948 Jim Andree * Düsseldorf 10.2.1912 — div. and had issue:

by 1st marriage:

XII   a.   **Bertram Friedrich Graf zu Castell-Rüdenhausen** * Golssen 12.7.1932 = Wien 10.10.1964 Felicitas Gräfin v. Auersperg * Wien 20.9.1944 and has issue:

XIII   a)   **Dominik Graf zu Castell-Rüdenhausen** * Wien 20.7.1965

XII   b.   **Konradin Friedrich Graf zu Castell-Rüdenhausen** * Berlin 10.10.1933 = Helsingfors 6.7.1961 Marta Catherina Lonegren * Helsingfors 17.4.1939 daughter of Bjarne Lonegren, and has issue:

XIII   a)   **Anne-Charlotte Catherina Victoria Gräfin zu Castell-Rüdenhausen** * Helsingfors 7.4.1962

          b)   **Carl Eduard Friedrich Hubertus Graf zu Castell-Rüdenhausen** * Helsingfors 15.3.1964

XII   c.   **Viktoria Adelheid Clementine Louise Gräfin zu Castell-Rüdenhausen** * Coburg 26.2.1935 = London 20.6.1960 Miles Huntingdon-Whiteley * Fareham 18.7.1929, and has issue:

XIII   a)   **Alice Louise Esther Margot Huntingdon-Whiteley** * London 22.7.1961

XIII   b)   **Beatrice Irene Helen Victoria Huntingdon-Whiteley** * London 6.9.1962

                          c)   **Leopold Maurice Huntingdon-Whiteley** * London 15.7.1965

by 2nd marriage:

XII   d.   **Calma Barbara Schnirring** * Valpariso 18.11.1938 = Fremont, Ohio 5.7.1961 Richard Berger * ... and has issue:

XIII   a)   **Sascha Berger** * Coburg 22.9.1961

                          b)   **Richard Berger** * Fremont, Ohio 7.7.1962

                          c)   **Victor Berger** * Fremont, Ohio ... 1963

XII   e.   **Dagmar Sibylla Schnirring** * Grosswusterwitz 22.11.1940 = Forcheim 26.2.1964 Heinrich Walz * ... and has issue:

XIII   a)   **Maria Walz** * München ... 8.1965

XII   f.   **Peter Michael Schnirring** * Grosswusterwitz 4.1.1943 + 6.2.1966

XI   (4)   **Dietmar Hubertus Friedrich Wilhelm Philipp Prince of Saxe-Coburg and Gotha** * Schloss Reinhardsbrunn 24.8.1909, ✕ Mosty, Russia 26.11.1943

        (5)   **Friedrich Josias Carl Eduard Ernst Kyrill Harald Prince of Saxe-Coburg and Gotha** * Schloss Callenburg 29.11.1918 = (1) Kassel 25.1.1942 **Victoria-Louise Gräfin zu Solms-Baruth** * Kassel 13.3.1921 daughter of Hans Graf zu Solms-Baruth – div. = (2) San Francisco 14.2.1948 Denyse de Muralt * Basle 14.12.1923 daughter of Gaston Robert de Muralt – div. = (3) ... Katherine Bremme * ...

by 1st marriage:

XII   a.   **Andreas Michael Arnim Siegfried Friedrich Hans Hubertus Prince of Saxe-Coburg and Gotha** * Kassel 21.3.1943

by 2nd marriage:

                   b.   **Maria Claudia Sibylla Princess of Saxe-Coburg and Gotha** * San Francisco 22.5.1949

                   c.   **Beatrice Charlotte Princess of Saxe-Coburg and Gotha** * Berne 15.7.1951

                   d.   **Adrian Vincenz Edward Prince of Saxe-Coburg and Gotha** * Coburg 18.10.1955

IX 9.   **Beatrice Mary Victoria Feodore Princess of Great Britain and Ireland** * Buckingham Palace 14.4.1857 + Balcombe Park 26.10.1944 = Osborne House 23.7.1885 Henry Prince of Battenberg * Milano 5.10.1858 + on board H.M.S. Blonde 20.1.1896, and had issue:

X   1)   **Alexander Albert Prince of Battenberg Marquis of Carisbrooke** * Windsor Castle 23.11.1886 + Kensington Palace 23.2.1960 = Chapel Royal, St. James's Palace 19.7.1917 Lady Irene Denison * London 4.7.1890 + London 16.7.1956, daughter of William Denison 2nd Earl of Londesborough and had issue:

XI   (1)   **Lady Iris Victoria Beatrice Grace Mountbatten** * Kensington Palace 13.1.1920 = (1) Haywards Heath 15.2.1941 Hamilton O'Malley * 19.10.1910 – div. = (2) Pound Ridge, N.J. 5.5.1957 Michael Kelly Bryan * 1916 – div. = (3) Toronto 11.12.1965 William Kemp * 1921 and has issue:

by 2nd marriage:

XII   a.   **Robin Bryan** * 20.12.1957

X   2)   **Victoria Eugenie Julia Ena Princess of Battenberg** * Balmoral Castle 24.10.1887 = Madrid 31.5.1906 **Alfonso XIII King of Spain** * Madrid 17.5.1886 + Roma 28.2.1941, and has issue see elsewhere

X 3) **Leopold Arthur Louis Prince of Battenberg**, later styled Lord Leopold Mountbatten * Windsor Castle 21.5.1889 + Kensington Palace 23.4.1922

4) **Maurice Victor Donald Prince of Battenberg** * Balmoral Castle 3.10.1891, ⚔ Sonnebeck 27.10.1914

VII **Ernest Augustus King of Hannover, Duke of Cumberland, Prince of Great Britain and Ireland** * Buckingham House 5.6.1771 + Schloss Herrenhausen 18.11.1851 = Neustrelitz 29.5.1815, London 29.8.1815 **Friederike Duchess of Mecklenburg-Strelitz** * Hannover 2.3.1778 + Hannover 29.6.1841 daughter of Karl II Duke of Mecklenburg-Strelitz, and widow of Prince Ludwig of Prussia, and of Friedrich Prinz zu Solms-Braunfels, and had issue:

VIII 1. **George V Frederick Alexander Charles Ernest Augustus King of Hannover, Duke of Cumberland, Prince of Great Britain and Ireland** * Berlin 27.5.1819 + Paris 12.6.1878 = Hannover 18.2.1843 **Marie Princess of Saxe-Altenburg** * Hildburghausen 14.4.1818 + Gmunden 9.1.1907 daughter of Joseph Duke of Saxe-Altenburg, and had issue:

IX 1) **Ernst August Wilhelm Adolf Georg Friedrich Crown Prince of Hannover, Duke of Cumberland, Prince of Great Britain and Ireland** * Hannover 21.9.1845 + Gmunden 14.11.1923 = Copenhagen 21.12.1878 **Thyra Princess of Denmark** * Kopenhagen 29.9.1853 + Gmunden 26.2.1933 daughter of Christian IX King of Denmark, and had issue:

X (1) **Alexandra Luise Marie Olga Elisabeth Therese Vera Princess of Hannover, Princess of Great Britain and Ireland** * Gmunden 29.9.1882 + Glücksburg 30.8.1963 = Gmunden 7.6.1904 **Friedrich Franz IV Grand Duke of Mecklenburg-Schwerin** * Palermo 9.4.1882 + Flensburg 17.11.1945, and had issue see elsewhere

(2) **Georg Wilhelm Christian Albert Edouard Alexander Friedrich Waldemar Ernst Adolf Prince of Hannover, Prince of Great Britain and Ireland, Earl of Armagh** * Gmunden 28.10.1880 + Nackel, Brandenburg 20.5.1912

(3) **Marie Louise Victoria Caroline Amelie Alexandra Augusta Friederike Princess of Hannover, Princess of Great Britain and Ireland** * Gmunden 11.10.1879 + Schloss Salem 31.1.1948 = Gmunden 10.7.1900 **Maximilian Margraf and Prince of Baden** * Baden-Baden 10.7.1867 + Konstanz 6.11.1929, and had issue see elsewhere

(4) **Olga Adelaide Louise Marie Alexandrine Agnes Princess of Hannover, Princess of Great Britain and Ireland** * Gmunden 11.7.1884 + Hubertihaus b. Gmunden 21.9.1958

(5) **Christian Friedrich Wilhelm Georg Peter Waldemar Prince of Hannover, Prince of Great Britain and Ireland** * Gmunden 4.7.1885 + Gmunden 3.9.1901

(6) **Ernst August Christian Georg Duke of Brunswick-Lüneburg, Prince of Hannover, Prince of Great Britain and Ireland, Earl of Armagh** * Penzing b. Wien 17.11.1887 + Schloss Marienburg 30.1.1953 = Berlin 24.5.1913 **Viktoria Luise Princess of Prussia** * Marmorpalais, Berlin 13.9.1892 daughter of Wilhelm II Emperor of Germany, and had issue:

XI a. **Ernst August Georg Wilhelm Christian Ludwig Franz Josef Nikolaus Duke of Brunswick-Lüneburg, Prince of Hannover, and of Great Britain and Ireland** * Brunswick 18.3.1914 = Schloss Marienburg 31.8. and Hannover 4.9.1951 **Ortrud Princess of Schleswig-Holstein-Sonderburg-Glücksburg** * Flensburg 19.12.1925 daughter of Albert Prince of Schleswig-Holstein-Sonderburg-Glücksburg, and has issue:

XII a) **Marie Viktoria Luise Hertha Friederike Princess of Hannover** * Hannover 26.11.1952

b) **Ernst August Albert Paul Otto Rupprecht Oskar Berthold Friedrich Ferdinand Christian Ludwig Prince of Hannover** * Hannover 26.2.1954

c) **Ludwig Rudolf Georg Wilhelm Philipp Friedrich Wolrad Maximilian Prince of Hannover** * Hannover 21.11.1955

d) **Olga Sophie Charlotte Anna Princess of Hannover** * Hannover 17.2.1958

e) **Alexandra Irene Margaritha Elisabeth Bathildis Princess of Hannover** * Hannover 18.2.1959

f) **Heinrich Julius Christian Otto Friedrich Franz Anton Günther Prince of Hannover** * Hannover 29.4.1961

XI		b.	**Georg Wilhelm Ernst August Friedrich Axel Prince of Hannover, Prince of Great Britain and Ireland** * Braunschweig 25.3.1915 = Salem 23.4.1946 **Sophie Princess of Greece and Denmark** * Corfu 26.6.1914 daughter of Andrew Prince of Greece and Denmark, and has issue:

XII

    a)   **Welf Ernst August Andreas Philipp Georg Wilhelm Ludwig Berthold Prince of Hannover** * Schloss Marienburg 25.1.1947

    b)   **Georg Paul Christian Prince of Hannover** * Schloss Salem 9.12.1949

    c)   **Friedrike-Elisabeth Viktoria Luise Alice Olga Theodora Helena Princess of Hannover** * Schloss Salem 15.10.1954

XI

    c.   **Friederike Luise Thyra Viktoria Margarete Sophie Olga Cecile Isabelle Christa Princess of Hannover, Princess of Great Britain and Ireland** * Blankenburg 18.4.1917 = Athens 9.1.1938 **Paul I King of Greece** * Athens 14.12.1901 + Athens 6.3.1964, and has issue see elsewhere

    d.   **Christian Oskar Ernst August Wilhelm Viktor Georg Heinrich Prince of Hannover** * Gmunden 1.9.1919 = Bruxelles 25.11.1963 Mireille Dutry * London 10.1.1946 daughter of Armand Dustry, and has issue:

XII

    a)   **Caroline Luise Mireille Irene Sophie Princess of Hannover** * 3.5.1965

XI

    e.   **Welf Heinrich Ernst August Georg Christian Berthold Friedrich Wilhelm Louis Ferdinand Prince of Hannover** * Gmunden 11.3.1923 = Büdingen 21.9.1960 **Alexandra Prinzessin zu Isenburg u. Büdingen** * Frankfurt-am-Main 23.10.1937 daughter of Otto Friedrich Fürst zu Isenburg u. Büdingen

IX   2)   **Friederike Sophie Marie Henriette Amelie Therese Princess of Hannover, Princess of Great Britain and Ireland** * Hannover 9.1.1848 * Biarritz 16.10.1926 = Windsor Castle 24.4.1880 Alfons Frhr. v. Pawel-Ramingen * Coburg 27.7.1843 + Biarritz 20.11.1932, and had issue:

X   (1)   **Victoria Georgine Beatrice Maude Anne Freiin. v. Pawel-Ramingen** * London 7.3.1881 + 27.3.1881

IX   3)   **Marie Ernestine Josephine Adolfine Henriette Therese Elisabeth Alexandra Princess of Hannover, Princess of Great Britain and Ireland** * Hannover 3.12.1849 + Gmunden 4.6.1904

22

VII   **Adolphus Frederick Duke of Cambridge, Prince of Great Britain and Ireland** * Buckingham House 24.2.1774 + Cambridge House, London 8.7.1850 = Kassel 7.5.1818, London 1.6.1818 **Augusta Princess of Hesse-Kassel** * Schloss Rumpenheim 25.7.1797 + St. James's Palace 6.4.1889 dau. of Friedrich Landgraf of Hesse-Kassel, and had issue:

VIII 1.   **George William Frederick Charles 2nd Duke of Cambridge, Prince of Great Britain and Ireland** * Hannover 26.3.1819 + Cambridge House 17.3.1904 = morganatically Clerkenwell 8.1.1840 Louisa Fairbrother * London 1816 + London 12.1.1890 dau. of Robert Baring, and had issue:

IX   1)   **George William Adolphus FitzGeorge** * London 27.8.1843 + Lucerne 2.9.1907 = Paris 25.11.1885 Rosa Baring * London 9.3.1854 + London 10.3.1927 dau. of William Baring, and had issue:

X   (1)   **George William Frederick FitzGeorge** * London 12.10.1892 + Tours 13.6.1960 = (1) 1918 Esther Vignon * 1888 + circa 1935 − div. = (2) 1934 France Bellanger * 1911 dau. of Robert Bellanger s.p.

   (2)   **Mabel Iris FitzGeorge** * London 23.9.1886 = (1) Chapel Royal St. James's Palace 12.12.1912 Robert Balfour * Stirling 7.3.1869 + Salcombe Regis 1.11.1942, = (2) London 12.8.1945 Vladimir Emmanuelovitch Prince Galitzine * St. Petersburg 5.6.1884 + London 13.7.1954, and has issue:

   by 1st marriage:

XI   a.   **Robert George Victor FitzGeorge Balfour** * London 15.9.1913 = Chapel Royal, St. James's Palace 4.12.1943 Mary Diana Christian * London 12.10.1914 dau. of Arthur Christian, and has issue:

XII   a)   **Diana Christian Mary FitzGeorge Balfour** * London 8.3.1946

   b)   **Robin Victor FitzGeorge Balfour** * London 5.6.1951

X   (3)   **George Daphné FitzGeorge** * London 23.2.1889 + Castiglione della Pescaia, Grosetto 1.6.1954 = London 8.12.1915 George Foster Earle * Cottingham 8.2.1890 + Baggrave Hall, Leicester 11.12.1965 − div. s.p.

IX   2)   **Sir Adolphus Augustus Frederick FitzGeorge** * London 30.1.1846 + London 17.12.1922 = (1) Hessle, Yorks 21.9.1875 Sophie Holden * 1857 + London 3.2.1920 dau. of Thomas Holden, = (2) Pimlico, Middlesex 28.10.1920 Margarita Watson * 1863 + London 26.2.1934 dau. of John Watson, and had issue:

   by 1st marriage:

X   (1)   **Olga Mary Adelaide FitzGeorge** * 11.6.1877 + Rouen 15.10.1920 = (1) London 18.12.1897 Sir Archibald Hamilton 5th Bart. * London 10.12.1876 + Selsey 18.3.1939 − div. = (2) London 5.1.1905 Robert Charlton Lane * London 26.1.1873 + Havant 23.5.1943 and had issue:

   by 1st marriage:

XI   a.   **George Edward Archibald Augustus FitzGeorge Hamilton** * London 30.12.1898 ✗ 18.5.1918

   b.   a daughter * & + 5.5.1902

   by 2nd marriage:

   a.   **Mary Alice Olga Sofia Jane Lane** * London 4.1.1919 = (1) Warlington 14.11.1939 Edward Hohler * London 22.1.1917 − div. = (2) London 14.5.1962 Ronald Scrivener * London 29.12.1919, and has issue:

   by 1st marriage:

XII   a)   **Olga Mary Hohler** * Windsor 11.10.1940

   b)   **Philippa Caroline Jane Hohler** * Harrogate 13.1.1942

XII		c)	**Frederick Christopher Gerald Hohler** * Windsor 30.8.1943
		d)	**Robert Henry Adolphus Hohler** * Maidstone, Kent 2.10.1947

IX   3)   **Sir Augustus Charles Frederick FitzGeorge** * London 12.6.1847 + London 30.10.1933

VIII   2.   **Augusta Caroline Charlotte Elisabeth Mary Sophia Louise Princess of Cambridge, Princess of Great Britain and Ireland** * Hannover 19.7.1822 + Neustrelitz 5.12.1916 = Buckingham Palace 28.6.1843 **Friedrich Wilhelm Grand Duke of Mecklenburg-Strelitz** * Neustrelitz 17.10.1819 + Neustrelitz 30.5.1904, and had issue see elsewhere

      3.   **Mary Adelaide Wilhelmine Elisabeth Princess of Cambridge, Princess of Great Britain and Ireland** * Hannover 27.11.1833 + White Lodge, Richmond 27.10.1897 = Kew 12.6.1866 **Francis Prince and Duke of Teck** * Wien 27.8.1837 + White Lodge, Richmond 20.1.1900, and had issue:

IX   1)   **Victoria Mary Augusta Louise Olga Pauline Claudine Agnes Princess of Teck** * Kensington Palace 26.5.1867 + Marlborough House 24.3.1953 = Chapel Royal, St. James's Palace 6.7.1893 **George V, King of Great Britain and Ireland, Emperor of India** * Marlborough House 3.6.1865 + Sandringham House 20.1.1936, and had issue see elsewhere

      2)   **Adolphus Charles Alexander Albert Edward George Philip Louis Ladislaus 2nd Duke of Teck and 1st Marquis of Cambridge** * Kensington Palace 13.8.1868 + Shotton Hall, Shrewsbury 24.10.1927 = Eaton Hall, Chester 12.12.1894 Lady Margaret Grosvenor * Eaton Hall 9.4.1873 + London 27.3.1929, daughter of Hugh Grosvenor 1st Duke of Westminster, and had issue:

X   (1)   **George Francis Hugh 2nd Marquis of Cambridge** * Grosvenor House, London 11.10.1895 = Woodhouse, Leicestershire 10.4.1923 Dorothy Westenra Hastings * Cirencester 18.5.1899, daughter of Hon. Osmond Westenra Hastings, and has issue:

XI   a.   **Lady Mary Ilona Margaret Cambridge** * London 24.9.1924 = Kirtling, Newmarket 9.11.1950 Peter Whitley * Singapore 22.10.1923, and has issue:

XII   a)   **Sarah Elisabeth Whitley** * London 30.11.1954

               b)   **Charles Francis Peter Whitley** * Brighton 10.9.1961

X   (2)   **Victoria Constance Mary Princess of Teck**, later known as Lady Mary Cambridge * White Lodge, Richmond 12.6.1897 = St. Margaret's, Westminster 14.6.1923 Henry Fitzroy Somerset 10th Duke of Beaufort * London 4.4.1900 s.p.

          (3)   **Helena Frances Augusta Princess of Teck**, later known as Lady Helena Cambridge * Grosvenor House 23.10.1899 = Windsor Castle 2.9.1919 John Evelyn Gibbs * London 22.12.1879 + Tetbury 11.10.1932 s.p.

          (4)   **Frederick Charles Edward Prince of Teck**, later known as Lord Frederick Cambridge * Wien 24.9.1907 ✕ France May 1940

X   3)   **Francis Joseph Leopold Frederick Prince of Teck** * Kensington Palace 9.1.1870 + London 22.10.1910

      4)   **Alexander Augustus Frederick William Alfred George Prince of Teck, Earl of Athlone** * Kensington Palace 14.4.1874 + Kensington Palace 16.1.1957 = Windsor Castle 10.2.1904 **Alice Princess of Albany, Princess of Great Britain and Ireland** * Windsor Castle 25.2.1883 daughter of Leopold Duke of Albany, and had issue:

XI   (1)   **May Helen Emma Princess of Teck**, later known as Lady May Cambridge * Claremont 23.1.1906 = Balcombe 24.10.1931 Sir Henry Abel-Smith * London 8.3.1900, and has issue:

XII   a.   **Anne Mary Sibylla Abel-Smith** * London 28.7.1932 = Windsor Castle 14.12.1957 David Lidell-Grainger * London 26.1.1930, and has issue:

24

XIII   a) **Ian Richard Peregrine Lidell-Grainger** * Edinburgh 23.2.1959

        b) **Charles Montague Lidell-Grainger** * Edinburgh 23.7.1960

        c) **Simon Rupert Lidell-Grainger** * Edinburgh 27.12.1962

        d) **Alice Mary Lidell-Grainger** * Edinburgh 3.3.1965

XII   b. **Richard Francis Abel-Smith** * London 11.10.1933 = London 29.4.1960 Marcia Kendrew * Fulmer Chase 27.1.1940 daughter of Sir Douglas Kendrew, and has issue:

XIII   a) **Katherine Emma Abel-Smith** * Windsor 11.3.1961

XII   c. **Elisabeth Alice Abel-Smith** * London 5.9.1936 = London 29.4.1965 Peter Wise * London 29.12.1929

XI (2) **Rupert Alexander George Augustus Prince of Teck**, later styled Viscount Tremanton * Claremont 24.8.1907 + Bellevue-sur-Saône 15.4.1928

   (3) **Maurice Francis George Prince of Teck** * Claremont 29.3.1910 + Schloss Reinhardsbrunn 14.9.1910

2 The Descendants of Henriette Anne Princess of England 1644-1670 and Philippe 1 Duc d'Orleans 1640-1701.

II   **Henriette Anne Princess of England, Scotland, and Ireland** * Exeter 16.6.1644 + St-Cloud 30.6.1670 = Palais-Royal 31.3.1661 Philippe I Duc d'Orleans * St-Germain-en-Laye 21.9.1640 + St-Cloud 9.6.1701, and had issue:

III 1.   **Marie Louise, Mlle. d'Orleans** * Palais Royal 27.3.1662 + Madrid 12.2.1689 = by proxy Fontainbleau 31.8.1679, and in person Burgos 18.11.1679 Carlos II King of Spain Madrid * 6.11.1661 + Madrid 1.11.1700, s.p.

     2.   **Philippe Charles d'Orleans Duc de Valois** * Fontainbleau 16.7.1664 + 8.12.1666

     3.   a daughter * & + Versailles 9.7.1665

     4.   **Anne Marie, Mlle. de Valois** * St-Cloud 27.8.1669 + Torino 26.8.1728 = by proxy Palais-Royal 10.4.1684 Vittorio Amadeo II King of Sardinia * Torino 14.5.1666 + Rivoli 31.10.1732, and had issue   *see overleaf*

III   **Anne Marie[1] Princess of Orleans** * St-Cloud 27.8.1669 + Torino 26.8.1728 = Palais Royal by proxy 10.4.1684 Vittorio Amadeo II King of Sardinia, Duke of Savoy * Torino 14.5.1666 + Rivoli 31.10.1732, and had issue:

IV   1.   **Marie Adelaide Princess of Savoy** * Torino 6.12.1685 + Versailles 12.2.1712 = Versailles 7.12.1697 Louis de Bourbon, Duc de Bourgogne * Versailles 6.8.1682 + Marly 18.2.1712, and had issue:

V   1)   **Louis Duc de Bretagne** * Versailles 25.6.1704 + Versailles 13.4.1705

    2)   **Louis Duc de Bretagne** * Versailles 8.1.1707 + Versailles 8.3.1712

    3)   **Louis XV King of France** * Versailles 15.2.1710 + Versailles 10.5.1774 = Fontainbleau 5.9.1725 Marie Leszczynska Princess of Poland * Breslau 23.6.1703 + Versailles 24.6.1768 dau. of Stanislaus I Leszczynski King of Poland, and had issue:

VI   (1)   **Louise Elisabeth de Bourbon Princess of France** * Versailles 14.8.1727 + Versailles 6.12.1759 = Alcalá 25.10.1739 Filippo de Borbón Duke of Parma * Madrid 15.3.1720 + Alessandria 18.7.1765, and had issue:

VII   a.   **Isabel Maria Luisa Antoinetta Ferdinanda Giuseppina Saveria Domenica Giovanna Princess of Parma, Infanta of Spain** * Madrid 31.12.1741 + Wien 27.11.1763 = Wien 6.10.1760 **Emperor Joseph II** * Schönbrunn 13.3.1741 + Wien 20.2.1790, and had issue see elsewhere

    b.   **Ferdinando Maria Filippo Lodovico Sebastiano Francesco Giacomo Duke of Parma, Plaisance and Guastalla** * Parma 20.1.1751 + Fontevio 9.10.1802 = Château de Colorno 19.7.1769 **Maria Amelia Archduchess of Austria** * Wien 26.2.1746 + Prag 18.6.1804 dau. of Emperor Franz I, and had issue:

VIII   a)   **Carolina Maria Teresa Giuseppa Princess of Bourbon-Parma** * 22.11.1770 + Dresden 1.3.1804 = 9.5.1792 **Maximilian Prince of Saxony** * Dresden 13.4.1759 + Dresden 3.1.1838 and had issue see elsewhere

    b)   **Lodovico I Duke of Parma, King of Etruria** * Plaisance 5.7.1773 + Firenze 27.5.1803 = Madrid 25.8.1795 **Maria Luisa Infanta of Spain** * San Ildefonso 6.7.1782 + Roma 13.3.1824 dau. of Carlos IV King of Spain, and had issue:

IX   (a)   **Carlo Lodovico II Duke of Parma** * Madrid 22.12.1799 + Nice 16.4.1883 = Torino 5.9.1820 **Maria Teresa Princess of Savoy** * Roma 19.9.1803 + San Martino 16.7.1879 dau. of Vittorio Emanuele I King of Sardinia, and had issue:

X   1a.   **Luisa Francesca di Paola Teresa Maria Anna Clothilde Beatrice Princess of Bourbon-Parma** * Lucca 29.10.1821 + 8.9.1823

    2a.   **Fernando Carlo III Giuseppe Maria Vittorio Baldasarre Duke of Parma** * Lucca 14.1.1823 + Parma 27.3.1854 = Frohsdorf 10.11.1845 **Louise Marie Princess of France** * Paris 21.9.1819 + Venezia 1.2.1864 dau. of Charles Ferdinand Duc de Berry, and had issue:

XI   1b.   **Margherita Maria Teresa Enrichetta Princess of Bourbon-Parma** * Parma 1.1.1847 + Viareggio 29.1.1893 = Frohsdorf 4.2.1867 **Don Carlos Duque de Madrid, Infant of Spain** * Laybach 30.3.1848 + Varese 18.7.1909, and had issue see elsewhere

---

1   In addition to the children given in the work Queen Anne Marie also had 1) a daughter * & + 6.6.1690 2) a daughter * & + 19.7.1691 and 3) a son * & + 9.11.1697

2b. **Roberto I Carlo Luigi Duke of Parma** * Firenze 9.7.1848 + Pianore, near Viareggio 16.11.1907 = (1) Roma 5.4.1869 **Maria Pia Princess of Bourbon-Sicily** * Gaeta 2.8.1849 + Biarritz 29.9.1882 dau. of Ferdinando II King of Naples and Sicily; = (2) Schloss Fischhorn 15.10.1884 **Maria Antonia Princess of Bragança, Infanta of Portugal** * Bronnbach 28.11.1862 + Schloss Berg, Luxembourg 14.5.1959 dau. of Miguel I Duke of Bragança, and had issue:

by 1st marriage

1c. **Maria Luisa Pia Teresa Ana Ferdinanda Francesca Antoinetta Margherita Giuseppina Carolina Bianca Lucia Apolonia Princess of Bourbon-Parma** * Roma 17.1.1870 + Sofia 31.1.1899 = Pianore 20.4.1893 **Ferdinand I King of Bulgaria** * Wien 26.2.1861 + Coburg 10.9.1948, and had issue see elsewhere

2c. **Ferdinando Maria Carlo Pio Luigi Francesco Giuseppe Pietro Paolo Roberto Antonio Prince of Bourbon-Parma** * Bozen 5.3.1871 + Cannes 14.4.1872

3c. **Luisa Maria Annunziata Enrichetta Teresa Princess of Bourbon-Parma** * Cannes 24.3.1872 + Brunnsee 22.6.1943

4c. **Enrico I Maria Alberto Ferdinando Carlo Pio Luigi Antonio Duke of Parma** * Wartegg 13.6.1873 + Pianore 10.5.1939

5c. **Maria Immacolata Luisa Francesca Praxedes Annunziata Teresa Pia Ana Ferdinanda Antoinetta Giuseppina Lucia Apolonia Filomena Clothilde Emerenciana Maria Giulia Princess of Bourbon-Parma** * Wartegg 21.7.1874 + Pianore 16.5.1914

6c. **Giuseppe I Maria Pietro Paolo Francesco Roberto Tomaso d'Aquino Andreas-Avellino Biago Mauro Carlo Stanislao Luigi Filippo Neri Leone Bernardo Ferdinando Duke of Parma** * Biarritz 30.6.1875 + Pianore 7.1.1950

7c. **Maria Teresa Pia Luisa Immacolata Ferdinanda Enrichetta Giuseppina Alfona Princess of Bourbon-Parma** * Biarritz 15.10.1876 + Brunnsee 25.1.1959

8c. **Maria Pia Antoinetta Carolina Princess of Bourbon-Parma** * Biarritz 9.10.1877 + Wartegg 29.1.1915

9c. **Beatrice Colomba Maria Immacolata Leonia Princess of Bourbon-Parma** * Biarritz 9.1.1879 + Brunnsee 11.3.1946 = Schwartzau 12.8.1906 **Conte Pietro Lucchesi Palli** * Roma 7.2.1870 + Brunnsee 5.12.1939, and has issue see elsewhere

10c. **Elie Roberto Carlos Maria Pio José Duke of Parma** * Biarritz 23.7.1880 + Friedberg Steiermk. 27.6.1959 = Wien 25.5.1903 **Maria Anna Archduchess of Austria** * Linz 6.1.1882 + Lausanne 25.2.1940 dau. of Friedrich Archduke of Austria, Duke of Teschen, and had issue:

1d. **Elisabetta Maria Anna Pia Luisa Princess of Bourbon-Parma** * Wien 17.3.1904

2d. **Carlo Luigi Federico Antonio Roberto Elias Maria Prince of Bourbon-Parma** * Wien 22.9.1905 + Baden b. Wien 26.9.1912

3d. **Maria Francesca Giuseppa Raniera Enrichetta Pia Luisa Princess of Bourbon-Parma** * Weilburg b. Baden 5.9.1906

XIII

4d. **Roberto II Ranieri Alexis Luigi Enrico Deodato Elias Pio Maria Duke of Parma** * Weilburg 7.8.1909

5d. **Francesco Alfonso Gabriele Luigi Enrico Roberto Pio Carlo Elias Maria Prince of Bourbon-Parma** * Weilburg 14.6.1913 + Magyar-Ovar 29.5.1939

6d. **Giovanna Isabella Alfonsina Pia Luisa Maria Princess of Bourbon-Parma** * Weilburg 8.7.1916 + Toledana 1.11.1949

7d. **Alice Maria Francesca Luisa Pia Ana Valeria Princess of Bourbon-Parma** * Wien 13.11.1917 = Wien 16.4.1936 **Alfonso Prince of Bourbon-Sicily, Infant of Spain** * Madrid 30.11.1901 + Madrid 3.2.1964, and has issue see elsewhere

8d. **Maria Cristina Albertina Enricheta Luisa Pia Carlota Princess of Bourbon-Parma** * Wien 7.6.1925

XII

11c. **Maria Anastasia Antoinetta Cristina Enrichetta Princess of Bourbon-Parma** * Biarritz 25.8.1881 + Biarritz 7.9.1881

12c. **Augusto Prince of Bourbon-Parma** * & + Biarritz 29.9.1882

by 2nd marriage:

13c. **Maria da Neves Adelaide Enrichetta Pia Antonia Princess of Bourbon-Parma** * Wartegg 5.8.1885 + Solesmes, Sarthe 6.2.1959

14c. **Sixte Ferdinando Maria Ignazio Alfonso Roberto Michael Francesco Carlo Luigi Saverio Giuseppe Antonio Pio Taddeo Giovanni Sebastiano Paolo Biagio Estanislao Benedetto Bernardo Marco Prince of Bourbon-Parma** * Wartegg 1.8.1886 + Paris 14.3.1934 = Paris 12.11.1919 **Hedwige de La Rochefoucauld** * Paris 15.2.1896 dau. of Armand de La Rochefoucauld 5th Duc de Doudeauville, and had issue:

XIII

1d. **Isabelle Marie Antoinette Louise Hedwige Princess of Bourbon-Parma** * Paris 14.3.1922 = Paris 23.6.1943 **Comte Roger de La Rochefoucauld** * Paris 8.10.1915, and has issue:

XIV

1e. **Eudes de La Rochefoucauld** * Paris 23.7.1944

2e. **Sixte de La Rochefoucauld** * Paris 8.2.1946

3e. **Hugues de La Rochefoucauld** * Paris 30.1.1948

4e. **Charles de La Rochefoucauld** * Paris 5.3.1950

5e. **Robert de La Rochefoucauld** * ... 1952

XII

15c. **Francesco Xavier Carlo Maria Anna Giuseppe Prince of Bourbon-Parma** * Camaiore 25.5.1889 = Lignières 12.11.1927 Marie Madeleine de Bourbon-Busset * Paris 23.3.1898 dau. of Georges de Bourbon-Busset Comte de Lignières, and has issue:

XIII

1d. **Marie Francoise Princess of Bourbon-Parma** * Paris 19.8.1928 = Paris 7.1.1960 Eduard Prinz v. Lobkowicz * New York 12.6.1926, and has issue:

1e.   **Marie Eduard Xavier Ferdinand August Gaspard Prinz v. Lobkowicz** * Paris 18.10.1960

2e.   **Maria Robert Emanuel Josef Michel Benoit Melchior Prinz v. Lobkowicz** * Paris 31.12.1961

3e.   **Marie Charles-Henri Hugues Xavier Benoit Michel Eduard Joseph Balthasar Prinz v. Lobkowicz** * Paris 17.5.1964

2d.   **Hugues (Carlos) Prince of Bourbon-Parma** * Paris 8.4.1930 = Roma 29.4.1964 **Irene Princess of the Netherlands** * Soestdijk 5.8.1939 dau. of Queen Juliana of the Netherlands

3d.   **Marie Therese Princess of Bourbon-Parma** * Paris 28.7.1933

4d.   **Cécile Marie Antonie Madeleine Jeanne Agnes Françoise Princess of Bourbon-Parma** * Paris 12.4.1935

5d.   **Marie des Neiges Princess of Bourbon-Parma** * Paris 29.4.1937

6d.   **Sixte Henri Prince of Bourbon-Parma** * Pau 22.7.1940

16c. **Francesca Giuseppa Maria Teresa Elisabetta Sofia Anna Luisa Eulalia Michaela Raffaela Gabriella Princess of Bourbon-Parma** * Schwartzau 22.4.1890

17c. **Zita Maria delle Gazie Adelgonda Michaela Raffaela Gabriella Giuseppina Antonia Luisa Agnese Princess of Bourbon-Parma** * Pianore 9.5.1892 = Schwartzau 21.10.1911 **Karl I Emperor of Austria, King of Hungary** * Persenbeug 17.8.1887 + Funchal 1.4.1922, and has issue see elsewhere

18c. **Felix Maria Vincenzo Prince of Bourbon-Parma** * Schwartzau 28.9.1893 = Luxembourg 6.11.1919 **Charlotte Grand Duchess of Luxembourg** * Schloss Berg 23.1.1896, and has issue see elsewhere

19c. **Rene Carlo Maria Giuseppe Prince of Bourbon-Parma** * Schwartzau 17.10.1894 + Kopenhagen 30.7.1962 = Kopenhagen 9.6.1921 **Margarethe Princess of Denmark** * Bernstorff 17.9.1895 dau. of Valdemar Prince of Denmark, and had issue:

1d.   **Jacques Marie Antoine Robert Valdemar Charles Felix Sixte Ansgar Prince of Bourbon-Parma** * Longwy 9.6.1922 = Kopenhagen 9.6.1947 **Birgitta Countess v. Holstein-Ledreborg** * Schloss Ledreborg 29.6.1922 dau. of Joseph Count v. Holstein-Ledreborg, and has issue:

1e.   **Philippe Prince of Bourbon-Parma** * Kopenhagen 22.1.1949

2e.   **Lorraine Princess of Bourbon-Parma** * Roskilde 27.7.1951

XIII	2d. **Anne Antoinette Francoise Charlotte Princess of Bourbon-Parma** * Paris 18.9.1923 = Athens 10.6.1948 **Michael King of Roumania** * Sinaia 25.10.1921, and has issue see elsewhere
	3d. **Michel Marie Xavier Valdemar Georges Robert Charles Aymard Prince of Bourbon-Parma** * Paris 4.3.1926 = Paris 9.6.1951 Yolande Princess de Broglie-Revel * Paris 26.4.1928 dau. of Joseph Prince de Broglie-Revel, and has issue:
XIV	1e. **Inès Princess of Bourbon-Parma** * Paris 9.5.1952
	2e. **Eric Prince of Bourbon-Parma** * Kopenhagen 28.8.1953
	3e. **Sybil Princess of Bourbon-Parma** * Paris 10.11.1954
	4e. **Victoire Princess of Bourbon-Parma** * Crespières 8.11.1957
	5e. **Charles Emanuel Prince of Bourbon-Parma** * 3.6.1961
XIII	4d. **André Prince of Bourbon-Parma** * Paris 6.3.1928 = Villefranche-sur-Mer 9.5.1960 Paulette Gacry * Paris 5.9.1935 dau. of Paul Gacry, and has issue:
XIV	1e. **Sophie de Bourbon-Parma** * 13.11.1961
XII	20c. **Maria Antonia Sofia Aloysia Giuseppa Michaela Gabriela Raffaela Anna Princess of Bourbon-Parma** * Schwartzau 7.11.1895
	21c. **Isabella Maria Anna Princess of Bourbon-Parma** * Schwartzau 14.6.1898
	22c. **Louis Carlo Leopoldo Roberto Prince of Bourbon-Parma** * Schwartzau 5.12.1899 = Roma 23.1.1939 **Maria Francesca Princess of Savoy** * Roma 26.12.1914 dau. of Vittorio Emanuele III King of Italy, and has issue:
XIII	1d. **Guido Sisto Luigi Roberto Vittorio Prince of Bourbon-Parma** * Cannes 7.8.1940 = Cannes 11.7.1964 Brigitte Peu-Duvallon * Cannes 13.8.1943 dau. of Victor Peu-Duvallon
	2d. **Remigio Francesco Saverio Luigi Roberto Vittorio Prince of Bourbon-Parma** * Cannes 14.7.1942
	3d. **Chantal Maria Elena Antoinetta Carlota Princess of Bourbon-Parma** * Cannes 24.11.1946
	4d. **Jean Bernard Rémy Prince of Bourbon-Parma** * Cannes 15.10.1961
XII	23c. **Enrichetta Anna Maria Immacolata Antonia Roberta Princess of Bourbon-Parma** * Pianore 8.3.1903
	24c. **Gaëtan Maria Giuseppe Pio Prince of Bourbon-Parma** * Pianore 3.6.1905 + Mandelieu, Cannes 9.3.1958 = Paris 29.4.1931 **Margarete Princess v. Thurn u. Taxis** * Château de Beloeil 8.11.1909 dau. of Alexander Prince v. Thurn u. Taxis, Duca di Castel-Duino and has issue:

XIII   1d.   **Diana Margharita Princess of Bourbon-Parma** * Paris 22.5.1932 = Krauchenwies b. Sigmaringen 16.4.1955 **Franz Joseph Prince of Hohenzollern-Sigmaringen** * Schloss Umkirch 15.3.1926 and has issue see elsewhere

XI   3b.   **Alicia Maria Carolina Ferdinanda Rachael Giovanna Filomena Princess of Bourbon-Parma** * Parma 27.12.1849 + Schwertberg 16.1.1935 = Frohsdorf 11.1.1868 **Ferdinand IV Grand Duke of Tuscany, Archduke of Austria** * Firenze 10.6.1835 + Salzburg 17.1.1908, and had issue see elsewhere

               4b.   **Enrico Carlo Luigi Giorgio Abraham Paolo Maria Prince of Bourbon-Parma, Comte de Bardi** * Parma 12.2.1851 + Menton 14.4.1905 = (1) Cannes 25.11.1873 **Maria Immacolata Princess of Bourbon-Sicily** * Napoli 21.1.1855 + Pau 23.8.1874 dau. of Ferdinando II King of Naples and Sicily = (2) Salzburg 15.10.1876 **Adelgundes Princess of Bragança, Infanta of Portugal** * Bronnbach 10.11.1858 + Gunten, Berne 15.4.1946 dau. of Miguel Duke of Bragança s.p.

IX   (b)   **Maria Luisa Carlota Princess of Bourbon-Parma** * Barcelona 2.10.1802 + Roma 18.3.1857 = (1) Dresden 7.11.1825 **Maximilian Prince of Saxony** * Dresden 13.4.1759 + Dresden 3.1.1838 = (2) 22.7.1849 Chevalier Francesco Rossi * ... + Venezia 30.9.1854 = (3) 19.2.1855 Conte Giovanni Vimercati * 21.12.1788 + ... s.p.

VIII   :)   **Maria Antonietta Giuseppina Walpurga Anna Luisa Vicenza Margherita Caterina Princess of Bourbon-Parma** * Parma 28.11.1774 + Roma 20.2.1841

          d)   **Carlota Maria Ferdinanda Teresa Anna Giuseppa Giovanna Luisa Vicenza Rosalia Princess of Bourbon-Parma** * Parma 7.9.1777 + Roma 5.4.1813

          e)   **Filippo Maria Lodovico Francesco Prince of Bourbon-Parma** * 22.3.1783 + 2.7.1786

          f)   **Antoinetta Luisa Princess of Bourbon-Parma** * Parma 21.10.1784 died young

          g)   **Maria Luisa Princess of Bourbon-Parma** * Parma 17.4.1787 + 22.11.1789

VII   c.   **Maria Luisa Teresa Princess of Bourbon-Parma** * Parma 9.12.1751 + Roma 2.1.1819 = San Ildefonso 4.9.1765 **Carlos IV King of Spain** * Portici 11.11.1748 + Roma 19.1.1819 and had issue see elsewhere

VI   (2)   **Anne Henriette de Bourbon Princess of France** * Versailles 14.8.1727 + Versailles 10.2.1752

       (3)   **Marie Louise de Bourbon Princess of France** * Versailles 28.7.1728 + Versailles 19.2.1733

       (4)   **Mgr. Louis Dauphin of France** * Versailles 4.9.1729 + Fontainbleau 20.12.1765 = (1) Versailles 23.2.1745 Maria Teresa Infanta of Spain * Madrid 11.6.1726 + Versailles 22.7.1746 dau. of Felipe V King of Spain = (2) Versailles 9.2.1747 **Maria Josepha Princess of Saxony** * Dresden 4.11.1731 + Versailles 13.3.1767 dau. of Friedrich August II Elector of Saxony, and had issue:

by 1st marriage:

VII   a.   **Marie Thérèse Princess of France** * Versailles 19.7.1746 + Versailles 27.4.1748

by 2nd marriage:

        b.   a child * & + 30.1.1748

        c.   a child * & + 10.5.1749

        d.   **Marie Zéphyrine Princess of France** * Versailles 26.8.1750 + Versailles 1.9.1755

        e.   **Louis Joseph Xavier Duc de Bourgogne** * Versailles 13.9.1751 + Versailles 22.3.1761

VII	f.	a daughter * & + 9.3.1752

g. **Xavier Marie Joseph Duc d'Acquitaine** * Versailles 8.9.1753 + Versailles 22.2.1754

h. **Louis XVI Auguste King of France** * Versailles 23.8.1754 + Paris 21.1.1793 = Versailles 16.5.1770 **Marie Antoinette Archduchess of Austria** * Wien 2.11.1755 + Paris 16.10.1793 dau. of Emperor Franz I, and had issue:

VIII

a) **Marie Thérèse Charlotte Princess of France** * Versailles 19.12.1778 + Frohsdorf .19.10.1851 = Kitau, Kurland 10.6.1799 **Louis Antoine Duc d'Angoulême** * Versailles 6.8.1775 + Goritz 3.6.1844, s.p.

b) **Louis Joseph Xavier François Dauphin of France** * Versailles 22.10.1781 + Château de Meudon 4.6.1789

c) **Louis (XVII) Charles Dauphin of France** * Versailles 27.3.1785 + The Temple 8.6.1795

d) **Sophie Hélène Béatrix Princess of France** * Versailles 9.7.1786 + Versailles 16.6.1787

VII

i. **Louis XVIII Stanislas Xavier King of France** * Versailles 17.11.1755 + Tuileries 16.9.1824 = Versailles 14.5.1771 **Marie Giuseppina Princess of Savoy** * Torino 2.9.1753 + Hartwell House, Aylesbury 13.11.1810 dau. of Vittorio Amadeo III King of Sardinia s.p.

j. **Charles X Philippe King of France** * Versailles 9.10.1757 + Schloss Graffenberg, Goritz 6.11.1836 = Versailles 16.11.1773 **Maria Teresa Princess of Savoy** * Torino 31.1.1756 + Graz 2.6.1805 dau. of Vittorio Amadeo III King of Savoy, and had issue:

VIII

a) **Louis Antoine Duc d'Angoulême** * Versailles 6.8.1775 + Goritz 3.6.1844 = Mitau 10.6.1799 **Marie Thérèse Princess of France** * Versailles 19.12.1778 + Frohsdorf 19.10.1851 dau. of Louis XVI King of France s.p.

b) a daughter * Versailles 5.8.1776 + 11.8.1776

c) **Charles Ferdinand Duc de Berry** * Versailles 24.1.1778 + Paris 14.2.1820 = Paris 17.6.1816 **Maria Carolina Princess of Bourbon-Sicily** * Napoli 5.11.1798 + Schloss Brunnsee 17.4.1870 dau. of Francesco I King of Naples and Sicily, and had issue:

IX

(a) **Louise Isabelle Princess of France** * Paris 13.7.1817 + 14.7.1817

(b) a son * & + Paris 13.9.1818

(c) **Louise Marie Thérèse Princess of France** * Paris 21.9.1819 + Palazzo Giustiniani, Venezia 1.2.1864 = Frohsdorf 10.11.1845 **Carlo III Duke of Parma** * Lucca 14.1.1823 + Parma 27.3.1854, and had issue see elsewhere

(d) **Henri (V) Charles Ferdinand Marie Dieudonné Comte de Chambord** * Tuileries Palace 29.9.1820 + Frohsdorf 24.8.1883 = Bruck a.d. Mur 16.11.1846 **Marie Therese Archduchess of Austria, Princess of Modena** * Modena 14.7.1817 + Goritz 25.3.1886 dau. of Francesco IV Duke of Modena, Archduke of Austria s.p.

VIII

d) **Sophie Princess of France** * Versailles 6.1.1783 + Choisy-le-Roi 22.6.1783

VII

k. **Marie Adélaide Clotilde Xavière Princess of France** * Versailles 23.9.1759 + Napoli 7.3.1802 = Chambéry 6.9.1775 **Carlo Emanuele IV King of Sardinia** * Torino 24.5.1751 + 6.10.1819 s.p.

l. **Élisabeth Philippine Marie Hélène Princess of France** * Versailles 3.5.1764 + Paris 10.5.1794

VI

(5) **Philippe Duc d'Anjou** * Versailles 30.8.1730 + Versailles 9.4.1733

(6) **Marie Adélaide Princess of France** * Versailles 23.3.1732 + Trieste 27.2.1800

(7)   **Victoire Louise Marie Thérèse Princess of France** * Versailles 11.5.1733 + Trieste 7.6.1799

(8)   **Sophie Philippine Élisabeth Justine Princess of France** * Versailles 27.7.1734 + Versailles 3.3.1782

(9)   **Thérèse Felicie Princess of France** * Versailles 16.5.1736 + Abbaye de Fontevrault 28.9.1744

(10) **Louise Marie Princess of France** * Versailles 15.7.1737 + Carmel St-Denis 23.12.1787

IV 2. **Maria Anna Princess of Savoy** * 14.8.1687 + 5.8.1690

    3. **Maria Luisa Gabriella Princess of Savoy** * Torino 17.9.1688 + Madrid 14.2.1714 = Figueras 2.11.1701
Felipe V King of Spain formerly Duc d'Anjou * Versailles 19.12.1683 + Madrid 9.7.1746 and had issue:

V   1) **Luis I King of Spain** * Madrid 25.8.1707 + Madrid 31.8.1724 = Lerma 18.8.1723 **Elisabeth Princess of Orleans** * Versailles 11.12.1709 + Palais du Luxembourg, Paris 16.6.1742 dau. of Philippe II Duc d'Orleans, s.p.

   2) **Felipe Luis Infant of Spain** * 7.7.1709 + 8.7.1709

   3) **Felipe Pedro Gabriel Infant of Spain** * Madrid 7.6.1712 + Madrid 29.12.1719

   4) **Ferdinando VI King of Spain** * Madrid 23.9.1713 + Villaviciosa 10.8.1759 = Badajoz 20.1.1729 Maria Barbara Princess of Bragança, Infanta of Portugal * Lisboa 4.12.1711 + Aranjeuz 27.8.1758 dau. of João V King of Portugal, s.p.

IV 4. **Vittorio Amadeo Giovanni Filippo Prince of Piedmont, Prince of Savoy** * 6.5.1699 + 22.3.1715

    5. **Carlo Emanuele III King of Sardinia** * Torino 27.4.1701 + Torino 20.2.1773 = (1) 16.2.1722 Anne Christine Pfalzgräfin v. Sulzbach * 5.2.1704 + 12.3.1723 dau. of Theodor Pfalzgraf v. Sulzbach; = (2) 23.7.1724 Polixene Landgräfin of Hesse-Rheinfels-Rotenburg * 21.9.1706 + Torino 13.1.1735 dau. of Ernst Leopold Landgraf of Hesse-Rheinfels-Rotenburg; = (3) 1.4.1737 **Elisabeth Therese Princess of Lorraine** * Lunéville 15.10.1711 + Torino 3.7.1741 dau. of Leopold Duke of Lorraine, and had issue:

by 1st marriage:

V   1) **Vittorio Amadeo Theodor Duke of Aosta, Prince of Savoy** * Torino 7.3.1723 + Torino 11.8.1725

by 2nd marriage:

   2) **Vittorio Amadeo III Maria King of Sardinia** * Torino 26.6.1726 + Torino 16.10.1796 = Oulx 31.5.1750 Maria Antoinetta Infanta of Spain * Seville 17.11.1729 + Château de Moncalieri 19.9.1785 dau. of Felipe V King of Spain, and had issue:

VI   (1) **Carlo Emanuele IV Fernando Maria King of Sardinia** * Torino 24.5.1751 + 6.10.1819 = Chambéry 6.9.1775 **Marie Adélaide Clothilde Princess of France** * Versailles 23.9.1759 + Napoli 7.3.1802 dau. of Louis Dauphin of France, s.p.

   (2) **Carlotta Isabella Maria Princess of Savoy** * Torino 16.7.1752 + Torino 17.4.1755

   (3) **Maria Giuseppina Luisa Princess of Savoy** * Torino 2.9.1753 + Hartwell House, Aylesbury 13.11.1810 = Versailles 14.5.1771 **Louis XVIII King of France** * Versailles 17.11.1755 + Tuileries 16.9.1824 s.p.

   (4) **Amadeo Alessandro Maria Duke of Monferrato, Prince of Savoy** * Torino 5.10.1754 + Torino 29.4.1755

   (5) **Maria Teresa Princess of Savoy** * Torino 31.1.1756 + Graz 2.6.1805 = Versailles 16.11.1773 **Charles X King of France** * Versailles 9.10.1757 + Goritz 6.11.1836, and had issue see elsewhere

   (6) **Maria Ana Carlota Gabriela Princess of Savoy** * Torino 17.12.1757 + Torino 11.10.1824 = Torino 19.3.1775 **Benedetto Duke of Chablais, Prince of Savoy** * Torino 21.6.1741 + Torino 4.1.1808 s.p.

   (7) **Vittorio Emanuele IV and I King of Sardinia** * Torino 24.7.1759 + Moncalieri 10.1.1824 = Torino 25.4.1789 **Maria Theresia Archduchess of Austria, Princess of Modena** * Milano 1.11.1773 + Genova 29.3.1832 dau. of Ferdinand Archduke of Austria, Duke of Modena, and had issue:

VII		a.	**Maria Beatrice Vittoria Giuseppina Princess of Savoy** * Torino 6.12.1792 + Cattajo 15.9.1840 = Cagliari 20.6.1812 **Francesco IV Duke of Modena, Archduke of Austria,** * Milano 6.10.1779 + Modena 21.1.1846, and had issue see elsewhere
		b.	**Maria Adelaide Clothilde Xaveria Borbonia Princess of Savoy** * Torino 1.10.1794 + 2.8.1795
		c.	**Carlo Emanuele Prince of Savoy** * Torino 3.9.1796 + Cagliari 9.8.1799
		d.	a daughter * 20.12.1800 + 10.1.1801
		e.	**Maria Teresa Fernanda Felicitas Gaetana Pia Princess of Savoy** * Roma 19.9.1803 + San Martino 16.7.1879 = Torino 5.9.1820 **Carlo Lodovico II Duke of Parma** * Madrid 22.12.1799 + Nice 16.4.1883, and had issue see elsewhere
		f.	**Maria Ana Ricarda Carlotta Margherita Pia Princess of Savoy** * Roma 19.9.1803 + Prag 4.5.1884 = Torino 5.9.1820 **Ferdinand I Emperor of Austria, King of Hungary** * Wien 19.4.1793 + Prag 29.6.1875 s.p.
		g.	**Maria Cristina Carlotta Giuseppina Gaetana Elisa Princess of Savoy** * Cagliari 14.11.1812 + Caserta 21.1.1836 = Voltri 21.11.1832 **Ferdinando II King of Naples and Sicily** * Palermo 12.1.1810 + Caserta 22.5.1859, and had issue see elsewhere

VI		(8)	**Maria Giuseppina Ferdinanda Princess of Savoy** * Torino 21.11.1760 + Torino 19.5.1768
		(9)	**Maurizio Giuseppe Maria Duke of Montferrat Prince of Savoy** * Torino 13.12.1762 + Torino 1.9.1799
		(10)	**Maria Carolina Antoinetta Princess of Savoy** * Torino 17.1.1764 + Dresden 28.12.1782 = Dresden 24.10.1781 **Anton I King of Saxony** * Dresden 27.12.1755 + Dresden 6.6.1836 s.p.
		(11)	**Carlo Felice I Giuseppe Maria King of Sardinia** * Torino 6.4.1765 + Torino 27.4.1831 = Palermo 6.4.1807 **Maria Cristina Princess of Bourbon-Sicily** * Caserta 17.1.1779 + Savonna 12.3.1849 dau. of Ferdinando I King of Naples and Sicily, s.p.
		(12)	**Giuseppe Benedetto Maria Placido Conte d'Asti, Prince of Savoy** * Torino 5.10.1766 + Cagliari 29.10.1802

V	3)	**Eleonora Maria Teresa Princess of Savoy** * Torino 28.2.1728 + Moncalieri 14.8.1781
	4)	**Maria Luisa Gabriela Princess of Savoy** * Torino 25.3.1729 + 22.6.1767
	5)	**Maria Felicite Princess of Savoy** * 19.3.1730 + Roma 13.5.1801
	6)	**Giovanni Carlo Emanuele Philiberto Duke of Aosta** * Torino 17.5.1731 + 23.4.1735
	7)	**Carlo Francesco Romauldo Duke of Chablais Prince of Savoy** * Torino 23.7.1733 + 28.12.1733

by 3rd marriage:

	8)	**Carlo Francesco Maria Augusto Prince of Savoy** * 1.12.1738 + 25.3.1745
	9)	**Vittoria Margharita Princess of Savoy** * 22.6.1740 + 14.7.1742
	10)	**Benedetto Maria Maurizio Duke of Chablais Prince of Savoy** * Torino 21.6.1741 + Torino 4.1.1808 = 19.3.1775 **Maria Anna Princess of Savoy** * Torino 17.12.1757 + Torino 11.10.1824 dau. of Vittorio Amadeo III King of Sardinia s.p.

| IV | 6. | **Emanuele Philberto Prince of Savoy** * 1 + 19.12.1705 |
| | 7. | a stillborn son 22.11.1709 |

3 The Descendants of Elisabeth Charlotte Countess Palatine of The Rhine 1652-1722 and Philippe 1 Duc d'Orleans 1640-1701.

III   **Elisabeth Charlotte Countess Palatine of the Rhine** * Heidelberg 27.5.1652 + St-Cloud 8.12.1722 = Metz 21.11.1671 **Philippe I de Bourbon Duc d'Orleans** * St-Germain-en-Laye 21.9.1640 + St-Cloud 9.6.1701 and had issue:

IV   1.   **Alexandre Louis d'Orleans Duc de Valois** * St-Cloud 2.6.1673 + Palais-Royal 16.3.1676

     2.   **Philippe II Duc d'Orleans** * St-Cloud 2.8.1674 + Versailles 2.12.1723 = Versailles 18.2.1692 **Françoise Marie de Bourbon, Mlle. de Blois** * Château de Maintenon 9.2.1677 + Paris 1.2.1749, natural dau. of Louis XIV King of France and Madame de Montespan, and had issue:

V   1)   a daughter, Mlle. de Valois * 17.12.1693 + 17.10.1694

     2)   **Marie Louise Élisabeth Princess of Orleans** * 20.8.1695 + Château de Muette 21.7.1719 = Versailles 6.7.1710 **Charles de Bourbon Duc de Berry** * Versailles 31.8.1686 + Marly 4.5.1714, and had issue:

VI   (1)   a daughter * & + Fontainbleau 21.7.1711

         (2)   **Charles de Berry Duc d'Alençon** * Versailles 26.3.1713 + 16.4.1713

         (3)   **Marie Louise Élisabeth de Berry** * Versailles 16.6.1714 + Versailles 17.6.1714

V   3)   **Louise Adélaide, Mlle. de Chartres, Princess of Orleans** * 13.8.1698 + 10.2.1743

     4)   **Charlotte Aglaé, Mlle. de Valois, Princess of Orleans** * 22.10.1700 + Paris 19.1.1761 = Tuileries 21.6.1720 **Francesco III Duke of Modena** * 2.7.1698 + Varese 22.2.1780, and had issue see elsewhere

     5)   **Louis I Duc d'Orleans** * Versailles 4.8.1703 + Paris 4.2.1752 = Sarri 18.6.1724 **Auguste Marie Margräfin of Baden** * Aschaffenburg 10.11.1704 + Palais-Royal 8.8.1726 dau. of Ludwig Wilhelm Margraf of Baden-Baden, and had issue:

VI   (1)   **Louis Philippe I Duc de Chartres, Duc d'Orleans** * Paris 12.5.1725 + St-Cloud 18.11.1785 = (1) Versailles 17.12.1743 **Louise Henriette de Bourbon-Conti** * Paris 20.6.1726 + Paris 9.2.1759 dau. of Louis Armand II Prince de Conti; = (2) 23.4.1773 Charlotte Beraud de la Haye de Riou 5.10.1738 + Paris 6.2.1806 dau. of Jean Beraud de la Haye, and had issue:

         by 1st marriage

VII   a.   a daughter * 12.7.1745 + St-Cloud 14.12.1745

         b.   **Louis Philippe II Joseph Duc d'Orleans** * St-Cloud 13.4.1747 + Paris 6.11.1793 = 5.4.1769 **Louise Marie Adélaide de Bourbon-Penthièvre** * Paris 13.3.1753 + Ivry-sur-Seine 23.6.1821 dau. of Louis de Bourbon Duc de Penthièvre, and had issue:

VIII   a)   **Louis Philippe I King of France** * Paris 6.10.1773 + Claremont, Surrey 26.8.1850 = Palermo 25.11.1809 **Maria Amelia Princess of Bourbon-Sicily** * Caserta 26.4.1782 + Claremont 24.3.1866 dau. of Ferdinando IV King of Naples and Sicily, see later

           b)   **Antoine Philippe d'Orleans Duc de Montpensier** * 3.7.1775 + Salt Hill, near Windsor 18.5.1807

           c)   **Louise Marie Adélaide Eugénie, Mlle. d'Orleans** * Palais-Royal 23.8.1777 + Tuileries 31.12.1847

           d)   a daughter * 23.8.1777 + 1.2.1782

           e)   **Alphonse Léodegar d'Orleans, Comte de Beaujolais** * Paris 7.10.1779 + Malta 14.5.1808

VII   c.   **Louise Marie Thérèse Bathilde Princess of Orleans** * St-Cloud 9.7.1750 + Paris 13.1.1822 = Versailles 24.4.1770 **Louis Henri Joseph Prince de Condé, Duc de Bourbon** * Paris 13.4.1756 + Château de Saint-Leu 27.8.1830, and had issue see elsewhere

VI   (2)   **Louise Madeleine Princess of Orleans** * Paris 5.8.1726 + 11.5.1728

V		6)	**Louise Élisabeth, Mlle. de Montpensier, Princess of Orleans** * Versailles 11.12.1709 + Paris 16.6.1742 = Lerma 20.1.1722 **Luis I King of Spain** * Versailles 25.8.1707 + Madrid 31.8.1724, s.p.
		7)	**Philippine Élisabeth, Mlle. de Beaujolais, Princess of Orleans** * Versailles 18.12.1714 + 21.5.1734
		8)	**Louise Diane, Mlle. de Chartres, Princess of Orleans** * Paris 27.6.1716 + Issy 26.9.1736 = Versailles 22.1.1732 **Louis François I Prince de Conti** * Paris 13.8.1717 + Paris 2.8.1776, and had issue see elsewhere

cAbAg

IV	3.		**Elisabeth Charlotte, Mlle. de Chartres, Princess of Orleans** * St-Cloud 13.9.1676 + Commercy 23.12.1744 = Fontainbleau 13.10.1698 Leopold Joseph Duke of Lorraine * Innsbruck 11.9.1679 + Lunéville 27.3.1729 and had issue:
V		1)	**Léopold Prince of Lorraine** * 26.8.1699 + Nancy 2.4.1700
		2)	**Elisabeth Charlotte Princess of Lorraine** * Nancy 21.10.1700 + 4.5.1711
		3)	**Louise Christine Princess of Lorraine** * 13.11.1701 + 18.11.1701
		4)	**Marie Gabriele Charlotte Princess of Lorraine** * 30.12.1702 + Lunéville 10.5.1711
		5)	**Louis Prince of Lorraine** * Lunéville 28.1.1704 + Lunéville 10.5.1711
		6)	**Joséphine Gabriele Princess of Lorraine** * Lunéville 16.2.1705 + 25.3.1708
		7)	**Gabriele Louise Princess of Lorraine** * 4.3.1706 + 13.6.1710
		8)	**Léopold Clemens Carl Prince of Lorraine** * Lunéville 25.4.1707 + Lunéville 4.6.1723
		9)	**François Etienne Duke of Lorraine** (Emperor Franz Stephan) * Nancy 8.12.1708 + Innsbruck 18.8.1765 = 12.2.1736 Empress Maria Theresia * Wien 13.5.1717 + Wien 29.11.1780 dau. of Emperor Karl VI and had issue see Chapter 4
		10)	**Eleonore Princess of Lorraine** * 4.7.1710 + 28.7.1710
		11)	**Elisabeth Therese Princess of Lorraine** * Lunéville 15.10.1711 + Torino 3.7.1741 = 1.4.1737 **Carlo Emanuele III King of Sardinia** * 27.4.1701 + Torino 20.2.1773, and had issue see elsewhere
		12)	**Charles Alexander Prince of Lorraine** * Lunéville 12.12.1712 + Château de Tervueren 4.7.1780 = 7.1.1744 Maria Anna Archduchess of Austria * 14.9.1718 + 16.12.1744 dau. of Emperor Karl VI, and had issue:
VI		(1)	a daughter * & + 6.10.1744
V		13)	**Anne Charlotte Princess of Lorraine** * Lunéville 17.5.1714 + Mons 7.11.1773
		14)	a son * & + December 1715

VIII **Louis Philippe I King of the French** * Paris 6.10.1773 + Claremont, Surrey 26.8.1850 = Palermo 25.11.1809 **Maria Amelia Princess of Bourbon-Sicily** * Caserta 26.4.1782 + Claremont 24.3.1866 dau. of Ferdinando IV King of Naples and Sicily, and had issue:

IX 1. **Ferdinand Philippe Louis Charles Henri Rosolin Duc d'Orleans** * Palermo 3.9.1810 + Sablonville 13.7.1842 = Fontainbleau 30.5.1837 **Helene Duchess of Mecklenburg-Schwerin** * Ludwigslust 24.1.1814 + Richmond, Surrey 18.5.1858 dau. of Friedrich Ludwig Hereditary Duke of Mecklenburg-Schwerin, and had issue:

X 1) **Louis Philippe Albert Comte de Paris** * Paris 24.8.1838 + Stowe House 8.9.1894 = Kingston-on-Thames 30.5.1864 **Marie Isabel Princess of Orleans, Infanta of Spain** * Seville 21.9.1848 + Villamanrique, Seville 23.4.1919 dau. of Antoine Duc de Montpensier, and had issue:

XI (1) **Marie Amélie Louise Hélène Princess of Orleans** * York House, Twickenham 28.9.1865 + Versailles 25.10.1951 = Lisboa 22.5.1886 **Carlos I King of Portugal** * Lisboa 28.9.1863 + Lisboa 1.2.1908, and had issue see elsewhere

(2) **Louis Philippe Duc d'Orleans** * York House, Twickenham 6.2.1869 + Palermo 28.3.1926 = Wien 5.11.1896 **Maria Dorothea Archduchess of Austria** * Alscút 14.6.1867 + Alscút 6.4.1932 dau. of Joseph Archduke of Austria, Palatine of Hungary — div. s.p.

(3) **Hélène Louise Henriette Princess of Orleans** * York House 13.6.1871 + Castellamare di Strabia 21.1.1951 = (1) Kingston-on-Thames 25.6.1895 **Emanuele Filberto Duke of Aosta, Prince of Savoy** * Genova 13.1.1869 + Torino 4.7.1931, = (2) ... 1936 Otto Campini * ... + ... and had issue by 1st marriage see elsewhere

(4) **Charles Prince of Orleans** * Paris 21.1.1875 + Paris 8.6.1875

(5) **Isabelle Marie Laure Mercédès Ferdinande Princess of Orleans** * Château d'Eu 7.5.1878 + Larache, Marocco 21.4.1961 = Twickenham 30.10.1899 **Jean Duc de Guise** * Paris 4.9.1874 + Larache 25.8.1940, and had issue see elsewhere

(6) **Jacques Marie Antoine Clément Prince of Orleans** * Château d'Eu 5.4.1880 + 22.1.1881

(7) **Louise Françoise Marie Laure Princess of Orleans** * Cannes 24.2.1882 + Seville 18.4.1958 = Wood Norton 16.11.1907 **Carlos Prince of Bourbon-Sicily, Infant of Spain** * Gries b. Bozen 10.11.1870 + Seville 11.11.1949, and had issue see elsewhere

(8) **Ferdinand François Philippe Marie Laurent Duc de Montpensier** * Château d'Eu 9.9.1884 + Château de Randan 30.1.1924 = Château de Randan 20.8.1921 Doña Maria Isabel González de Olañeta y Ibarreta, Marquesa de Valdeterrazo and a Grandee of Spain * Madrid 22.4.1895 + Madrid 11.7.1958 dau. of Don Ulpiano González de Olañeta y González de Ocampo Marques de Valdeterrazo s.p.

X 2) **Robert Philippe Louis Eugène Ferdinand Duc de Chartres** * Tuileries 9.11.1840 + Château de Saint-Firmin 5.12.1910 = Kingston-on-Thames 11.6.1863 **Françoise Princess of Orleans** * Château de Neuilly 14.8.1844 + Château de Saint-Firmin 28.10.1925 dau. of François Prince de Joinville, and had issue:

XI (1) **Marie Amélie Françoise Helene Princess of Orleans** * Morgan House, Ham Common, Richmond 13.1.1865 + Kopenhagen 4.12.1909 = Château d'Eu 22.10.1885 **Valdemar Prince of Denmark** * Bernstorff Castle 27.10.1858 + Kopenhagen 14.1.1939, and had issue see elsewhere

(2) **Robert Louis Philippe Ferdinand François Marie Prince of Orleans** * Morgan House 10.1.1866 + Château de Saint-Firmin 30.5.1885

(3) **Henri Philippe Marie Prince of Orleans** * Morgan House 15.10.1867 + Saigon 9.8.1901

(4) **Marguerite Louise Marie Françoise Princess of Orleans** * Morgan House 25.1.1869 + Château de la Forest, Montcresson 31.1.1940 = Chantilly 22.4.1896 Patrice de Mac-Mahon 2nd Duke of Magenta * Outreau 10.6.1855 + Paris 23.5.1927, and had issue:

XII	a.	**Marie Elisabeth de Mac-Mahon** * Lunéville 19.6.1899 + Voreppe, (Isère) 27.9.1951 = Paris 22.9.1924 Henry de Plan Comte de Sieyès de Veynes * Aix-en-Provence 6.2.1883 + Château de la Forest 20.6.1953, and had issue:

XIII	a)	**Marguerite Françoise Marie de Plan de Sieyès de Veynes** * Paris 22.2.1926 = Ollon-sur-Aigle, Suisse 28.1.1956 Jean-Louise Gilliéron * Genève 16.4.1916, and has issue:

XIV	(a)	**Irène Gilliéron** * Paris 5.2.1957
	(b)	**Arnaud Gilliéron** * Paris 5.5.1958

XIII	b)	**Isabelle Jeanne Henriette Marie de Plan de Sieyès de Veynes** * Paris 8.11.1927 + La Forest 28.4.1951
	c)	**François Xaver de Plan, Comte de Sieyès de Veynes** * Paris 16.7.1929

XII	b.	**Amélie Françoise Marie de Mac-Mahon** * Lunéville 11.9.1900 = Paris 5.2.1921 Almaric Lombard de Buffières Comte de Rambuteau * Plainpalais, près Genève 29.8.1890 + Buchenwald 13.12.1944, and has issue:

XIII	a)	**Françoise de Lombard de Buffières de Rambuteau** * Paris 21.5.1922 = Ozolles, (S-et-L.) ... 9.1946 Philippe Comte de Rodez-Bénavent * Paris 21.5.1922, and has issue:

XIV	(a)	**Marc Antoine de Rodez-Bénavent** * Mâcon, (S-et-L.) 20.7.1947
	(b)	**Hugues de Rodez-Bénavent** * Montpellier 13.8.1951
	(c)	**Marie-Amélie de Rodez-Bénavent** * Montpellier 30.8.1953

XIII	b)	**Philibert Patrice Marie Lombard de Buffières Comte de Rambuteau** * Paris 14.9.1923
	c)	**Comte Henri Philibert Marie Lombard de Buffières de Rambuteau** * Ozolles 20.7.1925 = St-Georges de Reneins (Rhône) 31.7.1956 Irmeline de Clarett de Fleurieu * Stockholm 18.10.1935 dau. of Comte Mederic de Fleurieu, and has issue:

XIV	(a)	**Jean Marie Almaric Lombard de Buffières de Rambuteau** * Villefranche-sur-Saône 20.6.1957
	(b)	**Marie Edla Rita Lombard de Buffières de Rambuteau** * Villefranche-sur-Saône 9.12.1958
	(c)	**Claude Lombard de Buffières de Rambuteau** * Villefranche-sur-Saône 13.12.1959
	(d)	**Philibert Lombard de Buffières de Rambuteau** * Villefranche-sur-Saône 25.3.1966

XIII	d)	**Comte Maurice Almaric Marie Lombard de Buffières de Rambuteau** * Paris 5.2.1927 = Paris ... 1954 Yolande de Mitry * 8.5.1929 dau. of Comte Emmanuel de Mitry, and has issue:

XIV	(a)	**Emmanuel Lombard de Buffières de Rambuteau** * Paris 12.12.1954
	(b)	**François Lombard de Buffières de Rambuteau** * Paris 19.6.1956
	(c)	**Aymar Lombard de Buffières de Rambuteau** * Paris 13.12.1957
	(d)	**Patrice Lombard de Buffières de Rambuteau** * Paris 21.8.1960
	(e)	**Marie Lorraine de Buffières de Rambuteau** * Paris 18.3.1964
	(f)	**Laurent Lombard de Buffières de Rambuteau** * Paris 7.10.1965

F. Winterhalter   *By gracious permission of H.M. The Queen*

4   Queen Victoria and the French Royal Family
at the Château d'Eu

Standing : Prince Leopold of Naples and Sicily, Prince of Salerno; King
Louis Philippe; François, Prince de Joinville; Prince Albert, the Prince
Consort; Prince August Ludwig of Saxe-Coburg and Gotha.
Seated : Hélène, Duchesse d'Orleans; Princess Clementine of Salerno;
Caroline, Duchesse d'Aumale *or* Françoise, Princesse de Joinville; Madame
Adélaide (sister to King Louis Philippe); Queen Victoria; Queen Marie
Amélie; Princess Clementine of Saxe-Coburg and Gotha.
Children : Robert, Duc de Chartres; Louis Philippe, Comte de Paris;
Ferdinand, Duc d'Alençon; Prince Ludwig August of Saxe-Coburg and
Gotha; Philipp, Duke of Württemberg; Prince Philipp of Saxe-Coburg
and Gotha.

XII	c.	**Maurice Jean Marie de Mac-Mahon 3rd Duc de Magenta** * Lunéville 13.11.1903 + Evreux 27.10.1954 = Sully-le-Château 25.8.1937 Marguerite de Riquet Comtesse de Caraman-Chimay * Paris 29.12.1913 dau. of Philippe de Riquet Prince de Caraman-Chimay, and has issue:

XII   c.   **Maurice Jean Marie de Mac-Mahon 3rd Duc de Magenta** * Lunéville 13.11.1903 + Evreux 27.10.1954 = Sully-le-Château 25.8.1937 Marguerite de Riquet Comtesse de Caraman-Chimay * Paris 29.12.1913 dau. of Philippe de Riquet Prince de Caraman-Chimay, and has issue:

XIII   a)   **Philippe Maurice Marie de Mac-Mahon 4th Duc de Magenta** * Paris 15.5.1938

         b)   **Nathalie Jeanne Marie de Mac-Mahon** * Paris 11.4.1939

         c)   **Anne Monique Marie de Mac-Mahon** * Sully-le-Château 9.8.1941 = 6.10.1963 Arnould Baron Thenard * Neuilly-sur-Seine 3.3.1940, and has issue:

XIV   (a)   **Jacques Thenard** * Paris 23.1.1965

            (b)   **Stanislas Thenard** * Paris 21.4.1966

XIII   d)   **Patrick Michel Marie Comte de Mac-Mahon** * Lausanne 11.9.1943 = Beaumont-le-Roger 11.6.1966 Beatrix de Blanquet du Chayla * Romans (Isère) 27.3.1945 dau. of Bernard de Blanquet de Chayla

         e)   **Véronique Henriette Marie de Mac-Mahon** * Sully-le-Château 5.6.1948

XI   **Jean Pierre Clément Marie Duc de Guise** * Paris 4.9.1874 + Larache Marocco 25.8.1940 = Kingston-on-Thames 30.10.1899 **Isabelle Princess of Orleans** * Château d'Eu 7.5.1878 + Larache 21.4.1961 dau. of Louis Philippe Comte de Paris, and had issue:

XII   a.   **Isabelle Françoise Hélène Marie Princess of Orleans** * Paris 27.11.1900 = (1) Chesnay, près Versailles 15.9.1923 Comte Bruno d'Harcourt * Vevey, Switzerland 20.9.1899 + Casablanca 29.4.1930; = (2) Jouy-en-Joas (S-et-O) 12.7.1934 Prince Pierre Murat * Paris 6.4.1900 + Rabat, Marocco 30.7.1948, and has issue:

by 1st marriage:

XIII   a)   **Comte Bernard François Gilbert Jean Marie d'Harcourt** * Larache 1.1.1925 + Larache 4.9.1958 = (1) ... Zénaide Rachewska * ... dau. of ... = (2) Paris 10.1.1951 Jeanne Marie de Contades * Paris 22.4.1928 dau. of Vicomte Jean de Contades, and had issue:

by 2nd marriage:

XIV   (a)   **Bruno d'Harcourt** * Boulogne-Billancourt 26.10.1951.

            (b)   **François d'Harcourt** * Boulogne-Billancourt 21.6.1953

XIII   b)   **Gilonne Jeanne Armande Anne Marie d'Harcourt** * Larache 1.1.1927 = Cany (Seine-Marit) 9.9.1950 Comte Antoine de Dreux-Brézé * Cany 22.8.1928, and has issue:

XIV   (a)   **Laure de Dreux-Brézé** * Cany 23.4.1951

            (b)   **Anne de Dreux-Brézé** * Boulogne-Billancourt 26.2.1952 + Cany 6.2.1953

            (c)   **Diane de Dreux-Brézé** * Boulogne-Billancourt 5.2.1954

            (d)   **Anne Pierre de Dreux-Brézé** * Neuilly-sur-Seine 12.9.1958 + 14.9.1958

XIII   c)   **Isabelle Henriette Christiane Gabrielle Marie d'Harcourt** * Larache 1.1.1927 = Paris 20.10.1945 Prince Louis Murat * Paris 4.9.1920, and has issue:

XIV   (a)   **Pierre Charles Marie Jean Joachim Napoléon Prince Murat** * Neuilly-sur-Seine 17.10.1949

            (b)   **Xavier Paul Marie Bruno Joachim Napoléon Prince Murat** * Casablanca 16.7.1951 + Fédala, Marocco 30.9.1951

XIV   (c)   **Leila Marie Isabelle Solange Monique Anne Princesse Murat** * Boulogne-Billancourt 17.3.1953

                    (d)   **Laura Marguerite Marie Cécile Gilonne Princesse Murat** * Boulogne-Billancourt 20.9.1954

XIII   d)   **Monique Gabrielle Marie d'Harcourt** * Paris 7.1.1929 = Paris 1.7.1948 Comte Alfred Boulay de la Meurthe * Paris 26.7.1925, and has issue:

XIV   (a)   **Gilonne Boulay de la Meurthe** * Neuilly-sur-Seine 25.4.1949

                    (b)   **Laure Boulay de la Meurthe** * Rabat 27.4.1951

                    (c)   **Yseult Boulay de la Meurthe** * Casablanca 19.4.1956

XII   b.   **Françoise Isabelle Louise Marie Princess of Orleans** * Paris 25.12.1902 + Paris 25.2.1953 = Palermo 11.2.1929 **Christopher Prince of Greece** * Pavlovsk 10.8.1888 + Athens 21.1.1940, and had issue see elsewhere

       c.   **Anne Hélène Marie Princess of Orleans** * Nouvion-en-Thiérache 5.8.1906 = Napoli 5.11.1927 **Amadeo Duke of Aosta, Prince of Savoy** * Torino 21.10.1898 + Nairobi 3.3.1942, and had issue see elsewhere

       d.   **Henri Robert Ferdinand Marie Louis Philippe Comte de Paris** * Château de Nouvion-en-Thiérache 5.7.1908 = Palermo 8.4.1931 **Isabel Princesse of Orleans and Bragança** * Château d'Eu 13.8.1911 dau. of Pedro Prince of Orleans and Bragança, and has issue:

XIII   a)   **Isabelle Marie Laure Victorie Princess of Orleans** * Woluwé-St-Pierre 8.4.1932 = Dreux 10.9.1964 Fredrich Karl Graf v. Schönborn-Buchheim * Schloss Schönborn 30.3.1938, and has issue:

XIV   (a)   **Damian Graf v. Schönborn-Buchheim** * Wien 17.7.1965

                    (b)   **Vinzenz Graf v. Schönborn-Buchheim** * Schloss Schönborn 28.11.1966

XIII   b)   **Henri Philippe Pierre Marie Comte de Clermont** * Woluwé Saint-Pierre 14.6.1933 = Dreux 5.7.1957 Marie Therese Duchess of Württenberg * Altshausen 12.11.1934 dau. of Philipp Duke of Württenberg, and has issue:

XIV   (a)   **Marie Isabelle Marguerite Anne Princess of Orleans** * Boulogne-Billancourt 3.1.1959

                    (b)   **François Henri Louis Marie Prince of Orleans** * Boulogne-Billancourt 7.2.1961

                    (c)   **Blanche Princess of Orleans** * Regensburg 10.9.1962

                    (d)   **Jean Prince of Orleans** * Boulogne-sur-Seine 19.3.1965

XIII   c)   **Hélène Astrid Léopoldine Marie Princess of Orleans** * Woluwé-St-Pierre 17.9.1934 = Dreux 17.1.1957 **Comte Evrard de Limburg-Stirum** * Huldenberg 31.10.1927, and has issue, see elsewhere

           d)   **François Gaston Michel Marie Prince of Orleans** * Woluwé-St-Pierre 15.8.1935, ✗ Taourirt, Algeria 11.10.1960

           e)   **Anne Marguerite Brigitte Marie Princess of Orleans** * Woluwé-St-Pierre 4.12.1938 = Dreux 12.5.1965 **Carlos Prince of Bourbon-Sicily** * Lausanne 16.1.1938

           f)   **Diane Françoise Maria da Gloria Princess of Orleans** * Petropolis 24.3.1940 = Schloss Altshausen 21.7.1960 **Carl Duke of Württemberg** * Fredrichshafen 1.8.1936, and has issue see page

46

XIII

    g)   **Michael Joseph Benoit Marie Prince of Orleans**   * Rabat 25.6.1941

    h)   **Jacques Jean Jaroslaw Marie Prince of Orleans**   * Rabat 25.6.1941

    i)   **Claude Marie Agnes Catherine Princess of Orleans** * Larache 11.12.1943 = 22.7.1964 **Amadeo, Duke of Aosta, Prince of Savoy** * Firenze 27.9.1943

    j)   **Jeanne de Chantal Alice Clotilde Marie Princess of Orleans** * Pampelune 9.1.1946

    k)   **Thibaud Louis Denis Humbert Prince of Orleans** 21.1.1948

IX   2.   **Louise Marie Thérèse Charlotte Isabelle Princess of Orleans** * Palermo 3.4.1812 + Ostend 11.10.1850 = Château de Compiègne 9.8.1832 **Léopold I King of Belgium, Prince of Saxe-Coburg and Gotha** * Coburg 16.12.1790 + Laeken Palace 10.12.1865, and had issue:

X   1)   **Louis Philippe Léopold Victor Ernest Prince of Belgium** * Bruxelles 24.7.1833 + Bruxelles 16.5.1834

    2)   **Léopold II Louis Philippe Marie Victor King of Belgium** * Bruxelles 9.4.1835 + Laeken Palace 17.12.1909 = Bruxelles 22.8.1853 **Maria Henriette Archduchess of Austria** * Buda 23.8.1836 + Spa 19.9.1902 dau. of Joseph Archduke of Austria, Palatine of Hungary; = (2) morganatically Bruxelles 15.12.1909 Blanche Delacroix Baroness de Vaugham, and had issue:

by 1st marriage:

XI   (1)   **Louise Marie Amélie Princess of Belgium** * Bruxelles 18.2.1858 + Wiesbaden 1.3.1924 = Bruxelles 4.2.1875 **Philipp Prince of Saxe-Coburg and Gotha** * Paris 28.3.1844 + Coburg 3.7.1921, and had issue see elsewhere

    (2)   **Léopold Ferdinand Élie Victor Albert Maria Prince of Belgium, Duke of Brabant** * Laeken 12.6.1855 + Bruxelles 22.1.1869

    (3)   **Stéphanie Clotilde Louise Hermine Marie Charlotte Princess of Belgium** * Laeken 21.5.1864 + Pannonhalma, Hungary 23.8.1945 = (1) Wien 10.5.1881 **Rudolf Crown Prince of Austria-Hungary** * Laxenburg 21.8.1858 + Mayerling 30.1.1889; = (2) Miramar 22.3.1900 Elemér Prince Lónyay de Nagy-Lónya et Vásáros-Namény * Bodrog-Olaszi 24.8.1863 + Budapest 20.7.1946, and had issue by 1st marriage, see elsewhere

    (4)   **Clémentine Albertine Marie Léopoldine Princess of Belgium** * Laeken 30.7.1872 + Nice 8.3.1955 = Château de Moncalieri 14.11.1910 **Victor Napoleon Prince Bonaparte** * Paris 18.7.1862 + Bruxelles 3.5.1926, and had issue see elsewhere

X   3)   **Philippe Eugène Ferdinand Marie Clément Baudouin Léopold Georges Prince of Belgium, Count of Flanders** * Laeken 24.3.1837 + Bruxelles 17.11.1905 = Berlin 25.4.1867 **Marie Luise Princess of Hohenzollern-Sigmaringen** * Sigmaringen 17.11.1845 + Bruxelles 26.11.1912 dau. of Karl Anton Fürst v. Hohenzollern-Sigmaringen, and had issue:

XI   (1)   **Baudouin Léopold Philippe Marie Charles Antoine Joseph Louis Prince of Belgium** * Bruxelles 3.6.1869 + Bruxelles 23.1.1891

    (2)   **Henriette Marie Charlotte Antoinette Princess of Belgium** * Bruxelles 30.11.1870 + Sierre, Valais, Suisse 28.3.1948 = Bruxelles 12.2.1896 **Philippe Emmanuel Duc de Vendôme** * Obermais b. Meran 18.1.1872 + Cannes 1.2.1931, and had issue see elsewhere

    (3)   **Joséphine Marie Stéphanie Victoire Princess of Belgium** * Bruxelles 30.11.1870 + Bruxelles 18.1.1871

    (4)   **Joséphine Caroline Marie Albertine Princess of Belgium** * Bruxelles 18.10.1872 + Namur 6.1.1958 = Bruxelles 28.5.1894 **Karl Anton Prince of Hohenzollern-Sigmaringen** * Schloss Sigmaringen 1.9.1868 + Namedy 21.2.1919, and had issue see elsewhere

    (5)   **Albert I Léopold Clément Marie Meinrad King of Belgium** * Bruxelles 8.4.1875 + Marche-les-Dames 17.2.1934 = München 2.10.1900 **Elisabeth Duchess in Bavaria** * Possenhofen 25.7.1875 + Château de Stuyvenberg 23.11.1965, dau. of Karl Theodor Duke in Bavaria, and had issue:

47

XII		a.	**Léopold III Philippe Charles Albert Meinrad Hubert Marie Michel King of Belgium** * Bruxelles 3.11.1901 = (1) Bruxelles 10.11.1926 **Astrid Princess of Sweden** * Stockholm 17.11.1905 + Küssnacht 29.8.1935 dau. of Karl Prince of Sweden; = (2) Laeken 6.12.1941 Mary Liliane Baels, Princess de Rethy * London 28.11.1916 dau. of Henri Baels, and had issue:

by 1st marriage:

XIII		a)	**Joséphine Charlotte Ingeborg Elisabeth Marie Josèphe Marguerite Astrid Princess of Belgium** * Bruxelles 11.10.1927 = Luxembourg 9.4.1953 **Jean Grand Duke of Luxembourg** * Schloss Berg 5.1.1921, and has issue see elsewhere
		b)	**Baudouin I Albert Charles Léopold Axel Marie Gustave King of Belgium** * Château de Stuyvenberg 7.9.1930 = Bruxelles 15.12.1960 Doña Fabiola de Mora y Aragon * Madrid 11.6.1928 dau. of Don Gonzalo de Mora y Fernández Marqués de Casa Riera
		c)	**Albert Félix Humbert Théodore Christian Eugène Marie Prince of Belgium, Prince of Liège** * Château de Stuyvenberg 6.6.1934 = Bruxelles 2.6.1959 Donna Paola Ruffo di Calabria * Forte dei Marmi 11.9.1937 dau. of Principe Don Fulco Ruffo di Calabria Duca di Guardia Lombarda, and has issue:

XIV		(a)	**Philippe Léopold Louis Marie Prince of Belgium** * Bruxelles 15.4.1960
		(b)	**Astrid Joséphine Fabrizia Elisabeth Paola Marie Princess of Belgium** * Bruxelles 5.6.1962
		(c)	**Laurent Benoit Baudouin Marie Prince of Belgium** * Bruxelles 19.10.1963

by 2nd marriage:

XIII		d)	**Alexandre Emmanuel Henri Albert Marie Léopold Prince of Belgium** * Laeken 18.7.1942
		e)	**Marie Christine Daphne Astrid Elisabeth Léopoldine Princess of Belgium** * Laeken 6.2.1951
		f)	**Marie Esmeralda Adelaide Liliane Anne Léopoldine Princess of Belgium** * Laeken 30.9.1956

XII		b.	**Charles Théodore Henri Antoine Meinrad Prince of Belgium, Count of Flanders** * Bruxelles 10.10.1903
		c.	**Marie José Charlotte Sophie Amélie Henriette Gabrielle Princess of Belgium** * Ostend 4.8.1906 = Roma 8.2.1930 **Umberto II King of Italy** * Racconigi 15.9.1904, and has issue, see elsewhere

X		4)	**Marie Charlotte Amélie Auguste Victoire Clémentine Léopoldine Princess of Belgium** * Laeken 7.6.1840 + Château de Bouchut 19.1.1927 = 27.7.1857 **Maximilian I Emperor of Mexico, Archduke of Austria** * Wien 6.7.1832 + Queretaro 19.6.1867, s.p.

IX	3.		**Marie Christine Caroline Adélaide Françoise Léopoldine Princess of Orleans** * Palermo 12.4.1813 + Palazzo Vitelli, Pisa 2.1.1839 = Trianon Palace 17.10.1837 **Friedrich Duke of Württemberg** * Riga 20.12.1804 + Bayreuth 28.10.1881 and had issue, see elsewhere
	4.		**Louis Charles Philippe Raphaël Duc de Nemours** * Palais Royal 25.10.1814 + Versailles 26.6.1896 = St-Cloud 27.4.1840 Victoire Princess of Saxe-Coburg and Gotha * Wien 14.2.1822 + Claremont 10.11.1857 dau. of Ferdinand Prince of Saxe-Coburg and Gotha and had issue:

X	1)		**Louis Philippe Marie Ferdinand Gaston Comte d'Eu** * Château de Neuilly 28.4.1842 + at sea on board the Massilia 28.8.1922 = Rio de Janeiro 15.10.1864 **Isabel Princess of Brazil and Bragança, Infanta of Portugal** * Rio de Janeiro 29.7.1846 + Château d'Eu 14.11.1921 dau. of Pedro II Emperor of Brazil, and had issue:

XI   (1) **Pedro de Alcántara Luis Filipe Maria Gastão Miguel Gabriel Rafael Gonzaga Prince of Orléans and Bragança** * Petropolis, Brazil 15.10.1875 + Petropolis 29.1.1940 = Versailles 14.11.1908 Marie Elisabeth Gräfin Dobrzensky v. Dobrzenicz * Chotébor, Boh. 7.12.1875 + Sintra, Portugal 11.6.1951 dau. of Johann Wenzel Graf Dobrzensky v. Dobrzenicz, and had issue:

XII   a.   **Isabel Maria Amélie Luisa Vitória Teresa Joana Princess of Orléans and Bragança** * Château d'Eu 13.8.1911 = Palermo 8.4.1931 **Henri Comte de Paris** * Château de Nouvion-en-Thiérache 5.7.1908, and has issue see elsewhere

         b.   **Pedro de Alcántara Gastão João Maria Filipe Lourenço Huberto Miguel Rafael Gabriel Gonzaga Prince of Orléans and Bragança** * Château d'Eu 19.2.1913 = Séville 18.12.1944 **Maria de la Esperanza Princess of Bourbon-Sicily, Infanta of Spain** * Madrid 14.6.1914, dau. of Carlos Prince of Bourbon-Sicily, Infant of Spain, and has issue:

XIII   a)   **Pedro de Alcántara Carlos João Lourenço Miguel Rafael Gabriel Gonzaga Prince of Orléans and Bragança** * Rio de Janiero 31.10.1945

            b)   **Maria da Glória Henriqueta Dolores Luca Michaela Rafaela Gabriela Gonzaga Princess of Orléans and Bragança** * Petropolis 13.12.1946

            c)   **Alfonso Duarte Francisco Marcos Miguel Rafael Gabriel Gonzaga Prince of Orléans and Bragança** * Petropolis 25.4.1948

            d)   **Manuel Alvaro Raniero Miguel Gabriel Rafael Gonzaga Prince of Orléans and Bragança** * Petropolis 17.6.1949

            e)   **Cristina Maria de Rosário Leopoldina Michaela Gabriela Rafaela Gonzaga Princess of Orléans and Bragança** * Petropolis 16.10.1950

            f)   **Francisco Humberto Miguel Rafael Gabriel Gonzaga Prince of Orléans and Bragança** * Petropolis 9.12.1956

XII   c.   **Maria Francisca Amélia Luisa Vitória Teresa Isabel Princess of Orléans and Bragança** * Château d'Eu 8.9.1914 = Petropolis 15.10.1942 **Dom Duarte Duke of Bragança, Infant of Portugal** * Seebenstein 23.9.1907, and has issue, see elsewhere

         d.   **João Maria Filipe Gabriel Prince of Orléans and Bragança** * Boulogne-sur-Seine 15.10.1916 = Sintra 29.4.1949 Fatima Scherifa Chirine * Cairo 19.4.1923 dau. of Ismail Chirine Bey, and has issue:

XIII   a)   **João Henrique Prince of Orléans and Bragança** * Rio de Janeiro 25.4.1954

XII   e.   **Teresa Maria Teodora Princess of Orléans and Bragança** * Boulogne-sur-Seine 18.6.1919 = Sintra 7.10.1957 Ernesto de Martorell y Caldero * ... and has issue:

XIII   a)   **Doña Elisabeth Maria Francisca Joana Pia e Todos os Santos de Orléans e Bragança de Martorell** * Estoril 14.2.1959

XI   (2) **Luis Maria Filipe Pedro de Alcántara Gastão Miguel Rafael Gonzaga Prince of Orléans and Bragança** * Petropolis 26.1.1878 + Cannes 26.3.1920 = Cannes 4.11.1908 **Maria delle Grazie Princess of Bourbon-Sicily** * Cannes 12.8.1878 dau. of Alfons Prince of Bourbon-Sicily, Duke of Caserta, and has issue:

XII   a.   **Pedro Henrique Alfonso Filipe Maria Gabriel Rafael Gonzaga Prince of Orléans and Bragança** * Boulogne-sur-Seine 13.9.1909 = Schloss Nymphenburg 19.8.1937 **Marie Elisabeth Princess of Bavaria** * Nymphenburg 9.9.1914 dau. of Franz Prince of Bavaria and has issue:

XIII   a)   **Luis Gastão Maria José Pio Prince of Orléans and Bragança** * Mandelieu 6.6.1938

            b)   **Eudo Maria Raniero Pedro José Prince of Orléans and Bragança** * Mandelieu 8.6.1939

XIII   c)   **Beltrão Maria José Pio Januário Prince of Orléans and Bragança** * Mandelieu 2.2.1941

               d)   **Isabel Maria Josefa Henriqueta Francisça Princess of Orléans and Bragança** * Bourboule (P-de-D.) 5.4.1944

               e)   **Pedro de Alcántara Henrique Maria Prince of Orléans and Bragança** * Petropolis 1.12.1945

               f)   **Fernando Diniz Maria José Prince of Orléans and Bragança** * Petropolis 2.2.1948

               g)   **Antonio João Maria José Prince of Orléans and Bragança** * Petropolis 24.6.1950

               h)   **Leonor Maria Josefa Filipa Michaela Gabriela Rafaela Gonzaga Princess of Orléans and Bragança** * Jacarézinho, Brazil 20.5.1953 + Paris 25.11.1954

               i)   **Francisço Maria José Rasso Miguel Gabriel Rafael Gonzaga Prince of Orléans and Bragança** * Jacarézinho 6.4.1955

               j)   **Alberto Maria João Miguel Gabriel Rafael Gonzaga Prince of Orléans and Bragança** * Jundiai do Sul, Brazil 23.6.1957

               k)   **Maria Teresa Adelgunde Luiza Josa Michaela Gabriela Rafaela Gonzaga Princess of Orléans and Bragança** * Jundiaí de Sul 14.7.1959

               l)   **Maria Gabriela Dorothea Isabel José Michaela Gonzaga Princess of Orléans and Bragança** * Jundiai de Sul 14.7.1959

XII   b.   **Luis Gastão Antonio Maria Filipe Prince of Orléans and Bragança** * Cannes 19.2.1911 + Neuilly-sur-Seine 8.9.1931

               c.   **Pia Maria Raniera Isabel Antoineta Vitória Teresa Amélia Gerarda Raimunda Ana Michaela Rafaela Gonzaga Princess of Orléans and Bragança** * Boulogne-sur-Seine 4.3.1913 = Paris 12.8.1948 Comte René de Nicolay * Château de Lude (Sarthe) 17.1.1910 + Paris 25.11.1954, and has issue:

XIII   a)   **Louis Jean de Nicolay** * Le Mans (Sarthe) 18.9.1949

               b)   **Robert de Nicolay** * Neuilly-sur-Seine 17.2.1952

XI   (3)   **Antonio Gastão Luis Felipe Francisço de Assis Maria Miguel Rafael Gabriel Gonzaga Prince of Orléans and Bragança** * Paris 9.8.1881 + Edmonton, London 29.11.1918

X   2)   **Ferdinand Philippe Marie Duc d'Alençon** * Château de Neuilly 12.7.1844 + Belmont, near Wimbledon 29.6.1910 = Possenhofen 28.9.1868 Sophie Duchess in Bavaria * Possenhofen 23.2.1847 + Paris 4.5.1897 dau. of Maximilian Duke in Bavaria and had issue:

XI   (1)   **Louise Victoire Marie Amélie Sophie Princess of Orleans** * Bushy Park 9.7.1869 + München 4.2.1952 = Nymphenburg 15.4.1891 **Alfons Prince of Bavaria** * München 24.1.1862 + München 8.1.1933, and had issue see elsewhere

               (2)   **Philippe Emmanuel Maximilian Marie Eudes Duc de Vendôme** * Obermais b. Meran 18.1.1872 + Cannes 1.2.1931 = Bruxelles 12.2.1896 **Henriette Princess of Belgium** * Bruxelles 30.11.1870 + Sierre, Valais, Suisse 28.3.1948 dau. of Philippe Count of Flanders, and had issue:

XII   a.   **Marie Louise Ferdinande Charlotte Henriette Princess of Orleans** * Neuilly 31.12.1896 = (1) Neuilly 12.1.1916 **Filipo Prince of Bourbon-Sicily** * Cannes 10.12.1885 + St. Johns, Canada 9.3.1949, − div. = (2) Chichester 12.12.1928 Walter Kingsland * New York 23.4.1888 + 20.7.1961, and had issue by 1st marriage, see elsewhere

               b.   **Sophie Joséphine Louise Marie Immaculée Gabrielle Philippine Henriette Princess of Orleans** * Neuilly 19.10.1898 + Château de Tourron 9.10.1928

               c.   **Geneviève Marie Jeanne Françoise Chantal Monique Louise Alberta Joséphine Gabrielle Emmanuela Henriette Princess of Orleans** * Neuilly 21.9.1901 = Neuilly 2.7.1923 Antoine Marquis de Chaponay * Paris 30.1.1893 + Rabat 9.9.1956, and has issue:

50

XIII   a)   **Pierre Emmanuel François Henri Baudouin de Chaponay** * Paris 24.1.1925 + on active service Gulf of Mexico 2.10.1943

         b)   **Henryanne Maria Pierre Emmanuelle Constance de Chaponay** * Cannes 8.5.1926

XII   d.   **Charles Philippe Emmanuel Ferdinand Louis Gérard Joseph Marie Ghislain Baudouin Christophe Raphael Antoine Expedit Henri Duc de Nemours** * Neuilly 4.4.1905 = Paris 24.9.1928 Marguerite Watson * Richmond 12.2.1899 dau. of Garret Watson s.p.

X   3)   **Marguerite Adélaide Marie Princess of Orleans** * Tuileries 16.2.1846 + Paris 24.10.1893 = Château de Chantilly 15.1.1872 Wladyslaw Prince Czartoryski * Warsaw 3.7.1828 + Boulogne-sur-Seine 23.6.1894 and had issue:

XI   (1)   **Adam Ludwik Prince Czartoryski** * Paris 5.11.1872 + Warsaw 21.6.1937 = Warsaw 31.8.1901 Maria Ludwika Krasińska * Warsaw 24.3.1883 + Cannes 23.1.1958 dau. of Count Ludwik Krasiński, and had issue:

XII   a.   **Izabella Malgorzata Maria Magdalena Antonina Jacenta Jósefa Ludwika Princess Czartoryska** * Warsaw 17.8.1902 + Cannes 8.3.1929 = Paris 25.8.1927 **Prince Gabriel of Bourbon-Sicily** * Cannes 11.1.1897, and had issue see elsewhere

         b.   **Elzbieta Bianka Maria Konstancja Princess Czartoryska** * Krasne 1.9.1905 = Goluchowo 26.6.1929 Count Stefan Zamoyski * Racewo 17.2.1904, and has issue:

XIII   a)   **Maria Helena Zamoyska** * Roma 12.2.1940

         b)   **Count Zdzislaw Zamoyski** * Washington 25.9.1943

         c)   **Count Adam Stefan Zamoyski** * New York 11.1.1949

XII   c.   **Jósef August Antoni Maria Pius Prince Czartoryski** * Warsaw 20.10.1907 + Seville 1.7.1946 = Ouchy-Lausanne 16.8.1937 **Maria de los Dolores Princess of Bourbon-Sicily** * Madrid 15.2.1909 dau. of Carlos Prince of Bourbon-Sicily, Infant of Spain, and has issue:

XIII   a)   **Adam Karol Prince Czartoryski** * Seville 2.1.1940

         b)   **Ludwik Piotr Prince Czartoryski** * Seville 13.3.1945 + Seville 3.5.1946

XII   d.   **Anna Maria Jolanata Gabriela Izabella Józefa Antonina Princess Czartoryska** * Goluchowo 6.1.1914 = Warsaw 12.8.1936 Wladyslaw Prince Radziwill * Brixen 21.6.1909 — div. and has issue:

XIII   a)   **Monika Magdalena Maria Aloiza Princess Radziwill** * Warsaw 21.6.1937 = Rio de Janeiro 26.11.1960 Manuel d'Ornellas Suarez * San Sebastian, Spain 29.4.1937, and has issue:

XIV   (a)   **Tomas Manuel d'Ornellas Radziwill** * Buenos Aires 13.9.1961

            (b)   **Veronica d'Ornellas Radziwill** * Buenos Aires 24.12.1962

            (c)   **Maria Cristina d'Ornellas Radziwill** * Lima, Peru 28.1.1966

XIII   b)   **Elzbieta Maria Gabriela Zofia Princess Radziwill** * Warsaw 6.1.1939 = Rio de Janeiro 18.7.1958 Antoni Potocki * Cracow 26.9.1924, and has issue:

XIV   (a)   **Inès Antonia Maria Jolanta Potocka** * Buenos Aires 29.1.1959

            (b)   **Marguerite Maria Gabriele Louise Potocka** * Rio de Janeiro 27.3.1960

            (c)   **Jan Antonio Rafael Ladislaus Potocki** * Rio de Janeiro 16.4.1961

            (d)   **Izabela Maria Gabriele Sophie Potocka** * Rio de Janeiro 16.6.1962

XIV (e) **Stefan Alexander Rafael Potocki** * Montreal 18.7.1965

XII e. **Wadyslaw Maria Piotr Alkantary Prince Czartoryski** * Goluchowo 30.8.1918 = Montana, Suisse 28.1.1949 **Elisabeth York** * Winterton, Lincs. 11.11.1925 dau. of Georg York s.p.

f. **Therese Maria Magdalena Joanna Elzbieta Princess Czartoryska** * Goluchowo 1.7.1923 = Bytom 24.12.1945 Jan Groda-Kowalski * Kordon 23.5.1917, and has issue:

XIII a) **Maria Barbara Groda-Kowalska** * Cracow 15.6.1946

b) **Magdalene Marie Groda-Kowalska** * Opole 5.6.1947

c) **Adalbert Thaddäus Johann Groda-Kowalski** * Opole 29.8.1948

XII g. **Ludwik Adam Maria Józef Antoni Jan Karol Rafael Prince Czartoryski** * Warsaw 14.12.1927 ✗ Warsaw 24.9.1944

XI (2) **Witold Kazikierz Filip Jan Prince Czartoryski** * Paris 10.3.1876 + Versailles 29.10.1911

X 4) **Blanche Marie Amélie Caroline Louise Victoire Princess of Orleans** * Claremont 28.10.1857 + Paris 4.2.1932

IX 5. **Françoise Louise Caroline Princess of Orleans** * Twickenham 28.3.1816 + Château de Neuilly 20.5.1818

6. **Marie Clémentine Caroline Léopoldine Clotilde Princess of Orleans** * Château de Neuilly 3.6.1817 + Wien 16.2.1907 = St-Cloud 20.4.1843 August Ludwig Prince of Saxe-Coburg and Gotha * Wien 13.6.1818 + Schloss Ebenthal 26.7.1881, and had issue:

X 1) **Philipp Ferdinand Marie August Raphael Prince of Saxe-Coburg and Gotha** * Paris 28.3.1844 + Coburg 3.7.1921 = Bruxelles 4.2.1875 **Louise Princess of Belgium** * Bruxelles 18.2.1858 + Wiesbaden 1.3.1924 dau. of Leopold II King of Belgium and had issue:

XI (1) **Leopold Clemens Philipp August Maria Prince of Saxe-Coburg and Gotha** * Szent-Anthal 19.7.1878 + Wien 27.4.1916

(2) **Dorothea Marie Henriette Auguste Luise Princess of Saxe-Coburg and Gotha** * Wien 30.4.1881 = Coburg 2.8.1898 **Ernst Güther Duke Schleswig-Holstein-Sonderburg-Augustenburg** * Dolzig 11.8.1883 + Primkenau 22.2.1921 s.p.

X 2) **Ludwig August Marie Eudes Prince of Saxe-Coburg and Gotha** * Château d'Eu 9.8.1845 + Carlsbad 14.9.1907 = Rio de Janiero 15.12.1864 **Leopoldina Princess of Bragança, Princess of Brazil** * Rio de Janeiro 13.7.1847 + Wien 7.2.1871 dau. of Emperor Pedro II of Brazil, and had issue:

XI (1) **Peter August Ludwig Maria Michael Gabriel Raphael Gonzaga Prince of Saxe-Coburg and Gotha** * Rio de Janeiro 19.3.1866 + Wien 6.7.1934

(2) **August Leopold Philipp Maria Michael Gabriel Raphael Gonzaga Prince of Saxe-Coburg and Gotha** * Rio de Janeiro 6.12.1867 + Schladming 11.10.1922 = Wien 30.5.1894 **Karoline Archduchess of Austria** * Alt-Münster 5.9.1869 + Budapest 12.5.1945 dau. of Karl Salvator Archduke of Austria, Prince of Tuscany, and had issue:

XII a. **August Klemens Karl Joseph Maria Michael Gabriel Raphael Gonzaga Prince of Saxe-Coburg and Gotha** * Pola 27.10.1895 + Gerasdorf 22.9.1909

b. **Klementine Maria Theresa Josepha Leopoldine Viktoria Raphaela Michaela Gabriela Gonzaga Princess of Saxe-Coburg and Gotha** * Pola 23.3.1897 = Coburg 17.11.1925 Eduard v. Heller * Cairo 21.3.1877, and has issue:

52

XIII   a)   **Marie Amelie v. Heller** * Bougy-Saint-Martin 9.8.1926 = Bougy-Saint-Martin 19.12.1949 **Carlo Felice Nicolis dei Conti di Robilant e Cereaglio** * Venezia 11.7.1927 and has issue, see elsewhere

       b)   **Athlone Alexander August Georg v. Heller** * Bougy-Saint-Martin 22.7.1938

XII   c.   **Maria Karoline Philomena Ignatia Pauline Josepha Michaela Gabriela Raphaela Gonzaga Princess of Saxe-Coburg and Gotha** * Pola 10.1.1899 + Schladming 6.6.1941

       d.   **Ranier Maria Joseph Florian Ignatius Michael Gabriel Raphael Gonzaga Prince of Saxe-Coburg and Gotha** * Pola 4.5.1900 disappeared in Budapest 7.1.1945 = (1) München 15.12.1930 Johanna Károlyi v. Károly-Patty * Salzburg 17.9.1906 dau. of Caroly Károlyi v. Károly-Patti = (2) Budapest 13.2.1940 Edith de Kozol * Budapest 31.5.1913, and had issue:

       by 1st marriage:

XIII   a)   **Johannes Heinrich Friedrich Werner Konrad Ranier Maria Prince of Saxe-Coburg and Gotha** * Innsbruck 28.3.1931 = München 24.10.1957 Freiin. Marie Gabriele v. Fürstenberg * Tinz 22.6.1921 dau. of Franz Xaver Frhr. v. Fürstenberg, and has issue:

XIV   (a)   **Felicitas Franziska Princess of Saxe-Coburg and Gotha** * 6.4.1958

XII   e.   **Philipp Josias Maria Joseph Ignatius Michael Gabriel Raphael Gonzaga Prince of Saxe-Coburg and Gotha** * Walterskirchen 18.8.1901 = Budapest ... 1945 Sarah Halas * ... and has issue:

XIII   a)   **Philipp Prince of Saxe-Coburg and Gotha** * ...

XII   f.   **Theresia Christiane Maria Josepha Ignatia Benizia Michaela Gabriela Raphaela Gonzaga Princess of Saxe-Coburg and Gotha** * Walterskirchen 23.8.1902 = Salzburg 6.10.1930 Lamoral Frhr. Taxis v. Bordogna u.Valnigra * Unter-Mais 7.12.1900 + Trento 28.1.1966 and has issue:

XIII   a)   **Dom Lamoral Carlos Tasso de Saxe-Coburg e Bragança** * Gmunden 16.7.1931 = São Paulo 15.12.1956 Doña Denyse Morse Paes de Almeida * São Paulo 27.4.1935 dau. of Sebastiao Pais de Almeida

       b)   **Doña Alice Carolina Teresa Francisça Clementina Antonia Josefina Maria Tasso de Saxe-Coburg e Bragança** * Schladming 7.6.1936 = Villazano di Trento 7.1.1956 Conte Michele Carlo di Formentini * Gorizia 3.1.1929, and has issue:

XIV   (a)   **Conte Leonardo Alessandro di Formentini** * Gorizia 28.10.1956

       (b)   **Isabella Teresa Cristina Leopoldina di Formentini** * Gorizia 3.1.1958

       (c)   **Conte Filippo di Formentini** * Gorizia 1.5.1964

XIII   c)   **Tassilo Philip Frhr. Taxis v. Bordogna u.Valnigra** * Gmunden 3.1.1939

       d)   **Maria Christina Freiin. Taxis v. Bordogna u.Valnigra** * Pergine di Trento 31.1.1945

XII   g.   **Leopoldine Blanka Maria Josepha Ignazia Pankrazia Michaela Gabriela Raphaela Gonzaga Princess of Saxe-Coburg and Gotha** * Schloss Gerasdorf 13.5.1905

       h.   **Ernst Franz Maria Joseph Ignatius Thaddeus Felix Michael Gabriel Raphael Gonzaga Prince of Saxe-Coburg and Gotha** * Schloss Gerasdorf 25.2.1907 = Ebenthal 4.9.1939 Irmgard Röll * Aue, Sachsen 22.1.1912

XI   (3)   **Joseph Ferdinand Franz Maria Michael Gabriel Raphael Gonzaga Prince of Saxe-Coburg and Gotha** * Rio de Janeiro 21.5.1869 + Wiener-Neustadt 13.8.1888

XI   (4)   **Ludwig Gaston Klemens Maria Michael Gabriel Raphael Gonzaga Prince of Saxe-Coburg and Gotha** * Schloss Ebenthal 15.9.1870 + Innsbruck 23.1.1942 = (1) München 1.5.1900 **Mathilde Princess of Bavaria** * Villa Amseè 17.8.1877 + Davos 6.8.1906 dau. of Ludwig III King of Bavaria; = (2) Bischofsteinitz 30.11.1907 Maria Anna Gräfin v.u. zu Trauttmansdorff-Weinsberg * Ober-Waltersdorf 27.5.1873 + Coburg 24.7.1948 dau. of Karl 4th Fürst v.u. zu Trauttmansdorff-Weinsberg, and had issue:

by 1st marriage:

XII   a.   **Antonius Maria Ludwig Klemens Eugen Karl Heinrich August Luitpold Leopold Franz Wolfgang Peter Joseph Gaston Alexander Alfons Ignatius Aloysius Stanislaus Prince of Saxe-Coburg and Gotha** * Innsbruck 17.6.1901 = Steyr 14.5.1938 Luise Mayrhofer * Graz 22.6.1903 dau. of Alois Mayrhofer

              b.   **Maria Immakulata Leopoldine Franziska Theresia Elisabeth Sancta-Angelica Nicolette Princess of Saxe-Coburg and Gotha** * Innsbruck 10.9.1904 + Varese 18.3.1940

by 2nd marriage:

XII   c.   **Josefine Maria Anna Leopoldine Amalie, Klementine Ludovica Theresia Gabriela Gonzaga Princess of Saxe-Coburg and Gotha** * Château de Vogelsang 20.9.1911 = Kitzbühel 12.5.1937 Frhr. v. Baratta-Dragono * Schloss Budischau 28.11.1901, — div. and has issue:

XIII   a)   **Maria Carolina Isabella Eugenie Florence Aloisia Josefa Augusta Freiin. v. Baratta-Dragono** * Wien 16.10.1937

              b)   **Richard-Pedro Clemens Friedrich Alois Maria Frhr. v. Baratta-Dragono** * Wien 16.4.1939

X   3)   **Maria Adelheid Amalie Clotilde Princess of Saxe-Coburg and Gotha** * Château de Neuilly 8.7.1846 * Alscút 3.6.1927 = Coburg 12.5.1864 **Joseph Karl Ludwig Archduke of Austria, Palatine of Hungary** * Pressburg 2.3.1833 + Fiume 13.6.1905, and had issue see elsewhere

      4)   **Maria Luise Franziska Amalie Princess of Saxe-Coburg and Gotha** * Coburg 23.10.1848 + Schloss Biederstein 6.5.1894 = Schloss Ebenthal b. Wien 20.9.1875 Maximilian Duke in Bavaria * München 7.12.1849 + Feldafing 12.6.1893, and had issue:

XI   (1)   **Siegfried August Maximilian Maria Duke in Bavaria** * Bamberg 10.7.1876 + München 12.3.1952

            (2)   **Christoph Joseph Clemens Maria Duke in Bavaria** * Schloss Biederstein 22.4.1879 + München 10.7.1963 = München 14.5.1924 Anna Sibig * Scholtzhausen b. Mallersdorf 18.7.1874 + 31.12.1957 s.p.

            (3)   **Luitpold Emanuel Ludwig Maria Duke in Bavaria** * Schloss Biederstein 30.6.1890

X   5)   **Ferdinand I Maximilian Karl Leopold Maria, King of Bulgaria, Prince of Saxe-Coburg and Gotha** * Wien 26.2.1861 + Coburg 10.9.1948 = (1) Villa Pianore, Lucca 20.4.1893 **Marie Luise Princess of Bourbon-Parma** * Roma 17.1.1870 + Sofia 31.1.1899 dau. of Robert Duke of Parma; = (2) Gera 1.3.1908 **Eleonore Princess Reuss** * Trebschen b. Züllichau 22.8.1860 + Euxinograd 12.9.1917 dau. of Heinrich IV Fürst Reuss-Kostritz, and had issue by 1st marriage:

XI   (1)   **Boris III Klemens Robert Maria Pius Ludwig Stanislaus Xaver King of Bulgaria** * Sofia 30.1.1894 + Sofia 28.8.1943 = Assisi 25.10.1930 **Giovanna Princess of Savoy** * Roma 13.11.1907 dau. of Vittorio Emmanuele III King of Italy, and had issue:

XII   a.   **Marie Luise Princess of Bulgaria** * Sofia 13.1.1933 = Cannes 20.2.1957 **Karl 7th Fürst zu Leiningen** * Coburg 2.1.1928 and has issue see elsewhere

             b.   **Simeon II King of Bulgaria** * Sofia 16.6.1937 = Lausanne 21.1.1962 Doña Margarita Gomez Acebo y Cojuela * Madrid 6.1.1935, dau. of Don Manuel Gomez Acebo y Modet Marqués de Cortina, and has issue:

XIII a) **Kardram Prince of Bulgaria** * Madrid 2.12.1962

b) **Kyril Prince of Bulgaria** * Madrid 11.7.1964

c) **Kubrat Prince of Bulgaria** * Madrid 5.11.1965

XI (2) **Cyril Heinrich Franz Ludwig Anton Karl Philipp Prince of Bulgaria** * Sofia 17.11.1895 + Sofia
1.2.1945

(3) **Euxodie Augusta Philippine Klementine Marie Princess of Bulgaria** * Sofia 17.1.1898

(4) **Nadejda Klementine Maria Pia Majella Princess of Bulgaria** * Sofia 30.1.1899 + Stuttgart 15.2.1958
= Bad Mergentheim 24.1.1924 **Albrecht Eugen Duke of Württemberg** * Stuttgart 8.1.1895
+ Schwäbisch-Gmund 24.6.1954, and has issue see elsewhere

IX 7. **François Ferdinand Philippe Louis Marie Prince de Joinville** * Château de Neuilly 14.8.1818 + Paris 16.6.1900
= Rio de Janeiro 1.5.1843 **Francisça Princess of Bragança, Princess of Brazil** * Rio de Janeiro 2.8.1824 + Paris
27.3.1898, dau. of Pedro I Emperor of Brazil, and had issue:

X 1) **Françoise Marie Amélie Princess of Orleans** * Château de Neuilly 14.8.1844 + Château de Saint-Firmin
28.10.1925 = Kingston-on-Thames 11.6.1863 **Robert Duc de Chartres** * Tuileries 9.11.1840 + Château
de Saint-Firmin 5.12.1910, and had issue see elsewhere

2) **Pierre Philippe Jean Marie Duc de Penthièvre** * Château de Saint-Cloud 4.11.1845 + 17.7.1919

3) **a daughter** * & + Claremont 30.10.1849

IX 8. **Charles Ferdinand Louis Philippe Emmanuel Duc de Penthièvre** * Palais Royal 1.1.1820 + Château de Neuilly
25.7.1828

9. **Henri Eugène Philippe Louis Duc d'Aumale** * Palais Royal 16.1.1822 + Zucco, Sicily 7.5.1897 = Napoli
25.11.1844 **Maria Carolina Princess of Bourbon-Sicily** * Wien 26.4.1822 + Twickenham 6.12.1869 dau. of
Leopoldo Prince of Bourbon-Sicily, Prince of Salerno, and had issue:

X 1) **Louis Philippe Marie Léopold, Prince de Condé** * St-Cloud 15.11.1845 + Sydney, Australia 24.5.1866

2) **Henri Léopold Philippe Duc de Guise** * St-Cloud 11.9.1847 + St-Cloud 17.10.1847

3) **François Paul Duc de Guise** * Palermo 11.1.1852 + Twickenham 15.4.1852

4) **François Louis Philippe Marie Duc de Guise** * Twickenham 5.1.1854 + Paris 25.7.1872

IX 10. **Antoine Marie Philippe Louis Duc de Montpensier** * Château de Neuilly 31.7.1824 + San Lucar de Barrameda
4.2.1890 = Madrid 10.10.1846 **Maria Luisa Infanta of Spain** * Madrid 30.1.1832 + Séville 2.2.1897 dau. of
Fernando VII King of Spain, and had issue:

X 1) **Doña Maria Isabel Francisça de Asis Antonia Luisa Fernanda Cristina Amelia Felipa Adelaide Josefa Elena
Enriqueta Carolina Justina Rufina Gasparina Melchiora Balthasara Matea de Orleans y Borbón, Infanta of
Spain** * Séville 21.9.1848 + Villamanrique, Séville 23.4.1919 = Kingston-on-Thames 30.5.1864 **Louis
Philippe Prince of Orleans, Comte de Paris** * Paris 24.8.1838 + Stowe House 8.9.1894, and had issue
see elsewhere

2) **Doña Maria Amelia Luisa Enriqueta de Orleans y Borbón, Infanta of Spain** * Séville 28.8.1851 + Séville
11.11.1870

3) **Doña Maria Cristina Francisça de Paula Antoineta de Orleans y Borbón, Infanta of Spain** * Séville
29.10.1852 + Séville 28.4.1879

4) **Doña Maria de la Regla Francisça de Asis Antonia Luisa Fernanda de Orleans y Borbón, Infanta of Spain**
* Séville 9.10.1856 + Séville 25.7.1861

5) **Don Fernando Maria Enrique Carlos de Orleans y Borbón, Infant of Spain** * San Lucar de Barrameda
29.5.1859 + Saint-Mesmin, près d'Orleans 3.12.1873

X	6)		**Doña Maria de la Mercedes Isabel Francisça de Asis Antonia Luisa Fernanda de Orleans y Borbón, Infanta of Spain** * Madrid 24.6.1860 + Madrid 26.6.1878 = Madrid 23.1.1878 **Alfonso XII King of Spain** * Madrid 28.11.1857 + El Pardo Madrid 25.11.1885 s.p.

7) **Don Felipe Raymundo Maria de Orleans y Borbón, Infant of Spain** * 12.5.1862 + 13.2.1864

8) **Don Antonio Maria Luis Felipe Juan Florencio de Orleans y Borbón, Infant of Spain, Duque de Galliera** * Séville 23.2.1866 + Paris 24.12.1930 = Madrid 6.3.1886 **Doña Maria Eulalia de Borbón y Borbón, Infanta of Spain** * Madrid 12.2.1864 + Irun 8.3.1958, dau. of Isabella II Queen of Spain, and had issue:

XI (1) **Don Alfonso Maria Francisço Antonio Diego de Orleans y Borbón, Infant of Spain, Duque de Galliera** * Madrid 12.11.1886 = Rosenau b. Coburg 15.7.1909 **Beatrice Princess of Saxe-Coburg and Gotha, Princess of Great Britain and Ireland** * Eastwell Park 20.4.1884 + San Lucar de Barrameda 13.7.1966 dau. of Alfred Duke of Saxe-Coburg and Gotha, Duke of Edinburgh, Prince of Great Britain and Ireland, and had issue:

XII a. **Don Alvaro Antonio Carlos Felipe Fernando de Orleans y Sajonia Coburgo Gotha Prince of Orleans, Duque de Galliera** * Coburg 20.4.1910 = morgantically Roma 10.7.1937 Carla Parodi Delfino ʌ* Milano 13.12.1909 dau. of Leopoldo Parodi Delfino, and had issue:

XIII a) **Doña Gerada de Orleans y Parodi Delfino** * Roma 25.8.1939

b) **Don Alfonso de Orleans y Parodi Delfino** * Roma 23.8.1941

c) **Doña Beatrix de Orleans y Parodi Delfino** * Séville 27.4.1943 = 25.4.1964 Conte Tomasso Farini * Torino 16.9.1938

d) **Don Alvaro de Orleans y Parodi Delfino** * Roma 1.3.1947

XII b. **Don Alfonso Maria Cristino Justo de Orleans y Sajonia Coburgo Gotha Prince of Orleans** * Madrid 28.5.1912 + X by the Communists Madrid 18.11.1936

c. **Don Ataulfo Carlos Isabelo Alejandro de Orleans y Sajonia Coburgo Gotha Prince of Orleans** * Madrid 20.10.1913

XI (2) **Don Luis Fernando Maria Zacarias de Orleans y Borbón, Infant of Spain** * Madrid 5.11.1888 + Paris 20.6.1945 = London 19.9.1930 Marie Constance Say * Verrières-le-Buisson 25.8.1857 + Paris 15.7.1943 dau. of Constant Say s.p.

(3) **Doña Roberta de Orleans y Borbón, Infanta of Spain** * & + Madrid 16.3.1890

X 9) **Don Luis Maria Felipe Antonia de Orleans y Borbón** * Séville 30.4.1867 + 21.5.1874

4 The Descendants of Emperor Franz´1 Duke of Lorraine
1708-1765 and Empress Maria Theresia 1717-1780.

V   **Franz Stephan Duke of Lorraine, Emperor Franz I, Holy Roman Emperor**   * Nancy 8.12.1708 + Innsbruck 18.8.1765 = 12.2.1736 Empress **Maria Theresia** * Wien 13.5.1717 + Wien 29.11.1780 dau. of Emperor Karl VI and had issue:

VI   1.   **Marie Elisabeth Amelia Antoinette Josefa Gabriele Johanna Agathe Archduchess of Austria** * Wien 5.2.1737 + Laxenburg 7.6.1740

     2.   **Marie Anna Josefine Antoinette Johanna Archduchess of Austria** * Wien 6.10.1738 + Wien 19.11.1789

     3.   **Marie Karoline Ernestine Antonia Johanna Josefa Archduchess of Austria** * Wien 12.1.1740 + Wien 25.1.1741

     4.   **Josef II Benoit August Johann Anton Michael Adam, Holy Roman Emperor** * Schönbrunn 13.3.1741 + Wien 20.2.1790 = (1) Wien 6.10.1760 **Maria Isabella Princess of Parma, Infanta of Spain** * Madrid 31.12.1741 + Wien 27.11.1763 dau. of Philip Duke of Parma; = (2) Schönbrunn 23.1.1765 **Maria Josefa Princess of Bavaria** * München 30.3.1739 + Wien 28.5.1767 dau. of Karl VIII Holy Roman Emperor, Elector of Bavaria, and had issue:

     by 1st marriage:

VII   1)   **Maria Theresia Elisabeth Archduchess of Austria** * Wien 20.3.1762 + Wien 23.1.1770

     2)   **Marie Christine Archduchess of Austria** * & + Wien 22.11.1763

VI   5.   **Marie Christine Josepha Johanna Antonia Archduchess of Austria** * Wien 13.5.1742 + Wien 24.6.1798 = Wien 8.4.1766 **Albrecht Prince of Saxony, Duke of Teschen,** * Moritzburg 11.7.1738 + Wien 10.2.1822 and had issue see elsewhere

     6.   **Marie Elisabeth Josepha Johanna Antoinette Archduchess of Austria** * Wien 13.8.1743 + Linz 22.9.1808

     7.   **Karl Josef Emmanuel Johann Nepomuk Anton Prokop Archduke of Austria** * Wien 1.2.1745 + Wien 18.1.1761

     8.   **Maria Amelie Josephine Johanna Antoinette Archduchess of Austria** * Wien 26.2.1746 + Prag 18.6.1804 = Colorno 19.7.1769 **Ferdinand Duke of Parma,** * Parma 20.1.1751 + Fontevivo 9.10.1802, and had issue see elsewhere

     9.   **Peter Leopold I Josef Holy Roman Emperor, Grand Duke of Tuscany etc.** * Schönbrunn 5.5.1747 + Wien 1.3.1792 = Innsbruck 5.8.1765 **Maria Luisa Infanta of Spain** * Napoli 24.11.1745 + Wien 15.5.1792 dau. of Carlos III King of Spain, and had issue:

VII   1)   **Marie Theresia Josepha Charlotte Johanna Archduchess of Austria** * Wien 14.1.1767 + Dresden 7.11.1827 = Wien 18.10.1787 **Anton I King of Saxony** * Dresden 27.12.1755 + Pillnitz 6.6.1836, and had issue see elsewhere

     2)   **Franz II Joseph Holy Roman Emperor** and since 1804 **Emperor of Austria, King of Hungary etc.** * Firenze 12.2.1768 + Wien 2.3.1835 = (1) Wien 6.1.1788 **Elisabeth Duchess of Württemberg** * Treptow 21.4.1767 + Wien 18.2.1790 dau. of Friedrich Eugen Duke of Württemberg; = (2) Wien 19.9.1790 **Maria Teresa Princess of Naples and Sicily** * Napoli 6.6.1772 + Wien 13.4.1804 dau. of Ferdinando I King of Naples and Sicily = (3) Wien 6.1.1808 **Marie-Ludovika Archduchess of Austria-Este, Princess of Modena** * Monza 14.12.1787 + Verona 7.4.1816 dau. of Ferdinand Archduke of Austria, and Maria Beatrice Duchess of Modena; = (4) Wien 10.11.1816 Charlotte Auguste Princess of Bavaria * Mannheim 8.2.1792 + Wien 9.2.1873 dau. of Maximilian I Joseph King of Bavaria, and had issue:

     by 1st marriage:

VIII   (1)   **Ludovika Elisabeth Franziska Archduchess of Austria** * Wien 18.2.1790 + Wien 24.6.1791

     by 2nd marriage:

     (2)   **Marie Luise Leopoldine Franziska Theresia Josepha Lucia Archduchess of Austria** after 1814 **Duchess of Parma** * Wien 12.12.1791 + Wien 17.12.1847 = (1) The Louvre, Paris 2.4.1810 Napoleon I Emperor of France * Ajaccio 15.8.1769 + Longwood House, St. Helena 5.5.1821; = (2) Château de Sala, Parma 7.9.1821 Adam Adalbert Graf von Neipperg * Wien 8.4.1775 + Parma 22.2.1829; = (3) Parma 17.2.1834 Charles René Comte de Bombelles * Versailles 6.11.1785 + Versailles 30.5.1856, and had issue:

by 1st marriage:

IX   a.   **Napoleon II François Joseph Charles, King of Rome** titular Emperor of France, known as **The Duke of Reichstadt** * Tuileries Palace 20.3.1811 + Schönbrunn 22.7.1832

by 2nd marriage:

b.   **Albertina Maria Gräfin von Montenuovo** * Parma 1.5.1817 + Parma ... 1867 = Parma 28.10.1833 Luigi Conte di Sanvitale, Conte di Fontanellato * ... 1798 + Parma ... 1876, and had issue:

X   a)   **Conte Alberto di Sanvitale, Conte di Fontanellato** * Parma 28.8.1834 + Parma 25.9.1907 = Bologna 5.9.1869 Nob. Laura Malvezzi de Medici dei Marchesi di Castel Guelfo * ... 1845 + Lisboa 13.11.1876 dau. of Conte Giovanni Malvezzi de Medici, Marchese di Castel Guelfo, and had issue:

XI   (a)   **Nob. Albertina di Sanvitale** * Parma 17.11.1870 = Parma 27.4.1893 Conte Federico Montecuccoli degli Erri Marchese di Vaglio * Modena 15.11.1862 + Modena 31.10.1926, and has issue:

XII   1a.   **Conte Raimondo Montecuccoli degli Erri, Marchese di Vaglio** * Modena 18.1.1909 = Modena 25.1.1932 Maria Cecilia dei Conti Bentivoglio * Modena 1.2.1908 dau. of Conte Francesco Bentivoglio, and has issue:

XIII   1b.   **Francesca Montecuccoli degli Erri** * Modena 16.12.1932 = Modena 24.6.1959 Gian Carlo Bobbio * ..., and has issue:

XIV   1c.   **Mario Bobbio** * Milano 27.3.1960

             2c.   **Carlo Bobbio** * Milano 11.9.1963

XIII   2b.   **Conte Federico Montecuccoli degli Erri** * Modena 17.5.1934 = Modena 30.6.1960 Maria Angela Sillingardi * Modena 3.8.1935 dau. of Gaetano Sillingardi, and has issue:

XIV   1c.   **Maria Cecilia Montecuccoli degli Erri** * Vicenza 15.6.1961

             2c.   **Maria Luisa Montecuccoli degli Erri** * Vicenza 20.6.1964

XIII   3b.   **Giulia Montecuccoli degli Erri** * Modena 25.10.1936

XI   (b)   **Conte Giovanni di Sanvitale** * Parma 8.5.1872 + Bologna 7.4.1951

       (c)   **Nob. Guglielmina di Sanvitale** * ... + ...

X   b)   **Conte Stefano di Sanvitale** * Parma 14.8.1838 + Parma 2.1.1914

IX   c.   **Wilhelm Albrecht 1 Fürst von Montenuovo** * Salagrande, Parma 8.8.1819 + Wien 6.4.1895 = Wien 18.5.1850 Juliana Gräfin Batthyány-Strattman * 10.6.1827 + Wien 19.11.1871 dau. of Johann Baptist Graf Batthyány-Strattman, and had issue:

X   a)   **Albertine Leopoldine Wilhelmine Julia Maria Prinzessin v. Montenuovo** * Wien 30.6.1853 + Schloss Chroberz 13.11.1895 = Schloss Schwaigern 5.8.1873 Zygmunt Count Wielopolski, Marquis Gonzaga-Myszkowski * Kraków 30.1.1833 + Berlin 27.2.1902, and had issue:

Thomas Lawrence   *By gracious permission of H.M. The Queen*

5 Emperor Franz II, 1768–1835

XI (a) **Aleksander Erwin Wilhelm Julian Maria Count Wielopolski** * Chroberz 3.3.1875 + Chroberz 3.3.1937 = (1) Warszawa 15.9.1900 Zofia Countess von dem Broele gen. Plater * Plinksze 24.5.1879 + Chroberz 28.5.1926 dau. of Konstanty Count von dem Broele gen. Plater; = (2) Warszawa 27.12.1926 Helena Countess von dem Broele gen. Plater * Szayejki ... 1883 + Pruszkow 20.7.1954 dau. of Wladislaw Count von dem Broele gen. Plater, and had issue:

by 1st marriage:

XII 1a. **Zygmunt Konstanty Aleksander Albert Count Wielopolski** * Chroberz 10.7.1901 = Warszawa 22.8.1928 Maria Tyszkiewicz * Wilno 3.2.1904 dau. of Józef Count Tyszkiewicz, and has issue:

XIII 1b. **Aleksander Maria Józef Count Wielopolski** * Chroberz 15.10.1929 = Kraków 30.8.1953 Jadwiga Jaroszyńska * Pzaclaw 16.6.1934 dau. of Antoni Jaroszyński, and has issue:

XIV 1c. **Joanna Wielopolska** * Kraków 25.6.1955

2c. **Zofia Wielopolska** * 21.4.1959

XIII 2b. **Krzysztof Maria Pawel Józef Zygmunt Count Wielopolski** * Ksiaz Wielki 19.9.1931

3b. **Maria Isabella Teresa Zofia Eleonora Wielopolska** * Chroberz 4.1.1936 = 6.7.1963 Janusz Malinowski * 1931

XII 2a. **Maria Zofia Alberta Paulina Wielopolska** * Chroberz 16.7.1904 = Chroberz 26.9.1928 Wladyslaw Count Tarnowski * Końskie 21.11.1899 + missing in Russia 1939-44, and has issue:

XIII 1b. **Juliusz Count Tarnowski** * Końskie 21.9.1929 = Kraków 6.4.1953 Helena Ponińska * Poznań 15.8.1934 dau. of Edward Graf Poniński, and has issue:

XIV 1c. **Wladyslaw Count Tarnowski** * Kraków 7.1.1954

XIII 2b. **Marek Maria Stanislaw Count Tarnowski** * Końskie 26.1.1932

3b. **Aleksander Count Tarnowski** * Końskie 17.8.1934 = 6.12.1958 Marie Jeleńska * Wilno 20.5.1935 dau. of Kasimir Jaleński, and has issue:

XIV 1c. **Jacek Wladyslaw Maria Count Tarnowski** * Gdańsk 15.1.1964

2c. **Tomasz Count Tarnowski** * Gdańsk 11.6.1966

XII 3a. **Alfred Feliks Count Wielopolski** * Chroberz 19.10.1905 = Raclawice 21.9.1935 Maria Salomea Woytkowska * Stuttgart 1.3.1916 dau. of Tadeusz Woytkowski, and has issue:

XIII 1b. **Jan Marcin Count Wielopolski** * Warszawa 12.11.1936

2b. **Zofia Salomea Wielopolska** * Warszawa 12.6.1938 = 22.12.1961 Krzysztof Nieszkowski * 1929

3b. **Agnieszka Maria Klementina Wielopolska** * Klemensówska 10.7.1941

4b. **Andrzej Count Wielopolski** * ... 1945

XII		4a.	**Zofia Maria Olga Wielopolska** * Chroberz 14.9.1906 = Ksiaz-Wielki 26.4.1934 Jan Count Szeptycki * Przylbice 31.12.1905, and has issue:
XIII		1b.	**Pawl Jerzy Aleksander Leon Maria Count Szeptycki** * Lvóv 10.2.1935 = Pretoria 15.8.1961 Teresa Raciborska * ... and has issue:
XIV		1c.	**Katarzyna Teresa Maria Szeptycka** * 10.10.1962
		2c.	**Leon Franciszek Maria Count Szeptycki** * 8.3.1964
		3c.	**Paul Jan Maria Count Szeptycki** * 1.4.1965
XIII		2b.	**Maria Zofia Alberta Szeptycka** * Dziewietniki 13.12.1937
		3b.	**Andrzej Cyryl Maria Count Szeptycki** * Dziewietniki 9.7.1939
XII		5a.	**Aleksander Karol Count Wielopolski** * Chroberz 12.12.1910 = Warszawa 12.2.1938 Anna Beata Manteuffel * Anińsk 18.11.1915 dau. of Ignacy Baron Manteuffel, and has issue:
XIII		1b.	**Hubert Count Wielopolski** * Warszawa 15.1.1940
		2b.	**Piotr Count Wielopolski** * Warszawa 9.1.1943
		3b.	**Ignacy Count Wielopolski** * Michrów 3.1.1945
XII		6a.	**Alberta Maria Teresa Wielopolska** * Kraków 8.3.1917 = Warszawa 18.9.1943 Gerard Labuda * Nowa Huta 30.12.1916, and has issue:
XIII		1b.	**Aleksander Idzi Labuda** * Chroberz 15.6.1944
		2b.	**Iwo Maria Labuda** * Poznań 13.6.1945
		3b.	**Adam Stanislaw Labuda** * Poznań 21.11.1946
		4b.	**Damian Gerard Labuda** * Poznań 27.9.1949
		5b.	**Anastazja Zofia Labuda** * Poznań 21.6.1953
XI	(b)		**Maria Malgorzata Paulina Wilhelmina Róza Leopoldyna Julia Wielopolska** * Chroberz 30.3.1876 + Philadelphia, U.S.A. 31.12.1963 = Warszawa 24.8.1895 Józafat Count Plater-Zyberk * St. Petersburg 26.10.1859 + Moskorzew 7.1.1933, and had issue:
XII		1a.	**Stanislaw Count Plater-Zyberk** * Warszawa 22.4.1897 + Kielce 6.1.1952 = (1) Radoszewnica 4.2.1933 Helena Ostrowska * ... + Radoszewnica ... 3.1943 dau. of Michal Ostrowski; = (2) Kielce 7.4.1947 Wanda Zabkiewicz * Wilno 6.7.1920 dau. of Michal Zabkiewicz, and had issue:
			by 1st marriage:
XIII		1b.	**Jerzy Count Plater-Zyberk** * Male Soleczniki 21.4.1934 + Dźwinów 17.1.1953
		2b.	**Elzbieta Izabella Plater-Zyberk** * Male Soleczniki 23.11.1935
		3b.	**Michal Count Plater-Zyberk** * Male Soleczniki 22.5.1937
			by 2nd marriage:
		4b.	**Malgorzata Plater-Zyberk** * Kielce 4.8.1948
		5b.	**Andrzej Count Plater-Zyberk** * Kielce 10.6.1951
XII		2a.	**Aleksander Andrzej Erwin Zygmunt Count Plater-Zyberk** * Bebra 2.5.1899

XII	3a.	**Jerzy Count Plater-Zyberk** * Bebra 22.4.1900 + Bystra 23.12.1933
	4a.	**Zygmunt Count Plater-Zyberk** * Bebra 20.7.1901
	5a.	**Paulina Plater-Zyberk** * Bebra 18.3.1904 = Moskorzew 8.1.1930 Jan Count Plater-Zyberk * Moszków 5.9.1894, and has issue:

XIII   1b.   **Malgorzata Maria Plater-Zyberk** * Moszków 4.3.1931 = Paris 8.6.1957 Leszek Firla * Gorlice 29.6.1932, and has issue:

XIV   1c.   **Helena Janina Paulina Maria Firla** * Genève 20.4.1958

                2c.   **Barbara Malgorzata Maria Firla** * Genève 6.8.1962

XIII   2b.   **Hubert Maria Count Plater-Zyberk** * Moszków 22.6.1932 = Yaoundé 3.8.1959 Countess Sophie Dzieduszycka * 29.12.1932 dau. of Count Stanislas Dzieduszycki, and had issue:

XIV   1c.   **Ingrid Plater-Zyberk** * Yaoundé, Africa 2.6.1961

                2c.   **Anna Plater-Zyberk** * Pointe Noire, Africa 19.7.1966

XIII   3b.   **Helena Maria Plater-Zyberk** * Moszków 26.10.1933 = Paris 5.5.1961 Claude Julien La Ferrière * Firminy 22.2.1932, and has issue:

XIV   1c.   **Gabriel La Ferrière** * Paris 9.2.1962

                2c.   **Jean La Ferrière** * Paris 26.3.1963

                3c.   **Hubert La Ferrière** * Paris 27.2.1966

XIII   4b.   **Eugeniusz Maria Count Plater-Zyberk** * Moszków 26.1.1936

       5b.   **Maria Alberta Plater-Zyberk** * Moszków 4.7.1937 = Paris 8.5.1965 Jean François Frégnac * Paris 12.9.1922 and has issue:

XIV   1c.   **Pauline Frégnac** * Paris 2.12.1966

XII   6a.   **Józafat Count Plater-Zyberk** * Królewiec 2.1.1906 = Gieranony 28.9.1938 Maria Meysztowicz * 13.2.1911 dau. of Edward Meysztowicz, and has issue:

XIII   1b.   **Maria Antonina Plater-Zyberk** * Wilno 9.7.1939 = 31.10.1964 **Godfrey v. Miller zu Aichholz** * 13.3.1933, and has issue see elsewhere

       2b.   **Józafat Maria Count Plater-Zyberk** * Jedrzejów 23.1.1941

       3b.   **Róza Maria Plater-Zyberk** * Jedrzejów 28.5.1943

       4b.   **Elzbieta Maria Plater-Zyberk** * Bry Mews, U.S.A. 20.12.1950

XII   7a.   **Maria Plater-Zyberk** * Bebra 1.6.1910 = Warszawa 26.4.1938 Tadeusz Count Czacki * Koniuchy 15.12.1905, and has issue:

XIII   1b.   **Anna Maria Czacka** * Poryck 8.2.1939 = Phoenixville, Pa. 12.9.1964 Georg Malik * 22.4.1932 and has issue:

XIV   1c.   **Julia Marie Elisabeth Malik** * Philadelphia 5.11.1965

XIII   2b.   **Malgorzata Maria Czacka** * Moskorzew 20.6.1941 = Phoenixville 4.4.1964 Joseph Victor Cygan * 7.4.1930, and has issue:

XIV   1c.   **Andrew-Victor Cygan** * Doylestown, Pa. 5.2.1965

                           2c.   **Monica Ann Cygan** * Noristown, Pa. 19.10.1966

XIII   3b.   **Stanislaw Tadeusz Count Czacki** * Moskorzew 15.12.1942

XI   (c)   **Maria Anna Paulina Julia Aniela Regina Roza Monika Franziska Wielopolska**
* Chroberz 8.9.1878 = Warszawa 16.10.1897 August Stanislaw Potocki
* Maluszyn 20.5.1868 + Moskorzew 1.11.1927, and has issue:

XII   1a.   **Alberta Maria Paulina Potocka** * Warszawa 10.2.1899 = Moskorzew
24.10.1922 Pawel Potocki * Chrzastów 4.7.1900 + Kraków 8.6.1945 s.p.

                           2a.   **Stanislaw Jan Zygmunt Franciszek Potocki** * Moskorzew 4.10.1902
= Kraków 8.1.1931 Joanna Potocka * Lvóv 21.9.1904 dau. of Andrzej
Potocki s.p.

XI   (d)   **Alfred Count Wielopolski** * Wien 17.11.1879 + Arusha 7.5.1955 = (1)
Torrigiani 12.11.1934 Caroline McMurtrie * 25.12.1868 + Nice ... 4.1939;
= (2) Philadelphia 2.2.1946 Catherine Merrick * Philadelphia 27.7.1900 dau. of
John Vaughan Merrick s.p.

       (e)   **Albert Krzysztof Julian Maria Józef Count Wielopolski** * Römerbad 7.8.1884
+ Brestovan 16.12.1939 = Jabloń 6.7.1910 Elzbieta Zamoyska * Warszawa
24.9.1888 dau. of Tomasz Count Zamoyski, and has issue:

XII   1a.   **Jan Count Wielopolski** * Spala 24.7.1911 missing in Russia 1939-1944

                           2a.   **Julia Wielopolska** * Spala 22.6.1912 = Brestovan 10.6.1944 Stefan Prenosil
* 14.9.1916, and has issue:

XIII   1b.   **Anna Prenosil** * Zlate 12.2.1946

                           2b.   **Eleonora Prenosil** * Bratislava 25.2.1948

                           3b.   **Jadwiga Prenosil** * Trnava 28.3.1951

XII   3a.   **Elzbieta Wielopolska** * Spala 8.10.1913 = Warszawa 15.11.1933 Wlodzimierz
Prince Swiatopolk Czetwertyński * Suchowola 21.11.1907 + Qualicum Beach,
B.C., Canada 12.9.1965, and has issue:

XIII   1b.   **Jerzy Prince Swiatopolk Czetwertyński** * Warszawa 15.9.1937
= 20.6.1964 Susan Marie Silvaggio * Seattle, Washington 30.5.1943
and has issue:

XIV   1c.   **Ann Elisabeth Princess Swiatopolk-Czetwertyńska** * Great Lakes,
Ill. U.S.A. 9.4.1966

XIII   2b.   **Krystyna Princess Swiatopolk Czetwertyńska** * Edinburgh 5.4.1947

XII   4a.   **Alberta Wielopolska** * Jablón 9.7.1915 = Brestovan 2.2.1946 Michal Pálka
* Liptovský Svätý Mikuláš 2.6.1902, and has issue:

XIII   1b.   **Elzbieta Pálka** * Bratislava 4.9.1946

                           2b.   **Darina Pálka** * Scarborough 21.10.1948

                           3b.   **Judyta Pálka** * Scarborough 15.12.1950

X   b)   **Alfred Adam Wilhelm Johann Maria 2 Fürst von Montenuovo** * Wien 16.9.1854
+ Wien 6.9.1927 = Wien 30.10.1879 Franziska Gräfin Kinsky v. Wchinitz u. Tettau
* Wien 26.12.1861 + Margarethen am Moos 13.7.1936 dau. of Ferdinand Fürst Kinsky
v. Wchinitz u. Tettau, and had issue:

XI   (a)   **Juliana Rosa Franziska Leopoldine Maria Prinzessin von Montenuovo**
* Margarethen am Moos 15.11.1880 + Schloss Berg 27.6.1961 = (1) Wien
20.5.1903 Dionys Graf Draskovich v. Trakostjan * Szent Kiraly 28.6.1875
+ Wien 8.3.1909 = (2) Bruck a.d. Leitha 5.2.1914 **Karl 5 Fürst zu Oettingen-
Oettingen u. Oettingen-Wallerstein** * Königssaal i. Böh. 27.4.1877 + München
24.5.1930, and had issue:

by 1st marriage:

XII   1a.   **Maria Franziska Juliana Johanna Gräfin Draskovich v. Trakostjan** * Wien
8.3.1904 = Berchtesgarden 3.9.1930 **Albrecht Duke of Bavaria** * München
3.5.1905, and has issue see elsewhere

XI   (b)   **Marie Felizia Franziska Wilhelmine Juliane Prinzessin v. Montenuovo** * Margarethen
20.10.1881 + Tegernsee 10.8.1954 = Wien 5.8.1909 **Franz Graf v. Ledebur-Wicheln**
* Petersburg i. Böh. 6.9.1877 + Wallerstein 24.5.1954 and has issue see elsewhere

(c)   **Ferdinand Bonaventura Franz Alfred Erwin Maximilian Marie 3 Fürst v. Montenuovo**
* Margarethen am Moos 29.5.1888 + Szob 2.5.1951 = Budapest 10.11.1927
Ilona Baroness Solymossy de Loos et Egervar * Nagy Teremi 18.4.1895 dau. of
Ladislaus Baron Solymossy de Loos et Egervar, and has issue:

XII   1a.   **Julia Franziska Ilona Maria Prinzessin v. Montenuovo** * Budapest 27.9.1930
= Budapest 11.5.1950 Gyula Mathé * Török-Kanisza 15.4.1904 s.p.

2a.   **Marie-Julie Johanna Gabrielle Prinzessin v. Montenuovo** * Budapest
29.9.1931 = Budapest 24.12.1955 Robert Reithauser * Budapest 1.12.1919

3a.   **Franziska Maria Johanna Gabrielle Prinzessin v. Montenuovo** * Budapest
24.5.1934 = Budapest 19.3.1955 Egon Nezsényi * Budapest 6.7.1914,
and has issue:

XIII   1b.   **Franziska Nezsényi** * Wien 23.9.1957

2b.   **Marie Julie Nezsényi** * Wien 20.6.1959

XI   (d)   **Franziska de Paula Maria Ludovika Juliane Wilhelmine Margarethe Prinzessin v.
Montenuovo** * Margarethen am Moos 22.8.1893 = Wien 11.4.1918 Leopold Prinz
von Lobkowicz * Unterberkovic 7.7.1888 + Prag 15.5.1933, and has issue:

XII   1a.   **Maria Julia Franziska Ida Kaspara Walpurga Prinzessin v. Lobkowicz** * Prag
25.11.1919 = Prag 26.1.1939 Johann Prinz v. Thurn u. Taxis * Schloss
Mzell 28.6.1908 + Freiburg i. Br 3.4.1959, and has issue:

XIII   1b.   **Maria Alexandra Franziska Gabriele Leonhardine Kaspara Ursula
Prinzessin v. Thurn u. Taxis** * Prag 21.10.1939 = München 20.9.1962
Franz Graf v. Colloredo-Mannsfeld * Paris 10.8.1938, and has issue:

XIV   1c.   **Antony Georg Ferdinand Maria Graf v. Colloredo-Mannsfeld**
* Wien 25.4.1964

2c.   **Teresita Maria Gräfin v. Colloredo-Mannsfeld** * Wien 27.12.1965

XIII   2b.   **Leopold Erich Maria Lamoral Leonhard Karl Anselm Kaspar Petrus Prinz v. Thurn u. Taxis** * Komotau 29.4.1943 + Graz 8.12.1957

           3b.   **Friedrich Leonhard Ignatius Josef Maria Lamoral Balthasar Prinz v. Thurn u. Taxis** * Linz 22.6.1950

           4b.   **Karl Ferdinand Maria Lamoral Leonhard Ignatius Anselm Prinz v. Thurn u. Taxis** * Linz 13.4.1952

           5b.   **Maximilian Anselm Andreas Paulinus Leonhard Lamoral Maria Prinz v. Thurn u. Taxis** * Linz 22.6.1955

XII   2a.   **Amalie Franziska Ida Melchiora Pauline Leonhardine Prinzessin v. Lobkowicz** * Unteřberkovic 25.1.1921 = Unteřberkovic 23.5.1944 Franz Prinz zu Schwarzenberg * Prag 24.3.1913, and has issue:

XIII   1b.   **Ludmila Maria de Victoria Franziska de Paula Eleonora Thaddea Leonharda Agnes de Bohemia Prinzessin zu Schwarzenberg** * Prag 25.7.1945

           2b.   **Isabelle Eleonore Maria Franziska Romana Leonharda Thaddea Sidonia Prinzessin zu Schwarzenberg** * Prag 22.6.1946

           3b.   **Johann v. Nepomuk Maria Heinrich Franz Leonhard Thaddäus Thomas de Aquino Prinz zu Schwarzenberg** * Chicago 19.2.1957

XII   3a.   **Leopoldine Bertha Marie Franziska Ida Balthasara Leonhardine Prinzessin v. Lobkowicz** * Unteřberkovic 14.11.1926 = Unteřberkovic 22.8.1945 Johann Graf Dobrzensky v. Dobrzenicz * Chotěboř 19.6.1911 and has issue:

XIII   1b.   **Johann Joseph Graf Dobrzensky v. Dobrzenicz** * Prag 14.6.1946

           2b.   **Zdislawa Marie Elisabeth Gräfin Dobrzensky v. Dobrzenicz** * Prag 23.5.1947

           3b.   **Helene Johanna Therese Gräfin Dobrzensky v. Dobrzenicz** * Château d'Eu 21.10.1948

           4b.   **Margarethe Rosa Isabelle Gräfin Dobrzensky v. Dobrzenicz** * Toronto 14.9.1952

           5b.   **Karl Kunata Lukas Graf Dobrzensky v. Dobrzenicz** * Toronto 4.6.1955

XII   4a.   **Rosa Maria Franziska Ida Kaspara Leonhardine Anselma Prinzessin v. Lobkowicz** * Prag 21.4.1929

XI   (c)   **Marie Sophie Wilhelmine Hyacinthe Prinzessin v. Montenuovo** * Wien 10.9.1859 + Wien 2.3.1911 = Wien 23.5.1878 Anton Graf Apponyi v. Nagy-Appony * Wien 29.12.1852 + Bad Ischl 4.2.1920, and had issue:

XII   1a.   **Julia Gräfin Apponyi v. Nagy-Appony** * Kis-Appony 13.9.1879 + ... = Jablonicz 31.10.1903 Heinrich Graf zu Herberstein * Gross-Opatowitz 17.1.1874 + ... and has issue:

XIII   1b.   **Marie Henriette Gräfin zu Herberstein** * Gross-Opatowitz 4.3.1914 = Budapest 21.7.1945 Mihály Graf Zichy zu Zich u. Vásonykeö * Budapest 5.7.1917, and has issue:

XIV   1c.   **Ferenc Graf Zichy zu Zich u. Vásonykeö** * ... 1946

XIV

        2c.   **László Graf Zichy zu Zich u. Vásonykeö** * ... 1947

        3c.   **Mihály Graf Zichy zu Zich u. Vásonykeö** * ... 1950

XIII

    2b.   **Johann Heinrich Graf zu Herberstein** * Gross-Opatowitz 28.2.1915
+ Budapest 4.11.1940

XII

  2a.   **Antal Graf Apponyi v. Nagy-Appony** * Marchegg 6.1.1883 + Lausanne
8.8.1954 = London 9.6.1912 Kitty Nelke * Englefield Green 27.7.1893,
and has issue:

XIII

    1b.   **Marie Juliane Katherine-Gabrielle Gräfin Apponyi v. Nagy-Appony**
* London 23.3.1913 + London 1.4.1952 = Sankt-Wolfgang 20.9.1934
Anthony Irby * London 21.3.1908, and had issue:

XIV

        1c.   **Paul Anthony Irby** * London 7.8.1935

        2c.   **George Anthony Peter Irby** * Windsor 3.6.1942

        3c.   **Charles Leonard Anthony Irby** * London 5.6.1945

XIII

    2b.   **Antal Eugen Paul Maria Hubert Heribert Graf Apponyi v. Nagy-Appony**
* Jablonicz 16.3.1915

    3b.   **Alexandrine Antoinette Marie Juliane Katherine Huberta Franziska
Gräfin Apponyi v. Nagy-Appony** * Ouchy-Lausanne 10.10.1919

VIII

  (3) **Ferdinand I Karl Leopold Joseph Franz Marcelin Emperor of Austria, King of Hungary** * Wien
19.4.1793 + Prag 29.6.1875 = Wien 27.2.1831 **Maria Anna Princess of Savoy** * Roma 19.9.1803
+ Prag 4.5.1884 dau. of Vittorio Emanuele I King of Sardinia s.p.

  (4) **Marie Caroline Leopoldine Franziska Theresia Josepha Medaros Archduchess of Austria** * Wien
8.6.1794 + Wien 16.3.1795

  (5) **Caroline Ludovika Leopoldine Archduchess of Austria** * Wien 4.12.1795 + Wien 30.6.1799

  (6) **Marie Leopoldina Josepha Caroline Archduchess of Austria** * Wien 22.1.1797 + Rio de Janeiro
11.12.1826 = Rio de Janeiro 6.11.1817 **Pedro I Emperor of Brasil** * Queluz 12.10.1798 + Queluz
24.9.1834, and had issue see elsewhere

  (7) **Marie Clementine Franziska Josepha Archduchess of Austria** * Wien 1.3.1798 + Château de Chantilly
3.9.1881 = Wien 28.7.1816 **Leopoldo Prince of Naples and Sicily, Prince of Salerno** * Napoli
2.7.1790 + Napoli 10.3.1851, and had issue see elsewhere

  (8) **Joseph Franz Leopold Archduke of Austria** * Wien 9.4.1799 + Wien 30.6.1807

  (9) **Caroline Ferdinande Theresia Josephine Demetria Archduchess of Austria** * Wien 8.4.1801
+ Dresden 22.5.1832 = Dresden 7.10.1819 **Friedrich August II King of Saxony** * Dresden
18.5.1797 + Brennbuchel 9.8.1854 s.p.

  (10) **Franz Karl Joseph Archduke of Austria** * Wien 7.12.1802 + Wien 8.5.1878 = Wien 4.11.1824
Sophie Princess of Bavaria * München 27.1.1805 + Wien 28.5.1872 dau. of Maximilian I Joseph
King of Bavaria, and had issue:

IX

  a. **Franz Joseph I Karl Emperor of Austria, King of Hungary etc.** * Schönbrunn 18.8.1830
+ Schönbrunn 21.11.1916 = Wien 24.4.1854 Elisabeth Duchess in Bavaria * München
24.12.1837 + Genève 10.9.1898 dau. of Maximilian Duke in Bavaria, and had issue:

X

  a) **Sophie Friederike Dorothea Marie Josephine Archduchess of Austria** * Laxenburg
5.3.1855 + 29.5.1857

  b) **Gisela Luise Marie Archduchess of Austria** * Laxenburg 12.7.1856 + München
27.7.1932 = Wien 20.4.1875 **Leopold Prince of Bavaria** * München 9.2.1846
+ München 28.9.1930, and had issue see elsewhere

X   c)   **Rudolf Franz Karl Joseph Crown Prince of Austria** * Laxenburg 21.8.1858 + Mayerling 30.1.1889 = Wien 10.5.1881 **Stephanie Princess of Belgium** * Château de Laeken 21.5.1864 + Pannonhalma, Hungary 23.8.1945 dau. of Leopold II King of The Belgians, and had issue:

XI   (a)   **Elisabeth Marie Henriette Stephanie Gisela Archduchess of Austria** * Laxenburg 2.9.1883 + Wien-Hütteldorf 22.3.1963 = (1) Wien 23.1.1902 Otto Prinz zu Windisch-Graetz * Graz 7.10.1873 + Lugano 25.12.1952; — div. = (2) Wien 4.5.1948 Leopold Petznek * Bruck a.d. Leitha 30.6.1881 + Wien 27.7.1956, and had issue:

by 1st marriage:

XII   1a.   **Franz Joseph Marie Otto Antonius Ignatius Oktavianus Prinz zu Windisch-Graetz** * Prag 22.3.1904 = Bruxelles 3.1.1934 Ghislaine Comtesse d'Arschot-Schoonhoven * Bruxelles 10.3.1912 dau. of Guillaume Comte d'Arschot-Schoonhoven, and has issue:

XIII   1b.   **Stephanie Marie Eva Prinzessin zu Windisch-Graetz** * Bruxelles 17.1.1939

2b.   **Guillaume Franz Joseph Maria Prinz zu Windisch-Graetz** * Nairobi 19.11.1950

XII   2a.   **Ernst Weriand Maria Otto Antonius Expeditus Anselmus Prinz zu Windisch-Graetz** * Prag 21.4.1905 + Wien 23.12.1952 = (1) Wien 17.10.1927 Ellen Skinner * Scheibbs 6.4.1906 dau. of Henry Skinner — div.; = (2) Schwarzenbach 11.5.1947 Eva Freiin. von Isbary * Wien 5.4.1921 dau. of Lothar Frhr. v. Isbary, and has issue:

by 1st marriage:

XIII   1b.   **Otto Ernst Wilhelm Prinz zu Windisch-Graetz** * Wien 5.12.1928 = Wien 27.4.1957 Johanna Gräfin v. Wimpffen * Budapest 26.5.1936 dau. of Franz Graf v. Wimpffen, and has issue:

XIV   1c.   **Henriette Raphaela Prinzessin zu Windisch-Graetz** * Salzburg 31.1.1958

2c.   **Désirée Eleonore Marie Felizitas Prinzessin zu Windisch-Graetz** * Salzburg 1.7.1959

3c.   **Philipp Amadeus Otto Ernst Prinz zu Windisch-Graetz** * Salzburg 22.6.1960

XIII   2b.   **Stephanie Maria Magdalena Prinzessin zu Windisch-Graetz** * Wien 1.1.1933 = St-Wolfgang 2.5.1956 Joseph Christoforetti * Kurtatsch b. Bozen 27.1.1919, and has issue:

XIV   1c.   **Angelika Maria Christoforetti** * Salzburg 16.11.1956

2c.   **Alexander Wilhelm Christoforetti** * Salzburg 18.1.1958

3c.   **Claudia Maria Christoforetti** * Salzburg 22.6.1960

4c.   **Nikolaus Josef Christoforetti** * 26.10.1962

by 2nd marriage:

XIII   3b.   **Eleonore Prinzessin zu Windisch-Graetz** * Wien 25.8.1947

4b.   **Elisabeth Prinzessin zu Windisch-Graetz** * Wien 24.10.1951

XII

3a. **Rudolf Johannes Maria Otto Joseph Antonius Andreas Prinz zu Windisch-Graetz** * Ploschkowitz 4.2.1907 + Wien 9.6.1939

4a. **Stephanie Eleonore Maria Elisabeth Kamilla Philomena Veronika Prinzessin zu Windisch-Graetz** * Ploschkowitz 9.7.1909 = (1) Bruxelles 22.7.1933 Pierre Comte d'Alcantara de Querrieu * Château d'Oydonek 2.11.1907 + in Oranienburg concentration camp 14.10.1944; = (2) Boitsfort 14.11.1945 Karl Axel Björklund * Rö Högsjö 21.12.1906, and has issue:

by 1st marriage:

XIII

1b. **Alvar Étienne Jean Othon Pierre Marie Joseph Pie François de Borgia Comte d'Alcantara de Querrieu** * Uccle 30.1.1935 = Helsinki 18.7.1956 Anita Damsten * Helsinki 15.12.1936 dau. of Peter Damsten, and has issue:

XIV

1c. **Patricia Stéphanie Anne Comtess d'Alcantara de Querrieu** * Bruxelles 19.1.1957

2c. **Frédéric Pierre Othon Jacques François de Borgia Comte d'Alcantara de Querrieu** * Bruxelles 9.4.1958

3c. **Véronique Comtesse d'Alcantara de Querrieu** * Bruxelles 27.5.1960

by 2nd marriage:

XIII

2b. **Björn Axel Björklund** * Uccle 20.10.1944

X

d) **Marie Valerie Mathilde Amalie Archduchess of Austria** * Ofen 22.4.1868' + Schloss Wallsee 6.9.1924 = Ischl 31.7.1890 **Franz Salvator Archduke of Austria, Prince of Tuscany** * Alt-Münster 21.8.1866 + Wien 20.4.1939, and had issue see elsewhere

IX

b. **Ferdinand Maximilian Joseph Emperor of Mexico, Archduke of Austria** * Wien 6.7.1832 + Queretaro, Mexico 19.6.1867 = Bruxelles 27.7.1857 **Marie Charlotte Princess of Belgium** * Laeken 7.6.1840 + Château de Bouchout, Belgium 19.1.1927 dau. of Léopold I King of the Belgians s.p.

c. **Karl Ludwig Joseph Marie Archduke of Austria** * Schönbrunn 30.7.1833 + Wien 19.5.1896 = (1) Dresden 4.11.1856 **Margarete Princess of Saxony** * Dresden 24.5.1840 + Monza 15.9.1858 dau. of Johann I King of Saxony; = (2) Venezia 21.10.1862 **Maria Annunciata Princess of Naples and Sicily** * Caserta 24.3.1843 + Wien 4.5.1871 dau. of Ferdinando II King of Naples and Sicily; = (3) Kleinheubach 23.7.1863 **Maria Teresa Princess of Bragança, Infanta of Portugal** * Kleinheubach 24.8.1855 + Wien 12.2.1944 dau. of Dom Miguel I Duke of Bragança, and had issue:

by 2nd marriage:

X

a) **Franz Ferdinand Karl Ludwig Joseph Maria Archduke of Austria** * Graz 18.12.1863 + (Assassinated) Sarejavo 28.6.1914 = morg. Reichstadt 1.7.1900 Sophie Gräfin Chotek v. Chotkowa u. Wognin, Herzogin v. Hohenberg * Stuttgart 1.3.1868 + Sarejavo 28.6.1914 dau. of Bohuslaw Graf Chotek v. Chotkowa u. Wognin, and had issue:

XI

(a) **Sophie Maria Franziska Antonia Ignatia Alberta Fürstin v. Hohenberg** * Konopischt 24.7.1901 = Schloss Tetschen 8.9.1920 Friedrich Graf v. Nostitz-Reineck * Prag 1.11.1893, and has issue:

XII

1a. **Erwein Maximilian Franz Peter Paul Hubertus Conrad Maria Graf v. Nostitz-Reineck** * Heinrchsgrün 29.6.1921 + Wysoki b. Charkow as Russian Prisoner of War 11.9.1949

XII		2a.	**Franz v. Assisi Friedrich Ernst Leopold Joseph Maria Graf v. Nostitz-Reineck** * Wien 2.2.1923 ✕ Berent 23.2.1945

XII   2a. **Franz v. Assisi Friedrich Ernst Leopold Joseph Maria Graf v. Nostitz-Reineck** * Wien 2.2.1923 ✕ Berent 23.2.1945

           3a. **Alois Karl Josef Maria Graf v. Nostitz-Reineck** * Wien 12.8.1925 = Schloss Zeil 12.9.1962 Marie Therese Gräfin v. Waldburg zu Zeil u. Trauchburg * Schloss Zeil 8.8.1931 dau. of Erich Fürst v. Waldburg zu Zeil u. Trauchburg and has issue:

XIII   1b. **Friedrich Erich Thaddäus Vincenz Jakob Alois Josef Maria Graf v. Nostitz-Reineck** * Graz 19.7.1963

               2b. **Monika Maria Theresia Walburga Henriette Gräfin v. Nostitz-Reineck** * Graz 15.4.1965

XII   4a. **Sophie Amalia Therese Quirina Henriette Lukretia Magdalena Maria Ignatia Gräfin v. Nostitz-Reineck** * Wien 4.6.1929 = Graz 18.8.1953 **Ernst Gordian Frhr. v. Gudenus** * Madrid 26.3.1916, and has issue see elsewhere

XI   (b) **Maximilian Karl Franz Michael Hubert Anton Ignatius Joseph Maria 2 Fürst u. Herzog v. Hohenberg** * Wien 29.9.1902 + Wien 8.1.1962 = Wolfegg 16.11.1926 **Maria Elisabeth-Bona Gräfin v. Waldburg zu Wolfegg u. Waldsee** * Waldsee 10.8.1904 dau. of Maximilian Fürst v. Waldburg u. Wolfegg u. Waldsee, and had issue:

XII   1a. **Franz Ferdinand Friedrich Ernst Josef Karl Leopold Mauritius Hubertus Maria 3 Fürst u. Herzog v. Hohenberg** * Arstetten 13.9.1927 = Luxembourg 9.5.1956 **Elisabeth Princess of Luxembourg, Princess of Bourbon-Parma and Nassau** * Schloss Berg 22.12.1922 dau. of Charlotte Grand Duchess of Luxembourg, and has issue:

XIII   1b. **Anna Charlotte Euphemie Marie Helene Fürstin v. Hohenberg** * Colmar Berg 18.8.1958

               2b. **Sophie Fürstin v. Hohenberg** * Colmar Berg 5.5.1960

XII   2a. **Georg Friedrich Maximilian Jaroslav Petrus Canisius Josef Markus Hubertus Maria Fürst v. Hohenberg** * Arstetten 25.4.1929 = Schloss Wald 8.9.1960 **Eleonore Prinzessin v. Auersperg-Breunner** * Goldegg 12.9.1928 dau. of Karl 10 Fürst v. Auersperg, and has issue:

XIII   1b. **Nikolaus Fürst v. Hohenberg** * Boulogne-sur-Seine 3.7.1961

               2b. **Henriette Fürstin v. Hohenberg** * Boulogne-sur-Seine 9.11.1962

XII   3a. **Albrecht Philipp Leopold Josef Andreas Hubertus Maria Fürst v. Hohenberg** * Arstetten 4.2.1931 = Wien 12.5.1962 Comtesse Leontine de Cassis-Faraone * Vught 3.8.1933 dau. of Comte Leo de Cassis-Faraone, and has issue:

XIII   1b. **Margarethe Fürstin v. Hohenberg** * Wien 19.6.1963

               2b. **Leo Fürst v. Hohenberg** * Wien 28.9.1964

               3b. **Johanna Fürstin v. Hohenberg** * Wien 29.4.1966

XII   4a. **Johann Andreas Josef Antonius Michael Severinus Alexander Hubertus Maria Fürst v. Hohenberg** * Arstetten 3.5.1933

           5a. **Peter Friedrich Benedikt Josef Emanuel Gerhard Judas Thaddäus Hubertus Maria Fürst v. Hohenberg** * Arstetten 26.3.1936

XII   6a.   **Gerhard Josef Anton Stephan Jakob Wenzel Pius Hartmann Hubertus Maria Fürst v. Hohenberg** * Wien 23.12.1941

XI   (c)   **Ernst Alphons Franz Ignaz Joseph Maria Anton Fürst v. Hohenberg** * Konopischt 27.5.1904 + Graz 5.3.1954 = Wien 25.5.1936 Marie Therese Wood * Wien 9.5.1910 dau. of George Jervis Wood, and has issue:

XII   1a.   **Franz Ferdinand Maximilian Georg Ernst Maria Josef Zacharius Ignaz Fürst v. Hohenberg** * Wien 14.3.1937

          2a.   **Ernst Georg Elemer Albert Josef Antonius Peregrinus Rupert Maria Fürst v. Hohenberg** * Wien 1.3.1944

X   b)   **Otto Franz Joseph Karl Ludwig Maria Archduke of Austria** * Graz 21.4.1865 + Wien 1.11.1906 = Dresden 2.10.1886 **Maria Josepha Princess of Saxony** * Dresden 31.5.1867 + Schloss Wildenwart 28.5.1944 dau. of Georg I King of Saxony, and had issue:

XI   (a)   **Karl I Franz Joseph Ludwig Hubert Georg Otto Maria Emperor of Austria, King of Hungary, etc.** * Persenbeug 17.8.1887 + Funchal, Madeira 1.3.1922 = Schwarzau am Steinfelde 21.10.1911 **Zita Princess of Bourbon-Parma** * Villa Pianore 9.5.1892 dau. of Robert I Duke of Parma, and has issue:

XII   1a.   **Franz Joseph Otto Robert Maria Anton Karl Max Heinrich Sixtus Xaver Felix Renatus Ludwig Gaetan Pius Ignatius Archduke of Austria** * Villa Wartholz b. Reichenau 20.11.1912 = Nancy 10.5.1951 **Regina Princess of Saxe-Meiningen** * Würzburg 6.1.1925 dau. of Georg Duke of Saxe-Meiningen, and has issue:

XIII   1b.   **Andrea Maria Archduchess of Austria** * Würzburg 30.5.1953

             2b.   **Monika Maria Roberta Antonia Raphaele Archduchess of Austria** * Würzburg 13.9.1954

             3b.   **Michaela Maria Madeleine Kiliana Elisabeth Archduchess of Austria** * Würzburg 13.9.1954

             4b.   **Gabriela Maria Charlotte Felicitas Elisabeth Antonia Archduchess of Austria** * Luxembourg 14.10.1956

             5b.   **Walburga Maria Franziska Helene Elisabeth Archduchess of Austria** * Berg 5.10.1958

             6b.   **Karl Thomas Robert Maria Franziskus Bahnam Archduke of Austria** * Starnberg 11.1.1961

             7b.   **Paul Georg Archduke of Austria** * Starnberg 16.12.1964

XII   2a.   **Adelheid Maria Josepha Sixta Antonia Roberta Ottonia Zita Charlotte Luise Immakulata Pia Theresia Beatrix Franziska Isabelle Henriette Maximiliana Genoveva Ignatia Marcus d'Aviano Archduchess of Austria** * Hetzendorf 3.1.1914

          3a.   **Robert Karl Ludwig Maximilian Michael Maria Anton Franz Ferdinand Joseph Otto Hubert Georg Pius Johannes Marcus d'Aviano Archduke of Austria** * Schönbrunn 8.2.1915 = Bourg-en-Bresse 28.12.1953 **Margherita Princess of Savoy-Aosta** * Capodimonte, Napoli 7.4.1930 dau. of Amadeo Prince of Savoy, Duke of Aosta, and had issue:

XIII   1b.   **Maria Beatrix Anna Felicitas Zita Charlotte Adelheid Christina Elisabeth Gennara Archduchess of Austria** * Boulogne-sur-Seine 11.12.1954

71

XIII		2b.	**Lorenz Otto Carl Amadeus Thadeus Maria Pius Andreas Marcus d'Aviano Archduke of Austria** * Boulogne-sur-Seine 16.12.1955

XIII

2b. **Lorenz Otto Carl Amadeus Thadeus Maria Pius Andreas Marcus d'Aviano Archduke of Austria** * Boulogne-sur-Seine 16.12.1955

3b. **Gerhard Thaddäus Anton Marcus d'Aviano Maria Umberto Otto Carl Amadeus Archduke of Austria** * Boulogne-sur-Seine 30.10.1957

4b. **Martin Carl Amadeo Maria Archduke of Austria** * Boulogne-sur-Seine 21.12.1959

5b. **Isabella Marie Laura Helena Antonia Zita Anna Gennara Archduchess of Austria** * Boulogne-sur-Seine 2.3.1963

XII

4a. **Felix Friedrich August Maria vom Siege Franz Joseph Peter Karl Anton Robert Otto Pius Michael Benedikt Sebastien Ignatius Marcus d'Aviano Archduke of Austria** * Schönbrunn 31.5.1916 = Beaulieu 19.11.1952 Anna-Eugenie Princesse et Duchesse d'Arenberg * Château d'Ellingen 5.7.1925 dau. of Robert Prince et Duc d'Arenberg, and has issue:

XIII

1b. **Maria del Pilar Sophie Valerie Charlotte Zita Johanna Marcus d'Aviano Caspara Archduchess of Austria** * Mexico City 18.10.1953

2b. **Carl Philipp Maria Otto Lukas Markus d'Aviano Melchior Archduke of Austria** * Mexico City 18.10.1954

3b. **Kinga Barbara Maria Carlota Jakobea Markus d'Aviano Balthasara Archduchess of Austria** * Schloss Guttenberg 13.10.1955

4b. **Raimund Joseph Carl Ludwig Maria Gabriel Markus d'Aviano Caspar** * Mexico City 28.1.1958

5b. **Myriam Adelheid Hugoline Omnes Sancti Marcus d'Aviano Melchiora Archduchess of Austria** * Mexico City 21.11.1959

6b. **István Franz-Leopold Johannes Maria Rudolph Theresius Marcus d'Aviano Balthasar Archduke of Austria** * Mexico City 22.9.1961

7b. **Viridis Aloisia Marie-Eleonore Elisabeth Marcus d'Aviano Caspara Archduchess of Austria** * Mexico City 22.9.1961

XII

5a. **Carl Ludwig Maria Franz Joseph Michael Gabriel Antonius Robert Stephan Pius Gregor Ignatius Marcus d'Aviano Archduke of Austria** * Baden b. Wien 10.3.1918 = Château de Beloeil 17.1.1950 **Yolande Princesse de Ligne** * Madrid 6.5.1923 dau. of Eugène 11 Prince de Ligne, and has issue:

XIII

1b. **Rudolf Maria Carl Eugen Anna Antonius Marcus d'Aviano Archduke of Austria** * Château de Beloeil 17.11.1950

2b. **Alexandra Maria Anna Philippa Othina Archduchess of Austria** * Château de Beloeil 10.7.1952

3b. **Carl Christian Maria Anna Rudolph Anton Marcus d'Aviano Archduke of Austria** * Château de Beloeil 26.8.1954

4b. **Maria Constanza Anna Rosario Roberta Archduchess of Austria** * Château de Beloeil 19.10.1957

XII

6a. **Rudolf Syringus Peter Karl Franz Joseph Robert Otto Antonius Maria Pius Benedikt Ignatius Laurentius Justiniani Marcus d'Aviano Archduke of Austria** * Villa Prangins 5.9.1919 = Tuxedo Park, N.Y. 22.6.1953 Xenia Besobrasow * Paris 11.6.1929 dau. of Serge Alexandrovitch Besobrasow, and has issue:

XIII

1b. **Maria-Anna Charlotte Zita Elisabeth Regina Therese Archduchess of Austria** * Uccle, Bruxelles 19.5.1954

XIII

2b. **Carl Peter Otto Serge Joseph Paul Leopold Heinrich Archduke of Austria** * Katana, Congo 5.11.1955

3b. **Simeon Carl Eugen Joseph Leopold Archduke of Austria** * Katana, Congo 29.6.1958

4b. **Johannes Carl Ludwig Clemens Maria Joseph Marcus d'Aviano Leopold Archduke of Austria** * Bruxelles 11.12.1962

XII

7a. **Charlotte Hedwig Franziska Josepha Maria Antonia Roberta Ottonia Pia Anna Ignatia Marcus d'Aviano Archduchess of Austria** * Villa Prangins 1.3.1921 = Pöcking am Starnberger See 25.7.1956 **Georg Duke of Mecklenberg** * Oranienbaum b. St. Petersburg 5.10.1899 + Sigmaringen 6.7.1963 s.p.

8a. **Elisabeth Charlotte Alphonsa Christina Theresia Antonia Josepha Roberta Ottonia Franziska Isabella Pius Marcus d'Aviano et omnes sancti Archduchess of Austria** * El Pardo, Madrid 31.5.1922 = Lignières 12.9.1949 Heinrich Prinz v.u. zu Liechtenstein * Graz 5.8.1916, and has issue:

XIII

1b. **Vincenz Karl Alfred Maria Michael et omnes sancti Prinz v.u. zu Liechtenstein** * Graz 30.7.1950

2b. **Michael Karl Alfred Prinz v.u. zu Liechtenstein** * Graz 10.10.1951

3b. **Charlotte Maria Benedikta Eleonore Adelheid et omnes sancti Prinzessin v.u. zu Liechtenstein** * Graz 3.7.1953

4b. **Christof Karl Alfred Maria Michael Hugo Ignatius et omnes sancti Prinz v.u. zu Liechtenstein** * Graz 11.4.1956

5b. **Karl Maria Alfred Michael Georg et omnes sancti Prinz v.u. zu Liechtenstein** * Graz 31.8.1957

XI

(b) **Maximilian Eugen Ludwig Friedrich Philipp Ignatius Joseph Maria Archduke of Austria** * Wien 13.4.1895 + Nice 19.1.1952 = Laxenburg 29.11.1917 Franziska Prinzessin zu Hohenlohe-Waldenburg-Schillingsfürst von Ratibor u. Corvey * Teplitz 21.6.1897 dau. of Konrad Prinz zu Hohenlohe-Waldenburg-Schillingsfürst v. Ratibor u. Corvey, and had issue:

XII

1a. **Ferdinand Karl Max Franz Otto Konrad Maria Joseph Ignatius Nikolaus Archduke of Austria** * Wien 6.12.1918 = Seefeld 10.4.1956 **Helene Gräfin zu Toerring-Jettenbach** * Winhöring 20.5.1937 dau. of Karl Theodor Graf zu Toerring-Jettenbach, and has issue:

XIII

1b. **Elisabeth Caecilia Helen Antonia Archduchess of Austria** * Essen 15.3.1957

2b. **Sophie Maria Germaine Franziska Archduchess of Austria** * Boulogne-sur-Seine 19.1.1959

3b. **Maximilian Heinrich Ferdinand Archduke of Austria** * Paris 8.2.1961

XII

2a. **Heinrich Karl Maria Archduke of Austria** * München 7.1.1925 = Münster i. W. 17.10.1961 **Ludmila Gräfin v. Galen** * Haus Assen 20.6.1939 dau. of Christoph Graf v. Galen, and has issue:

XIII

1b. **Philipp Joachim Franz Max Clemens Gallus Archduke of Austria** * Zürich 16.10.1962

2b. **Marie-Christine Franziska Sophie Archduchess of Austria** * Zürich 14.3.1964

XIII 3b.   **Ferdinand Archduke of Austria** * Zürich 28.5.1965

X c) **Ferdinand Karl Ludwig Joseph Johann Maria Archduke of Austria** * Wien 27.12.1868
+ München 10.3.1915 = morganatically, Chur 15.8.1909 Bertha Czuber * Prag 1879
+ ... dau. of Emanuel Czuber s.p.

d) **Margarete Sophie Marie Annunciata Theresia Caroline Luise Josephe Johanna
Archduchess of Austria** * Artstetten 13.5.1870 + Gmunden 24.8.1902 = Wien
24.1.1893 **Albrecht Duke of Württemberg** * Wien 23.12.1865 + Schloss Altshausen
29.10.1939, and had issue see elsewhere

by 3rd marriage:

e) **Maria Annunciata Adelheid Theresia Michaela Karoline Luise Pia Ignatia Archduchess of
Austria** * Reichenau 31.7.1876 + Vaduz 8.4.1961

f) **Elisabeth Amalia Eugenia Maria Theresia Karoline Luise Josepha Archduchess of Austria**
* Reichenau 7.7.1878 + Vaduz 13.3.1960 = Wien 20.4.1903 Aloys Prinz v.u. zu
Liechtenstein * Hollenegg 17.6.1869 + Vaduz 16.3.1955, and had issue:

XI (a) **Franz Josef II Maria Aloys Alfred Karl Johannes Heinrich Michael Georg Ignatius
Benediktus Gerhardus Majella Fürst v.u. zu Liechtenstein** * Frauenthal 16.8.1906
= Vaduz 7.3.1943 Georgine Gräfin v. Wilczek * Graz 24.10.1921 dau. of
Ferdinand Graf v. Wilczek, and has issue:

XII 1a. **Johannes Adam Ferdinand Alois Josef Maria Marko d'Aviano Pius Erbprinz
v.u. zu Liechtenstein** * Zürich 14.2.1945

2a. **Philipp Erasmus Alois Ferdinand Maria Sebaldus Prinz v.u. zu Liechtenstein**
* Zürich 19.8.1946

3a. **Nikolaus Ferdinand Maria Josef Raphael Prinz v.u. zu Liechtenstein**
* Zürich 24.10.1947

4a. **Nora Elisabeth Maria Assunta Josefine Georgine omnes sancti Prinzessin v.u.
zu Liechtenstein** * Zürich 31.10.1950

5a. **Franz Josef Wenzel Georg Maria Prinz v.u. zu Liechtenstein** * Zürich
19.11.1962

XI (b) **Maria Theresia Henriette Aloisia Alfreda Franziska Josepha Julie Adelheid Margarete
Annunziata Elisabeth Ignatia Benedikta Prinzessin v.u. zu Liechtenstein** * Wien
14.1.1908 = Wien 12.2.1944 **Arthur Graf Strachwitz v. Gross-Zauche u. Camminetz**
* Gross-Reichenau 18.12.1905, and has issue see elsewhere

(c) **Karl Alfred Maria Johannes Baptista Heinrich Aloys Georg Hartmann Ignatius
Benediktus Franz Joseph Rochus Prinz v.u. zu Liechtenstein** * Frauenthal
16.8.1910 = Schloss Persenbeug 17.2.1949 **Agnes Archduchess of Austria,
Princess of Tuscany** * Schloss Persenbeug 14.12.1928 dau. of Hubert Salvator
Archduke of Austria, Prince of Tuscany, and has issue:

XII 1a. **Dominik Volkmar Hubert Alois Maria Josef Thadäus Thomas Paulus Karl
Ignatius Severius Prinz v.u. zu Liechtenstein** * Wien 20.6.1950

2a. **Andreas Duarte Emanuel Ulrich Benedikt Josef Maria Karl Rafael Ignatius
Mathias Paulus Prinz v.u. zu Liechtenstein** * Wien 25.2.1952

3a. **Gregor Heinrich Augustinius Judas Thaddäus Josef Maria Pius Paulus
Antonius Stefan Salvator Prinz v.u. zu Liechtenstein** * Wien 18.4.1954

4a. **Alexandra Maria Christina Aloisia Ulrike Henriette Agnes Ignatia Pia Gabriela
Anastasia Prinzessin v.u. zu Liechtenstein** * Wien 25.12.1955

XII   5a.   **Maria Pia Prinzessin v.u. zu Liechtenstein** * Wien 6.8.1960

XI   (d)   **Georg Hartmann Maria Josef Franz de Paula Aloys Ignatius Benediktus Martin Prinz v.u. zu Liechtenstein** * Gr.-Ullersdorf 11.11.1911 = Schloss Altshausen 23.9.1948 **Marie Christine Duchess of Württemberg** * Tübingen 2.9.1924 dau. of Philipp Albrecht Duke of Württemberg, and has issue:

XII   1a.   **Margarita Maria Helene Rosa Aloisia Philippine Elisabeth Georgine Josefa Konrada Pia Ignatia Prinzessin v.u. zu Liechtenstein** * Wien 1.5.1950

           2a.   **Maria Assunta Elisabeth Philippine Rosa Helena Aloisia Georgine Josefa Benedikta Pia Ignatia Prinzessin v.u. zu Liechtenstein** * Wien 28.4.1952

           3a.   **Isabelle Marie Helene Caroline Alfreda Josefa Monika Pia Georgina Hemma Henriette Ignatia Prinzessin v.u. zu Liechtenstein** * Wien 17.5.1954

           4a.   **Christoph Alois Maria Ferdinand Josef Philipp Pius Konrad Thaddäus Ruppert Paulus Ignatius Prinz v.u. zu Liechtenstein** * Wien 15.1.1958

           5a.   **Marie Helene Diane Rosa Elisabeth Aloysia Philippine Josefa Gabriella Pia Antonia Ignatia Prinzessin v.u. zu Liechtenstein** * Wien 8.9.1960

XI   (e)   **Ulrich Dietmar Maria Franz Ferdinand Karl Alois Josef Ignatius Benediktus Johannes Augustinus Prinz v.u. zu Liechtenstein** * Gr.-Ullersdorf 29.8.1913

       (f)   **Marie Henriette Theresia Aloisia Franziska Sophie Josepha Michaela Adelheid Annunziata Elisabeth Ignatia Benedikta omnes sancti Prinzessin v.u. zu Liechtenstein** * Wien 6.11.1914 = Wien 24.8.1943 Peter Graf v.u. zu Eltz gen. Faust v. Stromberg * Wien 28.10.1909, and has issue:

XII   1a.   **Johann Erwein Maria Alois Josef Thaddäus Graf v.u. zu Eltz gen. Faust v. Stromberg** * Zürich 22.8.1946

           2a.   **Alexander Franz Josef Maria Jakob Dionysius Johann Nepomuk Graf v.u. zu Eltz gen. Faust v. Stromberg** * Zürich 9.10.1947

           3a.   **Franz Joseph Johann Nepomuk Maria Graf v.u. zu Eltz gen. Faust v. Stromberg** * Gmunden 6.8.1950

XI   (g)   **Aloys Heinrich Maria Franz Joseph Ferdinand Ignatius Benediktus Libertus Marko d'Aviano Prinz v.u. zu Liechtenstein** * Wien 20.12.1917

       (h)   **Heinrich Hartneid Maria Franz de Paula Johann Alois Joseph Ignatius Benediktus Hilarion Prinz v.u. zu Liechtenstein** * Gr.-Ullersdorf 21.10.1920

IX   d.   **Maria Anna Carolina Pia Archduchess of Austria** * Wien 27.10.1835 + Wien 5.2.1840

      e.   a son * & + 24.10.1840

      f.   **Ludwig Viktor Joseph Anton Archduke of Austria** * Wien 15.5.1842 + Wien 18.1.1919

VIII   (11)   **Marie Anne Franziska Theresia Josepha Medarde Archduchess of Austria** * Wien 8.6.1804 + Baden b. Wien 28.12.1858

     (12)   **Johann Nepomuk Karl Franz Joseph Felix Archduke of Austria** * Wien 30.8.1805 + Wien 19.2.1809

     (13)   **Amalia Theresia Archduchess of Austria** * Wien 6.4.1807 + Wien 9.4.1807

VII   3)   **Ferdinand III Joseph Johann Grand Duke of Tuscany, Archduke of Austria** * Firenze 6.5.1769 + Firenze 18.6.1824 = (1) Wien 19.9.1790 **Luisa Princess of Naples and Sicily** * Napoli 27.7.1773 + Wien 19.9.1802 dau. of Ferdinando I King of Naples and Sicily; = (2) Wien 6.5.1821 **Marie Ferdinande Princess of Saxony** * Dresden 27.4.1796 + Schloss Brandeis 3.1.1865 dau. of Maximilian Prince of Saxony, and had issue:

75

by 1st marriage:

VIII (1) **Caroline Ferdinanda Theresia Archduchess of Austria, Princess of Tuscany** * Firenze 2.8.1793 + Wien 4.1.1802

(2) **Franz Leopold Ludwig Archduke of Austria, Prince of Tuscany** * Firenze 15.12.1794 + Firenze 18.5.1800

(3) **Leopold II Johann Joseph Franz Ferdinand Karl Grand Duke of Tuscany, Archduke of Austria** * Firenze 3.10.1797 + Schloss Brandeis 29.1.1870 = (1) Firenze 16.11.1817 **Maria Anna Princess of Saxony** * Dresden 15.11.1799 + Pisa 24.3.1832 dau. of Maximilian Prince of Saxony; = (2) Napoli 7.6.1833 **Marie Antoinetta Princess of Naples and Sicily** * Palermo 19.12.1814 + Orth b. Gmunden 7.11.1898 dau. of Francesco I King of Naples and Sicily, and had issue:

by 1st marriage:

IX a. **Maria Caroline Auguste Elisabeth Vincentia Johanne Josepha Archduchess of Austria, Princess of Tuscany** * Firenze 19.11.1822 + Firenze 5.10.1841

b. **Auguste Ferdinande Luise Marie Johanne Josepha Archduchess of Austria, Princess of Tuscany** * Firenze 1.4.1825 + München 26.4.1864 = Firenze 15.4.1844 Luitpold Prince of Bavaria * Würzburg 12.3.1821 + München 12.12.1912, and had issue:

X a) **Ludwig III Leopold Joseph Marie Aloysius Alfred King of Bavaria** * München 7.1.1845 + Schloss Sárvár, Hungary 18.10.1921 = Wien 20.2.1868 **Marie Theresia Archduchess of Austria-Este, Princess of Modena** * Brünn 2.7.1849 + Schloss Wildenwart 3.2.1919 dau. of Ferdinand Archduke of Austria, Prince of Modena, and had issue:

XI (a) **Rupprecht Maria Luitpold Ferdinand Crown Prince of Bavaria** * München 18.5.1869 + Leutstetten b. Starnberg 2.8.1955 = (1) München 10.7.1900 **Marie Gabriele Duchess in Bavaria** * Tegernsee 9.10.1878 + Sorrento 24.10.1912 dau. of Karl Theodor Duke in Bavaria; = (2) Schloss Hohenberg b. Lenggries 7.4.1921 **Antoinette Princess of Luxembourg and Nassau** * Hohenberg 9.10.1899 + Lenzerheide, Suisse 31.7.1954 dau. of Wilhelm Grand Duke of Luxembourg, and has issue:

by 1st marriage:

XII 1a. **Luitpold Maximilian Ludwig Karl Prince of Bavaria** * Bamberg 8.5.1901 + Berchtesgarden 27.8.1914

2a. **Irmingard Maria Therese José Cäcilia Adelheid Michaela Antonia Adelgunde Princess of Bavaria** * Kreuth 21.9.1902 + Tegernsee 21.4.1903

3a. **Albrecht Luitpold Ferdinand Michael Duke of Bavaria** * München 3.5.1905 = Berchtesgarden 3.9.1930 **Marita Gräfin Draskovich v. Trakostjan** * Wien 8.3.1904 dau. of Dionys Graf Draskovich v. Trakostjan, and has issue:

XIII 1b. **Marie Gabriele Princess of Bavaria** * München 30.5.1931 = Nymphenburg 23.10.1957 Georg 7 Fürst v. Waldburg zu Zeil u. Trauchburg * Würzburg 5.6.1928, and has issue:

XIV 1c. **Maria Walburga Monika Charlotte Mathäa Gräfin v. Waldburg zu Zeil u. Trauchburg** * Ravensburg 21.9.1958

2c. **Maria Gabriele Walburga Cäcilia Theresia Gräfin v. Waldburg zu Zeil u. Trauchburg** * Ravensburg 22.11.1959

3c. **Maria Monika Sofie Walburga Nikoletta Gräfin v. Waldburg zu Zeil u. Trauchburg** * Ravensburg 22.3.1961

Photo Anton Sahm

Above left: 6   Duke Albrecht of
Bavaria and his family
Left to right: Prince Max Emanuel,
Duchess Marita, Duke Albrecht,
Prince Franz

Photo Gyenes

Above right: 7   Archduke Otto
and Archduchess Regina

Presse-Seeger

Left: 8   Crown Prince Hans
Adam of Liechtenstein and his
fiancée, Countess Maria
Kinsky *v.* Wchinitz u. Tettau

4c.   **Maria Erich Wunibald Aloysius Georg Erbgraf v. Waldburg zu Zeil u. Trauchburg** * Ravensburg 21.11.1962

2b.   **Marie Charlotte Princess of Bavaria** * München 30.5.1931
= Nymphenburg 3.9.1955 Paul 4 Fürst v. Quadt zu Wykradt u. Isny
* Isny 28.11.1930, and had issue:

1c.   **Alexander Albrecht Maria Ghislain Peter Paul Georg Mauritius Erbgraf v. Quadt zu Wykradt u. Isny** * München 18.1.1958

2c.   **Maria Anna Gabrielle Ghislaine Gräfin v. Quadt zu Wykradt u. Isny** * Friedrichshafen 8.4.1960

3b.   **Franz Prince of Bavaria** * München 14.7.1933

4b.   **Max Emanuel Prince of Bavaria** * München 21.1.1937

4a.   **Rudolf Friedrich Rupprecht Prince of Bavaria** * München 30.5.1909
+ München 26.6.1912

by 2nd marriage:

5a.   **Heinrich Franz Wilhelm Prince of Bavaria** * Schloss Hohenburg 28.3.1922
+ San Carlos de Bariloche, Argentina 14.2.1958 = St-Jean-de-Luz 31.7.1951
Anne de Lustrac * Neuilly-sur-Seine 28.9.1927 dau. of Jean Baron de Lustrac

6a.   **Irmingard Maria Josefa Princess of Bavaria** * Berchtesgarden 29.5.1923
= Schloss Nymphenburg 19.7.1950 **Ludwig Prince of Bavaria** * München
22.6.1913, and has issue see elsewhere

7a.   **Editha Maria Gabriele Anna Cunigunde Princess of Bavaria** * Schloss
Hohenburg 16.9.1924 = (1) Milano 12.11.1946 Tito Brunetti * Firenze
18.12.1906 + near Piacenza 13.7.1954; = (2) Tergensee 29.12.1959
Gustav Schimert * Budapest 28.11.1910, and has issue:

by 1st marriage:

1b.   **Serena Giovanna Sofia Antonia Brunetti** * Milano 22.12.1947

2b.   **Carlotta Hilda Maria Anna Brunetti** * Milano 10.6.1949

3b.   **Antonia Hilda Eugenia Assunta Brunetti** * Viareggio 12.6.1952

by 2nd marriage:

4b.   **Andreas Heinrich Rupprecht Marius Schimert** * München 26.5.1961

5b.   **Christian Philipp Gabriel Johannes Schimert** * 18.3.1963

8a.   **Hilda Hildegard Marie Gabriele Princess of Bavaria** * Berchtesgarden
24.3.1926 = Lima, Peru 12.2.1949 Juan Edgar Bradstock Lockett de Loayza
* Lima 13.3.1912, and has issue:

1b.   **Juan Bradstock Christopher Anthony Rupprecht Henry Lockett de
Wittelsbach** * Lima 10.4.1950

2b.   **Bradstock Miguel Maria Alexander Lockett de Wittelsbach** * Lima
3.5.1953

3b.   **Henry Maria Alexander Bradstock Luitpold Lockett de Wittelsbach**
* Rosswies 11.4.1958

4b.   **Marie Isabel Irmingard Hilda Charlotte Lockett de Wittelsbach**
* Rosswies 5.7.1960

XII	9a.	**Gabriele Adelgunde Marie Theresia Antonia Princess of Bavaria** * Berchtesgarden 10.5.1927 = Nymphenburg 18.6.1953 **Carl Erbprinz von Croÿ** * Düsseldorf 11.10.1914, and has issue see elsewhere
	10a.	**Sofie Marie Theresia Princess of Bavaria** * Starnberg 20.6.1935 = Berchtesgarden 20.1.1955 Jean-Engelbert Prince et Duc d'Arenberg * 's-Gravenhage 14.7.1921, and has issue:

XIII

    1b. **Léopold-Engelbert Evrard Rupprecht Gaspard Prince et Duc d'Arenberg** * Tervuren 20.2.1956

    2b. **Charles Louis Felix Melchior Prince et Duc d'Arenberg** * Tervuren 13.3.1957

    3b. **Marie-Gabrielle Elisabeth Princesse et Duchesse d'Arenberg** * Tervuren 2.6.1958

    4b. **Henri Antoine Marie Prince et Duc d'Arenberg** * Tervuren 20.5.1961

XI

(b) **Adelgunde Marie Auguste Therese Princess of Bavaria** * Villa Amsee b. Lindau 17.10.1870 + Sigmaringen 4.1.1958 = München 20.1.1915 **Wilhelm Fürst v. Hohenzollern-Sigmaringen** * Schloss Benrath 7.3.1864 + Sigmaringen 22.10.1927 s.p.

(c) **Maria Ludwiga Theresia Princess of Bavaria** * Villa Amsee 6.7.1872 + Lindau 10.6.1954 = München 31.5.1897 **Ferdinando Duke of Calabria, Prince of Naples and Sicily** * Roma 25.7.1869 + Lindau 7.1.1960, and had issue see elsewhere

(d) **Karl Maria Luitpold Prince of Bavaria** * Villa Amsee 1.4.1874 + München 9.5.1927

(e) **Franz Maria Luitpold Prince of Bavaria** * Schloss Leutstetten 10.10.1875 + Schloss Leutstetten 25.1.1957 = Schloss Weilburg, Baden b. Wien 8.7.1912 **Isabelle Prinzessin v. Croÿ** * Château de l'Hermitage 7.10.1890 dau. of Carl Alfred 12 Herzog v. Croÿ, and had issue:

XII

    1a. **Ludwig Karl Maria Anton Joseph Prince of Bavaria** * Schloss Nymphenburg 22.6.1913 = Schloss Nymphenburg 20.7.1950 **Irmingard Princess of Bavaria** * Berchtesgarden 29.5.1923 dau. of Rupprecht Crown Prince of Bavaria, and has issue:

XIII

    1b. **Luitpold Rupprecht Heinrich Prince of Bavaria** * Leutstetten 14.4.1951

XII

    2a. **Maria Elisabeth Franziska Josepha Therese Princess of Bavaria** * Nymphenburg 9.9.1914 = Nymphenburg 19.8.1937 **Pedro Henrique Prince of Orléans and Bragança** * Boulogne-sur-Seine 13.9.1909, and has issue see elsewhere

    3a. **Adelgunde Maria Antonia Elisabeth Josepha Princess of Bavaria** * Nymphenburg 9.6.1917 = Schloss Leutstetten 2.6.1948 Zdenko Frhr. v. Hoenning-O'Carroll * Sünching 6.8.1906, and has issue:

XIII

    1b. **Marie Gabrielle Radegundis Pia Theresia von Kinde Jesu Desideria Venazius Freiin. v. Hoenning O'Carroll** * Sünching 18.5.1949

    2b. **Franz Johann Nepomuk Pius Karl Cyprian Frhr. v. Hoenning O'Carroll** * Sünching 26.9.1950

    3b. **Hildegard Maria Margarete Theresia Oktavia Ludolfa Freiin. v. Hoenning O'Carroll** * Sünching 29.3.1952

4b.   **Joseph Bernhard Maria Gabriel Pius Johann Capistran Frhr. v. Hoenning O'Carroll** * Sünching 28.3.1953

5b.   **Maria Dorothea Rupertine Helene Pia Theresia Pitra Freiin. v. Hoenning O'Carroll** * Sünching 26.5.1956

XII   4a.   **Eleonore Therese Marie Josepha Gabriele Princess of Bavaria** * Nymphenburg 11.9.1918 = Nymphenburg 11.8.1951 Konstantin Graf v. Waldburg zu Zeil u. Trauchburg * Schloss Zeil 15.3.1909, and has issue:

XIII

1b.   **Maria Erich Franz Georg Wunibald Graf v. Waldburg zu Zeil u. Trauchburg** * Glashütte b. Wengen 25.9.1952

2b.   **Maria Elisabeth Therese Eleonora Walburga Monika Gräfin v. Waldburg zu Zeil u. Trauchburg** * Glashütte b. Wengen 6.1.1954

3b.   **Maria Georg Konstantin Franz Wunibald Ulrich Graf v. Waldburg zu Zeil u. Trauchburg** * München 1.5.1955

4b.   **Maria Eleonore Gabriele Theresia Walburga Elisabeth Gräfin v. Waldburg zu Zeil u. Trauchburg** * München 22.2.1957

5b.   **Maria Konstantin Karl Ludwig Wilibald Georg Graf v. Waldburg zu Zeil u. Trauchburg** * München 30.7.1958

6b.   **Maria Theresia Monika Walburga Gräfin v. Waldburg zu Zeil u. Trauchburg** * München 19.1.1960

XII   5a.   **Dorothea Therese Marie Franziska Princess of Bavaria** * Schloss Leutstetten 25.5.1920 = Sárvár, Hungary 3.8.1938 **Gottfried Archduke of Austria, Prince of Tuscany** * Linz 14.3.1902 and has issue see elsewhere

6a.   **Rasso Maximilian Rupprecht Prince of Bavaria** * Leutstetten 24.5.1926 = Schloss Wallsee 17.10.1955 **Theresia Archduchess of Austria, Princess of Tuscany** * Wallsee 9.1.1931 dau. of Theodor Salvator Archduke of Austria, Prince of Tuscany, and has issue:

XIII

1b.   **Maria-Theresia Anna Walburga Irmingard Princess of Bavaria** * Hohenschwangau 10.9.1956

2b.   **Franz-Josef Michael Maria Ignatius Prince of Bavaria** * Leutstetten 21.9.1957

3b.   **Elisabeth Maria Imaculata Anastasia Princess of Bavaria** * Leutstetten 22.1.1959

4b.   **Wolfgang Rupprecht Maria Theodor Prince of Bavaria** * Leutstetten 28.1.1960

5b.   **Benedikta Maria Gabrielle Princess of Bavaria** * Leutstetten 13.3.1961

6b.   **Christoph Ludwig Maria Prince of Bavaria** * Leutstetten 5.5.1962

7b.   **Gisela Princess of Bavaria** * Leutstetten 10.9.1964

XII   7a.   **Mathilde Maria Theresia Henriette Christine Luitpolda Princess of Bavaria** * Villa Amsee 17.8.1877 + Davos 6.8.1906 = München 1.5.1900 **Ludwig Gaston Prince of Saxe-Coburg and Gotha** * Ebenthal 15.9.1870 + Innsbruck 23.1.1942, and had issue see elsewhere

8a.   **Wolfgang Maria Leopold Prince of Bavaria** * Villa Amsee 2.7.1879 + München 31.5.1895

9a.   **Hildegarte Marie Christine Therese Princess of Bavaria** * München 5.3.1881 + Schloss Wildenwart 2.2.1948

XII		10a. **Wiltrud Maria Alice Princess of Bavaria** * München 10.11.1884 = Münster 26.11.1924 **Wilhelm 2 Herzog v. Urach, Graf v. Württemberg** * Monaco 3.3.1864 + Rapallo 24.3.1928, s.p.

10a. **Wiltrud Maria Alice Princess of Bavaria** * München 10.11.1884 = Münster 26.11.1924 **Wilhelm 2 Herzog v. Urach, Graf v. Württemberg** * Monaco 3.3.1864 + Rapallo 24.3.1928, s.p.

11a. **Helmtrud Marie Amalie Princess of Bavaria** * München 22.3.1886

12a. **Gundelinde Maria Josepha Princess of Bavaria** * München 26.8.1891 = Schloss Wildenwart 23.2.1919 **Johann Georg Graf v. Preysing-Lichtenegg-Moos** * Moos 17.12.1887 + München 17.3.1924, and has issue see elsewhere

X   b)   **Leopold Maximilian Joseph Maria Arnulf Prince of Bavaria** * München 9.2.1846 + München 28.9.1930 = Wien 20.4.1873 **Gisela Archduchess of Austria** * Laxenburg 12.7.1856 + München 27.7.1932 dau. of Franz Joseph Emperor of Austria, and had issue:

XI   (a)   **Elisabeth Maria Auguste Princess of Bavaria** * München 8.1.1874 = Genova 2.12.1893 Otto Graf v. Seefried auf Buttenheim * Bamberg 26.9.1870 + Schloss Stiebar 5.9.1951, and has issue:

XII   1a. **Elisabeth Marie Gräfin v. Seefried auf Buttenheim** * Znaim 10.6.1897

2a. **Auguste Maria Gabrielle Gräfin v. Seefried auf Buttenheim** * Znaim 20.6.1899 = Salzburg 12.6.1919 **Adalbert Prince of Bavaria** * Nymphenburg 3.6.1886, and has issue see elsewhere

3a. **Marie Valerie Gräfin v. Seefried auf Buttenheim** * Znaim 20.8.1901 = (1) München 24.6.1923 Rudolf Carl Frhr. v. Stengel * München 7.12.1899—marriage annulled; = (2) München 17.5.1933 Wilhelm Otto v. Riedemann * Hamburg 6.4.1903 + Oporto 19.9.1940 and has issue:

             by 1st marriage:

XIII   1b. **Heinrich Friedrich Maria Hermann Rudolf Otto Frhr. v. Stengel** * München 23.5.1924 X Russia 1.2.1943

             by 2nd marriage:

2b. **Anna Maria v. Riedemann** * München 31.8.1934

3b. **Maria Pia v. Riedemann** * Wien 17.3.1938

XII   4a. **Franz Joseph Otto Maria Graf v. Seefried auf Buttenheim** * Rozsahegy 29.7.1904 = Frankfurt 9.8.1941 Gabriele v. Schnitzler * München 3.11.1918 dau. of Georg v. Schnitzler, and has issue:

XIII   1b. **Franz Georg Graf v. Seefried auf Buttenheim** * Frankfurt-am-Main 15.5.1942

2b. **Ferdinand Otto Maria Graf v. Seefried auf Buttenheim** * Madrid 13.11.1944

3b. **Isabelle Valerie Gräfin v. Seefried auf Buttenheim** * Madrid 13.11.1949

4b. **Johann Stephan Hubert Franz Maria Graf v. Seefried auf Buttenheim** * Wien 3.8.1958

XI   (b)   **Auguste Maria Luise Princess of Bavaria** * München 28.4.1875 + Regensburg 25.6.1964 = München 15.11.1893 **Joseph Archduke of Austria, Palatine of Hungary** * Alscút 9.8.1872 + Rain b. Straubing 6.7.1962 and had issue see elsewhere

(c) **Georg Franz Josef Luitpold Maria Prince of Bavaria** * München 2.4.1880 + Roma 31.5.1943 = Schönbrunn 10.2.1912 **Isabella Archduchess of Austria** * Pressburg 17.11.1888 dau. of Friedrich Archduke of Austria, Duke of Teschen—marriage annulled s.p.

(d) **Konrad Luitpold Franz Joseph Maria Prince of Bavaria** * München 22.11.1883 = Château d'Aglie, Piedmont 8.1.1921 **Maria Bonna Princess of Savoy-Genoa** * Château d'Aglie 1.8.1896 dau. of Tomasso, Duke of Genoa, Prince of Savoy, and has issue:

1a. **Amalie Isabella Maria Gisela Margarethe Princess of Bavaria**[1] * München 15.12.1921 = Lugano 25.8.1949 Umberto Poletti * Milano 21.6.1921

2a. **Eugen Leopold Adelaide Thomas Maria Prince of Bavaria** * München 16.7.1925

c) **Therese Charlotte Marianne Augustine Princess of Bavaria** * München 12.11.1850 + Lindau 19.9.1925

d) **Franz Joseph Arnulf Adalbert Marie Prince of Bavaria** * München 6.7.1852 + Venezia 12.11.1907 = Wien 12.4.1882 Theresia Prinzessin v.u. zu Liechtenstein * Schloss Liechtenstein 28.7.1850 + München 13.3.1938 dau. of Aloys Fürst v.u. zu Liechtenstein, and has issue:

(a) **Heinrich Luitpold Prince of Bavaria** * München 24.6.1884 X Monte Sule 8.11.1916

c. **Maria Maximiliane Thekla Johanne Josepha Archduchess of Austria, Princess of Tuscany** * Firenze 9.1.1827 + Firenze 18.5.1834

by 2nd marriage:

d. **Maria Isabella Annunziata Johanne Josepha Umilta Appolonie Philomena Virginie Gabriela Archduchess of Austria, Princess of Tuscany** * Firenze 21.5.1834 + Bürgenstock, près Lucerne 14.7.1901 = Firenze 10.4.1850 **Francesco Prince of Naples and Sicily, Count of Trapani** * Napoli 13.8.1827 + Paris 24.9.1892, and has issue see elsewhere

e. **Ferdinand IV Salvator Marie Joseph Johann Baptist Franz Ludwig Gonzaga Raphael Ranier Januarius Grand Duke of Tuscany, Archduke of Austria** * Firenze 10.6.1835 + Salzburg 17.1.1908 = (1) Dresden 24.11.1856 **Anne Marie Princess of Saxony** * Dresden 4.1.1836 + Napoli 10.2.1859 dau. of Johann I King of Saxony; = (2) Frohsdorf 11.1.1868 **Alicia Princess of Bourbon-Parma** * Parma 27.12.1849 + Schwertberg 16.11.1935 dau. of Carlo III Duke of Parma, and had issue:

by 1st marriage:

a) **Marie Antoinette Leopoldine Annunziata Anne Amalie Josepha Johanna Immakulata Thekla Archduchess of Austria, Princess of Tuscany** * Firenze 10.1.1858 + Cannes 13.4.1883

by 2nd marriage:

b) **Leopold Ferdinand Salvator Marie Joseph Johann Baptist Zenobius Rupprecht Ludwig Karl Jacob Vivian Archduke of Austria, Prince of Tuscany** * Salzburg 2.12.1868 + 4.7.1953 = morg. (1) Veyrier b. Genève 25.7.1903 Wilhelmine Adamovic * Ludenburg 1.5.1877 + Wien ... — div.; = (2) Zurich 26.10.1907 Maria Ritter * ... — div.; = (3) Berlin ... 1933 Clara Pawloska * ...

---

1   It is believed that Signora Poletti has three children but the Author has been unable to discover any details about them.

X	c)	**Luise Antoinette Maria Theresia Josepha Johanna Leopoldine Caroline Ferdinande Alice Ernestine Archduchess of Austria, Princess of Tuscany** * Salzburg 2.9.1870 + Bruxelles 23.3.1947 = (1) Wien 21.11.1891 **Friedrich August III King of Saxony** * Dresden 25.5.1865 + Sibyllenort 18.2.1932 − div.; = (2) London 25.9.1907 Enrico Toselli * Firenze 15.3.1883 + Firenze 15.1.1926, and had issue by 1st marriage, see elsewhere

by 2nd marriage:

XI	(a)	**Carlo Emanuele Filiberto Toselli** * 7.5.1908

X	d)	**Joseph Ferdinand Salvator Maria Franz Leopold Anton Albert Johann Baptist Karl Ludwig Rupert Maria Auxiliatrix Archduke of Austria, Prince of Tuscany** * Salzburg 24.5.1872 + Wien 25.8.1942 = (1) Morganatically, Maria Plan b. Salzburg 2.5.1921 Rosa Kaltenbrunner * Linz 27.2.1878 + Salzburg 9.12.1929 − div.; = (2) Wien 27.1.1929 Gertrud Tomanek Edle v. Beyerfels * Brünn 13.4.1902 dau. of Aloys Tomanek Edler v. Beyerfels, and has issue:

by 2nd marriage:

XI	(a)	**Claude Marie Theresia Principessa di Firenze** * Wien 6.4.1930
	(b)	**Maximilian Franz Josef Karl Otto Heinrich Principe di Firenze** * Wien 17.3.1932

X	e)	**Peter Ferdinand Salvator Karl Ludwig Maria Joseph Leopold Rupert Pius Pancraz Archduke of Austria, Prince of Tuscany** * Salzburg 12.5.1874 + Sankt-Gilgen 8.11.1948 = Cannes 8.11.1900 **Maria Cristina Princess of Naples and Sicily** * Cannes 10.4.1877 + Sankt-Gilgen 4.10.1947 dau. of Alfonso, Count of Caserta, Prince of Naples and Sicily, and has issue:

XI	(a)	**Gottfried Maria Joseph Peter Ferdinand Hubert Anton Rupert Leopold Heinrich Ignaz Alfons Archduke of Austria, Prince of Tuscany** * Linz 14.3.1902 = Sárvár 3.8.1938 **Dorothea Princess of Bavaria** * Schloss Leutstetten 25.5.1920 dau. of Franz Prince of Bavaria, and has issue:

XII	1a.	**Elisabeth Maria Dorothea Josefa Theresia Ludmilla Archduchess of Austria, Princess of Tuscany** * Schloss Achberg 22.10.1939 = Salzburg 24.4.1965 Friedrich v. Braun * Regensburg 26.12.1934, and has issue:

XIII	1b.	**Bernadette v. Braun** * Bonn 21.7.1966

XII	2a.	**Alice Marie Christine Margarete Antoinette Josefa Rosa Helene Adelgunde Eleonore Archduchess of Austria, Princess of Tuscany** * Schloss Leutstetten 29.4.1941
	3a.	**Leopold Franz Peter Ferdinand Maria Joseph Gottfried Georg Karl Otto Rudolf Michael Archduke of Austria, Prince of Tuscany** * Schloss Leutstetten 25.10.1942 = Menetou-Salon (Cher) 26.7.1965 Laetitia de Belsunce d'Arenberg * Broumana 2.9.1941 dau. of Henri Marquis de Belsunce, and has issue:

XIII	1b.	**Sigismund Archduke of Austria** * Lausanne 21.4.1966

XII	4a.	**Marie Antoinette Christine Josefa Rosa Margarethe Pia Angela Theresia Gabriele Isabella Ludmilla Zita Ruperta Archduchess of Austria, Princess of Tuscany** * Sankt-Gilgen 16.9.1950

XI

(b) **Helene Marie Alice Christine Josepha Anna Margareta Madeleine Walburga Blandina Caecilie Philomena Carmela Ignazia Rita de Cascia Archduchess of Austria, Princess of Tuscany** * Linz 30.10.1903 + Tübingen 8.9.1924 = Altshausen 24.10.1923 **Philipp Duke of Württemberg** * Stuttgart 14.11.1893, and had issue see elsewhere

(c) **Georg Maria Ranier Joseph Peter Hubert Gottfried Eustach Rupert Ignaz Archduke of Austria, Prince of Tuscany** * Parsch b. Salzburg 22.8.1905 + Schloss Altshausen 21.3.1952 = Sankt-Gilgen 29.4.1936 **Marie Valerie Gräfin v. Waldburg zu Zeil** * Schloss Wallsee 28.6.1913 dau. of Georg Graf v. Waldburg zu Zeil, and had issue:

XII

1a. **Gontran Maria Georg Otto Joseph Peter Franz Leopold Karl Gabriel Walpurgis Ludwig Archduke of Austria, Prince of Tuscany** * Schloss Weissenberg 19.8.1937 + Wohlen 9.5.1943

2a. **Radbot Ferdinand Maria Johann Georg Gottfried Otto Joseph Anton Raphael Willibald Linus Archduke of Austria, Prince of Tuscany** * Muri, Suisse 23.9.1938

3a. **Marie Christine Elisabeth Franziska Klementine Helene Rosa Josepha Agnes Walburga Michaela Notgera Archduchess of Austria, Princess of Tuscany** * Muri, Suisse 8.4.1941 + Wohlen 4.1.1942

4a. **Walburga Rosa Maria Christine Elisabeth Clementine Helene Caroline Zita Stephanie Michaela Apollinaria Archduchess of Austria, Princess of Tuscany** * Muri, Suisse 23.7.1942

5a. **Verena Gertrud Maria Josepha Christine Elisabeth Georgine Walburga Paula Johanna Gabriele Aloysia Archduchess of Austria, Princess of Tuscany** * Muri, Suisse 21.6.1944 + Wohlen 5.1.1945

6a. **Johann Archduke of Austria, Prince of Tuscany** * & + 27.12.1946

7a. **Katharina Maria Christina Josefa Clementine Elisabeth Walburga Theresia Gertrud Georgine Agnes Gabriele Archduchess of Austria, Princess of Tuscany** * Muri, Suisse 24.4.1948

8a. **Agnes Maria Gertrud Elisabeth Josepha Pia Theresia Walburga Raphaela Archduchess of Austria, Princess of Tuscany** * Muri, Suisse 20.4.1950

9a. **Georg Maria Otto Joseph Leopold Philipp Michael Vitus Augustinus Archduke of Austria, Prince of Tuscany** * Schloss Syrgenstein 28.8.1952

XI

(d) **Rosa Maria Antonie Roberta Josepha Anna Walburga Carmela Ignazia Rita de Cascia Archduchess of Austria, Princess of Tuscany** * Parsch b. Salzburg 22.9.1906 = Friedrichshafen 1.8.1928 **Philipp Duke of Württemberg** * Stuttgart 14.11.1893, and has issue:

X f) **Heinrich Ferdinand Salvator Maria Joseph Leopold Karl Ludwig Albert Rupert Katharina v. Ricci Archduke of Austria, Prince of Tuscany** * Salzburg 13.2.1878 = morganatically ... Karolina Veronika Ludescher * Staudach b. Stams 6.12.1883 and has issue:

XI

(a) **Heinrich Habsburg-Lothringen** * München 27.8.1908 = St. Johann im Pongau 13.5.1939 Helvig Schütte * Kopenhagen 10.2.1910 dau. of Gudmund Schütte, and has issue:

XII

1a. **Ulrich Ferdinand Gudmund Habsburg-Lothringen** * Wolfsberg 3.10.1941 = Pustig 25.10.1964 Friederike v. Klinkowstzoem * Wien 31.3.1942 and has issue:

XIII

1b. **Eugen Habsburg-Lothringen** * 31.12.1964

XII			2a.	**Helvig Helle Habsburg-Lothringen** * Wolfsberg 29.12.1942
			3a.	**Christoph Heinrich Habsburg-Lothringen** * Wolfsberg 22.10.1944

XI   (b)   **Ottmar Habsburg-Lothringen** * München 7.8.1910 = Salzburg 19.12.1944 Helene Moser * Altenmarkt b. Salzburg 3.7.1920 dau. of Johannes Moser, and has issue:

XII   1a.   **Ulrike Margarethe Habsburg-Lothringen** * Salzburg 29.12.1945

             2a.   **Elisabeth Maria Habsburg-Lothringen** * Salzburg 20.1.1948

             3a.   **Albrecht Clemens Habsburg-Lothringen** * Salzburg 24.10.1951

XI   (c)   **Veronika Habsburg-Lothringen** * München 15.3.1912

X   g)   **Anna Maria Theresia Ferdinanda Adelheid Leopolda Ludovika Antonia Franziska Germana Henriette Hedwig Archduchess of Austria, Princess of Tuscany** * Lindau 17.10.1879 + Baden-Baden 30.5.1961 = Salzburg 12.2.1901 Johannes 7 Fürst zu Hohenlohe-Bartenstein u Jagstberg * Bartenstein 20.8.1863 + Bartenstein 19.8.1921, and had issue:

XI   (a)   **Maria Rosa Adelheid Therese Henriette Margarete Anna Prinzessin zu Hohenlohe-Bartenstein** * Bartenstein 21.12.1903 = Klein, Süssen 5.5.1923 Josef Hugo Waldenmeier * Salach 16.3.1895, − div. and has issue:

XII   1a.   **Eberhard Waldenmeier** * Magold, Württemberg 30.3.1924 = Syracuse Sicily July 1947 Maria Greca * Syracuse 1924 dau. of Virgilio Greca, and has issue:

XIII   1b.   **Carlo Waldenmeier** * Syracuse 12.4.1948

                2b.   **Rita Waldenmeier** * Syracuse 28.5.1950

                3b.   **Stephania Waldenmeier** * Syracuse ... 10.1951

                4b.   **Francisco Waldenmeier** * San Francisco 17.1.1960

                5b.   **Maria Theresia Waldenmeier** * San Francisco 22.1.1965

XII   2a.   **Wolfgang Waldenmeier** * Vollmaringen b. Horb 26.11.1925 = Ottenheim Kr. Lahr, Baden 21.12.1952 Elsa Walther * 1926 dau. of Arthur Walther, and has issue:

XIII   1b.   **Eberhard Waldenmeier** * Lahr, Baden 27.7.1953

                2b.   **Wolfgang Waldenmeier** * Lahr, Baden 16.2.1957

                3b.   **Joachim Waldenmeier** * Lahr, Baden 24.7.1958

XI   (b)   **Karl Ferdinand Otto Leopold Michael Maria Johannes 8 Fürst zu Hohenlohe-Bartenstein** * Bartenstein 20.10.1905 + Königshofen 7.5.1950 = Bartenstein 20.8.1936 Maria Clara Freiin. v. Meyern-Hohenberg * Wüstenahorn b. Coburg 7.11.1912 dau. of Hans Michael Frhr. v. Meyern-Hohenberg, and had issue:

XII   1a.   **Franziska Maria Elisabeth Germana Hildegard Anna Prinzessin zu Hohenlohe-Bartenstein** * Bartenstein 22.5.1927 = Bartenstein 4.6.1959 Alexander Frowein * Arnhem 9.11.1934, and has issue:

XIII   1b.   **Madeleine Frowein** * Hartford, Conn. U.S.A. 18.12.1960

XIII   2b.   **Henry Frowein** * Hartford, Conn. U.S.A. 17.12.1963

XII   2a.   **Henriette Marie Margarete Magdalena Therese Prinzessin zu Hohenlohe-Bartenstein** * Bartenstein 23.8.1938 = 20.4.1964 **Hans Veit Graf zu Toerring-Jettenbach** * München 11.1.1935, and has issue see elsewhere

       3a.   **Ferdinand Michael 9 Fürst zu Hohenlohe-Bartenstein** * Bartenstein 6.12.1942

XI   (c)   **Albrecht Maria Josef Ernst Georg Alexander Konrad 5 Fürst zu Hohenlohe-Jagstberg** * Bartenstein 9.9.1906 = München 22.10.1936 Therese Gräfin v. Geldern-Egmont * München 11.8.1911 dau. of Alfons Graf v. Mirbach Geldern-Egmont, and has issue:

XII   1a.   **Alexander Maria Ladislaus Johannes Carl Ludwig Erbprinz zu Hohenlohe-Jagstberg** * Schloss Haltenbergstetten 25.8.1937 = Fuschl 7.6.1963 **Michaela Prinzessin v. Schönburg-Waldenburg** * Berlin 9.3.1940 dau. of Hugo Prinz v. Schönburg-Waldenburg, and has issue:

XIII   1b.   **Antoinette Prinzessin zu Hohenlohe-Jagstberg** * München 24.2.1964

XII   2a.   **Johannes Maria Carl Alfons Friedrich Leopold Prinz zu Hohenlohe-Jagstberg** * Schloss Haltenbergstetten 2.12.1939

       3a.   **Eleonore Maria Irene Anna Elisabeth Margarethe Prinzessin zu Hohenlohe-Jagstberg** * Schloss Haltenbergstetten 17.10.1940

XI   (d)   **Elisabeth Adelheid Eleonore Germana Ernestine Maria Imaculata Prinzessin v. Hohenlohe-Bartenstein** * Bartenstein 8.12.1907 + Aigen Glas b. Salzburg 1.8.1927

      (e)   **Margarethe Henriette Maria Agnes Antonia Aloysia Prinzessin zu Hohenlohe-Bartenstein** * Bartenstein 14.2.1909

      (f)   **Friedrich August Hermann Maria Peter Rasso Prinz zu Hohenlohe-Bartenstein** * Lindau 3.9.1910 = Birnau, Bodensee 20.1.1959 Marie Claire Buet de Villars * Aubenas (Ardeche) 2.8.1916 dau. of Fernand Buet Marquis de Villars, and has issue:

XII   1a.   **Helena Maria Margarethe Franziska Anna Alix Rosa Elisabeth Katharina Prinzessin zu Hohenlohe-Bartenstein** * Heidelberg 22.3.1960

X   h)   **Margareta Maria Albertine Alice Ferdinanda Ludovika Antonia Leopolda Roberta Henrika Theresia Eduarda Archduchess of Austria, Princess of Tuscany** * Salzburg 13.10.1881 + Schwertberg 30.4.1965

     i)   **Germana Maria Theresia Antonia Leopolda Alice Ferdinanda Josepha Ludovika Caroline Ehrentraut Prota Archduchess of Austria, Princess of Tuscany** * Salzburg 11.9.1884 + Schwertberg 3.11.1955

     j)   **Robert Ferdinand Salvator Archduke of Austria, Prince of Tuscany** * Salzburg 15.10.1885 + Salzburg 2.8.1895

     k)   **Agnes Maria Theresia Ferdinanda Alice Antonia Josepha Ludovika Anna Amalie Germana Emanuela Archduchess of Austria, Princess of Tuscany** * Salzburg 26.3.1891 + Schwertberg 4.10.1945

IX   f.   **Maria Theresia Annunziata Johanne Josepha Luise Virginie Appolonie Philomena Archduchess of Austria, Princess of Tuscany** * Firenze 29.6.1836 + Firenze 5.8.1838

IX   g.   Maria Christine Annunziata Luise Anne Johanne Josepha Agatha Dorothee Philomena
                 Archduchess of Austria, Princess of Tuscany * Firenze 5.2.1838 + Firenze 1.9.1849

         h.   Karl Salvator Maria Joseph Johann Baptist Philipp Jakob Januarius Ludwig Gonzaga Ranier
                 Archduke of Austria, Prince of Tuscany * Firenze 30.4.1839 + Wien 18.1.1892 = Roma
                 19.9.1861 Maria Immaculata Princess of Naples and Sicily * Napoli 14.4.1844 + Wien
                 18.2.1899 dau. of Ferdinando II King of Naples and Sicily, and had issue:

X   a)   Marie Theresia Antoinette Immakulata Josepha Ferdinanda Leopoldine Franziska
                 Caroline Isabelle Januaria Aloysia Christine Anna Archduchess of Austria, Princess of
                 Tuscany * Alt-Bunzlau 18.9.1862 + Schloss Saybusch 10.5.1933 = Wien 28.2.1886
                 Karl Stephan Archduke of Austria * Gross-Sellowitz 5.9.1860 + Schloss Saybusch,
                 Poland 7.4.1933, and had issue see elsewhere

         b)   Leopold Salvator Marie Joseph Ferdinand Franz v. Assisi Karl Anton v. Padua Johann
                 Baptist Xaver Aloys Gonzaga Ranier Venceslaus Gallus Archduke of Austria, Prince of
                 Tuscany * Alt-Bunzlau 15.10.1863 + Wien 4.9.1931 = Frohsdorf 24.10.1889 Blanca,
                 Infanta of Spain * Graz 7.9.1868 + Viareggio 25.10.1949 dau. of Don Carlos Duke of
                 Madrid, and had issue:

XI   (a)   Maria de los Dolores Beatrix Carolina Blanka Leopoldina Margaretha Anna Josepha
                 Pia Raphaela Michaela Sixta Stanislawa Ignatia Hieronyma Gregoria Georgia Cäcilia
                 Carmino Barbara Archduchess of Austria, Princess of Tuscany * Lemberg 5.5.1891

         (b)   Maria Immakulata Carolina Margarita Blanka Leopoldina Beatrix Anna Josepha
                 Raphaela Michaela Stanislawa Ignatia Hieronyma Carmino Katherina Petra Cäcilia
                 Archduchess of Austria, Princess of Tuscany * Lemberg 9.9.1892 = Roma
                 14.7.1932 Nob. Igino Neri Serneri * Roma 22.7.1891 + Viareggio 1.5.1950 s.p.

         (c)   Margarita Raniera Maria Antonia Blanka Leopoldina Beatrix Anna Josepha Raphaela
                 Michaela Stanislawa Ignatia Alice Cäcilia Archduchess of Austria, Princess of Tuscany
                 * Lemberg 8.5.1894 = Schloss Sonnberg 27.11.1937 Francesco Marchese Taliani
                 de Marchio * Ascoli Piceno 22.10.1887 s.p.

         (d)   Ranier Karl Leopold Blanka Anton Margarete Beatrix Peter Joseph Raphael Michael
                 Ignaz Stephan Archduke of Austria, Prince of Tuscany * Zagreb 21.11.1895
                 + Wien 25.5.1930

         (e)   Leopold Maria Alfons Blanka Karl Anton Beatrix Raphael Michael Joseph Peter
                 Ignatzus Archduke of Austria, Prince of Tuscany * Zagreb 30.1.1897 + Willimantic,
                 Conn. U.S.A. 14.3.1958 = (1) Wien 12.4.1919 Dagmar Freiin. v. Nicolics-Podrinje
                 * Zagreb 15.7.1898 dau. of Wladimir Frhr. v. Nicolics-Podrinje − div.; = (2) ...
                 Alice Coburn * ... and had issue:

                 by 1st marriage:

XII   1a.   Gabrielle Habsburg-Lothringen * 12.2.1922 = ... Jan von der Muhl * ...

XI   (f)   Maria Antonia Roberta Blanka Leopoldina Beatrix Margarita Karoline Josepha
                 Raphaela Michaela Ignatia Aurelia Archduchess of Austria, Princess of Tuscany
                 * Zagreb 13.7.1899 = (1) Barcelona 16.7.1924 Don Ramón Orlandis y de Villalonga
                 * Palma de Mallorca 24.12.1896 + Palma de Mallorca 10.11.1936 = (2)
                 Montevideo ... 1942 Luis Perez Sucre * ... + ... and has issue:

                 by 1st marriage:

XII   1a.   Doña Blanca Maria de la Nieves Orlandis y Habsburgo * Palma de Mallorca
                         17.9.1926 = Buenos Aires 15.4.1948 Don Juan Ereñú y Ferreira * Rosario
                         de Santa Fe, Argentina 27.1.1908, and has issue:

XIII   1b.   Don Joaquin Alfonso Ereñú y Orlandis * Buenos Aires 25.6.1949

86

2b. **Doña Maria Antonia Ereñú y Orlandis** * Buenos Aires 13.6.1950

3b. **Don Carlos Alberto Ereñú y Orlandis** * Buenos Aires 8.9.1951

4b. **Doña Christina Eugenia Ereñú y Orlandis** * Buenos Aires 7.1.1958

5b. **Don Eugenio Ereñú y Orlandis** * Buenos Aires 20.5.1959

XII

2a. **Don Juan Orlandis y Habsburgo** * Palma de Mallorca 2.1.1928 = Buenos Aires ... 3.1951 Doña Hildegarde Bragagnolo y Daiqui Chevalier * Buenos Aires 25.7.1932 dau. of Don Teoboldo Bragagnolo, and has issue:

XIII

1b. **Doña Maria del Carmen Orlandis y Bragagnolo** * Barcelona 13.2.1952

2b. **Don Ramón Orlandis y Bragagnolo** * Viareggio 28.4.1953

3b. **Don Luis Felipe Orlandis y Bragagnolo** * Viareggio 13.6.1954

4b. **Doña Maria del Pilar Orlandis y Bragagnolo** * Viareggio 28.5.1955

5b. **Doña Hildegarda Orlandis y Bragagnolo** * Viareggio 28.5.1955

6b. **Doña Marta Orlandis y Bragagnolo** * La Amettla del Vallés, Prov. di Barcelona 6.1.1957

XII

3a. **Doña Isabel Orlandis y Habsburgo** * Palma de Mallorca 12.3.1931 = Palma de Mallorca 8.1.1954 Don Fausto Morell y Rovira * Palma de Mallorca 9.12.1916, and has issue:

XIII

1b. **Don Fausto Morell y Orlandis** * Palma de Mallorca 18.12.1954

2b. **Don Francisco Javier Morell y Orlandis** * Palma de Mallorca 5.12.1955

3b. **Don Carlos Morell y Orlandis** * Palma de Mallorca 24.1.1957

4b. **Doña Maria Immaculada Morell y Orlandis** * Palma de Mallorca 14.5.1958

XI

(g) **Anton Maria Franz Leopold Blanka Karl Joseph Ignaz Raphael Michael Margareta Nicetas Archduke of Austria, Prince of Tuscany** * 20.3.1901 = Sinaia 26.7.1931 **Ileana Princess of Roumania** * Bucarest 5.1.1909 dau. of Ferdinand I King of Roumania, — div., and has issue:

XII

1a. **Stefan Archduke of Austria, Princess of Tuscany** * Mödling 15.8.1932 = Milton, Mass. U.S.A. 28.8.1954 Jerrine Soper * Boston, Mass. 19.6.1931 dau. of Charles Soper, and has issue:

XIII

1b. **Christoph Archduke of Austria, Prince of Tuscany** * Boston, Mass. 26.1.1957

2b. **Ileana Archduchess of Austria, Princess of Tuscany** * Boston, Mass. 4.1.1958

3b. **Peter Archduke of Austria, Prince of Tuscany** * Boston, Mass. 19.2.1959

4b. **Constanza Archduchess of Austria, Princess of Tuscany** * Detroit, U.S.A. 2.10.1960

5b. **Anton Archduke of Austria, Prince of Tuscany** * 7.11.1964

XII

2a. **Maria Ileana Archduchess of Austria, Princess of Tuscany** * Mödling 18.12.1933 + Rio de Janeiro 11.1.1959 = Wien 7.12.1957 **Johann Graf Kottulin Kottulinsky** * Graz 3.1.1917 + Rio de Janeiro 11.1.1959, and had issue see elsewhere

XII		3a.	**Alexandra Archduchess of Austria, Princess of Tuscany** * Schloss Sonnberg 21.5.1935 = Salzburg 3.9.1962 **Eugen Eberhard Duke of Württemberg** * Carlsruhe, OSchl. 2.11.1930

3a. **Alexandra Archduchess of Austria, Princess of Tuscany** * Schloss Sonnberg 21.5.1935 = Salzburg 3.9.1962 **Eugen Eberhard Duke of Württemberg** * Carlsruhe, OSchl. 2.11.1930

4a. **Dominic Archduke of Austria, Princess of Tuscany** * Sonnberg 4.7.1937 = Houston, Texas 11.6.1960 Engel v. Voss * Houston, Texas 31.3.1937 dau. of Ernst v. Voss, and has issue:

XIII

    1b. **Sandor Archduke of Austria** * Wien 13.2.1965

XII

5a. **Maria Magdalena Archduchess of Austria, Princess of Tuscany** * Schloss Sonnberg 2.10.1939 = Mondsee 29.8.1959 Hans Frhr. v. Holzhausen * Windisch-Garten 1.9.1929, and has issue:

XIII

    1b. **Johann Friedrich Anton Frhr. v. Holzhausen** * Salzburg 29.7.1960

    2b. **Georg Ferdinand Frhr. v. Holzhausen** * Salzburg 16.2.1962

    3b. **Alexandra Maria Freiin. v. Holzhausen** * Salzburg 22.1.1963

XII

6a. **Elisabeth Archduchess of Austria, Princess of Tuscany** * Schloss Sonnberg 15.5.1942 = Mondsee 3.8.1964 Friedrich Sandhofer * ...

XI

(h) **Assunta Alix Ferdinanda Blanka Leopoldina Margaretha Beatrix Josepha Raphaela Michaela Philomena Archduchess of Austria, Princess of Tuscany** * Wien 10.8.1902 = Ouchy-Lausanne 17.9.1939 Joseph Hopfinger * Boryslaw, Galicia 14.4.1905 — div.

(i) **Franz Joseph Karl Leopold Blanka Adelgonde Ignatius Raphael Michael Vero Archduke of Austria, Prince of Tuscany** * Wien 4.2.1905 = London 22.7.1927 Marta Aloisia Baumer * Wien 30.9.1906 dau. of Alois Baumer s.p.

(j) **Karl Pius Maria Adelgonde Blanka Leopold Ignaz Raphael Michael Salvator Kyrill Angelus Barbara Archduke of Austria, Prince of Tuscany** * Wien 4.12.1909 + Barcelona 24.12.1952 = Wien 10.5.1938 Christa Satzger de Bálványos * Wien 4.12.1914 dau. of Géza Satzger de Bálványos — div., and had issue:

XII

1a. **Alexandra Blanca v. Habsburg-Lothringen** * Viareggio 20.1.1941 = Barcelona 1.2.1960 Don José Maria Riera de Leyva * Almeria 13.11.1934, and has issue:

XIII

    1b. **Doña Alejandra Matilde Riera y Habsburgo-Lothringen** * Lima, Peru 4.11.1960

XII

2a. **Immaculada Pia v. Habsburg-Lothringen** * Barcelona 3.7.1945

X

c) **Franz Salvator Maria Joseph Ferdinand Karl Leopold Anton v. Padua Johann Baptist Januarius Aloys Gonzaga Ranier Benedikt Berhard Archduke of Austria, Prince of Tuscany** * Alt-Münster 21.8.1866 + Wien 20.4.1939 = (1) Ischl 31.7.1890 **Marie Valerie Archduchess of Austria** * Ofen 22.4.1868 + Schloss Wallsee 6.9.1924 dau. of Franz Joseph Emperor of Austria; = (2) Wien 28.4.1934 Melanie Freiin. v. Riesenfels * Schloss Seisenegg 20.9.1898 dau. of Philipp Frhr. v. Riesenfels, and has issue:

XI

(a) **Elisabeth Franziska Marie Karoline Ignatia Archduchess of Austria, Princess of Tuscany** * Wien 27.1.1892 + Syrgenstein 29.1.1930 = Niederwallsee 19.9.1912 Georg Graf v. Waldburg zu Zeil u. Trauchburg * Hohenems 7.1.1878 + Schloss Syrgenstein 26.10.1955, and has issue:

88

1a. **Marie Valerie Klementine Franziska Elisabeth Walburga Gräfin v. Waldburg zu Zeil u. Trauchburg** * Wallsee 28.6.1913 = Sankt-Gilgen 29.4.1936 **Georg Archduke of Austria, Prince of Tuscany** * Parsch b. Salzburg 22.8.1905 + Schloss Altshausen 21.3.1952, and has issue see elsewhere

2a. **Klementine Marie Hedwig Elisabeth Agnes Walburga Gräfin v. Waldburg zu Zeil u. Trauchburg** * Wallsee 5.10.1914 + Syrgenstein 21.9.1941

3a. **Elisabeth Hedwig Maria Franziska Walburga Xaveria Gräfin v. Waldburg zu Zeil u. Trauchburg** * Wallsee 23.2.1917

4a. **Franz Joseph Vitus Xaver Georg Wunibald Graf v. Waldburg zu Zeil u. Trauchburg** * Chur 7.3.1927 = Pommersfelden 21.6.1956 Priscilla Gräfin v. Schönborn-Wiesentheid * München 5.2.1934 dau. of Clemens Graf v. Schönborn-Wiesentheid, and has issue:

XIII

    1b. **Maria Rosario Clara Dorothea Walburga Gräfin v. Waldburg zu Zeil u. Trauchburg** * Hohenems 2.4.1957

    2b. **Carolina Josepha Graziella Maria Walburga Gräfin v. Waldburg zu Zeil u. Trauchburg** * Hohenems 15.12.1958

    3b. **Elisabeth Maria Sophie Aloisia Walburga Gräfin v. Waldburg zu Zeil u. Trauchburg** * Hohenems 28.1.1960 + Hohenems 30.4.1966

    4b. **Franz-Clemens Marie Josef Willibald Graf v. Waldburg zu Zeil u. Trauchburg** * Hohenems 5.3.1962

    5b. **Stephan-Georg Manfred Rupert Wunibald Graf v. Waldburg zu Zeil u. Trauchburg** * Hohenems 3.8.1963

XI

(b) **Franz Carl Salvator Marie Joseph Ignaz Archduke of Austria, Prince of Tuscany** * Lichtenegg 17.2.1893 + Schloss Wallsee 10.12.1918

(c) **Hubert Salvator Ranier Maria Joseph Ignatius Archduke of Austria, Prince of Tuscany** * Lichtenegg 30.4.1894 = Schloss Anholt 25.11.1926 **Rosemary Prinzessin zu Salm-Salm** * Potsdam 13.4.1904 dau. of Emanuel Erbprinz zu Salm-Salm and has issue:

XII

1a. **Friedrich Salvator Franz Karl Ranier Gabriel Mathäus Vincentius Hubert Maria Joseph Ignatius Archduke of Austria, Prince of Tuscany** * Wien 27.11.1927 = Wien 18.6.1955 Margarethe Gräfin Kálnoky v. Köröspatak * Csicso 13.5.1926 dau. of Sándor Graf Kálnoky v. Köröspatak, and has issue:

XIII

    1b. **Leopold Salvator Hubert Maria Ranier Judas Thaddäus Alexander Maximilian Stephan Franziskus Pius Alois Archduke of Austria, Prince of Tuscany** * Wien 16.10.1956

    2b. **Maria Bernadette Christa Agnes Josepha Raphaela Archduchess of Austria, Princess of Tuscany** * Wien 10.2.1958

    3b. **Alexander Salvator Maria Josef Raphael Pius Archduke of Austria, Prince of Tuscany** * Wien 12.4.1959

    4b. **Katharina Mathilde Aloisia Maria Elisabeth Raphaela Archduchess of Austria, Princess of Tuscany** * Rorregg 1.11.1960

XII

2a. **Agnes Christina Franziska Caroline Theresia Raphaela Johanna Magdalena Huberta Josepha Ignatia Archduchess of Austria, Princess of Tuscany** * Schloss Persenbeug 14.12.1928 = Schloss Persenbeug 17.2.1949 **Karl Alfred Prinz v.u. zu Liechtenstein** * Frauenthal 16.8.1910, and has issue see elsewhere

3a. **Maria Margaretha Elisabeth Franziska Josepha Valeria Emanuela Michaela Philippa Rosa Huberta Ignatia Archduchess of Austria, Princess of Tuscany** * Wien 29.1.1930

4a. **Maria Ludowika Isabelle Alfonsa Anna Thadea Ferdinanda Katharina Huberta Marie Josepha Ignatia Archduchess of Austria, Princess of Tuscany** * Schloss Persenbeug 31.1.1931

5a. **Maria Adelheid Theodora Antonia Batholomea Leopolda Amalia Mathilde Markus d'Aviano Huberta Josepha Ignatia Archduchess of Austria, Princess of Tuscany** * Schloss Persenbeug 28.7.1933

6a. **Elisabeth Mathilde Karoline Alberta Jacobea Martina Helena Lucia Maria Josepha Huberta Ignatia Archduchess of Austria, Princess of Tuscany** * Schloss Persenbeug 18.3.1935 = Schloss Persenbeug 6.7.1959 **Heinrich Prinz v. Auersperg-Breunner** * Ainödt 21.5.1931, and has issue see elsewhere

7a. **Andreas Salvator Gabriel Gottfried Petrus Paulus Augustinus Severinus Maria Josephus Hubertus Ignatius Archduke of Austria, Prince of Tuscany** * Schloss Persenbeug 28.4.1936

8a. **Josepha Hedwig Georgia Henriette Barbara Agathe Stefana Mathia Koloman Maria Huberta Ignatia Archduchess of Austria, Princess of Tuscany** * Schloss Persenbeug 2.9.1937

9a. **Valerie Isabelle Maria Anna Alfonsa Dedieria Brigitte Sophia Thomasia Huberta Josepha Ignatia Archduchess of Austria, Princess of Tuscany** * Wien 23.5.1941 = Schloss Persenbeug 30.9.1966 **Maximilian Markgraf of Baden** * Schloss Salem 3.7.1933

10a. **Maria Alberta Dominika Benedikta Dorothea Felicitas Beatrix Simon Josophat Huberta Josepha Ignatia Archduchess of Austria, Princess of Tuscany** * Schloss Persenbeug 1.6.1944

11a. **Markus Emanuel Salvator Franziskus de Paula Stanislaus Gregorius Josaphat Florian Joseph Hubert Ignatius Archduke of Austria, Prince of Tuscany** * Schloss Persenbeug 2.4.1946

12a. **Johann Maximilian Salvator Benedictus Ambrosius Pius Lukas Wolfgang Maria Joseph Hubert Ignatius Archduke of Austria, Prince of Tuscany** * Schloss Persenbeug 18.9.1947

13a. **Michael Salvator Konrad Johannes Aloisius Franziskus Xaverius Barbabas Antonius Maria Josephus Hubertus Ignatius Archduke of Austria, Prince of Tuscany** * Schloss Persenbeug 18.9.1947

(d) **Hedwig Maria Immakulata Michaela Ignatia Archduchess of Austria, Princess of Tuscany** * Ischl 24.9.1896 = Schloss Wallsee 24.4.1918 Bernhard Graf zu Stolberg-Stolberg * Mankato, U.S.A. 20.1.1881 + Hall, Tirol 22.9.1952, and has issue:

1a. **Marie Elisabeth Valerie Josefa Anna Gräfin zu Stolberg-Stolberg** * Innsbruck 21.5.1919

2a. **Franz Josef Hubert Bernhard Stephan Martin Maria Graf zu Stolberg-Stolberg** * Schloss Wallsee 30.4.1920 = Kremsmünster 5.8.1957 Elisabeth Christiane Gräfin Kinsky v. Wchinitz u. Tettau * Mähr-Kromau 16.5.1926 dau. of Rudolf Graf Kinsky v. Wchinitz u. Tettau, and has issue:

1b. **Marie-Valerie Aglaë Hedwig Elisabeth Gräfin zu Stolberg-Stolberg** * Wien 6.6.1958

2b. **Marie-Christine Sybille Hedwig Elisabeth Gräfin zu Stolberg-Stolberg**
* Wien 20.7.1959

3b. **Marie-Antoinette Mathilde Hedwig Gräfin zu Stolberg-Stolberg** * Hall,
Tirol 8.9.1960

4b. **Marie-Sophie Elisabeth Hedwig Gräfin zu Stolberg-Stolberg** * Hall,
Tirol 14.12.1961

XII

3a. **Friedrich Leopold Martin Maria Graf zu Stolberg-Stolberg** * Wallsee
23.5.1921 = Werfen b. Salzburg 24.3.1948 Aloysia v. Pachmann * Zell am
See 24.7.1923 dau. of Ernst v. Pachmann, and has issue:

XIII

1b. **Christoph Bernhard Maria Graf zu Stolberg-Stolberg** * Zermatt 28.7.1948

2b. **Marie Elisabeth Emanuela Gräfin zu Stolberg-Stolberg** * Hall 19.12.1949

3b. **Peter Franziskus Theodor Raphael Blasius Maria Graf zu Stolberg-
Stolberg** * Hall 3.2.1951

4b. **Johannes Ernst Bonifaz Maria Graf zu Stolberg-Stolberg** * Hall
14.5.1952

5b. **Markus Eugenius Bernhard Maria Graf zu Stolberg-Stolberg**
* Innsbruck 19.5.1953

6b. **Eleonore Maria Gräfin zu Stolberg-Stolberg** * Hall 7.6.1959

XII

4a. **Bernhard Hubert Josef Martin Maria Graf zu Stolberg-Stolberg** * Stams
30.8.1922 + Wien 6.10.1958

5a. **Therese Marie Valerie Anne Hedwig Gräfin zu Stolberg-Stolberg** * Linsen
11.10.1923 = Hall 7.8.1945 **Paul Joseph Graf Wolff-Metternich zur Gracht**
* Strassburg 4.6.1916, and has issue see elsewhere

6a. **Carl Franz Georg Petrus Canisius Hubert Martin Maria Graf zu Stolberg-
Stolberg** * Reichen 7.6.1925 = Maria-Wörth, Karnten 22.8.1951 Edith
Winkelbaur * Wien 25.5.1923 dau. of Adolf Winkelbaur, and has issue:

XIII

1b. **Christin Friedrich Bernhard Adolf Franz Bonifatius Graf zu Stolberg-
Stolberg** * Wien 9.6.1952

2b. **Andreas Rudolf Hubert Martin Graf zu Stolberg-Stolberg** * Klagenfurt
8.10.1954

3b. **Claudia Maria Edina Hedwig Gräfin zu Stolberg-Stolberg** * Hall
25.5.1956

XII

7a. **Ferdinand Maria Immaculata Joseph Martin Hubert Graf zu Stolberg-Stolberg**
* Reichen 8.12.1926 = Bodenburg 23.4.1966 Jutta Freiin. v. Cramm
* Berlin-Charlottenburg 15.3.1938 dau. of Adalbert Frhr. v. Cramm

8a. **Anna Regina Emmanuela Maria Gräfin zu Stolberg-Stolberg** * Bad Ischl
20.12.1927 = Hall 9.10.1954 Chevalier Jack de Spirlet * Bruxelles
3.4.1930, and has issue:

XIII

1b. **Beatrice Marie Valerie Hedwig Ghislaine de Spirlet** * Zürich 21.6.1955

2b. **Isabelle Astrid Paule Marie de Spirlet** * Ixelles 26.6.1957

3b. **Marie Elisabeth Ferdinande Catherine Louise de Spirlet** * Ixelles
30.4.1960

4b. **Guy Bernard Pierre Eduard Jack Marie de Spirlet** * Ixelles 13.5.1962

XIII		5b.	**Nicolas Jean François Madelaine Marie de Spirlet** * Ixelles 10.10.1964

XII   9a. **Magdalena Maria Mathilde Emmanuela Walpurgis Gräfin zu Stolberg-Stolberg** * Hall 19.12.1930 = Hall 8.9.1958 Martin Frhr. v. Kripp zu Prunberg u. Krippach * Krippach 25.12.1924, and has issue:

XIII   1b. **Paul Berhard Bonifacius Joseph Georg Frhr. v. Kripp zu Prunberg u. Krippach** * Meran 24.4.1959

         2b. **Marie Agnes Hedwig Elisabeth Mathilde Freiin. v. Kripp zu Prunberg u. Krippach** * Meran 24.4.1959

         3b. **Johann Jakob Karl Martin Joseph Frhr. v. Kripp zu Prunberg u. Krippach** * Innsbruck 10.9.1960

         4b. **Sigmund Otto Bonifacius Antonius Joseph Frhr. v. Kripp zu Prunberg u. Krippach** * Meran 5.6.1962

         5b. **Franz-Xaver Friedrich Blasius Maria Joseph Frhr. v. Kripp zu Prunberg u. Krippach** * Meran 2.2.1964

XI   (e) **Theodor Salvator Petrus Realinus Maria Josef Ignatius Archduke of Austria, Prince of Tuscany** * Schloss Wallsee 9.10.1899 = Schloss Zeil 28.7.1926 Maria Therese Gräfin v. Waldburg zu Zeil u. Trauchburg * Neu-Trauchburg 18.10.1901 dau. of Georg 5 Fürst v. Waldburg zu Zeil u. Trauchburg, and has issue:

XII   1a. **Franz Salvator Georg Josef Maria Thaddäus Archduke of Austria, Prince of Tuscany** * Schloss Wallsee 10.9.1927 = Hochburg b. Ach. 26.4.1962 **Anna-Amelie Prinzessin v. Schönburg-Waldenburg** * Frankfurt a.d. Oder 22.1.1936 dau. of Georg Prinz v. Schönburg-Waldenburg

         2a. **Theresia Monika Maria Valerie Elisabeth Ludovika Walburga Anna Archduchess of Austria, Princess of Tuscany** * Schloss Wallsee 9.1.1931 = Schloss Wallsee 17.10.1955 **Rasso Prince of Bavaria** * Schloss Leutstetten 24.5.1926, and has issue see elsewhere

         3a. **Maria Immakulata Mathilde Elisabeth Gabriele Walburga Huberta Archduchess of Austria, Princess of Tuscany** * Schloss Wallsee 7.12.1933 = Wallsee 9.6.1959 Reinhart Graf v.u. zu Hoenbroech * Kellenberg 15.10.1926, and has issue:

XIII   1b. **Alexandra Maria Margarete Josefa Gräfin v.u. zu Hoensbroech** * Schloss Kellenberg 19.3.1960

         2b. **Franz Lothar Branco Ignatius Georg Graf v.u. zu Hoensbroech** * Schloss Kellenberg 23.4.1961

         3b. **Maria Consuelo Pia Felicitas Gräfin v.u. zu Hoensbroech** * Schloss Kellenberg 30.5.1962

         4b. **Donata Theodora Carlotta Maria Gräfin v.u. zu Hoensbroech** * Schloss Kellenberg 23.8.1963

         5b. **Elena Maria Victoria Ingeborg Gräfin v.u. zu Hoensbroech** * Schloss Kellenberg 1.5.1965

XII   4a. **Carl Salvator Otto Maximilian Johannes Maria Archduke of Austria, Prince of Tuscany** * Schloss Wallsee 23.6.1936

XI   (f)   **Gertrud Maria Gisela Elisabeth Ignatia Archduchess of Austria, Princess of Tuscany**
* Schloss Wallsee 19.11.1900 + Wangen, Allgäu 22.12.1962 = Bad Ischl
29.12.1931 Georg Graf v. Waldburg zu Zeil u. Trauchburg * Hohenems 7.1.1878
+ Schloss Syrgenstein 26.10.1955, and has issue:

XII   1a.   **Marie Sophie Josepha Elisabeth Walburga Gräfin v. Waldburg zu Zeil u.
Trauchburg** * Innsbruck 5.12.1932 = Maria-Thann 7.5.1957 **Wessel Frhr.
v. Loë** * Wissen 8.8.1928 and has issue see elsewhere

     2a.   **Josef Klemens Georg Vitus Willibald Konrad v. Parzham Graf v. Waldburg zu
Zeil u. Trauchburg** * Syrgenstein 12.4.1934 = Bergen b. Neuburg a.d. Donau
21.5.1960 Maria Benedikta Freiin. v. Redwitz * Wertheim-am-Main
12.4.1937 dau. of Alfons Frhr. v. Redwitz   and has issue:

XIII   1b.   **Vitus Franziskus Rupert Benedikt Jósef Wunibald Maria Graf v. Waldburg
zu Zeil u. Trauchburg** * München 17.3.1961

     2b.   **Marie-Christine Sophie Eugenie Walburga Benedikta Josefa Gräfin v.
Waldburg zu Zeil u. Trauchburg** * Ravensburg 2.7.1962

     3b.   **Alois Willibald Johann Baptist Paul Maria Graf v. Waldburg zu Zeil u.
Trauchburg** * Ravensburg 23.6.1963

XI   (g)   **Maria Elisabeth Therese Philomena Ignatia Archduchess of Austria, Princess of
Tuscany** * Wallsee 19.11.1901 + Innsbruck 29.12.1936

     (h)   **Clemens Salvator Leopold Benedikt Antonius Maria Joseph Ignatius Archduke of
Austria, Prince of Tuscany** * Schloss Wallsee 6.10.1904 = Wien 20.2.1930
Elisabeth Gräfin Rességuier de Miremont * Nisko, Galicia 28.10.1906 dau. of
Friedrich Graf Rességuier de Miremont, and has issue:

XII   1a.   **Marie Valerie Christiane Elisabeth Clementine Franziska Josepha Marcella
Prinzessin v. Altenburg** * Wien 16.1.1931 = Unterach a. Attersee
20.7.1959 **Mario Graf v. Ledebur-Wicheln** * Samaden 28.7.1931, and has
issue see elsewhere

     2a.   **Clemens Maria Franz Salvator Friedrich Christian Joseph Johannes a Mata
Prinz v. Altenburg** * Wien 8.2.1932 = Unterach 17.10.1964 Laurence de
Costa de Beauregard * Neuilly-sur-Seine 3.6.1942 dau. of Henry Marquis de
Costa de Beauregard, and has issue:

XIII   1b.   **Philipp Prinz v. Altenburg** * Salzburg 15.3.1966

XII   3a.   **Georg Adam Maria Friedrich Leopold Joseph Michael Prinz v. Altenburg**
* Wien 23.9.1933 = Salzburg 7.2.1963 Maria Roswitha Wickl * Prag
2.3.1941, and has issue:

XIII   1b.   **Aegidus Prinz v. Altenburg** * Salzburg 4.1.1964

XII   4a.   **Peter Friedrich Christian Clemens Maria Leopold Joseph Matthäus Prinz v.
Altenburg** * Wien 18.9.1935 = Nieder-Flanditz 2.10.1965 **Juliana Gräfin v.
Waldstein-Wartenberg** * Buchberg-am-Kamp 22.5.1940 dau. of Eugen Graf v.
Waldstein-Wartenberg

     5a.   **Christoph Theodor Johannes Leopold Joseph Maria Vitalis Prinz v. Altenburg**
* Wallsee 28.4.1937

     6a.   **Elisabeth Maria Christiane Magdalena Walburga Prinzessin v. Altenburg**
* Wien 11.12.1938

7a.   **Franz Joseph Georg Clemens Maria Leopold Prinz v. Altenburg** * Ischl 15.3.1941

8a.   **Nikolaus Gottfried Salvator Maria Joseph Leopold Johannes Vianney Prinz v. Altenburg** * Ischl 22.5.1942

9a.   **Johannes Maria Karl Salvator Leopold Ignatius Florian Prinz v. Altenburg** * Gmunden 21.1.1949

(i)   **Mathilde Maria Antonia Ignatia Archduchess of Austria, Princess of Tuscany** * Ischl 9.8.1906 = Hall 10.4.1947 Ernst Hefel * Schruns 25.11.1888 s.p.

(j)   **Agnes Archduchess of Austria** * & + Ischl 26.6.1911

d)   **Carolina Maria Immakulata Josepha Ferdinanda Theresia Leopoldine Antoinette Franziska Isabelle Luise Januaria Christine Benedikta Laurencia Justinianna Archduchess of Austria, Princess of Tuscany** * Alt-Münster 5.9.1869 + Budapest 12.5.1945 = Wien 30.5.1894 **August Leopold Prince of Saxe-Coburg and Gotha** * Rio de Janeiro 6.12.1867 + Schladming 11.10.1922, and had issue see elsewhere

e)   **Albrecht Salvator Marie Joseph Ferdinand Karl Anton Johannes Xaver Aloys Ranier Klemens Roman Archduke of Austria, Prince of Tuscany** * Alt-Bunzlau 22.11.1871 + Bozen 27.2.1896

f)   **Maria Antoinette Immakulata Josepha Ferdinande Theresia Leopoldine Franziska Caroline Isabella Januaria Luise Christine Appolonie Archduchess of Austria, Princess of Tuscany** * Wien 18.4.1874 + Arco 14.1.1891

g)   **Maria Immakulata Raniera Josepha Ferdinande Theresia Leopoldine Antoinette Henriette Franziska Caroline Aloysia Januaria Christine Philomena Rosalia Archduchess of Austria, Princess of Tuscany** * Baden b. Wien 3.9.1878 = Wien 29.10.1900 **Robert Duke of Württemberg** * Meran 14.1.1873 + Schloss Altshausen 12.4.1947 s.p.

h)   **Ranier Salvator Maria Joseph Ferdinand Leopold Karl Anton de Padua Franz v. Assisi Johann Baptist Xaver Aloys Gonzaga Stephan Protomartyr Alexander Archduke of Austria, Prince of Tuscany** * Wien 27.2.1880 + Arco 4.5.1889

i)   **Henriette Marie Immakulata Adelgunde Josepha Ferdinande Theresia Leopoldine Franziska Caroline Isabella Januaria Luise Christine Eleonore Archduchess of Austria, Princess of Tuscany** * Wien 20.2.1884 + Traunkirchen 13.8.1886

j)   **Ferdinand Salvator Franz v. Assisi Anton de Padua Johann Baptist Xaver Aloys Gonzaga Ranier Erasmus Archduke of Austria, Prince of Tuscany** * Baden b. Wien 2.6.1888 + Traunkirchen 28.7.1891

i.   **Maria Anne Caroline Annunziata Johanne Josepha Gabriela Theresia Margarete Philomena Archduchess of Austria, Princess of Tuscany** * Firenze 9.6.1840 + Firenze 13.7.1841

j.   **Ranier Salvator Marie Stephan Joseph Johann Philipp Jacob Antonius Zanobi Ludwig Gonzaga Archduke of Austria, Prince of Tuscany** * Firenze 1.5.1842 + Firenze 14.8.1844

k.   **Marie Luise Annunziata Anna Johanne Josepha Antoinette Philomena Appolonie Thomasa Archduchess of Austria, Princess of Tuscany** * Firenze 31.10.1845 + Hanau 27.8.1917 = Schloss Brandeis 31.5.1865 Karl 5 Fürst v. Isenburg * Birstein 29.7.1838 + Sclackenwerth 4.4.1899, and had issue:

X   a)   **Leopold Wolfgang Ernst Maria Ferdinand Karl Michael Anton Victor Ludwig Joseph Johann Baptist Franz Prinz v. Isenburg** * Offenbach 10.3.1866 + München 30.1.1933 = (1) Heidelberg 22.4.1902 **Olga Princess of Saxe-Weimar and Eisenach** * Stuttgart 8.9.1869 + Berchtesgarden 12.1.1924 dau. of Hermann Prince of Saxe-Weimar and Eisenach; = (2) Berchtesgarden 2.12.1924 Maria Josepha Gräfin Eckbrecht v. Dürckheim-Montmartin * München 27.10.1880 + Bad Homburg 14.12.1937 dau. of Ernst Graf Eckbrecht v. Dürckheim-Montmartin, and had issue:

by 1st marriage:

XI   (a)   **Wilhelm Karl Hermann Prinz v. Isenburg** * Darmstadt 16.1.1903 + Mühlheim 23.11.1956 = Wiesbaden 30.4.1930 Helene Gräfin v. Korff gen. Schmising-Kerssenbrock * Darmstadt 6.4.1900 dau. of Alfred Graf v. Korff gen. Schmising-Kerssenbrock s.p.

X   b)   **Maria Antoinette Charlotte Anna Sophie Adelheid Isabelle Eulalia Leopoldine Augustine Beatrice Aloisia Michaele Angela Prinzessin v. Isenburg** * Offenbach 10.2.1867 + Birstein 13.8.1943

     c)   **Maria Michelle Johanna Antonia Leopoldine Karolina Adelheid Eulalia Sophie Aloysia Anna Elisabeth Prinzessin v. Isenburg** * Birstein 24.6.1868 + Berlin 19.3.1919

     d)   **Franz Joseph Maria Leopold Anton Carl Aloys Victor Wolfgang Bonifacius 6 Fürst v. Isenburg** * Birstein 1.6.1869 + Frankfurt-am-Main 14.9.1939 = Darmstadt 19.5.1896 Friederike Prinzessin zu Solms-Braunfels * Bonn 29.3.1873 + Hanau 21.4.1927 dau. of Hermann Prinz zu Solms-Braunfels, and had issue:

XI   (a)   **Marie Luise Antoinette Eulalie Josepha Wilhelmine Prinzessin v. Isenburg** * Birstein 22.3.1897 = Birstein 14.8.1918 Wilhelm Hans Graf v. Oppersdorff * Oberlogau 22.1.1896, and has issue:

XII   1a.   **Franz Eduard Johannes Alexander Hubert Michael Maria Graf v. Oppersdorff** * Oberlogau 19.6.1919 = Schloss Haus, Regensburg 19.6.1955 **Marie Therese Prinzessin v. Thurn u. Taxis** * Schloss Taxis 10.9.1925 dau. of Franz Joseph 9 Fürst v. Thurn u. Taxis, and has issue:

XIII   1b.   **Ferdinande Franziska Maria Hedwig Elisabeth Luise Gabriele Margarethe Adelheid Gräfin v. Oppersdorff** * Regensburg 25.3.1956

          2b.   **Marie Gabriele Aloysia Margarethe Elisabeth Josephine Gräfin v. Oppersdorff** * Regensburg 25.3.1957

          3b.   **Franz Joseph Maria Albrecht Johann Bernhard Friedrich Anton Hubert Michael Graf v. Oppersdorff** * Regensburg 24.5.1958

          4b.   **Margarethe Marie Luise Elisabeth Helene Regina Hedwig Melanie Theodora Gräfin v. Oppersdorff** * Regensburg 9.11.1959

          5b.   **Michael Ferdinand Johannes Edouard Karl Anton Joachim Hubertus Joseph Maria Graf v. Oppersdorff** * Regensburg 18.6.1962

XII   2a.   **Hans Georg Eduard Franz Eusebius Alexander Michael Hubert Karl Maria Graf v. Oppersdorff** * Ober-Altwaltersdorf 27.11.1920 = Braunfels 30.8.1950 Maria Gabriele Prinzessin zu Solms-Braunfels * Braunfels 23.8.1918 dau. of Georg Friedrich 7 Fürst zu Solms-Braunfels, and has issue:

XIII   1b.   **Maria Viktoria Beatrice Luise Mathilde Irene Hedwig Candida Gräfin v. Oppersdorff** * Frankfurt-am-Main 3.2.1954

XIII		2b. **Hans Georg Franz Joseph Ferdinand Eduard Maria Graf v. Oppersdorff** * Frankfurt-am-Main 11.1.1957

XII   3a. **Joseph Ferdinand Hans Wilhelm Karl Eduard Michael Hubert Maria Graf v. Oppersdorff** * Ober-Altwaltersdorf 26.3.1922 = Birnau am Bodensee 10.9.1958 Maria Assunta Gräfin v. Schönburg-Glauchau * Wechselburg 19.5.1935 dau. of Karl Graf v. Schönburg-Glauchau, and has issue:

XIII   1b. **Marie Isabelle Antoinette Anna Luise Hedwig Candida Dorothea Josefa Gräfin v. Oppersdorff** * Köln 4.7.1959

    2b. **Maria Tatiana Monica Margarita Lioba Adelheid Carolina Henrietta Gräfin v. Oppersdorff** * Köln 24.2.1961

XII   4a. **Friedrich Karl Eduard Wilhelm Hans Franziskus Eusebius Michael Hubert Maria Graf v. Oppersdorff** * Oberlogau 30.1.1925 = Frankfurt-am-Main 28.2.1962 **Elisabeth Princess of Hesse-Kassel** * Roma 8.10.1940 dau. of Philipp Landgraf of Hesse-Kassel, and has issue:

XIII   1b. **Friedrich Philipp Wilhelm Hans Moritz Maria Graf v. Oppersdorff** * Frankfurt-am-Main 1.12.1962

    2b. **Alexander Wolfgang Johannes Georg Victor Emanuel Maria Graf v. Oppersdorff** * 3.8.1965

XI   (b) **Marie Alexandra Johanna Sophie Elisabeth Thomasa Gabriele Prinzessin v. Isenburg** * Birstein 21.12.1899 + Arcola, near Trieste 22.12.1945 = Birstein 14.6.1923 **Eduard Prinz zu Windisch-Graetz** * Gonobitz 15.7.1891, and has issue see elsewhere

    (c) **Joseph Franz Ferdinand Maria Karl Hermann Alexius Vincenz v. Paula 7 Fürst v. Isenburg** * Birstein 17.7.1901 + Birstein 9.12.1956 = Remplin 22.7.1939 Irene Countess Tolstoy * Tsarskoi Selo 26.1.1917 dau. of Alexander Count Tolstoy, and has issue:

XII   1a. **Irene Friederike Cecile Theresia Antoinette Helene Alexandra Sophie Anna Maria Luise Prinzessin v. Isenburg** * Birstein 30.9.1940 = Birstein 28.8.1961 Wilhelm Graf zu Stolberg-Stolberg * Ascherode 2.6.1927, and has issue:

XIII   1b. **Franz-Joseph Johannes Wilhelm Laurentius Maria Graf zu Stolberg-Stolberg** * Aachen 24.6.1962

    2b. **Isabel-Juliana Helene Therese Maria Annunciata Gräfin zu Stolberg-Stolberg** * Aachen 7.6.1963

    3b. **Irina Christiana Maria Gräfin zu Stolberg-Stolberg** * Aachen 21.4.1964

XII   2a. **Maria Annunciata Franziska Felizitas Caroline Sophie Gabriele Imagina Prinzessin v. Isenburg** * Birstein 14.9.1941

    3a. **Franz Alexander Karl Friedrich Christian Hubert Georg Gabriel Maria 8 Fürst v. Isenburg** * Birstein 22.7.1943

    4a. **Elisabeth Christiane Helene Huberta Margarethe Madelaine Maria Fatima Prinzessin v. Isenburg** * Birstein 5.4.1945

XI   (d) **Marie Sophie Eulalie Aloysia Paula Gabriele Prinzessin v. Isenburg** * Birstein 7.1.1903

XI

XII

XIII

XII

XIII

XII

XIII

XII

XIII

XI

CHAPTER IV
LORRAINE =
AUSTRIA

(e) **Marie Anna Agnes Michaela Prinzessin v. Isenburg** * Birstein 7.3.1904 = Birstein 17.4.1929 Georg Adam Graf v. Starhemberg * Eferding 10.4.1904, and has issue:

1a. **Franziska Sophie Marie Friederike Gräfin v. Starhemberg** * Eisenkappel 10.7.1930 = Eltville 23.5.1956 Karl Theodor Mayer * Wien 2.2.1924, and has issue:

1b. **Elisabeth Marie Franziska Anna Adele Mayer** * Washington D.C. 24.7.1957

2b. **Peter Georg Mayer** * Washington D.C. 4.10.1958

3b. **Christian Mayer** * Washington D.C. 7.8.1960

2a. **Sophie Marie Elisabeth Therese Franziska Alexandra Anna Gräfin v. Starhemberg** * Eisenkappel 14.9.1931 = Eisenkappel 14.5.1951 Alexander Graf Matz v. Spiegelfeld * Graz 2.9.1925, and has issue:

1b. **Georg Adam Alexander Franz Maria Mathias Graf Matz v. Spiegelfeld** * Wien 25.2.1952

2b. **Franz Xaver Ferdinand Maria Philipp Nery Graf Metz v. Spiegelfeld** * Wien 26.5.1953

3b. **Anna Alexandra Maria Gabrielle Franziska Sophie Gräfin Matz v. Spiegelfeld** * Wien 26.11.1954

4b. **Christian Ferdinand Georg Friedrich Gisbertus Franz Joseph Maria Graf Matz v. Spiegelfeld** * Wien 28.1.1956

5b. **Matthias Graf Matz v. Spiegelfeld** * 27.12.1960

3a. **Franz Joseph Salvator Ernst Rüdiger Georg Thaddäus Friedrich Maria Graf v. Starhemberg** * Bad Ischl 18.7.1933 = Maria-Wörth 25.6.1960 Itha Hauninger v. Haueningen * Wien 24.11.1938 dau. of Franz Hauninger Edler v. Haueningen, and has issue:

1b. **Georg Adam Graf v. Starhemberg** * Klagenfurt 7.4.1961

2b. **Franz Joseph Graf v. Starhemberg** * Klagenfurt 24.6.1963

3b. **Franziska Gräfin v. Starhemberg** * Klagenfurt 2.12.1964

4a. **Friederike Olivia Helene Luise Ludwiga Stefanie Maria Gräfin v. Starhemberg** * Rychvald 20.8.1936 = Eisenkappel 8.6.1955 **Karl Prinz v. Auersperg-Breunner** * Goldegg 26.4.1930, and has issue see elsewhere

5a. **Irene Gräfin v. Starhemberg** * Birstein 7.3.1940 = Eisenkappel 16.7.1959 Johannes Prinz v. Auersperg * Weitwörth b. Salzburg 29.1.1934, and has issue:

1b. **Vinzenz Prinz v. Auersperg** * Klagenfurt 17.7.1960

2b. **Gabrielle Prinzessin v. Auersperg** * Lisboa 6.6.1961

3b. **Ferdinand Prinz v. Auersperg** * Klagenfurt 21.11.1964

(f) **Maria Joseph Ferdinand Karl Valerius Ernst Hermann Heinrich Agnus Theophilus Mathias Prinz v. Isenburg** * Birstein 20.2.1906

X	e)	**Karl Joseph Maria Anton Leopold Victor Franz Michael Pius Aloys Simon Prinz v. Isenburg** * Offenbach 18.2.1871 + Rapallo 6.1.1951 = London 24.8.1895 Berthe Lewis * New Orleans 16.3.1872 + Santa Margherita, near Rapallo 22.4.1939 s.p.
	f)	**Viktor Karl Salvator Maria Leopold Anton Aloys Joseph Ranier Johann Casimir Prinz v. Isenburg** * Offenbach 29.2.1872 + Berlin 4.2.1946 = Nürnburg 11.4.1908 Leontine Rohrer Freifrau v. Rombach * Schlackenwerth 27.1.1886 + Berlin-Charlottenburg 7.11.1950 s.p.
	g)	**Alfons Maria Leopold Anton Karl Alois Joseph Franz Pius Johannes Michael Heinrich Prinz v. Isenburg** * Offenbach a.M. 6.2.1875 + Langenselbold 22.4.1951 = Petschau 1.12.1900 **Pauline Gräfin v. Beaufort-Spontin** * Paris 8.11.1876 + Langenselbold 11.12.1955 dau. of Friedrich Herzog v. Beaufort-Spontin, and has issue:
XI	(a)	**Margarete Marie Alfonsa Luisa Melanie Antoinette Paula Friederike Prinzessin v. Isenburg** * Langenselbold 16.10.1901
	(b)	**Maria Imagina Aloysia Friederike Tusnelda Wunibalde Lucia Bertha Prinzessin v. Isenburg** * Langenselbold 12.12.1902
	(c)	**Elisabeth Franziska Marie Melanie Norberta Prinzessin v. Isenburg** * Langenselbold 6.6.1904 = Langenselbold 19.5.1934 Johannes Eggen van Terlan * Gand 23.6.1888 + Bonn 28.12.1952, and has issue:
XII	1a.	**Maria Alphonsa Elisabeth Pauline Hortense Benoite Eggen van Terlan** * Carlsbad 17.6.1935 + Hanau 6.8.1938
	2a.	**Charles Paul Jean Lamoral Baudouin Marie Eggen van Terlan** * Hanau 18.7.1937
	3a.	**Helene Alphonsa Pauline Hortense Elisabeth Marie Felicie Eggen van Terlan** * Besancon 27.5.1942
XI	(d)	**Maria Ernst Hubertus Alfons Karl Friedrich Stephan Thomas Prinz v. Isenburg** * Langenselbold 26.12.1906 = Nairobi 8.2.1937 Fiona Davidson * Pretoria 17.2.1917 dau. of William Davidson, and has issue:
XII	1a.	**Maria Pauline Elisabeth Margarethe Stephanie Fiona Antoinette Princess of Isenburg** * Moshi, Tanganyika 23.11.1937 = Nairobi 3.8.1962 Francis Cain * South Sea 27.5.1934
	2a.	**Maria Karl Alfons Wilhelm Ernst Heinrich Johannes David Nikolaus Prince of Isenburg** * Moshi 6.12.1939 = Princeton, N.J. 5.6.1965 Valerie O'Dea * Washington D.C. 12.11.1942
	3a.	**Maria Franz Wilhelm Eugen Wolfgang Ernst Walter Ludwig Prince of Isenburg** * Moshi 4.6.1941
	4a.	**Maria Viktor Alexander Alphons Richard Heinrich Robert Kasimir Michael Johannes Prince of Isenburg** * Oldeani 2.6.1944
	5a.	**Maria Richard Leonhard Benedikt Anton Jakob Quentin Friedrich Ernst Prince of Isenburg** * Oldeani 3.2.1946
XI	(e)	**Maria Heinrich Leon Friedrich Karl Alphons Maximilian Prinz v. Isenburg** * Langenselbold 16.9.1913 + Tiflis as Russian Prisoner of War 13.1.1946
X	h)	**Maria Elisabeth Franziska Antoinette Leopoldine Karolina Aloysia Anne Sophie Camila Praxedes Prinzessin v. Isenburg** * Birstein 18.7.1877 + Hadamar 28.9.1943 = Birstein 27.6.1919 Georg Beyer * Castell b. Mayence 29.2.1880 + Hadamar 13.5.1941 s.p.

X   i)   **Adelaide Marie Sophie Carola Aloisia Leopoldine Antoinette Anna Franziska Eulalie Elisabeth Therese Josephine Tommasa Prinzessin v. Isenburg** * Birstein 31.10.1878 + Dourgne, Tarn 4.3.1936

IX   l.   **Ludwig Salvator Maria Joseph Johann Baptist Dominik Ranier Ferdinand Karl Zenobius Antonin Archduke of Austria, Prince of Tuscany** * Firenze 4.8.1847 + Schloss Brandeis 12.10.1915

            m.   **Johann Nepomuk Salvator Marie Joseph Johann Ferdinand Balthasar Ludwig Karl Zenobius Antonin Archduke of Austria, Prince of Tuscany** * Firenze 25.11.1852 + Lost at Sea 15.8.1890 (known as Johann Orth)

VIII   (4)   **Marie Luise Josephe Christine Rosa Archduchess of Austria, Princess of Tuscany** * Firenze 30.8.1799 + Firenze 15.6.1857

        (5)   **Maria Theresia Franziska Josepha Johanna Benedikta Archduchess of Austria, Princess of Tuscany** * Wien 21.3.1801 + Torino 12.1.1855 = Firenze 30.9.1817 **Carl Alberto I King of Sardinia** * Paris 29.10.1798 + Oporto 28.7.1849 s.p.

VII   4)   **Marie Anna Ferdinande Josepha Charlotte Johanna Archduchess of Austria** * Wien 21.4.1770 + Prag 1.10.1809

     5)   **Karl Ludwig Johann Joseph Laurencius Archduke of Austria, Duke of Teschen** * Firenze 5.9.1771 + Wien 30.4.1847 = Weilburg 17.9.1815 **Henriette Princess of Nassau-Weilburg** * Schloss Ermitage b. Bayreuth 30.10.1797 + Wien 29.12.1829 dau. of Friedrich Wilhelm Duke of Nassau-Weilburg, and had issue:

VIII   (1)   **Maria Theresia Isabella Archduchess of Austria** * Wien 31.7.1816 + Albano 8.8.1867 = Napoli 27.1.1837 **Ferdinando II King of Naples and Sicily** * Palermo 12.1.1810 + Caserta 22.5.1859, and had issue see elsewhere

        (2)   **Albrecht Friedrich Rudolf Archduke of Austria, Duke of Teschen** * Wien 3.8.1817 + Wien 18.2.1895 = München 1.5.1844 **Hildegarte Princess of Bavaria** * Würzburg 10.6.1825 + Wien 2.4.1864 dau. of Ludwig I King of Bavaria, and had issue:

IX   a.   **Maria Theresia Anna Archduchess of Austria** * Wien 15.7.1845 + Tübingen 8.10.1927 = Wien 18.1.1865 **Philipp Duke of Württemberg** * Neuilly-sur-Seine 30.7.1838 + Stuttgart 11.10.1917 and has issue see elsewhere

        b.   **Karl Albrecht Ludwig Archduke of Austria** * Wien 3.1.1847 + Wien 19.7.1848

        c.   **Mathilde Maria Adelgunde Archduchess of Austria** * Wien 25.1.1849 + Wien 6.6.1867

VIII   (3)   **Karl Ferdinand Archduke of Austria** * Wien 29.7.1818 + Gross-Seelowitz 20.11.1874 = Wien 18.4.1854 **Elisabeth Archduchess of Austria** * Ofen 17.1.1831 + Wien 14.2.1903 dau. of Joseph Archduke of Austria, Palatine of Hungary, and had issue:

IX   a.   **Franz Joseph Archduke of Austria** * Gross-Seelowitz 5.3.1855 + Gross-Seelowitz 13.3.1855

        b.   **Friedrich Maria Albrecht Wilhelm Karl Archduke of Austria, Duke of Teschen** * Gross-Seelowitz 4.6.1856 + Altenburg, Hungary 30.12.1936 = Château de l'Hermitage, Belgium 8.10.1878 **Isabelle Prinzessin v. Croÿ** * Dülmen 27.2.1856 + Budapest 5.9.1931 dau. of Rudolf Herzog v. Croÿ, and has issue:

X   a)   **Maria Christina Isabelle Natalie Archduchess of Austria** * Kraków 17.11.1879 + Anholt 6.8.1962 = Wien 10.5.1902 **Emanuel Erbprinz zu Salm-Salm** * Münster i. W. 30.11.1871 X Pinsk 19.8.1916 and had issue see elsewhere

X   b) **Maria Anna Isabelle Epiphanie Eugenie Gabriele Archduchess of Austria** * Linz 6.1.1882 + Lausanne 25.2.1940 = Wien 25.5.1903 **Eli Prince of Bourbon-Parma** * Biarritz 23.7.1880 + Freiburg, Steiermark 27.6.1959, and had issue see elsewhere

       c) **Maria Henrietta Caroline Gabriele Archduchess of Austria** * Pressburg 10.1.1883 + Mariazell 2.9.1956 = Baden b. Wien 3.6.1908 Gottfried Prinz zu Hohenlohe-Waldenburg-Schillingsfürst v. Ratibor u. Corvey * Wien 8.11.1867 + Wien 7.11.1932, and has issue:

XI   (a) **Marie Elisabeth Henriette Prinzessin zu Hohenlohe-Waldenburg-Schillingsfürst v. Ratibor u. Corvey** * Wien 27.9.1909

       (b) **Natalie Isabelle Marie Prinzessin zu Hohenlohe-Waldenburg-Schillingsfürst v. Ratibor u. Corvey** * Baden b. Wien 28.7.1911

       (c) **Friedrich Konrad Konstantin Gottfried Marie Prinz zu Hohenlohe-Waldenburg-Schillingsfürst v. Ratibor u. Corvey** * Wien 18.2.1913 + Twikbuli, near Kutais, Caucasus, as Russian Prisoner of War ... 12.1945

X   d) **Natalie Maria Theresia Archduchess of Austria** * Pressburg 12.1.1884 + Pressburg 23.3.1898

       e) **Stephanie Marie Isabelle Archduchess of Austria** * Pressburg 1.5.1886 + Ostend 29.8.1890

       f) **Gabriele Maria Theresia Archduchess of Austria** * Pressburg 14.9.1887 + Budapest 15.11.1954

       g) **Isabella Maria Theresia Christine Eugenie Archduchess of Austria** * Pressburg 17.11.1888 = Schönbrunn 10.2.1912 **Georg Prince of Bavaria** * München 2.4.1880 + Roma 31.5.1943 (marriage annulled) s.p.

       h) **Marie Alice Emanuele Agnes Anna Archduchess of Austria** * Pressburg 15.1.1893 + Halbthurn 1.7.1962 = Lucerne 8.5.1920 Friedrich-Heinrich Frhr. Waldbott v. Bassenheim * Tolcsva 17.9.1889 + Seefeld a. Pilsensee 16.12.1959, and had issue:

XI   (a) **Maria Immaculata Hedwig Isabella Freiin. Waldbott v. Bassenheim** * Hármashutta 27.7.1921 = Oberalting-Seefeld 10.12.1947 **Hans Heribert Graf zu Toerring-Jettenbach** * Winhöring 25.12.1903, and has issue see elsewhere

       (b) **Anton Friedrich Martin Bartolomäus Frhr. Waldbott v. Bassenheim** * Hármashutta 24.8.1922 = Wien ... Thea Schanderer * Wien 13.1.1938, and has issue:

XII   1a. **Christian Friedrich Anton Frhr. Waldbott v. Bassenheim** * Wien 19.4.1961

       2a. **Christine Maria Alice Freiin. Waldbott v. Bassenheim** * Eisenstadt 6.8.1963

       3a. **Peter Josef Frhr. Waldbott v. Bassenheim** * Eisenstadt 24.1.1966

       4a. **Alice Stefanie Freiin. Waldbott v. Bassenheim** * Eisenstadt 24.1.1966

XI   (c) **Paul Albrecht Friedrich Cyrille Maria Frhr. Waldbott v. Bassenheim** * Magyar-Ovár 9.2.1924 = Wolfsegg 16.6.1958 Marie Theresia Gräfin Capello v. Wickenburg * Gmunden 17.8.1929 dau. of Eduard Graf Capello v. Wickenburg s.p.

       (d) **Isabella Klementine Hedwig Theodore Maria Freiin. Waldbott v. Bassenheim** * Sátoraljaujhely 20.4.1926 = Leopoldville, Congo 23.4.1952 Pongrác Graf Somssich v. Sáard * Budapest 12.8.1920, and has issue:

XII   1a. **István László Friedrich Marie-Gobert Graf Somssich v. Sáard** * Leopoldville 23.5.1953

       2a. **Gabor Hans Heribert Pongrác Graf Somssich v. Sáard** * München 14.3.1955

3a. **Christoph László Paul Frederic Graf Somssich v. Sáard** * Usumbura,
Burundi 26.7.1960

(e) **Stephanie Elisabeth Alice Maria Freiin. Waldbott v. Bassenheim** * Sátoraljaujhely
19.11.1929 = München 27.9.1955 **Johann Graf zu Königsegg-Aulendorf**
* Königseggwald 13.4.1925, and has issue:

1a. **Isabelle Gabriele Maria Apollonia Eusebia Gräfin zu Königsegg-Aulendorf**
* München 23.7.1956

2a. **Maximilian Ulrich Philipp Eusebius Benno Graf zu Königsegg-Aulendorf**
* München 16.6.1958

3a. **Markus Maximilian Eusebius Johannes Graf zu Königsegg-Aulendorf**
* München 16.5.1963

(f) **Joseph Clemens Alexius Friedrich Polycarp Maria Frhr. Waldbott v. Bassenheim**
* Sátoraljaujhely 26.1.1931

h) **Albrecht Franz Joseph Karl Friedrich Georg Hubert Maria Archduke of Austria, Duke of
Teschen** * Weilburg b. Baden 24.7.1897 + Buenos Aires 23.7.1955 = (1) Brighton,
Sussex 16.8.1930 Irene Lelbach * Szabadka 22.12.1897 dau. of Johann Lelbach,
− div.; = (2) Pannonhalma 9.5.1938 Juliana Bocskay de Felsö-Bánya * Szelevény
1.11.1909 dau. of Béla Bocskay de Felsö-Bánya − div.; = (3) Buenos Aires ... Lydia
Strauss * ..., and had issue:

by 2nd marriage:

(a) **Charlotte Isabella Maria Christine Esther Katharina Pia Habsburg-Lothringen
Princess of Hungary** * Budapest 3.3.1940

(b) **Ildiko Katharina Isabella Henriette Alice Maria Habsburg-Lothringen Princess of
Hungary** * Budapest 19.2.1942

c. **Maria Christine Desideria Henriette Felicitas Raniera Archduchess of Austria** * Gross-Seelowitz
21.7.1858 + Madrid 6.2.1929 = Madrid 29.11.1879 **Alfonso XII King of Spain** * Madrid
28.11.1857 + El Pardo, Madrid 25.11.1885, and had issue see elsewhere

d. **Karl Stephan Eugen Viktor Felix Maria Archduke of Austria** * Gross-Seelowitz 5.9.1860
+ Schloss Saybusch 7.4.1933 = Wien 28.2.1886 **Maria Theresia Archduchess of Austria,
Princess of Tuscany** * Alt-Bunzlau 18.9.1862 + Schloss Saybusch 10.5.1933 dau. of Karl
Salvator Archduke of Austria, Prince of Tuscany, and had issue:

a) **Eleonora Maria Immakulata Christina Josepha Sosthenesia Archduchess of Austria**
* Pola 28.11.1886 = Schloss Saybusch 9.1.1913 Alfons v. Kloss * Trieste 9.6.1880
+ Wien 25.8.1953, and has issue:

(a) **Albrecht Karl Stephan v. Kloss** * Pola 13.10.1913 = Baden 4.9.1942 Erika Kaiser
* Baden 13.10.1920 dau. of Guido Kaiser, and has issue:

1a. **Karl Stephan v. Kloss** * Baden 4.10.1943

2a. **Maria Elisabeth Franziska v. Kloss** * Baden 3.12.1944

3a. **Barbara Eleonore v. Kloss** * Baden 5.6.1946

(b) **Karl Albrecht v. Kloss** * Wien 15.2.1915 X Kotanie, Poland 5.9.1939

(c) **Ranier Albrecht v. Kloss** * Baden 12.10.1916 = Pfaffstätten 17.1.1944
Cornelia Schoute * Wormerveer, Holland 15.1.1920 dau. of Cornelius Schoute,
and has issue:

XII		1a.	**Elisabeth v. Kloss** * Engelstein 26.2.1945
		2a.	**Georg v. Kloss** * Baden 5.9.1954

XI   (d)   **Ernst Jerome v. Kloss** * Baden 19.1.1919 = Wiener-Neustadt 11.7.1953 Rixta Maria Hartig * Wiener-Neustadt 27.4.1925 dau. of Julius Eugen Hartig, and has issue:

XII		1a.	**Florian v. Kloss** * Wien 12.3.1954
		2a.	**Thomas v. Kloss** * Wien 29.12.1956
		3a.	**Nikolaus v. Kloss** * Wien 24.9.1957
		4a.	**Andrea v. Kloss** * Wien 24.12.1958

XI   (e)   **Alfons Salvator v. Kloss** * Pola 3.5.1920 = Schloss Engelstein 12.7.1947 Theresia Gräfin v. Coreth zu Coredo * Kittsee 12.3.1923 dau. of Max Graf v. Coreth zu Coredo, and has issue:

XII		1a.	**Andreas v. Kloss** * Wien 5.5.1948
		2a.	**Johannes v. Kloss** * Graz 21.11.1949
		3a.	**Alfons v. Kloss** * Graz 19.9.1953

XI   (f)   **Friedrich Anton v. Kloss** * Schloss Saybusch 13.2.1922 ✕ Stalingrad February 1943

         (g)   **Maria Theresia Franziska v. Kloss** * Baden 7.5.1925 = Schloss Engelstein 20.4.1949 Walter Kaiser * Mährisch-Schönberg 5.10.1918, and has issue:

XII		1a.	**Martin Kaiser** * Zwettl 20.4.1950
		2a.	**Michael Guido Joseph Kaiser** * Engelstein 23.3.1951
		3a.	**Marius Kaiser** * Engelstein 7.4.1952
		4a.	**Claudia Kaiser** * Engelstein 7.10.1954
		5a.	**Christian Kaiser** * Engelstein 2.10.1957

XI   (h)   **Stephan Maximilian v. Kloss** * Baden 23.11.1933 = Baden 3.9.1955 Ingrid Morocutti * Klagenfurt 24.5.1936 dau. of Wolfgang Morocutti, and has issue:

XII		1a.	**Michaela v. Kloss** * Baden 3.6.1956
		2a.	**Marina v. Kloss** * Baden 28.1.1958
		3a.	**Christoph v. Kloss** * Baden 18.2.1959
		4a.	**Marcus v. Kloss** * Baden 12.6.1960

X   b)   **Renata Maria Caroline Raniera Theresia Philomena Desideria Macaria Archduchess of Austria** * Pola 2.1.1888 + Schloss Balice b. Kraków 16.5.1935 = Schloss Zywiec, Poland 16.1.1909 Hieronim Prince Radziwill * Cannes 6.1.1885 + in the Russian Deportation 6.4.1945, and had issue:

XI   (a)   **Maria Teresa Kanuta Karolina Dominika Renata Princess Radziwill** * Balice 19.1.1910

         (b)   **Dominik Ranier Karl Hieronim Maria Nikolaj Alfons Prince Radziwill** * Balice 23.1.1911 = (1) Paris 30.5.1938 **Eugénie Princess of Greece and Denmark** * Paris 10.2.1910 dau. of George Prince of Greece and Denmark, — div.; = (2) Roma 8.1.1947 Lida Bloodgood * New York 1.2.1923 dau. of Johan van Schaick Bloodgood, and has issue:

by 1st marriage:

XII

1a. **Tatiana Maria Renata Eugenia Elzbieta Malgorzata Princess Radziwill**
* Rouen 28.8.1939 = Athens 26.3.1966 Jean Fruchard * 1.4.1937

2a. **Jerzy Andrzej Dominik Hieronim Piotr Leon Prince Radziwill** * Cape Town
4.11.1942

by 2nd marriage:

3a. **Lida Maria Renata Princess Radziwill** * Cape Town 11.7.1954

4a. **Maria Ludwika Jadwiga Princess Radziwill** * Cape Town 23.1.1956

XI

(c) **Karol Hieronim Celestyn Maria Konstanty Stanislaw Prince Radziwill** * Balice
3.5.1912 = Buenos Aires 21.3.1949 Doña Maria Luisa de Alvear * Buenos Aires
11.7.1913 dau. of Don Eugenio de Alvear s.p.

(d) **Olbracht Hieronim Maria Karol Izydor Stanislaw Prince Radziwill** * Balice
10.5.1914 + Davos 23.6.1932

(e) **Eleonora Maria Aniela Alberta Renata Karolina Princess Radziwill** * Balice
2.8.1918 = Balice 21.4.1938 Benedykt Count Tyszkiewicz * Czerwony Dwór
2.8.1904 + Lódz 6.2.1956 s.p.

(f) **Leon Hieronim Stanislaw Karol Maria Tadeusz Prince Radziwill** * Balice 28.10.1922

X

c) **Karl Albrecht Nikolaus Leo Gratianus Archduke of Austria** * Pola 18.12.1888
+ Oestervik, Stockholm 17.3.1951 = Schloss Saybusch 8.11.1920 Alice Ankarcrona
* Tullgarn, Sweden 18.12.1889 dau. of Carl Gustaf Ankarcrona, and has issue:

XI

(a) **Karl-Stefan Maximilian Ferdinand Narcissus Maria Prinz v. Altenburg** * Balice
29.10.1921 = Genève 18.9.1952 Marie-Louise af Petersens * Stockholm 4.11.1910
dau. of August af Petersens, and has issue:

XII

1a. **Maria-Christina Ninfa Renata Margarita Isabella Clara Eugenia Anselma
Prinzessin v. Altenburg** * Stockholm 21.4.1953

2a. **Karl-Albrecht Ferdinand Leopold Philipp Joseph Rafael Maria Prinz v.
Altenburg** * Stockholm 24.10.1956 + Zürich 26.5.1957

XI

(b) **Maria-Christina Immaculata Elisabeth Renata Alice Gabriela Prinzessin v. Altenburg**
* Saybusch 8.12.1923

(c) **Karl-Albrecht Maximilian Leon Maria Dominique Prinz v. Altenburg** * Saybusch
4.8.1926 + Saybusch 19.12.1928

(d) **Renata Maria Theresia Alice Elisabeth Prinzessin v. Altenburg** * Saybusch
13.4.1931 = Stockholm 26.6.1957 Don Eduardo de Zulueta y Dato * Paris
10.12.1924, and has issue:

XII

1a. **Don Carlos Eduardo Ernesto Maria George Rámon Anthony de Zulueta y
Altenburg** * New York 19.10.1958

2a. **Don Ernesto Maria Jaime Antonio Rámon Cristóbal de Zulueta y Altenburg**
* New York 7.7.1961

3a. **Doña Isabelle Maria Cristina Immaculada Renata Tomasa de Zulueta y
Altenburg** * Madrid 7.3.1965

X

d) **Mechtildis Maria Christina Leona Theresia Rosario Nikosia Archduchess of Austria**
* Pola 11.10.1891 = Schloss Saybusch 11.1.1913 Olgierd Prince Czartoryski * Sielec
25.10.1888, and has issue:

XI		(a)	**Konstanty Stefan Aleksander Adam Gracjan Prince Czartoryski** * Sielec 9.12.1913 = Rio de Janeiro 21.12.1941 Karolina Plater-Zyberk * Minsk Litewski 7.12.1917 dau. of Henryk Count Plater-Zyberk, and has issue:

XII   1a. **Karol Henryk Prince Czartoryski** * Rio de Janeiro 9.12.1942 = 29.8.1964 Aline Ternynck * 1940 dau. of René Ternynck and has issue:

XIII   1b. **Maria Dolores Dorota Princess Czartoryska** * São Paulo 16.9.1965

XII   2a. **Krzysztof Hubert Prince Czartoryski** * Rio de Janeiro 25.8.1946

XI   (b) **Cecylia Teresa Immakulata Ilona Felicyta Elzbieta Helena Princess Czartoryska** * Sielec 9.4.1915 = London 25.6.1947 Jerzy Rostworowski * Warszawa 10.9.1910 and has issue:

XII   1a. **Isabella Maria Teresa Adelajda Rostworowska** * London 30.3.1948

     2a. **Karol Stefan Rostworowski** * Rio de Janeiro 27.5.1950

     3a. **Jerzy Olgierd Rostworowski** * Rio de Janeiro 12.2.1953

     4a. **Malgorzata Rostworowska** * São Paulo 20.12.1956

XI   (c) **Izabella Maria Karolina Zuzanna Róza Marcelina Cypriana Dezyderia Felicja Mechtylda Princess Czartoryska** * Sielec 8.8.1917 = Balice 8.12.1942 Rafal Count Bninski * Dobczyn 27.2.1918 + Warszawa 13.10.1943, and has issue:

XII   1a. **Karol Andrzej Rafal Antoni Józef Aleksander Konstanty Maria Count Bninski** * Warszawa 15.11.1943

XI   (d) **Aleksander Chrystian Antoni Józef Prince Czartoryski** * Sielec 21.10.1919

X   e) **Leo Karl Maria Kyrill Method Archduke of Austria** * Pola 5.7.1893 + Bestwina 28.4.1939 = Wien 4.10.1922 Maria Klothilde v. Thuillieres Gräfin v. Montjoye-Vaufrey et de la Roche * Meidling 6.11.1893 dau. of Karl de Thuillieres Graf v. Montjoye-Vaufrey et de la Roche, and had issue:

XI   (a) **Maria Desiderata Theresa Fidelis Irene Gräfin v. Habsburg-Lothringen** * Lissa b. Posen 3.8.1923 = Wien 6.4.1947 Wolfgang Graf Hartig * Melk 13.8.1922 and has issue:

XII   1a. **Karl Johann Leo Maria Franz de Paula Wolfgang Edmund Graf Hartig** * Wien 8.6.1949

     2a. **Andreas Maria Franz de Paula Wolfgang Edmund Leopold Graf Hartig** * Wien 6.2.1952

XI   (b) **Mechtildis Maria Irene Fidelis Gräfin v. Habsburg-Lothringen** * Lissa 14.8.1924 = Wien 29.4.1948 Manfred Graf u. Markgraf v. Piatti * Loosdorf 22.7.1924, and has issue:

XII   1a. **Andrea Maria Anna Alexandra Theckla Gabriele Gräfin v. Piatti** * Wien 3.2.1949

     2a. **Alfons Maria Ferdinand Leo Karl Judas Thaddäus Josef Graf v. Piatti** * Wien 13.9.1950

     3a. **Michael Graf v. Piatti** * Wien 23.1.1955

XII

       4a.   **Ferdinand Graf v. Piatti** * Wien 23.3.1962

       5a.   **Benedikt Graf v. Piatti** * Wien 21.1.1966

XI

   (c)   **Elisabeth Irene Maria Fidelis Gräfin v. Habsburg-Lothringen** * Wien 13.3.1927

   (d)   **Leo-Stephan Maria Carl Wolfgang Rudolf Fidelis Graf v. Habsburg-Lothringen**
* Zywiec Poland 12.6.1928 = Wien 31.3.1962 Gabriele Kunert * Warnsdorf,
Böh. 15.6.1935 dau. of Julius Kunert, and has issue:

XII

       1a.   **Maria Isabella Klara Gräfin v. Habsburg-Lothringen** * Reading, Pa, U.S.A.
21.12.1962

       2a.   **Albrecht Stanislaus Bernhard Mathias Manfred Graf v. Habsburg-Lothringen**
* St. Gallen 6.9.1963

XI

   (e)   **Hugo Carl Maria Leo Fidelis Graf v. Habsburg-Lothringen** * Zywiec 27.9.1930

X

   f)   **Wilhelm Franz Joseph Karl Archduke of Austria** * Pola 10.2.1895 + Wladimir-Wolensk,
near Kiev in a Russian Concentration Camp 1954

IX

   e.   **Eugen Ferdinand Pius Bernhard Felix Maria Archduke of Austria** * Gross-Seelowitz
21.5.1863 + Meran 30.12.1954

   f.   **Eleonore Archduchess of Austria** * Gross-Seelowitz 19.11.1864 + Gross-Seelowitz 9.12.1864

VIII

   (4)   **Friedrich Ferdinand Leopold Archduke of Austria** * Wien 14.5.1821 + Wien 5.10.1847

   (5)   **Rudolf Archduke of Austria** * Wien 25.9.1822 + Wien 24.10.1822

   (6)   **Maria Caroline Luise Christine Archduchess of Austria** * Wien 10.9.1825 + Baden b. Wien
17.7.1915 = Wien 21.2.1852 **Ranier Archduke of Austria** * Wien 11.1.1827 + Wien 27.1.1913,
and had issue see elsewhere

   (7)   **Wilhelm Franz Karl Archduke of Austria** * Wien 21.4.1827 + Weikersdorf b. Wien 29.7.1894

VII

   6)   **Alexander Leopold Johann Joseph Archduke of Austria** * Poggio Imperiale 14.8.1772 + Laxenburg
12.7.1795

   7)   **Albrecht Johann Joseph Archduke of Austria** * Firenze 19.12.1773 + Firenze 22.7.1774

   8)   **Maximilian Johann Joseph Archduke of Austria** * Firenze 23.12.1774 + Firenze 9.3.1778

   9)   **Joseph Anton Johann Archduke of Austria, Palatine of Hungary** * Firenze 9.3.1776 + Budapest
13.1.1847 = (1) Gatschina 30.10.1799 **Alexandra Pavlovna Grand Duchess of Russia** * Tsarskoie Selo
9.8.1783 + Budapest 16.3.1801 dau. of Paul I Petrovitch Emperor of Russia; = (2) Schaumburg
30.8.1815 **Hermine Princess of Anhalt-Bernburg-Schaumburg** * Hoym 2.12.1797 + Budapest 14.9.1817
dau. of Viktor II Karl Duke of Anhalt-Bernburg-Schaumburg; = (3) Kircheim 24.8.1819 **Maria Dorothea
Duchess of Württemberg** * Karlsruhe 1.11.1797 + Budapest 30.3.1855 dau. of Friedrich Eugen Duke of
Württemberg, and had issue:

by 1st marriage:

VIII

   (1)   **Alexandrine Archduchess of Austria** * & + Budapest 8.3.1801

by 2nd marriage:

   (2)   **Hermine Amalie Maria Archduchess of Austria** * Budapest 14.9.1817 + Wien 13.2.1842

   (3)   **Stephan Franz Viktor Archduke of Austria** * Budapest 14.9.1817 + Menton 19.2.1867

by 3rd marriage:

   (4)   **Franziska Maria Elisabeth Archduchess of Austria** * Budapest 31.7.1820 + Budapest 23.8.1820

   (5)   **Alexander Archduke of Austria** * Budapest 6.6.1825 + Budapest 12.11.1837

(6) **Elisabeth Franziska Maria Archduchess of Austria** * Budapest 17.1.1831 + Wien 14.2.1903 = (1)
Wien 4.10.1847 **Ferdinand Archduke of Austria, Prince of Modena** * Modena 20.7.1821 + Brünn
15.12.1849; = (2) Wien 18.4.1854 **Karl Ferdinand Archduke of Austria** * Wien 29.7.1818
+ Gross-Seelowitz 20.11.1874, and had issue by both marriages see elsewhere

(7) **Joseph Ludwig Karl Archduke of Austria, Palatine of Hungary** * Pressburg 2.3.1833 + Fiume
13.6.1905 = Coburg 12.5.1864 **Maria Adelheid Princess of Saxe-Coburg and Gotha** * Neuilly-sur-
Seine 8.7.1846 + Alscút 3.6.1927 dau. of August Prince of Saxe-Coburg and Gotha, and had issue:

a. **Elisabeth Clementine Clothilde Maria Amalie Archduchess of Austria** * Alscút 18.3.1865
+ 7.1.1866

b. **Maria Dorothea Amalie Archduchess of Austria** * Alscút 14.6.1867 + Alscút 6.4.1932
= Wien 5.11.1896 **Philippe Duc d'Orléans** * York House, Twickenham 6.2.1869 + Palermo
28.3.1926 — div. s.p.

c. **Margarethe Clementine Maria Archduchess of Austria** * Alscút 6.7.1870 + Regensburg
2.5.1955 = Budapest 15.7.1890 Albrecht 8 Fürst v. Thurn u. Taxis * Regensburg 8.5.1867
+ Regensburg 22.1.1952, and had issue:

a) **Franz Joseph Maximilian Maria Antonius Ignatius Lamoral 9 Fürst v. Thurn u. Taxis**
* Regensburg 21.12.1893 = Schloss Bronnbach 23.11.1920 **Maria Isabel Princess of
Bragança, Infanta of Portugal** * Kleinheubach 19.11.1894 dau. of Dom Miguel Duke of
Bragança, and has issue:

(a) **Gabriel Albert Maria Michael Franz Joseph Gallus Lamoral Erbprinz v. Thurn u.
Taxis** * Schloss Haus b. Regensburg 16.10.1922 ✗ Stalingrad 17.12.1942

(b) **Helene Maria Maximiliana Emanuela Michaela Gabriela Raphaela Prinzessin v.
Thurn u. Taxis** * Schloss Haus 27.5.1924 = Regensburg 29.4.1947 Rudolf
Erwein Graf v. Schönborn-Wiesentheid * Würzburg 1.10.1918 and has issue:

1a. **Albert Ernst Graf v. Schönborn-Wiesentheid** * Würzburg 20.2.1948

2a. **Johann Philipp Graf v. Schönborn-Wiesentheid** * Würzburg 3.7.1949

3a. **Gabriela Helene Gräfin v. Schönborn-Wiesentheid** * Würzburg 16.10.1950

4a. **Peter Andreas Graf v. Schönborn-Wiesentheid** * Regensburg 10.11.1954

(c) **Maria Theresia Michaela Raphaela Gabriela Carolina Ludovica Prinzessin v. Thurn u.
Taxis** * Schloss Taxis 10.9.1925 = Schloss Haus 19.6.1955 **Franz Eduard Graf v.
Oppersdorff** * Oberlogau 19.6.1919, and has issue see elsewhere

(d) **Maria Ferdinanda Eudoxia Michaela Gabriela Raphaela Prinzessin v. Thurn u. Taxis**
* Schloss Haus 19.12.1927 = Regensburg 15.7.1950 **Franz Joseph Prince of
Hohenzollern-Sigmaringen** * Schloss Umkirch 15.3.1926 (marriage annulled) s.p.

b) **Karl August Joseph Maria Maximilian Lamoral Antonius Ignatius Benediktus Valentin
Prinz v. Thurn u. Taxis** * Schloss Garatshausen 23.7.1898 = Schloss Taxis 18.8.1921
Maria Ana Princess of Bragança, Infanta of Portugal * Schloss Fischhorn 3.9.1899 dau.
of Dom Miguel Duke of Bragança, and has issue:

(a) **Clothilde Alberta Maria Franziska Xaveria Andrea Prinzessin v. Thurn u. Taxis**
* Regensburg 30.11.1922 = Regensburg 7.11.1944 Johann Moritz Prinz v.u. zu
Liechtenstein * Waldstein b. Peggau 6.8.1914, and has issue:

1a. **Dietmut Margarete Maria Benedicta Anna Prinzessin v.u. zu Liechtenstein**
* Wien 1.4.1949

2a. **Gundaker Albert Alfred Petrus Prinz v.u. zu Liechtenstein** * Wien 1.4.1949

Österreichische Nationalbibliothek

9   Archduke Joseph, Palatine
     of Hungary, 1776–1847

Österreichische Nationalbibliothek

10   Archduke Karl, Duke of
      Teschen, 1771–1847

Österreichische Nationalbibliothek

11   Archduke Johann, 1782–1859

Österreichische Nationalbibliothek

12   Napoleon II, Duke of
Reichstadt, with the Emperor
Franz Joseph and Princess
Caroline of Salerno, later
Duchesse d'Aumale

3a. **Alfred Heinrich Michael Benedikt Maria Prinz v.u. zu Liechtenstein** * Wien 17.9.1951

4a. **Adelgunde Maria Anna Therese Mafalda Eleonore Prinzessin v.u. zu Liechtenstein** * Wien 10.8.1953

5a. **Karl Emmeran Duarte Johannes Theobold Benedikt Prinz v.u. zu Liechtenstein** * Regensburg 1.7.1955

6a. **Maria Eleonore Bernadette Hildegard Prinzessin v.u. zu Liechtenstein** * Wien 14.11.1958

(b) **Mafalda Theresia Franziska Josepha Maria Prinzessin v. Thurn u. Taxis** * Regensburg 6.3.1924 = München 22.12.1961 Franz Prinz v. Thurn u. Taxis * Schloss Lissa 15.4.1915, and has issue:

1a. **Daria Maria Gabriele Prinzessin v. Thurn u. Taxis** * München 6.3.1962

(c) **Johannes Baptista de Jesus Maria Ludwig Miguel Friedrich Bonifazius Lamoral Prinz v. Thurn u. Taxis** * Schloss Höfling b. Regensburg 5.6.1926

(d) **Albert Maria Raimund Ildefons Paul Polycarpe Lamoral Prinz v. Thurn u. Taxis** * Regensburg 23.1.1929 + Regensburg 21.2.1935

c) **Ludwig Philipp Maria Friedrich Joseph Maximilian Antonius Ignatius Lamoral Prinz v. Thurn u. Taxis** * Regensburg 2.2.1901 + Schloss Niederaichbach 22.4.1933 = Schloss Hohenburg b. Lenggries 14.11.1922 **Elisabeth Princess of Luxembourg and Nassau** * Luxembourg 7.3.1901 + Schloss Hohenburg 2.8.1950 dau. of Wilhelm Grand Duke of Luxembourg, and has issue:

(a) **Anselm Albert Ludwig Maria Lamoral Prinz v. Thurn u. Taxis** * Jagdhaus Tiergarten b. Regensburg 14.4.1924 X Solotaja 25.2.1944

(b) **Iniga Anna Margarete Wilhelmine Luise Prinzessin v. Thurn u. Taxis** * Schloss Niederaichbach 25.8.1925 = Regensburg 20.5.1948 **Eberhard Fürst v. Urach, Graf v. Württemberg** * Stuttgart 24.1.1907, and has issue see elsewhere

d) **Max Emanuel Maria Siegfried Joseph Antonius Ignatius Lamoral Prinz v. Thurn u. Taxis** * Regensburg 1.3.1902

e) **Elisabeth Helene Maria Valerie Franziska Maximiliane Antonie Prinzessin v. Thurn u. Taxis** * Regensburg 15.12.1903 = Regensburg 16.6.1923 **Friedrich Christian Margraf of Meissen, Prince of Saxony** * Dresden 31.12.1893, and has issue see elsewhere

f) **Raphael Ranier Karl Maria Joseph Antonius Ignatius Hubertus Lamoral Prinz v. Thurn u. Taxis** * Regensburg 30.5.1906 = Regensburg 24.5.1924 **Margarete Prinzessin v. Thurn u. Taxis** * Berlin 19.10.1913 dau. of Maximilian Theodor Prinz v. Thurn u. Taxis, and has issue:

(a) **Max Emanuel Maria Albert Paul Isabella Klemens Lamoral Prinz v. Thurn u. Taxis** * Schloss Bullachberg b. Füssen 7.9.1935

g) **Philipp Ernst Maria Adalbert Joseph Maximilian Antonius Ignatius Stanislaus Lamoral Prinz v. Thurn u. Taxis** * Schloss Prüfening 7.5.1908 + Schloss Hohenberg 23.7.1964 = Schloss Taxis 8.9.1929 **Eulalia Prinzessin v. Thurn u. Taxis** * Schloss Biskupitz 21.12.1908 dau. of Friedrich Prinz v. Thurn u. Taxis, and has issue:

(a) **Albert Friedrich Maria Lamoral Kilian Prinz v. Thurn u. Taxis** * Schloss Prüfening 5.7.1930 = Birkenstein 30.7.1962 Alexandra Baronesse v. der Ropp * Königsburg i. Pr. 31.10.1932 dau. of Schweter Baron v. der Ropp

XI   (b) **Margarete Eleonore Maria Franziska Antonius v. Padua Prinzessin v. Thurn u. Taxis** * Schloss Hohenberg 1.12.1933

        (c) **Antonia Maria Margareta Theresia vom Kinde Jesu Prinzessin v. Thurn u. Taxis** * Schloss Hohenberg 28.1.1936

IX   d. **Joseph August Viktor Clemens Maria Archduke of Austria** * Alscút 9.8.1872 + Rain b. Straubing 6.7.1962 = München 15.11.1893 **Auguste Princess of Bavaria** * München 28.4.1875 + Regensburg 25.6.1964 dau. of Leopold Prince of Bavaria, and has issue:

X   a) **Joseph Franz Leopold Anton Ignatius Maria Archduke of Austria** * Brünn 28.3.1895 + Carcavelos, Portugal 25.9.1957 = Schloss Sibyllenort 4.10.1924 **Anna Princess of Saxony** * Lindau 4.5.1903 dau. of Friedrich August III King of Saxony, and had issue:

XI   (a) **Margit Archduchess of Austria** * Budapest 17.8.1925 = Tihany 17.8.1943 Alexander Czech-Erba Odescalchi Principe de Monteleone * Budapest 23.3.1914, and has issue:

XII   1a. **Sybilla Erba Odescalchi** * Stockholm 7.4.1945

XI   (b) **Ilona Archduchess of Austria** * Budapest 20.4.1927 = Sigmaringen 30.4.1946 **Georg Alexander Duke of Mecklenburg** * Nice 27.8.1921, and has issue see elsewhere

        (c) **Anna Theresia Gabriella Archduchess of Austria** * Budapest 19.4.1928

        (d) **Joseph Arpád Benedikt Ferdinand Franz Maria Gabriel Archduke of Austria** * Budapest 8.2.1933 = Bronnbach 12.9.1956 **Maria Aloysia Prinzessin zu Löwenstein-Wertheim-Rosenberg** * München 6.11.1935 dau. of Karl 8 Fürst zu Löwenstein-Wertheim-Rosenberg, and has issue:

XII   1a. **Joseph Karl Archduke of Austria** * München 7.8.1957 + München 8.8.1957

        2a. **Monika-Helena Maria Carolina Stephanie Elisabeth Immakolata Benedicta Dominica Archduchess of Austria** * München 14.9.1958

        3a. **Joseph Karl Maria Arpád Stephan Pius Ignatius Aloysius Cyrillus Archduke of Austria** * München 18.3.1960

        4a. **Maria Christine Regina Stephanie Immacolata Carolina Monika Ägidia Archduchess of Austria** * München 1.9.1961

        5a. **Andreas-Augustinus Maria Arpád Aloys Konstantin Pius Ignatius Peter Archduke of Austria** * München 29.4.1963

XI   (e) **István Dominik Anton Umberto Archduke of Austria** * Budapest 1.7.1934

        (f) **Maria Kinga Beatrix Archduchess of Austria** * Budapest 27.8.1938 = Regensburg ... 1959 Ernst Kiss * ... and has issue:

XII   1a. **Mátyás Kiss** * ... 1964

XI   (g) **Géza Ladislaus Euseb Gebhard Rafael Albert Maria Archduke of Austria** * Budapest 14.11.1940 = Freibourg 7.7.1965 Monika Decker * Frankfurt-am-Main 1.12.1939 dau. of Walther Decker

        (h) **Michael Kalman Pius Matthias Ludwig Emmerich Martin Archduke of Austria** * Budapest 5.5.1942 = Bronnbach 13.4.1966 **Christine Prinzessin zu Löwenstein-Wertheim-Rosenberg** * Würzburg 18.9.1940 dau. of Karl 8 Fürst zu Löwenstein-Wertheim-Rosenberg

X   b)   **Gisela Augustine Anna Maria Archduchess of Austria** * Kistapolcsány 5.7.1897
+ Volosca 30.3.1901

     c)   **Sophie Klementine Elisabeth Klotilde Maria Archduchess of Austria** * Volosca
11.3.1899

     d)   **László Luitpold Joseph Anton Ignaz Maria Archduke of Austria** * Volosca 3.1.1901
+ Budapest 29.8.1946

     e)   **Mátyás Joseph Albrecht Anton Ignaz Maria Archduke of Austria** * Budapest 26.6.1904
+ Kistapolocsány 7.10.1905

     f)   **Magdalena Maria Raniera Archduchess of Austria** * Kistapolocsány 6.9.1909

IX   e.   **László Philipp Marie Vincent Archduke of Austria** * Alscút 16.7.1875 + Budapest 6.9.1895

     f.   **Elisabeth Henriette Clotilde Maria Viktoria Archduchess of Austria** * Alscút 9.3.1883
+ Regensburg 8.2.1958

     g.   **Clotilde Maria Amalie Philomena Raniera Archduchess of Austria** * Fiume 9.5.1884 + Alscút
14.12.1903

VIII   (8)   **Maria Henriette Anna Archduchess of Austria** * Budapest 23.8.1836 + Spa, Belgium 19.9.1902
= Bruxelles 22.8.1853 **Leopold II King of The Belgians** * Bruxelles 9.4.1835 + Laeken 17.12.1909,
and had issue see elsewhere

VII   10)   **Marie Klementine Josepha Johanna Fidelis Archduchess of Austria** * Poggio Imperiale 24.4.1777
+ Napoli 15.11.1801 = Foggia 25.6.1797 **Francesco I King of Naples and Sicily** * Napoli 19.8.1777
+ Napoli 8.11.1830, and had issue see elsewhere

     11)   **Anton Viktor Joseph Johann Raimund Archduke of Austria** * Poggio Imperiale 31.8.1779 + Wien
2.4.1835

     12)   **Maria Amalia Josepha Johanna Catherine Theresia Archduchess of Austria** * Firenze 15.10.1780 + Wien
25.12.1798

     13)   **Johann Baptist Joseph Fabian Sebastian Archduke of Austria** * Firenze 20.1.1782 + Wien 11.5.1859
= morg. 18.2.1827 Anna Maria Josephine Plöchel Gräfin v. Meran * Bad Aussee 9.1.1804 + Bad Aussee
4.8.1855 dau. of Jakob Plöchel, and had issue:

VIII   (1)   **Franz Ludwig Johann Baptist Graf v. Meran** * Wien 11.3.1839 + Abbazia 27.3.1891 = Ottenstein
8.7.1862 Theresia Gräfin v. Lamberg * Pressburg 16.8.1836 + Grundlsee 11.9.1913 dau. of Franz
Graf v. Lamberg, and had issue:

IX   a.   **Anna Maria Johanna Therese Gräfin v. Meran** * Graz 12.4.1864 + Leitmeritz 31.3.1935
= Graz 9.4.1892 Alphons v. Stefenelli-Prenterhof-Hohenmaur * Padua 27.10.1863
+ Klagenfurt 12.11.1894 = (2) Graz 2.12.1896 Johann Ritter v. Radey * Marburg,
Steiermark 4.6.1863 + Salzburg 8.6.1955, and had issue:

     by 1st marriage:

X   a)   **Johann v. Stefenelli-Prenterhof-Hohenmaur** * Graz 26.2.1893 + Villach 27.8.1947
= Wien 27.1.1932 Renata Rein * Sisek 25.11.1902 dau. of Mauro Rein — div. and
had issue:

XI   (a)   **Hannes v. Stefenelli-Prenterhof-Hohenmaur** * Wien 19.10.1932 = Hannover
24.8.1963 Heidi Herrman * Herrmanshagen 9.9.1937 dau. of Franz Herrman, and
has issue:

XII   1a.   **Nicole Theresa v. Stefenelli-Prenterhof-Hohenmaur** * Vancouver 6.12.1966

X   b)   **Franz v. Stefenelli-Prenterhof-Hohenmaur** * Laibach 23.4.1933

by 2nd marriage:

X   c)   **Konstantin v. Radey** * Stry, Galizien 10.5.1898 = 18.3.1942 Margit Gräfin Széchényi v. Sárvár-Felsövidék * Horpacs 7.2.1905 + Salzburg 14.11.1954 dau. of Peter Graf Széchényi v. Sárvár-Felsövidék s.p.

     d)   **Therese v. Radey** * Prelouc 7.11.1900

     e)   **Rudolf v. Radey** * Pardubitz,Böh. 28.12.1906 + Leitmeritz, Böh. 1.11.1928

     f)   **Johann Georg v. Radey** * Pardubitz 24.2.1907 ✗ Virograd-Warwarowska 12.1.1944 = Goldegg 24.4.1943 Agathe Prinzessin v. Auersperg * Goldegg 25.9.1918 dau. of Adolf Erbprinz v. Auersperg, and had issue:

XI   (a)   **Johann Georg v. Radey** * Schloss Goldegg 5.2.1944

IX   b.   **Maria Johanna Anna Gräfin v. Meran** * Graz 9.8.1865 + Graz 7.2.1933

     c.   **Johann Baptist Stephan Joseph Franz Polycarp Graf v. Meran** * Graz 26.1.1867 + Graz 13.4.1947 = Graz 4.2.1891 Ladislaja Gräfin v. Lamberg * Móor 20.5.1870 + Graz 17.3.1952 dau. of Philipp Karl Graf v. Lamberg, and had issue:

X   a)   **Franz Philipp Johannes Graf v. Meran** * Graz 3.12.1891 = Salzburg 31.12.1923 Wilhelmine Prinzessin v. Auersperg * Weitwörth 4.10.1894 dau. of Eduard Prinz v. Auersperg, and has issue:

XI   (a)   **Marie Cäcilia Franziska Ladislaja Agnes Gräfin v. Meran** * Graz 3.12.1924 = Stainz 12.10.1949 Karl Ernst Graf v.u. zu Trauttmansdorff-Weinsberg * Pottenbrunn 6.10.1927, and has issue:

XII   1a.   **Ferdinand Karl Josef Franz Viktor Graf v.u. zu Trauttmansdorff-Weinsberg** * Graz 28.7.1950

     2a.   **Andreas Otto Michael Franz Graf v.u. zu Trauttmansdorff-Weinsberg** * Graz 17.11.1951

     3a.   **Isabella Wilhelmine Gräfin v.u. zu Trauttmansdorff-Weinsberg** * Graz 8.7.1953

     4a.   **Charlotte Maria Josefa Gräfin v.u. zu Trauttmansdorff-Weinsberg** * Graz 24.8.1955

     5a.   **Marie Theresia Ladislaja Augusta Gräfin v.u. zu Trauttmansdorff-Weinsberg** * Graz 28.8.1960

     6a.   **Eleonore Sophie Maria Gräfin v.u. zu Trauttmansdorff-Weinsberg** * Graz 26.5.1962

XI   (b)   **Ladislaja Maria Huberta Walburga Fidelis Gräfin v. Meran** * Graz 3.1.1926 = (1) Stainz 23.2.1957 Johann Frhr. Economo v. San Serff * Wien 15.7.1917 — div.; = (2) Seewiessen St. Leonard Trauung 24.10.1965 Karl Albrecht Erbprinz zu Hohenlohe-Schillingsfürst * Wien 30.4.1926, and has issue:

by 2nd marriage:

XII   1a.   **Marie Aglae Wilhelmine Rosa Johanna Ladislaja Gabriele Agathe Prinzessin zu Hohenlohe-Waldenburg-Schillingsfürst v. Ratibor u. Corvey** * Schillingsfürst 22.4.1966

XI   (c)   **Karoline Wilhelmine Theresia Anna Maria Gräfin v. Meran** * Stainz 13.3.1929 = 16.5.1960 Johann Keil * 27.2.1926, and has issue:

XII

1a.   **Matthias Julius Franz Alexander Maria Keil** * Graz 7.12.1960

2a.   **Martina Margaritta Johanna Wilhelmine Ladislaja Maria Keil** * Graz 7.12.1960

3a.   **Hans Christian Ludwig Gabriel Keil** * Graz 2.3.1962

XI

(d)   **Franziska Theresia Johanna Maria Gräfin v. Meran** * Graz 7.7.1933 = 7.10.1962 Jean Riollot * 27.2.1926, and has issue:

XII

1a.   **Guillemette Marie Therese Johanna Franziska Berta Riollot** * 24.2.1964

XI

(e)   **Johannes Karl Franz Josef Konrad Graf v. Meran** * Graz 24.10.1934 = 18.6.1959 Ingrid Messner * Stainz 16.1.1939, and has issue:

XII

1a.   **Johanna Maria Karolina Wilhelmine Gräfin v. Meran** * Graz 10.10.1959

2a.   **Katharina Eleonore Anna Maria Gräfin v. Meran** * Graz 18.3.1961

3a.   **Maria Therese Franziska Augustina Gräfin v. Meran** * Brandhof 28.8.1962

4a.   **Franz Graf v. Meran** * Stainz 22.4.1964

5a.   **Fritz Graf v. Meran** * Stainz 9.6.1965

X

b)   **Marie Theresia Gräfin v. Meran** * Stainz 21.4.1893 = Graz 4.2.1912 Karl Kunata Graf Kottulinsky * Chotěboř 16.9.1877 + Neudau 3.10.1939, and has issue:

XI

(a)   **Johann Adalbert Kunata Georg Maria Graf Kottulinsky** * Neudau 24.4.1913 = Neudau 19.4.1938 Cecile-Maria Freiin. v. Ottenfels gen. v. Gschwind * Wien 8.8.1912 dau. of Franz Frhr. v. Ottenfels gen. v. Gschwind, and has issue:

XII

1a.   **Franz-Karl Kunata Maria Graf Kottulinsky** * Graz 5.3.1939

2a.   **Kunata Johann Graf Kottulinsky** * Graz 18.8.1940

3a.   **Madeleine Maria Gräfin Kottulinsky** * Graz 11.11.1941 = Neudau 25.5.1962 **Clemens Prinz v. Croÿ** * Berlin 5.7.1934, and has issue see elsewhere

4a.   **Elisabeth Gräfin Kottulinsky** * Graz 6.6.1943

5a.   **Adalbert Graf Kottulinsky** * Neudau 12.9.1944 + Neudau 13.9.1944

6a.   **Hans Graf Kottulinsky** * Neudau 19.12.1947

XI

(b)   **Kunata Johann Ignazius Josef Graf Kottulinsky** * Neudau 6.7.1914 = Neudau 29.9.1945 Margarethe Prinzessin v. Rohan * Sichrow 21.7.1923 dau. of Alain Fürst v. Rohan, Duc de Montabazon et Bouillon, and has issue:

XII

1a.   **Marie Luise Gräfin Kottulinsky** * Graz 1.12.1946

2a.   **Margarete Maria Gräfin Kottulinsky** * Neudau 5.11.1949

XI

(c)   **Jaroslaw Franz Josef Ignazius Maria Graf Kottulinsky** * Graz 3.1.1917 + Rio de Janeiro 11.1.1959 = Wien 7.12.1957 **Maria Ileana Archduchess of Austria** * Mödling 18.12.1933 + Rio de Janeiro 11.1.1959 dau. of Anton Archduke of Austria, Prince of Tuscany, and had issue:

XII

1a.   **Ileana Gräfin Kottulinsky** * 25.8.1958

XI

(d)   **Josef Albrecht Kunata Johann Ignazius Maria Graf Kottulinsky** * Graz 26.9.1919 ✗ Hohenstein b. Berlin 20.4.1945 = Weissenegg 15.2.1944 Wilhelmine Gräfin v.u. zu Trauttmansdorff-Weinsberg * Wien 7.2.1920 dau. of Karl Graf v.u. zu Trauttmansdorff-Weinsberg, and had issue:

XII   1a.   **Maria Isabelle Gräfin Kottulinsky** * Kogl 9.12.1944

XI   (e)   **Theodora Maria Elisabeth Ladislaja Ignazia Gräfin Kottulinsky** * Neudau 6.10.1921 = Neudau 4.7.1944 Leopold-Zeno Graf v. Goëss * Graz 2.9.1916, and has issue:

XII   1a.   **Maria Theresia Theodora Hemma Ladislaja Elisabeth Johanna Erasma Gräfin v. Goëss** * Ebenthal 24.5.1945

                 2a.   **Johann Peter Zeno Kunata Josef Leopold Anton Alois Maria Saurau Graf v. Goëss** * Ebenthal 13.6.1946

                 3a.   **Johann Josef Leopold Zeno Maria Immaculata Amadeus Graf v. Goëss** * Ebenthal 8.12.1948

                 4a.   **Carl Anton Johann Leopold Zeno Kunata Franz v. Paula Kreszenz Graf v. Goëss** * Ebenthal 2.4.1951

                 5a.   **Hemma-Christiane Marie Theodora Ignazia Gregoria Gräfin v. Goëss** * Ebenthal 12.3.1957

X   c)   **Philipp Heinrich Franz Johann Graf v. Meran** * Stainz 11.7.1894 + Stainz 19.5.1950 = Thannhausen 3.8.1921 **Maria-Anna Gräfin v.u. zu Eltz gen. Faust v. Stromberg** * Klagenfurt 11.6.1900 dau. of Karl Graf v.u. zu Eltz gen. Faust v. Stromberg, and had issue:

XI   (a)   **Anna Maria Ladislaja Karoline Gräfin v. Meran** * Csákberény 3.6.1922 = Graz 17.3.1951 **Gordian Frhr. v. Gudenus** * Sutthaisen 9.10.1915, and has issue see elsewhere

         (b)   **Maria Christina Johanna Theresia Gräfin v. Meran** * Csákberény 2.7.1923 = Zollikon, Kanton Zürich 30.6.1954 Friedrich Rothenbühler * Burgdorf, Kanton Bern 14.12.1914, and has issue:

XII   1a.   **Friedrich Stephan Rothenbühler** * Zürich 20.5.1958

XI   (c)   **Franz Stephan Johann Maria Assunta Graf v. Meran** * Csákberény 15.8.1924 = Usa-River, Tanzania 15.6.1964 Uta Strohschneider * Wien 22.5.1938, dau. of Harald Strohschneider

         (d)   **Philipp Karl Franz Johann Ignaz Graf v. Meran** * Csákberény 11.12.1926

         (e)   **Maximilian Joseph Ottokar Johann Graf v. Meran** * Csákberény 20.4.1930 = Wien 16.9.1961 Caroline Prinzessin zu Schwarzenberg * Berlin 16.2.1937 dau. of Johann Prinz zu Schwarzenberg, and has issue:

XII   1a.   **Philipp Karl Graf v. Meran** * Innsbruck 2.8.1962

                 2a.   **Johannes Christoph Graf v. Meran** * Innsbruck 26.8.1963

XI   (f)   **Eleonore Magdalene Ottkara Theresia Gräfin v. Meran** * Csákberény 20.4.1930

X   d)   **Johann Franz Philipp Graf v. Meran** * Stainz 8.2.1896 = Szent-Tamás 6.7.1919 Ilona Gräfin Almásy de Zsadány et Török-Szent-Miklós * Koloszvár 9.1.1894 + Wien 20.12.1966 dau. of Imre Graf Almásy de Zsadány et Török-Szent-Miklós, and had issue:

XI   (a)   **Maria Ladislaja Helene Gräfin v. Meran** * Körösladány 9.3.1920 = Körösladány 1944 Béla de Rudnó et Divék-Újfalu * Wien 26.10.1918, and has issue:

XII   1a.   **Lajos de Rudnó et Divék-Újfalu** * Nagykonyi,Kom. Tolna 11.8.1945

112

2a. **Sándor de Rudnó et Divék-Újfalu** * Kaposvár, Kom. Somegy 27.11.1946

3a. **Ilona de Rudnó et Divék-Újfalu** * Kaposvár 15.1.1948

4a. **János de Rudnó et Divék-Újfalu** * Kaposvár 23.1.1949

5a. **András de Rudnó et Divék-Újfalu** * Kaposvár 14.6.1950

6a. **Tamás de Rudnó et Divék-Újfalu** * Kaposvár 14.6.1950

7a. **Mária Katalin de Rudnó et Divék-Újfalu** * Kaposvár 10.5.1953

8a. **Erzsébet de Rudnó et Divék-Újfalu** * Kaposvár 5.11.1955 + Kaposvár 13.11.1955

9a. **Gábor de Rudnó et Divék-Újfalu** * Salzburg 28.11.1957

10a. **Beatrice de Rudnó et Divék-Újfalu** * Salzburg 11.3.1959

XI

(b) **Johann Baptist Stephan Emmerich Ladislaus Graf v. Meran** * Körösladány 14.10.1921

(c) **Helene Maria Ladislaja Gräfin v. Meran** * Körösladány 8.9.1927 = Glanegg 2.4.1951 Maurizio Lodi-Fè * Salonika 1.6.1918, and has issue:

XII

1a. **Michel Lodi-Fè** * Roma 24.1.1952

2a. **Alessandro Lodi-Fè** * Roma 28.7.1953

3a. **Caterina Lodi-Fè** * Roma 27.5.1956

4a. **Nicola Lodi-Fè** * Roma 30.8.1959

X

e) **Maria-Anna Gräfin v. Meran** * Brandhof 14.8.1897 = Graz 1.2.1919 Friedrich Adalbert Frhr. Mayr v. Melnhof * Himberg 7.7.1892 + 3.3.1956, and has issue:

XI

(a) **Maria-Anna Freiin. Mayr v. Melnhoff** * Glanegg 9.12.1919 = Glanegg 12.3.1942 Ludwig Stanislaus 6 Fürst zu Sayn-Wittgenstein-Sayn * Kopenhagen 4.5.1915 + Sayn 9.1.1962, and has issue:

XII

1a. **Marie Yvonne Helena Walburga Anna Leonille Prinzessin zu Sayn-Wittgenstein-Sayn** * Glanegg 9.12.1942 = Salzburg 21.5.1962 Alfons Graf v. Coreth zu Coredo * Hochscharten 19.2.1930, and has issue:

XIII

1b. **Constantin Alexander Alfons Botho Ludwig Maria Graf Coreth zu Coredo** * Salzburg 27.6.1963

2b. **Maximilian Peter Alfons Maria Graf Coreth zu Coredo** * Salzburg 29.10.1965

XII

2a. **Alexander Konrad Friedrich Heinrich 7 Fürst zu Sayn-Wittgenstein-Sayn** * Salzburg 1.11.1943

3a. **Elisabeth Prinzessin zu Sayn-Wittgenstein-Sayn** * Glanegg 1.4.1948

4a. **Therese Maria Leonilla Prinzessin zu Sayn-Wittgenstein-Sayn** * Sayn 25.4.1952

5a. **Peter Heinrich Stanislas Maria Prinz zu Sayn-Wittgenstein-Sayn** * Sayn 22.1.1954

XI

(b) **Ladislaja Freiin. Mayr v. Melnhoff** * Salzburg 23.12.1920 = (1) Glanegg 29.9.1942 Konrad Prinz zu Hohenlohe-Ingelfingen * Berne 16.8.1919 X Nikolskoie 16.5.1943; = (2) Salzburg 25.7.1946 Johann Jakob Graf v.u. zu Eltz gen. Faust v. Stromberg * Kleinheubach 22.9.1921, and has issue:

by 2nd marriage:

XII   1a. **Maria de Mercede Lidvine Sophie Anna Walburga Thekla Gräfin v.u. zu Eltz gen. Faust v. Stromberg** * Glanegg 12.5.1947

                     2a. **Maria de Mercede Karl Johannes v. Nepomuk Friedrich Sebastianus Philipp Jakob Graf v.u. zu Eltz gen. Faust v. Stromberg** * Eltville 1.5.1948

                     3a. **Maria de Mercede Michael Friedrich Sebastianus Paulinus Johannes v. Nepomuk Graf v.u. zu Eltz gen. Faust v. Stromberg** * Eltville 22.6.1949

                     4a. **Maria Assunta Sophie Ladislaja Walpurga Thekla Gräfin v.u. zu Eltz gen. Faust v. Stromberg** * Eltville 9.11.1950

                     5a. **Maria de Mercede Christiane Josephine Thekla Walpurga Barbara Gräfin v.u. zu Eltz gen. Faust v. Stromberg** * Eltville 27.11.1951

                     6a. **Maria de Mercede Johanna Thekla Walpurga Gräfin v.u. zu Eltz gen. Faust v. Stromberg** * Eltville 18.4.1954

                     7a. **Maria de Mercede Georg Johann v. Nepomuk Graf v.u. zu Eltz gen. Faust v. Stromberg** * Eltville 26.9.1956

                     8a. **Maria de Mercede Johannes v. Nepomuk Friedrich Franziskus Graf v.u. zu Eltz gen. Faust v. Stromberg** * Eltville 2.10.1957

                     9a. **Maria Benedicta Walpurga Thekla Gräfin v.u. zu Eltz gen. Faust v. Stromberg** * Eltville 26.8.1962

XI   (c) **Margarete Theodora Freiin. Mayr v. Melnhof** * Glanegg 25.1.1923 = Glanegg 3.3.1946 Hermann Ritter v. Jedina * Pola 28.8.1911, and has issue:

XII   1a. **Johann Hermann Friedrich Ritter v. Jedina** * Glanegg 26.11.1946

                     2a. **Isabella Maria Klothilde v. Jedina** * Glanegg 17.3.1949

XI   (d) **Friedrich Franz Frhr. Mayr v. Melnhof** * Glanegg 5.7.1924 = Kitzbühel 16.12.1948 Maria Anna Gräfin v. Orsini u. Rosenberg * Klagenfurt 20.8.1927 dau. of Johann Andreas 5 Fürst v. Orsini u. Rosenberg, and has issue:

XII   1a. **Maria-Theresia Freiin. Mayr v. Melnhof** * Salzburg 2.2.1950

                     2a. **Friedrich Johann Frhr. Mayr v. Melnhof** * Salzburg 10.11.1952

                     3a. **Theodora Ladislaja Freiin. Mayr v. Melnhof** * Salzburg 2.8.1954

                     4a. **Catherina Maria Freiin. Mayr v. Melnhof** * Salzburg 24.2.1956

                     5a. **Heinrich Frhr. Mayr v. Melnhof** * Salzburg 10.4.1957 + Zürich 30.10.1957

                     6a. **Sophie Freiin. Mayr v. Melnhof** * Salzburg 22.12.1958

                     7a. **Stephanie Freiin. Mayr v. Melnhof** * Salzburg 27.12.1961

                     8a. **Paul Frhr. Mayr v. Melnhof** * 4.7.1963 + 12.7.1963

XI   (e) **Therese Maria Freiin. Mayr v. Melnhof** * Glanegg 21.9.1926 = Glanegg 12.5.1949 **Heinrich Graf v. Hoyos** * Horn 6.11.1924, and has issue see elsewhere

            (f) **Gabriele Klara Huberta Maria Freiin. Mayr v. Melnhof** * Glanegg 16.10.1928 = Glanegg 24.9.1953 Ernst Wagner-Schilling * Valparaiso 15.1.1924, and has issue:

XII   1a. **Andrés Jakob Wagner Mayr-Melnhof** * Santiago de Chile 23.8.1955

                     2a. **Pablo Federico Heinrich Wagner Mayr-Melnhof** * Santiago de Chile 17.9.1956

XII   3a.   **Daniela Huberta Maria Wagner Mayr-Melnhof** * Santiago de Chile 2.8.1960

4a.   **Christián Rule Ernesto Wagner Mayr-Melnhof** * Santiago de Chile 13.11.1963

XI   (g)   **Elisabeth Maria Huberta Klementine Freiin. Mayr v. Melnhof** * Glanegg 4.11.1930 = Schloss Glanegg 24.8.1960 Stephan v. Visy * Baksa, Hungary 1.8.1906, and has issue:

XII   1a.   **Marina v. Visy** * Glanegg 27.5.1961

2a.   **Barbara v. Visy** * Morristown N.J. U.S.A. 15.9.1962

3a.   **Stephan v. Visy** * Camden, South Carolina 25.2.1964

XI   (h)   **Huberta Maria Theresia Franziska Freiin. Mayr v. Melnhof** * Glanegg 9.3.1932 = Schloss Glanegg 4.8.1963 Emanuel Frhr. v. Pereira-Arnstein * Berlin-Wilmersdorf 27.9.1931, and has issue:

XII   1a.   **Michelle Gabrielle Maria Freiin. v. Pereira-Arnstein** * Alexandria, Virginia, U.S.A. 15.7.1964

2a.   **Desiré Maria Elisabeth Freiin. v. Pereira-Arnstein** * & + Alexandria, Va, 17.7.1965

XI   (i)   **Johanna Maria Paula Freiin. Mayr v. Melnhof** * Glanegg 23.10.1935 = Schloss Glanegg 15.7.1957 Johann v. Oswald * Hannover 1.1.1925, and has issue:

XII   1a.   **Yvonne Maria Theresia Huberta Georgina v. Oswald** * Salzburg 23.4.1958

2a.   **Gabriela Maria-Anna Elisabeth Petra v. Oswald** * Salzburg 19.10.1959

3a.   **Madeleine Marie Christine Hedwig v. Oswald** * Salzburg 14.4.1961

4a.   **Nicole Marie Charlotte Johanna v. Oswald** * Salzburg 8.3.1963

X   f)   **Ladislaja Maria Gräfin v. Meran** * Stainz 8.10.1899 = Graz 29.12.1928 Johann Graf de la Fontaine u. d'Harnoncourt-Unverzagt * Wien 17.4.1896, and has issue:

XI   (a)   **Johann Nikolaus Graf de la Fontaine u. d'Harnoncourt-Unverzagt** * Berlin 6.12.1929 = Graz 27.6.1953 Alice Hoffelner * Wien 26.9.1930 dau. of Leopold Hoffelner, and has issue:

XII   1a.   **Elisabeth Juliana Gräfin de la Fontaine u. d'Harnoncourt-Unverzagt** * Wien 29.5.1954

2a.   **Philipp Karl Graf de la Fontaine u. d'Harnoncourt-Unverzagt** * Wien 20.9.1955

3a.   **Eberhard Kurt Graf de la Fontaine u. d'Harnoncourt-Unverzagt** * Wien 28.12.1957

4a.   **Franziskus Maximilian Graf de la Fontaine u. d'Harnoncourt-Unverzagt** * Wien 10.10.1961

XI   (b)   **Philipp Hubert Emmerich Maria Eberhard Graf de la Fontaine u. d'Harnoncourt-Unverzagt** * Berlin 9.2.1931

(c)   **Juliana Emilie Ladislaja Huberta Gräfin de la Fontaine u. d'Harnoncourt-Unverzagt** * Graz 1.10.1932 = Grundlsee 5.7.1955 Kurt Theiner * Wien 5.12.1928, and has issue:

XII   1a.   **Johann Nikolaus Theiner** * Wien 7.8.1957

XII		2a.	**Andreas Franz Theiner** * 12.1.1959
		3a.	**Renatus Theiner** * 24.12.1960

XI   (d)   **Karl Hubert Kunata Graf de la Fontaine u. d'Harnoncourt-Unverzagt** * Graz 12.8.1934 = Graz 5.4.1964 Gerda List * Graz 18.10.1939 dau. of Hans List, and has issue:

XII   1a.   **Isabella Ladislaja Dagmar Gräfin de la Fontaine u. d'Harnoncourt-Unverzagt** * Graz 4.3.1965

XI   (e)   **Franz Hubert Emmerich Graf de la Fontaine u. d'Harnoncourt-Unverzagt** * Graz 2.8.1937 = Graz 5.9.1965 Marion Fogarassy * Zagreb 4.4.1941 dau. of Viktor Fogarassy, and has issue:

XII   1a.   **Ladislaja Thaddea Maria Ildiko Gräfin de la Fontaine u. d'Harnoncourt-Unverzagt** * Graz 5.6.1966

X   g)   **Eleonore Maria Gräfin v. Meran** * Graz 18.5.1901

       h)   **Marie Valerie Gräfin v. Meran** * Graz 14.10.1902 = Graz 1.8.1921 Johann Anton Graf v. Goëss * Klagenfurt 31.1.1892, and has issue:

XI   (a)   **Maria-Anna Ladislaja Antonia Gabrielle Theresia Josepha Propera Gräfin v. Goëss** * Graz 25.6.1922 = Gradisch 10.10.1945 Georg Holm v. Reutter * Wien 25.12.1919, and has issue:

XII		1a.	**Marie Valerie Thaddea Leopoldine Eleonore v. Reutter** * Graz 28.10.1948
		2a.	**Georg Thaddäus Holm Johann Ewald Ernst v. Reutter** * Hollererhof 12.1.1949
		3a.	**Aglaée Beatrice Eleonore Marie Theresia v. Reutter** * Hollererhof 14.10.1955
		4a.	**Elisabeth Franziska Thaddea Jeanette Wilhelmine v. Reutter** * Hollererhof 27.1.1957

XI   (b)   **Maria Franziska Ladislaja Antonia Leopoldine Josefa Theodora Gräfin v. Goëss** * Graz 9.11.1923 = Gradisch 3.5.1951 **Eberhard Graf v. Küenberg** * München 6.2.1925, and has issue see elsewhere

       (c)   **Johann Zeno Leopold Anton Maria Josef Rupertus Primus-Felicianus Graf v. Goëss** * Gradisch 1.6.1925 = Terlan 22.4.1952 **Antonia Gräfin v. Enzenberg zum Freyen u. Jöchelsthurn** * Liebenaich 17.11.1927 dau. of Sighard Graf v. Enzenberg zum Freyen u. Jöchelsthurn, and has issue:

XII		1a.	**Marie Theresia Sidonia Antonia Martina Juliana Gräfin v. Goëss** * Klagenfurt 30.1.1953
		2a.	**Karl Georg Johann Anton Maria Graf v. Goëss** * Klagenfurt 4.3.1954
		3a.	**Johann Ulrich Zeno Maria Wilhelm Graf v. Goëss** * Klagenfurt 25.6.1955
		4a.	**Elisabeth Franziska Maria Desirée Gräfin v. Goëss** * Klagenfurt 23.5.1957
		5a.	**Michael Graf v. Goëss** * Klagenfurt 4.8.1961

XI   (d)   **Johann Ulrich Anton Maria Josef Konrad Nikolaus Graf v. Goëss** * Graz 26.11.1926 = Wien 11.8.1960 Maria Margarete Gräfin v. Abensperg u. Traun * Wien 14.5.1937 dau. of Johann Adam Graf v. Abensperg u. Traun, and has issue:

XII   1a.   **Maria Johanna Margarethe Gräfin v. Goëss** * Wien 3.3.1962

               2a.   **Johann Anton Adam Graf v. Goëss** * Wien 25.12.1963

               3a.   **Ernst Ulrich Graf v. Goëss** * Wien 27.1.1966

XI   (e)   **Eleonore Marie Antonia Josefa Nepomucena Philippine Gräfin v. Goëss**
* Ebenthal 16.5.1928 = Gradisch 20.7.1947 Heinrich 6 Fürst v. Orsini u. Rosenberg
* Welzenegg 29.1.1925, and has issue:

XII   1a.   **Ladislaja Maria Anna Henriette Hippolitta Josepha Gräfin v. Orsini u.
Rosenberg** * Klagenfurt 26.7.1948

               2a.   **Johannes Andreas Alois Heinrich Anton Josef Maria Erbgraf v. Orsini u.
Rosenberg** * Klagenfurt 26.8.1949

               3a.   **Ferdinand Friedrich Andreas Heinrich Josef Maria Graf v. Orsini u. Rosenberg**
* Klagenfurt 28.5.1953

               4a.   **Markus Antonius Andreas Heinrich Josef Maria Graf v. Orsini u. Rosenberg**
* Klagenfurt 8.8.1955

               5a.   **Matthias Johannes Andreas Heinrich Josef Maria Graf v. Orsini u. Rosenberg**
* Klagenfurt 8.8.1955

               6a.   **Henriette Josefine Sophia Maria Gräfin v. Orsini u. Rosenberg** * Klagenfurt
15.5.1957

               7a.   **Andrea Franziska Josefa Maria Gräfin v. Orsini u. Rosenberg** * Klagenfurt
21.5.1958

XI   (f)   **Franz-Anton Johann Maria Joseph Judas Thaddäus Ingebert et omnes sancti Graf v.
Goëss** * Klagenfurt 22.10.1929 = Grafenstein 16.1.1956 Elisabeth Anne Nichols
* Birmingham, Alabama 23.12.1930 dau. of Morgan Nichols, and has issue:

XII   1a.   **Maria del Pilar Elisabeth Hemma Gräfin v. Goëss** * Wien 9.6.1956

               2a.   **Henriette Gräfin v. Goëss** * Wien 21.1.1958

               3a.   **Caroline Gräfin v. Goëss** * Wien 11.5.1961

               4a.   **Olivia Maria Gräfin v. Goëss** * Wien 11.3.1964

               5a.   **Amanda Maria Gräfin v. Goëss** * Chattanooga, U.S.A. 11.11.1966

XI   (g)   **Ernst-Friedrich Johann Maria Josef Benedictus Adam Zeno Gregor Graf v. Goëss**
* Klagenfurt 12.3.1932 = Dyck 12.10.1961 **Gabrielle Altgrafin zu Salm-
Reifferscheidt-Krautheim u. Dyck** * Bonn 9.11.1941 dau. of Franz Joseph 6 Fürst
u. Altgraf zu Salm-Reifferscheidt-Krautheim u. Dyck, and has issue:

XII   1a.   **Sveva Cäcilia Gräfin v. Goëss** * Klagenfurt 16.8.1962

               2a.   **Philippa Cäcilia Gräfin v. Goëss** * Klagenfurt 8.7.1964

               3a.   **Moritz-Heinrich Graf v. Goëss** * Klagenfurt 5.6.1966

XI   (h)   **Hemma Nicolasine Maria Antonia Clementine Gräfin v. Goëss** * Klagenfurt
23.11.1934 = Gurk 30.8.1959 Heinrich Graf Marenzi v. Tagliano u. Talgate
* Wien 26.12.1930, and has issue:

XII   1a.   **Stephan Maria Heinrich Franz Anton Johannes Graf Marenzi v. Tagliano u.
Talgate** * Klagenfurt 24.6.1960

               2a.   **Douglas Maria Anatol Franz Anton Gabriel Graf Marenzi v. Tagliano u.
Talgate** * Wien 17.10.1963

XI	(i)	**Georg Johann Douglas Alexander Graf v. Goëss** * Klagenfurt 24.4.1938 = 15.10.1966 Veronika Freiin. von Haerdtl * Klagenfurt 28.2.1943 dau. of Thomas Frhr. v. Haerdtl
	(j)	**Andreas Anton Graf v. Goëss** * Klagenfurt 9.9.1946

X   g)   **Karl Hubert Graf v. Meran** * Brandhof 12.9.1907

IX   d.   **Franz Peter Johann Graf v. Meran** * Graz 5.10.1868 + Bad Aussee 10.11.1949 = Wien 7.6.1902 Marie Johanna Prinzessin v.u. zu Liechtenstein * Burgstall 21.8.1877 + Wien 11.1.1939 dau. of Aloys Prinz v.u. zu Liechtenstein, and had issue:

X   a)   **Maria Henriette Therese Aloysia Benedikta Gräfin v. Meran** * Graz 25.6.1904 = Graz 30.8.1927 Karl Prinz v. Auersperg-Breunner * Goldegg 16.1.1895, and has issue:

XI   (a)   **Eleonore Marie Gobertine Henriette Prinzessin v. Auersperg-Breunner** * Goldegg 12.9.1928 = Schloss Wald 8.9.1960 **Georg Fürst v. Hohenberg** * Arstetten 25.4.1929, and has issue see elsewhere

    (b)   **Karl Marie Franz Gobertus Prinz v. Auersperg-Breunner** * Goldegg 26.4.1930 = Eisenkappel 8.6.1955 **Friederike Gräfin v. Starhemberg** * Reichwaldau 20.8.1936 dau. of Georg Adam Graf v. Starhemberg, and has issue:

XII   1a.   **Franz-Joseph Karl Georg Heinrich Maria Gobertus Prinz v. Auersperg-Breunner** * Buenos Aires 20.7.1956

    2a.   **Sophie Irene Henriette Marie Gobertina Prinzessin v. Auersperg-Breunner** * Buenos Aires 17.4.1958

    3a.   **Karl Georg Adolf Maria Gobertus Prinz v. Auersperg-Breunner** * Wien 17.2.1960

    4a.   **Stephanie Prinzessin v. Auersperg-Breunner** * Buenos Aires 17.4.1964

XI   (c)   **Heinrich Weikhard Rudolf Gobertus Felix Maria Prinz v. Auersperg-Breunner** * Ainödt 21.5.1931 = Schloss Persenbeug 6.7.1959 **Elisabeth Archduchess of Austria, Princess of Tuscany** * Schloss Persenbeug 18.3.1935 dau. of Hubert Salvator Archduke of Austria, Prince of Tuscany, and has issue:

XII   1a.   **Johann Weikhard Karl Thaddäus Severin Gobertus Maria Prinz v. Auersperg-Breunner** * Buenos Aires 23.10.1961

    2a.   **Isabel Maria Ernestina Silvester Thaddäa Leopoldina Gobertina Prinzessin v. Auersperg-Breunner** * Wien 31.12.1962

    3a.   **Maximilian Andreas Karl Blasius Thaddäus Gobertus Maria Prinz v. Auersperg-Breunner** * Wien 3.2.1964

XI   (d)   **Ernestine Johanna Maria Gobertina Laurentia Prinzessin v. Auersperg-Breunner** * Ainödt 5.9.1932

    (e)   **Johanna Agathe Maria Gobertina Prinzessin v. Auersperg-Breunner** * Ainödt 4.5.1934 = Schloss Wald 2.9.1959 Johann Maximilian Graf v.u. zu Trauttmansdorff-Weinsberg * Wien 20.2.1929, and has issue:

XII   1a.   **Johannes Markus Graf v.u. zu Trauttmansdorff-Weinsberg** * Wien 23.11.1960

    2a.   **Désirée Theresia Gräfin v.u. zu Trauttmansdorff-Weinsberg** * Wien 4.3.1962

    3a.   **Johanna Daria Gräfin v.u. zu Trauttmansdorff-Weinsberg** * Wien 23.10.1963

(f) **Aglaë Marie Eleonore Gobertina Prinzessin v. Auersperg-Breunner** * Wald 27.7.1937 = Schloss Wald 12.1.1961 Stephan v. Friedberg * Wien 14.2.1932, and has issue:

    1a. **Matthias Maria Erhard Karl v. Friedberg** * Wien 24.10.1961

    2a. **Ulrich Maria Heinrich v. Friedberg** * Wien 30.3.1963

(g) **Marianne Henriette Eleonore Gobertina Prinzessin v. Auersperg-Breunner** * Zseliz, Hungary 15.12.1943

b) **Therese Maria Josefa Franziska Aloysia Ignatia Gräfin v. Meran** * Székesfehérvár 13.1.1906 = Graz 9.4.1931 Ferdinand Graf v. Westphalen zu Fürstenberg * Przemysl 7.2.1899 s.p.

c) **Aloys Franz Josef Johann Maria Ignaz Graf v. Meran** * Székesfehérvár 4.4.1907 = Pöchlarn 13.9.1942 Elisabeth Freiin. v. Tinti * Bonn 15.10.1917 dau. of Friedrich Frhr. v. Tinti, and has issue:

(a) **Franz Johann Heinrich Bartholomäus Ignaz Maria Graf v. Meran** * Pöchlarn 11.6.1946

(b) **Maria Theresia Johanna Ignatia Gräfin v. Meran** * Pöchlarn 16.4.1948

(c) **Henriette Paula Ignatia Maria Gräfin v. Meran** * Pöchlarn 3.3.1951

(d) **Elisabeth Gräfin v. Meran** * Pöchlarn 27.7.1955

d) **Heinrich Franz Josef Maria Ignatius Benediktus Graf v. Meran** * Székesfehérvár 26.4.1908

e) **Albrecht Josef Clemens Maria Franz Graf v. Meran** * Stainz 4.4.1912

f) **Johann Josef Franz Maria Ignatius Clemens Graf v. Meran** * Graz 30.5.1920 = Lugano 3.5.1950 Maria Wendula Eichmann * Berne 4.4.1921 dau. of Otto Eichmann, and has issue:

(a) **Josef Ferdinand Wilhelm Otto Maria Franz Johann Graf v. Meran** * Chur, Switzerland 8.4.1951

(b) **Georg Maria Alois Karl Heinrich Johann Franz Graf v. Meran** * Chur 12.8.1953

(c) **Anna Maria Gräfin v. Meran** * Chur 29.5.1957

e. **Karoline Johanna Anna Gräfin v. Meran** * Graz 21.9.1870 + Wien 8.9.1944 = Bad Aussee 24.7.1893 Heinrich Frhr. v. Doblhoff-Dier * Weikersdorf 6.3.1868 + Weikersdorf 8.5.1926, and had issue:

a) **Heinrich Johann Franz Joseph Elias Frhr. v. Doblhoff-Dier** * Loeben 20.7.1894

b) **Maria Theresia Karoline Philippine Freiin. v. Doblhoff-Dier** * Loeben 23.8.1896

c) **Franz Karl Heinrich Venerandus Frhr. v. Doblhoff-Dier** * Loeben 14.11.1897 X Treviso 16.7.1916

d) **Johann Rudolf Heinrich Franz Paul Frhr. v. Doblhoff-Dier** * Loeben 10.1.1901 + Salzburg 4.5.1948

f. **Rudolf Johann Franz Graf v. Meran** * Graz 9.12.1872 + Salzburg 17.9.1959 = Goldegg 18.1.1917 Johanna Prinzessin v. Auersperg * Goldegg 14.7.1890 dau. of Karl 9 Fürst v. Auersperg, and has issue:

a) **Rudolf Karl Franz Graf v. Meran** * Innsbruck 20.12.1917 = Wolfegg 10.11.1951 **Marie Therese Gräfin v. Blanckenstein** * Battelau 31.5.1929 dau. of Karl Graf v. Blanckenstein, and has issue:

XI		(a)	**Ladislaja Eleonore Johanna Gräfin v. Meran** * Buenos Aires 26.10.1952
		(b)	**Adolf Graf v. Meran** * Buenos Aires 6.10.1953
		(c)	**Johanna Gräfin v. Meran** * Veinticino de Mayo, Argentina 29.1.1955
		(d)	**Rudolf Graf v. Meran** * Veinticino de Mayo, Argentina 1.2.1956
		(e)	**Andreas Graf v. Meran** * Buenos Aires 24.5.1957
		(f)	**Gabriele Gräfin v. Meran** * Buenos Aires 19.11.1958
		(g)	**Maria Anna Gräfin v. Meran** * Buenos Aires 9.10.1959
		(h)	**Karl Graf v. Meran** * Buenos Aires 12.10.1960 + Buenos Aires 15.10.1960
		(i)	**Heinrich Graf v. Meran** * Nueva Palmira, Uruguay 14.11.1961
		(j)	**Christine Isabel Gräfin v. Meran** * Buenos Aires 14.6.1963
		(k)	**Hemma Isabel Maria Gräfin v. Meran** * Buenos Aires 21.7.1965

X   b)   **Adolf Karl Franz Rudolf Graf v. Meran** * Goldegg 21.5.1919 = Salzburg 18.4.1961 Ada Kindermann * Wien 29.3.1922 dau. of Heinrich Kindermann, and has issue:

XI   (a)   **Johannes Heinrich Rudolf Gobertus Graf v. Meran** * Salzburg 15.10.1961

        (b)   **Cornelia Elisabeth Eleonore Magdalena Gräfin v. Meran** * Salzburg 14.11.1963

X   c)   **Caroline Eleonore Theresia Johanna Gräfin v. Meran** * Losensteinleiten 15.11.1920 = Salzburg 7.9.1946 Christian Witt v. Dörring * Wien 2.8.1914, and has issue:

XI   (a)   **Johanna Witt v. Dörring** * Grossarl 8.1.1947

        (b)   **Aglaé Witt v. Dörring** * Gmunden 1.1.1949

        (c)   **Karl Witt v. Dörring** * Gmunden 4.6.1951

        (d)   **Theodor Christian Witt v. Dörring** * Gmunden 2.1.1953

        (e)   **Eleonore Witt v. Dörring** * Gmunden 9.3.1955

        (f)   **Franz Witt v. Dörring** * Radstadt 3.9.1956

        (g)   **Johann Georg Witt v. Dörring** * Radstadt 15.12.1957

IX   g.   **Albrecht Johann Franz Graf v. Meran** * Graz 11.12.1874 + Grundlsee 9.7.1928

VII   14)   **Ranier Joseph Johann Michael Franz Hieronymus Archduke of Austria, Viceroy of Lombardy** * Pisa 30.9.1783 + Bozen 16.1.1853 = Prag 28.5.1820 **Maria Francesca Princess of Savoy-Carignan** * Paris 13.4.1800 + Bozen 25.12.1850 dau. of Carlo Emanuele Prince of Savoy Carignan, and had issue:

VIII   (1)   **Maria Karoline Auguste Elisabeth Margarethe Dorothee Archduchess of Austria** * Milano 6.2.1821 + Milano 23.1.1844

        (2)   **Adelheid Franziska Marie Raniera Elisabeth Clotilde Archduchess of Austria** * Milano 3.6.1822 + Torino 20.1.1855 = Stupinigi, near Torino 12.4.1842 **Vittorio Emanuele II King of Sardinia** * Torino 14.3.1820 + Roma 9.1.1878 and had issue see elsewhere

        (3)   **Leopold Ludwig Maria Franz Julius Eustorgius Gerhard Archduke of Austria** * Milano 6.6.1823 + Hörnstein 24.5.1898

        (4)   **Ernst Karl Felix Maria Ranier Gottfried Cyriak Archduke of Austria** * Milano 8.8.1824 + Arco 4.4.1899

        (5)   **Sigismund Leopold Ranier Maria Ambrosius Valentin Archduke of Austria** * Milano 7.1.1826 + Wien 15.12.1891

VIII (6) **Ranier Ferdinand Maria Johann Evangelist Franz Ignaz Archduke of Austria** * Wien 11.1.1827 + Wien 27.1.1913 = Wien 21.2.1852 **Marie Caroline Archduchess of Austria** * Wien 10.9.1825 + Baden 17.7.1915 dau. of Karl Archduke of Austria, Duke of Teschen s.p.

(7) **Heinrich Anton Maria Ranier Karl Gregor Archduke of Austria** * Milano 9.5.1828 + Wien 30.11.1891 = Bozen 4.2.1868 Leopoldine Hofmann Gräfin v. Waideck * Krems 29.11.1842 + Wien 29.11.1891 dau. of Ignaz Hofmann, and had issue:

IX a. **Maria Raniera Gräfin v. Waideck** * Lucerne 21.7.1872 + Gries b. Bozen 17.2.1936 = Wien 26.7.1892 **Don Enrico Conte Lucchesi Palli 11 Principe di Campofranco** * Brunnsee 19.8.1861 + Schloss Alleg 1.3.1924, and has issue see elsewhere

VIII (8) **Maximilian Karl Maria Ranier Joseph Marcellus Archduke of Austria** * Milano 16.1.1830 + Milano 16.3.1839

VII 15) **Ludwig Joseph Anton Johann Archduke of Austria** * Firenze 13.12.1784 + Wien 21.12.1864

16) **Rudolf Johann Joseph Ranier Archduke of Austria** * Pisa 8.1.1788 + 1831

VI 10. **Karoline Archduchess of Austria** * & + Schönbrunn 17.9.1748

11. **Johanna Gabrielle Josephine Antonia Archduchess of Austria** * Wien 4.2.1750 + Wien 23.12.1762

12. **Josefa Gabrielle Johanna Antonia Anna Archduchess of Austria** * Wien 19.3.1751 + Schönbrunn 15.10.1767

13. **Maria Karoline Luise Josephine Johanna Antonia Archduchess of Austria** * Schönbrunn 13.8.1752 + Schloss Hetzendorf b. Schönbrunn 8.9.1814 = Caserta 12.5.1768 **Ferdinando I King of Naples and Sicily** * Napoli 12.1.1751 + Napoli 4.1.1825, and had issue see elsewhere

14. **Ferdinand Karl Anton Joseph Johann Stanislas Archduke of Austria** * Schönbrunn 1.6.1754 + Wien 24.12.1806 = Milano 15.10.1771 **Marie Beatrice Princess of Modena** * Modena 6.4.1750 + Wien 14.11.1829 dau. of Herkules III Duke of Modena, and had issue:

VII 1) **Josef Franz Archduke of Austria-Este, Prince of Modena** * & + 1772

2) **Marie Therese Josefa Johanna Archduchess of Austria-Este, Princess of Modena** * Milano 1.11.1773 + Genova 29.3.1832 = Torino 25.4.1789 **Vittorio Emanuele I King of Sardinia** * Torino 24.7.1759 + Moncalieri 10.1.1824, and had issue see elsewhere

3) **Josefa Ferdinande Johanna Ambroise Archduchess of Austria-Este, Princess of Modena** * 13.5.1775 + 20.8.1777

4) **Marie Leopoldine Josefa Johanna Archduchess of Austria-Este, Princess of Modena** * Milano 10.12.1776 + Wasserburg-am-Inn 23.6.1848 = (1) 15.2.1795 Karl Theodor Elector Palatine of The Rhine, Elector of Bavaria * Drogenbusch, Bruxelles 11.12.1724 + München 16.2.1799; = (2) München 14.11.1804 Ludwig Graf v. Arco * München 30.1.1773 + München 20.8.1854, and had issue:

by 2nd marriage:

VIII (1) **Aloys Nikolaus Ambros Graf v. Arco** * Stepperg 6.12.1808 + Anif 10.9.1891 = (1) Wien 9.10.1830 Irene Markgräfin v. Pallavicini * Allgyö, Hungary 2.9.1811 + Wien 31.1.1877 dau. of Eduard Markgraf v. Pallavicini; = (2) 30.7.1877 Pauline Oswald * 31.3.1851 + München 17.2.1902, and had issue (subsequently legitamised)

by 2nd marriage:

IX a. **Sophie Arco Gräfin v. Stepperg** * München 11.6.1868 + Thannbach 26.11.1952 = München 11.3.1890 Ernst Graf von Moy de Sons * München 17.10.1860 + München 19.5.1922 s.p.

VIII (2) **Maximilian Joseph Bernhard Graf v. Arco-Zinneberg** * Stepperg 13.12.1811 + Meran 13.11.1885 = München 3.6.1833 Leopoldine Gräfin v. Waldburg-Zeil u. Trauchburg * Rottweil 26.6.1811 + Meran 10.2.1886 dau. of Franz Fürst v. Waldburg-Zeil u. Trauchburg, and had issue:

IX	a.	**Marie Christiane Franziska Gräfin v. Arco-Zinneberg** * 23.5.1834 + Billigheim 31.3.1892 = München 17.7.1856 Carl Graf v. Leiningen-Billigheim * Heidelberg 7.3.1823 + Billigheim 23.7.1900, and had issue:

X   a)   **Leopoldine Gräfin v. Leiningen-Billigheim** * Nieder-Walluf 9.4.1857 + München 5.9.1917 = Billigheim 5.5.1885 Gottfried Frhr. v. Vequel-Westernach * München 15.7.1847 + Hohenkammer 29.5.1898, and had issue:

XII   (a)   **Karl Borramäus Wenzeslaus Gottfried Maria Ludwig Arsacius Frhr. v. Vequél-Westernach** * Hohenkammer 13.10.1886 X Lille 4.10.1914

      (b)   **Therese Marie Gabriele Anna Elisabeth Josepha Helene Freiin. v. Vequel-Westernach** * Hohenkammer 22.1.1888 = München 11.2.1908 Kurt v. Rodenberg * München-Gladbach 13.1.1877 + München 12.2.1931, and had issue:

XII   1a.   **Gabriele v. Rodenberg** * Darmstadt 29.11.1908 = 11.2.1938 Fritz v. Bomhard * 4.1.1910 X 18.1.1945, and has issue:

XIII   1b.   **Christa v. Bomhard** * München 10.12.1938

XII   2a.   **Ruth v. Rodenberg** * Darmstadt 30.5.1910

      3a.   **Ingeborg v. Rodenberg** * Altdamm b. Stettin 24.8.1913 = ... Carl Alfred Scheel * Marburg 4.12.1904, and has issue:

XIII   1b.   **Jan Marcel Scheel** * 17.3.1938

XI   (c)   **Maria Leopoldine Mechtilde Sophia Afra Theodolinde Freiin. v. Vequel-Westernach** * Hohenkammer 13.11.1889 = Hohenkammer 4.5.1909 Julius Lermer * Osterhofen 23.9.1872 + Wildthurn 12.6.1948, and has issue:

XII   1a.   **Hans Lermer** * Wildthurn 4.12.1919 = (1) Wildthurn 5.6.1949 Elfriede Specht * Mamming 31.5.1931 − div.; = (2) München 2.9.1958 Margrit Holltrotter * Chemnitz 25.12.1937, and has issue:

by 1st marriage:

XIII   1b.   **Michael Lermer** * Wildthurn 28.5.1950

by 2nd marriage:

      2b.   **Gudula Alrune Lermer** * Wildthurn 3.2.1959

      3b.   **Christoph Lermer** * Wildthurn 9.8.1962

XI   (d)   **Mechtilde Maria Viktoria Sophia Notburga Frieda Clara Felicitas Freiin. v. Vequel-Westernach** * Hohenkammer 10.7.1894

X   b)   **Karl Polykarpus Wenceslas Johann Ludwig Maria Graf v. Leiningen-Billigheim** * Niederwalluf 18.7.1860 + Billigheim 22.1.1899 = München 8.8.1898 Christine Blahva * Wien 19.4.1873 + München 9.6.1934 s.p.

      c)   **Mechtilde Maria Pia Gräfin v. Leiningen-Billigheim** * Billigheim 17.8.1870 + Rottenburg a.d. Laaber 14.4.1946 = Billigheim 8.2.1893 Maximilian Frhr. v. Cetto * München 8.10.1869 + Oberlauterbach 11.3.1961, and had issue:

XI   (a)   **Marie Augusta Gabriele Freiin. v. Cetto** * Oberlauterbach 21.7.1894 + Oberlauterbach 18.9.1895

      (b)   **Leopoldine Maria Freiin. v. Cetto** * Oberlauterbach 6.9.1895

XI   (c)   **Ernst Karl Wenzeslaus Polykarp Joseph Maria Frhr. v. Cetto**   * Oberlauterbach
18.4.1897 ✗ Douamont-Verdun 8.6.1916

      (d)   **Gabriele Marie Freiin. v. Cetto**   * Oberlauterbach 6.4.1898

      (e)   **Anton Wilhelm Joseph Maria Frhr. v. Cetto**   * Oberlauterbach 1.6.1901
+ Oberlauterbach 29.5.1963 = Dennenlöhe 21.7.1940 Rosemarie Freiin. v.
Süsskind-Schwendi * Dennenlöhe 17.1.1913 dau. of Ludwig Frhr. v. Süsskind-
Schwendi, and has issue:

XII   1a.   **Mechtildis Brigitta Freiin. v. Cetto**   * Nürnberg 10.2.1942

      2a.   **Veronika Irmingard Maria Freiin. v. Cetto**   * Rottenburg a.d. Laaber 9.1.1946

      3a.   **Anton Maximilian Kurt Ludwig Frhr. v. Cetto**   * Oberlauterbach 24.11.1947

XI   (f)   **Wilhelmine Maria Josepha Freiin. v. Cetto**   * Oberlauterbach 12.6.1904

      (g)   **Max Emanuel Frhr. v. Cetto**   * München 29.10.1908 + Oberlauterbach 26.12.1921

IX   b.   **Therese Anna Ludovica Gräfin v. Arco-Zinneberg**   * 13.12.1835 + Adendorf 20.6.1906
= München 6.6.1854 Maximilian August Graf v. Loë * Wissen 20.6.1817 + Wissen 29.6.1879

X   a)   **Maximilian Hubert Sophia Graf v. Loë**   * 29.9.1855 + ... 1885

      b)   **Friedrich-Leopold Aloysius Maria Hubertus Graf v. Loë**   * Wissen 28.5.1861 + Gries b.
Bozen 14.4.1899 = Tantenhausen 14.6.1888 Paula Gräfin v. Korff gen. Schmising
* Münster i. W. 14.7.1863 + Burg Adendorf 11.2.1942 dau. of Clemens Graf v. Korff
gen. Schmising and had issue:

XI   (a)   **Degenhard-Bertram Klemens Hubert Aloysius Joseph Maria Graf v. Loë**   * Wissen
8.4.1889 ✗ 21.8.1915

      (b)   **Klemens Friedrich Ferdinand Hubertus Aloysius Joseph Maria Frhr. v. Loë**
* Wissen 5.7.1890 ✗ 11.10.1914

      (c)   **Maria Mathilde Therese Ferdinande Georgia Walpurga Huberta Aloysia Josepha
Freiin. v. Loë**   * Wissen 1.1.1895 = Frankfurt-am-Main 19.3.1919 **Johannes Frhr.
v. Gumppenberg** * Pöttmes 26.6.1891 + Genève 16.11.1959, and has issue see
elsewhere

      (d)   **Felix Maximilian Ludwig Georg Aloysius Hubertus Joseph Maria Graf v. Loë**
* Wissen 1.9.1896 ✗ Schwaneburg 25.7.1944 = Anholt 8.9.1925 **Isabella
Prinzessin zu Salm-Salm** * Potsdam 13.2.1903 dau. of Emanuel Erbprinz zu Salm-
Salm, and had issue:

XII   1a.   **Friedrich Paul Emanuel Christoph Hubertus Maria Graf v. Loë**   * Wissen
8.6.1926 = Vosswinkel 2.10.1957 Inez Freiin. v. Boeselager * Hann-Münden
6.2.1935 dau. of Maximilian Frhr. v. Boeselager, and has issue:

XIII   1b.   **Raphael Felix Maximilian Pius Maria Frhr. v. Loë**   * Wissen 30.8.1958

      2b.   **Wessel Martin Wolfgang Philipp Maria Frhr. v. Loë**   * Wissen 10.11.1959

      3b.   **Winfried Johannes Benedikt Maria Frhr. v. Loë**   * Wissen 29.7.1961

      4b.   **Paula Freiin. v. Loë**   * Wissen 17.5.1963

      5b.   **Augustinus Frhr. v. Loë**   * Wissen 12.6.1966

XII   2a.   **Christine Maria Georgia Ignatia Freiin. v. Loë**   * Wissen 31.7.1927 = Wissen
30.8.1949 Johannes Prinz zu Löwenstein-Wertheim-Rosenberg * Kleinheubach
8.7.1919, and has issue:

123

XIII		1b.	**Maria Michael Aloysius Felix Thomas Cyriacus Bernhard Johannes Prinz zu Löwenstein-Wertheim-Rosenberg** * Wissen 20.12.1950
		2b.	**Maria Karl Emanuel Ludger Petrus Prinz zu Löwenstein-Wertheim-Rosenberg** * Weeze 18.1.1952
		3b.	**Maria Felix Friedrich Johannes Pius Faustinus Prinz zu Löwenstein-Wertheim-Rosenberg** * Weeze 15.2.1954
		4b.	**Maria Isabella Josephine Ulrike Ludmilla Christine Prinzessin zu Löwenstein-Wertheim-Rosenberg** * Steinebach-am-Ammersee 2.11.1956
		5b.	**Maria Josephine Sophie Konrada Monika Afra Prinzessin zu Löwenstein-Wertheim-Rosenberg** * Steinebach-am-Ammersee 23.4.1958
		6b.	**Maria Martin Carl Wolfgang Franz Rasso Prinz zu Löwenstein-Wertheim-Rosenberg** * Steinebach-am-Ammersee 15.4.1961

XII		3a.	**Clemens Wessel Albrecht Cyriakus Joseph Hubertus Maria Frhr. v. Loë** * Wissen 8.8.1928 = Maria Thann 7.5.1957 **Sophie Gräfin v. Waldburg-Zeil** * Innsbruck 5.12.1932 dau. of Georg Graf v. Waldburg-Zeil and has issue:

XIII		1b.	**Georg Friedrich Benedikt Maria Frhr. v. Loë** * Meckenheim 18.4.1958
		2b.	**Felix Franz Martin Frhr. v. Loë** * Bad Godesberg 30.8.1960
		3b.	**Philipp Joseph Bonifatius Christophorus Maria Frhr. v. Loë** * Bad Godesberg 11.10.1961
		4b.	**Maria Annunciata Freiin. v. Loë** * Bad Godesberg 15.2.1963
		5b.	**Agnes Freiin. v. Loë** * Bad Godesberg 25.4.1966

XII		4a.	**Maria Elisabeth Leopoldine Josepha Theresa Freiin. v. Loë** * Wissen 15.3.1930 = Wissen 22.9.1954 Philipp Frhr. Wambolt v. Umstadt * Frischau 15.8.1918 s.p.
		5a.	**Paula Therese Franziska Maria Freiin. v. Loë** * Wissen 1.3.1931 + Köln 29.10.1950
		6a.	**Franz Raphael Viktor Hubertus Christoph Maria Frhr. v. Loë** * Wissen 24.10.1936
		7a.	**Maria Rosa Maximiliane Klothilde Huberta Freiin. v. Loë** * Wissen 3.6.1939

X	c)		**Luise Maria Friederike Huberta Ignatia Freiin. v. Loë** * 30.7.1863 + Ahrensberg 24.6.1921
	d)		**Mathilde Klementine Maria Beatrix Johanna Huberta Elisabeth Gabriele Margarete Freiin. v. Loë** * Wissen 22.2.1865 + München 11.1.1937 = Wissen 2.8.1887 Georg Frhr. v. Gumppenberg * Brückenhausen 21.5.1852 + Pöttmes 30.7.1930 and had issue:

XI	(a)		**Maria-Theresia Huberta Aloysia Johanna Freiin. v. Gumppenberg** * Pöttmes 7.7.1888 = Pöttmes 10.9.1907 Maximilian-Joseph Graf Deym v. Střitež * Arnstorf 27.1.1880 + Arnstorf 5.9.1934, and had issue:

XII		1a.	**Joseph Maria Hans Georg Johann Nepomuk Wenzeslaus Graf Deym v. Střitež** * Arnstorf 12.9.1908 = Arnstorf 19.5.1937 Maria Teresia Freiin. v. Fürstenberg * Kadi-Köi, Turkey 6.11.1906 dau. of Friedrich Frhr. v. Fürstenberg, and has issue:

XIII		1b.	**Joseph Maria Johann Nepomuk Leodegar Franz v. Assisi Hubert Viktorinus Wenzeslaus Graf Deym v. Střitež** * Arnstorf 2.10.1938

124

2b. **Leopold Maria Friedrich Jakob Christoph Pantaleon Hubert Viktorinus Johann Nepomuk Wenzeslaus Graf Deym v. Střitež** * Arnstorf 25.7.1940 = Holthausen 13.8.1966 Dagmar Freiin. v. Fürstenberg * Eberswalde 6.7.1938 dau. of Leopold Frhr. v. Fürstenberg

3b. **Ferdinand Maria Sebastian Paulus Hubertus Viktorinus Johann Nepomuk Wenzeslaus Graf Deym v. Střitež** * Arnstorf 20.1.1942 = Arnstorf 20.8.1966 Waltraud Kathrein v. Andersill * Oetz 11.6.1943 dau. of Albert Ritter Kathrein v. Andersill

4b. **Michael Maria Franz Xaver Apollinarius Viktorinus Johannes Nepomuk Wenzeslaus Graf Deym v. Střitež** * Arnstorf 20.7.1943

5b. **Christoph Maria Joseph Erwin Degenhard Silvester Hubert Viktorinus Johann Nepomuk Wenzeslaus Graf Deym v. Střitež** * Arnstorf 28.12.1944

6b. **Bernhard Maria Elimar Maternus Andreas Hubert Viktorinus Nepomuk Wenzeslaus Graf Deym v. Střitež** * Arnstorf 14.9.1946

7b. **Benedikt Oktavio Maria Graf Deym v. Střitež** * Arnstorf 6.8.1953

2a. **Hans Georg Maria Joseph Johann Nepomuk Wenzeslaus Robert Viktorinus Graf Deym v. Střitež** * München 17.4.1910 + Arnstorf 3.10.1931

3a. **Maria-Theresia Mathilde Josepha Johanna Nepomucena Wenzeslawa Viktorina Gräfin Deym v. Střitež** * Arnstorf 19.9.1911 = Arnstorf 17.4.1937 Karl Ludwig Graf v. Dreschel * München 15.6.1907 s.p.

4a. **Johann Nepomuk Maria Joseph Viktorinus Bonifazius Graf Deym v. Střitež** * Arnstorf 13.5.1913 X Rastoje, Russia 11.8.1941 = Zákány, Kom Somogy 30.5.1938 Maria Antoinetta Gräfin Zichy zu Zich u. Vásonykeö * Wien 6.7.1913 dau. of Edmund Graf Zichy zu Zich u. Vásonykeö, and had issue:

1b. **Gabriele Maria Theresia Nepomucena Wenzeslawa Gräfin Deym v. Střitež** * Budapest 31.10.1939 = Jablonec 27.7.1963 Lajos Farkas * Mostova, Slovakia 25.9.1940, and has issue:

    1c. **Thomas Ludwig Joseph Maria Farkas** * Jablonec 14.10.1964

2b. **Johann Christoph Maria Joseph Ludwig Wenzeslaus Viktorinus Graf Deym v. Střitež** * Budapest 13.5.1941 = 30.12.1963 Ilona Lengyel * Yajka 28.5.1938, and has issue:

    1c. **Katharina Josephine Sybille Wenzeslawa Gräfin Deym v. Střitež** * Jablonec 21.6.1965

5a. **Viktorinus Maria Joseph Hugo Wenzeslaus Johann Nepomuk Ignatius Graf Deym v. Střitež** * Arnstorf 11.1.1915 X Gruel, Russia 15.8.1941

6a. **Anna Maria Josepha Agnes Katharina Johanna Nepomucena Wenzeslawa Viktorina Gräfin Deym v. Střitež** * Arnstorf 19.1.1917 = Arnstorf 19.4.1941 Dietrich Graf v. Soden-Fraunhofen * Nürnberg 28.7.1910 + Stuttgart 15.12.1961, and had issue:

1b. **Brigitta Maria Theresia Barbara Anna Adelheid Gräfin v. Soden-Fraunhofen** * Mariakirchen 14.12.1942

2b. **Wolfgang Maria Karl Alfred Dietrich Maximilian Johannes Baptist Ephraim Graf v. Soden-Fraunhofen** * Erdweg 11.6.1944

<table>
<tr><td>XIII</td><td></td><td>3b.</td><td>**Mechtild Maria Franziska Xaveria Brigitta Antonia Dietrica Maximiliane Gräfin v. Soden-Fraunhofen** * Erdweg 15.1.1946</td></tr>
</table>

XIII
    3b. **Mechtild Maria Franziska Xaveria Brigitta Antonia Dietrica Maximiliane Gräfin v. Soden-Fraunhofen** * Erdweg 15.1.1946

    4b. **Maria Nives Theresia Anna Brigitta Ursula Gräfin v. Soden-Fraunhofen** * Erdweg 5.12.1949

    5b. **Irma Benedikta Maria Josepha Brigitta Anna Sophie Gräfin v. Soden-Fraunhofen** * Erdweg 7.6.1953

XII
    7a. **Elisabeth Maria Theresia Josepha Agnes Katharina Johanna Nepomucena Wenzeslawa Viktorina Gräfin Deym v. Střitež** * Arnstorf 10.12.1919 = Roma 3.9.1964 Eugen Diem * München 17.6.1909 s.p.

    8a. **Agnes Maria Paula Viktorina Johanna Nepomucena Wenzeslawa Gräfin Deym v. Střitež** * Arnstorf 21.10.1924 + Arnstorf 5.11.1924

    9a. **Franz Xaver Maria Johann v. Kreuz Petrus Canisius Maximilian Viktorinus Johannes Nepomuk Wenzeslaus Graf Deym v. Střitež** * Arnstorf 12.10.1925 + München 3.8.1962 = Innsbruck 5.4.1961 **Monica Gräfin v. Spiegelfeld** * Tijukas (Brasil) 14.1.1927 dau. of Sigmund Graf v. Spiegelfeld, and had issue:

XIII
    1b. **Martin Leopold Thaddäus Johannes Nepomuk Viktorinus Wenzeslaus Franz Graf Deym v. Střitež** * Landshut 12.1.1962

XII
    10a. **Katharina Maria Paula Petronella Viktorina Johanna Nepomucena Wenzeslawa Gräfin Deym v. Střitež** * Arnstorf 30.5.1927 = Mariakirchen 12.6.1948 Gustav Graf v. Preysing-Lichtenegg * Nieder-Raunau 15.9.1919, and had issue:

XIII
    1b. **Iniga Maria Theresia Katherina Franziska Monika Johanna Elisabeth Alexandra Pia Gräfin v. Preysing-Lichtenegg** * Mariakirchen 3.5.1949

    2b. **Johann Stanislaus Maria Anton Ives Christoph Ignatius Konrad Damian Jabok Rupert Graf v. Preysing-Lichtenegg** * Mariakirchen 19.2.1952

XII
    11a. **Genofeva Maria Oda Stephana Katherina Viktorina Nepomucena Wenzeslawa Gräfin Deym v. Střitež** * Arnstorf 24.1.1929 = Arnstorf 19.4.1951 Rudolf Riederer Frhr. v. Paar zu Schönau * München 12.9.1925, and has issue:

XIII
    1b. **Maria Mercedes Elisabeth Franziska Therese Riederer Freiin. v. Paar zu Schönau** * München 29.1.1952

    2b. **Adelheid Huberta Maria Viola Justina Riederer Freiin. v. Paar zu Schönau** * Mallersdorf 20.9.1954

    3b. **Peter Canisius Franz Maximilian Johann Nepomuk Riederer Frhr. v. Paar zu Schönau** * Grafeling 15.6.1957

    4b. **Barbara Elisabeth Maria Gisela Riederer Freiin. v. Paar zu Schönau** * München 7.5.1962

XI
    (b) **Elisabeth Maria Dominika Josepha Huberta Friederika Magdalena Freiin. v. Gumppenberg** * Pöttmes 27.5.1889

    (c) **Johannes Heinrich Maria Ludwig Herbert Joseph Aloys Frhr. v. Gumppenberg** * Pöttmes 26.6.1891 + Genève 16.11.1959 = Frankfurt-am-Main 19.2.1919 **Maria Mathilde Freiin. v. Loë** * Wissen 1.1.1895 dau. of Friedrich Graf v. Loë, and had issue:

XII

1a.   **Sebastian Thomas Maria Joseph Johannes Hubert Georg Paulus Frhr. v. Gumppenberg** * Pöttmes 29.12.1919 = Pöttmes 12.4.1948 Hildegard Witt * Hamburg 6.10.1929, dau. of Franz Witt

2a.   **Friedrich Felix Christoph Ignatius Maria Blasius Frhr. v. Gumppenberg** * Pöttmes 1.2.1921

3a.   **Maria-Theresia Helene Huberta Johanna Freiin. v. Gumppenberg** * Pöttmes 18.8.1922 = Pöttmes 3.3.1943 Wernher Frhr. v. Schönau-Wehr * Stuttgart 26.10.1916, and has issue:

XIII

1b.   **Elisabeth Theresia Gunhild Gabriele Freiin. v. Schönau-Wehr** * Stuttgart 10.3.1944

2b.   **Albrecht Hyrus Egbert Sebastian Frhr. v. Schönau-Wehr** * Schrobenhausen 15.7.1945 + Augsburg 28.10.1945

3b.   **Gabriele Maria Barbara Therese Freiin. v. Schönau-Wehr** * Stuttgart 7.5.1947

4b.   **Johannes Hyrus Moritz Maria Frhr. v. Schönau-Wehr** * Augsburg 2.1.1949

5b.   **Katherina Mathilde Inga Eleonore Freiin. v. Schönau-Wehr** * Augsburg 22.2.1951

XII

4a.   **Christoph Joseph Judas Thaddeus Maria Hubertus Frhr. v. Gumppenberg** * Pöttmes 25.9.1924 = Grünwald 3.10.1953 Carin Freiin. v. Mauchenheim gen. Bechtolsheim * München 26.3.1927 dau. of Georg Frhr. v. Mauchenheim gen. Bechtolsheim

5a.   **Franz-Georg Appollinaris Dietrich Maria Frhr. v. Gumppenberg** * Pöttmes 23.7.1926 + Freiburg i. Br. 5.10.1958

XI

(d)   **Hildegard Christiane Maria Johanna Huberta Afra Freiin. v. Gumppenberg** * 13.12.1894 + Pöttmes 3.5.1919

X

e)   **Ludwig Dietrich Joseph Maria Hubert Pachalis Frhr. v. Loë** * Wissen 31.3.1866 + Düsseldorf 19.6.1919

f)   **Georg Felix Maria Hubertus Aloysius Christian Frhr. v. Loë** * Wissen 14.6.1868 + Adendorf 27.9.1942 = Tatenhausen 26.11.1902 Paula Gräfin v. Korff gen. Schmising * Münster i. W. 14.7.1863 + Adendorf 11.2.1942 dau. of Clemens Graf v. Korff gen. Schmising, and had issue:

XI

(a)   **Therese Josepha Aloysia Huberta Freiin. v. Loë** * Wissen 23.9.1903 = Adendorf 14.5.1929 Edmund Frhr. v. Loë * Mheer 16.5.1888 + Adendorf 11.4.1938 s.p.

(b)   **Dietrich Lewin Antonius Maria Hubertus Aloysius Joseph Frhr. v. Loë** * Wissen 14.6.1905 + Kevaer 31.12.1925

IX

c.   **Sophie Leopoldine Ludovica Gräfin v. Arco-Zinneberg** * Zeil 14.11.1836 + Wolfegg 21.12.1909 = München 19.4.1860 Franz Fürst v. Waldburg zu Wolfegg u. Waldsee * Wolfegg 11.9.1833 + Wolfegg 14.12.1906, and had issue:

X

a)   **Friedrich Leopold Maria Joseph Michael Aloysius Willibald Graf v. Waldburg zu Wolfegg u. Waldsee** * Waldsee 29.9.1861 + Ditton Hall 21.4.1895

b)   **Maximilian Wunibald Maria Joseph Servatius Fürst v. Waldburg zu Wolfegg u. Waldsee** * Waldsee 13.5.1863 + Chur 27.9.1950 = Hořin b. Melnik 26.7.1890 Sidonie Prinzessin v. Lobkowicz * Drhovl 12.8.1869 + Wolfegg 24.7.1941 dau. of Georg Christian Fürst v. Lobkowicz, and had issue:

XI	(a)	**Franz Xaver Maria Ludwig Joseph Andreas Willibald Aloysius Alfons Fürst v. Waldburg zu Wolfegg u. Waldsee** * Waldsee 25.8.1892 = Wechselburg 6.5.1920 Adelheid Gräfin v. Schönburg-Glauchau * Wechselburg 28.7.1900 dau. of Joachim Graf v. Schönburg-Glauchau, and had issue:

XII   1a. **Maximilian Willibald Maria Franz Xaver Benedikt Johann Baptist Erbgraf v. Waldburg zu Wolfegg u. Waldsee** * Waldsee 22.6.1924 = Wien 8.2.1955 Ida Gräfin Khuen v. Belasi * Prag 1.5.1928 dau. of Heinrich Graf Khuen v. Belasi, and has issue:

XIII   1b. **Maria Katherina Walburga Ida Oktavia Leonarda Theresia Johanna Gräfin v. Waldburg zu Wolfegg u. Waldsee** * Ravensburg 18.3.1956

       2b. **Johannes Baptist Franz Xaver Willibald Maria Joseph Philipp Jen Leonhard Graf v. Waldburg zu Wolfegg u. Waldsee** * Ravensburg 9.3.1957

       3b. **Jacob Heinrich Wunibald Maria Joseph Rupert Leonhard Graf v. Waldburg zu Wolfegg u. Waldsee** * Ravensburg 9.3.1957

       4b. **Thomas Georg Willibald Maria Johannes Vianney Leonhard Graf v. Waldburg zu Wolfegg u. Waldsee** * Ravensburg 28.7.1960

       5b. **Maria Adelheid Franziska Josefa Leonharda Walburga Gräfin v. Waldburg zu Wolfegg u. Waldsee** * Ravensburg 31.8.1963

XII   2a. **Maria Oktavia Monika Colette Christophora Sophie Johanna Walburga Gräfin v. Waldburg zu Wolfegg u. Waldsee** * Wechselburg 1.8.1926 = Waldsee 6.5.1958 Dietrich Graf v. Brühl * Königsburg i. Pr. 1.12.1925 and has issue see elsewhere

       3a. **Otto Joachim Maria Joseph Wunibald Petrus Canisius Georg Christophorus Felix Graf v. Waldburg zu Wolfegg u. Waldsee** * Waldsee 30.5.1928

       4a. **Maria Sidonia Josepha Walburga Ignatia Coletta Ursula Gräfin v. Waldburg zu Wolfegg u. Waldsee** * Waldsee 20.10.1929 = Waldsee 28.9.1955 Leopold Graf v. Walderdorff * Kürn 7.4.1928, and has issue:

XIII   1b. **Birgitta Maria Adelheid Melanie Kunigunde Gräfin v. Walderdorff** * Regensburg 2.7.1956 + 16.2.1962

       2b. **Marguerita Anna Maria Oktavia Henriette Apollinaris Gräfin v. Walderdorff** * Kürn 19.8.1957

       3b. **Georg Philipp Graf v. Walderdorff** * 3.5.1959

       4b. **Helene Gräfin v. Walderdorff** * 27.3.1963

XII   5a. **Gebhard Heinrich Maria Willibald Benedikt Eucharius Graf v. Waldburg zu Wolfegg u. Waldsee** * Waldsee 8.12.1930

       6a. **Ferdinand Ludwig Joseph Maria Wunibald Konrad Christophorus Graf v. Waldburg zu Wolfegg u. Waldsee** * Waldsee 17.12.1933 = Aurach b. Kitzbühel 8.6.1964 **Emma Prinzessin v. Croÿ** * Sutton, Surrey 30.12.1943 dau. of Prinz Alexander v. Croÿ, and has issue:

XIII   1b. **Richard Heinrich Gebhard Wunibald Bernard Graf v. Waldburg zu Wolfegg u. Waldsee** * Augsburg 20.5.1965

XI   (b)   **Georg Maria Joseph Willibald Stephan Gerhard Graf v. Waldburg zu Wolfegg u. Waldsee** * Waldsee 25.12.1893 X Josafowa a.d. Dubisa 30.5.1915

XI (c) **Friedrich Maria Joseph Wunibald Petrus Claver Philippus-Neri Graf v. Waldburg zu Wolfegg u. Waldsee** * Waldsee 25.5.1895 X Somme 20.4.1916

(d) **Maria Anna Walburga Antonia Elisabetha Bona Theresia Gräfin v. Waldburg zu Wolfegg u. Waldsee** * Waldsee 1.10.1896 + Prassberg, Allgau 9.7.1954 = Wolfegg 26.4.1923 Albrecht Graf v. Spreti * München 3.8.1890 + Prassberg, Allgau 8.3.1956, and had issue:

XII 1a. **Bernhard-Ludwig Georg Friedrich Joseph Sidonius Maria Graf v. Spreti** * Pähl 23.6.1924 + Kisslegg 8.10.1948 = Augsburg 5.12.1944 Elisabeth Holzmann * Kisslegg 18.11.1921, and had issue:

XIII 1b. **Herbert Maximilian Heinrich Graf v. Spreti** * Kisslegg 27.4.1946

XII 2a. **Maximilian Albrecht Petrus Canisius Ferdinand Hubertus Joseph Maria Graf v. Spreti** * Pähl 12.10.1925 X Breslau 20.3.1944

3a. **Rudolf-Joseph Heinrich Franz v. Assisi Maria Graf v. Spreti** * Pähl 29.3.1929

XI (e) **Maria Sophie Franziska Walburga Gräfin v. Waldburg zu Wolfegg u. Waldsee** * Waldsee 10.10.1899

(f) **Joseph Maria Ludwig Wunibald Alfons Graf v. Waldburg zu Wolfegg u. Waldsee** * Waldsee 18.5.1901

(g) **Maria Henriette Walburga Gräfin v. Waldburg zu Wolfegg u. Waldsee** * Waldsee 17.9.1902 = Wolfegg 23.2.1922 **Carl Adam Graf v. Wuthenau-Hohenthurm** * Dresden 15.11.1896, and has issue see elsewhere

(h) **Johannes Nepomuk Maria Wunibald Anton Laurentius Graf v. Waldburg zu Wolfegg u. Waldsee** * Waldsee 10.8.1904 + Kisslegg 18.5.1966 = Mileschau-am-Donnersberg 19.9.1938 **Franziska Gräfin v. Ledebur-Wicheln** * Mileschau 18.6.1913 dau. of Eugen Graf v. Ledebur-Wicheln, and had issue:

XII 1a. **Eleonore Henriette Walburga Therese Maria Gräfin v. Waldburg zu Wolfegg u. Waldsee** * Petersburg 15.7.1939 = Kisslegg 16.5.1962 Mario Graf v. Matuschka * Oppeln 27.2.1931, and has issue:

XIII 1b. **Stephanie Gräfin v. Matuschka** * Salzburg 22.6.1963

2b. **Michael Graf v. Matuschka** * Salzburg 8.12.1964

XII 2a. **Friedrich Maximilian Willibald Johann Nepomuk Michael Anton Maria Graf v. Waldburg zu Wolfegg u. Waldsee** * Prag 29.10.1940

3a. **Eugen Wunibald Hubert Augustinus Lukas Maria Graf v. Waldburg zu Wolfegg u. Waldsee** * Krzemusch b. Dux 18.10.1943

4a. **Franz Willibald Ignatius Lukas Sanoti Graf v. Waldburg zu Wolfegg u. Waldsee** * Wolfegg 1.11.1946

5a. **Elisabeth Marie Walburga Magdalena Rosa Gräfin v. Waldburg zu Wolfegg u. Waldsee** * Wolfegg 19.2.1948

6a. **Maria Sidonia Walburga Katherina Gräfin v. Waldburg zu Wolfegg u. Waldsee** * Wolfegg 19.2.1948

7a. **Monika Maria Anna Antonia Walburga Gräfin v. Waldburg zu Wolfegg u. Waldsee** * Kisslegg 2.2.1952

XI		(i)	**Maria Elisabeth Bona Walburga Josefa Laurentia Gräfin v. Waldburg zu Wolfegg u. Waldsee** * Waldsee 10.8.1904 = Wolfegg 16.11.1926 **Maximilian 2 Herzog v. Hohenberg** * Wien 29.9.1902 + Wien 8.1.1962, and had issue see elsewhere

(j)   a son * & + 1908

(k)   **Heinrich Maria Willibald Benedikt Albrecht Philipp Ulrich Graf v. Waldburg zu Wolfegg u. Waldsee** * Wolfegg 16.9.1911 = Sigmaringen 4.1.1942 **Maria Antonia Prinzessin v. Hohenzollern-Sigmaringen** * Sigmaringen 19.2.1921 dau. of Friedrich Viktor Fürst v. Hohenzollern-Sigmaringen, and has issue:

XII

1a.   **Maria Sidonia Margarete Elisabeth Walburga Caspara Meinrada Barbara Gräfin v. Waldburg zu Wolfegg u. Waldsee** * Freiburg i. Br. 4.12.1942

2a.   **Maria Sophie Therese Viktoria Walburga Elisabeth Gräfin v. Waldburg zu Wolfegg u. Waldsee** * Krauchenwies 9.7.1946

3a.   **Maria Friedrich Maximilian Wunibald Meinrad Michael Gebhard Konstantin Graf v. Waldburg zu Wolfegg u. Waldsee** * Wolfegg 21.5.1948

4a.   **Maria Josef Anton Willibald Fidelis Petrus Canisius Graf v. Waldburg zu Wolfegg u. Waldsee** * Heinrichsburg 15.12.1950

5a.   **Maria Margarete Theresa Walburga Dionysia Gräfin v. Waldburg zu Wolfegg u. Waldsee** * Heinrichsburg 26.2.1953

6a.   **Maria Anna Adelheid Jacobe Walburga Petrusa Bernhardine Gräfin v. Waldburg zu Wolfegg u. Waldsee** * Heinrichsburg 20.8.1954

7a.   **Maria Hubert Willibald Pius Johannes Nepomuk Graf v. Waldburg zu Wolfegg u. Waldsee** * Heinrichsburg 25.6.1956

8a.   **Maria Theresia Viktoria Walburga Franziska Epiphania Gräfin v. Waldburg zu Wolfegg u. Waldsee** * Heinrichsburg 8.1.1958

9a.   **Maria Jaokobe Walburga Meinrada Sebastiana Gräfin v. Waldburg zu Wolfegg u. Waldsee** * Heinrichsburg 20.1.1960

10a. **Ludmila Walburga Martha Ida Johanna Vianney Gräfin v. Waldburg zu Wolfegg u. Waldsee** * Biberach a.d. Riss 29.7.1964

X

c)   **Joseph August Maria Paul Willibald Graf v. Waldburg zu Wolfegg u. Waldsee** * Waldsee 14.3.1864 + Waldsee 29.4.1922

d)   **Elisabeth Bona Maria Walpurga Josepha Gräfin v. Waldburg zu Wolfegg u. Waldsee** * Waldsee 3.12.1867 + Weinsberg 16.2.1947 = Wolfegg 5.9.1893 Anton Graf v. Stolberg-Wernigerode * Tervueren 23.8.1864 + Peterswaldau 4.2.1905, and had issue:

XI

(a)   **Franz Xaver Maria Joseph Martin Anton Hubertus Ignatius Sebastian Georg Willibald Vincenz v. Paul Leo Graf v. Stolberg Wernigerode** * Peterswaldau 19.7.1894 + Gostynie, Poland as Prisoner of War 4.5.1947 = München 31.5.1922 **Barbara Princess of Naples and Sicily** * Schloss Nymphenberg 14.12.1902 dau. of Ferdinand Prince of Naples and Sicily, Duke of Calabria, and had issue:

XII

1a.   **Elisabeth Bona Maria Alfonsa Ferdinanda Josefa Antonie Juliane Gräfin v. Stolberg-Wernigerode** * Peterswaldau 17.4.1923 = Lindau 26.1.1944 Rüdiger Graf v. Stillfried-Rattonitz * Silbitz 14.7.1923, and has issue:

XIII

1b.   **Barbara Gräfin v. Stillfried-Rattonitz** * Moos 22.12.1948 + Lindau 29.3.1951

2b.   **Maria Gabriele Christine Gräfin v. Stillfried-Rattonitz** * Lindau 13.8.1950

130

XIII   3b.   **Maria Pia Gräfin v. Stillfried-Rattonitz** * Lindau 20.4.1956

XII   2a.   **Maria Josefa Gabriele Antonia Gebharda Gräfin v. Stolberg-Wernigerode**
                * Peterswaldau 11.5.1924

          3a.   **Ferdinand Anton Maria Christian Friedrich Leopold Franz Josef Pius
                Gabriel Graf v. Stolberg-Wernigerode** * Peterswaldau 4.7.1925

          4a.   **Sophie Marie Antonie Henrike Thaddea Gabriele Gräfin v. Stolberg-
                Wernigerode** * Peterswaldau 21.12.1926

XI   (b)   **Maria Anna Sophie Clothilde Josepha Elisabetha Bona Cäcilia Agnes Franziska
                Walburga Candida Gräfin v. Stolberg-Wernigerode** * Peterswaldau 3.10.1895
                + St. Antoniushaus b. Waldbreitbach 2.2.1946

          (c)   **Joseph Ludwig Maria Friedrich Leopold Martin Wunibald Gabriel Graf v. Stolberg-
                Wernigerode** * Gries 23.3.1900 X Gablenz 14.4.1945

X   e)   **Ludwig Maria Josef Wunibald Petrus Pius Graf v. Waldburg zu Wolfegg u. Waldsee**
          * Waldsee 27.10.1871 + Baden-Baden 24.6.1906 = Salzburg 17.4.1902 Anna Gräfin v.
          Galen * Meran 17.11.1881 dau. of Hubert Graf v. Galen, and had issue:

XI   (a)   **Marie Sophie Huberta Sidonia Walburga Gräfin v. Waldburg zu Wolfegg u. Waldsee**
                * Kisslegg 22.4.1904 = Wolfegg 31.1.1928 **Georg Graf Henckel Frhr. v. Donnersmarck**
                * Grambschütz 5.8.1902, and has issue see elsewhere

          (b)   **Hubert Maria Aloysius Wunibald Pius Graf v. Waldburg zu Wolfegg u. Waldsee**
                * Kisslegg 7.1.1906 = Adldorf 12.9.1933 **Anna Elisabeth Gräfin v. Arco-Valley**
                * Adldorf 10.8.1909 dau. of Maximilian Graf v. Arco-Valley, and has issue:

XII   1a.   **Ludwig Karl Maximilian Hubert Willibald Modestus Graf v. Waldburg zu
                Wolfegg u. Waldsee** * Pähl 15.6.1934 = Überacken 7.9.1960 **Stephanie
                Prinzessin v. Schönburg-Waldenburg** * Gusow 22.9.1938 dau. of Georg Prinz v.
                Schönburg-Waldenburg, and has issue:

XIII   1b.   **Elisabeth Pauline Anna Amelie Marie Waldburga Gräfin v. Waldburg zu
                     Wolfegg u. Waldsee** * Möckmühl 7.6.1962

              2b.   **Hubertus Georg Karl Maria Willibald Johannes Graf v. Waldburg zu
                     Wolfegg u. Waldsee** * Möckmühl 15.5.1964

XII   2a.   **Maximilian Otto Wunibald Maria Hubert Agapitus Graf v. Waldburg zu Wolfegg
                u. Waldsee** * Adldorf 18.8.1935 = Unsleben 16.7.1960 **Henriette Freiin. v.
                Habermann** * Würzburg 8.11.1937 dau. of Hugo Frhr. v. Habermann, and has
                issue:

XIII   1b.   **Christoph Hubertus Willibald Maria Maximilian Eusebius Graf v.
                     Waldburg zu Wolfegg u. Waldsee** * München 2.12.1961

XII   3a.   **Franz Ferdinand Maria Hubert Willibald Johannes Graf v. Waldburg zu
                Wolfegg u. Waldsee** * Augsburg 8.2.1937

          4a.   **Karl Ernst Maria Hubert Wunibald Dionys Graf v. Waldburg zu Wolfegg u.
                Waldsee** * Augsburg 17.11.1940

          5a.   **Maria Assunta Walburga Adelheid Anna Huberta Gräfin v. Waldburg zu
                Wolfegg u. Waldsee** * Tagmersheim 1.11.1950

X	f)	**Heinrich Maria Willibald Josef Stanislaus Graf v. Waldburg zu Wolfegg u. Waldsee** * Wolfegg 30.3.1874 + Sonthofen 19.2.1949 = Buckfast 7.6.1934 Frederica Marwin * Jaffrey, New Hampshire, U.S.A. 7.6.1899 s.p.

IX d. **Helene Sophie Therese Gräfin v. Arco-Zinneberg** * Zinneberg 8.11.1837 + Traunegg 4.3.1897 = München 20.10.1856 Heinrich Frhr. v.u. zu Franckenstein * Offenburg 31.5.1826 + Wien 15.10.1883, and had issue:

X a) **Margarete Leopoldine Maria Josephine Gabriele Domenika Freiin. v.u. zu Franckenstein** * München 6.7.1869 + Linz 30.3.1938 = Traunegg b. Wels 16.7.1891 **August Graf v.u. zu Eltz gen. Faust v. Stromberg** * Linz 29.3.1866 + Tillysburg 10.9.1921, and had issue see elsewhere

   b) **Konrad Maria Leopold Josef Hubertus Ignatius Aloysius Theodor Frhr. v.u. zu Franckenstein** * Traunegg 1.7.1875 + Heiligenkreuz 11.12.1938 = Wispach 2.5.1906 Anna Gräfin Esterházy v. Galántha * Salzburg 16.2.1886 dau. of Daniel Graf Esterházy v. Galántha, and had issue:

XI (a) **Heinrich Maria Franz Konrad Joseph Daniel Casimir Benediktus Bonifazius Aloysius Stanislaus Johannes Raphael Paul Arbogast Frhr. v.u. zu Franckenstein** * Traunegg 16.7.1908 = Mirskofen 23.10.1934 Maria Pia Freiin. v. Fürstenberg * Paderborn 22.3.1905 + Maltepe, Turkey 5.12.1961 dau. of Friedrich Frhr. v. Fürstenberg; = (2) Istanbul 19.4.1966 Christine Miras * Istanbul 15.8.1917, and has issue :

    by 1st marriage:

XII 1a. **Conrad Maria Arbogast Heinrich Hubertus Friedrich Joseph Tarcisius Johannes-Chrysostomus Anton Pius Stephan Achilles Odilo Placidus Euphemius Frhr. v.u. zu Franckenstein** * Kadiköy, Turkey 27.8.1935 = Salzburg 10.10.1964 Ingrid Müller * Hallein, Salzburg 15.10.1941 dau. of Wilhelm Müller, and has issue:

XIII 1b. **Nicolaus Frhr. v.u. zu Franckenstein** * München 22.5.1966

XII 2a. **Arbogast-Maria Eugen Leopold Joachim Heinrich Joseph Conrad Placidus Tarcisius Odilo Pankratius Friedrich Thomas Johannes Hubertus Emanuel Frhr. v.u. zu Franckenstein** * Istanbul 12.12.1937

    3a. **Maria-Pia Odette Anna Eugenie Praxedes Ive Helene Therese Agnes Elisabeth Ludovika Margarethe Godleva Freiin. v.u. zu Franckenstein** * Istanbul 15.10.1939

    4a. **Maria-Gratia Guendoline Johanna Anna Euphemia Fotini Praxedes Elisabeth Helene Godleva Margarethe Ludovica Afra Henriette Huberta Agnes Freiin. v.u. zu Franckenstein** * Istanbul 21.5.1941

    5a. **Rhabanus-Maurus Frhr. v.u. zu Franckenstein** * Istanbul 5.1.1943

    6a. **Johannes der Täufer Maria Joseph Arbogast Heinrich Conrad Rochus Tarcisius Frhr. v.u. zu Franckenstein** * Istanbul 26.4.1946

XI (b) **Joseph Maria Konrad Michael Benedikt Maurus Placidius Aloysius Hieronymus Frhr. v.u. zu Franckenstein** * Traunegg 30.9.1910 = 23.2.1942 Kay Boyle * St. Pulis, Minnesota 19.2.1903, and has issue:

XII 1a. **Felicitas Freiin. v.u. zu Franckenstein** * New York 3.12.1942

    2a. **Johannes Frhr. v.u. zu Franckenstein** * 23.12.1943

132

XI

    (c) **Ludwig Maria Conrad Franz Joseph Benedikt Stanislaus Paul Maria Frhr. v.u. zu Franckenstein** * Traunegg 12.11.1914 + Vrsac, Yugoslavia 9.9.1945 = Bregenz 15.2.1943 Dorothea v. Kobbe * Lindau 28.10.1921 dau. of Hans v. Kobbe, and had issue:

XII

        1a. **Ludwig Erkinger Maria Frhr. v.u. zu Franckenstein** * Bregenz 13.8.1944

        2a. **Josef Ferdinand Maria Frhr. v.u. zu Franckenstein** * Bregenz 13.8.1944

XI

    (d) **Maria-Helene Margarethe Josepha Benedikta Praxedes Theresia Sophie Agnes Hildegardis Rosario Freiin. v.u. zu Franckenstein** * Traunegg 2.10.1917 + Hall, Tirol 14.5.1963

    (e) **Anna Maria Johanna Emanuela Margarethe Alacoque Helene Therese Sophie Benedikta Ignatia Agnes Aloysia Elisabeth Praxedes Freiin. v.u. zu Franckenstein** * Traunegg 8.6.1920

X

    c) **Franz Leopold Maria Maximilian Joseph Nikolaus Hugo Frhr. v.u. zu Franckenstein** * Meran 9.4.1879 + Windischgarsten 27.2.1943 = Prag 8.2.1911 Edina Gräfin v. Kolowrat-Krakowsky-Liebsteinsky * Reichenau, Böh. 19.10.1885 + Lambach 8.2.1959 dau. of Zdenko Graf v. Kolowrat-Krakowsky-Liebsteinsky, and had issue:

XI

    (a) **Franz Maria Konrad Heinrich Zdenko Joseph Ignatius Aloysius Salvator Frhr. v.u. zu Franckenstein** * Sonnwend 21.7.1912 + Windischgarsten ... 1950

    (b) **Olga Maria Margarethe Edina Franziska Leontine Josefa Ignatia Bonaventura Freiin. v.u. zu Franckenstein** * Sonnwend 14.7.1914 = ... 1958 ... v. Ekhel

IX

    e. **Ludwig Graf v. Arco-Zinneberg** * München 3.1.1840 + München 20.11.1882 = (1) Krieckenbeck 30.10.1872 Adolfine Gräfin v. Schaesberg * 6.8.1854 + Maxlrain 23.5.1874 dau. of Julius Graf v. Schaesberg; = (2) Prag 10.2.1879 Josephine Prinzessin v. Lobkowicz * Wien 10.2.1853 + Maxlrain 24.11.1898 dau. of Joseph Prinz v. Lobkowicz, and had issue:

    by 1st marriage:

X

    a) **Walburga Gräfin v. Arco-Zinneberg** * Maxlrain 20.9.1873 + St. Johann bei Pfatter 25.8.1958 = Maxlrain 24.7.1893 Otto Graf v.u. zu Lerchenfeld auf Köfering u. Schönberg * München 2.10.1869 + Salzburg 5.10.1938, and had issue:

XI

    (a) **Ludwig Maximilian Hugo Heinrich Joseph Ferdinand Konrad Franziskus Philipp Urban Graf v.u. zu Lerchenfeld auf Köfering u. Schönberg** * Bamberg 25.5.1894 ✗ Bersnicourt près Reims 14.5.1917

    (b) **Josef Hugo Ferdinand Ludwig Max Emmeran Otto Leopold Franz Hippolyt Johann Stanislaus Graf v.u. zu Lerchenfeld auf Köfering u. Schönberg** * Bamberg 6.5.1895 + München 27.7.1936 = Tetschen 5.7.1922 Sophie Gräfin Thun v. Hohenstein * Prag 28.11.1901 — div. dau. of Jaroslav Fürst Thun v. Hohenstein, and had issue:

XII

        1a. **Ludwig Hugo Graf v.u. zu Lerchenfeld auf Köfering u. Schönberg** * Tetschen 20.3.1923 = Wolbeck 1.9.1948 Sibylle Gräfin v. Merveldt * Westerwinkel 16.6.1923 dau. of Franziskus Graf v. Merveldt, and has issue:

XIII

        1b. **Isabelle Maria Walburga Sophie Helene Huberta Michaela Gräfin v.u. zu Lerchenfeld auf Köfering u. Schönberg** * Köfering 11.1.1950

        2b. **Philippus Neri Johannes Peter Maria Joseph Franz Ludwig Hugo Hubertus Michael Emmeran Graf v.u. zu Lerchenfeld auf Köfering u. Schönberg** * Köfering 25.5.1952

XIII		3b. **Daisy Marie Elisabeth Huberta Michaela Julia Gräfin v.u. zu Lerchenfeld auf Köfering u. Schönberg** * Köfering 22.5.1953 + Köfering 15.12.1965

XI   (c)   **Hugo Otto Emmeran Maria Josef Ludwig Adolf Ferdinand Alexis Graf v.u. zu Lerchenfeld auf Köfering u. Schönberg** * Köfering 16.7.1896 + St. Johann b. Pfatter 16.2.1960 = Zeist 23.9.1931 Jkvr. Telma Pauw van Wieldrecht * Haus Silvana, Boschen Duin 18.10.1907 dau. of Jkr. Henry Pauw van Wieldrecht, − div. s.p.

           (d)   **Heinrich Maria Otto Emmeran Ludwig Graf v.u. zu Lerchenfeld auf Köfering u. Schönberg** * Köfering 23.7.1897 = Wien 18.5.1932 Sarlota Gräfin Bethlen v. Bethlen * Klausenburg 31.5.1897 + 13.10.1964 dau. of Ödön Graf Bethlen v. Bethlen s.p.

           (e)   **Marie Clara Josepha Walburga Anna Sidonia Emmerentia Adolfine Isabella Johanna Felizitas Gräfin v.u. zu Lerchenfeld auf Köfering u. Schönberg** * St. Johann 16.5.1899

           (f)   **Sophie Josepha Maria Rosalia Walburga Adolfine Emmerentia Anna Gabriele Gräfin v.u. zu Lerchenfeld auf Köfering u. Schönberg** * St. Johann 16.6.1900 + Dornach 15.1.1951 = Belgrade 27.4.1930 Alexander Raceta * Burda 23.9.1897, and had issue:

XII   1a.   **Draginja Sujesana Raceta** * Belgrade 10.1.1931

XI   (g)   **Rosa Sidonia Wilhelmine Walburga Gräfin v.u. zu Lerchenfeld auf Köfering u. Schönberg** * Köfering 12.5.1910 = St. Johann 9.10.1945 Vittorio Schwarz * Teplitz-Schönau 15.7.1894, s.p.

      by 2nd marriage:

X   b)   **Maria Sidonia Gräfin v. Arco-Zinneberg** * Maxlrain 26.7.1880 + Ostrowine 11.4.1928 = München 5.2.1902 Ferdinand Frhr. v. Twickel * Lüttinghof 2.11.1863 + Ettal 1.12.1938, and had issue:

XI   (a)   **Maria Immaculata Zdenka Anna Hedwig Josephine Benedikta Walburga Freiin. v. Twickel** * München 8.12.1901 = (1) Ostrowine 11.4.1923 August Graf Droste zu Vischering * Vischering 17.7.1898 + Darfeld 3.4.1931; = (2) Vischering 2.9.1943 Friedrich Karl Graf v. Westphalen zu Fürstenberg * Laër 22.4.1898, and had issue:

           by 1st marriage:

XII   1a.   **Max Ferdinand Maria Rosario Klemens August Heinrich Zdenko Hubertus Antonius Georgius Dionysius Graf Droste zu Vischering** * Vischering 9.9.1924 X Guben 8.3.1945

XI   (b)   **Johannes Maria Leo Ferdinand Alfons Hubertus Cajus Markus Frhr. v. Twickel** * Ostrowine 22.4.1903 = (1) Wien 15.5.1944 Maria Johanna Gräfin v. Waldstein * Iglau 15.1.1922 + Trebitsch 10.7.1945 dau. of Joseph Graf v. Waldstein; = (2) Westerwinkel 21.4.1949 Maria Gräfin v. Merveldt * Lembeck 5.7.1922 dau. of Ferdinand Graf v. Merveldt, and has issue:

           by 1st marriage:

XII   1a.   **Maria Zdenka Freiin. v. Twickel** * Trebitsch 21.4.1945

           by 2nd marriage:

              2a.   **Ludovika Maria Ida Josefa Walburga Freiin. v. Twickel** * Lembeck 20.3.1950

3a. **Ferdinand Johannes Markus Josef Michael Hubertus Frhr. v. Twickel**
* Lembeck 16.4.1951

4a. **Walburga Elisabeth Sidonia Michaela Freiin. v. Twickel** * Lembeck 28.9.1952

5a. **Markus Maria Johannes Carl Pius Frhr. v. Twickel** * Lembeck 23.7.1954
+ Recklinghausen 8.10.1954

6a. **Theresia Alexandra Flora Freiin. v. Twickel** * Lembeck 24.11.1955
+ Westerwinkel 29.8.1956

7a. **Polyxena Patricia Josefine Hedwig Freiin. v. Twickel** * Gelsenkirchen
13.3.1959

8a. **Christine Nikola Elisabeth Zdenka Walburga Freiin. v. Twickel** * Gelsenkirchen
9.1.1963

(c) **Maria Elisabeth Walburga Josephine Hedwig Adolfine Mamertina Bonifacia Freiin. v.
Twickel** * Ostrowine 11.5.1904 = Ettal 17.6.1943 Richard Frhr. v. Geymüller
* Kamenitz a.d. L. 2.4.1894 missing since 15.5.1945, and had issue:

1a. **Rudolf Frhr. v. Geymüller** * Kamenitz 2.9.1944

2a. **Maria Zdenka Freiin. v. Geymüller** * Bad Ischl 6.11.1945

3a. **Johannes Frhr. v. Geymüller** * Bad Ischl 6.11.1945

(d) **Maria Huberta Theresia Hedwig Petrus Freiin. v. Twickel** * Ostrowine 16.10.1905

(e) **Maria Immaculata Sophia Josephine Theresia Hedwig Anna Christian Walburga
Eusebia Freiin. v. Twickel** * Ostrowine 11.12.1906

(f) **Maria Monica Rosario Adolfine Theresia Josepha Magdalene Remigia Placida Freiin.
v. Twickel** * Ostrowine 1.10.1908 = Ettal 25.3.1943 Ludwig Frhr. v. Leonrod
* München 17.9.1906 X Berlin 26.8.1944; = (2) Schmiechen 31.7.1948 Hans
Wiedersperger Frhr. v. Wiedersperg-Leonrod * Pardubitz 10.5.1903, and has issue:

by 2nd marriage:

1a. **Ferdinand Maria Johannes Jakobinus Rupertus Rasso Wilhelm Friedrich
Wiedersperger Frhr. v. Wiedersperg-Leonrod** * München 25.7.1950

2a. **Maria Assumpta Josefine Polyxene Clara Sidonie Monika Wiedersperger
Freiin. v. Wiedersperg-Leonrod** * München 8.8.1953

(g) **Maria Josefine Anna Hedwig Walburga Elisabeth Milburga Freiin. v. Twickel**
* Ostrowine 19.2.1910

(h) **Ludwig Joseph Maria Ferdinand Hubertus Georg Ignatius Antonius Thomas
Eustachis Frhr. v. Twickel** * Ostrowine 20.9.1911 + Eisenach 13.3.1945
= Coughton Court 20.6.1939 Anna Barbara Throckmorton * London 10.10.1911
dau. of Richard Courtenay Brabazon Throckmorton, and had issue:

1a. **Johannes Robert Frhr. v. Twickel** * Berlin 25.7.1940

2a. **Alexander Frhr. v. Twickel** * Choustnak, Böh. 14.11.1941

3a. **Ludwig Frhr. v. Twickel** * & + March 1945

(i) **Ignatius von Loyala Josef Maria Hubertus Aloysius Ferdinand Antonius v. Padua
Friedrich Leopold Frhr. v. Twickel** * Ostrowine 10.6.1918 X North Italy
5.4.1945

(j) **Maria Theresia Gertrudis Margarete Alacoque Hedwig Walburga Marcella Philippa
Katharina v. Siena Freiin. v. Twickel** * Ostrowine 25.4.1920 = Ettal 20.5.1948
Karl Frhr. v. Moreau * München 10.7.1916 s.p.

X	c)	**Maria Josef Maximilian Antonius Ludwig Melchior Graf v. Arco-Zinneberg** * Maxlrain 3.9.1881 + München 23.11.1924 = (1) Wien 29.4.1907 Wilhelmine Prinzessin v. Auersperg * Rothenhaus 14.6.1884 + Maxlrain 1.12.1919 dau. of Engelbert Prinz v. Auersperg; = (2) Wien 2.6.1921 Christiane Gräfin v. Clam-Gallas * Grafenstein 5.9.1884 + Tannenmühle 26.10.1947 dau. of Franz Graf v. Clam-Gallas, and had issue:

by 1st marriage:

XI	(a)	**Maria Maximilian Joseph Ludwig Engelbert Gabriel Ignatius Antonius Franziskus Leonhard Viktor Wilhelm Petrus v. A. Caspar Graf v. Arco-Zinneberg** * München 23.3.1908 + Wien 19.5.1937
	(b)	**Maria Engelbert Servatius Ignatius Stanislaus Ludwig Johannes Nepomuk Melchior Graf v. Arco-Zinneberg** * München 13.5.1909 = Regensburg 2.5.1946 Eugenie Gräfin Schaffgotsch gen. Semperfrei v.u. zu Kynast u. Greiffenstein * Remolkwitz 16.1.1921 dau. of Hans Ulrich Graf Schaffgotsch gen. Semperfrei v.u. zu Kynast u. Greiffenstein and has issue:

XII	1a.	**Andreas Graf v. Arco-Zinneberg** * 20.2.1959
	2a.	**Ulrich Graf v. Arco-Zinneberg** * 18.3.1963

XI	(c)	**Marie-Gabrielle Ludwiga Josephine Sidonie Walpurga Elisabeth Franziska Sophie Monika Balthasare Gräfin v. Arco-Zinneberg** * München 25.8.1910 = München 10.7.1934 Anton Graf v. Arco-Valley * St. Martin 5.2.1897 + Salzburg 29.6.1945, and had issue:

XII	1a.	**Maria Wilhelmine Gabrielle Emilie Leopoldine Franziska Gräfin v. Arco-Valley** * Pähl 3.12.1935
	2a.	**Maria Ludmilla Christiane Gertrud Gabrielle Pia Gräfin v. Arco-Valley** * Pähl 5.5.1937
	3a.	**Maria Antonia Gräfin v. Arco-Valley** * Pähl 20.8.1940 = St. Martin 2.8.1966 Michael Graf v. Spaur u. Flavon * Milano 19.1.1939
	4a.	**Max Joseph Graf v. Arco-Valley** * Pähl 26.4.1942 + St. Martin 16.7.1942
	5a.	**Leopoldine Gräfin v. Arco-Valley** * Pähl 19.6.1943

XI	(d)	**Maria Ferdinand Ignatius Joseph Ludwig Wilhelm Antonius Franziskus Valentin Caspar Graf v. Arco-Zinneberg** * München 11.2.1912
	(e)	**Maria Ludwig Gottfried Engelbert Ignatius Franziskus Konrad Aloysius Judas Thaddäus Katherina Melchior Graf v. Arco-Zinneberg** * München 25.11.1913 X Projawino, Russia 18.2.1942 = Moos 25.1.1940 **Maria Theresia Gräfin v. Preysing-Lichtenegg-Moos** * Moos 23.3.1922 dau. of Johann-Georg Graf v. Preysing-Lichtenegg-Moos, and had issue:

XII	1a.	**Rupprecht-Maximilian Maria Ludwig Joseph Georg Konrad Thaddäus Hubertus Felix Sebastian Caspar Graf v. Arco-Zinneberg** * Pähl 14.1.1941

XI	(f)	**Maria Rosario Josephine Pazifica Sidonia Gräfin v. Arco-Zinneberg** * München 2.10.1915
	(g)	**Maria Oldaricus-Philipp Kaspar Graf v. Arco-Zinneberg** * Maxlrain 12.12.1917 = Nieder-Altaich 26.9.1943 **Maria Theresia Gräfin v. Preysing-Lichtenegg-Moos** * Moos 23.3.1922 dau. of Johann Georg Graf v. Preysing-Lichtenegg-Moos, and widow of brother, and had issue:

XII   1a.   **Maria Ludwig Karl Hieronymus Oldaricus Georg Joseph Sylverius Peter Paul Melchior Graf v. Arco-Zinneberg** * Moos 20.6.1944 + Moos 14.8.1944

         2a.   **Ripprand Maria Franz Ulrich Gaspare del Buffalo Christophorus Jakob Kaspar Graf v. Arco-Zinneberg** * München 25.7.1955

XI   (h)   **Walburga Gräfin v. Arco-Zinneberg** * Maxlrain ... 11.1919 + Maxlrain ... 1.1920

by 2nd marriage:

         (i)   **Maria Sophie Wilhelmine Josephine Franziska Clotilde Anna Elisabeth Eusebia Balthasara Gräfin v. Arco-Zinneberg** * München 15.12.1922 = Tannenmühle 9.6.1946 Adolf Graf v.u. zu Trauttmansdorff-Weinsberg * Prag 1.6.1925, and has issue:

XII   1a.   **Maria Wilhelmine Theresa Ida Christine Gräfin v.u. zu Trauttmansdorff-Weinsberg** * Wien 3.2.1947

         2a.   **Marie Therese Christiane Josefine Ulrike Gräfin v.u. zu Trauttmansdorff-Weinsberg** * Innsbruck 4.7.1948

         3a.   **Marie-Antoinette Ida Gertrude Eugenie Eva Gräfin v.u. zu Trauttmansdorff-Weinsberg** * Dippethub 24.12.1953

         4a.   **Joseph Adolf Engelbert Graf v.u. zu Trauttmansdorff-Weinsberg** * Alt-Lengbach 14.10.1958

X   d)   **Ferdinand Maria Joseph Maximilian Ludwig Antonius Aemilian Balthasar Graf v. Arco-Zinneberg** * Maxlrain 10.9.1882 + München 2.5.1940 = (1) Heltorf 15.8.1922 Maria Gräfin v. Spee * Ahrenthal 1.6.1890 + München 17.2.1928 dau. of Wilhelm Graf v. Spee; = (2) Kirchheim 3.10.1929 Marie Gräfin v. Fugger-Glött * Kirchheim 29.4.1894 + München 13.3.1935 dau. of Carl Ernst 1st Fürst Fugger v. Glött, and had issue:

by 1st marriage:

XI   (a)   **Melanie Maria Josephine Elisabeth Ernestine Wilhelmine Huberta Kaspar Donata Adelaide Gräfin v. Arco-Zinneberg** * München 8.6.1923

         (b)   **Ludwig Maria Joseph Ferdinand Johannes Baptista Hubertus Melchior Thaddäus Pius Constantinus Romanus Graf v. Arco-Zinneberg** * München 11.3.1925 ⚔ Leitmeritz 4.2.1945

         (c)   **Wilhelm Emmanuel Maria Ferdinand Ludwig Joseph Hubertus Balthasar Aegidius Marcellus Graf v. Arco-Zinneberg** * München 1.11.1926 missing in Russia since January 1945

by 2nd marriage:

         (d)   **Karl Antonius v. Padua Maria Ernst Ludwig Joseph Ferdinand Konrad v. Parzham Petrus Canisius Kaspar Anastasius Bernhardus Graf v. Arco-Zinneberg** * München 18.8.1931 = Majern Kr. Neunberg 6.4.1961 **Hedwig Gräfin Henckel v. Donnersmarck** * Grambschütz 16.6.1935 dau. of Georg Graf Henckel v. Donnersmarck, and has issue:

XII   1a.   **Marie-Gabriele Gräfin v. Arco-Zinneberg** * Stuttgart 28.5.1962

         2a.   **Anna-Sophie Gräfin v. Arco-Zinneberg** * Stuttgart 10.6.1964

XI   (e)   **Albert Magnus Maria Karl Ludwig Ferdinand Antonius v. Padua Konrad v. Parzham Melchior Martin Marinus Graf v. Arco-Zinneberg** * München 12.11.1932 = Kirchheim 10.5.1961 Elisabeth Freiin. v. Hertling * München 4.6.1932 dau. of Georg Frhr. v. Hertling and has issue:

XII		1a. **Ulrich Maria Joseph-Ernst Georg Ferdinand Albertus Magnus Rupertus Graf v. Arco-Zinneberg** * Krumbach 8.12.1963

IX f. **Karl Maria Rupert Ludwig Theobold Graf v. Arco-Zinneberg** * Zinneberg 1.7.1841 + Blühenbach b. Gastein 25.8.1873 = Gracht 20.7.1867 Mathilde Gräfin Wolff-Metternich zur Gracht * Bonn 14.5.1840 + Graz 8.6.1925, dau. of Friedrich Graf Wolff-Metternich zur Gracht and had issue:

X a) **Mathilde Leopoldine Irene Elisabeth Maria Huberta Theresia Gräfin v. Arco-Zinneberg** * Görz 16.1.1869 + Grado 28.9.1942 = ... Arthur Trankel * ... + ...

IX g. **Irene Gräfin v. Arco-Zinneberg** * Zinneberg 18.12.1842 + Neckarhausen 1.11.1917 = München 8.8.1861 Friedrich Graf v. Oberndorff * Mannheim 15.2.1829 + Bregenz 4.8.1913, and had issue:

X a) **Franz Albert Alfred Maria Fortunatus Graf v. Oberndorff** * Neckarhausen 25.7.1862 + Karlsruhe 1.5.1920 = Gracht 6.7.1889 **Therese Gräfin Wolff-Metternich zur Gracht** * Frauenthal 2.3.1864 + St. Blasien 3.11.1920 dau. of Max Graf Wolff-Metternich zur Gracht, and had issue:

XI (a) **Hedwig Maria Theresia Irene Fortunata Gräfin v. Oberndorff** * Neckarhausen 20.7.1890 + Neckarhausen 8.3.1933

(b) **Friedrich Anton Maria Fortunatus Graf v. Oberndorff** * Neckarhausen 20.12.1891 = Weinheim 25.1.1920 Margarete-Marie Freiin. v. Berckheim * Weinheim 25.9.1897 + Neckarhausen 1.5.1954 dau. of Sigmund Graf v. Berckheim, and has issue:

XII 1a. **Franz-Xaver Anton Sigmund Berhard Maria Fortunatus Gebhard Graf v. Oberndorff** * Neckarhausen 18.7.1921 X Hungary 11.1.1945

2a. **Johannes Vincenz Karl Georg Hubertus Maria Fortunatus Bonaventura Graf v. Oberndorff** * Neckarhausen 18.7.1922 X Russia 3.10.1941

3a. **Wolfgang Peter Antonius Philipp Kaspar Melchior Balthasar Maria Fortunatus Graf v. Oberndorff** * Neckarhausen 7.1.1925

4a. **Maria Elisabeth Adolfine Therese Irene Margarethe Monica Fortunata Gräfin v. Oberndorff** * Neckarhausen 4.4.1928

5a. **Walburga Sidonia Alfreda Theresia Constantia Maria Fortunata Gräfin v. Oberndorff** * Neckarhausen 27.7.1932 = Neckarhausen 8.9.1950 Wittigo-Johann Graf v. Einsiedel * Vietnitz 28.11.1919, and has issue:

XIII 1b. **Sandro Florian Beccone Graf v. Einsiedel** * Heidelberg 31.7.1951

2b. **Andreas Jean-Paul Hubertus Maria Graf v. Einsiedel** * Heidelberg 28.1.1953

3b. **Georgina Margarit Florence Maria Gräfin v. Einsiedel** * Heidelberg 5.6.1954

4b. **Fabian Graf v. Einsiedel** * 20.1.1959

XII 6a. **Georg Hubertus Carolus Petrus Konrad v. Parzham Franziskus Maria Fortunatus Graf v. Oberndorff** * Mannheim 27.4.1938 + Heidelberg 3.3.1965

XI (c) **Irene Maria Fortunata Gräfin v. Oberndorff** * Neckarhausen 5.1.1895 + Schönburg,Württ 21.12.1920

138

X   b)   **Antonia Maria Fortunata Gräfin v. Oberndorff** * Neckarhausen 27.9.1863
+ Neckarhausen 21.10.1951

c)   **Maximilian Karl Maria Fortunatus Graf v. Oberndorff** * Neckarhausen 30.8.1867
+ Klein Togo 1.6.1900

d)   **Wolfgang Peter Maria Fortunatus Karl Graf v. Oberndorff** * Neckarhausen 25.7.1871
+ Münster 21.8.1906 = Wiessentheid 15.5.1906 Maria Gräfin v. Schönborn-Wiesentheid
* Wiesentheid 20.1.1872 + Wiesentheid 9.7.1920 dau. of Arthur Graf v. Schönborn-
Wiesentheid s.p.

IX   h.   **Anna Christiane Irene Renate Gräfin v. Arco-Zinneberg** * München 28.2.1844 + Roma
17.4.1927 = München 12.5.1866 Alfred Graf zu Stolberg-Stolberg * Brauna 18.11.1835
+ at Sea 1.10.1880 and had issue:

X   a)   **Friedrich Leopold Christian Petrus Maria Graf zu Stolberg-Stolberg** * Gimborn
1.7.1868 + Ullstadt 4.9.1955 = Ahrenthal 26.4.1922 Maria Gräfin v. Spee * Wesel
23.6.1895 dau. of Lepold Graf v. Spee, and had issue:

XI   (a)   **Friedrich Leopold Alfred Hermann Christian Josef Petrus Johannes Evangalist
Maria Graf zu Stolberg-Stolberg** * Brauna 28.2.1923 + Sandar b. Tiflis 8.10.1924

(b)   **Pius Maria Leopold Alfred Josef Petrus Paulus Johannes Evangalist Patrick Martinus
Hubertus Michael Graf zu Stolberg-Stolberg** * Brauna 8.10.1924 = Frankfurt-am-
Main 26.5.1962 Gudrun Bock * Wilhelmshafen 29.12.1940 dau. of Arnim Bock,
and has issue:

XII   1a.   **Patrick Valentin Pius Michael Meinolf Graf zu Stolberg-Stolberg** * Bensheim
27.5.1963

XI   (c)   **Georg Ferdinand Aloysius Alfred Petrus Johannes Evangalist Antonius Lukas Maria
Graf zu Stolberg-Stolberg** * Brauna 14.10.1927 = Ullstadt 25.6.1959 **Marie-
Gabrielle Freiin. v.u. zu Franckenstein** * Ullstadt 1.8.1931 dau. of Georg Frhr. v.u.
zu Franckenstein, and has issue:

XII   1a.   **Christoph-Thaddäus Moritz Georg Aloysius Friedrich-Leopold Maria Graf zu
Stolberg-Stolberg** * Bad Reichenhall 15.6.1960

2a.   **Friedrich-Leopold Johannes Thaddäus Franziskus Joseph Maria Graf zu
Stolberg-Stolberg** * Salzburg 16.3.1962

XI   (d)   **Alfred Adam Friedrich-Leopold Martinus Meinrad Petrus Johannes Evangalist
Bonifatius Thomas v. Aquino Maria Graf zu Stolberg-Stolberg** * Brauna 18.1.1929
= Würzburg 14.12.1961 Anneliese Ernst * Ahrweiler 23.4.1926 dau. of Anton
Ernst

X   b)   **Maria Pia Paula Georgia Elisabeth Huberta Gräfin zu Stolberg-Stolberg** * Gimborn
14.8.1870 + Knocke-sur-Mer, Belgium 1.4.1913 = Brauna 21.6.1894 Moritz Frhr. v.u.
zu Franckenstein * Ullstadt 18.3.1869 + Grambschütz 24.1.1931, and had issue:

XI   (a)   **Anna-Maria Leopoldine Sophie Elisabeth Julie Josepha Rosario Agnes Therese
Benedikte Ignatia Antonie Huberta Aloysia Freiin. v.u. zu Franckenstein**
* München 30.3.1896

(b)   **Johann Georg Karl Arbogast Maria Joseph Antonius Aloysius Benediktus Hubert
Bernhard Alfred Frhr. v.u. zu Franckenstein** * Nördlingen 20.8.1898 + 28.3.1965
= Wien 1.12.1925 Karoline Princess v. Schönburg-Hartenstein * Wien 23.12.1898
dau. of Johannes Prinz v. Schönburg-Hartenstein, and had issue:

XII	1a.	**Marie Sophie Franziska Caroline Anna Antonia Pia Rita Juda Thaddea Elisabeth Freiin. v.u. zu Franckenstein** * Ullstadt 11.10.1926 = Offenburg 25.3.1957 Reinhard v. Schiller * Klein-Kloden 17.11.1923, and has issue:

XIII

      1b. **Johannes v. Schiller** * Cali-Valle, Columbia 6.12.1957

      2b. **Michael v. Schiller** * Cali-Valle, Columbia ... 11.1958

      3b. **Katherina v. Schiller** * Cali-Valle, Columbia ... 10.1961

XII

2a. **Marie Elisabeth Walburga Martha Rita Petra Paula Franziska Karoline Sophie Benedikta Pia Leopoldine Freiin. v.u. zu Franckenstein** * Würzburg 9.3.1928 = Ullstadt 26.6.1959 **Gottfried Frhr. v. Twickel** * Havixbeck 26.3.1929, and has issue see elsewhere

3a. **Maria Walburga Helene Irmgard Anna Renate Irene Scholastika Marta Rita Gabriele Freiin. v.u. zu Franckenstein** * Würzburg 26.7.1929 = Ullstadt 10.5.1954 Peter Frhr. v. Aretin * Münchsdorf 25.6.1923, and has issue:

XIII

      1b. **Carl Pius Maria Georg Judas Thaddäus Antonius Romauld Frhr. v. Aretin** * Würzburg 7.2.1955

      2b. **Alexandra Maria Elisabeth Caroline Walburga Therese Freiin. v. Aretin** * Würzburg 22.9.1956

      3b. **Georg Erwein Andreas Maria Paulus Johannes Frhr. v. Aretin** * Würzburg 30.11.1957

XII

4a. **Maria Gabriele Leopoldine Rita Judas Thaddäa Scholastika Petra Freiin. v.u. zu Franckenstein** * Ullstadt 1.8.1931 = Ullstadt 26.6.1959 **Georg Graf zu Stolberg-Stolberg** * Brauna 14.10.1927 and has issue see elsewhere

5a. **Maria Pia Benedikta Ernestine Freiin. v.u. zu Franckenstein** * Ullstadt 28.8.1933 + München 7.4.1963

6a. **Heinrich Moritz Maria Johannes Arbogast Carl Benediktus Judas Thaddäus Jacobus Konrad Pius Frhr. v.u. zu Franckenstein** * Würzburg 15.1.1939

XI

(c) **Maria Immaculata Leopoldine Crescentia Josepha Antonia Agnes Benedikta Augustine Bernharda Katherina Rosa Franziska Elisabeth Petra Paula Freiin. v.u. zu Franckenstein** * Nördlingen 9.3.1901

(d) **Johann Heinrich Maria Joseph Hubert Georg Alfred Benedikt Stanislaus Thomas Frhr. v.u. zu Franckenstein** * Nördlingen 8.11.1902 = Innsbruck 20.4.1953 Theresa Riccabona v. Reichenfels * Innsbruck 10.4.1909 dau. of Josef Heinrich Riccabona v. Reichenfels s.p.

(e) **Marie Elisabeth Sophie Magdalene Hedwig Josepha Franziska Antonia Scholastika Johanna Freiin. v.u. zu Franckenstein** * Nördlingen 6.3.1905 + Ullstadt 4.4.1919

X

c) **Leopoldine Walburga Maria Pia Huberta Franziska Gräfin zu Stolberg-Stolberg** * Gimborn 13.9.1872 + Schloss Neuburg a.d. Kammel 2.1.1948

d) **Sophie Maria Pia Frederica Adolfine Huberta Gräfin zu Stolberg-Stolberg** * Brauna 31.5.1874 + Gotschdorf 22.1.1945 = Brauna 9.10.1901 Johannes Edgar Graf Henckel v. Donnersmarck * Kaulwitz 24.6.1861 + Grambschütz 17.10.1911, and had issue:

XI   (a)   **Georg Maria Nives Lazarus Petrus Dominikus Joseph Johannes Alfred Friedrich Leopold Hubertus Graf Henckel v. Donnersmarck** * Grambschütz 5.8.1902 = Wolfegg 31.1.1928 **Sophie Gräfin v. Waldburg zu Wolfegg u. Waldsee** * Kisslegg 22.4.1904 dau. of Ludwig Graf v. Waldburg zu Wolfegg u. Waldsee, and had issue:

XII

1a.   **Anna Maria Sophie Huberta Ludowika Walburgis Eleonora Katherina Cosima Gräfin Henckel v. Donnersmarck** * Grambschütz 14.12.1928 + Burg Maubach 12.11.1954 = Stepperg 6.8.1953 **Franz Graf v. Spee** * Schleiden 14.3.1923, and had issue see elsewhere

2a.   **Maria Theresia Anna Huberta Sophia Pia Georgia Bonifacia Cosima Gräfin Henckel v. Donnersmarck** * Grambschütz 6.6.1930 = München 9.6.1954 **Karl Albrecht Frhr Griessenbeck v. Griessenbach** * Griessenbeck 19.4.1924, and has issue:

XIII

1b.   **Christoph Frhr. Griessenbeck v. Griessenbach** * Landshut 24.3.1955

2b.   **Angela Frhr. Griessenbeck v. Griessenbach** * Landshut 11.2.1956

3b.   **Felix Frhr. Griessenbeck v. Griessenbach** * Landshut 26.4.1958

XII

3a.   **Maria Immaculata Eleonore Carla Elisabeth Barbara Katherina Antonia Sophia Benedikta Huberta Johanna Walburga Gabriele Hedwig Gräfin Henckel v. Donnersmarck** * Grambschütz 4.12.1931 = Stepperg 18.4.1963 Athanasios Remoundos * Athens 27.7.1921, and has issue:

XIII

1b.   **Johannes Athanasios Remoundos** * Athens 17.2.1966

XII

4a.   **Peter Maria Ludwig Johannes Edgar Georg Friedrich Lazarus Alfred Hubertus Albert Leopold Graf Henckel v. Donnersmarck** * Grambschütz 18.11.1933 = Ingolstadt 21.7.1962 Christine Schreyögg * Ingolstadt 5.3.1937 dau. of Georg Schreyögg

5a.   **Hedwig Maria Elisabeth Sophia Anna Benedikta Luitgarde Walburgis Katherina Pia Gräfin Henckel v. Donnersmarck** * Grambschütz 16.6.1935 = Mauern Kr. Neunberg 6.4.1961 **Karl Graf v. Arco-Zinneberg** * München 18.8.1931, and has issue see elsewhere

6a.   **Maria Ursula Anna Huberta Sophie Franziska Gabriele Walpurgis Elisabeth Katherina Graf Henckel v. Donnersmarck** * Grambschütz 2.4.1938 = Stepperg 30.8.1965 Johannes Frhr. v. Ow * München 16.7.1928, and has issue:

XIII

1b.   **Katherina Elisabeth Freiin. v. Ow** * Horb a. N. 28.8.1966

XII

7a.   **Karla Margaretha Maria Ludwiga Renata Huberta Anna Sophia Benedikta Pia Gräfin Henckel v. Donnersmarck** * Grambschütz 4.4.1940 = Mauern 6.4.1961 Felix Frhr. v. Loë * Bandung, Java 9.4.1924, and has issue:

XIII

1b.   **Ferdinand Maria Frhr. v. Loë** * Saarbrücken 21.5.1962

2b.   **Maximilian Frhr. v. Loë** * Ludwigshafen 1.6.1965

3b.   **Stephanie Freiin. v. Loë** * Ludwigshafen 7.6.1966

XII

8a.   **Elisabeth Huberta Maria Hedwig Theresia Irene Monika Sophia Afra Georgia Gräfin Henckel v. Donnersmarck** * Grambschütz 15.10.1941 = Stepperg 19.6.1965 Ludolf Frhr. v. Schorlemer * Grundhof 12.2.1919, and has issue:

XIII   1b. **Ursula Maria Freiin. v. Schorlemer** * Luxembourg 5.5.1966

XI   (b) **Anna-Maria Immaculata Antonie Eleonore Sophie Johanna Katharina Leopoldine Domenica Magdalena Huberta Paula Jacobea Hedwig Elisabeth Josepha Gräfin Henckel v. Donnersmarck** * Grambschütz 28.4.1904 + Albano, Roma 5.9.1925

       (c) **Marie-Eleonore Maximiliane Sophie Catherina Johanna Josepha Huberta Aloysia Gräfin Henckel v. Donnersmarck** * Grambschütz 22.3.1906

       (d) **Alfred Maria Friedrich Leopold Johannes Lazarus Hubertus Graf Henckel v. Donnersmarck** * Grambschütz 4.6.1911 ✗ Taganrog 8.12.1941

IX   i. **Mechtilde Amalie Maria Christiane Gräfin v. Arco-Zinneberg** * München 3.2.1845 + Schramberg 26.7.1874 = Schorn 10.8.1868 Ferdinand Graf v. Bissengen u. Nippenberg * Wieten 6.3.1837 + Schramberg 6.1.1919, and had issue:

X   a) **Maria Ludovica Leopoldine Theresia Gräfin v. Bissengen u. Nippenberg** * Schramberg 25.6.1869 + Strassburg 31.10.1914

       b) **Maria Cajetan Stanislaus Graf v. Bissengen u. Nippenberg** * Schramberg 20.8.1870 + Hohenstein 7.10.1956 = München 4.6.1921 Elisabeth Freiin. v. Aretin * Kissengen 30.6.1886 + Hohenstein 24.10.1957 dau. of Anton Frhr. v. Aretin s.p.

       c) **Margarethe Maria Walburga Leopoldine Pia Gräfin v. Bissengen u. Nippenberg** * Schramberg 2.7.1871 + Schramberg 4.4.1889

       d) **Maria Elisabeth Josepha Pia Aloysia Gräfin v. Bissengen u. Nippenberg** * Schramberg 11.7.1873 + Potsdam 20.12.1904 = Schramberg 30.9.1902 Konrad Frhr. v. Stotzingen * Steisslingen 14.6.1873 + Konstanz 30.10.1933, and had issue:

XI   (a) **Maria Mechtilde Catolica Ferdinande Josepha Antonia Wilhelmine Freiin. v. Stotzingen** * Potsdam 14.12.1903

       (b) **Margarethe Elisabeth Josepha Antonia Wilhelmine Freiin. v. Stotzingen** * Potsdam 20.12.1904

IX   j. **Nikolaus Aloysius Constantin Graf v. Arco-Zinneberg** * 8.1.1848 + 16.9.1870

    k. **Maximilian Konstantin Friedrich Alfons Graf v. Arco-Zinneberg** * München 19.2.1850 + München 24.1.1916 = Pera 28.6.1875 Olga Freiin. v. Werther * Kopenhagen 12.4.1853 + München 31.1.1937 dau. of Karl Frhr. v. Werther, and had issue:

X   a) **Leopoldine Sophie Maria Gräfin v. Arco-Zinneberg** * Waldsee 18.4.1876 + Bonn 7.6.1956 = München 15.4.1902 Anton Graf v. Spee * Heltorf 5.8.1866 + Maubach 12.2.1924, and had issue:

XI   (a) **Veronika Helene Benedikta Mechtildis Huberta Maria Gräfin v. Spee** * Leyenburg 27.2.1904

       (b) **Ambrosius Franz Antonius Hubertus Maria Graf v. Spee** * Berlin 23.2.1905

       (c) **Antonia Nikolausine Maria Immaculata Huberta Eulalia Gräfin v. Spee** * Berlin-Lichterfelde 10.12.1906 + Eisenkirchen 20.1.1951

       (d) **Julitta Maria Sophie Leopoldine Hedwig Huberta Gräfin v. Spee** * Berlin-Lichterfelde 17.10.1909

       (e) **Margarethe Hugoline Marie Agnes Franziska Brigitta Huberta Gräfin v. Spee** * Berlin-Lichterfelde 7.10.1911

       (f) **Degenhart Bertram Alois Maximilian Joseph Anton Hubertus Maria Graf v. Spee** * Berlin-Lichterfelde 10.10.1919 missing in Russia since 10.1.1942

142

X

b) **Helene Maria Gräfin v. Arco-Zinneberg** * Schönburg 26.10.1877 + Nieder-Arnbach 22.12.1961 = München 23.10.1899 Hans-Albrecht Graf v. Harrach zu Rohrau u. Thannhausen * Firenze 11.2.1873 + Nieder Arnbach 22.10.1963, and has issue:

XI

(a) **Marie-Elisabeth Leopoldine Innocentia Gräfin v. Harrach zu Rohrau u. Thannhausen** * München 28.7.1900 + Nieder Arnbach 26.3.1957 = München 12.1.1922 Maximilian Frhr. v. Pfetten-Arnbach * Arnbach 7.11.1897, and had issue:

XII

1a. **Nicolas Andreas Marquard Johannes Theodor Maria Felix Frhr. v. Pfetten-Arnbach** * München 26.7.1927 = Haiming b. Piesing 27.8.1951 Rosalie Freiin. v. Ow * München 30.7.1930 dau. of Anton Frhr. v. Ow s.p.

2a. **Cajetan Christoph Marquard Maximilian Maria Ludwig Ferdinand Frhr. v. Pfetten-Arnbach** * München 12.7.1930 = 14.4.1964 Henriette Gräfin v. Khuen v. Belasi * Nustar 17.2.1937 dau. of Heinrich Graf Khuen v. Belasi, and has issue:

XIII

1b. **Nicolas Christoph Marquard Maria Maximilian Leonhard Frhr. v. Pfetten-Arnbach** * München 25.9.1966

XII

3a. **Ursula Maria Melanie Johanna Candida Thaddäa Helene Freiin. v. Pfetten-Arnbach** * München 13.10.1933 = Nieder Arnbach 20.10.1955 Nikolaus v. Stumm * Marburg a.d. Lahn 7.6.1928, and has issue:

XIII

1b. **Ferdinand Maria Cajetan Carl Alexander Boris Maximilian v. Stumm** * München 19.2.1957

2b. **Johannes v. Stumm** * 27.7.1959

3b. **Maria Stefanie v. Stumm** * 15.8.1960

4b. **Vera v. Stumm** * 22.4.1964

XII

4a. **Sebastian Maria Egon Marquard Camillo Pius Benedikt Frhr. v. Pfetten-Arnbach** * München 18.7.1939 = Berlin 22.6.1964 Renate Riesopp * Berlin 15.12.1941 dau. of Martin Riesopp and has issue:

XIII

1b. **Thomas Nicolas Kilian Marquard Frhr. v. Pfetten-Arnbach** * 6.4.1965

XI

(b) **Helene Jucunde Maria Gräfin v. Harrach zu Rohrau u. Thannhausen** * Firenze 25.11.1901 = München 20.5.1924 Maximilian Frhr. v. Mauchenheim gen. Bechtolsheim * Stockholm 5.2.1891 + Hardberg 30.10.1961, and had issue:

XII

1a. **Christoph Clemens Maria Maximilian Aloysius Hubertus Mavico Frhr. v. Mauchenheim gen. Bechtolsheim** * München 27.7.1925 = Murnau 25.11.1954 Marie-José Arlabosse Français de Nantes * Chappa-Loakay, Indo-China 25.8.1925 dau. of Marcel Comte Arlabosse Français de Nantes, and has issue:

XIII

1b. **Marie-Hélène Theresia Rita Freiin. v. Mauchenheim gen. Bechtolsheim** * Murnau 8.8.1955

2b. **Carola Maria Louise Karin Freiin. v. Mauchenheim gen. Bechtolsheim** * Murnau 8.10.1956

3b. **Marcus Maximilian Christoph-Clemens Maria Mavico Frhr. v. Mauchenheim gen. Bechtolsheim** * Murnau 31.10.1958

4b. **Isabelle Freiin. v. Mauchenheim gen. Bechtolsheim** * 21.5.1962

XII		2a. **Georg Heinrich Maria Hubertus Thaddäus Mavico Frhr. v. Mauchenheim gen. Bechtolsheim** * München 27.8.1926 = München 7.9.1957 Denise Lauschmann * Budapest 4.10.1931 dau. of Dénes Lauschmann, and has issue:

XIII   1b. **Beatrix Denise Charlotte Helene Marie Elisabeth Freiin. v. Mauchenheim gen. Bechtolsheim** * München 17.10.1959

XII   3a. **Franz-Felix Maria Joseph Maximilian Konrad Thaddäus Mavico Frhr. v. Mauchenheim gen. Bechtolsheim** * Pähl 29.3.1933

XI   (c) **Mechtildis Maria-Gerda Gräfin v. Harrach zu Rohrau u. Thannhausen** * Firenze 31.3.1905

      (d) **Barbara Maria Sophie Eleonore Renata Gräfin v. Harrach zu Rohrau u. Thannhausen** * Firenze 20.9.1907

      (e) **Irene Maria Rosario Pauline Gräfin v. Harrach zu Rohrau u. Thannhausen** * Tiefhartmannsdorf 2.10.1910 = München 20.8.1934 John Osmael Scott-Ellis 9th Baron Howard de Walden * London 27.11.1912, and had issue:

XII   1a. **Hon. Mary Hazel Caridwen Scott-Ellis** * London 12.8.1935 = London 20.11.1957 Joseph Graf Czernin v.u. zu Chudenitz * Prag 9.8.1924, and had issue:

XIII
      1b. **Charlotte Mary Sidonia Czernin** * London 28.11.1958
      2b. **Henriette Mary Rosario Czernin** * London 10.1.1960
      3b. **Alexandra Mary Romana Czernin** * London 6.11.1961
      4b. **Philippa Mary Loretta Czernin** * London 3.7.1963
      5b. **Peter John Joseph Czernin** * London 1.1.1966

XII   2a. **Hon. Blanche Susan Fionodbhar Scott-Ellis** * London 6.10.1937 = London 8.2.1961 David Buchan of Auchmacoy * Olney, Bucks 18.9.1929, and has issue:

XIII
      1b. **Sophia Jane Elisabeth Buchan** * London 5.3.1962
      2b. **John Charles Augustus David Buchan** * London 1.3.1963
      3b. **James Alexander Stephen Buchan** * London 27.9.1964
      4b. **Thomas Richard Sinclair Buchan** * London 22.1.1966

XII   3a. **Hon. Jessica Jane Vronwy Scott-Ellis** * Chirk Castle 6.8.1941 = London 12.7.1966 Adrian White * Berkhamstead 29.6.1940

      4a. **Hon. Camilla Anne Bronwen Scott-Ellis** * London 1.4.1947

X   c) **Mechtilde Christiane Maria Gräfin v. Arco-Zinneberg** * Schönburg 8.3.1879 + London 4.6.1958 = (1) München 22.8.1904 **Karl Fürst Lichnowsky** * Kreuzenort 8.3.1860 + Kuchelna 27.2.1928; = (2) London 1.12.1937 Ralph Harding Peto * London 11.2.1877 + London 5.9.1945, and had issue by 1st marriage see elsewhere

      d) **Nikolas Antonius Ludwig Joseph Maria Graf v. Arco-Zinneberg** * Schönburg 11.1.1881 + Passau 19.5.1958

      e) **Maria-Sophie Gabriele Walpurga Gräfin v. Arco-Zinneberg** * Schönburg 25.11.1882 + Mondsee 4.3.1965 = München 30.11.1907 Otto Graf v. Almeida * München 6.2.1887 + Mondsee 8.1.1956, and had issue:

XI   (a)   **Paul Johann Carl Balthasar Maria Graf v. Almeida** * Mondsee 6.1.1909 + 25.11.1959 = Alkoven 30.5.1947 Ruth Lankes * Essen 21.4.1921 dau. of Artur Lankes and has issue:

XII   1a.   **Nicolette Elisabeth Helene Franziska Gräfin v. Almeida** * Salzburg 7.5.1948

                      2a.   **Mario Otto Carlos Ludwig Christian Graf v. Almeida** * Salzburg 18.7.1950

                      3a.   **Peter Manuel Artur Friedrich Simon Graf v. Almeida** * Mondsee 30.4.1952

XI   (b)   **Micheline Hanna Helene Huberta Gräfin v. Almeida** * München 12.2.1911

               (c)   **Ludwig Otto Johann Rolf Graf v. Almeida** * München 9.12.1913

X   f)   **Alois Hubertus Karl Maria Graf v. Arco-Zinneberg** * Meran 24.1.1886 + München 18.11.1965 = München 15.11.1916 Lidwine Freiin. Wamboldt v. Umstadt * Birkenau 23.3.1893 + München 2.12.1957 — div., and had issue:

XI   (a)   **Peter Andreas Thaddeus Graf v. Arco-Zinneberg** * Schönburg 30.11.1917 = Isny 18.8.1951 Margarete Söhnl * Aussig 3.9.1916 dau. of Otto Franz Söhnl, and has issue:

XII   1a.   **Diana Giovanna Lidwine Maria Gräfin v. Arco-Zinneberg** * München 30.8.1952

                     2a.   **Andrea Gertrud Maria Christine Gräfin v. Arco-Zinneberg** * München 25.4.1955

XI   (b)   **Ursula Maria Helene Gräfin v. Arco-Zinneberg** * Schönburg 2.3.1919 = München 12.12.1952 Benedikt Georgii * München 2.11.1922, and has issue:

XII   1a.   **Monica Georgii** * München 4.10.1953

                     2a.   **Pia Georgii** * München 2.8.1955

XI   (c)   **Susanne Antoinetta Anna Gräfin v. Arco-Zinneberg** * Schönburg 11.7.1921 = San Juan, Porto Rico 27.10.1952 Jochem Heidsieck * Amsterdam 28.8.1911, and has issue:

XII   1a.   **Teresa Maria Lidwine Heidsieck** * New York 15.8.1953

XI   (d)   **Sophie Maria Anna Therese Gräfin v. Arco-Zinneberg** * Schönburg 26.2.1928

X   g)   **Hubert Graf v. Arco-Zinneberg** * München 6.5.1888 + München 16.5.1888

           h)   **Anna Mathilde Maria Valentine Gräfin v. Arco-Zinneberg** * Schönburg 14.2.1890 + München 6.10.1953 = München 26.6.1912 Rudolf Graf v. Marogna-Redwitz * München 15.10.1888 ✕ Berlin-Tegel 12.10.1944, and had issue:

XI   (a)   **Elisabeth Helene Gräfin v. Marogna-Redwitz** * München 27.6.1949 = Hittenkirchen 3.2.1948 Christian v. Loeben * Leipzig 9.2.1911, and has issue:

XII   1a.   **Huberta Helene Mechtildis v. Loeben** * München 27.6.1949

                     2a.   **Rudolf Franz Georg v. Loeben** * Aschau-Chiemsee 21.7.1951

XI   (b)   **Rudolf Ludwig Franz Maximilian Philipp Graf v. Marogna-Redwitz** * München 23.10.1914 ✕ Kursk 9.7.1942

(c)   **Hubert Franz Alois Rudolf Graf v. Marogna-Redwitz** * München 26.1.1919
X Charkow 13.4.1942

X   i)   **Elisabeth Maria Josephine Leopoldine Gräfin v. Arco-Zinneberg** * München 15.11.1891
+ Berlin 26.3.1938 = München 7.9.1918 Gustav Frhr. v. Schrenck-Notzing * München
29.5.1894 + München 1.7.1957 s.p.

IX   l.   **Franz Graf v. Arco-Zinneberg** * München 12.1.1851 + Henry Chapelle 12.5.1914

       m.   **Christiane Maximiliane Gräfin v. Arco-Zinneberg** * München 27.11.1852 + München
30.9.1923 = München 4.5.1878 Konrad Graf v. Preysing-Lichtenegg-Moos * Zeil 16.3.1843
+ München 6.6.1903, and had issue:

X   a)   **Johann Max Emanuel Maria Joseph Stanislaus Pius Graf v. Preysing-Lichtenegg-Moos**
* München 4.4.1879 + München 10.12.1913 = Grünau 29.11.1905 Ernestine Freiin.
Herring v. Frankensdorf * Gmunden 17.7.1885 dau. of Ernst Frhr. Herring v.
Frankensdorf s.p.

       b)   **Johann Kaspar Maximilian Maria Joseph Franz Xaver Aloysius Peter Paul Leo Graf v.
Preysing-Lichtenegg-Moos** * München 28.6.1880 + Niewkerke 14.4.1918

       c)   **Maria-Immaculata Leopoldine Josepha Margaretha Gräfin v. Preysing-Lichtenegg-Moos**
* Moos 1.7.1881 + München 5.3.1951

       d)   **Anna Maria Josepha Ignatia Theresia Liboria Gräfin v. Preysing-Lichtenegg-Moos**
* Moos 23.7.1882 + Preeshan 15.5.1919

       e)   **Elisabeth Sophie Maria Anna Josepha Margarethe Leopolda Gräfin v. Preysing-Lichtenegg-
Moos** * Moos 15.11.1883 + Natternberg 27.2.1932 = München 22.11.1905 Ernst Graf
v. Harrach zu Rohrau u. Thannhausen * Hradek, Böh. 26.10.1879, and had issue:

XI   (a)   **Christiane Marie Therese Elisabeth Leopoldine Ernestine Maximiliane Gräfin v.
Harrach zu Rohrau u. Thannhausen** * Wien 12.10.1916 = London 4.6.1952
Arthur Trethowen Battagel * Watford 30.6.1908, and has issue:

XII   1a.   **Elisabeth Christiana Battagel** * Worthing, Sussex 25.12.1953

XI   (b)   **Ernst Leonhard Otto Georg Johann Konrad Maria Schnee Hubertus Graf v. Harrach
zu Rohrau u. Thannhausen** * München 5.8.1919 = Klagenfurt 7.10.1948
Hermine Neukirchner * Kindberg 2.10.1923, and has issue:

XII   1a.   **Christiane Anna Elisabeth Gräfin v. Harrach zu Rohrau u. Thannhausen**
* Santiago de Chile 27.12.1949

       2a.   **Ernst Georg Franz Christian Graf v. Harrach zu Rohrau u. Thannhausen**
* Santiago de Chile 22.6.1951

X   f)   **Josepha Maria Anna Ludovica Borromäa Gräfin v. Preysing-Lichtenegg-Moos** * Moos
1.11.1884 + München 6.2.1921

       g)   **Mechtilde Maria Josepha Anna Marcellina Gräfin v. Preysing-Lichtenegg-Moos** * Moos
9.1.1886 + München 23.1.1916 = München 14.10.1909 Johann Theodor Graf v.
Preysing-Lichtenegg-Moos * Mittelstetten 17.5.1884 + Brixen 26.2.1965 s.p.

       h)   **Johann Georg Heribert Maria Joseph Benedikt Ignatius Christian Graf v. Preysing-
Lichtenegg-Moos** * Moos 17.12.1887 + München 17.3.1924 = (1) München 18.9.1915
Anna Maria Gräfin v.u. zu Lerchenfeld auf Köfering u. Schönberg * St. Gilla 27.2.1885
+ St. Gilla 13.4.1916 dau. of Maximilian Graf v.u. zu Lerchenfeld auf Köfering u.
Schönberg; = (2) Wildenwart 23.2.1919 **Gundelinde Princess of Bavaria** * München
26.8.1891 dau. of King Ludwig III of Bavaria, and had issue:

by 2nd marriage:

XI

(a) **Johann Kaspar Warmund Konrad Simon Thaddäus Raimund Gebhard Nemegion Pantaleon Sigmund Maria Graf v. Preysing-Lichtenegg-Moos** * Moos 19.12.1919 X Zug 14.2.1940

(b) **Maria Theresia Christiane Anna Leopoldine Auguste Elisabeth Notburga Thaddäa Creszentia Walburga Josepha Angela Annunciata Gräfin v. Preysing-Lichtenegg-Moos** * Moos 23.3.1922 = (1) Moos 25.1.1940 **Ludwig Graf v. Arco-Zinneberg** * München 25.11.1913 X Projawino 18.2.1942; = (2) Nieder-Altaich 26.9.1943 **Odalricus Graf v. Arco-Zinneberg** * Maxlrain 12.12.1917, and has issue by both marriages see elsewhere

X

i) **Johannes Baptist Kaspar Maria Joseph Peter Paul Claver Graf v. Preysing-Lichtenegg-Moos** * Moos 30.6.1889 X Hallu 11.8.1918

j) **Johann Christoph Maximilian Maria Joseph Stanislaus Graf v. Preysing-Lichtenegg-Moos** * Moos 13.11.1891 + Arco 30.1.1911

VIII

(3) **Caroline Gräfin v. Arco** * Stepperg 26.12.1814 + Stepperg 18.1.1815

VII

5) **Francesco IV Joseph Karl Ambrosius Stanislaus Duke of Modena, Archduke of Austria-Este** * Milano 6.10.1779 + Modena 21.1.1846 = Cagliari 20.6.1812 **Maria Beatrix Princess of Savoy** * Torino 6.12.1792 + Cattajo 15.9.1840 dau. of Vittorio Emanuele I King of Sardinia, and had issue:

VIII

(1) **Maria Theresia Beatrice Gaëtane Archduchess of Austria-Este, Princess of Modena** * Modena 14.7.1817 + Goritz 25.3.1886 = Brück 16.11.1846 **Henri Comte de Chambord** titular King of France * Tuileries Palace 29.9.1820 + Frohsdorf 24.8.1883 s.p.

(2) **Francesco V Ferdinand Geminian Duke of Modena, Archduke of Austria-Este** * Modena 1.6.1809 + Wien 20.11.1875 = München 30.3.1842 **Adelgunde Princess of Bavaria** * Würzburg 19.3.1823 + München 28.10.1914 dau. of Ludwig I King of Bavaria, and had issue:

IX

a. **Anne Beatrice Archduchess of Austria-Este, Princess of Modena** * Gries b. Bozen 19.10.1848 + Modena 8.7.1849

VIII

(3) **Ferdinand Karl Viktor Archduke of Austria-Este, Prince of Modena** * Modena 20.7.1821 + Brünn 15.12.1849 = Schönbrunn 4.10.1847 **Elisabeth Archduchess of Austria** * Buda 17.1.1831 + Wien 14.2.1903 dau. of Joseph Archduke of Austria, Palatine of Hungary, and had issue:

IX

a. **Maria Theresia Henriette Dorothee Archduchess of Austria-Este, Princess of Modena** * Brünn 2.7.1849 + Schloss Wildenwart 3.2.1919 = Wien 20.2.1868 **Ludwig III King of Bavaria** * München 7.1.1845 + Schloss Sárvár, Hungary 18.10.1921, and had issue see elsewhere

VIII

(4) **Maria Beatrice Anna Franziska Archduchess of Austria-Este, Princess of Modena** * Modena 13.2.1824 + Goritz 18.3.1906 = Modena 6.2.1847 **Don Juan de Borbón, Infant of Spain** * Aranjeuz 15.5.1822 + Brighton, England 21.11.1887, and had issue see elsewhere

VII

6) **Ferdinand Karl Joseph Archduke of Austria-Este, Prince of Modena** * 25.4.1781 + 5.11.1850

7) **Maximilian Joseph Johann Ambrosius Karl Archduke of Austria-Este, Prince of Modena** * 14.7.1782 + Ebenzweir 1.6.1863

8) **Marie Antoinette Archduchess of Austria-Este, Princess of Modena** * 21.10.1784 + 8.4.1786

9) **Karl Ambrosius Joseph Johann Baptist Archduke of Austria-Este, Prince of Modena** * 2.11.1785 + 2.9.1809

VII 10) **Maria Ludovika Beatrice Antoinette Josepha Johanna Archduchess of Austria-Este, Princess of Modena**
* Monza 14.12.1787 + Verona 7.4.1816 = Wien 6.1.1808 **Franz II Emperor of Austria, King of Hungary,** formerly Holy Roman Emperor * Firenze 12.2.1768 + Wien 2.3.1835, and had issue see elsewhere

VI 15. **Marie Antoinette Anne-Josephine Johanna Archduchess of Austria** * Wien 2.11.1755 + Paris 16.10.1793 = Versailles 16.5.1770 **Louis XVI King of France** * Versailles 23.8.1754 + Paris 21.1.1793 and had issue: see elsewhere

16. **Maximilian Franz Xaver Joseph Johann Anton de Paul Wenceslas Archduke of Austria** * Wien 8.12.1756 + Wien 27.6.1801

5 The Descendants of Luise Marie Countess Palatine of The Rhine 1647-1679 and Carl Theodor Otto Fürst zu Salm 1645-1710

III **Luise Marie Countess Palatine of the Rhine** * Paris 23.7.1647 + Aachen 11.3.1679 = Paris 20.3.1671 Carl Theodor Otto 4th Fürst zu Salm * Anholt 27.7.1645 + Aachen 10.11.1710, and had issue:

IV 1. **Luise Prinzessin zu Salm** * 23.3.1672 + ... 1707

2. a daughter * & + 6.9.1673

3. **Ludwig Otto 5th Fürst zu Salm** * Aachen 24.10.1674 + Anholt 23.11.1738 = Anholt 20.7.1700 Albertine Prinzessin v. Nassau-Hadamar * Hadamar 6.7.1679 + Anholt 24.4.1716 dau. of Moritz Heinrich Fürst v. Nassau-Hadamar and had issue:

V 1) **Dorothea Franziska Agnes Prinzessin zu Salm** * Anholt 21.1.1702 + Anholt 25.1.1751 = Anholt 25.3.1719 Nicolaus Leopold Fürst zu Salm since 1738 1st Fürst zu Salm-Salm * Nancy 25.1.1701 + Schloss Hoogstraeten 4.2.1770, and had issue:

VI (1) **Gabrielle Marie Christine Prinzessin zu Salm-Salm** * 8.1.1720 + Thorn ... 1792

(2) **Ludwig Carl Otto 2nd Fürst zu Salm-Salm** * 22.8.1721 + 29.7.1778 = Seraing 30.10.1775 Maria Anna Felizitas Gräfin v. Horion * 12.5.1743 + Senones 9.5.1800 s.p.

(3) **Wilhelm Florentin Claud Lamoral Prinz zu Salm-Salm** * 2.3.1723 X Freiburg 4.1.1744

(4) **Elisabeth Ludovika Maria Prinzessin zu Salm-Salm** * 14.8.1724 + ...

(5) **Luise Franziska Wilhelmine Prinzessin zu Salm-Salm** * Schloss Hoogstraeten 2.3.1725 + Köln 19.2.1764 = Anholt 19.3.1743 Johann Wilhelm Graf von Manderscheid * Köln 14.2.1708 + Köln 2.11.1772, and had issue see Chapter 6

(6) **Marie Christine Prinzessin zu Salm-Salm** * 14.8.1728 + 8.10.1779

(7) **Marie Elisabeth Josepha Prinzessin zu Salm-Salm** * Schloss Hoogstraeten 4.4.1729 + Schloss Schönborn 4.3.1775 = Anholt 1.8.1751 Erwein Graf von Schönborn-Heussenstamm * Mainz 17.1.1727 + Wien 25.7.1801, and had issue see Chapter 7

(8) **Maria Franziska Josepha Prinzessin zu Salm-Salm** * 28.10.1731 + Wien 5.9.1806 = Anvers 1.7.1761 Georg Adam 1st Fürst von Starhemberg * London 10.8.1724 + Wien 19.4.1807, and had issue see Chapter 8

(9) **Friedrich Ernst Maximilian Wild-u. Rheingraf zu Salm-Salm, Herzog von Hoogstraeten** * Anholt 28.11.1732 + Anvers 14.9.1773 = Hoogstraeten 16.3.1757 **Ludovika Prinzessin von Hessen Rheinfels-Rotenburg** * Rotenburg a.d. Fulda 18.4.1729 + Anholt 6.1.1800 dau. of Joseph Erbprinz von Hessen-Rheinfels-Rotenburg, and had issue:

VII a. **Nicolaus Leopold Ludwig Prinz zu Salm-Salm** * 1.6.1760 + 16.3.1768

b. **Constantin Alexander Joseph 3rd Fürst zu Salm-Salm**, see later

c. **Ludwig Johann Nepomuk August Prinz zu Salm-Salm** * 25.3.1765 + 23.10.1765

d. **Georg Adam Franz Prinz zu Salm-Salm** * 29.5.1766 + 12.7.1834

e. **Wilhelm Florentin Friedrich Prinz zu Salm-Salm** * 26.9.1769 + 2.3.1824

f. **Ludwig Otto Oswald Prinz zu Salm-Salm** * 2.7.1772 + 5.2.1822 = ... Felicitas Morano * ... + ...

g. **Maria Anna Henriette Prinzessin zu Salm-Salm** * 31.10.1773 + 18.1.1776

VI (10) **Carl Alexander Prinz zu Salm-Salm** * 15.10.1735 + Lisboa 1.2.1796 = 14.5.1766 Maria Charlotte Freiin. Leers v. Leersbach * 10.4.1753 + ... and had issue:

VII a. **Franz August Ludwig Prinz zu Salm-Salm** * 1.8.1773 + 22.6.1809

VI (11) **Auguste Sophie Prinzessin zu Salm-Salm** * 15.10.1735 + 30.1.1775

VI   (12)   **Josepha Prinzessin zu Salm-Salm** * Anholt 26.12.1736 + Schillingsfürst 25.10.1790 = Senones 29.10.1771 Carl Albrecht Fürst zu Hohenlohe-Schillingsfürst * Schillingsfürst 22.9.1719 + Schillingsfürst 25.1.1793, s.p.

(13)   **Marie Josephine Henriette Prinzessin zu Salm-Salm** * 20.12.1737 + ... 1774

(14)   **Maria Anna Prinzessin zu Salm-Salm** * Anholt 17.2.1740 + Heussenstamm 4.7.1816 = by Proxy, Malines 6.11.1758 Don Pedro de Alcántara de Toledo y Silva Pimental Enriquez Hurtado de Mendoza 12 Duque del Infantado * Madrid 27.12.1729 + bei Frankfurt-am-Main 1.6.1790, and had issue see Chapter 9

(15)   **Emanuel Heinrich Nicolaus Leopold Prinz zu Salm-Salm** * 22.5.1742 + 26.5.1808

(16)   **Franz Joseph Prinz zu Salm-Salm** * 30.11.1743 + ...

(17)   **Wilhelm Felix Johannes Prinz zu Salm-Salm** * 10.3.1745 + Hambach, Oberpfalz 14.9.1810

V   2)   **Elisabeth Alexandrine Felicite Charlotte Gotfriede Prinzessin zu Salm** * Anholt 21.7.1704 + Bruxelles 27.12.1739 = Anholt 18.3.1721 Claude Lamoral II Prince de Ligne * 7.8.1685 + Beloeil 7.4.1766, and had issue see Chapter 10

3)   **Christine Anna Luise Oswaldine Prinzessin zu Salm** * Anholt 29.4.1707 + Schloss Hoogstraeten 19.8.1775 = (1) Anholt 9.3.1726 Joseph Erbprinz v. Hessen-Rheinfels-Rotenburg * 23.9.1705 + Rotenburg a.d. Fulda 24.6.1744 = (2) Anholt 12.7.1753 Nicolaus Leopold Fürst zu Salm-Salm * Nancy 25.1.1701 + Schloss Hoogstraeten 4.2.1770, and had issue:

by 1st marriage:

VI   (1)   **Viktoria Prinzessin v. Hessen-Rheinfels-Rotenburg** * 25.2.1728 + Paris 1.7.1792 = Saverne 23/24.12.1745 Karl Prince de Rohan-Soubise * 16.7.1715 + 1.7.1787 s.p.

(2)   **Ludovika Prinzessin v. Hessen-Rheinfels-Rotenburg** * Rotenburg a.d. Fulda 18.4.1729 + Anholt 6.1.1800 = Hoogstraeten 16.3.1757 **Maximilian Wild-u. Rheingraf zu Salm-Salm, Herzog v. Hoogstraeten** * Anholt 28.11.1732 + Anvers 14.9.1773, and had issue see above

(3)   **Leopoldine Dorothea Prinzessin v. Hessen-Rheinfels-Rotenburg** * 1.10.1731 died young

(4)   **Ernst Prinz v. Hessen-Rheinfels-Rotenburg** * 28.5.1735 + 6.6.1742

IV   4.   **Luise Apollonia Prinzessin zu Salm** * 21.1.1677 + 22.5.1678

5.   a son * & + 16.7.1675

6.   **Eleonore Christine Elisabeth Prinzessin zu Salm** * 14.3.1678 + Bruxelles 23.3.1757 = by Proclamation 17.8.1713 Conrard Albert Duc d'Ursel * 10.2.1665 + Namur 3.5.1738, and had issue see Chapter 11

VII **Constantin Alexander Joseph Johann Nepomuk 3rd Fürst zu Salm-Salm** * Hoogstraeten 22.11.1762 + Karlsruhe 25.2.1828 = (1) Püttlingen 31.12.1782 Victoria Felicitas Prinzessin zu Löwenstein-Wertheim-Rochefort * Nancy 2.1.1769 + Senones 29.11.1786 dau. of Theodor Alexander Prinz zu Löwenstein-Wertheim-Rochefort; = (2) Vinac, Böhemia 4.2.1788 **Maria Walpurga Gräfin v. Sternberg-Manderscheid** * Prag 11.5.1770 + Düsseldorf 16.6.1808 dau. of Christian Graf v. Sternberg-Manderscheid; = (3) 's-Gravenhage 12.6.1810 Catherina Bender * Frankfurt-am-Main 19.1.1791 + 13.3.1831 dau. of Christoph Bender, and had issue:

by 1st marriage:

VIII 1. **Maria Victoria Prinzessin zu Salm-Salm** * 1.8.1784 + 3.4.1786

2. **Wilhelm Florentin Ludwíg Carl 4th Fürst zu Salm-Salm** * Senones 17.3.1786 + Anholt 2.8.1846 = Schloss Napoleonshöhe b. Kassel 21.7.1810 Flamina Rossi * Ajaccio 21.7.1795 + 20.12.1840 dau. of Nicolo Rossi, and had issue:

IX 1) **Alfred Constantin Alexander 5th Fürst zu Salm-Salm** * Anholt 27.12.1814 + Anholt 5.10.1886 = Roeulx 13.6.1836 Auguste Princesse de Croy * Bruxelles 7.8.1815 + Cleve 10.3.1886 dau. of Ferdinand Prince de Croy, and had issue:

X (1) **Mathilde Wilhelmine Marie Constance Prinzessin zu Salm-Salm** * Anholt 19.4.1837 + Bruxelles 19.4.1898

(2) **Nikolaus Leopold Joseph Marie 6th Fürst zu Salm-Salm** * Anholt 18.7.1838 + Anholt 16.2.1908 = Schönau-Teplitz 13.5.1855 **Eleonore Prinzessin von Croy** * 13.5.1855 + Berlin 20.3.1903 dau. of Alexis Prinz v. Croy s.p.

(3) **Adelheid Franziska Marie Christine Alice Prinzessin zu Salm-Salm** * Anholt 21.1.1840 + Paderborn 25.8.1916 = Anholt 30.11.1871 **Philipp Prinz von Croy** * Düsseldorf 1.3.1840 + Düsseldorf 29.6.1913 and had issue see elsewhere

(4) **Marie Eleonore Maximiliane Augustine Prinzessin zu Salm-Salm** * Anholt 13.4.1843 + Achern, Baden 3.6.1908

(5) **Carl Theodor Alfred Marie Paul Aimé Prinz zu Salm-Salm** * Anholt 6.3.1845 + 16.1.1923

(6) **Alfred Ferdinand Stephan Maria 7th Fürst zu Salm-Salm** * Anholt 13.3.1846 + Anholt 20.4.1923 = Wien 18.10.1869 Rosa Gräfin v. Lützow * Hamburg 31.3.1850 + Borohradek 5.2.1927 dau. of Franz Graf v. Lützow, and had issue:

XI a. **Emanuel Alfred Leopold Franz Erbprinz zu Salm-Salm** * Münster i. W. 30.11.1871 ✗ Pinsk 19.8.1916 = Wien 10.5.1902 **Christine Archduchess of Austria** * Cracow 17.11.1879 + Anholt 6.8.1962, dau. of Friedrich Archduke of Austria, and had issue:

XII a) **Isabelle Maria Rosa Katherina Antonia Prinzessin zu Salm-Salm** * Potsdam 13.2.1903 = Anholt 8.9.1925 **Felix Graf von Loë** * Wissen 1.9.1896 ✗ Schwaneburg 25.7.1944, and has issue see elsewhere

b) **Rosemary Friederike Isabelle Eleonore Henriette Antonia Prinzessin zu Salm-Salm** * Potsdam 13.4.1904 = Anholt 25.11.1926 **Hubert Salvator Archduke of Austria** * Lichtenegg 30.4.1894, and has issue see elsewhere

c) **Nikolaus Leopold Heinrich Alfred Emanuel Friedrich Antonius 8th Fürst zu Salm-Salm** * Potsdam 14.2.1906 = (1) München 19.7.1928 Ida Fürstin von Wrede * München 26.2.1909 dau. of Carl Philipp 4th Fürst von Wrede — div.; = (2) Hamburg-Eimsbüttel 19.10.1950 Eleonore v. Zitzewitz * Prebendow 24.11.1919 dau. of Wilhelm Siegfried v. Zitzewitz — div.; = (3) Bern 23.3.1962 Maria Moret * Grolley-Fribourg 23.6.1930 dau. of Léon Moret, and has issue:

by 1st marriage:

XIII (a) **Konstanze Maria Theresia Jakobea Kaspara Prinzessin zu Salm-Salm** * Anholt 25.7.1929

153

XIII   (b)   **Alfred Franz Emanuel Christophorus Bruno Melchior Erbprinz zu Salm-Salm** * Anholt 6.10.1930 ✗ in an Air Raid, Anholt 21.3.1945

       (c)   **Carl Philipp Josef Petrus Coelestinus Balthasar Erbprinz zu Salm-Salm** * Anholt 19.5.1933 = München 8.2.1961 Erika von Morgen * Berlin 19.3.1935 dau. of Ernst v. Morgen, and has issue:

XIV   1a.   **Emanuel Philipp Nikolaus Johann Felix Prinz zu Salm-Salm** * Münster i. W. 6.12.1961

                 2a.   **Philipp Petrus Andreas Antonius Joachim Prinz zu Salm-Salm** * Münster i. W. 5.7.1963

XIII   (d)   **Anna Huberta Maria Alfonsa Kaspara Prinzessin zu Salm-Salm** * Anholt 2.8.1935

       (e)   **Margarethe Cecile Johanna Alfonsa Melchiara Prinzessin zu Salm-Salm** * Anholt 2.8.1935 = Petersburg b. Bonn 23.9.1957 György Szolnoki-Scheftsik * Törökszentmiklos 11.7.1926 + Paris 30.4.1965, and has issue:

XIV   1a.   **Stephan Jean Georges Scheftsik de Szolnok** * Orleans 10.5.1958

                 2a.   **Portia Isadora Constance Scheftsik de Szolnok** * Orleans 15.1.1960

                 3a.   **Cécile Scheftsik de Szolnok** * Orleans 9.7.1961

                 4a.   **Jean Stephan Georges Scheftsik de Szolnok** * Orleans 2.8.1963

by 2nd marriage:

XIII   (f)   **Ludwig-Wilhelm Carl Emanuel Jörg Nikolaus Prinz zu Salm-Salm** * Hamburg 15.4.1953

by 3rd marriage:

       (g)   **Christian-Nikolaus Lucius Piero Angelus Prinz zu Salm-Salm** * Genève 25.8.1964

XII   d)   **Cäcilie Marie Alphonsine Emmanuele Antonia Prinzessin zu Salm-Salm** * Potsdam 8.3.1911 = Anholt 27.5.1930 Franz Joseph 6th Fürst u. Altgraf zu Salm-Reifferscheidt-Krautheim u. Dyck * Wien 7.4.1899 + Bonn 13.6.1958, and has issue:

XIII   (a)   **Marie Christine Erwine Isabella Innocentia Thaddäa Altgräfin u. Prinzessin zu Salm-Reifferscheidt-Krautheim u. Dyck** * Alfter 4.1.1932 = Alfter b. Bonn 27.7.1955 Peter Graf Wolff-Metternich zur Gracht * Göttingen 5.3.1929, and has issue:

XIV   1a.   **Georgina Cäcilia Sophia Paula Maria Apollonia Gräfin Wolff-Metternich zur Gracht** * Bonn 18.10.1956

                 2a.   **Helene Christine Salome Maria Apollonia Gräfin Wolff-Metternich zur Gracht** * Bonn 22.10.1957

                 3a.   **Maria del Pilar Emanuela Johanna Thomasine Apollonia Gräfin Wolff-Metternich zur Gracht** * Bonn 21.12.1959

                 4a.   **Simeon Peter Stanislas Heinrich Maria-Apollonia Graf Wolff-Metternich zur Gracht** * Kassel 30.4.1965

XIII   (b)   **Marie Anne Friederike Christine Leopoldine Emmanuela Helena Altgräfin u. Prinzessin zu Salm-Reifferscheidt-Krautheim u. Dyck** * Alfter 18.8.1933 = London 27.7.1964 Hon. Alexander Geddes * Dublin 24.9.1910 and has issue:

XIV   1a.   **Camilla Johanna Geddes** * London 10.12.1966

154

XIII   (c)   **Rosemary Ferdinande Dorothea Mathea Michaela Josepha Thaddäa Altgrafin u. Prinzessin zu Salm-Reifferscheidt-Krautheim u. Dyck** * Alfter 24.2.1937 = Alfter b. Bonn 11.9.1959 Johannes Graf Huyn * Warsaw 3.7.1930, and has issue:

XIV   1a.   **Johannes Joseph Felix Maria Victor Franziskus Xavier Graf Huyn** * Tokio 28.7.1960

       2a.   **Marie-Christine Helena Irmgard Cäcilia Ignatia Immaculata Gräfin Huyn** * Tokio 27.11.1961

       3a.   **Franz Ferdinand Christian Paul Joseph Maria Emanuel Graf Huyn** * Bonn 16.3.1964

       4a.   **Maria Assunta Ernestine Michaela Katherina Natalie Gräfin Huyn** * Bonn 30.4.1965

XIII   (d)   **Isabella Marie Franziska Gabrielle Pia Altgrafin u. Prinzessin zu Salm-Reifferscheidt-Krautheim u. Dyck** * Alfter 19.2.1939 = Dyck 2.10.1962 Franz Albrecht Metternich-Sándor 4th Herzog v. Ratibor 4th Fürst v. Corvey, Prinz zu Hohenlohe-Schillingsfürst * Rauden 23.10.1920, and has issue:

XIV   1a.   **Victor Erbprinz v. Ratibor u. Corvey, Prinz zu Hohenlohe-Schillingsfürst** * Wien 31.3.1964

       2a.   **Tassilo Ferdinand Prinz v. Ratibor u. Corvey, Prinz zu Hohenlohe-Schillingsfürst** * Wien 23.10.1965

XIII   (e)   **Gabrielle Louisanne Huberta Theodora Maria Immaculata Altgrafin u. Prinzessin zu Salm-Reifferscheidt-Krautheim u. Dyck** * Bonn 9.11.1941 = Dyck 12.10.1961 Ernst Friedrich Graf v. Goëss * Klagenfurt 12.3.1932, and has issue see elsewhere

       (f)   **Cäcilie Christine Caroline Maria Immaculata Michaela Thaddäa Altgrafin u. Prinzessin zu Salm-Reifferscheidt-Krautheim u. Dyck** * Bonn 14.12.1943

XI   b.   **Marie Emma Henriette Franziska Prinzessin zu Salm-Salm** * Anholt 20.2.1874

    c.   **Henriette Franziska Alexia Prinzessin zu Salm-Salm** * Anholt 21.6.1875 + Bozen 2.7.1961 = Anholt 15.1.1907 **Don Carlo Lucchesi Palli, 12 Principe di Campofranco** * Brunnsee 22.12.1868 + Portobuffole 18.8.1951, and had issue see elsewhere

    d.   **Franz Emmanuel Konstantin Prinz zu Salm-Salm** * Anholt 30.8.1876 + Loburg b. Coesfeld 10.1.1964 = Prag 16.11.1912 Maria Anna Freiin. v.u. zu Dalberg * Datschitz, Böh. 11.3.1891 dau. of Karl Frhr. v.u. zu Dalberg, and has issue:

XII   a)   **Marie Gabriele Prinzessin zu Salm-Salm** * Loburg 31.8.1913 = Loburg 18.9.1934 = Josef Erwein Graf v. Deroy Frhr. v. Fürstenberg * Cadi-Keuy b. Istanbul 21.1.1908 and has issue:

XIII   (a)   **Erasmus-Elmar Hubertus Theodor Johannes Evang. Ludwig Friedrich Maria Frhr. v. Fürstenberg** * Landshut 9.11.1936 = Singen 2.5.1962 **Marie Antonia Gräfin Vetter v. der Lille** * Innsbruck 1.4.1932 dau. of Rudolf Graf Vetter v. der Lille, and has issue:

XIV   1a.   **Friedrich Leopold Frhr. v. Fürstenberg** * Landshut 4.2.1963

       2a.   **Ferdinand Frhr. v. Fürstenberg** * Landshut 30.8.1964

       3a.   **Maria Anna Gabriele Freiin. v. Fürstenberg** * Landshut 11.9.1965

XIII   (b)   **Maria-Elisàbeth Anna Odette Gabriele Freiin. v. Fürstenberg** * Landshut 12.2.1938 = Weinhenstephan b. Landshut 29.4.1964 **Felix Graf Vetter von der Lille** * Innsbruck 6.3.1928

         (c)   **Amélie Christine Maria Freiin. v. Fürstenberg** * Landshut 19.4.1941

         (d)   **Franz-Georg Ulrich Erwein Frhr. v. Fürstenberg** * Landshut 4.7.1942

         (e)   **Erwein Maria Joseph Frhr. v. Fürstenberg** * Landshut 14.8.1944

         (f)   **Eleonore Elisabeth Maria Freiin. v. Fürstenberg** * Landshut 1.12.1948

XII   b)   **Maria Christine Rosa Prinzessin zu Salm-Salm** * Charlottenburg 21.11.1914

      c)   **Auguste Franziska Karoline Prinzessin zu Salm-Salm** * Charlottenburg 14.1.1916 = Oggersheim 20.12.1953 Kurt Brubach * Nothweiler 24.9.1921, and has issue:

XIII   (a)   **Brigitta Christiane Maria Brubach** * 20.11.1954

         (b)   **Franz Nikolaus Sylvester Brubach** * 31.12.1955

XII   d)   **Franz Karl Alfred Emanuel Aloysius Josef Maria Prinz zu Salm-Salm** * Münster i. W. 22.2.1917 = Heimerzheim 30.10.1951 Maria Freiin. v. Boeselager* Heimerzheim 3.12.1923 dau. of Albert Frhr. Boeselager, and has issue:

XIII   (a)   **Michael Alfred Wolfgang Dietrich Hendrik Antonius Maria Prinz zu Salm-Salm** * Heimerzheim 16.1.1953

         (b)   **Maria Katherina Anna Antonia Gabriele Huberta Prinzessin zu Salm-Salm** * Heimerzheim 2.4.1954

         (c)   **Jeanne Marie-Therese Eleonore Antoinette Prinzessin zu Salm-Salm** * Heimerzheim 18.8.1955

         (d)   **Adelheid Christiane Johanna Albertine Antonia Maria Prinzessin zu Salm-Salm** * Heimerzheim 21.6.1958

         (e)   **Antoinette Sophie Flaminia Alexandra Maria Prinzessin zu Salm-Salm** * Heimerzheim 28.7.1959

         (f)   **Christiane Flaminia Nathalie Elisabeth Antonia Huberta Maria Prinzessin zu Salm-Salm** * Wallhausen 6.3.1962

         (g)   **Franziskus-Hendrick Philipp Alfred Hermann Wolfgang Heribert Stephan Joseph Maria Prinz zu Salm-Salm** * Wallhausen 23.12.1963

XII   e)   **Alfred Constantin Augustinus Johannes Baptist Joseph Maria Prinz zu Salm-Salm** * Loburg 16.2.1920 ✕ Normandy 30.7.1944

      f)   **Elisabeth Henriette Maria Felizitas Pia Prinzessin zu Salm-Salm** * Loburg 8.2.1922

      g)   **Maria Anna Prinzessin zu Salm-Salm** * Loburg 20.4.1924

XI   e.   **Rosa Mathilde Charlotte Leopoldine Prinzessin zu Salm-Salm** * Anholt 16.3.1878 + Kassel-Wilhelmshöhe 28.8.1963 = Frankfurt-am-Main 16.10.1911 **Karl Graf zu Solms-Laubach** * Arnsburg 22.3.1870 + Kassel 24.2.1945, and had issue:

XII   a)   **Marcus Hans Donatus Alfred Wilhelm Graf zu Solms-Laubach** * Freiburg i. Br. 25.9.1913

      b)   **Karl Otto Ernst Benigne Franz Graf zu Solms-Laubach** * 12.4.1915 + Kassel 15.1.1927

XI   f.   **Alfred Florentin Konstantin Prinz zu Salm-Salm** * Anholt 29.11.1879 + Rhede 19.1.1952

      g.   **Auguste Flaminia Ferdinanda Prinzessin zu Salm-Salm** * Anholt 6.1.1881 + Herrnstein 31.5.1946 = Münster i. W. 15.2.1911 **Felix Graf Droste zu Vischering u. Nesselrode-Reichenstein** * Herten 28.2.1871 + Herrnstein 8.10.1953, and had issue see elsewhere

XI   h.   **Eleonore Henriette Christine Prinzessin zu Salm-Salm** * Kleve 23.2.1887 = Hamburg 27.5.1925 Carl Rieniets * Anvers 2.2.1891 + Johannesburg 9.1.1957

X   (7)   **Emanuel Maria Johann Prinz zu Salm-Salm** * Anholt 6.7.1847 + Verona, of wounds received at the Battle of Custozza, 26.6.1866

(8)   **Wilhelm Florentin Felix Leopold Marie Prinz zu Salm-Salm** * Anholt 30.8.1848 + Münster i. W. 19.6.1894

(9)   **Maximilian Emil Franz August Marie Prinz zu Salm-Salm** * Anholt 4.11.1849 + Firenze 24.3.1874

(10)   **Euphemia Maximiliane Marie Constanze Prinzessin zu Salm-Salm** * Anholt 1.6.1851 + Münster i. W. 17.2.1931

(11)   **Nathalie Rudolfine Marie Flaminia Prinzessin zu Salm-Salm** * Anholt 16.12.1853 + Gracht 14.3.1913 = Anholt 9.1.1872 Ferdinand Graf Wolff-Metternich zur Gracht * Gracht 2.7.1845 + Gracht 25.5.1938, and had issue:

XI   a.   **Alfred Levin Hubert Marie Graf Wolff-Metternich zur Gracht** * Beck 24.10.1872 + Köln 29.1.1932 = (1) Haag 15.5.1906 Marie Gräfin v.u. zu Hoensbroech * Haag 11.3.1879 + Hohenhonnef 31.12.1911 dau. of Wilhelm Graf v.u. zu Hoensbroech; = (2) Bonn 7.10.1913 Hedwige Freiin. v. Loë * Heerlen 9.12.1888 dau. of Franz Frhr. v. Loë s.p.

b.   **Paul Hubert Maria Leopold Graf Wolff-Metternich zur Gracht** * Anholt 16.9.1873 + Gracht 6.11.1953 = London 11.8.1914 Christine Fane * Halifax 3.8.1881 + Köln 30.4.1962 dau. of Sir Charles Fane, and has issue:

XII   a)   **Peter Charles Ferdinand Maria Graf Wolff-Metternich zur Gracht** * Brookside, Sutton Courtenay 30.7.1915 X Ukraine 18.10.1941 = München 8.9.1939 Leila Bridget Dunn * Kingston, Surrey 15.8.1919 dau. of Sir James Dunn, and had issue:

XIII   (a)   **Tassilo Peter Franziskus Paul Maria Graf Wolff-Metternich zur Gracht** * München 29.8.1940

XII   b)   **Monika Maria Christina Flaminia Gräfin Wolff-Metternich zur Gracht** * Beck 17.12.1919 = Gracht 16.4.1947 Karl Heinrich Prinz zu Sayn-Wittgenstein-Berleburg * Kassel 31.10.1919, and has issue:

XIII   (a)   **Hubertus Maximilian Casimir Thomas Maria Prinz zu Sayn-Wittgenstein-Berleburg** * Bonn 21.12.1948

(b)   **Stephanie Maria Prinzessin zu Sayn-Wittgenstein-Berleburg** * Bonn 3.6.1950

(c)   **Andreas Wolfgang Josef Maria Prinz zu Sayn-Wittgenstein-Berleburg** * Bonn 24.12.1952

(d)   **Maria Christina Therese Prinzessin zu Sayn-Wittgenstein-Berleburg** * Bonn 20.10.1955

XI   c.   **Fritz Maximilian Constantin Hubertus Maria Graf Wolff-Metternich zur Gracht** * Beck 4.9.1874 + Gracht 26.3.1913 = Berlin 4.7.1901 Clara Schrenck * Frankfurt a.d. Oder 16.7.1869 + Berlin 14.4.1938 s.p.

d.   **Marie Josephine Sophie Emma Gräfin Wolff-Metternich zur Gracht** * Beck 15.3.1876 + Trier 28.11.1946

e.   **Levin Anton Hubert Maria Graf Wolff-Metternich zur Gracht** * Beck 12.10.1877 + Frauenthal 27.1.1944 = Köln 15.1.1913 Lidwina Freiin. Geyr v. Schweppenberg * Müddersheim 2.4.1881 + Capellen b. Euskirchen 1.10.1959 dau. of Friedrich Frhr. Geyr v. Schweppenberg, and had issue:

XII		a)	**Sophie Maria Anna Flaminia Josefine Huberta Gräfin Wolff-Metternich zur Gracht** * Eupen 31.10.1913 = Köln 28.12.1939 Hermann Frhr. von Boeselager * Heimerzheim 16.3.1913, and has issue:

XIII

- (a) **Markus Antonius Michael Frhr. v. Boeselager** * Bonn 11.2.1941
- (b) **Adelheid Marion Freiin. v. Boeselager** * Bonn 17.12.1942
- (c) **Maria-Anna Marion Freiin. v. Boeselager** * Bonn 17.9.1945
- (d) **Antonius Maria Philipp Frhr. v. Boeselager** * Capellen 16.6.1947
- (e) **Lidwine Monica Clementine Gertrud Maria Freiin. v. Boeselager** * Capellen 15.11.1951
- (f) **Hermann Josef Frhr. v. Boeselager** * 25.2.1955

XII

b) **Ferdinand Maria Anton Hubertus Joseph Graf Wolff-Metternich zur Gracht** * Eupen 28.2.1915—missing in Russia since 12.7.1943

c) **Karl Friedrich Alfred Hubert Josef Maria Graf Wolff-Metternich zur Gracht** * Eupen 19.10.1916 = Capellen 12.11.1947 Wilhelmine Gräfin Henckel v. Donnersmarck * Romolkwitz 2.1.1921 dau. of Karl Graf Henckel v. Donnersmarck, and has issue:

XIII

- (a) **Levin Michael Karl Edgar Maria Graf Wolff-Metternich zur Gracht** * Gelsenkirchen-Horst 17.7.1949
- (b) **Ferdinand Michael Paul Maria Josef Maria Graf Wolff-Metternich zur Gracht** * Gelsenkirchen-Horst 3.2.1953
- (c) **Hieronymus Michael Levin Hermann-Josef Aloysius Maria Graf Wolff-Metternich zur Gracht** * Gelsenkirchen-Horst 21.6.1955
- (d) **Carl-Joseph Johannes Liborius Michael Levin Maria Graf Wolff-Metternich zur Gracht** * Gelsenkirchen-Horst 9.8.1957
- (e) **Theresia Gräfin Wolff-Metternich zur Gracht** * 12.7.1960

XII

d) **Michael Erwein Levin Ladislaus Josef Maria Graf Wolff-Metternich zur Gracht** * Eupen 21.7.1920 = Kiedrich 29.7.1954 Ingemarie Freiin. v. Ritter zu Groenesteyn * Wiesbaden 7.8.1923 dau. of Egon Frhr. v. Ritter zu Groenesteyn s.p.

XI

f. **Josephine Hedwige Maria Huberta Gräfin Wolff-Metternich zur Gracht** * Haus Beck 10.4.1879 + Bonn 17.2.1941

g. **Ferdinand Maria Paul Leopold Hubert Graf Wolff-Metternich zur Gracht** * Beck 30.5.1881 ✗ Bellicourt 29.9.1918

h. **Joseph Maria Paul Clemens Hubert Graf Wolff-Metternich zur Gracht** * Beck 28.4.1884 + Heppingen 24.4.1943 = Strassburg 6.7.1915 Maria Freiin. Zorn v. Bulach * Osthausen 4.7.1891 dau. of Hugo Frhr. Zorn v. Bulach, and has issue:

XII

a) **Paul Joseph Hugo Ferdinand Alfred Alexander Graf Wolff-Metternich zur Gracht** * Strassburg 4.6.1916 = Hall i. Tirol 7.8.1945 Therese Gräfin zu Stolberg-Stolberg * Linsen 11.10.1923 dau. of Bernard Graf zu Stolberg-Stolberg, and has issue:

XIII

- (a) **Michael Donatus Joseph Hugo Bernhard Karl Maria Graf Wolff-Metternich zur Gracht** * Heppingen 10.5.1946
- (b) **Franz Joseph Matern Paul Maria Graf Wolff-Metternich zur Gracht** * Heppingen 7.10.1947

XIII   (c)   **Paul Christoph Martin Laurentius Kuno Maria Graf Wolff-Metternich zur Gracht**
                * Heppingen 14.4.1952

          (d)   **Theresa-Margarita Flaminia Hedwig Walburga Maria Consuelo Gräfin Wolff-Metternich zur Gracht** * 29.3.1956

          (e)   **Maria Valerie Gräfin Wolff-Metternich zur Gracht** * 26.6.1960

XII   b)   **Anna Marie Mercedes Flaminia Odilie Eleonore Gräfin Wolff-Metternich zur Gracht**
             * Strassburg 21.7.1918 = Heppingen 29.9.1942 Franz-Egon Frhr. v. Fürstenburg
             * Ehreshoven 21.11.1906 − div., and has issue:

XIII   (a)   **Peter Guido Joseph Cosmas Maria Frhr. v. Fürstenburg** * Heppingen 31.8.1945

XII   c)   **Flaminia Mathilde Odilie Maria Gräfin Wolff-Metternich zur Gracht** * Bonn 21.11.1922
             = Durbach ... François Lévêque de Vilmorin * Verrières-le-Buisson (S.-et-O.) 26.8.1922, and has issue:

XIII   (a)   **Nathalie Annemarie Caroline Lévêque de Vilmorin** * Strasbourg 28.10.1951

          (b)   **Vincent Denis Hugues Marie Frédéric Lévêque de Vilmorin** * Dürbach 30.7.1954

          (c)   **Hugues Jean Joseph Marie Benigne Lévêque de Vilmorin** * Heidelberg 25.7.1963

XII   d)   **Maria de las Mercedes Christina Odilia Gräfin Wolff-Metternich zur Gracht** * Bonn
             12.9.1924 = (1) Freiburg 14.10.1947 Weyprecht Graf Rüdt v. Collenberg * Strassburg
             22.1.1916 − div.; = (2) Durbach 28.4.1959 Sven Frhr. Marschall v. Bieberstein
             * Freiburg 11.3.1929, and has issue:

             by 1st marriage:

XIII   (a)   **Benedetta Gräfin Rüdt v. Collenberg** * Freiburg 11.4.1948

XII   e)   **Hugo Ferdinand Paul Josef Arthur Maria Graf Wolff-Metternich zur Gracht** * Heppingen
             10.12.1926 ✕ Pyritz 4.2.1945

XI   i   **Eleonore Marie Huberta Anna Gräfin Wolff-Metternich zur Gracht** * Beck 29.7.1888
          + Müddersheim 7.2.1929 = Gracht 1.10.1912 Friedrich-Karl Frhr. Geyr v. Schweppenberg
          * Müddersheim 30.6.1877 + Düren 16.2.1966, and had issue:

XII   a)   **Flaminia Constance Maximiliane Antonia Freiin. Geyr v. Schweppenberg** * Müddersheim
             19.7.1913 = 27.4.1955 Hermann Berressem * Sayn 13.12.1923 s.p.

      b)   **Sophie Mathilde Maria Huberta Antonia Freiin. Geyr v. Schweppenberg** * Müddersheim
             27.12.1914 = Müddersheim 10.5.1951 Wilfried Stegemann * Charlottenburg 4.3.1918,
             and has issue:

XIII   (a)   **Eleonore Stegemann** * Düsseldorf 15.5.1952

          (b)   **Wilhelm Stegemann** * Düsseldorf 24.7.1953

XII   c)   **Friedrich-Karl Johannes Maria Antonius Frhr. Geyr v. Schweppenberg** * Müddersheim
             21.12.1916−missing since 1945

      d)   **Theodor Kuno Hubertus Antonius Amadeus Maria Frhr. Geyr v. Schweppenberg**
             * Müddersheim 8.8.1918 = Hönningen a. Rh. 19.4.1944 Wilhelmine Gräfin v. Westerholt
             u. Gysenberg * Ariendorf 26.7.1920 dau. of Friedrich Graf v. Westerholt u. Gysenberg,
             and has issue:

XIII		(a)	**Antonius Paul Alexander Ildenfons Hubertus Maria Frhr. Geyr v. Schweppenberg** * Hönningen a. Rh. 16.8.1948
		(b)	**Johanna Cornelia Elisabeth Sofie Antonia Maria Freiin. Geyr v. Schweppenberg** * Hönningen a. Rh. 19.12.1950
		(c)	**Monika Friederike Sophie Antonia Maria Freiin. Geyr v. Schweppenberg** * Hönningen a. Rh. 9.4.1958
XII		e)	**Karl Peter Maria Antonius Hubertus Amandus Frhr. Geyr v. Schweppenberg** * Müddersheim 5.1.1920 ✗ Russia 29.12.1943
		f)	**Egon Alfred Marie Margareta Amandus Hubertus Frhr. Geyr v. Schweppenberg** * Müddersheim 14.9.1921 ✗ Villagrappa, Italy 12.11.1944

XI	j.		**Franziskus Florentin Maria Hubertus Ignatius Sylvester Graf Wolff-Metternich zur Gracht** * Beck 31.12.1893 = Schloss Herdingen 5.11.1925 Alix Freiin. v. Fürstenberg * Dahlhausen 17.3.1900 dau. of Engelbert Graf v. Fürstenberg-Herdingen, and has issue:

XII		a)	**Franziskus Johann Adolf Engelbert Ferdinand Hubertus Maria Graf Wolff-Metternich zur Gracht** * Bonn 15.8.1926
		b)	**Winfried Maria Paul Constantin Franziskus Ferdinand Engelbert Hubert Hadrian Graf Wolff-Metternich zur Gracht** * Bonn 8.9.1928 = Roma 28.5.1960 Catherine Wirts * 8.10.1932, and has issue:

XIII		(a)	**Moritz Graf Wolff-Metternich zur Gracht** * 6.7.1961
		(b)	**Katherina Gräfin Wolff-Metternich zur Gracht** * 22.4.1964
		(c)	**Paul Graf Wolff-Metternich zur Gracht** * 8.10.1965

XII		c)	**Teresia Maria Franziska Flaminia Emanuela Elisabeth Gräfin Wolff-Metternich zur Gracht** * Bonn 24.12.1930 = Altenberg 8.9.1953 Clemens Graf v.u. zu Hoensbroech * Schloss Haag 26.5.1926, and has issue:

XIII		(a)	**Maria Bernadette Agnes Franziska Pentecosta Pia Gräfin v.u. zu Hoensbroech** * Geldern 25.5.1954
		(b)	**Maria Theresa Alix Isabelle Pentecosta Pia Gräfin v.u. zu Hoensbroech** * Geldern 26.5.1956
		(c)	**Michael Maria Rüdiger Pius Heinrich Pentecoustus Graf v.u. zu Hoensbroech** * Geldern 25.5.1957
		(d)	**Martinus Maria Johannes Patrick Josef James Andreas Graf v.u. zu Hoensbroech** * Geldern 30.11.1960

XII		d)	**Antonius Franziskus Sebastianus Maria Graf Wolff-Metternich zur Gracht** * Bonn 13.6.1933

IX	2)		**Emil Georg Maximilian Joseph Prinz zu Salm-Salm** * 6.4.1820 + Rhede 27.6.1858 = 9.1.1851 Wilhelmine v. Ising * 3.7.1822 + Rhede 26.2.1887, and had issue:

X		(1)	**Florentin Andrew Rudolf Clemens Marie Prinz zu Salm-Salm** * 15.1.1852 ✗ Gravelotte 18.8.1870
		(2)	**Alexander Felix Emil Everard Waldemar Marie Prinz zu Salm-Salm** * 7.3.1853 + 17.7.1892 = 4.10.1883 Louisa Romanes * Craigerne, Scotland 29.4.1860 + Graudenz 12.12.1909 dau. of Robert Romanes s.p.
		(3)	**Claire Clementine Friederike Flaminia Olga Marie Prinzessin zu Salm-Salm** * Rhede b. Bocholt 25.9.1854 + Emms 11.8.1903 = Rhede 18.7.1876 Alexander von Padberg * Münster i. W. 18.12.1832 + Hildesheim 27.9.1912, and had issue:

XI   a.   **Wolfgang Alexander Maria Wilhelm Johannes v. Padberg** * Kassel 19.10.1878 + 6.11.1958
= Berlin 2.4.1908 Vera Bandelow * Herischdorf b. Warmbrunn 24.3.1885 dau. of
Friedrich Bandelow and had issue:

XII   a)   **Ursula v. Padberg** * Frankfurt a.d. Oder 6.11.1908 + 10.11.1918

        b)   **Ruth v. Padberg** * Frankfurt a.d. Oder 21.4.1911 = Bonn 14.10.1937 Peter Wirts
* 31.3.1895 s.p.

        c)   **Hans Wolfgang v. Padberg** * Frankfurt a.d. Oder 29.10.1914 = (1) 2.3.1940
Edith Kumpick * 11.2.1914 dau. of Otto Kumpick; = (2) 22.6.1949 Ursula Tank
* 3.2.1923 dau. of Wilhelm Tank, and has issue:

           by 2nd marriage:

XIII   (a)   **Jürgen v. Padberg** * Bad Godesberg 28.3.1950

           (b)   **Susanne v. Padberg** * Bonn 11.4.1951

           (c)   **Gabriele v. Padberg** * Bonn 12.1.1953

           (d)   **Alexander v. Padberg** * Bonn 8.10.1954

           (e)   **Wolfgang v. Padberg** * Bonn 1.4.1957

           (f)   **Felicitas v. Padberg** * Luxemburg 4.5.1962

XII   d)   **Harro Kurt Alexander v. Padberg** * Frankfurt/Oder 1.1.1918 = Hamburg 8.6.1943
Liselotte Struck * 26.1.1923 dau. of Hans Struck, and has issue:

XIII   (a)   **Harro Hans-Egon Wolfgang v. Padberg** * Hamburg 16.8.1945

           (b)   **Thomas Alexander Hubertus v. Padberg** * Hamburg 10.9.1946

           (c)   **Uwe v. Padberg** * Hamburg 3.9.1953

           (d)   **Bernd v. Padberg** * Hamburg 3.9.1953

XII   e)   **Rosemarie Irene Erdmuthe v. Padberg** * Frankfurt/Oder 1.1.1918 = Bonn 24.7.1943
Heinz Gebelhoff * 9.12.1915 and has issue:

XIII   (a)   **Elke Vera Erdmuthe Gebelhoff** * Bonn 20.8.1946

           (b)   **Ulrich Heinz Erdmann Gebelhoff** * Düsseldorf 20.4.1949

           (c)   **Ulrike Irene Erdmuthe Gebelhoff** * Düsseldorf 20.4.1949

XI   b.   **Eberhard Wilhelm Maria Aloisius v. Padberg** * Kassel 11.8.1880 + Wien 23.2.1925
= Hildesheim 4.11.1919 Paula Wildberger * Zurich 14.3.1885 + Wien ... 1929 s.p.

        c.   **Robert Gustav Friedrich v. Padberg** * Kassel 28.10.1881 + Berlin-Spandau 27.3.1937
= Hildesheim 5.2.1907 Frieda v. der Becke * Puebla, Mexico 3.12.1880 + Berlin-Spandau
15.2.1944 and had issue:

XII   a)   **Herma-Erika v. Padberg** * Berlin 1.8.1910 + Berlin 3.7.1940

        b)   **Jobst-Ekkehard v. Padberg** * Berlin 1.10.1915 = (1) Idafehn/Oldenburg 20.2.1949
Leonie Leuder * Wichmannsdorf/Mecklenburg 7.11.1924 + Bochum 7.8.1960 dau. of
Carl Leuder, = (2) Hattingen 25.2.1961 Ingrid Leuder * Redewisch, Kr. Grevesmühlen
7.7.1927 dau. of Joachim Leuder, and has issue:

           by 1st marriage:

XIII   (a)   **Lutz v. Padberg** * Essen 22.2.1950

           (b)   **Norbert v. Padberg** * Hattingen 14.9.1947

by 2nd marriage:

XIII   (c)   **Andrea v. Padberg** * Winz-Niederwenigern 24.5.1962

XI   d.   **Maria Elisabeth v. Padberg** * Frankfurt/Oder 16.2.1883 + Hildesheim June 1939

        e.   **Elisabeth Hedwig Olga Maria v. Padberg** * Frankfurt/Oder 7.7.1884 + Essen-Bredeney 1.12.1937 = (1) Hannover 26.4.1909 Johann Ulrich Frhr. v. Cramer * Magdeburg 24.3.1881 ✗ Oleche vor Lodz 22.11.1914; = (2) Berlin 17.5.1917 Hans Fusban * Krefeld 5.4.1885, and had issue:

by 1st marriage:

XII   a)   **Johann Ulrich Frhr. v. Cramer** * Charlottenburg 29.1.1910 ✗ Northern France 9.6.1940

        b)   **Albrecht Wolfgang Eberhardt Frhr. v. Cramer** * Charlottenburg 28.5.1913 ✗ Leningrad 2.3.1944

by 2nd marriage:

        c)   **Gisela Fusban** * Gelsenkirchen 22.5.1918 = Norseeinsel Spiekerog 11.6.1949 Jacobus Reimers * 22.7.1912, and has issue:

XIII   (a)   **Elisabeth Reimers** * Gummersbach 20.4.1959

           (b)   **Jacobus Reimers** * Gummersbach 11.10.1960

XII   d)   **Harald Fusban** * Essen 8.6.1922 = Krefeld 22.9.1956 Inge Kruse * Essen 5.2.1925 dau. of Theodor Kruse, and has issue:

XIII   (a)   **Elisabeth Angela Hedwig Fusban** * Essen 23.10.1950

           (b)   **Tobias Hans Harald Fusban** * Heiligenhaus 20.10.1957

           (c)   **Daniel Theodor Fusban** * Heiligenhaus 29.9.1958

XI   f.   **Adelheid Maria v. Padberg** * Frankfurt/Oder 9.3.1886 = Hildesheim 5.10.1913 Hans Rath * Juchel, Westpreussen 16.7.1872 + Bisperode b. Hameln 22.7.1951, and has issue:

XII   a)   **Hansgünther Rath** * Magdeburg 11.2.1918 ✗ Russia 1.11.1943

        b)   **Rose-Maria Rath** * Dörtmund 23.7.1921 = London 15.6.1951 Ludwig v. Lany * Tanganyika 18.3.1908, and has issue:

XIII   (a)   **Peter-Hans v. Lany** * Limuru, Tanganyika 14.8.1952

           (b)   **Joy v. Lany** * Limuru 17.6.1959

XI   g.   **Hildegarde Albertine Eugenie v. Padberg** * Frankfurt/Oder 12.2.1892 + Hildesheim 10.5.1941

IX   3)   **Felix Constantin Alexander Johann Nepomuk Prinz zu Salm-Salm** * 25.12.1828 ✗ St-Privat 18.8.1870 = Washington, U.S.A. 30.8.1862 Agnes Joy * Swanton, Vermont, U.S.A. 25.12.1840 + Herrenalb 20.12.1912 s.p.

VIII 3.   **Christian Philipp August Felix Prinz zu Salm-Salm** * & + 1791

      4.   **Georg Leopold Maximilian Christian Prinz zu Salm-Salm** * 12.4.1793 + 20.11.1836 = 29.4.1828 Marie Gräfin v. Sternberg * 4.5.1802 + 14.10.1870 dau. of Leopold Graf v. Sternberg, and had issue:

IX   1)   **Constantin Prinz zu Salm-Salm** * 27.3.1829 + 18.1.1839

IX 2) **Franziska Marie Johanna Caroline Aloisia Prinzessin zu Salm-Salm** * 4.8.1833 + Gries 3.3.1908 = Prag 18.6.1853 **Alexis Prince von Croy** * Prag 13.1.1825 + Nauheim 20.8.1898, and had issue see elsewhere

VIII 5. **Eleonore Wilhelmine Luise Prinzessin zu Salm-Salm** * Meinberg 6.12.1794 + Schloss Dülmen 6.1.1871 = Schloss Anholt 21.7.1819 Alfred 10th Herzog von Croy * Aachen 22.12.1789 + Dülmen 14.7.1861, and had issue:

IX 1) **Leopoldine Augustine Jeanne Françoise Prinzessin von Croy** * Dülmen 9.8.1821 + Firenze 26.5.1907 = Dülmen 14.7.1841 Emmanuel Prince de Croy * Bruxelles 13.12.1811 + Château de Roeulx 16.1.1865, and had issue:

X (1) **Alfred Emmanuel Prince de Croy** * Dülmen 18.3.1842 + Brügge 21.5.1888 = London 12.1.1875 Elisabeth Parnall * Landhearn 29.12.1855 + Bellignies 7.9.1912 dau. of Charles Parnall, and had issue:

XI a. **Marie Elisabeth Louise Princesse de Croy** * London 26.11.1875

   b. **Léopold Marie Charles Edouard Emmanuel Prince de Croy-Solre** * San Remo 20.2.1877 + Château Saint-Benin-d'Azy (Nièvre) 22.12.1965 = Paris 23.10.1918 Jacqueline Denyse de Lespinay * Chantonnay, Vendée 9.3.1889 dau. of Zenobe Alexis Marquis de Lespinay, and had issue:

XII a) **Elisabeth Marie Claire Léopoldine Jacqueline Princesse de Croy** * Château de Saint-Benin-d'Azy 13.12.1921

   b) **Marie Dorothée Constance Denyse Isabella Princesse de Croy** * Château de Saint-Benin-d'Azy 19.8.1924

   c) **Claire-Constance Emmanuele Marie Princesse de Croy** * Château de Saint-Benin-d'Azy 22.9.1925 = Saint-Benin-d'Azy 22.7.1955 Richard Tyser * London 16.1.1930, and has issue:

XIII (a) **Angela Tyser** * Johannesburg 20.2.1956

   (b) **Charles Robert Tyser** * Oxford 16.1.1959

   (c) **James David Tyser** * Oxford 18.3.1960

XII d) **Léopold Emmanuel Marie Reginald Johann Elias Prince de Croy-Solre** * Château de Saint-Benin-d'Azy 17.11.1926 = Bruxelles 24.11.1956 Monique Minette d'Oulhaye * Bruxelles 25.4.1923 dau. of Marc d'Oulhaye, and has issue:

XIII (a) **Emanuel Léopold Jean Reginald Marie Gobert Prince de Croy** * Uccle 28.8.1957

   (b) **Henri Jean Hubert Marie Gobert Prince de Croy** * Nevers (Nièvre) 28.9.1958

   (c) **Jacqueline Constance Marie Elisabeth Gobertine Princesse de Croy** * Uccle 10.5.1960

   (d) **Eléonore Princesse de Croy** * 13.8.1964

XII e) **Florence Paula Thérèse Marie Léopoldine Princesse de Croy** * Château de Saint-Benin-d'Azy 14.12.1927 = Saint-Benin-d'Azy 23.7.1955 **Léopold Comte de Lannoy** * Wolouwé-St. Pierre 10.11.1926, and has issue see elsewhere

   f) **Cathérine Hélène Isabella Marie Léopoldine Princesse de Croy** * Château de Saint-Benin-d'Azy 1.4.1929

   g) **Jacqueline Rose Marie Denyse Léopoldine Princesse de Croy** * Château de Saint-Benin-d'Azy 8.8.1930 = Saint-Benin-d'Azy 23.6.1962 Silvano de Freitas Branca Visconde do Porto da Cruz * Funchal 29.9.1925, and has issue:

XIII   (a)   **Rodrigo Croy de Freitas Branca** * Lisboa 23.7.1963

                     (b)   **Mafalda Croy de Freitas Branca** * Nevers 22.4.1966

XII   h)   **Emmanuele Thérèse Marie Anne Léopoldine Princesse de Croy** * Château de Saint-Benin-d'Azy 22.2.1932

XI   c.   **Reginald Charles Alfred Arthur Prince de Croy** * London 26.9.1878 + Bruxelles 13.4.1961 = Bruxelles 25.10.1920 **Isabelle Princesse de Ligne** * Bruxelles 23.9.1889 dau. of Ernest 10th Prince de Ligne, and had issue:

XII   a)   **Yolande Marie Ernestine Emma Isabelle Princesse de Croy** * Bruxelles 22.2.1924

               b)   **Diane Marie Léopoldine Jacqueline Ernestine Emmanuela Princesse de Croy** * Bruxelles 25.1.1927

X   (2)   **Edouard Louis Gustave Emmanuel Prince de Croy** * Roeulx 13.9.1843 + Saffig 3.4.1914

         (3)   **Gustave Fernand Guillaume Alfred Prince de Croy** * Dülmen 19.5.1845 + Château de Roeulx 3.9.1889 = Paris 15.6.1868 Eugenie Louise de Croix * Paris 28.3.1842 + Dree 5.5.1916 dau. of Charles Comte de Croix, and had issue:

XI   a.   **Marguerite Constance Louise Marie Princesse de Croy** * Roeulx 1.10.1869 + Lugny-les-Charolles 23.9.1950 = Paris 28.6.1893 Théodule Comte de Grammont * Villersexel (H-S) 10.11.1865 + Lugny-les-Charolles (S-et-L) 23.12.1940, and had issue:

XII   a)   **Antoine Pierre Marie Théodule Louis Gustave Emmanuel Christoph Marquis de Grammont** * Paris 7.8.1897 = 20.10.1927 Anne-Marie Budes de Guébriant * St-Pol-de-Léon 6.8.1906 dau. of Hervé-Marie Budes Comte de Guébriant, and has issue:

XIII   (a)   **Marguerite Marie Jeanne Théodoline Aymardine Antoinette de Grammont** * Paris 12.6.1929 = Paris 14.6.1952 Christian Comte de Villoutreys * Paris 19.2.1925, and has issue:

XIV   1a.   **Jean François Marie Pierre Humbert de Villoutreys** * Paris 6.5.1953

                       2a.   **Thierry Marie Christian Antoine de Villoutreys** * Paris 8.6.1954

                       3a.   **Amaury de Villoutreys** * Paris 22.12.1963

XIII   (b)   **Bernard Alain Jean Marie Théodule Comte de Grammont** * Lugny-les-Charolles 1.10.1932

                 (c)   **Marie Hélène Léonie Mathilde de Grammont** * Paris 13.11.1933 = Paris 5.12.1960 Arnaud de Thomasson * Paris 9.12.1930, and has issue:

XIV   1a.   **Jean Marie Michel de Thomasson** * Paris 25.11.1961

                       2a.   **Eric Bernard de Thomasson** * Paris 19.11.1962

                       3a.   **Yves de Thomasson** * Paris 20.5.1966

XII   b)   **Alexandrine Aline Stéphanie Théodoline Marguerite Marie de Grammont** * Paris 25.1.1900

               c)   **Michel Emmanuel Marie Théodule Antoine Jean Comte de Grammont-Crillon** * Paris 28.12.1901 = Paris 5.5.1931 Henriette des Acres de l'Aigle * Paris 17.7.1910 dau. of Charles des Acres Marquis de l'Aigle, and has issue:

XIII   (a)   **Béatrice de Grammont** * Paris 5.3.1932 = Choisy-au-Bac 4.10.1955 Bertrand Marquis de Bouillé * Paris 2.7.1923, and has issue:

164

XIV   1a.   **Anne Olive de Bouillé** * Neuilly-sur-Seine 10.4.1957

     2a.   **Pierre de Bouillé** * Neuilly-sur-Seine 29.6.1958

     3a.   **Alix Rosalie de Bouillé** * Neuilly-sur-Seine 22.4.1963

XIII   (b)   **Comte Charles Emmanuel de Grammont** * Paris 4.1.1934

     (c)   **Elisabeth de Grammont** * Paris 18.11.1939 = Paris 7.3.1964 Comte Louis du Pouget de Nadaillac * Paris 9.6.1936

     (d)   **Ariane-Marie de Grammont** * Paris 24.1.1943 = Paris 7.10.1966 Jean Pierre le Clement de Saint Marcq * Bruxelles 21.10.1941

XII   d)   **Monique Marie Théodulee Aymardine Emma Antoinette Jeanne de Grammont** * Paris 16.4.1905 = Paris 15.11.1930 Comte Gaston du Chastel de la Howarderie * Bruxelles 22.1.1897, and has issue:

XIII   (a)   **Comte Jean Baptiste Gaston Marie Théodule Eugène du Chastel de la Howarderie** * Paris 14.4.1932 = Le-Plessis-Biron 20.10.1954 Yvonne Schaeffer * Beauvais 26.8.1934, dau. of Pierre Schaeffer and has issue:

XIV   1a.   **Comtesse Dominique Marie Alix Madeleine Charlotte Monique Renée du Chastel de la Howarderie** * Namur 25.5.1956

     2a.   **Comtesse Marylène Charlotte Monique du Chastel de la Howarderie** * Namur 13.3.1959

XIII   (b)   **Comtesse Marie Salvatrix Bernadette Anne Thérèse Elisabeth Marguerite du Chastel de la Howarderie** * Lugny-les-Charolles 14.10.1935 = Beret-Plage 18.8.1963 Marcel Coufourié * ... and has issue:

XIV   1a.   **Jean-Marc Coufourié** * 25.3.1965

XIII   (c)   **Comte Patrick Emmanuel Marie Antoine Pierre Gaston Ghislain du Chastel de la Howarderie** * St-Michel-de-Livet 12.8.1943

     (d)   **Comtesse Alix Henriette Marie Espérance Antoinette Louise du Chastel de la Howarderie** * Compiègne (Oise) 24.12.1950

XI   b.   **Auguste Marie Gustave Étienne Charles Emmanuel Prince de Croy** * Roeulx 18.10.1872 + Paris 4.6.1932 = Héverlé 2.12.1896 Marie Salvatrix Princesse et Duchesse d'Arenberg * Héverlé 26.4.1874 + Château de Roeulx 9.5.1956 dau. of Engelbert-August 8th Duc d'Arenberg, and had issue:

XII   a)   **Eléonore Dorothée Sophie Léopoldine Amélie Antoinette Marie Gabrielle Princesse de Croy** * Héverlé 19.9.1897 = Paris 25.4.1925 Comte Guy de La Rochefoucauld * Paris 14.5.1894 + Paris 23.1.1952, and has issue:

XIII   (a)   **Agnes de La Rochefoucauld** * Paris 15.3.1926

     (b)   **Comte Marc de La Rochefoucauld** * Paris 26.4.1927 = 29.4.1954 Claude-Chantal Pighetti de Rivasso * Paris 2.3.1930 dau. of Stephane Comte Pighetti de Rivasso, and has issue:

XIV   1a.   **Marie Dominique de La Rochefoucauld** * Chamonix 1.8.1957

     2a.   **Marie Josefa de La Rochefoucauld** * Chamonix 4.2.1963

     3a.   **Marie Benedicte de La Rochefoucauld** * Chamonix 25.12.1965

XIII   (c)   **Eliane de La Rochefoucauld** * Paris 22.7.1928

XII   b)   **Etienne Gustave Emmanuel Antoine Engelbert Marie Prince de Croy-Roeulx**
* Bruxelles 8.9.1898 = Paris 12.7.1922 **Alyette de Pomereu** * Paris 4.3.1903 dau.
of Robert Marquis de Pomereu and has issue:

XIII   (a)   **Rodolphe Etienne Alexandre Antoine Marie Prince de Croy** * Paris 8.4.1924
= Bailleul 15.12.1945 Odile de Bailleul * Paris 5.8.1926 dau. of Joseph Marquis
de Bailleul, and has issue:

XIV   1a.   **Olivier Robèrt Etienne Prince de Croy** * Paris 1.6.1948

                     2a.   **Alyette Princesse de Croy** * Paris 13.4.1951

XIII   (b)   **Philippe Robèrt Marie Prince de Croy** * Paris 13.5.1928

XII   c)   **Emmanuel Engelbert Prince de Croy** * & + Roeulx 2.2.1904

        d)   **Alexandre Etienne Emmanuel Marie François Gabriel Gérard Prince de Croy** * Roeulx
12.10.1905 + Château de Dree 3.5.1929

        e)   **Marie Claire Emma Engelberte Antoinette Princesse de Croy** * Roeulx 25.9.1907 = Roeulx
14.6.1926 **Amaury Prince de Merode** * Everbergh 3.10.1902 and has issue see elsewhere

        f)   **Gustave Théodule Fernand Josèphe Antoine Marie Prince de Croy** * Roeulx 21.8.1911
= Bruxelles 24.6.1959 Renée Lelarge * Huy 9.5.1908, dau. of Oscar Lelarge

XI   c.   **Constance Léopoldine Philippine Marie Princesse de Croy** * Paris 15.4.1876 + Château
Berlandet-lès-Echelles 10.10.1943 = Paris 7.7.1903 Comte Elzéar de Sabran-Pontevès
* Villeneuve-Loubet 17.2.1865 + Villecresnes (S-et-O.) 20.11.1940 and had issue:

XII   a)   **Marie Josèphe Delphine Guillemette Louise Antoinette Sybille de Sabran-Pontevès**
* Paris 18.3.1905 + Angers 15.9.1923

        b)   **Marie Josèphe Delphine Stéphanette de Sabran-Pontevès** * Paris 28.3.1906

        c)   **Marie Joseph Elzéar Gustave Jean Foulques Duc de Sabran-Pontevès** * Curbigny (S-et-L)
11.2.1908 = Paris 11.1.1936 Roselyne Monca Amat de Vallambrosa * Paris 19.9.1910
dau. of Comte Amedee Moncat Amat de Vallambrosa and has issue:

XIII   (a)   **Charles-Elzéar Marquis de Sabran-Pontevès** * Villecresnes 30.4.1937

             (b)   **Jean-Henri Elzéar Comte de Sabran-Pontevès** * Villecresnes 15.1.1939 = Paris
27.2.1965 Marie Isabelle Decazes * Cauderan (Gironde) 4.7.1941 dau. of Elie
Duc Decazes et de Glücksbierg, and has issue:

XIV   1a.   **Laure de Sabran-Pontevès** * Neuilly-sur-Seine 26.2.1966

XIII   (c)   **Géraud Amie de Sabran-Pontevès** * Villecresnes 18.3.1940 + Le Puy (Haute-Loire)
21.1.1941

             (d)   **Gersende de Sabran-Pontevès** * Ansouis (Vauclause) 29.7.1942

             (e)   **Comte Géraud de Sabran-Pontevès** * Ansouis 27.8.1943

13　Prince Léopold de Croÿ-Solre,
1877–1965

14　Prince Etienne de Croÿ-Roeulx

XII   d)   **Marie Josèphe Delphine Théoduline Jeanne Marguerite de Sabran-Pontevès** * Curbigny 25.9.1909 = Paris 25.5.1943 François Marquis de Vaulserre * Hagondange (Moselle) 2.7.1892 s.p.

         e)   **Marie Josèphe Delphine Isabelle de Sabran-Pontevès** * Curbigny 14.9.1915 = Villecresnes 31.8.1939 Bertrand Baron de Lacger Camplong * Orleans 20.9.1914 + St-Cloud 9.3.1951, and has issue:

XIII   (a)   **Baron Antoine Louis de Lacger Camplong** * Castres (Tarn) 19.7.1940

              (b)   **Anne Dauphine de Lacger Camplong** * Castres 6.11.1943

              (c)   **François de Lacger Camplong** * Castres 6.11.1943 + Castres 1.2.1944

              (d)   **Isabeau Françoise de Lacger Camplong** * Neuilly-sur-Seine 31.1.1945

XI   d.   **Alix Maximiliane Marie Princesse de Croy** * Roeulx 9.8.1884 = Paris 22.1.1907 René de la Croix Comte de Castries * 4.4.1876 + Paris 16.10.1950, and has issue:

XII   a)   **Maximilian Marie François de Paule Gabriel Gustave Antoine de la Croix Comte de Castries** * Roeulx 21.12.1908 = Paris 12.7.1946 Marie-Henriette de Tulle de Villefranche * Paris 9.3.1917 dau. of Henri Marquis de Villefranche, and has issue:

XIII   (a)   **Gabriel de la Croix de Castries** * Paris 28.8.1951

XII   b)   **Sabine Marie Jeanne Stéphanie Ghislaine de la Croix de Castries** * Paris 8.6.1910 + Château de Roeulx 11.1.1920

XI   e.   **Pauline Marie Magdalene Princesse de Croy** * Roeulx 11.1.1887

X   (4) & (5)   Twin Girls * & + Roeulx 24.4.1846

         (6)   **Emma Henriette Marie Léopoldine Princesse de Croy** * Roeulx 27.2.1858 + Pau ... 4.1934

IX   2)   **Rudolf Maximilian Constantin 11th Herzog von Croy** * Dülmen 13.3.1823 + Cannes 8.2.1902 = (1) Beloeil 15.9.1853 **Nathalie Princesse de Ligne** * Beloeil 31.5.1853 + Trazégnies 23.7.1863 dau. of Eugène 8th Prince de Ligne, = (2) Beauraing 22.9.1884 **Marie Prinzessin zu Salm-Salm** * Frankfurt-am-Main 21.1.1842 + Dülmen 18.6.1891 dau. of Franz Prinz zu Salm-Salm, and had issue:

by 1st marriage:

X   (1)   **Eugenie Eleonore Marie Louise Hedwige Prinzessin v. Croy** * Dülmen 11.10.1854 + Wien 12.6.1889 = Dülmen 17.6.1879 Paul 10th Fürst Esterházy v. Galántha * Wien 11.3.1843 + Lokkenhaus 22.8.1898, and has issue:

XI   a.   **Rudolf Paul Eugen Prinz Esterházy v. Galántha** * Hütteldorf 27.5.1880

X   (2)   **Isabelle Hedwige Franziska Natalie Prinzessin v. Croy** * Dülmen 27.2.1856 + Budapest 5.9.1931 = Schloss l'Hermitage, Belgium 8.10.1878 **Friedrich Archduke of Austria, Herzog v. Teschen** * Gross-Seelowitz 4.6.1856 + Altenburg, Hungary 30.12.1936, and had issue see elsewhere

         (3)   **Clementine Ferdinande Anne Prinzessin v. Croy** * Dülmen 9.7.1857 + Château de la Berlière 3.8.1893 = Dülmen 11.5.1880 Adhémar Comte d'Oultremont * Bruxelles 9.7.1845 + Paris 9.7.1910, and had issue:

XI   a.   **Emmanuel Octave Eugène Comte d'Oultremont** * Cannes 8.3.1881 + Duras 3.11.1958 = Bruxelles 11.2.1909 Antoinette Comtesse d'Oultremont * Bruxelles 19.7.1885 + Duras 20.8.1966 dau. of Eugène Comte d'Oultremont, and had issue:

XII		a)	Henriette Clémentine Antoinette Marie Ghislaine Comtesse d'Oultremont * Bruxelles 20.5.1910 = Duras 12.4.1934 **René Comte de Liedekerke de Pailhe** * Eysden 21.8.1906 s.p.
		b)	Clémentine Isabelle Antoinette Eugénie Marie Ghislaine Comtesse d'Oultremont * Bruxelles 5.4.1913 = Duras 16.4.1947 Edouard Comte de Liedekerke * Jehay-Bodegnée 6.9.1909, and has issue:

XIII

    (a) **Pierre Rasse Antoine Marie Ghislain Oscar Comte de Liederkerke** * Verlaine 31.12.1947 + Verlaine 2.2.1948

    (b) **Etienne Emmanuel Rasse Marie Ghislain Comte de Liederkerke** * Duras 16.1.1949

    (c) **Bertrand Henri Gérard Marie Ghislain Comte de Liederkerke** * Duras 18.8.1952

XII   c)   **Isabelle Marie Georgine Antoinette Comtesse d'Oultremont** * Bruxelles 11.7.1919

XI   b.   **Rodolphe Charles Alfred Henri Comte d'Oultremont** * Hontaing-lez-Leuze 24.11.1882 + 4.6.1921

X   (4)   **Carl Alfred 12 Herzog v. Croy** * Bruxelles 29.1.1859 + Schloss Karapancsa, Hungary 28.9.1906 = Bruxelles 25.4.1888 Marie-Ludmilla Princesse et Duchesse d'Arenberg * Héverlé 29.6.1870 + La Solitude, près Bruxelles 9.9.1953 dau. of Engelbert-August 8 Duc d'Arenberg, and had issue:

XI   a.   **Karl Rudolf Engelbert Philipp Leo 13 Herzog v. Croy** * Bruxelles 11.4.1889 = (1) Versoix b. Genève 27.10.1913 Nancy Leishman * Pittsburg 2.10.1894 dau. of John Leishman — div.; = (2) München 22.10.1924 Helene Lewis * Albany N.Y. 14.2.1898 — div.; = (3) Berlin 28.1.1933 Marie Louise Wiesner * Wandsbeck 22.6.1904 + Nordkirchen 13.2.1945; = (4) Düsseldorf 17.2.1949 Hildegard v. Guérard * Düsseldorf 26.1.1915 dau. of Theodor v. Guérard, and has issue:

by 1st marriage:

XII   a)   **Carl Emanuel Ludwig Petrus Eleonore Alexander Rudolf Engelbert Benno Erbprinz v. Croy** * Düsseldorf 11.10.1914 = Nymphenburg 18.6.1953 **Gabrielle Princess of Bavaria** * Berchtesgarden 10.5.1927 dau. of Rupprecht Crown Prince of Bavaria, and has issue:

XIII

    (a) **Marie-Theresa Antonia Nancy Charlotte Prinzessin v. Croy** * Dülmen 29.3.1954

    (b) **Rudolf Carl Rupprecht Prinz v. Croy** * Dülmen 8.7.1955

    (c) **Stefan Clemens Philipp Prinz v. Croy** * Merfeld 17.5.1959

XII   b)   **Antoinette Emma Laurenzia Charlotte Ludmilla Juliette Martha Helene Sabina Prinzessin v. Croy** * Berlin 27.10.1915 = (1) Nordkirchen 14.6.1943 Jürgen v. Goerne * Allenstein 12.2.1908 — div.; = (2) Hamburg ... 1947 Frederick Nelson Tucker * London 3.12.1919 — div. s.p.

     c)   **Maria-Luise Natalie Engelberta Ludmilla Prinzessin v. Croy** * Dülmen 18.12.1919 = (1) New York 11.3.1941 Richard Metz * New York 19.6.1912 — div.; = (2) New York 27.11.1952 Nelson Slater * Webster, Mass 7.7.1893, and has issue:

by 1st marriage:

XIII

    (a) **Valerie Metz** * New York 23.1.1945

by 3rd marriage:

XII   d)   **Clemens Franz Carl Anselm Prinz v. Croy** * Berlin 5.7.1934 = Neudau 25.5.1962 **Madeleine Gräfin Kottulinsky** * Graz 11.11.1941 dau. of Hans Graf Kottulinksy, and has issue:

168

XIII   (a)   **Carl Clemens Prinz v. Croy** * Graz 5.3.1963

             (b)   **Cecile Marie-Louise Charlotte Brigitte Prinzessin v. Croy** * Graz 21.2.1964

XI   b.   **Isabella Antonie Eleonore Natalie Klementine Prinzessin v. Croy** * Schloss L'Hermitage 7.10.1890 = Schloss Weilburg, Baden b. Wien 8.7.1912 **Franz Prince of Bavaria** * Leutstetten 10.10.1875 + Leutstetten 25.1.1947, and has issue see elsewhere

   c.   **Engelbert Ernst Eugen Prinz v. Croy** * Schloss L'Hermitage 9.11.1891 = Wien 27.11.1929 Marie Benedikta Prinzessin zu Schwarzenberg * Provitin 27.3.1900 dau. of Johann 9 Fürst zu Schwarzenberg s.p.

   d.   **Anton Prosper Clemens Prinz v. Croy** * Bruxelles 6.1.1893 = (1) Marienloh 23.5.1922 Rosalie v. Heyden-Linden * Fürstenberg 5.8.1894 + Münster i. W. 28.3.1942 dau. of Bogislav v. Heyden-Linden; = (2) Buchberg-am-Kamp 15.5.1944 **Wilhelmine Prinzessin v. Croy** * Wien 18.5.1906 dau. of Klemens Prinz v. Croy, and has issue:

by 1st marriage:

XII   a)   **Maria Elisabeth Ludmilla Josepha Prinzessin v. Croy** * Paderborn 10.3.1923 = Grumsmühlen 23.6.1944 Matthias Graf v. Schmettow * Potsdam 22.10.1918, and has issue:

XIII   (a)   **Wolfgang Bernhard Gottfried Anton Graf v. Schmettow** * Lingen a.d. Emms 14.3.1945

             (b)   **Rosalie Therese Brigitta Elisabeth Gräfin v. Schmettow** * Grumsmühlen 12.5.1948

             (c)   **Nikolaus Engelbert Albert Johannes Graf v. Schmettow** * Bochum 21.7.1953

             (d)   **Isabelle Maria-Theresia Colette Leonie Gräfin v. Schmettow** * Bruxelles 28.4.1960

XII   b)   **Carl-Alfred Friedrich Bogislaus Joseph Prinz v. Croy** * Marienloh 4.3.1924 = Haus Seelen über Xanten 7.5.1952 Huberta Freiin. v. Wolff gen Metternich * Haus Seelen 2.2.1928 dau. of Karl-Reinhard Frhr. v. Wolff gen Metternich s.p.

   c)   **Engelbert Emmanuel Alexander Joseph Prinz v. Croy** * Grumsmühlen 22.7.1925 ✗ missing in Russia 1945

   d)   **Clemens Anton Philipp Joseph Prinz v. Croy** * Grumsmühlen 7.9.1926 = Ehreshoven 27.7.1955 **Marie Therese Gräfin v. Schaesberg** * Berlin 11.12.1927 dau. of Walter Graf v. Schaesberg, and has issue:

XIII   (a)   **Eugen-Alexander Prinz v. Croy** * Mülheim a.d. Ruhr 22.4.1956

             (b)   **Philippe Prinz v. Croy** * Mülheim 8.9.1957

             (c)   **Albrecht Alexander Prinz v. Croy** * Mülheim 8.5.1959

             (d)   **Engelbert Alexander Prinz v. Croy** * Leverskusen 5.6.1962

XII   e)   **Margaretha Maria Christina Emmanuela Henriette Anna Katharina Prinzessin v. Croy** * Grumsmühlen 11.10.1930 = Grumsmühlen 7.6.1956 **Heinrich Graf v. Schaesberg** * Berlin 12.2.1922, and has issue see elsewhere

   f)   **Sophia Magdalena Maria Monica Prinzessin v. Croy** * Paderborn 28.3.1932 = Bruxelles 9.11.1957 **Tanguy le Gentil Vicomte de Rosmorduc** * Bruxelles 12.11.1927, and has issue see elsewhere

by 2nd marriage:

   g)   **Anton Egon Clemens Prinz v. Croy** * Grumsmühlen 27.8.1945

X   (5)   **Natalie Constance Henriette Prinzessin v. Croy** * Trazégnies 14.7.1863 + Düren 2.9.1957 = Dülmen 4.9.1883 Henri Comte de Merode 5 Prince de Grimberghe 8 Prince de Rubempré et d'Everberghe * Paris 28.12.1856 + Lausanne 13.7.1908, and had issue:

XI		a.	**Marie-Rodolphine Nathalie Ghislaine Comtesse de Merode** * Bruxelles 28.9.1884 = Westerloo 8.9.1910 **Don Luigi Massimo-Lancellotti Principe di Prossedi** * Frascati 29.7.1881 and has issue see elsewhere

XI   a.   **Marie-Rodolphine Nathalie Ghislaine Comtesse de Merode** * Bruxelles 28.9.1884 = Westerloo 8.9.1910 **Don Luigi Massimo-Lancellotti Principe di Prossedi** * Frascati 29.7.1881 and has issue see elsewhere

           b.   **Henriette Charlotte Eugénie Marie Ghislaine Comtesse de Merode** * Bruxelles 29.12.1885 = Westerloo 11.5.1920 Guillaume Comte d'Hemricourt de Grunne * Bauffe 14.10.1888, and has issue:

XII   a)   **Colette Nathalie Léonie Françoise Thérèse Madeleine Joséphine Marie Ghislaine Comtesse d'Hemricourt de Grunne** * Forest 16.12.1924 = Westerloo 12.10.1948 Baudouin Comte Cornet d'Elzius du Chenoy de Wal d'Espiennes * Bruxelles 12.3.1921 s.p.

                     b)   **Jeanne Marie Eugénie Thérèse Josephine Ghislaine Comtesse d'Hemricourt de Grunne** * Forest 11.6.1929 = Genève 17.5.1962 Alexis Prince Guédroïtz * Pancevo, Yugoslavia 9.6.1923, and has issue:

XIII   (a)   **Nicholas Prince Guédroïtz** * Bruxelles 5.7.1963

XI   c.   **Charles Werner Marie Gabriel Joseph Ghislain Prince de Merode Prince de Rubempré** * Bruxelles 28.11.1887 = Paris 10.11.1919 Marguerite Marie de Laguiche * Paris 8.5.1895 dau. of Peter Marquis de Laguiche s.p.

IX   3)   **Alexis Wilhelm Zephrin Victor Prinz v. Croy** * Paris 13.1.1825 + Bad Nauheim 20.8.1898 = Prag 18.6.1853 **Franziska Prinzessin zu Salm-Salm** * Pohořelic 4.8.1833 + Gries b. Bozen 3.3.1908 dau. of Georg Prinz zu Salm-Salm, and had issue:

X   (1)   **Marie Rosine Franziska Prinzessin v. Croy** * Dülmen 11.5.1854 + Gries b. Bozen 20.4.1901

        (2)   **Eleonore Leopoldine Aloisia Prinzessin v. Croy** * 13.5.1854 + Berlin 20.3.1904 = Schönau-Teplitz 13.5.1855 **Nikolaus Leopold Fürst zu Salm-Salm** * Anholt 18.7.1838 + Anholt 16.2.1908 s.p.

        (3)   **Max Rudolf Karl Dietrich Anna Prinz v. Croy** * Schweckhausen, Westf. 16.1.1864 + Slabetz 20.5.1920 = Křimic, Böh. 6.10.1908 Caroline Prinzessin v. Lobkowicz * Konopischt 4.10.1873 + Isareck 11.2.1951 dau. of Franz Prinz v. Lobkowicz, and had issue:

XI   a.   **Alexis Franz Antonius Maximilian Carolus Benediktus Mathias Maria Prinz v. Croy** * Slabetz 24.2.1910 = Petschau, Böh. 7.10.1931 **Elisabeth Gräfin v. Beaufort-Spontin** * Wien 15.11.1911 dau. of Heinrich Herzog v. Beaufort-Spontin, and has issue:

XII   a)   **Maximilian Heinrich Karl Maria Prinz v. Croy** * Slabetz 9.9.1932 = Altötting 29.11.1958 Asja Lukic * ... dau. of ... and has issue:

XIII   (a)   **Alexis Prinz v. Croy** * München 24.9.1959

XII   b)   **Albrecht Maria Johann Gerhard Michael Prinz v. Croy** * Slabetz 24.6.1938

                  c)   **Maria Anna Eleonore Antonia Mathea Prinzessin v. Croy** * Slabetz 20.9.1939 = Aicha 4.4.1964 Tamás Vass de Bihar * Penc, Hungary 15.5.1936, and has issue:

XIII   (a)   **Elisabeth Maria Eva Vass de Bihar** * 9.8.1964

XII   d)   **Anna Maria Friederike Alberta Prinzessin v. Croy** * Slabetz 24.2.1943 = Aicha ü. Vilshofen 6.10.1962 **Wolfram Frhr. v. Strachwitz** * Maserwitz 10.8.1933, and has issue see elsewhere

                  e)   **Johannes Marie Michael Prinz v. Croy** * Osterhofen 12.2.1955 + Passau 14.2.1955

XI   b.   **Franz de Paul Alfred Maximilian Aloys Marie Prinz v. Croy** * Slabetz 31.5.1911 ✕ Holland 26.9.1944

XI   c.   **Max Ignaz Anton Gerhard Benedikt Karl Maria Prinz v. Croy** * Slabetz 12.6.1912 = Prag 23.5.1938 Karoline Gräfin v. Busseul * Subotica 8.5.1918 dau. of Raoul Graf v. Busseul and has issue:

XII   a)   **Huberta Maria Prinzessin v. Croy** * Petschau 15.10.1939

           b)   **Josef Maria Prinz v. Croy** * Petschau 7.7.1941

           c)   **Alfred Maria Prinz v. Croy** * Petschau 3.2.1945

XI   d.   **Alfred Franz Johann Nepomuk Maximilian Karl Gerard Benoit Marie Prinz v. Croy** * Slabetz 17.12.1913 ✕ b. Pustoschka, Russia 23.11.1943

IX   4)   **Emma Auguste Prinzessin v. Croy** * Dülmen 26.6.1826 + Paris 7.1.1909

      5)   **Georges Victor Prince de Croy** * Château d'Hermitage 30.6.1828 + Paris 15.4.1879 = Paris 22.1.1862 Marie de Durfort-Civrac de Lorge * Paris 15.1.1841 + Château de Chambray (Eure) 28.12.1910 dau. of Emerie de Durfort-Civrac Duc de Lorge, and had issue:

X   (1)   **Louis Guillaune Laurent Victor Prince de Croy** * Château de L'Hermitage Condé-sur-L'Escaut (Nord) 22.9.1862 + Paris 28.5.1931 = Paris 24.11.1887 Hortense de L'Espine * Paris 25.2.1867 + Paris 28.8.1932 dau. of Comte Marie Emil de L'Espine s.p.

     (2)   **Marie-Eléonore Georgine Louise Princesse de Croy** * Bruxelles 6.1.1864 + Champfleury (Nièvre) 7.1.1962 = Paris 26.5.1887 René Vicomte de Chevigné * Poitiers 13.9.1851 + Château de Flesselles (Somme) 27.2.1899, and had issue:

XI   a.   **Marie Louise Alphonsine de Chevigné** * Paris 12.2.1889 + Epinay-sur-Orge 22.11.1940

       b.   **Anne Marie Josèphe Henriette de Chevigné** * Le Havre 6.9.1891 + Bordeaux 28.12.1962

       c.   **Anne Marie Joseph Guillaume Vicomte de Chevigné** * Angers (M-et-L.) 25.10.1893 ✕ Vaux (Somme) 20.6.1916

X   (3)   **Marie Elisabeth Pauline Anne Princesse de Croy** * Bruxelles 27.9.1865 + Paris 12.3.1947 = Paris 11.2.1889 Charles Comte de Bruce * Château d'Harzillemont á Hagnicourt (Ardennes) 30.3.1862 + Paris 9.1.1946, and had issue:

XI   a.   **Comte Robert Marie Hervé Charles Prosper de Bruce** * Château d'Harzillemont 18.11.1889 ✕ Verdun 11.9.1917

       b.   **Edouard Marie Louis Georges David Comte de Bruce** * Paris 24.6.1896 = Paris 3.2.1931 Anne d'Estampes * Paris 14.9.1903 dau. of Robert Marquis d'Estampes, and has issue:

XII   a)   **Comte Robert Marie Joseph de Bruce** * Paris 11.5.1932 = Château de St-Fargeau 15.10.1955 Beryl Anisson du Perron * Paris 26.2.1935 dau. of Alexandre Anisson du Perron, and has issue:

XIII   (a)   **Edouard de Bruce** * Paris 19.3.1957

           (b)   **Jacques de Bruce** * Paris 19.10.1958

           (c)   **Richard de Bruce** * Paris 26.5.1961

XII   b)   **Comte Charles Edouard Marie de Bruce** * Paris 4.7.1933 = Paris 8.9.1962 **Sylviane de Rochechouart de Mortemart** * Entrains-sur-Nohain 21.1.1940 dau. of Charles de Rochechouart 13 Duc de Mortemart, and has issue:

XIII   (a)   **Carlotta de Bruce** * Boulogne-sur-Seine 5.6.1963

X	(4)			**Jeanne Marie Emma Augustine Princesse de Croy** * Dülmen 9.10.1870 * Chambray (Eure) 29.5.1966 = Paris 20.6.1894 Herbert d'Espagne Marquis de Venevelles * Château de l'Assessoye 1.9.1864 + Paris 27.1.1923, and had issue:

X   (4)   Jeanne Marie Emma Augustine Princesse de Croy * Dülmen 9.10.1870 * Chambray (Eure) 29.5.1966 = Paris 20.6.1894 Herbert d'Espagne Marquis de Venevelles * Château de l'Assessoye 1.9.1864 + Paris 27.1.1923, and had issue:

XI   a.   **Fernand Marie Georges Gérard d'Espagne de Venevelles Marquis de Venevelles** * Paris 5.8.1895 + Sancoins 4.1.1945

    b.   **Georges Marie Louis Herbert d'Espagne de Venevelles Marquis de Venevelles** * Paris 21.2.1898 = Paris 4.2.1936 Marguerite des Isnards * 19.12.1910 dau. of Charles Marquis des Isnards, and has issue:

XII   a)   **Rosalie d'Espagne de Venevelles** * Paris 5.12.1936 = Paris 6.5.1961 Christoph Graf v. Degenfeld-Schönburg * Wien 9.4.1929, and has issue:

XIII   (a)   **Franz Joseph Christoph Johannes Maria Graf v. Degenfeld-Schönburg** * Heilbronn-am-Neckar 25.9.1962

    (b)   **Stephan Godehard Christoph Johannes Maria Graf v. Degenfeld-Schönburg** * Heilbronn-am-Neckar 15.5.1964

    (c)   **Georges Johannes Christoph Pascal Maria Graf v. Degenfeld-Schönburg** * Heilbronn-am-Neckar 16.4.1966

XII   b)   **Marguerite Marie d'Espagne de Venevelles** * Paris 12.7.1938

    c)   **Henri d'Espagne Comte de Venevelles** * Paris 11.10.1942

    d)   **Comte Alain d'Espagne de Venevelles** * Paris 1.1.1946

XI   c.   **Anne Marie Isabelle Eléonore d'Espagne de Venevelles** * Paris 4.5.1906 = 9.10.1930 Alain Budes Vicomte de Guébriant * Livry (S.-et-M.) 5.8.1905 + St-Pol-de-Léon 4.8.1944, and has issue:

XII   a)   **Aliette Jeanne Marie Léonie Budes de Guébriant** * Paris 6.8.1931 = Paris 3.7.1959 Comte Charles Henri de Cossé-Brissac * Paris 16.3.1936, and has issue:

XIII   (a)   **Marie Henriette de Cossé-Brissac** * Paris 23.4.1961

    (b)   **Anne Françoise de Cossé-Brissac** * Paris 5.6.1962

XII   b)   **Roland Georges Hervé Jean Budes Vicomte de Guébriant** * Paris 10.7.1936

X   (5)   **François Marie Emmanuel Josephe Prince de Croy** * Paris 18.3.1873 + 3.2.1950 = Paris 9.10.1908 Valentine Marie Louise de Chaponay * Château de Lascours (Gard) 28.4.1885 dau. of Jean de Chaponay, and has issue:

XI   a.   **Maximilienne Jeanne Françoise Marie Raymonde Princesse de Croy** * Sedan (Ardennes) 11.10.1909 = Paris 19.6.1933 Aymar Comte de La Tour du Pin Chambly * Paris 2.11.1906 and has issue:

XII   a)   **Comte François de La Tour du Pin Chambly** * Boulogne-Billancourt 1.3.1934

    b)   **Comte Olivier de La Tour du Pin Chambly** * Boulogne-Billancourt 21.2.1935 = 26.12.1964 Catherine de Guigné * Annecy 22.7.1942 dau. of Jacques Comte de Guigné, and has issue:

XIII   (a)   **Laurent de La Tour du Pin Chambly** * 26.2.1966

XII   c)   **Marie-Phylis de La Tour du Pin Chambly** * Paris 3.12.1936 = Paris 23.12.1959 Comte Renaud de Failly * Paris 13.1.1935, and has issue:

172

XIII   (a)   **Christophe de Failly** * Paris 18.1.1962

           (b)   **Isabelle de Failly** * 1.8.1965

XII   d)   **Dominique de La Tour du Pin Chambly** * Boisset-et-Gaujac (Gard) 4.12.1940 = Paris 18.4.1963 Comte Hervé de La Crenne de Verdun * 4.7.1935, and has issue:

XIII   (a)   **Geoffroy de La Crenne de Verdun** * Paris 16.2.1965

XI   b.   **François Emmanuel Georges Marie Pierre Prince de Croy** * Château de Juigné-sur-Mayenne 15.8.1913 = Indo-China 1.12.1941 Cecile Dumont * ... and has issue:

XII   a)   **Isabelle Princesse de Croy** * Indo-China 7.2.1943

XI   c.   **Humbert Marie François Antoine Louis Prince de Croy** * Château de Lascours (Gard) 20.1.1915 X 1944

        d.   **Simone Marie Mathilde Armande Princesse de Croy** * Château de Lascours (Gard) 6.11.1917 = Château de Lascours ... 10.1942 Comte Joachim de Pierre de Bernis * Aigues-Mortes (Gard) 18.12.1912 + Quincandon 4.12.1965, and has issue:

XII   a)   **Comte François Henri de Pierre de Bernis** * Quincandon 27.7.1943

        b)   **Comte Pierre de Pierre de Bernis** * Quincandon 5.1.1945

        c)   **Bertrand de Pierre de Bernis** * Quincandon 20.2.1948

        d)   **Catherine de Pierre de Bernis** * Quincandon 14.9.1953

XI   e.   **Robert Marie François Georges Prince de Croy** * Paris 4.6.1920

X   6)   **Anne Françoise Princesse de Croy** * Dülmen 24.1.1831 + Igls 2.7.1887 = Dülmen 30.7.1864 Fortuné Guigues de Moreton de Chabrillan Comte de Chabrillan * Fontainbleau 11.9.1828 + Paris 18.2.1900, and has issue:

XI   (1)   **Comte Guillaume Guigues de Moreton de Chabrillan** * Paris 24.4.1867 + Fontaine-Française 31.12.1895

     (2)   **Léonor Alfred Aynard Fortuné Guigues de Moreton de Chabrillan Marquis de Chabrillan** * Cannes 16.1.1869 + Paris 8.1.1950 = Paris 18.10.1893 Clémentine Félicité de Lévis-Mirepoix * Paris 17.12.1874 + Paris 25.11.1948 dau. of Comte Adrien de Lévis-Mirepoix, and had issue:

XI   a.   **Anne Marie Guigues de Moreton de Chabrillan** * Paris 15.8.1894 = Paris 7.5.1919 Armand Comte de Caumont La Force * Paris 7.6.1881 + Fontaine-Française (C.-d'Or) 23.9.1950, and had issue:

XII   a)   **Jean Bertrand Jacques Adrien Nompar Comte de Caumont La Force** * Paris 4.2.1920 = Paris 7.12.1948 Elisabeth de Castellane * Paris 9.7.1928 dau. of Boniface Marquis de Castellane, and has issue:

XIII   (a)   **Olivier de Caumont La Force** * Paris 27.7.1949

           (b)   **Isabelle de Caumont La Force** * Paris 23.7.1952

           (c)   **Cordelia de Caumont La Force** * Paris 30.7.1955

           (d)   **Laurence de Caumont La Force** * Paris 8.8.1961

           (e)   **Xavier de Caumont La Force** * Paris 19.12.1963

XII   b)   **Comte Robert-Henri Aynard François Nompar de Caumont La Force** * Paris 16.7.1925 = Paris 27.4.1955 Françoise Dior * Paris 7.4.1932 dau. of Raymond Dior — div. and has issue:

173

| XIII | | | (a) | **Christiane de Caumont La Force** * Paris 4.11.1957 |

| XII | | c) | | **Elisabeth Blanche Isabelle de Caumont La Force** * Paris 5.7.1927 = Paris 21.9.1946 Bernard Comte d'Harcourt * Paris 4.1.1919, and has issue: |

XIII

        (a)   **Lesline d'Harcourt** * Saint-Eusoge (Yonne) 4.9.1947

        (b)   **Aude d'Harcourt** * Saint-Eusoge 28.10.1949

        (c)   **Jean d'Harcourt** * Saint-Eusoge 9.6.1952

        (d)   **Christian d'Harcourt** * Paris 22.10.1954

XI   b.   **Robert Guigues de Moreton de Chabrillan Comte de Chabrillan** * Paris 3.3.1896 + Bissau, Portuguese Guinea 31.8.1925

      c.   **Isabelle Guiges de Moreton de Chabrillan** * Paris 25.8.1897 + Meillant (Cher) 8.12.1938 = Paris 28.6.1922 Comte Henri de Rochechouart de Mortemart * Paris 8.1.1896 + Meillant 7.2.1940 s.p.

IX   7)   **Berthe Rosine Ferdinande Prinzessin v. Croy** * Dülmen 12.5.1833 + Drensteinfurt 7.2.1906 = Düsseldorf 16.4.1863 Ignaz Frhr. v. Landsberg-Velen * Münster i. W. 9.2.1830 + Drensteinfurt 28.10.1915, and had issue:

X   (1)   **Helene Eleonore Freiin. v. Landsberg-Velen** * Dülmen 14.1.1864 + Drensteinfurt 29.1.1886 = Drensteinfurt 16.4.1885 Arthur Graf Strachwitz v. Gross-Zauche u. Camminetz * Gleiwitz 23.6.1846 + Gr-Reichenau 3.1.1919 s.p.

    (2)   **Marie Hermine Rudolpha Freiin. v. Landsberg-Velen** * Steinfurt 13.2.1865 + Falkenberg 19.3.1937 = Münster i. W. 14.6.1892 Johannes Nepomuk Graf v. Praschma Frhr. v. Bilkau * Falkenberg 22.12.1867 + Falkenberg 28.11.1935, and had issue:

XI   a.   **Joseph Friedrich Johannes Marie Hubertus Frhr. v. Bilkau** * Münster i. W. 22.3.1893 + Kansas City 15.3.1948 = (1) Paderborn 17.3.1918 Erna Thiele * St. Petersburg 18.5.1896 – div.; = (2) Kansas City 8.10.1927 Mabel Rice * 12.10.1908 dau. of Elton A. Rice, and had issue:

by 1st marriage:

XII   a)   **Gonzalo Frhr. v. Bilkau** * Mexico 11.5.1920 + Hollywood 14.2.1934

by 2nd marriage:

      b)   **Jeanine Freiin. v. Bilkau** * Kansas City 31.12.1928 = Kansas City 25.11.1950 Raymond Bailey * Harrisburg, Missouri 7.6.1925, and has issue:

XIII

        (a)   **Bradford Jerome Bailey** * Kansas City 26.11.1952

        (b)   **Susan Jeannine Bailey** * Glendale, California 13.10.1955

        (c)   **Cheri Lynn Bailey** * Louisville, Kentucky 14.8.1957

        (d)   **Robyn Renée Bailey** * Temple, Texas 10.12.1959

XII   c)   **Jacqueline Marie Freiin. v. Bilkau** * 24.11.1930 + Kansas City 13.2.1932

XI   b.   **Elisabeth Maria Ignatia Gräfin v. Praschma** * Gläsen 16.1.1895 + Bad Godesberg 7.12.1963

      c.   **Emanuela Gräfin v. Praschma** * 6.12.1895 + 15.12.1895

      d.   **Engelbert Maria Antonius Emanuel Graf v. Praschma** * Rogau 26.8.1898 + Rybnik 31.1.1941 = Mooiplaats, Transvaal 25.6.1930 Dorothy-Eva Ferreira * Johannesburg 16.2.1900, and had issue:

XII   a)   **Engelbert Maria Eric Emanuel Graf v. Praschma** * Bronkhorstpruit 26.5.1933
= 4.9.1965 Monica Mundell Jennings * Springs, Transvaal 21.3.1937

       b)   **Peter Hubert Maria Graf v. Praschma** * Johannesburg 17.7.1934 = Bellair, Durban
10.11.1962 Dawn Nesta Dawson * Malvern, Natal 29.1.1936, and has issue:

XIII   (a)   **Kim Maria Therese Gräfin v. Praschma** * Johannesburg 1.12.1964

XII   c)   **Helene Maria Emma Gräfin v. Praschma** * Hamburg 9.8.1936

       d)   **Friedrich Theodore Maria Graf v. Praschma** * Görlitz 7.1.1938

XI   e.   **Friedrich Leopold Maria Valentin Emanuel Oskar Graf v. Praschma** * Drensteinfurt 12.6.1900
= Rauden b. Ratibor 29.4.1937 Sophie Prinzessin v. Ratibor u. Corvey Prinzessin zu
Hohenlohe-Schillingsfürst * Rauden 22.12.1912 dau. of Viktor 3 Herzog v. Ratibor, 3 Fürst v.
Corvey, and has issue:

XII   a)   **Marie Elisabeth Engelberta Felizitas Gräfin v. Praschma** * Falkenberg 6.3.1938

       b)   **Johannes Victor Maria Michael Graf v. Praschma** * Rauden 8.5.1939

       c)   **Michael Maria Albrecht Philippus Benjamin Graf v. Praschma** * Corvey 19.4.1955

XI   f.   **Helene Maria Mathilde Friederica Laurenzia Hedwig Gräfin v. Praschma** * Rogau 7.8.1901
= Falkenberg 25.6.1925 Joseph Graf v. Francken-Sierstorpff * Endersdorf 23.5.1898, and
has issue:

XII   a)   **Maria Anna Johanna Olga Gräfin v. Francken-Sierstorpff** * Falkenberg 5.1.1927
= Ariendorf 24.10.1946 Max Gisbert Frhr. Geyr v. Schweppenberg * Ingenraedt
17.4.1904 — div., and has issue:

XIII   (a)   **Hubertus Frhr. Geyr v. Schweppenberg** * Neweid 11.6.1947 + Ariendorf
9.7.1947

           (b)   **Cornelia Freiin. Geyr v. Schweppenberg** * Ariendorf 23.9.1948

XII   b)   **Maria Elisabeth Johanna Eleonora Anna Gräfin v. Francken-Sierstorpff** * Franzdorf
28.3.1930 = Kalkum 3.1.1957 Egbert v. Kleist * Centa, Spanish Morocco 5.4.1926

       c)   **Alexander Maria Friedrich Barnabas Kasimir Graf v. Francken-Sierstorpff** * Neisse
4.3.1935 = Kasteel Amstenrade 18.6.1963 Agnes Comtesse Marchant d'Ansembourg
* Amsterdam 28.5.1935 dau. of Maximilian Comte Marchant d'Ansembourg

XI   g.   **Maria Pia Gabriele Gräfin v. Praschma** * Rogau 26.2.1903 missing in Russia ...

       h.   **Antonia Maria Casparine Gräfin v. Praschma** * Rogau 5.11.1904 missing in Russia ...

       i.   **Ignatz Maria Cajus Constantin Graf v. Praschma** * Rogau 22.2.1908 = Stettin-Altdamm
2.1.1940 Dorothea Sterzel * Freiburg i. Br. 19.2.1920 dau. of Paul Sterzel, and has issue:

XII   a)   **Marion Dorothea Gräfin v. Praschma** * Klötze 8.1.1941

       b)   **Maria Ranier Joachim Ignatz Graf v. Praschma** * Ilnau 17.5.1943

       c)   **Andreas Maria Michael Graf v. Praschma** * Willesbadessen 2.3.1946

       d)   **Isabella Maria Hedwig Pia Gräfin v. Praschma** * Kalbeck 16.9.1948

       e)   **Marie-Antoinette Sybille Gräfin v. Praschma** * Kalbeck 14.3.1951

XI		j.	**Maria Renata Josepha Friederike Gräfin v. Praschma** * Rogau 3.5.1909 = Falkenberg 3.5.1943 Anton Graf v. Francken-Sierstorpff * Endersdorf 9.8.1908 s.p.

X   (3)   **Engelbert Philipp Maria Frhr. von Landsberg-Velen** * Drensteinfurt 11.10.1866 + Drensteinfurt 19.1.1951

             (4)   **Emma Freiin. v. Landsberg-Velen** * Düsseldorf 7.2.1868 + Breslau 5.3.1940 = Steinfurt 23.6.1888 Arthur Graf Strachwitz v. Gross-Zauche u. Camminetz * Gleiwitz 23.6.1846 + Gr.-Reichenau 3.1.1919, and had issue:

XI   a.   **Helene Maria Ignatia Mathilde Gräfin Strachwitz v. Gross-Zauche u. Camminetz** * Gr.-Reichenau 20.5.1889

          b.   **Alexander Maria Hubertus Hyacinthus Graf Strachwitz v. Gross-Zauche u. Camminetz** * Gr.-Reichenau 29.11.1894 + Reno, Nevada 11.7.1962 = Berlin 24.2.1927 Friederike von Bredow * Berlin 2.11.1906 dau. of Leopold v. Bredow, and has issue:

XII   a)   **Frances Emanuela Maria Gräfin Strachwitz v. Gross-Zauche u. Camminetz** * Berlin 23.5.1928

          b)   **Christian Alexander Maria Graf Strachwitz v. Gross-Zauche u. Camminetz** * Gr.-Reichenau 1.7.1931

          c)   **Rosy Monika Maria Gräfin Strachwitz v. Gross-Zauche u. Camminetz** * Berlin 6.6.1933 = Reno, Nevada 24.8.1960 Hermann Schlueter * Negley, Ohio 9.3.1934, and has issue:

XIII   (a)   **Christopher Timothy Schlueter** * Argentina, Newfoundland 24.12.1961

          (b)   **Patricia Schlueter** * Brunswick, Georgia ... 3.1963

XII   d)   **Hubertus Eberhard Engelbert Maria Graf Strachwitz v. Gross-Zauche u. Camminetz** * Berlin 21.11.1937 = Norfolk, Virginia 11.6.1966 Mary Jo White * Norfolk, Virginia 8.12.1942

          e)   **Isabella Antonia Maria Gräfin Strachwitz v. Gross-Zauche u. Camminetz** * Berlin 9.11.1943

          f)   **Barbara Hedwig Maria Gräfin Strachwitz v. Gross-Zauche u. Camminetz** * Berlin 9.11.1943

XI   c.   **Rudolf Alfred Emanuel Maria Graf Strachwitz v. Gross-Zauche u. Camminetz** * Gr.-Reichenau 3.1.1896 = Ob.-Gläsersdorf 27.3.1943 Barbara Greene * São Paolo 28.9.1907 dau. of Edward Greene, and has issue:

XII   a)   **Rupert Graham Joseph Graf Strachwitz v. Gross-Zauche u. Camminetz** * Lucerne 30.4.1947

          b)   **Helene Alexandra Gräfin Strachwitz v. Gross-Zauche u. Camminetz** * Buenos Aires 2.6.1951

XI   d.   **Stanislas Maria Adalbert Hubertus Graf Strachwitz v. Gross-Zauche u. Camminetz** * Gr.-Reichenau 8.1.1899 = (1) Birlinghoven 11.2.1932 Maria Hagan * Köln 12.8.1889 + Köln 3.11.1943 dau. of Louis Hagan = (2) München 9.5.1956 Anne-Marie Schmidt * Berlin 11.11.1917 dau. of Erich Schmidt and has issue:

          by 2nd marriage:

XII   a)   **Maria Christina Gräfin Strachwitz v. Gross-Zauche u. Camminetz** * München 31.1.1957 + München 20.10.1957

XI   e.   **Maria Agnes Alice Engelberta Aloysia Gräfin Strachwitz v. Gross-Zauche u. Camminetz** * Gr.-Reichenau 11.4.1900

176

XI   f.   **Arthur Emmanuel Ernst Anton Graf Strachwitz v. Gross-Zauche u. Camminetz** * Gr.-Reichenau 18.10.1905 = Wien 12.2.1944 **Marie Therese Prinzessin v.u. zu Liechtenstein** * Wien 14.1.1908 dau. of Aloys Prinz v.u. zu Liechtenstein, and has issue:

XII   a)   **Antonius Peter-Georg Stanislaus Alois Judas-Thaddäus Graf Strachwitz v. Gross-Zauche u. Camminetz** * Zürich 25.11.1944

       b)   **Stanislaus Peter Alois Judas-Thaddäus Maria Graf Strachwitz v. Gross-Zauche u. Camminetz** * Bern 23.5.1946

       c)   **Stephanie Emma Elisabeth Maria-Annunciata Antonia Gräfin Strachwitz v. Gross-Zauche u. Camminetz** * San Sebastian 14.9.1948

X   (5)   **Alfred Friedrich Frhr. v. Landsberg-Velen** * Château de Roeulx 20.12.1872 + Münster i. W. 10.11.1954 = Breslau 7.1.1904 Johanna Freiin. v. Ketteler * Koppitz 20.7.1881 + Münster i. W. 7.7.1954 dau. of Otto Frhr. v. Ketteler, and had issue:

XI   a.   **Elisabeth Bertha Freiin. v. Landsberg-Velen** * Münster i. W. 8.1.1905 = Münster i. W. 8.9.1926 Mauritz Frhr. v. Strachwitz * Gruschewitz 12.12.1898 + Asbest, as Russian Prisoner of War 10.12.1953, and has issue:

XII   a)   **Marie-Elisabeth Freiin. v. Strachwitz** * Breslau 24.10.1927 = Drensteinfurt 20.2.1954 Wolfgang Graf zu Stolberg-Stolberg * Paskau 5.8.1922 and has issue:

XIII   (a)   **Otto Hubert Friedrich Mauritz Maria Graf zu Stolberg-Stolberg** * Frankfurt-am-Main 6.3.1955

       (b)   **Clemens Antonius Herbert Graf zu Stolberg-Stolberg** * Frankfurt-am-Main 23.3.1958

XII   b)   **Mauritz-Bodo Johann Friedrich Hyazinth Frhr. v. Strachwitz** * Breslau 21.7.1929 = München 3.10.1951 Margot Erdmann * München 27.3.1928 dau. of Konrad Erdmann, and has issue:

XIII   (a)   **Mauritz Ferdinand Alexander Wolfram Frhr. v. Strachwitz** * München 10.10.1951

       (b)   **Juliane Katherina Elisabeth Johanna Freiin. v. Strachwitz** * München 17.10.1952

       (c)   **Michael-Florentin Frhr. v. Strachwitz** * München 12.2.1956

       (d)   **Johann Friedrich Alexander Kurt Otto Frhr. v. Strachwitz** * München 3.10.1959

XII   c)   **Wolfram Alfred Kurt Heinrich Frhr. v. Strachwitz** * Maserwitz 10.8.1933 = Schloss Aicha 6.10.1962 **Anna Prinzessin v. Croy** * Slabetz 24.2.1943 dau. of Alexis Prinz v. Croy, and has issue:

XIII   (a)   **Wolfram Frhr. v. Strachwitz** * Detmold 9.7.1963

       (b)   **Caroline Freiin. v. Strachwitz** * Detmold 12.7.1964

XII   d)   **Helga Rosario Marie Elisabeth Freiin. v. Strachwitz** * Breslau 4.5.1935 = Drensteinfurt 18.6.1957 Alexander Frhr. v. Elverfeldt * Niedermarsberg Kr. Brilon 19.3.1929, and has issue:

XIII   (a)   **Alexander Mauritius Ludwig Maria Frhr. v. Elverfeldt** * Neheim-Hüsten 12.5.1959

       (b)   **Georg Sigismund Maria Frhr. v. Elverfeldt** * Arolsen 15.5.1960

       (c)   **Wolfram Maria Frhr. v. Elverfeldt** * Wimbern 27.2.1962

       (d)   **Alice Freiin. v. Elverfeldt** * Korbach 25.8.1963

XIII		(e)	**Dominik Frhr. v. Elverfeldt** * Korbach 26.9.1966

XI   b.   **Maria-Rosario Regina Freiin. v. Landsberg-Velen** * Obernigk 4.9.1906 = Bad Oeynhausen 12.5.1932 Gustav Scanzoni v. Lichtenfels * Zinneberg 3.10.1885, and has issue:

XII
- a) **Sonja Maria Rosario Isabella Scanzoni v. Lichtenfels** * München 20.8.1938
- b) **Silvelin Carlotta Scanzoni v. Lichtenfels** * München 31.10.1939
- c) **Oda Maria Mignon Scanzoni v. Lichtenfels** * Siegsdorf 10.3.1944

XI   c.   **Maria Helen Regina Freiin. v. Landsberg-Velen** * Münster i. W. 6.1.1909 = Drensteinfurt 12.4.1949 Friedrich Newzella * Troppau 16.5.1900, and has issue:

XII
- a) **Mario Newzella** * Troppau 15.3.1940
- b) **Christian Newzella** * Troppau 6.6.1941
- c) **Michael Newzella** * Troppau 7.11.1942
- d) **Gottfried Newzella** * Troppau 2.11.1944

XI   d.   **Gabriele Olga Christine Freiin. v. Landsberg-Velen** * Münster i. W. 21.12.1910 = Hermsdorf 25.11.1943 Constantin Graf Hoyos * Breslau 11.1.1907, and has issue:

XII
- a) **Maria Rosario Thaddea Gräfin Hoyos** * Drensteinfurt 4.6.1947
- b) **Isabella Felicitas Gabriele Gräfin Hoyos** * Drensteinfurt 24.3.1949
- c) **Nathalie Maria Carmen Gräfin Hoyos** * Drensteinfurt 27.9.1950

XI   e.   **Hedwig Maria Olga Freiin. v. Landsberg-Velen** * Münster i. W. 20.9.1916 = Münster i. W. 28.9.1939 Olaf Scanzoni v. Lichtenfels * Darmstadt 24.7.1913, and has issue:

XII
- a) **Christoph Scanzoni v. Lichtenfels** * Caracas 17.7.1940 = Caracas 9.9.1965 Graciela Dupouy * Caracas 9.1.1940 dau. of Walter Dupouy, and has issue:

XIII
- (a) **Christobal Otto Scanzoni v. Lichtenfels Dupouy** * Caracas 14.6.1966

XII
- b) **Alexandra Scanzoni v. Lichtenfels** * Caracas 20.2.1949

XI   f.   **Ingaz Wessel Max Michael Frhr. v. Landsberg-Velen** * Alsbach 29.9.1921 = Elkofen 24.6.1948 Margarete Gräfin v. Rechberg u. Rothenlöwen zu Hohenrechberg * Elkofen 28.5.1926 dau. of Wolfgang Graf v. Rechberg u. Rothenlöwen zu Hohenrechberg, and has issue:

XII
- a) **Engelbert Alexander Frhr. v. Landsberg-Velen** * München 7.6.1949
- b) **Elisabeth Andrea Freiin. v. Landsberg-Velen** * München 6.10.1951
- c) **Marie Antoinette Freiin. v. Landsberg-Velen** * 27.9.1954
- d) **Marie Gabrielle Freiin. v. Landsberg-Velen** * 9.11.1959

X   (6)   **Gabriele Freiin. v. Landsberg-Velen** * Steinfurt 11.5.1874 + Breslau 30.11.1922

    (7)   **Emanuel Eugen Klemens Ignaz Maria Frhr. v. Landsberg-Velen** * Drensteinfurt 5.3.1876 + Georghausen 13.12.1963 = Alsbach 6.9.1904 Marie Freiin. v. Fürstenberg * Heiligenhofen 22.4.1884 + Köln 23.11.1948 dau. of Egon Frhr. v. Fürstenberg, and has issue:

XI   a.   **Maria Antoinette Sophie Ignatia Freiin. v. Landsberg-Velen** * Köln 5.6.1905 = Berg Gladbach 28.6.1941 Gustav Neumann * Köln-Mühlheim 18.12.1893, and has issue:

178

XII   a)   **Ute Doris Sieglinde Neumann** * Köln 14.10.1941

XI   b.   **Franz-Egon Frhr. v. Landsberg-Velen** * Georghausen 17.10.1906 = Köln 30.11.1939 Ilse Burkhart * Krefeld 9.12.1906 dau. of Hans Burkhart s.p.

          c.   **Lewina Freiin. v. Landsberg-Velen** * Georghausen 26.9.1908 + Georghausen 5.8.1909

          d.   **Emanuel Antonius Marie Alfred Sofie Frhr. v. Landsberg-Velen** * Georghausen 26.5.1910 = Honeburg 29.5.1946 Eleonore Freiin. Ostman v. der Leye * Honeburg 24.10.1923 dau. of Franz Ludwig Frhr. Ostman v. der Leye, and has issue:

XII   a)   **Marion Elisabeth Franziska Freiin. v. Landsberg-Velen** * Osnabrück 5.4.1947

          b)   **Roswitha Clementine Isabella Freiin. v. Landsberg-Velen** * Osnabrück 22.8.1949

          c)   **Dorothée Huberta Ingeborg Freiin. v. Landsberg-Velen** * Lindlar 11.6.1955

XI   e.   **Wolfgang Ignaz Emma Antonius Frhr. v. Landsberg-Velen** * Georghausen 4.11.1911 = Köln 1.2.1941 Marianne Eicken * Köln 10.3.1916 dau. of Hermann Eicken, and has issue:

XII   a)   **Michael Frhr. v. Landsberg-Velen** * Köln 12.11.1941

          b)   **Georg Frhr. v. Landsberg-Velen** * Lindlar 28.12.1943

XI   f.   **Maria Therese Freiin. v. Landsberg-Velen** * Georghausen 7.5.1914 + Georghausen 20.1.1915

          g.   **Zita Marieluise Helene Antonie Freiin. v. Landsberg-Velen** * Bonn 20.3.1917 = Georghausen 24.4.1946 Guido Frhr. v. Fürstenberg * Köln 22.8.1917, and has issue:

XII   a)   **Gerold Heinrich Antonius Apollinaris Frhr. v. Fürstenberg** * Werdohl 13.6.1950

          b)   **Gudula Antonia Freiin. v. Fürstenberg** * Werdohl 18.12.1951

          c)   **Dagobert Antonius Frhr. v. Fürstenberg** * Werdohl 2.4.1953

X   (8)   **Franziska Antonia Hermine Maria Emma Engelberta Freiin. v. Landsberg-Velen** * Drensteinfurt 11.6.1877 + 24.9.1964 = Drensteinfurt 29.8.1911 Friedrich Theodor Graf zu Stolberg-Stolberg * Thomaswaldau 14.12.1877 + Gamburg a.d. Tauber 28.3.1954, and has issue:

XI   a.   **Maria Christine Bertha Emmanuela Engelberta Gräfin zu Stolberg-Stolberg** * Kiowitz 27.1.1916

          b.   **Maria Regina Pacis Bernardina Regina Antonia Gräfin zu Stolberg-Stolberg** * Kiowitz 7.9.1917

X   (9)   **Hermann Joseph Frhr. v. Landsberg-Velen** * Steinfurt 11.3.1879 X Chateroux 6.10.1914

IX   8)   **Gabrielle Henriette Wilhelmine Prinzessin v. Croy** * Dülmen 5.1.1835 + Lucerne ... 9.1905 = Dülmen 28.1.1874 Ludovic Prince de Polignac * 24.3.1827 + Bouzareah, Algeria 13.1.1904 s.p.

      9)   **Albert Prinz v. Croy** * Dülmen 16.5.1837 + Dülmen 21.4.1838

    10)   **Clotilde Prinzessin v. Croy** * Dülmen 2.11.1840 + Dülmen 29.3.1841

VIII 6.   **Johanna Wilhelmine Auguste Prinzessin zu Salm-Salm** * Anholt 5.8.1796 + Düsseldorf 22.11.1868 = Anholt 28.7.1824 Philipp Prinz von Croy * Wien 26.11.1801 + Bad Ems 2.7.1871, and had issue:

IX   1)   **Luise Constantine Nathalie Johanna Auguste Prinzessin v. Croy** * Anholt 2.6.1825 + Meran 8.1.1890 = Potsdam 20.6.1848 Count Constantine de Benckendorff * 10.10.1817 + Paris 29.1.1858 and had issue:

X   (1)   **Alexander Philipp Constantine Louis Count de Benckendorff** * Berlin 1.8.1849 + London 29.12.1916 = St. Petersburg 16.10.1879 Sophie Petrovna Countess Schouvaloff * 16.10.1857 + Ipswich 28.5.1928 dau. of Count Peter Pavlovitch Schouvaloff and had issue:

XI	a.	**Constantine Count de Benckendorff** * Baden-Baden 15.9.1880 + London 25.9.1959 = Moscow 1922 Maria Korchinska * Moscow 17.2.1895 dau. of Lucian Korczyński, and had issue:

XI   a.   **Constantine Count de Benckendorff** * Baden-Baden 15.9.1880 + London 25.9.1959 = Moscow 1922 Maria Korchinska * Moscow 17.2.1895 dau. of Lucian Korczyński, and had issue:

XII   a)   **Nathalie Countess de Benckendorff** * Moscow 8.9.1923 = London 27.11.1946 Thomas Humphrey Brooke * South Crosland, Near Huddersfield 31.1.1914, and has issue:

XIII   (a)   **Sophie Brooke** * York 5.9.1947

         (b)   **Helen Brooke** * Woking 27.3.1949 + Carcavelos, Portugal 10.7.1966

         (c)   **Thomas Joshua Brooke** * Ipswich 21.8.1964

XII   b)   **Alexander Count de Benckendorff** * Claydon, Ipswich 19.7.1925 = London 28.6.1952 Esther Norma Capadose * 8.7.1924 dau. of Anton Capadose, and has issue:

XIII   (a)   **Constantine Count de Benckendorff** * London 30.8.1953

         (b)   **Alexander Count de Benckendorff** * Aberdeen 11.9.1957

XI   b.   **Peter Count de Benckendorff** * St. Petersburg 1/13.1.1882 ✗ 27.5.1915 = 1909 Helene Dmitrievna Narischkine * 8.12.1879 + Paris 25.12.1965 dau. of Dmitri Constantinovitch Narischkine s.p.

         c.   **Nathalie Louise Countess de Benckendorff** * Nice 3.6.1886 = London 28.4.1911 Sir Jaspar Ridley * Ponteland 6.1.1887 + Ipswich 1.10.1951, and has issue:

XII   a)   **Katherine Sophy Ridley** * London 19.3.1912 = London 22.6.1941 Eugene Lampert * München 1.5.1914, and has issue:

XIII   (a)   **Alexander Lampert** * Oxford 16.8.1943 = Oxford 3.4.1965 Sally Box * Hampton Lucy, Wellesbourne, Warwickshire 8.4.1944 dau. of Anthony William Box, and has issue:

XIV   1a.   **Gregory Lampert** * Oxford 14.8.1965

XIII   (b)   **Nicholas Lampert** * Oxford 25.8.1945

XII   b)   **Jaspar Alexander Maurice Ridley** * London 20.4.1913 ✗ Italy 13.12.1943 = London 8.6.1939 Cressida Bonham-Carter * London 22.4.1917 dau. of Sir Maurice Bonham-Carter, and had issue:

XIII   (a)   **Adam Nicholas Ridley** * Hitchin 14.5.1942

XII   c)   **Constantine Anthony Ridley** * London 9.3.1916

         d)   **Oliver John Ridley** * London 14.10.1918

         e)   **Patrick Conrad Peter Ridley** * London 17.3.1931 + in an accident in Wales 11.5.1952

X   (2)   **Paul Leopold Johann Stephan Count de Benckendorff** * Berlin 10.4.1853 + 28.1.1921 = St.Petersburg 27.9/9.10.1897 Princess Marie Sergievna Dolgorouky * St. Petersburg 2/14.12.1847 + ... dau. of Prince Serge Alexevitch Dolgorouky s.p.

         (3)   **Nathalie Marie Helene Alexa Countess de Benckendorff** * Schandau/Elbe 7.9.1854 + Trachenberg 9.3.1931 = Berlin 18.6.1872 Hermann 5 Fürst v. Hatzfeldt Herzog zu Trachenberg * Trachenberg 4.2.1848 + Trachenberg 14.1.1933, and had issue:

Sargent   *By courtesy of Countess Benckendorff*

15   Count Alexander de Benckendorff, 1849–1916

XI   a.   **Hermann Ludwig Felix Maria Franz 6 Fürst v. Hatzfeldt, Herzog zu Trachenberg** * Gusswitz 14.1.1874 + Baden-Baden 24.10.1959 = Wien 9.1.1912 Elisabeth v. Tschirschky u. Bögendorff * Wien 3.11.1889 dau. of Heinrich v. Tschirschky u. Bögendorff and has issue:

XII   a)   **Hermann Krafft Maria August Siegfried Graf v. Hatzfeldt zu Trachenberg** * Bruxelles 24.11.1912 ✕ Woronesch, Russia 4.7.1942

     b)   **Huberta Maria Elisabeth Hedwige Alexandra Gräfin v. Hatzfeldt zu Trachenberg** * Washington D.C. 18.10.1916 = Trachenberg 16.7.1941 Hermann Graf v. Saurma-Jeltsch * Tworkau 16.10.1906, and has issue:

XIII   (a)   **Johanna Elisabeth Clothilde Sophie Huberta Hedwig Anna Maria Gräfin v. Saurma-Jeltsch** * Wien 10.5.1942 = Salaberg 16.8.1962 Hermann-Dietrich Frhr. v. Mylius * Schloss Eberhardtsreuth 11.6.1928, and has issue:

XIV   1a.   **Dietrich Edmund Hermann Georg Alexander Hubertus Maria Frhr. v. Mylius** * München 16.4.1963

     2a.   **Christian Franz Hermann Stephan Paulus Maria Frhr. v. Mylius** * Damascus 19.4.1964

     3a.   **Maria Agnes Elisabeth Huberta Hedwig Freiin. v. Mylius** * München 2.12.1966

XIII   (b)   **Johann Carl Friedrich Heinrich Maximilian Hermann Maria Graf v. Saurma-Jeltsch** * Salaberg 17.2.1945

XII   c)   **Natalie Henriette Marie Elisabeth Gräfin v. Hatzfeldt zu Trachenberg** * Berlin 14.2.1918

     d)   **Carl Heinrich Hermann Melchior Maria Fürst v. Hatzfeldt, Herzog zu Trachenberg** * Berlin 21.2.1921 = Düsseldorf 26.9.1952 Charlotte Zeglat * Heidelkrug/Ostpreussen 9.3.1922, and has issue:

XIII   (a)   **Carl Adrian Petrus Alexander Hermann Kraft Konstantin Maria Graf v. Hatzfeldt zu Trachenberg** * Mülheim/Ruhr 25.9.1954

     (b)   **Nikolaus Alexis Beatus Melchior Franziskus Maria Graf v. Hatzfeldt zu Trachenberg** * Mülheim 21.4.1958

     (c)   **Maximilian Cajetan Igor Eugen Heinrich Karl Maria Graf v. Hatzfeldt zu Trachenberg** * Mülheim 10.7.1959

     (d)   **Alexandra Theodora Natalie Elisabeth Ludovica Maria Gräfin v. Hatzfeldt zu Trachenberg** * Mülheim 24.3.1961

     (e)   **Boris Oliver Philip Antonius Harald Gothard Maria Graf v. Hatzfeldt zu Trachenberg** * Essen 10.8.1965

XII   e)   **Edmund Anton Otto Maria Graf v. Hatzfeldt zu Trachenberg** * Amsterdam 18.11.1923 = Neuhall 2.6.1954 Sophie Freiin. Spies v. Bullesheim * Haus Hall 2.8.1927 dau. of Franz Egon Frhr. Spies v. Bullesheim s.p.

     f)   **Friedrich Hermann Krafft Alexander Carl Borromäus Hubertus Maria Graf v. Hatzfeldt zu Trachenberg** * Trachenberg 22.10.1928 = Bonn 2.5.1964 Anna Maria Helene Freiin. v. Münchhausen * Berlin 7.10.1933 dau. of Thankmar Frhr. v. Münchhausen, and has issue:

XIII   (a)   **Sebastian Hermann Edmund Hieronymus Graf v. Hatzfeldt zu Trachenberg** * Bonn 7.7.1965

     (b)   **Marie Sophie Natalie Elisabeth Gräfin v. Hatzfeldt zu Trachenberg** * Bonn 30.9.1966

XI		b. **Alexander Maria Hermann Melchior Graf v. Hatzfeldt zu Trachenberg** * Berlin 10.2.1877 + Schloss Schönstein 27.11.1953 = Tokio 19.12.1904 Hanna Aoki * Tokio 16.12.1879 + Wissen 24.6.1953 dau. of Guizo Viscount Aoki, and had issue:

XII   a) **Hissa Elisabeth Natalie Olga Ilsa Gräfin v. Hatzfeldt zu Trachenberg** * Pommerswitz 26.2.1906 = München 28.4.1927 Erwein Graf v. Neipperg * Schwaigern 15.1.1897 + Stuttgart-Vaihingen 5.12.1957, and has issue:

XIII   (a) **Maria Immakulata Hanna Elisabeth Benedicta Euphrasia Gräfin v. Neipperg** * München 13.3.1928 = Johannesberg 14.7.1956 Klaus Werner Meilchen * Kaiserlautern 30.9.1920, and has issue:

XIV
- 1a.   **Maria Hissa Eugenie Meilchen** * Johannesburg 16.5.1957
- 2a.   **Maria Josefine Nathalie Meilchen** * Stuttgart 11.4.1960
- 3a.   **Maria Melchior Albert Meilchen** * Berlin 13.4.1964

XIII   (b) **Marie Hedwig Gabrielle Nathalie Benedicta Lioba Laurentia Gräfin v. Neipperg** * Seeshaupt 10.8.1929 = Cairo 11.4.1955 Anthony James Williams * London 28.5.1923, and has issue:

XIV
- 1a.   **Henrietta Ann Williams** * Cairo 13.4.1956
- 2a.   **James Kilian Williams** * New York 16.1.1958
- 3a.   **Adam Benedict Nicholas Williams** * Buenos Aires 16.8.1959
- 4a.   **Katherine Antonia Williams** * London 12.10.1961

XIII   (c) **Maria Anton-Hermann Alexander Konrad Georg Benedict Ephraim Graf v. Neipperg** * Trebnitz 19.6.1932 + ... 5.1966

       (d) **Maria Nathalie Gabrielle Benedikta Bernhardine Gräfin v. Neipperg** * Stuttgart 20.5.1948

X   (4) **Olga Marie Stephanie Pauline Countess de Benckendorff** * Stuttgart 11.10.1857 + Roma 26.1.1926 = Oechtrich 12.10.1882 Alessandro Guiccioli Marchese Ca' del Bosco * Venezia 5.3.1843 + ... s.p.

IX   2) **Leopold Emmanuel Ludwig Prince von Croy** * 5.5.1827 + Wien 15.8.1894 = (1) Venezia 20.1.1864 **Beatrice Gräfin Nugent** * Napoli ... 1822 + Wien 26.3.1880 dau. of Laval Graf Nugent; = (2) Politschan 5.5.1881 Rose Gräfin v. Sternberg * Gyöngyös 16.3.1836 + Wien 15.5.1918 dau. of Jaroslav Graf v. Sternberg s.p.

   3) **Alexander Gustav August Prinz v. Croy** * 21.8.1828 + Schloss Buckberg-am-Kamp 5.12.1887 = Laër 4.8.1863 Elisabeth Gräfin v. Westphalen zu Fürstenberg * Münster i. W. 14.6.1834 + Buchberg 30.10.1910 dau. of Klemens Graf v. Westphalen zu Fürstenberg, and had issue:

X
- (1) **Cunegonde Johanna Clementine Maria Therese Prinzessin v. Croy** * Buchberg 30.5.1864 + Habichen ... 4.1931
- (2) **Carl Philip Anne Clemens Prinz v. Croy** * Buchberg 6.6.1866 + Gars 4.2.1923
- (3) **Elisabeth Marie Stephanie Josephine Prinzessin v. Croy** * Marienlohe 2.8.1868 + Gars-am-Kamp 22.10.1960
- (4) **Wilhelm Hubert Ernst Prinz v. Croy** * Buchberg 6.10.1869 + Tulln 18.4.1918 = Arad 15.9.1898 Desideria Rónay de Zombor * Kis-Zombor 11.5.1874 + Graz 6.9.1935 and had issue:

XI   a.   **Stephan Alexander Maria Wilhelm Prinz v. Croy** * Paulis, Hungary 7.8.1899 + Tulsa, Oklahoma 3.9.1966 = Houston, Texas 21.6.1928 Virginia Taylor * Beaumont, Texas 2.1.1904 dau. of Oscar Homer Taylor s.p.

    b.   **Dorothea Elisabeth Maria Anna Prinzessin v. Croy** * Pörtschach 19.10.1900 + 9.2.1966 = Billignies 11.8.1926 Louis Olry Lusson * Ardmore, Pennsylvania 26.3.1893, and had issue:

XII   a)   **Louis Jean Etienne Lusson** * Ardmore, Pa. 3.5.1927 = Bayamon, Puerto Rico 12.5.1951 Carmen Luz Cintron * Naranjito, Puerto Rico 5.7.1932, and has issue:

XIII   (a)   **Louis Michael Lusson** * San Juan, Puerto Rico 27.4.1952

      (b)   **Henry Gil Lusson** * San Juan 30.11.1955

      (c)   **Richard Charles Lusson** * Bayamon 20.4.1958

XII   b)   **Charles Pierre Lusson** * Philadelphia 30.10.1929

    c)   **Henry de Croy Lusson** * Philadelphia 2.12.1930 = Virginia Beach, Va. 1957 Elsie George * Nashville, Tennessee 26.5.1938, and has issue:

XIII   (a)   **Cheryl Anne Lusson** * Norfolk, Virginia 22.9.1958

      (b)   **Juanita Marie Lusson** * Norfolk, Virginia 8.5.1961

XII   d)   **Marie Elisabeth Lusson** * Eustis, Florida 6.11.1933 = Wayne, Pa. 26.9.1953 Evan John McCorkle * Philadelphia 17.6.1931, and has issue:

XIII   (a)   **Mark Evan McCorkle** * Washington, D.C. 2.9.1954

      (b)   **Cynthia Marie McCorkle** * Bryn Marr, Pa. 26.8.1958

      (c)   **Barbara Elizabeth McCorkle** * Montgomery Co. 17.10.1959

      (d)   **Amelia Therese McCorkle** * Montgomery Co. 29.7.1962

XII   e)   **Dorothée May Lusson** * Eustis, Florida 6.11.1933 = Elkton, Maryland 1953 Gordon Weed Mella * Palo Alto, California 22.8.1931, and has issue:

XIII   (a)   **Richard Alan Mella** * Philadelphia 25.2.1954

      (b)   **Bruce William Mella** * St. Albans, N.Y. 15.7.1956 + Jamaica, N.Y. 19.10.1956

      (c)   **Glen David Mella** * Chelsea, Massachusetts 30.10.1957

      (d)   **Gordon James Mella** * Naples, Italy 21.10.1960

XI   c.   **Helene Elisabeth Maria Anna Prinzessin v. Croy** * Pörtschach 30.7.1902

    d.   **Elisabeth Kunigunde Maria Anna Prinzessin v. Croy** * Wildon 23.3.1904 X Wien, 17.9.1944 = Graz 30.10.1924 Sepp Brandl * ... − div., and had issue:

XII   a)   **Dorly Brandl** * Graz 29.8.1926 = (1) 13.5.1948 Franz Weber * Wilden 17.3.1920 − div.; = (2) 2.5.1955 Willy Rath * Graz 10.12.1929, and has issue:

       by 1st marriage:

XIII   (a)   **Franz Wolfgang Weber** * Graz 2.10.1949

       by 2nd marriage:

      (b)   **Manfred Willibald Josef Rath** * Graz 22.10.1957

XII   b)   **Clemens Brandl** * 23.1.1929

XI   e.   **Maria Helene Leopoldine Elisabeth Anna Prinzessin v. Croy** * Graz 11.1.1912

X   (5)   **Leopold Stephan Marie Prinz v. Croy** * Buchberg 11.10.1871 + Buchberg 23.10.1934

         (6)   **Klemens Maria Hubertus Joseph Alexander Prinz v. Croy** * Buchberg-am-Kamp 31.3.1873 + Wien 23.11.1926 = Wien 31.1.1903 Christiane Prinzessin v. Auersperg * Slatinan, Böh. 24.11.1878 + Carlslust 16.5.1945 dau. of Franz Josef Fürst v. Auersperg, and had issue:

XI   a.   **Franz Alexander Marie Clemens Anton Georg Prinz v. Croy** * Buchberg 8.11.1903 + Innsbruck 5.9.1918

          b.   **Marie Elisabeth Christiane Wilhelmine Antonia Kunigunde Prinzessin v. Croy** * Buchberg 17.6.1905 = Buchberg 20.4.1933 Eugen Graf v. Waldstein-Wartenberg * St. Pölten 20.1.1905, and has issue:

XII   a)   **Franz Josef Eugen Clemens Maria Graf v. Waldstein-Wartenberg** * Wien 16.5.1934

          b)   **Clemens Eugen Josef Leopold Maria Graf v. Waldstein-Wartenberg** * Wien 17.6.1935

          c)   **Maria-Christiane Immaculata Juliane Elisabeth Gräfin v. Waldstein-Wartenberg** * Wien 8.12.1936

          d)   **Vincenz Josef Eugen Clemens Maria Graf v. Waldstein-Wartenberg** * Wien 9.6.1938

          e)   **Juliane Maria Christiane Hermine Elisabeth Gräfin v. Waldstein-Wartenberg** * Buchberg 22.5.1940 = Nieder-Flanditz 2.10.1965 **Peter Prinz v. Altenburg** * Wien 18.9.1935

          f)   **Georg Max Eugen Clemens Antonius Johannes Graf v. Waldstein-Wartenberg** * Buchberg 17.12.1942

          g)   **Carl Eugen Clemens Josef Maria Graf v. Waldstein-Wartenberg** * Carlslust 22.11.1947

XI   c.   **Wilhelmine Maria Christiane Elisabeth Antonia Prinzessin v. Croy** * Wien 18.5.1906 = Buchberg 15.5.1944 **Anton Prinz v. Croy** * Bruxelles 6.1.1893, and has issue see elsewhere

          d.   **Maria Gabriele Wilhelmine Karoline Christiane Antonia Prinzessin v. Croy** * Wien 11.4.1908 + 27.11.1958

          e.   **Karl Franz Antonius Alexander Kaspar Melchior Balthasar Prinz v. Croy** * Wien 7.1.1912 = Graz 7.9.1939 Barbara Freiin. Söll v.u. zu Teissenegg * Graz 24.1.1906 + 27.11.1958 dau. of Ferdinand Frhr. Söll v.u. zu Teissenegg, and has issue:

XII   a)   **Ferdinand Maria Carl Clemens Franz Judas Thaddäus Prinz v. Croy** * Buchberg 23.6.1940

          b)   **Elisabeth Maria Brigitte Christiane Barbara Prinzessin v. Croy** * Buchberg 21.12.1941 = 4.6.1966 Albrecht Frhr. v. dem Bongart * Wien 9.9.1940

          c)   **Christiane Maria Elvira Antonia Thaddäa Prinzessin v. Croy** * Buchberg 11.2.1945

XI   f.   **Franziska Maria Elisabeth Wilhelmine Christiane Antonie Martina Prinzessin v. Croy** * Wien 30.1.1917 = Buchberg 30.5.1943 Josef Graf v. Schall-Riacour * Gaussig 30.9.1908 + Dresden 15.4.1944, and has issue:

XII   a)   **Christiane Maria Annunciata Josefine Benedikta Thaddäa Gräfin v. Schall-Riacour** * Gaussig 21.3.1944

XI   g.   **Agathe Maria Elisabeth Christiane Antonie Prinzessin v. Croy** * Wien 15.8.1920 = Kitzbühel 30.10.1955 Johannes Hasslwandter * Kitzbühel 15.8.1911 s.p.

X   (7)   **Alexander Marie August Stephan Klemens Prinz v. Croy** * Buchberg-am-Kamp 31.3.1873 + Bad Ischl 10.7.1937 = Wien 19.11.1909 Mathilde Gräfin v. Stockau * Wien 27.4.1881 + Bad Ischl 20.4.1949 dau. of Georg Graf v. Stockau, and had issue:

XI   a.   **Anton Philipp Maria Josef Ignatius Georg Alexander Prinz v. Croy** * Königsfeld 1.9.1909
= Rauden 11.11.1940 Klementine Prinzessin v. Ratibor u. Corvey, Prinzessin zu Hohenlohe-
Schillingsfürst * Rauden b. Ratibor 24.4.1918 dau. of Victor 3 Herzog v. Ratibor, 3 Fürst v.
Corvey, and had issue:

XII   a)   **Alexandra Marie Sibylle Sofie Prinzessin v. Croy** * Schloss Rauden 31.12.1941
= Corvey 15.9.1963 Carl-Alexander Graf v. Bismarck-Schönhausen * London 20.2.1935,
and has issue:

XIII   (a)   **Claudia Anna Katharine Mona Gräfin v. Bismarck-Schönhausen** * Hamburg
6.7.1964

XII   b)   **Franz Clemens Prinz v. Croy** * Schloss Corvey 25.9.1946

XI   b.   **Elisabeth Marie Evelyne Prinzessin v. Croy** * Königsfeld 14.2.1911 = Wien 12.5.1942
Heimdall Graf zu Stolberg-Wernigrode * Potsdam 23.12.1904 X, bei Stalingrad 9.12.1942 s.p.

        c.   **Alexander Georg Maria Josef Ignatius Prinz v. Croy** * Königsfeld 27.11.1912 = London
17.2.1938 Anne Elspeth Campbell * London 16.8.1917 dau. of William Campbell of
Glendarnuel, and has issue:

XII   a)   **Charlotte Alexandra Maria Clotilde Prinzessin v. Croy** * London 31.12.1938
= Langenburg 5.6.1965 **Kraft Fürst zu Hohenlohe-Langenburg** * Schwabisch Hall
25.6.1935, and has issue see elsewhere

           b)   **Emma Rosanne Prinzessin v. Croy** * Sutton, Sussex 30.12.1943 = Aurach b. Kitzbühel
8.6.1964 **Ferdinand Graf zu Waldburg Wolfegg u. Waldsee** * Waldsee 17.12.1933, and
has issue see elsewhere

           c)   **Maximilian Richard Alexander Prinz v. Croy** * London 2.6.1946

XI   d.   **Eveline Maria Franziska Elisabeth Ignatia Aloysia Prinzessin v. Croy** * Altenbuch 5.6.1914
= Wien 15.5.1940 Oswald Graf v. Kielmansegg * Wiener-Neustadt 30.12.1908, and has issue:

XII   a)   **Alexander Maria Eduard Karl Leopold Josef Oswald Servatius Graf v. Kielmansegg**
* Wien 13.3.1941

           b)   **Maria Mathilde Gabriele Elisabeth Gräfin v. Kielmansegg** * Wien 6.8.1942

           c)   **Elisabeth Maria Gabriele Floriana Bernadine Gräfin v. Kielmansegg** * Bad Ischl
6.11.1946

           d)   **Cunigunde Maria Anna Gräfin v. Kielmansegg** * Wien 4.10.1948

           e)   **Gabriele Maria Assunta Pia Leopoldine Gräfin v. Kielmansegg** * Wien 15.8.1950

           f)   **Georg Christian Maria Paul Egon Leopold Graf v. Kielmansegg** * Wien 30.6.1952

XI   e.   **Maria-Rosa Aloisia Mathilde Prinzessin v. Croy** * Altenbuch 29.3.1916 = Wien 31.1.1942
Gotthard Graf Schaffgotsch gen. Semperfrei v.u. zu Kynast u. Greiffenstein * Warmbrunn
5.9.1914, and has issue:

XII   a)   **Friedrich Alexander Johannes Christoph Leopold Gotthard Maria Graf Schaffgotsch gen.
Semperfrei v.u. zu Kynast u. Greiffenstein** * Bad Warmbrunn 22.1.1943

           b)   **Gotthard Wilhelm-Hans Oswald Karl Hubertus Maria Graf Schaffgotsch gen. Semperfrei
v.u. zu Kynast u. Greiffenstein** * Warmbrunn 26.4.1944

           c)   **Alexander Hans-Ulrich Carl Hubertus Gotthard Maria Graf Schaffgotsch gen. Semperfrei
v.u. zu Kynast u. Greiffenstein** * Nürnburg 18.8.1945

XII		d)	Elisabeth Mathilde Blanca Maria Hedwig Gräfin Schaffgotsch gen. Semperfrei v.u. zu Kynast u. Greiffenstein * München 17.9.1947
		e)	Hans Ulrich Gotthard Maria Graf Schaffgotsch gen. Semperfrei v.u. zu Kynast u. Greiffenstein * Garmisch-Partenkirchen 24.12.1949

X   (8)   **Marie Angelike Amelie Johanna Philippine Prinzessin v. Croy** * Laër 15.7.1874 + Buchberg ... 1874

IX   4)   **Stephanie Prinzessin v. Croy** * Anholt 7.10.1831 + Eltville 22.6.1906

      5)   **Amelie Prinzessin v. Croy** * Düsseldorf 15.11.1835 + Steyl, Netherlands 15.5.1897

      6)   **Marie Prinzessin v. Croy** * Düsseldorf 2.2.1837 + Berlin 1.4.1915 = Paris 2.5.1859 Karl 5 Fürst Lichnowsky * Grätz 19.12.1819 + Grätz 18.10.1901, and had issue:

X   (1)   **Karl Max 6 Fürst Lichnowsky** * Kreuzenort 8.3.1860 + Kuchelna 27.2.1928 = München 22.8.1904 **Mechtilde Gräfin v. Arco-Zinneberg** * Schönburg 8.3.1879 + London 4.6.1958 dau. of Maximilian Graf v. Arco-Zinneberg, and had issue:

XI   a.   **Wilhelm Dionysos Hermann Carl Max 7 Fürst Lichnowsky** * Grätz 1.7.1905 = Cap d'Ail 22.5.1936 Etelka Plachota * Pressburg 12.9.1908 dau. of Alfred Plachota, and has issue:

XII   a)   **Christiane Maria Gräfin Lichnowsky** * Troppau 6.2.1937

                          b)   **Felix Michael Fürst Lichnowsky** * Troppau 17.2.1940

                          c)   **Lucia Margit Gräfin Lichnowsky** * Troppau 11.9.1941

XI   b.   **Leonore Marie Helen Leodine Mechtilde Gräfin Lichnowsky** * Grätz 28.8.1906

                c.   **Michael Max Leopold Nikolaus Graf Lichnowsky** * Kuchelna 9.12.1907 = (1) London 2.3.1932 Mildred Withstandley * New York 10.11.1899 − div.; = (2) Rio de Janeiro 13.11.1953 Elisabeth v. Umnoff * Baden-Baden 17.6.1924 dau. of Nikolai v. Umnoff s.p.

X   (2)   **Maria Caroline Johanna Eleonore Louise Stephanie Amelie Gräfin Lichnowsky** * Grätz 6.9.1861 + Berlin 3.12.1933 = Grätz 26.9.1886 Wilhelm Graf v. Redern * Darmstadt 19.2.1842 + Berlin 1.12.1909, and had issue:

XI   a.   **Wilhelm Heinrich Victor Herbert Carl Graf v. Redern** * Berlin 13.2.1888 ✗ Ypres 14.12.1914

                b.   **Viktoria Maria Gräfin v. Redern** * Berlin 12.3.1889 = Berlin 29.11.1917 Ernst 5 Fürst zu Lynar, Graf v. Redern * Roma 31.3.1875 + Berlin 4.2.1934, and had issue:

XII   a)   **Maria-Amelia Elisabeth Margareta Hermine Gräfin zu Lynar** * Berlin 27.9.1918 = Görlsdorf 18.12.1944 Ignaz Graf v.u. zu Hoensbroech * Haanhof 26.11.1918, and has issue:

XIII   (a)   **Hubertus Ferdinand Ernst Wilhelm Graf v.u. zu Hoensbroech** * Unkel a. Rh. 13.10.1945

                              (b)   **Michael Wilhelm Walter Graf v.u. zu Hoensbroech** * Unkel a. Rh. 11.3.1947

                              (c)   **Manfred Gabriel Johannes Graf v.u. zu Hoensbroech** * Unkel a. Rh. 24.9.1948

                              (d)   **Christiane Ferdinande Anna Gräfin v.u. zu Hoensbroech** * Unkel a. Rh. 19.3.1951

                              (e)   **Elisabeth Friederike Maria Gräfin v.u. zu Hoensbroech** * Bonn 12.11.1956

XII   b)   **Margarete Johanna Elisabeth Gräfin zu Lynar** * Berlin 4.11.1919 = (1) Görlsdorf 19.10.1939 Karl Graf v.u. zu Hoensbroech * Münster i. W. 13.4.1911 ✗ Narvik 7.7.1941; = (2) Kreuth b. Heideck 18.10.1946 Wilhelm Moessinger * Frankfurt-am-Main 19.9.1919, and has issue:

by 2nd marriage:

XIII   (a)   **Yvonne Moessinger** * Frankfurt-am-Main 21.9.1947

                 (b)   **Irene Moessinger** * Frankfurt-am-Main 14.10.1949

XII   c)   **Elisabeth Gabriele Gräfin zu Lynar** * Görlsdorf 17.5.1922 = Oettingen 10.10.1946
Alois 10 Fürst zu Oettingen-Oettingen u. Oettingen-Spielberg * Kreuth 3.9.1920, and
has issue:

XIII   (a)   **Franziska Romana Theresia Notgera Prinzessin zu Oettingen-Oettingen u.
Oettingen-Spielberg** * München 14.10.1947

                 (b)   **Alexandra Pia Notgera Prinzessin zu Oettingen-Oettingen u. Oettingen-Spielberg**
* Oettingen 9.10.1948

                 (c)   **Albrecht Ernst Otto Joseph Maria Notger Erbprinz zu Oettingen-Oettingen u.
Oettingen-Spielberg** * München 7.2.1951

                 (d)   **Gabriele Elisabeth Aloisia Notgera Prinzessin zu Oettingen-Oettingen u. Oettingen-
Spielberg** * München 22.7.1953

                 (e)   **Margarita Agnes Maria Notgera Prinzessin zu Oettingen-Oettingen u. Oettingen-
Spielberg** * München 31.7.1957

XII   d)   **Alexandra Georgina Natalie Karoline Gräfin zu Lynar** * Görlsdorf 25.7.1924 = Aurich
30.3.1945 Wolf-Dietrich Steffan * Emden 31.1.1916, and has issue:

XIII   (a)   **Hans Steffan** * Pforzheim 12.11.1949

                 (b)   **Michael Steffan** * Pforzheim 21.2.1951

XII   e)   **Ernst Wilhelm Alexander Georg Rochus Manderup 6 Fürst zu Lynar** * Görlsdorf
25.7.1924 = Frankfurt-am-Main 10.2.1956 Ingrid Bretzke * Stettin 22.11.1924 dau.
of Ulrich Bretzke, and has issue:

XIII   (a)   **Beatrice Marie Amely Gräfin zu Lynar** * Frankfurt-am-Main 22.6.1958

                 (b)   **Josefa Alexandra Leonore Gräfin zu Lynar** * Berlin 25.3.1960

                 (c)   **Francisca Gräfin zu Lynar** * Berlin 14.2.1964

XII   f)   **Alexander Heinrich Walter Franz Graf zu Lynar** * Lindenau 21.7.1928

XI   c.   **Maria Wilhelmine Gabriele Hermine Elisabeth Gräfin v. Redern** * Görlsdorf 17.10.1890
+ Köln 14.7.1953

          d.   **Margarethe Helene Marie Louise Hermine Victoria Johanna Paula Gräfin v. Redern** * Görlsdorf
24.9.1893 + Düsseldorf 24.12.1944 = Berlin 8.1.1920 Wolfgang Graf v. Schaesberg
* Tannheim 8.5.1888 + Starnberg 14.4.1961, and had issue:

XII   a)   **Karl Max Rudolf Wilhelm Heinrich Hubertus Maria Graf v. Schaesberg** * Ingenraedt
25.6.1921 = Mülheim-Speldorf 19.4.1956 Eva Maria Bollert * Duisburg 5.10.1932
dau. of Max Bollert, and has issue:

XIII   (a)   **Pia Maria Margarethe Elisabeth Gräfin v. Schaesberg** * Mülheim 6.9.1958

XII   b)   **Rudolf Victor Graf v. Schaesberg** * Ingenraedt 2.9.1922 = Odenthal 29.1.1955
Monica Freiin. v. Thielmann * Jacobsdorf Kr. Falkenberg 3.4.1927 dau. of Stephan
Frhr. v. Thielmann, and has issue:

XIII   (a)   **Alice Margarethe Pia Maria Gräfin v. Schaesberg** * Köln 5.11.1955

XIII		(b)	**Michael Josef Heinrich Hubertus Maria Graf v. Schaesberg** * Köln 15.5.1958
		(c)	**Nadine Margaretha Josephine Maria Gräfin v. Schaesberg** * Leverkusen-Schlebusch 11.2.1961
		(d)	**Antonio Josef Caspar Maria Graf v. Schaesberg** * Leverkusen-Schlebusch 21.4.1962

XII   c)   **Elisabeth Maria Therese Margarete Gräfin v. Schaesberg** * Berlin 29.5.1927 = München 4.10.1956 Pedro Botas Menendez * ... — div., and has issue:

XIII   (a)   **Andreas Botas Schaesberg** * 18.8.1957

XI   e.   **Hermine Victoria Marie Gräfin v. Redern** * Berlin 11.4.1899 = Berlin 22.4.1920 Walter Graf v. Schaesberg * Tannheim 3.9.1890, and has issue:

XII   a)   **Eugen Karl Joseph Walter Hermine Hubertus Maria Graf v. Schaesberg** * Berlin 1.2.1921 ⚔ (missing), Hurtgenwald 16.9.1944

     b)   **Heinrich Julius Wilhelm Walter Hubertus Maria Graf v. Schaesberg** * Berlin 12.2.1922 = Grumsmühlen 7.6.1956 **Margaretha Prinzessin v. Croy** * Grumsmühlen 11.10.1930 dau. of Anton Prinz v. Croy, and has issue:

XIII   (a)   **Johannes Friedrich Walter Alfred Josef Maria Graf v. Schaesberg** * München 22.10.1960

     (b)   **Georg Clemens Heinrich Joseph Maria Graf v. Schaesberg** * München 21.6.1962

     (c)   **Christoph Rudolf Antonius Heinrich Joseph Maria Graf v. Schaesberg** * München 26.6.1963

     (d)   **Marie Elisabeth Henriette Bernadette Gräfin v. Schaesberg** * München 12.6.1965

XII   c)   **Marie Therese Elisabeth Huberta Gräfin v. Schaesberg** * Berlin 11.12.1927 = Engelskirchen 27.7.1955 **Clemens Prinz v. Croy** * Grumsmühlen 7.9.1926, and has issue see elsewhere

     d)   **Karl Anton Hubertus Maria Graf v. Schaesberg** * Berlin 12.4.1934

X   (3)   **Margarethe Eleonore Marie Caroline Gräfin Lichnowsky** * Grätz 24.9.1863 + Wien 8.4.1954 = Grätz 14.7.1897 Karl Graf v. Brzezie-Lanckoronski * Wien 4.11.1848 + Wien 15.7.1933 and has issue:

XI   a.   **Caroline Marie Adelheid Franziska Xaverine Margarete Edine Gräfin v. Brzezie-Lanckoronski** * Buchberg 11.8.1898

     b.   **Adelheid Marie Caroline Leonie Margarete Amelie Gräfin v. Brzezie-Lanckoronski** * Wien 5.2.1903

IX   7)   **August Philipp Prinz von Croy** * Düsseldorf 1.3.1840 + Düsseldorf 29.6.1913 = Anholt 30.11.1871 **Adelheid Prinzessin zu Salm-Salm** * Anholt 21.1.1840 + Paderborn 25.8.1916 dau. of Alfred Fürst zu Salm-Salm, and had issue:

X   (1)   **Emanuel Ludwig Marie Prinz von Croy** * Berlin 14.7.1874 + ... 11.1949

     (2)   **Marie Leopoldine Franziska Prinzessin v. Croy** * Nieder-Walluf 27.6.1876 + 12.3.1947

VIII   7.   **Auguste Luise Marie Prinzessin zu Salm-Salm** * 29.1.1798 + 10.3.1837

     8.   **Sophie Prinzessin zu Salm-Salm** * 1.11.1799 + ...

188

VIII 9. **Franz Friedrich Philipp Prinz zu Salm-Salm** * Herten 5.7.1801 + Bonn 31.12.1842 = Kleinheubach
24.3.1841 Marie Josephine Prinzessin zu Löwenstein-Wertheim-Rosenberg * Neustadt a. Main 9.8.1814
+ Kreuznach 9.6.1876 dau. of Constantin 4 Fürst zu Löwenstein-Wertheim-Rosenberg, and had issue:

IX 1) **Marie Eleonore Crescence Catherine Prinzessin zu Salm-Salm** * Frankfurt-am-Main 21.1.1842
+ Dülmen 18.6.1891 = (1) Frankfurt-am-Main 4.4.1866 **Don Mariano Téllez Girón y Beaufort-Spontin
12 Duque de Ousna 15 Duque del Infantado** * Madrid 19.7.1814 + Château de Beauraing 2.6.1882;
= (2) Beauraing 22.9.1884 **Rudolf Herzog v. Croy** * Dülmen 13.3.1823 + Cannes 8.2.1902 s.p.

by 3rd marriage:

VIII 10. **Otto Ludwig Oswald Graf v. Salm-Hoogstraeten** * Anholt 30.8.1810 + Tegernsee 11.5.1869 = (1) Dresden
20.11.1834 Ernestine Freiin. v. Varnbuler * 9.10.1814 + 29.7.1839 = (2) 12.8.1848 Pauline Freiin. v. Speth
* 26.1.1830 + Brixen April 1915 dau. of Friedrich Frhr. v. Speth s.p.

11. **Eduard August Georg Graf v. Salm-Hoogstraeten** * 8.9.1812 + Görz 18.5.1886 = 27.9.1845 Sophie v. Rohr
* 30.5.1824 + Görz 11.1.1891 and had issue:

IX 1) **Constantin Carl Gustav Graf v. Salm-Hoogstraeten** * 17.7.1846 + 7.12.1868

2) **Philipp Otto Ludwig Graf v. Salm-Hoogstraeten** * 10.8.1847 + 25.2.1880

VIII 12. **Rudolf Hermann Wilhelm Florentin August Graf v. Salm-Hoogstraeten** * Anholt 9.9.1817 + Vorde 2.12.1869
= 4.10.1839 Emilie Gräfin v. Borcke * Hütte 9.2.1822 + Heidelust b. Wesel 27.2.1874 dau. of Heinrich Graf v.
Borcke, and had issue:

IX 1) **Marie Florentine Ottilia Henriette Amelie Gräfin v. Salm-Hoogstraeten** * 26.8.1840 + ... = 9.5.1880
Amely de Petersen * ...

2) **Manfred August Albrecht Anton Heinrich Graf v. Salm-Hoogstraeten** * 6.4.1843 + Düsseldorf 10.10.1903
= Aachen 23.10.1874 Christine Schaaf * Aachen 5.6.1840 + Düsseldorf ..., and had issue:

X (1) **Maria Rudolf Johann Manfred Graf v. Salm-Hoogstraeten** * Aachen 30.9.1877 + Neuss 3.8.1944
= Düsseldorf 28.5.1903 Sophie Heuschen * Düsseldorf 14.3.1876 + Düsseldorf 31.12.1934 dau.
of Peter Heuschen, and had issue:

XI a. **Manfred Rudolf Kreuzwndisch Maria Graf v. Salm-Hoogstraeten** * Düsseldorf 31.8.1911
= Fraustadt 16.9.1944 Ruth Drozella * 19.2.1923, and has issue:

XII a) **Angela Maria Gräfin v. Salm-Hoogstraeten** * Neuss 6.6.1946

b) **Barbara Maria Gräfin v. Salm-Hoogstraeten** * Neuss 16.6.1947

c) **Manfred Rudolf Maria Graf v. Salm-Hoogstraeten** * Neuss 28.10.1949

IX 3) **Hermann Ludwig Eduard Rudolf Constantin Maria Graf v. Salm-Hoogstraeten** * Ahaus 16.10.1844 + ...

4) **Constantine Sophie Amelia Hermine Gräfin v. Salm-Hoogstraeten** * 16.12.1846 + ...

5) **Pauline Alfrède Auguste Amelia Katherine Gräfin v. Salm-Hoogstraeten** * 8.2.1849 + ... = 16.5.1872
Franz Stotten * ... + ... 1879

6) **Maximilian Emil Rudolf Hugues Marie Graf v. Salm-Hoogstraeten** * 1.11.1850 X près Amiens January
1871

7) **Felix Ferdinand Adrian Constantin Alexander Carl Conrad Graf v. Salm-Hoogstraeten** * 3.2.1853 + ...

8) **Conrad Gisbert Wilhelm Florentin Graf v. Salm-Hoogstraeten** * 13.10.1855 + ...

VIII 13. **Albrecht Friedrich Ludwig Johann Graf v. Salm-Hoogstraeten** * Anholt 3.9.1819 + Meran 2.4.1904 = Aurich
13.8.1843 Luise Gräfin v. Bohlen * Aurich 21.2.1819 + München 20.10.1875 dau. of Carl Graf v. Bohlen, and
had issue:

IX   1)   **Hermann Emil Constantin Graf v. Salm-Hoogstraeten** * A-Burstscheid 16.3.1844 + Meran 4.2.1905

            2)   **Augusta Ottilie Gräfin v. Salm-Hoogstraeten** * Aachen 27.9.1845 + Wien 17.11.1928

            3)   **Otto Ludwig Wilhelm Johann Graf v. Salm-Hoogstraeten** * Münster i. W. 9.5.1848 + Baden b. Wien 23.4.1907 = Homburg 12.6.1886 Ida Freiin. v. Erlanger * London 3.10.1865 + Baden b. Wien 26.4.1914 dau. of Viktor Frhr. v. Erlanger, and had issue:

X   (1)   **Wilhelm Ludwig Graf v. Salm-Hoogstraeten** * Klemenovo 22.4.1887 = München 11.2.1915 Katherina Benker * München 6.4.1891 + Puchheim 11.6.1963 dau. of Johann Benker, and has issue:

XI   a.   **Hermann Wilhelm Salm-Hoogstraeten** * München 25.3.1913 = München 19.9.1938 Gertraud Annemarie Atzenhofer * München 30.4.1917 dau. of Josef Atzenhofer, and has issue:

XII   a)   **Gertraud Ulrike Salm-Hoogstraeten** * München 21.2.1940

                      b)   **Helga Sieglinde Salm-Hoogstraeten** * München 25.6.1941

                      c)   **Irmingard Alwine Salm-Hoogstraeten** * München 2.12.1948

XI   b.   **Wilhelm Hermann Salm-Hoogstraeten** * Steinberg b. Graz 6.11.1917 = (1) Rattingen 31.12.1943 Friederike Schömehl * Rattingen 17.9.1920 + Rattingen 18.3.1945 dau. of Wilhelm Schömehl; = (2) Puchheim 13.10.1951 Elisabeth Stahl * Aschaffenburg 17.1.1924 dau. of Karl Stahl, and has issue:

                by 1st marriage:

XII   a)   **Ulrike Katherina Salm-Hoogstraeten** * Rattingen 20.2.1945

                by 2nd marriage:

                      b)   **Hans Rudolf Salm-Hoogstraeten** * München 2.4.1956

X   (2)   **Hermann Albrecht Eduard Graf Salm-Hoogstraeten** * Klemenovo 12.3.1888 + Caracas, Venezuela 18.3.1952 = Medgyesfalva 27.11.1917 Eleonore Gräfin v. Bissingen u. Nippenberg * Kecskemet 28.5.1896 dau. of Otto Graf v. Bissingen u. Nippenberg, − div. s.p.

IX   4)   **Alfred Wilhelm Karl Alexander Graf v. Salm-Hoogstraeten** * Münster i. W. 25.5.1851 + Wien 17.6.1919 = Reichenau 26.5.1884 Adolfine Freiin. v. Erlanger * London 9.10.1863 + Budapest ... 1944 dau. of Viktor Frhr. v. Erlanger, and had issue:

X   (1)   **Ludwig Albrecht Constantin Maria Graf v. Salm-Hoogstraeten** * Homburg 24.2.1885 + Budapest 23.7.1944 = (1) Reichenau 30.6.1909 Anne-Marie v. Kramsta * Frankenthal 22.5.1887 − div.; = (2) New York 8.1.1924 Millicent Rogers * New York 2.2.1902 + Albuquerque, New Mexico 12.1.1953 − div., dau. of Henry Huddleston Rogers, and had issue:

              by 2nd marriage:

              a.   **Peter Alfred Constantine Maria Graf v. Salm-Hoogstraeten** * New York 27.9.1925

X   (2)   **Otto Viktor Alfred Maria Graf v. Salm-Hoogstraeten** * Trautenberg 25.8.1886 + Rapallo... 1941 = New York 26.5.1915 Maud Coster * New York 30.4.1895, and had issue:

XI   a.   **Luise Maria Gräfin v. Salm-Hoogstraeten** * New York 25.2.1917 + Portschach 17.6.1951

           b.   **Henry Alexander Graf v. Salm-Hoogstraeten** * New York 17.3.1919

X   (3)   **Alfred Ludwig Arthur Maria Graf v. Salm-Hoogstraeten** * Trautenberg 8.2.1888 + London 10.9.1946 = Wien 8.8.1933 Rose Bless * ... dau. of Marcus Bless s.p.

        (4)   **Alexander Franz Albrecht Maria Graf v. Salm-Hoogstraeten** * Trautenberg 24.6.1890 X 24.7.1918

VIII 14.   **Hermann Johann Ignaz Friedrich Graf v. Salm-Hoogstraeten** * Paris 13.6.1821 + Bonn 24.9.1902

6 The Descendants of Luise Franziska Prinzessin zu Salm-Salm 1725-1764 and Johann Graf v. Manderscheid-Blankenheim 1708-1772.

VI   **Luise Franziska Prinzessin zu Salm-Salm** * Schloss Hoogstraeten 2.3.1725 + Köln 19.2.1764 = Anholt 15.11.1742 Johann Wilhelm Graf v. Manderscheid-Blankenheim * Köln 14.2.1708 + Köln 2.11.1772, and had issue:

VII   1.   **Auguste Dorothea Gräfin v. Manderscheid-Blankenheim** * Köln 28.1.1744 + Wien 19.11.1811 = Blankenheim 7.11.1762 Philipp Christian Graf v. Sternberg * Wien 5.3.1732 + Wien 14.5.1811, and had issue:

VIII   1)   **Franz Josef Graf v. Sternberg-Manderscheid** * Prag 4.9.1763 + Prag 8.4.1830 = Gollersdorf 23.9.1787 **Marie Franziska Gräfin v. Schönborn-Heussenstamm** * Wien 28.7.1763 + Prag 20.10.1825 dau. of Eugen Erwein Graf v. Schönborn-Heussenstamm, and had issue:

IX   (1)   **Leopoldine Gräfin v. Sternberg-Manderscheid** * Prag 10.7.1791 + Čech 15.12.1870 = Zasmuk 23.10.1811 **Franz Graf v. Silva-Tarouca** * Wien 27.4.1773 + Čech 2.12.1835 and had issue see elsewhere

          (2)   **Auguste Gräfin v. Sternberg-Manderscheid** * Prag 18.6.1793 + Pförten 21.7.1820 = Prag 19.6.1816 **Friedrich August Graf v. Brühl** * Pförten 19.11.1791 + Pförten 25.5.1856, and had issue:

X   a.   **Christine Gräfin v. Brühl** * Prag 28.3.1817 + Prag 23.10.1902 = Prag 11.7.1839 Erwein Graf v. Schönborn * Wien 17.5.1812 + Prag 12.1.1881, and had issue:

XI   a)   **Karl Friedrich Josef August Maria Erwein Franz Graf v. Schönborn** * Prag 10.4.1840 + Neuhof b. Neukirchen 29.5.1908 = (1) Konopischt 11.9.1861 Johann Prinzessin v. Lobkowicz * Konopischt 16.6.1840 + Malesitz 5.8.1872 dau. of Johann Prinz v. Lobkowicz; = (2) Brezina 13.9.1875 Zdenka Gräfin v. Sternberg * Wien 16.4.1846 + Schloss Malesitz 16.9.1915 dau. of Zdenko Graf v. Sternberg, and had issue:

             by 1st marriage:

XII   (a)   **Johann Nepomuk Maria Friedrich Karl Josef Eugen Richard Graf v. Schönborn** * Prag 3.4.1864 + Prag 7.6.1912 = Prag 17.6.1889 Anna Gräfin v. Wurmbrand-Stuppach * Wien 23.4.1868 + Prag 2.3.1938 dau. of Heinrich Graf v. Wurmbrand-Stuppach, and has issue:

XIII   1a.   **Maria Karl Johann Aloysius Andreas Heinrich Erwein Graf v. Schönborn** * Prag 28.11.1890 + München 31.8.1952 = (1) Prag 9.6.1914 Elisabeth Gräfin v. Nostitz-Rieneck * Teplitz 18.5.1890 dau. of Heinrich Graf v. Nostitz-Rieneck – div.; = (2) Prag 11.11.1929 Vera Prinzessin zu Hohenlohe-Waldenberg-Schillingsfürst-Kaunitz * Görz 22.5.1882 + Prag 1.12.1940 dau. of Egon Prinz zu Hohenlohe-Waldenberg-Schillingsfürst-Kaunitz; = (3) Friedberg, OSchles. 15.8.1944 Alexandra Völkker * Hamburg 28.3.1904 dau. of Siegfried Völkker – div.; = (4) Hamburg 11.2.1949 Gabriele Freiin. v. Seydlitz-Kurzbach * Hamburg 1.4.1920 dau. of Richard Frhr. v. Seydlitz-Kurzbach, and had issue:

                by 1st marriage:

XIV   1b.   **Maria Johanna Nepomucena Olga Desideria Philippa Gräfin v. Schönborn** * Lukawitz 23.5.1915 = Salzburg 27.11.1937 Ferdinand Frhr. v. Skal u. Gross-Ellguth * Endersdorf 9.7.1903 – div., s.p.

               2b.   **Maria Hugo-Damian Adalbert Josef Hubertus Graf v. Schönborn** * Lukawitz 22.9.1916 = Prag 10.5.1942 Eleonore Freiin. v. Doblhoff * Brünn 14.4.1920 dau. of Herbert Frhr. v. Doblhoff, and has issue:

XV   1c.   **Johann Philipp Maria Karl Herbert Ferdinand Graf v. Schönborn** * Prag 27.1.1943

                2c.   **Christof Maria Michael Hugo Damian Peter Adalbert Graf v. Schönborn** * Skalken 22.1.1945

XV		3c. **Barbara Maria Anna Michaela Elisabeth Gräfin v. Schönborn** * Graz 23.9.1947
		4c. **Michael Anatol Maria Hugo Karl Graf v. Schönborn** * Schruns 2.11.1954
XIV		3b. **Maria Anna Elisabeth Cyrilla Franziska v Paula Gräfin v. Schönborn** * Prag 29.3.1919

XIII   2a. **Eugenie Maria Sidonia Anna Johanna Klothilde Gräfin v. Schönborn** * Prichowic 3.6.1892 = Dlažkovic b. Trebnitz 22.6.1920 Victor Brabetz * Prag 21.11.1876 + Dlažkovic 9.1.1933, and has issue:

XIV   1b. **Susanne Brabetz** * Prag 16.8.1921 = Hamburg 18.8.1948 Werner Scheling * Hamburg 23.10.1920 and has issue:

XV   1c. **Peter Scheling** * Hamburg 3.7.1950

             2c. **Thomas Scheling** * Hamburg 9.2.1952

XIV   2b. **Peter Brabetz** * Prag 2.5.1925 ⚔ Schlesien 10.2.1945

XIII   3a. **Heinrich Maria Johann Maria Adalbert Alexander Aloys Graf v. Schönborn** * Prag 13.2.1895 = Prag-Karolinental 7.10.1936 Margarethe Gerstenberger * Graslitz 29.7.1910 dau. of Bruno Gerstenberger, and has issue:

XIV   1b. **Alexander Maria Karl Heinrich Franz Graf v. Schönborn** * Prag 29.1.1938

             2b. **Maria Elisabeth Anna Henriette Dionysia Gräfin v. Schönborn** * Prag 9.10.1940 = Los Angeles 27.1.1962 James Specht * Los Angeles 13.6.1938

             3b. **Maria Lothar Franz Maria Hugo Damian Eduard Graf v. Schönborn** * Prag 9.6.1943

XII   (b) **Maria Freidrich Karl Johann Joseph Eugen Franz v. Assisi Graf v. Schönborn** * Malesitz 4.10.1865 + Wien 23.8.1919 = Prag 21.5.1898 Sofie Cantacuzène * Loham, Kr. Bogen 11.10.1871 + Bad Tölz 7.12.1959 dau. of Constantin Prince Cantacuzène, and had issue:

XIV   1a. **Maria Paul Franz v. Paula Perceval Christinus Anton Demetrius Alois Joseph Theodosius Graf v. Schönborn** * Egern 29.5.1900

XII   (c) **Maria Joseph Leopold Ottmar Eugen Carl Graf v. Schönborn** * Malesitz 15.11.1866 + Berlin 17.3.1914

      (d) **Maria Franz Dominik Karl Graf v. Schönborn** * Malesitz 4.8.1870 + Burg Schleinitz 17.9.1942 = (1) Korompa 15.4.1896 Gabriele Gräfin Chotek v. Chotkowa u. Wognin * Korompa 11.3.1868 + Korompa 18.12.1933 dau. of Rudolf Graf Chotek v. Chotkowa u. Wognin; = (2) Graz 30.10.1937 Friederike v. Schlözer * Wien 1.3.1908–missing in Jugoslavia since 1945–dau. of Georg v. Schlözer, and had issue:

by 1st marriage

XIII   1a. **Marie Henriette Johanna Gabriele Franziska Josepha Antonia Aloysia Gräfin v. Schönborn** * Wien 2.1.1897 = Burg Schleinitz 31.5.1924 Alessandro Marchese Pallavicino * Parma 2.7.1898 + Roma 7.12.1965, and had issue:

XIV

1b. **Marchesa Gabriele Pallavicino** * Wien 14.4.1925 = Roma 27.12.1954 François Luc de Chevigny * ... and had issue:

XV

    1c. **Balthasar Luc de Chevigny** * Paris 16.6.1963

XIV

2b. **Marchesa Marie Louise Pallavicino** * Wien 23.4.1927

3b. **Marchese Sandro Pallavicino** * Wien 8.11.1936

4b. **Marchesa Teresa Pallavicino** * Wien 8.11.1936

XIII

2a. **Maria Johanne Christine Josepha Antonia Ignatia Gräfin v. Schönborn** * Korompa 15.9.1899 = Wien 15.6.1928 Walter Breitenfeld * Wien 17.12.1884 and has issue:

XIV

1b. **Elisabeth Maria Therese Johanne Breitenfeld** * 18.3.1929 = London 7.6.1952 Michael Skinner * Rochester, Kent 17.6.1927, and has issue:

XV

    1c. **Sophia Skinner** * London 11.4.1957

XIV

2b. **Hubert Breitenfeld** * 24.11.1930 = London 12.7.1953 Norma Turnbull * Blyth, Northumberland 11.8.1935, dau. of George Turnbull, and has issue:

XV

    1c. **Richard John Maria Breitenfeld** * London 25.12.1954

    2c. **Robert Anthony Maria Breitenfeld** * London 24.10.1959

XIV

3b. **Walburga Breitenfeld** * 17.10.1932

XII

(e) **Marie Christine Caroline Anne Therese Johanne Gräfin v. Schönborn** * Malesitz 11.6.1872 + Schloss Tochowice 14.9.1918 = Prag 2.7.1890 Friedrich Prinz v. Schwarzenberg * Worlik 30.1.1862 + Tochowice 2.10.1936 s.p.

by 2nd marriage

(f) **Marie Therese Cunegonde Christine Johanne Agnes Ernestine Sidonie Caroline Gräfin v. Schönborn** * Prag 1.10.1878 + Worlik 7.2.1949

(g) **Zdenko Maria Aloys Karl Wilhelm Graf v. Schönborn** * Prag 10.2.1879 + Krumbach 11.2.1960 = Prag 9.5.1905 Marie Gräfin v. Coudenhove * Seehof 22.2.1886 + Rheydt 20.1.1940 dau. of Gerolf Graf v. Coudenhove, and had issue:

XIII

1a. **Christine Marie Sidonie Gisela Gräfin v. Schönborn** * Stanislau 29.4.1906 = Wien 15.9.1930 Rudolf Graf v. Benigni in Müldenberg * Wien 29.12.1905, and has issue:

XIV

1b. **Johanna Maria Christine Gräfin v. Benigni in Müldenberg** * Wien 14.8.1931

2b. **Heinrich Theodor Sigmund Rudolf Graf v. Benigni in Müldenberg** * Steyr 4.4.1934 = 7.11.1959 Christine v. Küster * 19.3.1939 dau. of Joachim v. Küster, and has issue:

XV

    1c. **Monika Gräfin v. Benigni in Müldenberg** * Wien 4.10.1960

    2c. **Wolfgang Graf v. Benigni in Müldenberg** * Wien 18.7.1962

    3c. **Michael Graf v. Benigni in Müldenberg** * Wien 17.2.1964

XIV		3b. **Marie-Christine Gabriele Gräfin v. Benigni in Müldenberg** * Ulm 4.7.1936

XIII   2a.   **Henriette Marie Gisela Mathilde Gräfin v. Schönborn** * Chlum 9.9.1907 = Mariazell 8.5.1930 Karl Graf Braida v. Ronsecco u. Cornigliano * Sitzenthal 1.6.1902, and has issue:

XIV   1b.   **Sophia Marie-Christine Josephine Gräfin Braida v. Ronsecco u. Cornigliano** * Wien 22.4.1931

                                2b.   **Maximilian Eugen Karl Josef Maria Graf Braida v. Ronsecco u. Cornigliano** * Wien 13.5.1932 = 18.10.1961 Gertrud Grohmann * 8.4.1931 and has issue:

XV   1c.   **Christian Graf Braida v. Ronsecco u. Cornigliano** * 23.9.1962

                                     2c.   **Max Graf Braida v. Ronsecco u. Cornigliano** * 11.5.1964

XIV   3b.   **Eugen Graf Braida v. Ronsecco u. Cornigliano** * 12.10.1940

XIII   3a.   **Gabriele Maria Laurentia Gräfin v. Schönborn** * Chlum 5.9.1909 = Prag 16.8.1930 Friedrich Graf v. Mensdorff-Pouilly * Kulm 25.6.1896 and has issue:

XIV   1b.   **Maria Sidonia Elisabeth Anna Josefa Gräfin v. Mensdorff-Pouilly** * München 4.6.1931 = Fürstenfeld 16.2.1954 Michael Graf v.u. zu Trauttmansdorff-Weinsberg * Wien 16.3.1915 and has issue:

XV   1c.   **Friedrich Karl Graf v.u. zu Trauttmansdorff-Weinsberg** * Graz 18.12.1954

                                     2c.   **Josef Graf v.u. zu Trauttmansdorff-Weinsberg** * Graz 31.3.1956

                                     3c.   **Marie Gabriele Gräfin v.u. zu Trauttmansdorff-Weinsberg** * Graz 13.4.1957

                                     4c.   **Bernadette Gräfin v.u. zu Trauttmansdorff-Weinsberg** * Graz 11.6.1958

                                     5c.   **Elisabeth Gräfin v.u. zu Trauttmansdorff-Weinsberg** * Graz 7.1.1964

XIV   2b.   **Anna Elisabeth Marie Johanna Gräfin v. Mensdorff-Pouilly** * Oberstadion 16.6.1932 = Fürstenfeld 25.8.1966 Klemens Frhr. v. Schlorlemer * Overhagen 15.11.1932

                                3b.   **Emanuel Albertus Magnus Graf v. Mensdorff-Pouilly** * Ulm 16.1.1934

                                4b.   **Sophie Veronika Maria Gräfin v. Mensdorff-Pouilly** * Ulm 29.5.1937 = 9.5.1963 **Wolfgang Graf v. Korff gen Schmising Kerssenbrock** * Schurgast 22.4.1933 and has issue see elsewhere

                                5b.   **Eugen Theobold Arthur Maria Graf v. Mensdorff-Pouilly** * Prag 11.6.1942

XIII   4a.   **Gerolf Max Karl Zdenko Rudolf Hieronymus Maria Graf v. Schönborn** * Chlum 30.9.1915 = (1) München 5.11.1942 Blanka Knapp * Biberach a.d. Riss 24.5.1916 + Seon 24.10.1943 dau. of Alfons Knapp = (2) Wiesbaden 22.8.1953 Johanna-Maria Alberts * Braunschweig 22.6.1924 dau. of Maximilian Alberts

XIII

5a. **Zdenko Friedrich Franz Edmund Theophil Cajetan Maria Graf v. Schönborn**
* Prag 22.4.1917 = (1) München 5.12.1939 Ingeborg v. Bomhard * München
9.5.1918 dau. of Nikolaus v. Bomhard — div.; = (2) Oberstadion 29.11.1947
Maria Johanna Hirsch * Regensburg 17.7.1922 dau. of Georg Hirsch — div.
= (3) München 13.12.1954 Katherina Märkl * Würzburg 19.3.1911 dau. of
Josef Märkl, and has issue:

by 1st marriage:

XIV

1b. **Alexander Friedrich Graf v. Schönborn** * München 5.6.1941
= Aschausen u. Mockmühl 12.9.1966 Mechtild Gräfin v. Zepplin-
Aschausen * Heidelberg 20.10.1937 dau. of Friedrich-Hermann Graf
v. Zepplin-Aschausen

2b. **Angelika Elisabeth Gräfin v. Schönborn** * Oberstadion 24.8.1942

XII

(h) **Maria Adalbert Erwein Karl Laurenz Graf v. Schönborn** * Malesitz 16.8.1881
+ Klattau 18.1.1946 = (1) Horakow 18.6.1907 Rosine Gräfin Czernin v.u. zu
Chudenitz * Prag 14.10.1880 + Skočic b. Wodnan 23.9.1926 dau. of Josef Graf
Czernin v.u. zu Chudenitz = (2) Prag 1.6.1941 Selina Freiin. v. Ringhoffer
* Horka a.d. Iser 8.9.1911 + Prag 19.10.1953 dau. of Alfred Frhr. v. Ringhoffer,
and had issue:

by 1st marriage:

XIII

1a. **Maria Josefine Rosine Zdenka Aloisia Gräfin v. Schönborn** * Linz 1.6.1908

2a. **Maria Karl Zdenko Adalbert Markus Graf v. Schönborn** * Linz 25.4.1910
= (1) Wuppertal-Barmen 25.4.1935 Ilse Pfarr * Wuppertal-Langerfeld
2.12.1908 dau. of Georg Otto Pfarr — div.; = (2) Burg a.d. Wupper
1.2.1961 Annelore Dicke * Wuppertal 11.3.1923 dau. of Julius Dicke, and
has issue:

by 1st marriage:

XIV

1b. **Edda Maria Paula Charlotte Gräfin v. Schönborn** * Wuppertal-Barmen
21.2.1938 = Bonn 13.9.1955 Wolf van Riesenbeck * Wuppertal
8.11.1931, and has issue:

XV

1c. **Bergith van Riesenbeck** * Bad Godesberg 31.12.1955

2c. **Maren van Riesenbeck** * Bad Godesberg 21.1.1958

3c. **Götz Nicolas van Risenbeck** * Wuppertal 28.11.1961

XI

b) **Friedrich Erwein Maria Karl Franz Johann Thomas Graf v. Schönborn** * Dlažkovic
11.9.1841 + Wien 21.12.1907 = Wien 30.1.1869 **Therese Gräfin Czernin v.u. zu
Chudenitz** * 19.12.1843 + Wien 26.4.1910 dau. of Jaromir Graf Czernin v.u. zu
Chudenitz s.p.

c) **Erwein Friedrich Stephan Graf v. Schönborn** * 12.9.1842 + 9.1.1849

d) **Franz Marie Carl Erwein Paul Graf v. Schönborn** * Prag 24.1.1844 + Falkenau
25.6.1899—Cardinal von Schönborn

e) **Anna Marie Auguste Franziska Caroline Aloisia Gräfin v. Schönborn** * Dlažkovic
20.6.1845 + Wien 17.11.1909 = Prag 31.1.1866 Ernst Ferdinand Frhr. v. Gudenus
* Horn 8.9.1833 + Graz 28.10.1914, and had issue:

XII

(a) **Gordian Maria Ernst Ambrousius Erwein Johannes Nepomucenus Frhr. v. Gudenus**
* Thannhausen 7.12.1866 + Thannhausen 31.1.1957 = Prag 12.6.1900 Rosa
Prinzessin v. Lobkowicz * Prag 24.12.1867 + Thannhausen 15.5.1951 dau. of
Joseph Prinz v. Lobkowicz, s.p.

XII	(b)	**Erwein Ernst Maria Frhr. v. Gudenus** * Thannhausen 14.9.1869 + Thannhausen 17.12.1953 = Graz 20.1.1914 Sidonia Freiin. v. Morsey gen Picard * Hohenbrugg 19.7.1892 dau. of Franz Frhr. v. Morsey gen Picard, and had issue:

XIII   1a. **Elisabeth Maria Anna Christina Paula Leonhardine Freiin. v. Gudenus** * Madrid 27.12.1914 = Thannhausen 10.9.1935 Paul Graf Czernin v.u. zu Chudenitz * Roma 6.5.1904; + Graz 6.7.1955 and has issue:

XIV

               1b. **Jaromir Otto Graf Czernin v.u. zu Chudenitz** * Graz 23.7.1936

               2b. **Maria Sidonia Gräfin Czernin v.u. zu Chudenitz** * Graz 20.4.1940

               3b. **Marie Lucie Gräfin Czernin v.u. zu Chudenitz** * Graz 16.5.1941 = Wien 13.6.1966 Alexander Graf Hoyos * Berlin 5.3.1941

               4b. **Marie Elisabeth Gräfin Czernin v.u. zu Chudenitz** * 14.11.1944

XIII   2a. **Ernst Gordian Paul Franz Xaver Josef Ignaz Jakob Isidor Pelagius Leonhard Maximilian Maria Emanuel Frhr. v. Gudenus** * Madrid 26.3.1916 = Thannhausen 18.8.1953 Sophie Gräfin v. Nostitz-Rieneck * Wien 4.6.1929 dau. of Friedrich Graf v. Nostitz-Rieneck, and has issue:

XIV

               1b. **Sophie Maria Amelie Florence Norberta Leonarda Margaretha Henriette Michaela Freiin. v. Gudenus** * Graz 6.6.1954

               2b. **Maria Sidonia Freiin. v. Gudenus** * Graz 20.8.1955

               3b. **Erwein Friedrich Maria Gordian Andreas Balthasar Leonhard Josef Felix Frhr. v. Gudenus** * Thannhausen 30.8.1958

               4b. **Ferdinand Frhr. v. Gudenus** * Thannhausen 27.7.1960

XII   (c) **Marie Christine Johanna Nepomucena Hyacintha Karolina Anna Freiin. v. Gudenus** * Lukawitz 16.8.1870 + Schwarzenraben 19.1.1959 = Prag 2.10.1895 **Karl Graf u. Edler Herr v.u. zu Eltz gen. Faust von Stromberg** * Linz a.d. Donau 13.5.1867 + Schwarzenraben 1.2.1940, and had issue see elsewhere

       (d) **Theresia Maria Christiane Johanna Eutropia Freiin. v. Gudenus** * Thannhausen 14.12.1871 + Graz 9.3.1943

       (e) **Maria Wilhelmine Anna Johanna Freiin. v. Gudenus** * Thannhausen 15.9.1873 + Graz-Wetzelsdorf 4.1.1949 = Graz 18.9.1900 Ferdinand Graf zu Stolberg-Wernigrode * Tervueren 20.1.1867 + Paderborn 30.12.1939 and had issue:

XIII   1a. **Anna Maria Klothilde Franziska Alberta Amelia Elisabeth Mathilde Ferdinande Therese Johanna Nepomucena Vinzentia Veronika Eulalia Gräfin zu Stolberg-Wernigrode** * Störmede 10.12.1903

XII   (f) **Ernst Ferdinand Friedrich Maria Telesphor Frhr. v. Gudenus** * Thannhausen 5.1.1875 + Meran 22.12.1957 = Sutthausen b. Osnabrück 19.5.1914 Maria Rosario Freiin. v. Korff * Sutthausen 18.10.1893 dau. of Gottfried Frhr. v. Korff, and had issue:

XIII   1a. **Gordian Frhr. v. Gudenus** * Sutthausen 9.10.1915 = Graz 17.3.1951 **Anna Gräfin v. Meran** * Csákberény 3.6.1922 dau. of Philipp Graf v. Meran, and has issue:

XIV

               1b. **Philipp Ernst Frhr. v. Gudenus** * Wien 10.1.1952

               2b. **Gordian Franz Frhr. v. Gudenus** * Wien 11.4.1953

               3b. **Anna Maria Freiin. v. Gudenus** * Roma 4.3.1957

XIII

2a. **Maria Theresia Paula Freiin. v. Gudenus** * Meran 19.4.1921

3a. **Gottfried Erwein Frhr. v. Gudenus** * Meran 22.2.1924

XII

(g) **Paula Maria Johanna Freiin. v. Gudenus** * Thannhausen 28.10.1880 + Budapest 19.12.1944 = Thannhausen 5.10.1904 Josef Graf v. Stubenberg * Székelyhid 27.5.1865 + Wien 11.11.1932, and had issue:

XIII

1a. **Joseph-Wolfgang Maria Ernst Johann v. Nepomucek Carl Anton Gregor Graf v. Stubenberg** * Székelyhid 9.5.1906 X Russia 4.12.1944

2a. **Anna Maria Johanna Josefa Antonia Gräfin v. Stubenberg** * Székelyhid 11.3.1908 = Sacueni-Bihor 26.10.1935 Gabriel Baron Pilars de Pilar * Struga b. Warsaw 19.2.1904, and has issue:

XIV

1b. **Josef Baron Pilars de Pilar** * Berlin 11.9.1936 = 27.9.1960 Béatrice Lamotte d'Argy * La Moncelle 25.11.1938 dau. of Charles Lamotte d'Argy, and had issue:

XV

1c. **Carole Baronin Pilars de Pilar** * Bad Godesberg 6.8.1961

2c. **Roderick Baron Pilars de Pilar** * Bad Godesberg 10.2.1963

3c. **Josephine Baronin Pilars de Pilar** * Wiesmoor 8.7.1965

XIV

2b. **Antonius Baron Pilars de Pilar** * Berlin 21.9.1937

3b. **Carl Ernst Baron Pilars de Pilar** * Berlin 21.8.1939 = 24.11.1962 Petra von Johnston * Köln 2.12.1937 dau. of Mortimer v. Johnston, and has issue:

XV

1c. **Charles Johannes Gabriel Baron Pilars de Pilar** * Wasserburg am. Inn 20.8.1966

XIV

4b. **Roderick Baron Pilars de Pilar** * Berlin 28.8.1940 = Stockholm 28.8.1965 Gunvor Baroness Leijonhufvud * Stockholm 7.10.1941 dau. of Stig Abraham Baron Leijonhufvud, and has issue:

XV

1c. **Erik Baron Pilars de Pilar** * München 16.2.1966

XIV

5b. **Paul Baron Pilars de Pilar** * Lippstadt 9.2.1947

6b. **Gabriel Baron Pilars de Pilar** * Lippstadt 22.12.1949

XIII

3a. **Ernst Maria Anton Johann v. Nepomucek Carl Eleutherius Graf v. Stubenberg** * Wien 20.2.1911 = Chotěboř 16.10.1939 Anna Maria Gräfin Dobřžensky v. Dobřženicz * Chotěboř 25.9.1912 dau. of Johann Graf Dobřžensky v. Dobřženicz and has issue:

XIV

1b. **Johann Josef Maria Ernst Wolfgang Paul Graf v. Stubenberg** * Prag 4.10.1940

XIII

4a. **Paul Karl Johann v. Nepomucek Gordian Anton Josef Maria Petrus Graf v. Stubenberg** * Székelyhid 1.8.1914 + Roumania in the deportation, 1945

5a. **Elisabeth Anna Maria Gordiana Paula Josefa Dominica Gräfin v. Stubenberg** * Székelyhid 4.8.1915 = Sacueni-Bihor 10.2.1943 Elemér v. Malanotti * Wien 1.5.1916 s.p.

XIII   6a. **Therese Maria Anna Josefa Johanna v. Nepomucena Antonia Gordiana Alexandra Gabriele Gräfin v. Stubenberg** * Székelyhid 3.5.1918

XI   f)   **Hugo Graf v. Schönborn** * ... 1846 + 27.5.1847

      g)   **Maria Elisabeth Auguste Josephine Erweine Christine Ange Gräfin v. Schönborn** * Teplitz 4.9.1848 + Roth-Schönberg 7.6.1905 = Prag 26.10.1871 Egon v. Schönberg-Roth-Schönberg * Wilsdruff 14.4.1845 + Dresden 10.12.1908, and had issue:

XII   (a)   **Joseph Maria Michael Erwin Benno Ägid Johann Nepomuk v. Schönberg-Roth-Schönberg** * Lukawitz Böh., 1.9.1873 + Starnberg 24.4.1957 = Dresden 17.4.1907 Elisabeth Gräfin v. Montgelas * Roma 1.2.1884 + Dresden 25.3.1944 dau. of Eduard Graf v. Montgelas, and had issue:

XIII   1a. **Maria Immaculata Josepha Elisabeth Michaela Anna Thaddea Antonia Franziska v. Schönberg-Roth-Schönberg** * Dresden 3.4.1917 = (1) Dietramszell 23.9.1939 Joseph Wilhelm Schilcher * Dietramszell 17.9.1910 − div. = (2) Leoni 10.10.1944 dau. of Wolfram Müller * Immenstadt 12.5.1907, and has issue:

by 1st marriage:

XIV   1b. **Johannes Schilcher** * 18.7.1941

by 2nd marriage:

2b. **Elisabeth Müller** * 4.5.1946

XII   (b)   **Elisabeth Maria Emilia Michaela Eustachia v. Schönberg-Roth-Schönberg** * Roth-Schönberg 20.9.1874 + Dresden 7.7.1919

         (c)   **Maria Christina Michaela Angela Leodegara v. Schönberg-Roth-Schönberg** * Roth-Schönberg 2.10.1876 + Dresden-Goppeln 8.8.1963

         (d)   **Wilhelmine Maria Michaela Johanna de Matha Monika v. Schönberg v. Roth-Schönberg** * Prag 8.2.1878 + Bertholdstein 2.1.1958

         (e)   **Theresia Elisabeth Anna Maria Michaela Erwina Emmanuela Marcella v. Schönberg-Roth-Schönberg** * Wilsdruff 16.1.1881 + Wien 22.11.1942

         (f)   **Maria-Anna Elisabeth Annunciata Josepha Michaela Christina v. Schönberg-Roth-Schönberg** * Wilsdruff 25.3.1882

         (g)   **Michael Joseph Maria Ernst Wilhelm Peter Paul Johannes v. Schönberg-Roth-Schönberg** * Roth-Schönberg 25.6.1883 = Dresden 28.9.1911 Elinor von Weber * Bautzen 19.2.1889 dau. of Kurt Anton v. Weber, and has issue:

XIII   1a. **Maria-Elisabeth Alice Michaela Ursula v. Schönberg-Roth-Schönberg** * Dresden 26.10.1912 = Dresden 25.5.1939 Hermann Moers * Bonn 5.3.1908 and has issue:

XIV   1b. **Michael Wilhelm Hermann Moers** * Bonn 31.10.1940

2b. **Hans Peter Georg Maria Moers** * Görlitz 18.8.1943

3b. **Wilhelm Leo Maria Moers** * Freiburg/Sachsen 3.7.1945

4b. **Joachim Wilhelm Hermann Moers** * Köln 16.4.1950

XIII   2a. **Franz de Paula Ernst Joseph Maria Michael Hermann v. Schönberg-Roth-Schönberg** * Leipzig 7.4.1914 = Köslin 3.4.1941 Elisabeth Quade * Funkenhagen, Kr. Köslin 20.12.1910 dau. of Otto Quade

XIII   3a.   **Pius Michael Maria Johannes Dietrich Leo v. Schönberg-Roth-Schönberg**
* Leipzig 4.5.1915 = Donauwörth 30.12.1950 Erica Schauer * Gasbach b.
Geislingen 31.7.1923 dau. of Alfred Schauer and has issue:

XIV   1b.   **Monica Elisabeth Gabriele v. Schönberg-Roth-Schönberg** * Donauwörth
23.9.1953

          2b.   **Anna Maria Monica v. Schönberg-Roth-Schönberg** * Donauwörth
14.1.1955

          3b.   **Franz Michael Ulrich v. Schönberg-Roth-Schönberg** * Donauwörth
9.5.1956

          4b.   **Hans Ulrich Michael v. Schönberg-Roth-Schönberg** * Donauwörth
1.4.1961

          5b.   **Regine Fidèle Marianne v. Schönberg-Roth-Schönberg** * Heimenkirch
2.5.1962

XIII   4a.   **Maria Monika Paula Michaela Notpurga v. Schönberg-Roth-Schönberg**
* Leipzig 13.9.1917 = Dresden 11.9.1942 Hans Carl Graf Finck v.
Finckenstein * Dresden 18.9.1914, and has issue:

XIV   1b.   **Frieda Elisabeth Charlotte Gräfin Finck v. Finckenstein** * Görlitz
12.10.1944

          2b.   **Alexander Graf Finck v. Finckenstein** * Piene 23.9.1946
+ Braunschweig 4.11.1946

XI   h)   **Marie Leopoldine Josephe Erweine Gräfin v. Schönborn** * 15.2.1850 + 8.9.1852

     i)   **Maria Wilhelmine Elisabeth Caroline Sidonie Gräfin v. Schönborn** * Dlažkovic
25.6.1851 + Prag 1.9.1911

     j)   **Josef Graf v. Schönborn** * 8.8.1852 + 24.9.1852

     k)   **Adalbert Joseph Maria Franz August Graf v. Schönborn** * Dlažkovic 2.7.1854 + Haid
11.10.1924 = Haid, Böh. 10.9.1889 Adelheid Prinzessin zu Löwenstein-Wertheim-
Rosenberg * Kleinhuebach 17.7.1865 + Prag 6.9.1941 dau. of Karl 6th Fürst zu
Löwenstein-Wertheim-Rosenberg, and had issue:

XII   (a)   **Maria Christina Cäcilia Ludmilla Elisabeth Aloysia Gräfin v. Schönborn** * Prag
22.11.1890 + Abbei St. Gabriel in Bertholdstein 23.1.1933

     (b)   **Maria Joseph Karl Erwein Aloys Benedikt Franz Peter Paul Johannes Sebastian
Graf v. Schönborn** * Prag 25.1.1892 ✗ Miedzyrecze, Poland, 14.8.1915

     (c)   **Marie Agnes Sophie Gertrud Gräfin v. Schönborn** * Prag 16.11.1893
= Hertenstein 30.7.1921 Aladár Boroviczény b. Kisvárda * Jalkovec, Hungary
1.7.1890 + Wien 7.4.1963, and had issue:

XIII   1a.   **Károly György Maria Boroviczény v. Kisvárda** * Budapest 9.10.1922
= Budapest 30.7.1946 Irén Dénes de Arapatak * Ujvidék, Hungary
12.1.1923 dau. of Josef Dénes de Arapatak and has issue:

XIV   1b.   **György Imre Maria Boroviczény v. Kisvárda** * Budapest 14.2.1948

          2b.   **Orsolya Maria Franziska Agnes Boroviczény v. Kisvárda** * Budapest
6.6.1953

XIII	2a.	**Imre Johannes Maria Aladár Elemér Boroviczény v. Kisvárda** * Wien 24.6.1929 = Santiago de Compostela, Spain 24.9.1959 Aida Méndex Miaja * Santiago de Compostela 16.6.1930 dau. of Don Eduardo Méndez Curiel, and has issue:

XIV	1b.	**Eduard Aladár Imre Maria Antonio Boroviczény v. Kisvárda** * Graz 1.10.1960
	2b.	**Agnes Boroviczény v. Kisvárda** * Wien 7.4.1962
	3b.	**Erzsebet Boroviczény v. Kisvárda** * Madrid 23.3.1964
	4b.	**Károly Boroviczény v. Kisvárda** * Madrid 28.2.1965

XIII	3a.	**Ferenc Xaver Maria Benedictus Adalbert Karl Boroviczény v. Kisvárda** * Wien 23.3.1932 = Graz 2.9.1961 Maria Elisabeth Künigl Gräfin zu Ehrenburg * Wien 10.6.1936 dau. of Karl Künigl Graf zu Ehrenburg, and has issue:

XIV	1b.	**Kristóf Boroviczény v. Kisvárda** * Graz 23.7.1963
	2b.	**István Boroviczény v. Kisvárda** * Graz 8.11.1964

XII	(d)	**Maria Benedikta Wilhelmine Anna Eusebia Alfonsa Gräfin v. Schönborn** * Prag 29.10.1896 + Prag 6.4.1957 = Haid 19.11.1927 Franz Graf Kinsky v. Wchinitz u. Tettau * Wien 23.5.1878 + Chlumec 10.12.1935 s.p.
	(e)	**Maria Erwein Karl Hroznata Bernhard Maurus Graf v. Schönborn** * Prag 15.1.1899
	(f)	**Maria Franz v. Paula Wenzel Salvator Antonius v. Padua Paulus Erem. Graf v. Schönborn** * Prag 15.1.1899 + Prag 15.7.1964

XI	l)	**Philipp Graf v. Schönborn** * 21.8.1856 + ...
	m)	**Maria Paula Zoë Elisabeth Augustine Vincente Gräfin v. Schönborn** * Prag 22.1.1861 + Prag 9.2.1922 = Prag 6.5.1882 Zdenko Prinz v. Lobkowicz * Wien 5.5.1858 + Harrachsdorf, Böh. 13.8.1933, and had issue:

XII	(a)	**Marie Joseph Zdenko Ferdinand Erwein Petrus v. Alcantara Pachalis Kaspar Prinz v. Lobkowicz** * Prag 14.4.1884 + Wien-Schönbrunn 6.4.1918
	(b)	**Maria Immaculata Zdenko Christina Petra v. Alcantara Melchiora Judith Prinzessin v. Lobkowicz** * Prag 10.12.1885 + Prag 23.6.1964
	(c)	**Maria Erwein Karl Petrus v. Alcantara Romanus Damianus Balthasar Prinz v. Lobkowicz** * Prag 28.2.1887 = Vukovár 24.5.1923 Antoinette Gräfin v.u. zu Eltz gen. Faust v. Stromberg * Vukovár 17.5.1899 dau. of Jakob Graf v.u. zu Eltz, gen. Faust v. Stromberg, and has issue:

XIII	1a.	**Maria Paula Barbara Kaspara Petra v. Alcantara Friederika Thoma v. Aquin Walpurga Thekla Karolina Prinzessin v. Lobkowicz** * Vukovár 6.3.1924
	2a.	**Maria Sidonia Sophie Melchiora Petra v. Alcantara Valentina Faustina Prinzessin v. Lobkowicz** * Vukovár 14.2.1925
	3a.	**Maria Anna Lidwina Balthasara Petra v. Alcantara Gratiana Vladimira Liberta Prinzessin v. Lobkowicz** * Vukovár 18.12.1928

XII	(d)	**Maria Christine Philomena Vilibalda Elisabeth Antonia Petra v. Alcantara Kaspara Prinzessin v. Lobkowicz** * Unterbeřkovic 7.7.1890
	(e)	**Marie Wenzel Eusebius August Joseph Petrus v. Alcantara Anton Cresentius Melchior Prinz v. Lobkowicz** * Theresienstadt 17.4.1893 + Hetzendorf 4.11.1915

XII

    (f) **Maria Anna Bertha Josephine Paula Polykarpa Ignatia Petra v. Alcantara Balthasara Prinzessin v. Lobkowicz** * Postelberg, Böh. 25.1.1896 + Prag 28.5.1964

X

    b. **Franziska Gräfin v. Brühl** * Pförten 13.7.1818 + Düsseldorf 25.11.1844 = Prag 26.2.1840 August Wilhelm Graf v. Spee * Düsseldorf 18.4.1813 + Heltorf 23.8.1882, and had issue:

XI

    a) **Franz Friedrich August Hubert Pascalis Graf v. Spee** * Düsseldorf 11.4.1841 + Heltorf 7.3.1921 = Herten 17.9.1867 **Anna Gräfin Droste zu Vischering v. Nesselrode-Reichenstein** * Herten 15.11.1843 + Heltorf 29.3.1900, dau. of Felix Graf Droste zu Vischering v. Nesselrode-Reichenstein s.p.

    b) **Elisabeth Friederike Sophie Auguste Maria Huberta Gräfin v. Spee** * Düsseldorf 10.9.1842 + Dinklage 26.3.1920 = Heltorf 7.5.1861 Ferdinand Graf v. Galen * Münster i. W. 31.8.1831 + Dinklage, 5.1.1906 and had issue:

XII

    (a) **Elisabeth Fernande Anna Franziska Antonia Huberta Gräfin v. Galen** * Münster i. W. 5.3.1862 + Assen 1.1.1870

    (b) **Maria Anna Gräfin v. Galen** * Münster i. W. 4.8.1863 + Wien 19.6.1930

    (c) **Friedrich Matthias Graf v. Galen** * Münster i. W. 20.5.1865 + Dinklage 10.11.1919 = Gevelinghausen 4.9.1894 Paula Freiin. v. Wendt * Gevelinghausen 7.5.1873 + Dinklage 26.4.1959 dau. of Karl Frhr. v. Wendt, and had issue:

XIII

    1a. **Maria Elisabeth Josepha Sophia Anna Franziska Margarete Huberta Gräfin v. Galen** * Assen 13.7.1895

XII

    (d) **Augustinus Aloysius Graf v. Galen** * Assen 1.10.1866 + Bonn 20.11.1912 = Münster i. W. 12.11.1896 Levina Gräfin v. Korff gen. Schmising Kerssenbrock * Steinhausen 30.4.1867 + Bonn 14.9.1941 dau. of Klemens Graf v. Korff gen. Schmising Kerssenbrock, and had issue:

XIII

    1a. **Ferdinand Joseph Fidelis Raphael Antonius Hubertus Maria Graf v. Galen** * Sigmaringen 4.9.1898 ✗ Couroy, près Reims 21.7.1918

    2a. **Elisabeth Clementine Josepha Theresia Antonia Huberta Maria Gräfin v. Galen** * Düsseldorf 17.11.1899 = Assen 4.8.1920 Anton Frhr. v. Salis-Soglio * Wetzlar 6.5.1892 and has issue:

XIV

    1b. **Josefa Maria Lewina Antonia Adelheid Elisabeth Huberta Freiin. v. Salis-Soglio** * Münster i. W. 11.8.1922 = Gemünden 28.8.1947 Benedikt Frhr. v. Boeselager * Höllinghofen 2.3.1920 and has issue:

XV

    1c. **Antonius Wolfgang Hermann Joseph Hubertus Maria Frhr. v. Boeselager** * Wimbern, Kr. Iserlohn 12.9.1948

    2c. **Maximilian Leopold Christophorus Michael Hubertus Maria Frhr. v. Boeselager** * Hagen i. W. 25.11.1949

    3c. **Maria Benedicta Adelheid Antonia Josepha Freiin. v. Boeselager** * Gemünden 12.5.1951

    4c. **Maria Helene Pia Henriette Bernadette Freiin. v. Boeselager** * Hagen i. W. 22.11.1954 + Köln 19.8.1959

    5c. **Michael Philipp Ferdinand Antonius Hubertus Frhr. v. Boeselager** * Gemünden 4.9.1960

XIV	2b.	**Adelheid Maria Theresia Bernada Antonia Freiin. v. Salis-Soglio** * Gemünden 1.9.1923 = Maria-Laach 20.4.1960 Maximilian Frhr. Heereman von Zuvdtwyck * Surenberg 29.12.1893, and has issue:
XV	1c.	**Maria Bernadette Elisabeth Helene Freiin. Heereman von Zuydtwyck** * Riesenbeck Kr. Tecklenburg 20.2.1961
	2c.	**Maximilian Sigismund Frhr. Heereman von Zuydtwyck** * Riesenbeck 17.10.1962
XIV	3b.	**Antonius Augustinus Stephanus Thaddäus Michael Aloysius Maria Frhr. von Salis-Soglio** * Gemünden 26.12.1924 X b. Koskowo, Russia 24.8.1944
	4b.	**Pia Maria Alexandra Klementine Antonia Freiin. von Salis-Soglio** * Gemünden 21.8.1926 = Gemünden 26.7.1950 Karl Frhr. von Hövel * Westerholt 23.10.1915, and has issue:
XV	1c.	**Maria Anna Freiin. von Hövel** * Siegen 2.10.1953 + Junkerthal 8.2.1954
	2c.	**Friedrich Antonius Mariano Hubertus Pius Frhr. von Hövel** * Junkerthal 14.6.1955
	3c.	**Elisabeth Maria Antonia Pia Freiin. von Hövel** * Junkerthal 3.2.1957
	4c.	**Hermann-Joseph Mariano Pius Benedikt Frhr. von Hövel** * Junkerthal 18.2.1959
XIV	5b.	**Monika Paula Elisabeth Antonia Maria Freiin. von Salis-Soglio** * Gemünden 11.5.1929 = Gemünden 11.8.1955 Rudolf Frhr. von Lüninck * Halle a. S. 22.2.1923, and has issue:
XV	1c.	**Maria Theresia Mechtilde Antonia Josepha Freiin. von Lüninck** * Rothestein 12.8.1956
	2c.	**Mechtilde Elisabeth Antonia Josepha Maria Freiin. von Lüninck** * Rothestein 13.6.1957
	3c.	**Georg Antonius Gottfried Josef Maria Hubertus Frhr. von Lüninck** * Rothestein 21.5.1960
	4c.	**Elisabeth Antonia Josefa Huberta Maria Freiin. von Lüninck** * Rothestein 28.5.1961
	5c.	**Christophorus Frhr. von Lüninck** * Rothestein 25.10.1964
XIV	6b.	**Maria Ferdinande Theodora Helene Antonia Freiin. von Salis-Soglio** * Gemünden 2.11.1932 = Gemünden 7.8.1958 Franz Sigismund Frhr. v. Elverfeldt-Ulm zu Erbach * Canstein 13.6.1932 and has issue:
XV	1c.	**Maria-Anna Magda Pia Alexandra Paula Freiin. v. Elverfeldt-Ulm zu Erbach** * Frankfurt-am-Main 3.5.1959
	2c.	**Friedrich-Christian Max Anton Manfred Maria Frhr. v. Elverfeldt-Ulm zu Erbach** * Frankfurt-am-Main 27.12.1960
	3c.	**Clemens-August Ludwig Maria Gallus Bonifatius Frhr. v. Elverfeldt-Ulm zu Erbach** * Freiburg 5.6.1962 + Göttingen 28.6.1963
	4c.	**Max Augustinus Hubertus Maria Frhr. v. Elverfeldt-Ulm zu Erbach** * Freiburg 3.12.1963

XV

        5c.   **Antonius Christoph Franz Maria Frhr. v. Elverfeldt-Ulm zu Erbach**
            Freiburg/Brsg. 14.1.1966

XIV

     7b. **Maria Elisabeth Klementine Antonia Freiin. von Salis-Soglio**
         * Gemünden 2.11.1932 = Gemünden 28.8.1962 Gottfried Frhr. von
         Lüninck * Rothestein 22.2.1932, and has issue:

XV

        1c.   **Hedwig Freiin. von Lüninck** * Meschede 3.6.1963

        2c.   **Carl Ferdinand Frhr. von Lüninck** * Olsberg 13.5.1964

XIII

     3a. **Maria Maximiliana Josepha Margareta Marka Antonia Huberta Gräfin v. Galen**
         * Prüm 25.4.1901 = Assen 24.5.1923 Clemens Graf v. Korff gen. Schmising
         * Münster i. W. 26.6.1898 + Tatenhausen 23.12.1966, and had issue:

XIV

     1b. **Augusta Maria Gräfin v. Korff gen. Schmising** * Tatenhausen 21.1.1925

     2b. **Ferdinande Eleonore Gräfin v. Korff gen. Schmising** * Tatenhausen
         29.5.1926 + München 22.1.1960 = Tatenhausen 12.8.1952 Ulrich
         Frhr. Teuffel von Birkensee' * Karlsruhe i. B. 26.5.1925, and had issue:

XV

        1c.   **Benedikt Heinrich Mariano Clemens August Thaddäus Joseph**
            Frhr. Teuffel von Birkensee * Münster i. W. 18.9.1953

        2c.   **Christine Katharina Maria Augusta Thaddäa Josepha Freiin.**
            Teuffel von Birkensee * Tatenhausen 20.9.1954

        3c.   **Patricia Pia Maria Maximiliana Thaddäa Ulrike Josepha Freiin.**
            Teuffel von Birkensee * Tatenhausen 26.8.1956

XIV

     3b. **Guda Helene Gräfin v. Korff gen. Schmising** * Tatenhausen
         9.8.1927 = Tatenhausen 9.5.1957 Carl Sylvius v. Aulock * Breslau
         12.7.1919, and has issue:

XV

        1c.   **Andreas Maximilian Johannes von Aulock** * Bad Rothenfelde
            22.5.1958

        2c.   **Regina Ludwiga Ferdinande Helene von Aulock** * Bad Rothenfelde
            22.3.1960

        3c.   **Stephan Ferdinand Gebhart Rupert von Aulock** * Bad Rothenfelde
            22.3.1960

        4c.   **Carl Wolfgang Christian Alfred von Aulock** * Halle, Wetf.
            17.1.1964 + Schleswig 1.4.1965

XIV

     4b. **Ronna Mathilde Gräfin v. Korff gen. Schmising** * Tatenhausen
         12.4.1929 + Tatenhausen 20.11.1934

     5b. **Max Joseph Graf v. Korff gen. Schmising** * Tatenhausen 27.11.1932

     6b. **Degenhard Graf v. Korff gen. Schmising** * Tatenhausen 1.4.1935
         + Tatenhausen 4.4.1935

XIII

     4a. **Helene Maria Paula Josepha Antonia Huberta Gräfin von Galen** * Prüm
         25.8.1903 = Münster i. W. 9.7.1925 Clemens Graf v. Korff gen.Schmising-
         Kerssenbrock * Schurgast 5.7.1899 X Boronow 18.1.1945, and has issue:

XIV

     1b. **Ferdinand Joseph Caspar Levin Antonius Hubertus Maria Anna**
         Eustachius Graf v. Korff gen. Schmising-Kerssenbrock * Schurgast
         20.9.1926 = Hannover-Kleefeld 5.6.1953 Inga Verene Benecke
         * Hannover 2.4.1928 dau. of Otto Benecke and has issue:

XV	1c.	**Philipp-Ferdinand Rupert Johannes-Heinrich Maria Clemens Otto Fidelis Graf v. Korff gen. Schmising-Kerssenbrock** * München 24.4.1954
	2c.	**Bardo Ruppert Maria Wolfgang Harold Graf v. Korff gen. Schmising-Kerssenbrock** * München 10.6.1955
	3c.	**Marianus Florian Rupert Ingo Rembert Michael Protus Graf v. Korff gen. Schmising-Kerssenbrock** * München 11.9.1957
	4c.	**Valentin Nepomuk Rupert Gabriel Christoph Maria Johannes Graf v. Korff gen. Schmising-Kerssenbrock** * München 15.5.1961
	5c.	**Sebastian Rupert Max Josef Ludowik Alexander Ignatius Benedikt Graf v. Korff gen. Schmising-Kerssenbrock** * München 21.3.1963
XIV	2b.	**Christoph Bernhard Elisabeth Antonius Hubertus Maria Anna Porphyrus Graf v. Korff gen. Schmising-Kerssenbrock** * Schurgast 26.2.1928
	3b.	**Joachim Caspar Otto Elisabeth Antonius Hubertus Maria Anna Aegidius Graf v. Korff gen. Schmising-Kerssenbrock** * Schurgast 1.9.1929
	4b.	**Rembert Antonius Hubertus Maria Anna Bonifatius Graf v. Korff gen. Schmising-Kerssenbrock** * Schurgast 5.6.1931
	5b.	**Wolfgang Maria Karl Egon Hubertus Anna Soter Cajus Graf v. Korff gen. Schmising-Kerssenbrock** * Schurgast 22.4.1933 = 9.5.1963 **Veronika Gräfin v. Mensdorff-Pouilly** * Ulm 29.5.1937 dau. of Friedrich Graf v. Mensdorff-Pouilly, and has issue:
XV	1c.	**Isabelle Maria Helene Judica Gräfin v. Korff gen. Schmising-Kerssenbrock** * Köln 15.3.1964
	2c.	**Theresita Maria Mandela Hieronyma Gräfin v. Korff gen. Schmising-Kerssenbrock** * München-Gladbach 20.7.1965
	3c.	**Bernadette Marie Gabrielle Sidonie Regina Gräfin v. Korff gen. Schmising-Kerssenbrock** * München-Gladbach 30.10.1966
XIV	6b.	**Gisela Caroline Clementine Josepha Antonia Huberta Maria Anna Martina Gräfin v. Korff gen. Schmising-Kerssenbrock** * Schurgast 12.11.1935 = 18.9.1961 Wolff Frhr. v. dem Bongart * Pfaffendorf 19.7.1931, and has issue:
XV	1c.	**Gerard Frhr. v. dem Bongart** * Amberg 26.7.1962
	2c.	**Titus Frhr. v. dem Bongart** * Amberg 19.8.1964
	3c.	**Andreas Frhr. v. dem Bongart** * Amberg 23.12.1966
XIII	5a.	**Christoph Bernhard Paulus Conrad Gottfried Antonius Hubertus Maria Graf v. Galen** * Bonn 11.1.1907 = Kosteleč nad Orlici 28.7.1931 Marie-Sophie Gräfin Kinsky v. Wchinitz u. Tettau * Alderkosteletz 24.2.1909 dau. of Franz Graf Kinsky v. Wchinitz u. Tettau, and has issue:
XIV	1b.	**Pauline Franziska Maria Josepha Antonia Huberta Peter u. Paul Leonie Gräfin v. Galen** * Neuengraben 29.6.1932 = Assen 18.10.1955 Friedrich Graf v.u. zu Trauttmansdorff-Weinsberg * Bischofsteinitz 21.6.1926, and had issue:

1c.   **Maria Theresia Gräfin v.u. zu Trauttmansdorff-Weinsberg**
    * Hamilton, Ontario 28.7.1956

2c.   **Ferdinand Graf v.u. zu Trauttmansdorff-Weinsberg** * Hamilton,
    Ontario 1.11.1957

3c.   **Andreas Graf v.u. zu Trauttmansdorff-Weinsberg** * Hamilton,
    Ontario 15.10.1962

2b.   **Hedwig Maria Antonia Gabriele Huberta Josepha Johanna Felicie
Bernadette Gräfin v. Galen** * Neuengraben 8.2.1934 = Assen
12.7.1956 Rudolf de Longueval Graf von Buquoy * Gratzen
6.10.1927, and has issue:

1c.   **Johanna Maria Ferdinande Huberta Theresia Bernadette de
Longueval Gräfin v. Buquoy** * Bonn 1.8.1957

2c.   **Marie Bernadette Henriette Ferdinande Martina Huberta de
Longueval Gräfin v. Buquoy** * Bonn 5.11.1958

3c.   **Karl Georg Maria Christoph Bernhard Hubertus Hieronymus
Bonaventura de Longueval Graf v. Buquoy** * Bonn 20.7.1961

4c.   **Markus de Longueval Graf v. Buquoy** * Bonn 20.5.1963

3b.   **Ferdinand Joseph Conrad Levin Friedrich Karl Thomas Johannes Judas
Thaddäus Antonius Hubertus Maria Calistus Mauritius Graf v. Galen**
* Neuengraben 14.10.1935 = 15.1.1966 Anita Hempst * Offenbach/
Main 11.4.1938

4b.   **Johanna Paula Alphonsa Josepha Antonia Huberta Maria de Mercede
Cosmas u. Damian Gräfin v. Galen** * Assen 24.9.1936 = Assen
8.9.1956 Clemens August Graf v. Westphalen zu Fürstenberg
* Fürstenberg 23.3.1927, and has issue see elsewhere

5b.   **Maria Theresia Maximiliane Josepha Antonia Huberta Anselma Fidelis
Gräfin v. Galen** * Assen 21.4.1938 = Assen 23.2.1963 Comte Marc
Antoine d'Oultremont * Matran, Suisse 20.7.1927 and has issue:

1c.   **Comtesse Tatiana d'Oultremont** * Paris 5.3.1964

2c.   **Comtesse Ludmilla d'Oultremont** * Marseilles 26.7.1965

6b.   **Ludmilla Wladmiria Antonia Maria Huberta Silveria Wilhelmine
Cornelia Gräfin v. Galen** * Assen 20.6.1939 = Münster i. W.
17.10.1961 Heinrich Archduke of Austria * München 7.1.1925, and
has issue see elsewhere

6a.   **Maria Magdalena Hedwig Josepha Huberta Antonia Gräfin v. Galen** * Bonn
1.5.1908 = Münster i. W. 16.1.1934 Herbert Frhr. von Canstein * Dortmund
7.3.1902 ✕ Rhede b. Bocholt 24.3.1945, and has issue:

1b.   **Aeliane Gabriele Bernarda Huberta Maria Sophia Freiin. von Canstein**
* Dortmund 15.5.1935 = Münster i. W. 8.5.1957 Franz Joseph Frhr.
v. Weichs zur Wenne * Godelheim i. W. 11.2.1920, and has issue:

1c.   **Susanna Maria Magdalena Freiin. v. Weichs zur Wenne** * Thuyne
b. Lingen 15.4.1958

2c.   **Maximilian Hubertus Herbert Frhr. v. Weichs zur Wenne**
* Münster i. W. 10.5.1959

XV		3c.	**Maria Therese Freiin. v. Weichs zur Wenne** * Münster i. W. 23.6.1963
XIV		2b.	**Roswitha Lucia Freiin. v. Canstein** * Siegen i. W. 26.9.1936 = Münster i. W. 2.5.1956 Clemens Ludwig Frhr. Ostman von der Leye * Honeburg b. Osnabrück 28.2.1925

<table>
<tr><td>XII</td><td>(e)</td><td colspan="2">Maria Franziska Gräfin v. Galen * Dinklage 12.12.1867 + St. Louis U.S.A. 25.8.1928</td></tr>
<tr><td></td><td>(f)</td><td colspan="2">Maria Gräfin v. Galen * Dinklage 13.3.1869 + Dinklage 23.11.1876</td></tr>
<tr><td></td><td>(g)</td><td colspan="2">Wilhelm Emanuel Graf v. Galen * Münster i. W. 14.12.1870 + Freiburg, Switzerland 2.9.1949</td></tr>
<tr><td></td><td>(h)</td><td colspan="2">Gertrud Agnes Gräfin v. Galen * Dinklage 11.8.1872 + Gevelinghausen 20.11.1943 = Assen 1.10.1901 Konrad Frhr. v. Wendt * Gevelinghausen 24.4.1872 + Gevelinghausen 19.1.1945, and had issue:</td></tr>
</table>

XIII		1a.	**Maria Franziska Agnes Agatha Anna Antonia Huberta Freiin. v. Wendt** * Gevelinghausen 11.9.1905
		2a.	**Maria Elisabeth Magdalena Sophie Agathe Antonia Huberta Freiin. v. Wendt** * Gevelinghausen 8.4.1908 = Gevelinghausen 1.6.1932 Werner Frhr. von Canstein * Dortmund 11.1.1899, and had issue:
XIV		1b.	**Elisabeth Agnes Martha Katharina Agatha Huberta Maria Rabana Freiin. v. Canstein** * Haus Ewig b. Kraghammer 7.6.1933 = Greissem 5.9.1964 Rudolf v. Schleiber * Hülhoven 1.11.1932, and has issue:
XV		1c.	**Agnes Maria Monika v. Schleiber** * Geilenkirchen 11.7.1965
XIV		2b.	**Nothburga Bernardine Martha Monika Agatha Huberta Maria Rabana Freiin. v. Canstein** * Haus Ewig 13.9.1937 = Greissem 17.7.1962 Gottlieb von Stockhausen * Aschendorf/Ems 14.2.1935, and has issue:
XV		1c.	**Ada von Stockhausen** * Aschendorf/Ems 13.10.1963
		2c.	**Uta von Stockhausen** * Papenburg 25.7.1965
XIV		3b.	**Maria Monika Pia Ulrike Antonia Huberta Freiin. v. Canstein** * Schellenstein b. Bigge 16.12.1939
		4b.	**Agatha Maria Magdalena Josepha Freiin. v. Canstein** * Greissem 28.6.1950
XIII		3a.	**Carl Joseph Paulus Pankratius Antonius Hubertus Maria Frhr. v. Wendt** * Gevelinghausen 9.5.1911 X b. Rshew, Russia, 16.8.1942 = Neugattersleben 16.7.1936 Anna Therese v. Alvensleben * Victoria, British Colombia 13.6.1913 dau. of Bodo Graf v. Alvensleben, and has issue:
XIV		1b.	**Karl Joseph Conrad Ferdinand Antonius Hubertus Maria Frhr. v. Wendt** * Münster i. W., 28.4.1937 = Maria-Laach 23.8.1960 Hilke Heinemann * Berlin 26.9.1938 dau. of Hans Friedrich Heinemann, and has issue:
XV		1c.	**Karl Ludwig Max Hans Frhr. v. Wendt** * Bielefeld 19.12.1960
		2c.	**Thomas Karl Antonius Hubertus Frhr. v. Wendt** * Olsberg 14.7.1962

XV   3c.   **Benita Caroline Antonia Freiin. v. Wendt** * Olsberg 2.9.1965

XIV   2b.   **Ferdinande Agnes Anna Antonia Huberta Maria Agatha Freiin. v. Wendt** * Schellenstein 26.1.1939 = Lemgo, Lippe 20.10.1962 Frank Barboza * Paget, Bermuda 10.7.1937, and has issue:

XV   1c.   **Caroline Ada Marie Barboza** * Detmold 3.3.1963

                 2c.   **Susan Manuella Patricia Barboza** * Schoetmar, Lippe 24.3.1964

                 3c.   **Georgia Joan Frances Barboza** * Lemgo, Lippe 12.6.1965

XIV   3b.   **Maria Einsiedeln Clementine Huberta Antonia Therese Freiin. v. Wendt** * Schellenstein 3.2.1941

XII   (i)   **Joseph Graf v. Galen** * Dinklage 15.9.1873 + Dinklage 16.3.1876

        (j)   **Paula Ursula Gräfin v. Galen** * Dinklage 2.5.1876 + Coesfeld i. W. 21.5.1923

        (k)   **Klemens-August Joseph Graf v. Galen** * Dinklage 16.3.1878 + Münster i. W. 22.3.1946 Cardinal von Galen

        (l)   **Franz Joseph Emanuel Augustinus Antonius Hubertus Maria Graf v. Galen** * Dinklage 11.12.1879 + Darfeld 9.10.1961 = Münster i. W. 19.9.1907 Antonia Freiin. v. Weichs zur Wenne * Bladenhorst 2.6.1885 dau. of Franziskus Frhr. v. Weichs zur Wenne, and had issue:

XIII   1a.   **Maria Elisabeth Caroline Gräfin v. Galen** * Assen 20.6.1908 + Münster i. W. 2.10.1908

           2a.   **Mariaschnee Mathilde Caroline Elisabeth Antonia Huberta Gräfin v. Galen** * Berlin-Lichterfelde 11.11.1909 = Merfeld b. Dülmen 27.11.1941 Maximilian Frhr. von Boeselager * Eggermühlen 9.7.1907 X bei Friedeberg Neumark 30.1.1945, and has issue:

XIV   1b.   **Adelheid Mariaschnee Michaela Clemens August Freiin. v. Boeselager** * Eggermühlen 29.9.1942

                2b.   **Christine Elisabeth Berta Franz v. Assisi Freiin. v. Boeselager** * Eggermühlen 10.1.1944

                3b.   **Maria Klara Antonia Nikolaus Freiin. v. Boeselager** * Eggermühlen 9.10.1945

XIII   3a.   **Franz Joseph Georg Antonius Hubertus Graf v. Galen** * Berlin-Lichterfelde 15.6.1911 + Siberia,as Russian P.O.W. 30.10.1945 = Goldegg i. Pongau 29.6.1944 Margarete Gräfin v. Galen * Goldegg 2.9.1908 dau. of Ferdinand Graf v. Galen s.p.

           4a.   **Georg Bernhard Clemens Paul Hubertus Antonius Maria Graf v. Galen** * Münster i. W. 20.8.1912 = Londrina, Brasil 29.12.1939 Hildegard v. Chappius * Saarburg 29.4.1908 dau. of Herbert v. Chappius and has issue:

XIV   1b.   **Friedrich Alexander Franz Herbert Christoph Maria Graf v. Galen** * Rolandia, Brasil 26.2.1941

                2b.   **Adelheid Antonia Gertrud Elisabeth Eva Maria Gräfin v. Galen** * Rolandia, Brasil 26.6.1942

                3b.   **Hubertus Augustinus Gert-Ewald Joseph Maria Graf v. Galen** * Rolandia, Brasil 5.1.1944

                4b.   **Stephan Clemens Matthias Hubertus Maria Graf v. Galen** * Rolandia, Brasil 16.11.1945

XIII		5a.	**Christoph Bernhard Joseph Sebastian Antonius Hubertus Maria Graf v. Galen** * Münster i. W. 30.8.1914 = Würzburg 22.10.1952 Marie Elisabeth Gräfin v. Bredow * Klessen b. Friesack 20.5.1930 dau. of Joachim Graf v. Bredow, and has issue:

<table>
<tr><td>XIV</td><td>1b.</td><td>Michael Graf v. Galen * Rolandia, Brasil 2.10.1953</td></tr>
<tr><td></td><td>2b.</td><td>Gabriele Gräfin v. Galen * Rolandia, Brasil 21.8.1955</td></tr>
</table>

XIII   6a. **Friedrich Matthias Franz Graf v. Galen** * Dinklage 12.9.1919 + Dinklage 27.6.1926

            7a. **Ferdinand Graf v. Galen** * Dinklage 18.11.1921 + Dinklage 17.12.1921

            8a. **Matthias Bernhard Constantin Leopold Josaphat Antonius Hubertus Maria Graf v. Galen** * Dinklage 13.11.1923 X Forli, Italy 4.9.1944

            9a. **Wilhelm Clemens Augustinus Nikolaus Konrad Antonius Hubertus Maria Graf v. Galen** * Dinklage 6.12.1923 + Münster i. W. 29.5.1956

            10a. **Clemens August Adolf Jakobus Petrus Canisius Liborius Irenäus Antonius Hubertus Maria Graf v. Galen** * Dinklage 23.7.1925 X bei Roben 22.3.1945

XII   (m) **Maria Monika Graf v. Galen** * Dinklage 4.5.1886 + Münster i. W. 20.6.1896

XI   c) **Franziska Sophia Maria Huberta Caecilia Gräfin v. Spee** * Düsseldorf 22.11.1844 + Pförten 6.10.1847

X   c. **Friedrich Stephan Graf v. Brühl** * Pförten 26.12.1819 + Pförten 5.4.1893 = Heltorf 28.7.1846 Paula Gräfin v. Spee * Düsseldorf 13.6.1826 + Pförten 31.5.1889 dau. of Franz Anton Graf v. Spee, and had issue:

XI   a) **Marie Sophie Auguste Franziska Huberta Vincencia Gräfin v. Brühl** * Pförten 19.7.1847 + Pförten 10.4.1865

           b) **Marie Friedrich Franz Johannes Moritz Cyriakus Hubertus Graf v. Brühl** * Pförten 8.8.1848 + Pförten 11.7.1911 = Prag 26.5.1874 Bertha Prinzessin v. Lobkowicz * Wien 27.8.1851 + Pförten 9.12.1887 dau. of Joseph Prinz v. Lobkowicz, and had issue:

XII   (a) **Marie Friedrich Joseph Hubertus Michael Rupertus Graf v. Brühl** * Pförten 27.3.1875 + Herten 24.1.1949 = Münster i. W. 2.7.1903 Mathilde Freiin. von Twickel * Hameren 30.3.1877 + Münster i. W. 23.10.1957 dau. of August Frhr. v. Twickel, and had issue:

XIII   1a. **Maria Sophia Anna Bertha Josepha Huberta Margaretha Dominika Coletta Gräfin v. Brühl** * Pförten 4.8.1909 = Pförten 3.9.1935 Karl Graf v. Nostitz-Rieneck * Prag 6.3.1901 + Schruns, Voralberg 5.6.1961, and has issue:

XIV   1b. **Mathilde Marie Caroline Anna Colette Margaretha Gräfin v. Nostitz-Rieneck** * Plan. b. Marienbad, Böh. 12.6.1936

                  2b. **Friedrich Maria Joseph Karl Laurentius Wenzel Graf v. Nostitz-Rieneck** * Plan 10.8.1938

                  3b. **Joseph Maria Erwein Bernhard Karl Graf v. Nostitz-Rieneck** * Plan 20.8.1941

                  4b. **Hugo Graf v. Nostitz-Rieneck** * Plan 8.2.1943

                  5b. **Rosa Gräfin v. Nostitz-Rieneck** * Plan 9.8.1945

XIII 　　　　2a. **Marie Bertha Sidonia Josepha Margaretha Coletta Elisabeth Benedicta Huberta Mathilde Gräfin v. Brühl** * Pförten 14.3.1912 = Herten 14.4.1948 Moritz Graf v. Schall-Riacour * Gaussig 1.6.1910 + Hamm i. W. 19.5.1955, and had issue:

XIV 　　　　　　1b. **Adam Petrus Friedrich Andreas Maria Mauritius Graf von Schall-Raicour** * Kirchellen 17.9.1949

XIII 　　　　3a. **Marie Friedrich August Franziskus Hubertus Benedikt Johannes v. Nepomuk Graf v. Brühl** * Pförten 15.5.1913 = Breslau 10.3.1942 Marie Elisabeth Gräfin v. Korff gen Schmising-Kerssenbrock * Gross-Stein 22.10.1917 dau. of Ferdinand Graf v. Korff gen Schmising-Kerssenbrock, and has issue:

XIV 　　　　　　1b. **Aloysia Christiane Maria Augustina Gräfin v. Brühl** * Breslau 12.12.1942

　　　　　　2b. **Marie Friedrich Leopold Joseph Hyazinth Graf v. Brühl** * Breslau 26.8.1944

　　　　　　3b. **Marie Gangolf-Hubertus Augustinus Ludgerus Graf v. Brühl** * Billerbek 3.11.1946

　　　　　　4b. **Marie Ferdinand-Joseph Hermann Alexander Graf v. Brühl** * Billerbek 11.2.1949

　　　　　　5b. **Elisabeth-Stephanie Anna Carola Maria Gräfin v. Brühl** * Billerbek 19.11.1952

　　　　　　6b **Alexandra-Maria Josepha Hedwig Gräfin v. Brühl** * Billerbek 2.1.1955

XIII 　　　　4a. **Maria de Viktoria Margarethe Huberta Coletta Gräfin v. Brühl** * Pförten 14.9.1914 = Pförten 9.4.1940 Georg Graf v. Nostitz-Rieneck * Prag 13.3.1904, and has issue:

XIV 　　　　　　1b. **Franz Otto Christian Maria Joseph Graf v. Nostitz-Rieneck** * Forst, NLausitz 22.12.1940

　　　　　　2b. **Ferdinand Maria Georg Eduard Friedrich Graf v. Nostitz-Rieneck** * Prag 16.11.1943

　　　　　　3b. **Anna Georgine Maria Barbara Friederike Gräfin v. Nostitz-Rieneck** * Plan b. Marienbad 6.5.1945

　　　　　　4b. **Robert Maria Ulrich Georg Andreas Benediktus Graf v. Nostitz-Rieneck** * Wien 9.6.1949

XIII 　　　　5a. **Maria Josepha Paula Margaretha Coletta Mathilde Gräfin v. Brühl** * Pförten 13.3.1917 = Herten 20.11.1956 Hermann Frhr. v. Fürstenberg * Siedlinghausen 10.5.1900, and has issue:

XIV 　　　　　　1b. **Hildegard Maria Pia Coletta Freiin. v. Fürstenberg** * Meschede 5.4.1958

XIII 　　　　6a. **Maria Margaretha Elisabeth Bertha Anna Coletta Gräfin v. Brühl** * Pförten 3.7.1918 = Münster i. W. 14.6.1950 Joseph Frhr. v. Nagel-Doornick * Wickrath 5.2.1911, and has issue:

XIV 　　　　　　1b. **Sophie Elisabeth Mathilde Ida Colette Freiin. v. Nagel** * Lippstadt 24.5.1951

211

XIV

2b.   **Augustina Bertha Marie-Luise Margarethe Freiin. v. Nagel** * Belecke 29.9.1952

3b.   **Annette Maria Gertrud Josepha Colette Freiin. v. Nagel** * Belecke 5.6.1954

4b.   **Johanna Maria Irene Benedicta Colette Dominika Freiin. v. Nagel** * Belecke 4.8.1956

XII

(b)   **Maria Joseph Ferdinand Alfred Leopold Paschalis Hubertus Graf v. Brühl** * Pförten 17.5.1876 + Pförten 7.12.1887

(c)   **Maria Anna Bertha Huberta Fides Sidonia Gräfin v. Brühl** * Pförten 5.10.1877 = Pförten 25.10.1904 Otto Graf v. Westerholt u. Gysenberg * Sythen 22.6.1875 + b. Sythen 2.5.1920, and has issue:

XIII

1a.   **Maria-Bertha Theresia Gräfin v. Westerholt u. Gysenberg** * Sythen 16.10.1907 = Sythen 14.5.1929 Aloysius Graf v. Korff gen. Schmising-Kerssenbrock * Brincke 10.9.1891 + Bielefeld 5.6.1960 s.p.

2a.   **Sidonia Gräfin v. Westerholt u. Gysenberg** * Sythen 16.2.1909 = Sythen 31.7.1934 Wilderich Frhr. Geyr v. Schweppenburg * Bonn 7.1.1906 + b. Brockhagen 28.6.1954 s.p.

XII

(d)   **Paula Gräfin v. Brühl** * Pförten 11.7.1879 + Pförten 12.11.1882

(e)   **Maria Johannes Mauritius Joseph Felix Hubertus Graf v. Brühl** * Pförten 21.2.1881 + Kufstein 10.1.1947 = Schwerin 8.8.1921 Hertha Booth * Berlin 8.3.1892 + Bad Hall, Tirol 11.5.1960, dau. of Arthur Booth s.p.

(f)   **Maria Georg August Ferdinand Hubert Anton Peter Lukas Graf v. Brühl** * Pförten 18.10.1882 = Gr-Köln, Ostpr. 23.9.1924 Jeanne v. Stockhausen * Gumbinnen 1.6.1885 + Lüdinghausen 19.11.1957 dau. of Klemens v. Stockhausen, and has issue:

XIII

1a.   **Maria Dietrich Georg Franz Johannes Mauritius Petrus Canisius Graf. v. Brühl** * Königsberg i. Pr. 1.12.1925 = Bad Waldsee 6.5.1958 **Maria Octavia Gräfin v. Waldburg zu Wolfegg u. Waldsee** * Weschelburg 1.8.1926 dau. of Franz Ludwig Fürst v. Waldburg zu Wolfegg u. Waldsee, and has issue:

XIV

1b.   **Jeanne Maria Immaculata Berta Clara Walburga Raphaela Gräfin v. Brühl** * Bonn 22.2.1959

2b.   **Mauritius Georg Max Michael Lazarus Blasius Graf v. Brühl** * Marseilles 3.2.1960

3b.   **Philipp Joseph Gabriel Johannes Vianney Victor Maria Graf v. Brühl** * Marseilles 1.3.1961 + Marseilles 13.4.1961

4b.   **Marie Christine Gräfin v. Brühl** * Accra, Ghana 31.12.1962

5b.   **Henriette Gräfin v. Brühl** * Accra, Ghana 8.4.1963

XIII

2a.   **Maria Friedrich Clemens Thomas Hubertus Michael Graf v. Brühl** * Allenstein 29.12.1926 X b. Alt-Wartenburg 24.1.1945

3a.   **Maria Regina Bertha-Clara Margarete Gräfin v. Brühl** * Allenstein 1.10.1928

4a.   **Maria Alfred-Wilhelm August Otto Casimir Graf v. Brühl** * Allenstein 11.2.1931

XII

(g) **Maria August Hubert Alfred Alfred Paul Franz Graf v. Brühl** * Pförten 10.1.1884
+ Ostend, died of wounds, 12.1.1946 = Siegburg 14.4.1920 Alexia Freiin. v. Loë
* Siegburg 11.7.1889 dau. of Eugen Frhr. v. Loë and has issue:

XIII

1a. **Marianne Agnes Friederike Margarete Veronika Bertha Gräfin v. Brühl**
* Münster i. W. 13.1.1921

2a. **Ida Maria Agnes Felicitas Huberta Margarete Josepha Raphaela Monika Klara
Gräfin v. Brühl** * Münster i. W. 14.1.1925

3a. **Maria Zdenka Clementine Bertha Alexia Margarethe Josepha Huberta
Walburga Gräfin v. Brühl** * Paderborn 6.5.1930 = Johannesburg 1.7.1961
Hermann Frhr. Heereman v. Zuydtwyck * Kochschütz 23.8.1913 and has
issue:

XIV

1b. **Roger Franziskus Augustinus Frhr. Heereman v. Zuydtwyck**
* Fricksburg O.F.S. 1.7.1962

2b. **Verena Elisabeth Alexia Freiin. Heereman v. Zuydtwyck** * Rüthen,
Westf. 13.9.1965

XII

(h) **Maria Vincenz Sidonius August Jakob Franz Hubertus Graf v. Brühl** * Pförten
30.7.1885 = Hohenpähl 21.10.1919 Henriette Gräfin v. Spreti * München
10.5.1893 dau. of Bernhard Graf v. Spreti, and has issue:

XIII

1a. **Marie Gabrielle Bertha Franziska Paula Gräfin v. Brühl** * Potsdam
16.8.1920 = Willing b. Bad Aibling 14.3.1944 Herbert Guinand * Odessa
2.1.1915 and has issue:

XIV

1b. **Ludwig Guinand** * Willing 27.12.1944

2b. **Vera Maria Guinand** * Stuttgart 12.9.1946

3b. **Margarethe Guinand** * Stuttgart 28.11.1947 + Stuttgart 20.12.1947

4b. **Susanne Guinand** * Grötzingen 14.10.1950

XIII

2a. **Marie Christine Ida Sidonia Josepha Elisabeth Angela Gräfin v. Brühl**
* Hohenpähl 14.9.1921 = Willing b. Bad Aibling 4.8.1951 Sylvester Griek
* Krischen 31.12.1909, and has issue:

XIV

1b. **Sibylle Maria Elfriede Griek** * Fürstenfeldbruck 31.1.1953

2b. **Claudia Maria Agnes Griek** * Fürstenfeldbruck 1.1.1954

3b. **Martin Vincenz Maria Griek** * Fürstenfeldbruck 9.12.1956

4b. **Ulrike Maria Griek** * Fürstenfeldbruck 2.12.1958

XIII

3a. **Maria Ludwig Friedrich Berhard Albrecht Rudolf Alfred Thaddäus Graf v.
Brühl** * Willing 2.4.1924 X b. Sredne Jegorlyk, Russia 6.8.1942

4a. **Maria Heinrich Gordian Vincenz Philipp Anton Graf v. Brühl** * Willing
11.8.1929 = Gauting b. München 16.6.1956 Hildegard Seidl * München
6.9.1931 dau. of Friedrich Seidl, and has issue:

XIV

1b. **Elisabeth Anna Bertha Desiree Gertrud Henriette Gräfin v. Brühl**
* München 8.7.1959

2b. **Maria Josephine Monika Marianne Gräfin v. Brühl** * München
19.4.1962

XII		(i) **Maria Sidonia Elisabeth Huberta Josepha Anna Agnes Desideria Gräfin v. Brühl** * Pförten 10.2.1887 + Wulfen 12.2.1963 = Pförten 23.6.1920 Heribert Graf v. Spee * Düsseldorf 3.12.1863 + Düsseldorf 25.2.1939, and had issue:

<blockquote>

XIII

1a. **Maria Bertha Friederike Gräfin v. Spee** * Düsseldorf 6.5.1921 + Düsseldorf 15.6.1921

2a. **Balthasar Friedrich Heribert Maria Joseph Benedikt Johannes Baptist Anton Aloysius Hubertus Graf v. Spee** * Düsseldorf 21.6.1923 X b. Solobadka-Bobruisk, Russia 24.6.1944

3a. **Maria Elisabeth Paula Agnes Franziska Romana Bertha Augusta Kaspara Benedicta Philippa Benita Bartholomea Huberta Gräfin v. Spee** * Düsseldorf 23.8.1925, + Rees 11.12.1959

</blockquote>

XI

c) **Maria Franz Johannes Mauritius August Sylvester Hubertus Graf v. Brühl** * Pförten 31.12.1849 + Glogau 2.2.1911 = Prag 21.4.1887 Marianne Prinzessin v. Lobkowicz * Prag 3.12.1861 + Dresden 11.11.1925 dau. of Moritz 9th Fürst v. Lobkowicz, and had issue:

XII

(a) **Maria Anna Paula Bertha Josephine Huberta Theresia Gräfin v. Brühl** * Potsdam 21.12.1887 + Dresden 1.2.1912

(b) **Paula Elisabeth Wilhelmine Christine Caroline Maria Josepha Theodora Huberta Gräfin v. Brühl** * Potsdam 8.11.1888 = Berlin 11.5.1910 Friedrich Leopold Graf zu Stolberg-Stolberg * Paskau 27.8.1883, and has issue:

XIII

1a. **Marianne Paula Elisabeth Clara Wilhelmine Huberta Agnes Gräfin zu Stolberg-Stolberg** * Kaminietz 16.2.1911

2a. **Johannes Ev. Hubertus Maria Friedrich Günther Joseph Anton Aloysius Gregor Graf zu Stolberg-Stolberg** * Kaminietz 9.3.1912 X près St-Leger, France 8.9.1944

3a. **Friedrich Paul Johannes Maria Aloysius Joseph Graf zu Stolberg-Stolberg** * Kaminietz 11.5.1913 X b. Pilgramdorf 13.3.1945

4a. **Ferdinand Maria Joseph Andreas Hubertus Aloysius Xaverius Sidonius Graf zu Stolberg-Stolberg** * Dresden 30.11.1914 X Mährisch-Ostrau-Wiktowitz 31.1.1945

5a. **Otto Maria Josef Andreas Hubertus Aloysius Xaverius Alfred Graf zu Stolberg-Stolberg** * Dresden 30.11.1914 X b. Metz 17.9.1944

6a. **Eleonore Gräfin zu Stolberg-Stolberg** * Kaminietz 30.10.1918 + Kaminietz 12.12.1918

7a. **Franz v. Assisi Karl Josef Aloysius Maria Graf zu Stolberg-Stolberg** * Kaminietz 24.3.1922 X b. Borissow, Russia 29.6.1944

8a. **Joseph Graf zu Stolberg-Stolberg** * Kaminietz 24.3.1922 + Kaminietz 6.4.1922

9a. **Carl Maria Josef Johannes Aloysius Hilarius Graf zu Stolberg-Stolberg** * Kaminietz 11.1.1926 = (1) Tutzing 15.7.1954 Erna Reino van Gogh * Breda 7.5.1924 dau. of Anton van Gogh, — div.; = (2) Frankfurt-am-Main 23.7.1958 Nora Epstein * 24.11.1920 dau. of Alexander Epstein, and has issue:

by 2nd marriage:

XIV

1b. **Alexandra Paula Friederike Marianne Nora Gräfin zu Stolberg-Stolberg** * Frankfurt-am-Main 3.1.1959

XII   (c)   **Sophie Maria Anna Carola Sidonia Ferdinandine Leopoldine Huberta Josepha Stephania Gräfin v. Brühl** * Potsdam 24.12.1889

         (d)   **Christine Friederike Stephania Paula Franziska Augusta Maria Anna Josepha Huberta Gräfin v. Brühl** * Potsdam 24.12.1889

         (e)   **Friedrich Johannes Mauritius Maria Joseph Ferdinand Sebastian Hubertus Kalixtus Graf v. Brühl** * Potsdam 16.4.1891 ✕ Laon 31.8.1918

         (f)   **Maria Wilhelmine Josepha Huberta Antonia Ignatia Gräfin v. Brühl** * Potsdam 30.7.1895 = Dresden 25.6.1924 Carl Graf v. Zedtwitz-Liebenstein * Tharandt 26.12.1891, and has issue:

XIII   1a.   **Marianne Josefine Huberta Antonia Athanasia Gräfin v. Zedtwitz-Liebenstein** * Dresden 30.4.1925 = Wien 20.1.1951 Hans-Joachim v. Zastrow * Neusalz 15.10.1911, and has issue:

XIV   1b.   **Christopher John Maria v. Zastrow** * Nakuru, Kenya 16.5.1953

                     2b.   **David Charles v. Zastrow** * Nakuru, Kenya 28.11.1954

XIII   2a.   **Thaddäus Graf v. Zedtwitz-Liebenstein** * Dresden 5.8.1926 + ... 9.1926

               3a.   **Ottokar Graf v. Zedtwitz-Liebenstein** * Dresden 13.7.1928 + ... 3.1930

XI   d)   **Maria Ferdinand Adalbert Gangolf Stephan Alexander Hubertus Graf v. Brühl** * Pförten 3.5.1851 + Berlin 13.2.1911

        e)   **Maria Franz Leopold August Petrus Hubertus Graf v. Brühl** * Pförten 18.11.1852 + Freiburg i. Br. 10.1.1928 = Schloss Moos b. Lindau 10.11.1897 Aloysia Gräfin v. Quadt zu Wykradt u. Isny * Paris 17.6.1869 + Freiburg i. Br. 5.11.1952,dau. of Friedrich Graf v. Quadt zu Wykradt u. Isny, and had issue:

XII   (a)   **Marie Friedrich Franz Joseph Graf v. Brühl** * Moos 4.9.1898 ✕ La Folie Ferme, près Montdidier 9.4.1918

         (b)   **Maria Joseph Ferdinand Graf v. Brühl** * Sigmaringen 23.3.1900 + Freiburg i. Br. 21.4.1929

         (c)   **Maria Anna Julia Paula Gräfin v. Brühl** * Sigmaringen 20.6.1902

         (d)   **Maria Elisabeth Leopoldine Gräfin v. Brühl** * Sigmaringen 25.6.1905

         (e)   **Maria Hedwig Gräfin v. Brühl** * Sigmaringen 16.7.1908 + Freiburg i. Br. 19.8.1931

         (f)   **Maria Heinrich Alfred Fidelis Joseph Graf v. Brühl** * Sigmaringen 19.3.1912 ✕ El Alamein 1.7.1942

XI   f)   **Maria Huberta Gräfin v. Brühl** * & + Pförten 22.7.1854

        g)   **Maria Leopold Friedrich Bernward Johannes Hubertus Graf v. Brühl** * Pförten 29.5.1856 + Breslau 5.3.1920

        h)   **Maria Elisabeth Augusta Paula Philippine Huberta Gräfin v. Brühl** * Pförten 12.5.1858 + Pförten 7.3.1911

        i)   **Maria Christine Paula Barbara Rufina Secunda Huberta Gräfin v. Brühl** * Pförten 10.7.1860 + Pförten 14.3.1924

        j)   **Maria Alfred Nikolaus Benno Markus Hubertus Graf v. Brühl** * Pförten 25.4.1862 + Weizenrodau 28.2.1922 = Prag 12.9.1908 Therese Prinzessin v. Lobkowicz * Vraz b. Pisek, Böh. 18.10.1876 + Holzen 21.6.1958 dau. of Georg Christian Fürst v. Lobkowicz, and had issue:

XII		(a)	**Maria Georg Alfred Friedrich Stephan Gaudenz Hubertus Magnus Graf v. Brühl** * Düsseldorf 6.9.1910 + Reichertswalde 27.7.1919

XII   (a)   **Maria Georg Alfred Friedrich Stephan Gaudenz Hubertus Magnus Graf v. Brühl** * Düsseldorf 6.9.1910 + Reichertswalde 27.7.1919

            (b)   **Maria Anna Paula Elisabeth Polyxena Gräfin v. Brühl** * Düsseldorf 31.1.1912

            (c)   **Maria Ferdinand Alfred Friedrich Beda Hubertus Bonifatius Graf v. Brühl** * Düsseldorf 3.6.1913 ✕ missing in Russia 6.7.1944

            (d)   **Maria Paula Christina Elisabeth Theresia Rosa Sophie Gräfin v. Brühl** * Wolfegg 31.8.1915

XI   k)   **Maria Heinrich Graf v. Brühl** * & + Pförten 30.9.1864

            l)   **Maria Paul Graf v. Brühl** * Pförten 31.5.1871 + Pförten 26.6.1871

IX   (3)   **Christiane Gräfin v. Sternberg-Manderscheid** * 28.3.1798 + 21.12.1840 = 16.9.1838 Leopold Graf zu Stolberg-Stolberg * 24.2.1799 + 9.8.1840, and had issue:

X   a.   **Franz Joseph Friedrich Leopold Graf zu Stolberg-Stolberg** * 19.12.1840 + 9.3.1878 = 19.11.1872 Marie Magdalena Gräfin v.u. zu Hoensbroech * 22.7.1850 + 23.7.1878 dau. of Franz Egon Graf v.u. zu Hoensbroech, and had issue:

XI   a)   **Marie Monika Mathilde Petra Paula Gräfin zu Stolberg-Stolberg** * El Bihar, Algeria 9.11.1877 + Tournai 12.2.1904

IX   (4)   **Erwine Gräfin v. Sternberg-Manderscheid** * 27.8.1803 + 29.6.1840 = 4.10.1828 Olivier Graf von Wallis * Prag 15.1.1800 + Kolleschowitz 31.5.1878, and had issue:

X   a.   **Eleonore Gräfin v. Wallis** * 8.7.1829 + Smichow b. Prag 9.7.1881

            b.   **Carl Olivier Graf v. Wallis** * Prag 26.7.1837 + Kolleschowitz 3.11.1917 = Wien 5.5.1873 Sophie Gräfin Paar * 12.5.1850 + Wien 10.6.1874 dau. of Carl 4th Fürst Paar s.p.

            c.   **Franz Olivier Graf v. Wallis** * 26.9.1838 + Ebelsberg 1.2.1895 = Fünfkirchen 29.9.1879 Margarete v. Rodakowska * Venezia 13.2.1857 + Gallneukirchen 10.5.1929, dau. of Josef v. Rodakowski s.p.

IX   (5)   **Marie Franziska Gräfin v. Sternberg-Manderscheid** * 2.11.1805 + 27.5.1847 = (1) 10.11.1829 Joseph August Prinz v. Lobkowicz * 19.4.1799 + 20.3.1832; = (2) 17.8.1837 Carl Graf O'Hergerty * Dublin 18.3.1801 + Tillysburg 21.12.1882 and had issue:

by 1st marriage:

X   a.   **Marie Prinzessin v. Lobkowicz** * Billin 10.11.1830 + St-Florian 2.10.1913

by 2nd marriage:

            b.   **Patrick Graf O'Hergerty** * Canterbury 1.8.1838 + Debreczin 5.6.1867

            c.   **Aldelm Graf O'Hergerty** * Canterbury 15.10.1839 + Tillysburg 25.3.1854

            d.   **Caroline Gräfin O'Hergerty** * Salzburg 8.9.1840 + Tillysburg 18.6.1879

            e.   **Erwine Gräfin O'Hergerty** * Tillysburg ... 1841 + Linz 19.12.1879

            f.   **Franziska Gräfin O'Hergerty** * Tillysburg 2.7.1842 + St-Florian 5.5.1918

            g.   **Ida Gräfin O'Hergerty** * Tillysburg 24.1.1844 + St-Florian 5.9.1927 = Tillysburg 23.5.1865 Franz Graf u. Edler Herr v.u. zu Eltz gen. Faust von Stromberg * Pavia 15.3.1823 + Linz 16.9.1891 and had issue:

XI   a)   **August Carl Franz Maria Graf v.u. zu Eltz gen. Faust von Stromberg** * Linz 29.3.1866 + Tillysburg 10.9.1921 = Traunegg b. Wels 16.7.1891 **Margarete Freiin. v.u. zu Franckenstein** * Gmunden 6.7.1869 + Linz 30.3.1938 dau. of Heinrich Frhr. v.u. zu Franckenstein and had issue:

216

XII   (a)   **Helene Maria Ida Josepha Margarethe Ignazia Monika Gräfin v.u. zu Eltz gen. Faust v. Stromberg** * Enns 3.5.1892 + Lisboa 14.2.1943 = Tillysburg 24.5.1919 Dom José Luis da Saldanha da Gama * Torres Novas 3.1.1893 + Lisboa 5.5.1958, and had issue:

XIII

      1a.   **Dom Alexander Augusto Eltz da Saldanha da Gama** * Wien 5.5.1920 + Galamares 21.8.1960 = Lisboa 21.6.1947 Eleonor Schluter * 10.10.1914 s.p.

      2a.   **Dom Vasco Eltz da Saldanha da Gama** * Persenburg 10.10.1921 = Quinta dos Lagares de El Rei 25.11.1947 Doña Eugenia Vaz d'Almada * 28.4.1921 and has issue:

XIV

          1b.   **Dom José d'Almada da Saldanha da Gama** * 25.2.1947

          2b.   **Dom Laurenço d'Almada da Saldanha da Gama** * 18.2.1948

          3b.   **Dom Alvaro d'Almada da Saldanha da Gama** * 25.4.1949

          4b.   **Doña Isabel d'Almada da Saldanha da Gama** * 25.4.1949

          5b.   **Doña Elena d'Almada da Saldanha da Gama** * 17.8.1950

XIII

      3a.   **Dom Gastão Jose Eltz da Saldanha da Gama** * Lisboa 15.7.1924 = 21.4.1953 Doña Aline van Waterschoodt Pinti da Rocha * 15.12.1920 dau. of Americo Pinti da Rocha s.p.

XII   (b)   **Franz Maria Joseph Heinrich August Aloysius Hubert Anton Ignatius Maurus Graf v.u. zu Eltz gen. Faust von Stromberg** * Traunegg 6.9.1893 + Tillysburg 3.10.1941 = Clam 18.8.1923 Franziska Gräfin v.u. zu Clam-Martinic * Essling 30.7.1897 dau. of Gottfried Graf v.u. zu Clam-Martinic, and had issue:

XIII

      1a.   **August Gottfried Maria Franz Heinrich Joseph Judas-Thaddäus Graf v.u. zu Eltz gen. Faust von Stromberg** * Tillysburg 15.7.1924

      2a.   **Sophie Maria Margarethe Franziska Rosa Ida Gräfin v.u. zu Eltz gen. Faust von Stromberg** * Tillysburg 31.8.1925 = Tillysburg 3.6.1963 Kalman Alexander von Lónyay-Jasztrabszky v. Nagy Lónya u. Vásarosnamény * Budapest 21.4.1925

      3a.   **Heinrich Leopold Maria Franz August Judas Thaddäus Graf v.u. zu Eltz gen. Faust von Stromberg** * Tillysburg 15.11.1926 = 's-Gravenhage 27.4.1963 Clara Barones Snouckaert van Schauburg * 's-Gravenhage 19.9.1933 dau. of Marten Baron Snouckaert van Schauburg

XII   (c)   **Heinrich Konrad Maria Paul August Aloysius Timotheus Balthasar Graf v.u. zu Eltz gen. Faust von Stromberg** * Olmutz 24.1.1896 = Montreal 17.12.1955 Janet Thomson Stevenson * Bathgate, West Lothian 30.9.1910 dau. of Peter Stevenson s.p.

     (d)   **Karl-August Maria Joseph Kuno Aloysius Arbogast Graf v.u. zu Eltz gen. Faust von Stromberg** * Tillysburg 21.7.1897 = Czell-Dömölk 2.6.1923 Paula v. Szögyény-Marich de Magyar-Szögyén et Szolgaegyháza * Czell-Dömölk 15.2.1897 dau. of Franz v. Szögyény-Marich de Magyar-Szögyén et Szolgaegyháza, and had issue:

XIII

      1a.   **Franz August Karl Aloysius Paul Alexander Graf v.u. zu Eltz gen. Faust von Stromberg** * Steinamanger 2.4.1924 = (1) Budapest 29.4.1951 Johanna Urbán de Monyoró * Budapest 11.6.1923 dau. of Gáspár Urbán de Monyoró; = (2) Budapest 26.5.1959 Marianne Hubnay de Hubó * Budapest 30.12.1933 dau. of Sandor Hubnay de Hubó, and has issue:

by 1st marriage:

XIV   1b. **Johanna Maria Ilona Paula Benedicta Gräfin v.u. zu Eltz gen. Faust von Stromberg** * Balassagyarmat 9.8.1953

XIII   2a. **Maria Irma Paula Margarethe Ida Karoline Valerie Susanna Gräfin v.u. zu Eltz gen. Faust v. Stromberg** * Czelldölmölk 11.8.1925 = Donnerskirchen 24.1.1959 Antál v. Rainprecht * Veszprém 15.3.1908

XII   (e) **Maria Ida Josepha Ignatia Emma Laurentia Helene Leopoldine Margarethe Gräfin v.u. zu Eltz gen. Faust v. Stromberg** * Tillysburg 14.11.1898 + Friedrichshafen 1.6.1943 = Friedrichshafen 1.6.1940 Franz Frhr. v. Hornstein * Bittingen 25.4.1884 s.p.

     (f) **Franziska Christine Emma Maria Immaculata Josepha Caroline Charitas Rosa Ignatia Margarethe Gräfin v.u. zu Eltz gen. Faust v. Stromberg** * Tillysburg 15.12.1899 = Tillysburg 4.5.1922 Johann Frhr. v. Pranckh * Reichenhall 23.4.1888 ✗ b. Kaisersberg 24.1.1945, and had issue:

XIII   1a. **Pilgrim Johannes Sigmund Gottlieb August Joseph Maria Frhr. v. Pranckh** * Pux 22.2.1923 = Koblenz 25.5.1954 Maria Gräfin Vetter v. der Lilie * Hautzenbichl 13.9.1932 dau. of Ferdinand Graf Vetter v. der Lilie, and has issue:

XIV   1b. **Pilgrim Johann Ferdinand Frhr. v. Pranckh** * Hautzenbichl 11.8.1955

     2b. **Barbara Freiin. v. Pranckh** * Hautzenbichl 24.7.1956

     3b. **Franziska Freiin. v. Pranckh** * Hautzenbichl 21.1.1958

     4b. **Ferdinand Frhr. v. Pranckh** * Hautzenbichl 1.5.1959

XIII   2a. **Margarethe Cordula Clara Maria Ida Freiin. v. Pranckh** * Pux 11.1.1925 = Pux 23.8.1949 Rudolf v. Lennkh zu Bergheim u. Gansheim * Klagenfurt 3.4.1925, and has issue:

XIV   1b. **Hans Maria Rudolf v. Lennkh zu Burgheim u. Gansheim** * Wien 27.7.1951

     2b. **Rudolf Maria Pilgrim v. Lennkh zu Burgheim u. Gansheim** * Wien 19.2.1953

     3b. **Maximilian Maria Leo v. Lennkh zu Burgheim u. Gansheim** * Hof 11.4.1955

     4b. **Friedrich v. Lennkh zu Burgheim u. Gansheim** * Schwarzbach 30.9.1956

     5b. **Elisabeth v. Lennkh zu Burgheim u. Gansheim** * Lend 13.12.1960

     6b. **Peter v. Lennkh zu Burgheim u. Gansheim** * Lend 10.6.1963

XIII   3a. **Franz Georg Sigmund Gottlieb August Frhr. v. Pranckh** * Pux 13.3.1926 = Gröbming 8.5.1951 Sofia Gieselbrecht * Kranzbach 15.11.1928 dau. of Georg Gieselbrecht, and has issue:

XIV   1b. **Georg Rupprecht Frhr. v. Pranckh** * Pux 17.2.1952

     2b. **Gertrudis Hildegard Freiin. v. Pranckh** * Pux 15.12.1953

     3b. **Elisabeth Freiin. v. Pranckh** * Pux 13.6.1957

     4b. **Klara Freiin. v. Pranckh** * 26.10.1961

XIII   4a.   **Clara Benedicta Freiin. v. Pranckh**   *   Klagenfurt 21.3.1930

   5a.   **Maria Eleonora Katharina Freiin. v. Pranckh**   *   Klagenfurt 12.5.1931
= 18.11.1961 Alfred Greiter   *   15.5.1928, and has issue:

XIV   1b.   **Veronika Greiter**   *   Linz 1.11.1962

    2b.   **Eleonore Greiter**   *   Linz 27.10.1964

XII   (g)   **Christiane Maria Josefa Ignatia Helene Aloysia Pulcherina Margarethe Gräfin v.u. zu Eltz gen. Faust v. Stromberg**   *   Tillysburg 10.9.1901 = Tillysburg 28.5.1923 Franz Graf v.u. zu Lerchenfeld auf Köfering u. Schönberg   *   St-Gilla 2.6.1890 s.p.

   (h)   **Maximilian Maria Joseph Conrad Aloysius August Antonius Ignatius Vincentius Heinrich Graf v.u. zu Eltz gen. Faust v. Stromberg**   *   Tillysburg 22.1.1903
+ Viechtach 7.8.1954 = (1) Wolfring 2.7.1929 Elisabeth v. Coulon   *   München 22.12.1905 dau. of Carl v. Coulon − div.; = (2) München 10.5.1939 Maria Helena Edler v. Poschinger   *   München 19.1.1903 dau. of Benedikt Edler v. Poschinger, and had issue:

by 1st marriage:

XIII   1a.   **Hubertus Graf v.u. zu Eltz gen. Faust v. Stromberg**   *   Valdivia, Chile 8.9.1930 = Wolfring 21.8.1965 Dorothy Edle v. Scheibler   *   Brudersdorf bei Nabburg 15.1.1946 dau. of Bernhard Baron v. Scheibler, and has issue:

XIV   1b.   **Carl Graf v.u. zu Eltz gen. Faust v. Stromberg**   *   Nabburg 27.7.1966

XIII   2a.   **Marie Lise Gräfin v.u. zu Eltz gen. Faust v. Stromberg**   *   Amberg 8.9.1932
= Siegenthan 26.7.1961 Martin Lautenschlager   *   Siegenthan 9.3.1925, and has issue:

XIV   1b.   **Christiane Lautenschlager**   *   Siegenthan 3.5.1962

    2b.   **Maria Theresia Lautenschlager**   *   Siegenthan 30.6.1963

    3b.   **Elisabeth Lautenschlager**   *   Siegenthan 26.7.1964

by 2nd marriage:

XIII   3a.   **Georg Benedikt Graf v.u. zu Eltz gen. Faust v. Stromberg**   *   Zwiesel 3.8.1940 + Passau 17.8.1940

   4a.   **Diana Margarethe Angela Gabriele Gräfin v.u. zu Eltz gen. Faust v. Stromberg**   *   München 14.1.1942 = Lindberg 22.10.1965 Jürgen Kammer   *   Bad Nauheim 9.1.1939

XII   (i)   **Sophie Maria Josepha Helene Anna Ignatia Dorothea Margarethe Gräfin v.u. zu Eltz gen. Faust v. Stromberg**   *   Tillysburg 6.2.1906 = Linz 28.5.1935 Heinrich Graf v. Salburg   *   Leonstein 4.8.1905, and has issue:

XIII   1a.   **Max Joseph Norbert August Gregor Pius Graf v. Salburg**   *   Altenhof 12.3.1936

   2a.   **Monika Maria Christiane Margarete Helene Wilhelmine Gräfin v. Salburg**   *   Altenhof 5.7.1937 = Altenhof 7.2.1966 Karl Graf Draskovich v. Traskostjan   *   Wien 20.1.1923

   3a.   **Norbert Joseph Heinrich Pius Graf v. Salburg**   *   Linz 6.7.1940

   4a.   **Georg Josef Norbert Franz Graf v. Salburg**   *   Linz 7.10.1942

   5a.   **Stefan Josef Theodor Constantin Graf v. Salburg**   *   Altenhof 1.10.1945

XI	b)		**Karl Franz Maria Graf v.u. zu Eltz gen. Faust v. Stromberg** * Linz 13.5.1867 + Schwarzenraben 1.2.1940 = Prag 2.10.1895 **Christine Freiin. v. Gudenus** * Lukawitz, Böh. 16.8.1870 + Schwarzenraben 19.1.1959 dau. of Ernst Frhr. v. Gudenus, and had issue:

XII

(a) **Maria Ida Christine Margareta Ignatia Josepha Antonia Gräfin v.u. zu Eltz gen. Faust v. Stromberg** * Klagenfurt 20.7.1896 + Roma 7.4.1954

(b) **Maria Franz Seraphicus Ernst Leopold Joseph Aloysius Graf v.u. zu Eltz gen. Faust v. Stromberg** * Klagenfurt 15.11.1898 + Gleiwitz 31.8.1926

(c) **Maria-Anna Christine Theresia Antonia Monica Franziska de Paula Gräfin v.u. zu Eltz gen. Faust v. Stromberg** * Klagenfurt 11.6.1900 = Thannhausen 3.8.1921 **Philipp Graf von Meran** * Stainz 11.7.1894, and has issue see elsewhere

(d) **Maria Theresia Christina Karolina Gräfin v.u. zu Eltz gen. Faust v. Stromberg** * Wien 8.11.1902

(e) **Maria Rosa Ignazia Christina Gräfin v.u. zu Eltz gen. Faust v. Stromberg** * Wien 5.9.1907 = St-Florian 3.5.1933 Wilderich Frhr. von Ketteler * Störmede 27.3.1901, and has issue:

XIII   1a. **Karl Joseph Wilderich Paulus Margareta Maria Ignatius Frhr. v. Ketteler** * Schwarzenraben 19.3.1934 = 18.9.1962 Alke Lahmann * Berlin 25.10.1936 dau. of Lüder Lahmann, and has issue:

XIV   1b. **Joachim Frhr. v. Ketteler** * Nürnberg 27.12.1962

    2b. **Martin Frhr. v. Ketteler** * Nürnberg 15.5.1965

XIII   2a. **Clemens August Wilderich Christophorus Florianus Ignatius Maria Frhr. v. Ketteler** * Münster i. W. 20.7.1935 = 2.8.1962 Maria Paula Gräfin Kinsky v. Wchinitz u. Tettau * Königgratz 26.7.1939 dau. of Friedrich Carl Graf Kinsky v. Wchinitz u. Tettau and has issue:

XIV   1b. **Alexandra Freiin. v. Ketteler** * Münster i. W. 13.7.1963

    2b. **Carl Frhr. v. Ketteler** * Münster i. W. 4.1.1965

    3b. **Mariann Freiin. v. Ketteler** * Münster i. W. 29.7.1966

XIII   3a. **Paula Maria Godeleva Margaretha Christine Ferdinande Freiin. v. Ketteler** * Münster i. W. 7.4.1937 = 26.4.1962 Gustav Frhr. v. Fürstenberg * Mersine 8.7.1927, and has issue:

XIV   1b. **Marie-Christine Freiin. v. Fürstenberg** * Warendorf 2.12.1963

    2b. **Franz Frhr. v. Fürstenberg** * Warendorf 13.11.1964

    3b. **Resi Freiin. v. Fürstenberg** * Warendorf 14.12.1965

XIII   4a. **Christine Maria Franziska Michaela Paula Clementine Margarete Huberta Freiin. v. Ketteler** * Münster i. W. 15.11.1938 = 26.4.1962 Philippe Lamotte d'Argy * 21.7.1937, and has issue:

XIV   1b. **Sophie Lamotte d'Argy** * Charleville 21.3.1963

    2b. **Antoine Lamotte d'Argy** * Charleville 1.7.1964

XIII   5a.   **Franciscus v. Assisi Antonius Michael Carolus Hubertus Maria Frhr. v. Ketteler**
       * Münster i. W. 23.5.1940 = 9.5.1964 Sophie Freiin. Heereman v. Zuydtwyck
       * Hannover 12.7.1941 dau. of Sylvester Frhr. Heereman v. Zuydtwyck, and
       has issue:

XIV   1b.   **Maximilian Friedrich Frhr. v. Ketteler** * Paderborn 25.3.1965

               2b.   **Wilderich Frhr. v. Ketteler** * Paderborn 15.5.1966

XIII   6a.   **Maria Anna Margarethe Ignatia Wilderike Maximiliane Freiin. v. Ketteler**
       * Münster i. W. 17.10.1942

         7a.   **Maria Ida Anna Wilderike Michaela Freiin. v. Ketteler** * Schwarzenraben
       8.6.1945

         8a.   **Wilderich Augustinius Ludwig Wilhelm Gottfried Liborius Maria Frhr. v.**
       Ketteler * Schwarzenraben 28.5.1947

         9a.   **Wilhelm Emanuel Michael Maximilian Christophorus Hubertus Maria**
       Schezzelo Frhr. v. Ketteler * Schwarzenraben 1.8.1950

XI   c)   **Franz August Joseph Maria Graf v.u. zu Eltz gen. Faust v. Stromberg** * Linz 25.7.1868
     + Marienbad 26.6.1921 = Wien 21.11.1896 Anna Maria Gräfin v. Blome * Genève
     11.2.1871 + Salzburg 9.1.1960 dau. of Gustav Graf v. Blome, and had issue:

XII   (a)   **Josephine Maria Franziska Anna Ida Gräfin v.u. zu Eltz gen. Faust v. Stromberg**
     * Olmütz 13.10.1897 = Mühllacken 11.2.1919 Franz Frhr. v. Seyfferitz
     * Rovereto 3.12.1894 + Rotheau an der Traisen 31.3.1958 − div.,
     and has ıssue:

XIII   1a.   **Josef Franz Maria Paul Theobold Ulrich Frhr. v. Seyfferitz** * Linz
       18.5.1920

XII   (b)   **Franz Paul August Maria Joseph Graf v.u. zu Eltz gen. Faust v. Stromberg**
     * Pesenbach 6.2.1900 = (1) Buenos Aires 8.2.1923 Josephine Schramm * ...
     1897 − div.; = (2) Baden b. Wien 26.10.1930 Hilda Batson * 24.12.1896
     + Salzburg 10.5.1961 dau. of Richard Batson; = (3) 4.10.1962 Ingeborg Schandl
     * Wien 22.5.1913 dau. of Hadmar Schandl, and has issue:

     by 2nd marriage:

XIII   1a.   **Anita Josefine Maria Gräfin v.u. zu Eltz gen. Faust v. Stromberg** * Nice
       12.12.1932 = Alm b. Saalfelden 14.7.1960 Johannes Baar v. Baarenfas
       * Rohrbach b. Weistrach 18.12.1925

XII   (c)   **Rosa Maria Josepha Ida Gräfin v.u. zu Eltz gen. Faust v. Stromberg** * Pesenbach
     20.2.1902 = Linz 25.10.1924 Albert Graf Saint-Julien-Walsee * Bregenz
     26.6.1889 + Wien 15.12.1936 s.p.

XI   d)   **Rosa Maria Anna Josepha Ida Gräfin v.u. zu Eltz gen. Faust v. Stromberg** * Linz
     7.8.1870 + Linz 21.4.1907

X   h.   **Emma Gräfin O'Hergerty** * Tillysburg 5.5.1845 + St-Florian 10.4.1929

VIII   2)   **Johann Wilhelm Graf v. Sternberg-Manderscheid** * 25.1.1765 + ...

      3)   **Maximilian Graf v. Sternberg-Manderscheid** * 16.6.1766 + 23.6.1779

      4)   **Leopold Graf v. Sternberg-Manderscheid** * 2.8.1767 + 27.9.1768

VIII	5)	**Auguste Gräfin v. Sternberg-Manderscheid** * 19.11.1768 + ...	

6) **Marie Walpurgis Gräfin v. Sternberg-Manderscheid** * Prag 11.5.1770 + Düsseldorf 16.6.1806 = Vinac, Böh. 4.2.1788 **Constantin 3rd Fürst zu Salm-Salm** * Hoogstraeten 22.11.1762 + Karlsruhe 25.2.1828 and had issue see elsewhere

7) **Philipp Graf v. Sternberg-Manderscheid** * 7.2.1773 + 5.9.1778

8) **Christian Graf v. Sternberg-Manderscheid** * 7.2.1773 + 21.3.1773

9) **Georg Graf v. Sternberg-Manderscheid** * 23.10.1775 + 20.8.1787

10) **Joseph Graf v. Sternberg-Manderscheid** * 25.10.1776 + 7.12.1776

VII 2. **Felicitas Johanna Maria Charlotte Gräfin v. Manderscheid-Blankenheim** * Blankenheim 4.11.1753 + Herten 19.7.1828 = Burgel 22.7.1777 Johann Franz Joseph Graf zu Nesselrode-Reichenstein * Oberhausen-Osterfeld 2.9.1755 + Herten 24.10.1824, and had issue:

VIII 1) **Johann Wilhelm Karl Graf zu Nesselrode-Reichenstein** * 5.7.1778 + 31.2.1822 = 31.10.1802 Caroline Auguste Gräfin zu Nesselrode-Ehreshoven * 17.6.1787 + Wrestorf 8.2.1846 dau. of Carl Franz Graf zu Nesselrode-Ehreshoven s.p.

2) **Marie Caroline Charlotte Therese Josefine Gräfin zu Nesselrode-Reichenstein** * Herten 13.9.1779 + Münster i. W. 21.1.1858 = Herten 24.9.1799 Adolf Heidenreich Graf Droste zu Vischering * Vörhelm 1.6.1769 + Darfeld 30.12.1826, and had issue:

IX (1) **Johann Felix Bernhardinus Heidenricus Salesius Dominicus Josephus Maria Graf Droste zu Vischering v. Nesselrode-Reichenstein** * Münster i. W. 4.8.1808 + Herten 2.5.1865 = Hinnenburg 2.5.1835 Marie Theresia Gräfin v. Bocholtz Asseburg * Hinnenburg 25.9.1815 + Hinnenburg 24.6.1894 dau. of Hermann Graf v. Bocholtz Asseburg, and had issue:

X a. **Johann Hermann Heidenreich Bernhard Hubertus Diederich Graf Droste zu Vischering v. Nesselrode-Reichenstein** * Münster i. W. 24.5.1837 + Herten 7.2.1904 = Schellenberg 19.10.1869 Elisabeth Freiin. v. Vittinghof gen. Schell zu Schellenberg * Schellenberg 3.11.1846 + Münster i. W. 9.8.1916 dau. of Friedrich Frhr. v. Vittinghof gen. Schell zu Schellenberg, and had issue:

XI a) **Felix Maximilian Hermann Johann Bernhard Heidenreich Hubertus Maria Joseph Graf Droste zu Vischering v. Nesselrode-Reichenstein** * Herten 28.2.1871 + Herrnstein 8.10.1953 = Münster i. W. 15.2.1911 **Augusta Prinzessin zu Salm-Salm** * Anholt 6.1.1881 + Herrnstein 31.5.1946 dau. of Alfred 7th Fürst zu Salm-Salm, and had issue:

XII (a) **Clemens Johann Hermann Heinrich Bernhard Heidenreich Hubertus Maria Graf Droste zu Vischering v. Nesselrode-Reichenstein** * Herten 29.4.1912 = Kettenburg 27.9.1945 Marina Freiin. v. Kettenburg * Bremen 20.6.1921 dau. of Kuno Frhr. v. Kettenburg and has issue:

XIII 1a. **Felix Adolf Freidrich Heidenreich Hubertus Maria Graf Droste zu Vischering v. Nesselrode-Reichenstein** * Herten 13.8.1946

2a. **Hubertus Kuno Heidenreich Gregor Maria Graf Droste zu Vischering v. Nesselrode-Reichenstein** * Herten 17.11.1947

3a. **Dietrich Franz Karl Faustinus Hubertus Maria Graf Droste zu Vischering v. Nesselrode-Reichenstein** * Herten 15.2.1949

4a. **Bertram Felix Winfrid Hubertus Maria Graf Droste zu Vischering v. Nesselrode-Reichenstein** * Herten 5.6.1951

222

XII

(b) **Alfred Carl Adolf Friedrich Bernhard Heidenreich Maria Graf Droste zu Vischering v. Nesselrode-Reichenstein** * Herten 1.11.1913 ✗ b. Poroschkowo, Russia 24.9.1941

(c) **Adolf Friedrich Hubertus Bernhard Heidenreich Maria Graf Droste zu Vischering v. Nesselrode-Reichenstein** * Anholt 9.11.1914 ✗ b. Glowno, Poland 11.9.1939

(d) **Antonia Franziska Johanna Huberta Maria Gräfin Droste zu Vischering v. Nesselrode-Reichenstein** * Herten 12.10.1916 = Herrnstein 7.5.1951 Alexander Frhr. v. Susskind-Schwendi * Berlin 24.9.1903, and has issue:

XIII

1a. **Elisabeth Constance Antonia Freiin. v. Susskind-Schwendi** * Neuilly-sur-Seine 17.12.1952

XII

(e) **Constantia Hedwig Huberta Maria Gräfin Droste zu Vischering v. Nesselrode-Reichenstein** * Herten 28.7.1918

XI

b) **Clothilde Maria Huberta Josephe Apollinaria Gräfin Droste zu Vischering v. Nesselrode-Reichenstein** * 26.2.1873 + 28.4.1892

c) **Hedwig Josepha Huberta Apollinaria Theresia Gräfin Droste zu Vischering v. Nesselrode-Reichenstein** * Herten 31.12.1874 + Darfeld 5.10.1956

d) **Maria Theresia Huberta Antonia Franziska Gräfin Droste zu Vischering zu Nesselrode-Reichenstein** * Herten 13.6.1876 + 1.3.1962

e) **Maria Klementine Huberta Gräfin Droste zu Vischering v. Nesselrode-Reichenstein** * Münster i. W. 14.11.1880

f) **Adolf Friedrich Heidenreich Johann Hubertus Apollinaris Graf Droste zu Vischering v. Nesselrode-Reichenstein** * Herten 20.10.1885 + Herten 21.1.1936

X

b. **Franziska Hedwig Maximiliane Clementine Huberta Gräfin Droste zu Vischering v. Nesselrode-Reichenstein** * Herten 14.4.1839 + Gracht 27.5.1883 = Herten 7.8.1860 Max Werner Graf Wolff-Metternich zur Gracht * 31.12.1837 + 2.6.1883, and had issue:

XI

a) **Marie Mathilde Gräfin Wolff-Metternich zur Gracht** * 4.8.1862 + 16.4.1902 = 7.8.1883 Dietrich Frhr. v. Loë * Wissen 7.12.1850 + Köln 10.4.1926 s.p.

b) **Maria Therese Gräfin Wolff-Metternich zur Gracht** * Frauenthal 2.2.1864 + St-Blasien 3.11.1920 = Gracht 6.7.1889 **Franz Graf v. Oberndorff** * Neckarhausen 25.7.1862 + Karlsruhe 1.5.1920, and had issue see elsewhere

c) **Anna Gräfin Wolff-Metternich zur Gracht** * Beck 5.5.1869 + Kr. Nettersheim 28.2.1933 = Burg Wisem b. Troisdorf-am-Rh. 27.5.1890 Johann Friedrich Frhr. v. Solemancher-Antweiler * Grunhaus 24.5.1862 + 5.1.1940, and had issue:

XII

(a) **Johann Friedrich Karl Maximilian Georg Josef Maria Frhr. v. Solemancher-Antweiler** * Deutz 3.4.1891 ✗ 23.3.1918

(b) **Johann Maximilian Werner Paul Georg Joseph Maria Frhr. v. Solemancher-Antweiler** * Deutz 30.1.1892 = Köln 3.11.1937 Anneliese Mosler * Wilhelmshaven 28.6.1900 + Rheinbach 10.3.1960 and had issue:

XIII

1a. **Elisabeth Freiin. v. Solemancher-Antweiler** * Bonn 15.1.1940 + Bonn 3.2.1940

2a. **Friedrich Frhr. v. Solemancher-Antweiler** * Bonn 18.3.1941 + Bonn 31.3.1941

XII

(c) **Maria Hedwig Maximiliane Friederike Anna Freiin. v. Solemancher-Antweiler** * Halberstadt 22.8.1895 + Bechta, Oldenburg 26.11.1931

XI		d)	**Elisabeth Gräfin Wolff-Metternich zur Gracht** * 18.5.1876 + 28.4.1899
		e)	**Dietrich Max Felix Maria Hubertus Graf Wolff-Metternich zur Gracht** * 22.6.1878 + 19.4.1899

<table>
<tr><td>X</td><td>c.</td><td>Anna Maria Auguste Huberta Gräfin Droste zu Vischering v. Nesselrode-Reichenstein * Herten 15.11.1843 + Heltorf 29.3.1900 = Herten 17.9.1867 Franz Graf von Spee * Düsseldorf 11.4.1841 + Heltorf 7.3.1921 s.p.</td></tr>
<tr><td></td><td>d.</td><td>Antonie Bernardina Huberta Adolfina Ida Maria Theresia Gräfin Droste zu Vischering v. Nesselrode-Reichenstein * Herten 4.9.1846 + Hinnenburg 29.10.1920 = Münster i. W. 17.11.1874 Hermann Graf v. Bocholtz-Asseburg * Hinnenburg 4.2.1841 + Rustenhof 4.1.1889, and had issue:</td></tr>
</table>

XI

a) **Diederich Busso Wilhelm Franz Hermann Anton Maria Hubertus Graf v. Bocholtz-Asseburg** * Wallhausen 22.8.1878 + Hinnenburg 28.11.1906

b) **Hermann Werner Adolf-Wilhelm Hubertus Maria Graf v. Bocholtz-Asseburg** * Wallhausen 1.3.1880 X Chivy 26.9.1914 = Alsbach 14.7.1908 Maria Theresia Gräfin Wolff-Metternich zur Gracht * Leerbach 21.1.1888 + Hannover 30.9.1954 dau. of Levinus Graf Wolff-Metternich zur Gracht and had issue:

XII

(a) **Dietrich Busso Antonius Levinus Hermann Joseph Hubertus Gregor Maria Graf v. Bocholtz-Asseburg** * Hinnenburg 17.11.1909 = Paderborn 25.1.1938 Charlotte Antoinette Gräfin v. Plettenberg * Oels 22.6.1901 dau. of Paul Graf v. Plettenberg s.p.

(b) **Max Constantin Pius Franziskus Hubertus Maria Graf v. Bocholtz-Asseburg** * Hinnenburg 5.5.1911 X Bobruisk, Russia 20.6.1943

(c) **Wilhelm Anton Friedrich Vincenz Benediktus Sixtus Hubertus Maria Graf v. Bocholtz-Asseburg** * Hinnenburg 6.8.1913 + Münster i. W. 8.4.1950 = Hinnenburg 21.6.1949 Clementine Gräfin v. Preysing-Lichtenegg * Ulm 18.5.1916 + Tillet b. Bastogne, Belgium 24.2.1955 dau. of Anton Graf v. Preysing-Lichtenegg s.p.

XI

c) **Maria Theresia Maximiliana Huberta Rosalia Gräfin v. Bocholtz-Asseburg** * Hainhausen 1.9.1881 + Paderborn 10.11.1916

d) **Wilhelmine Marie Johanna Hedwig Gräfin v. Bocholtz-Asseburg** * Hainhausen 6.5.1883

e) **Hedwig Gräfin v. Bocholtz-Asseburg** * Hainhausen 20.10.1884 + Bad Lippspringe 11.12.1965

f) **Hubertus Maximilian Maria Josef Graf v. Bocholtz-Asseburg** * Hainhausen 20.10.1884 = Malens 6.1.1921 Hildegard Pachten * Anvers 21.8.1877 + Kufstein 2.3.1951 s.p.

g) **Klementine Maria Hermana Franziska Gräfin v. Bocholtz-Asseburg** * Hainhausen 31.5.1887

X   e. **Maria Hermengilde Sophie Ferdinande Wilhelmine Huberta Gräfin Droste zu Vischering v. Nesselrode-Reichenstein** * Münster i. W. 1.7.1848 + Schellenberg 8.5.1890 = Herten 27.7.1869 Maximilian Frhr. von Vittinghof gen. Schell zu Schellenberg * Schellenberg 12.6.1840 + Calbeck 5.11.1898, and had issue:

XI

a) **Alexandra Klothilde Auguste Maria Huberta Freiin. v. Vittinghof gen. Schell zu Schellenberg** * Schellenberg 15.12.1871 + Locarno 6.2.1942 = Münster i. W. 9.10.1900 Dietrich Frhr. v. Boeselager * Höllinghofen 22.2.1867 + Locarno-Minusio 10.3.1920 s.p.

b) **Maria Theresia Huberta Hermanne Erica Freiin. v. Vittinghof gen. Schell zu Schellenberg** * Schellenberg 8.1.1873 + Niesen 12.11.1957

XI   c)   **Friedrich August Max Anton Hubert Frhr. v. Vittinghof gen. Schell zu Schellenberg**
** Schellenberg 17.4.1874 + Niesen 5.1.1959 = Harff 7.6.1900 Rudolfine Freiin. v.
Mirbach * Ziadlowitz 24.12.1875 + Duisburg-Hamborn 4.5.1945 dau. of Ernst Graf v.
Mirbach-Harff and had issue:*

XII   (a)   **Wilhelmine Maria Josefine Huberta Freiin. v. Vittinghof gen. Schell zu Schellenberg**
** Schellenberg 5.4.1901 = Calbeck 15.7.1926 Clemens Frhr. v. Oer * Egelborg
b. Legden 25.8.1895, and has issue:*

XIII   1a.   **Adolf Wilhelm Antonius Hubertus Maria Frhr. v. Oer** * Münster i. W.
3.4.1927

        2a.   **Maria Anna Antonia Magdalena Sophia Freiin. v. Oer** * Münster i. W.
3.4.1927 = Legden 17.5.1951 Wolfgang Graf v. Plettenberg * Düsseldorf
22.1.1922, and has issue:

XIV   1b.   **Clemens August Friedrich Christian Michael Graf v. Plettenberg**
* Bad Kreuznach 4.7.1952

        2b.   **Marie Elisabeth Gräfin v. Plettenberg** * Bad Kreuznach 4.9.1953

        3b.   **Georg Felix Hubertus Graf v. Plettenberg** * Bad Kreuznach 16.10.1954

        4b.   **Walter Egbert Matthias Graf v. Plettenberg** * Bad Kreuznach
20.11.1955 + Mainz 4.4.1956

        5b.   **Ida Margarete Anna Gräfin v. Plettenberg** * Bad Kreuznach 13.4.1957

        6b.   **Franz Graf v. Plettenberg** * Bad Kreuznach 8.5.1961

XIII   3a.   **Maria Rudolfine Adelheid Antonia Freiin. v. Oer** * Münster i. W. 14.10.1930

        4a.   **Antonius Emanuel Theodor Maria Frhr. v. Oer** * Münster i. W. 25.12.1932

XII   (b)   **Maximilian Franz Friedrich Maria Hubertus Frhr. v. Vittinghof gen. Schell zu
Schellenberg** * Schellenberg 16.2.1903

        (c)   **Friedrich Wilhelm Alexander Maria Hubertus Frhr. v. Vittinghof gen. Schell zu
Schellenberg** * Schellenberg 8.7.1904 ✕ Polotzk 15.7.1941 = Enfield, Co. Meath
21.4.1937 Margaret O'Brien * San Francisco 27.9.1910 dau. of William O'Brien,
and had issue:

XIII   1a.   **Maria Immaculata Margaret Theodora Patricia Rudolfine Freiin. v. Vittinghof
gen. Schell zu Schellenberg** * Münster i. W. 31.5.1938 = Calbeck 27.9.1961
Adolf Frhr. Spies v. Büllesheim * Ratheim, Kr. Erkelenz 4.6.1929, and has
issue:

XIV   1b.   **Wilhelm Franz Frhr. Spies v. Büllesheim** * Aachen 7.3.1963

        2b.   **Margaret Sophie Daisy Freiin. Spies v. Büllesheim** * Aachen
19.6.1964

        3b.   **Mary Anna Freiin. Spies v. Büllesheim** * Aachen 20.10.1965

        4b.   **Antoinette Noëlle Freiin. Spies v. Büllesheim** * Aachen 19.12.1966

XIII   2a.   **Margaret Friederike Maria Therese Freiin. v. Vittinghof gen. Schell zu
Schellenberg** * Münster i. W. 14.7.1939 = Niesen 28.8.1964 Ludwig Frhr.
v. Elverfeldt * Canstein 14.2.1935, and has issue:

XIV   1b.   **Marguerite Marie Freiin. v. Elverfeldt** * Paderborn 13.10.1965

XII	(d)	**Theodor Franziskus Alexander Ernst Antonius Maria Hubertus Frhr. v. Vittinghof gen. Schell zu Schellenberg** * Schellenberg 30.4.1909
	(e)	**Felix Maria Carl Georg Antonius Aloysius Hubertus Frhr. v. Vittinghof gen. Schell zu Schellenberg** * Calbeck 3.10.1910 = Madrid 25.4.1950 Aileen O'Brien * San Francisco 4.1.1913 dau. of William O'Brien s.p.
	(f)	**Johannes Nepomuk Hubertus Benediktus Antonius Maria Frhr. v. Vittinghof gen. Schell zu Schellenberg** * Calbeck 23.2.1912 ✕ Liwny, Russia 9.7.1942
	(g)	**Maria Rizza Franziska Huberta Freiin. v. Vittinghof gen. Schell zu Schellenberg** * Calbeck 14.12.1913

XI	d)	**Franziska Maria Dorothea Aloysia Huberta Katharina Freiin. v. Vittinghof gen. Schell zu Schellenberg** * Schellenberg 25.11.1875 + Blumenthal b. Aals 21.8.1937
	e)	**Maximilian Maria Felix Hubert Frhr. v. Vittinghof gen. Schell zu Schellenberg** * Schellenberg 10.6.1882 + Ehreshoven 15.8.1939 = Mettlach 23.1.1906 Rizza Freiin. v. Liebig * Reichenberg, Böh. 20.6.1873 + Ahrenthal b. Sinzig 25.12.1948 dau. of Theodor Frhr. v. Liebig, and had issue:

XII	(a)	**Marie Angela Adelina Huberta Josefa Freiin. v. Vittinghof gen. Schell zu Schellenberg** * Bonn 21.7.1909 = Haus Saareck b. Mettlach 23.1.1935 Hubertus Graf v. Spee * Wesel 25.3.1910, and had issue:

XIII	1a.	**Roderich Maximilian Leopold Hubertus Graf v. Spee** * Koblenz 23.10.1935 = Haus Stockhausen 2.5.1961 Margarit v. Stockhausen * Arnsberg 21.3.1935 dau. of Max v. Stockhausen, and has issue:

XIV	1b.	**Maria Franziska Gräfin v. Spee** * Bad Godesberg 29.10.1961
	2b.	**Dominik Anton Wolfgang Hubertus Graf v. Spee** * Bad Godesberg 6.12.1962

XIII	2a.	**Wolfgang Hubertus Franziskus Graf v. Spee** * Koblenz 22.11.1937
	3a.	**Beatrice Gräfin v. Spee** * & + Ahrenthal 13.5.1942
	4a.	**Heinrich Alexander Hubertus Paul Joseph Graf v. Spee** * Bad Godesberg 27.2.1950

XII	(b)	**Alexandra Maria Ludwina Josephina Huberta Freiin. v. Vittinghof gen. Schell zu Schellenberg** * Bonn 7.7.1914 = Erpel b. Linz, Rh. 14.1.1941 Alfonso Marchese Tacoli dei Marchesi di San Possidoni * Birkfield 7.2.1915 ✕ Valona, Albania 19.3.1944, and had issue:

XIII	1a.	**Johannes Maria Angelica Hubertus Christophorus Marchese Tacoli dei Marchesi di San Possidoni** * Remagen 14.2.1944
	2a.	**Elisabeth Flaminia Theodora Maria Dolores Marchesa Tacoli dei Marchesi di San Possidoni** * Remagen 14.2.1944

XI	f)	**Maria Antonia Franziska Huberta Freiin. v. Vittinghof gen. Schell zu Schellenberg** * Schellenberg 25.10.1885 + Sacre Coeur Riedenburg 23.5.1963
	g)	**Felix Maria Maximilian Hubertus Frhr. v. Vittinghof gen. Schell zu Schellenberg** * Schellenberg 21.8.1887 + Niesen 3.9.1925 = Münster i. W. 26.10.1910 Elvire Freiin. v. Twickel * Kervel 11.9.1887 + Düsseldorf 14.5.1952 dau. of Ferdinand Frhr. v. Twickel, and has issue:

XII   (a)   **Hubertus Friedrich Ferdinand Maximilian Antonius Frhr. v. Vittinghof gen. Schell zu Schellenberg** * Paderborn 3.12.1911

X   f.   **Dietrich Heidenreich Bernhard Hubertus Graf Droste zu Vischering v. Nesselrode-Reichenstein** * 11.3.1850 + 22.10.1880

     g.   **Max Felix Heidenreich Bernhard Johann Dietrich Hubertus Anna Maria Graf Droste zu Vischering v. Nesselrode-Reichenstein** * 14.3.1853 + Münster i. W. 25.7.1888

     h.   **Adolf Heidenreich Bernhard Clemens August Hubertus Graf Droste zu Vischering v. Nesselrode-Reichenstein** * 9.11.1854 + Münster i. W. 8.12.1905

     i.   **Huberta Maria Wilhelmine Clementine Rosine Liboria Aloysia Gräfin Droste zu Vischering v. Nesselrode-Reichenstein** * Münster i. W. 29.11.1862 + Havixbeck 16.4.1946 = Herten 21.9.1891 Klemens Frhr. v. Twickel * Lüttinghof 18.8.1861 + Münster i. W. 19.5.1916, and had issue:

XI   a)   **Johann Rudolf Klemens August Sebastian Maria Benedikt Aloysius Hubertus Cyriakus Donatus Anton Frhr. v. Twickel** * Stovern 20.1.1893 = Vischering 8.1.1920 Margarethe Gräfin Droste zu Vischering * Vischering 18.7.1896 dau. of Maximilian Graf Droste zu Vischering, and had issue:

XII   (a)   **Huberta Maria Felizitas Sophie Helene Agnes Freiin. v. Twickel** * Havixbeck 24.2.1921 = Havixbeck 10.9.1943 Ferdinand Graf v. Spee * Borken 27.12.1908 and has issue:

XIII   1a.   **Stephan Rudolf Hubertus Maria Konrad Liborius Graf v. Spee** * Ahausen 23.7.1944

     2a.   **Georg Maria Hubertus Graf v. Spee** * Ahausen 9.12.1945

     3a.   **Marie Elisabeth Margarethe Huberta Anna Christine Gräfin v. Spee** * Ahausen 6.11.1947

     4a.   **Madeleine Sophie Maria Huberta Walburga Gräfin v. Spee** * Ahausen 25.2.1949

     5a.   **Walburga Maria Assunta Huberta Katherina Gräfin v. Spee** * Heggen 21.11.1950

XII   (b)   **Sophia Elisabeth Maria Huberta Freiin. v. Twickel** * Havixbeck 5.5.1922

     (c)   **Margarethe Maria Theresia Huberta Freiin. v. Twickel** * Havixbeck 8.8.1923 = Havixbeck 26.4.1951 Alexander Baron van Hövell tot Westerflier * Elst b. Nijmegen 10.4.1917, and has issue:

XIII   1a.   **Canisius Maximilian Anthonius Maria Baron van Hövell tot Westerflier** * Vardingholt 4.2.1952

     2a.   **Christophorus Rudolf Joseph Maria Baron van Hövell tot Westerflier** * Vardingholt 5.8.1953

     3a.   **Margarethe Maria Therese Mechteld Barones van Hövell tot Westerflier** * Rhede 2.8.1954

     4a.   **Maria Josephina Theresia Barones van Hövell tot Westerflier** * Rhede 13.11.1955 + Rhede 25.1.1956

     5a.   **Thomas Alexander Willem Maria Baron van Hövell tot Westerflier** * Rhede 16.12.1956

     6a.   **Bernadette Maria Sophie Franziska Barones van Hövell tot Westerflier** * Rhede 20.2.1958

XIII	7a.	**Elisabeth Maria Alexandra Augusta Barones van Hövell tot Westerflier** * Rhede 29.4.1959
	8a.	**Alexandra Maria Elisabeth Johanna Barones van Hövell tot Westerflier** * Rhede 11.9.1962
	9a.	**Antonia Maria Josefa Angela Barones van Hövell tot Westerflier** * Rhede 5.9.1963
	10a.	**Johannes Michael Ignatius Maria Baron van Hövell tot Westerflier** * Rhede 28.3.1965
	11a.	**Raphael Josef Maximilian Maria Baron van Hövell tot Westerflier** * Rhede 28.3.1965

XII   (d)   **Clemens August Maria Aloysius Hubertus Dyonisius Frhr. v. Twickel** * Havixbeck 2.2.1925

           (e)   **Max-Georg Augustinius Hubertus Petrus Canisius Aloysius Frhr. v. Twickel** * Havixbeck 22.8.1926

           (f)   **Gottfried Ludgerus Hubertus Aloysius Josef Frhr. v. Twickel** * Havixbeck 26.3.1929 = Üllstadt 26.6.1959 **Marie Elisabeth Freiin. v.u. zu Franckenstein** * Würzburg 9.3.1928 dau. of Georg Frhr. v.u. zu Franckenstein, and has issue:

XIII	1a.	**Friedrich Franz Andreas Aloysius Maria Frhr. v. Twickel** * Münster i. W. 21.6.1960
	2a.	**Elisabeth Maria Paula Agatha Freiin. v. Twickel** * Münster i. W. 7.7.1961
	3a.	**Johanna Freiin. v. Twickel** * Münster i. W. 20.7.1963
	4a.	**Theresia Freiin. v. Twickel** * Münster i. W. 26.10.1965

XII   (g)   **Jan-Rudolf Maria Aloysius Hubertus Michael Frhr. v. Twickel** * Havixbeck 17.7.1930

           (h)   **Bonifatius Maria Hubertus Maximilian Georg Petrus Canisius Frhr. v. Twickel** * Havixbeck 7.7.1933

XI   b)   **Johann Hermann Felix Heidenrich Maria Aloysius Ignatius Wiho Cajus Cyriakus Walpurgis Judas-Thaddäus Frhr. v. Twickel** * Stovern 20.4.1895

           c)   **Ludgerus Augustinus Antonius de Padua Maria Joseph Hubertus Cyriakus Genoveva Titus Walburgis Judas-Thaddäus Wiho Emanuel Donatus Frhr. v. Twickel** * Stovern 3.1.1900 + Warstein 23.2.1947 = Schloss Haag 16.9.1930 Eleonore Gräfin v.u. zu Hoensbroech * Münster i. W. 4.5.1909 dau. of Franz Lothar Graf v.u. zu Hoensbroech, and has issue:

XII   (a)   **Franz-Josef Maria Hubertus Frhr. v. Twickel** * Vogelsang 2.7.1931 = Mettlach 25.1.1963 Gabriele Freiin. v. Schönberg * Wurzen 1.12.1935 dau. of Friedrich Frhr. v. Schönberg, and has issue:

XIII	1a.	**Renata Bertha Maria Imakulata Elinor Friederike Freiin. v. Twickel** * Geldern 12.12.1963
	2a.	**Eugen Ferdinand Josef Andreas Maria Frhr. v. Twickel** * Geldern 10.11.1966

XII   (b)   **Ferdinand Rudolf Hubertus Maria Frhr. v. Twickel** * Vogelsang 18.2.1934 = Geldern 25.2.1960 Brigitte Lauffs * Geldern 2.4.1938 dau. of Carl Lauffs, and has issue:

XIII   1a.   **Isabelle Karla Maria Elinor Euthymia Freiin. v. Twickel** * Krefeld-Uerdingen 13.10.1962

            2a.   **Ferdinande Franziska Maria Judas Thaddäus Freiin. v. Twickel** * Krefeld-Uerdingen 3.11.1963

            3a.   **Ludgerus Peter Maria Jordan Frhr. v. Twickel** * Krefeld-Uerdingen 22.5.1964

            4a.   **Hubertus Rudolf Maria Frhr. v. Twickel** * Krefeld-Uerdingen 26.5.1966

            5a.   **Madeleine Johanna Karola Maria Freiin. v. Twickel** * Krefeld-Uerdingen 26.5.1966

XII   (c)   **Hans Hermann Hubertus Maria Frhr. v. Twickel** * Vogelsang 18.2.1934 = Handorf 5.6.1963 Maria Astrid Freiin. v. Fürstenberg * Münster i. W. 6.3.1940 dau. of Oswald Frhr. v. Fürstenberg, and has issue:

XIII   1a.   **Kyrill Oswald Ludgerus Petrus Maria Frhr. v. Twickel** * Münster i. W. 14.3.1964

            2a.   **Marie Desirée Friederike Christina Luise Freiin. v. Twickel** * Münster i. W. 23.8.1965

XII   (d)   **Paul Clemens Hubertus Maria Frhr. v. Twickel** * Vogelsang 6.10.1935 = 16.10.1964 Anna Monika Gräfin v. Praschma, Gräfin v. Korff gen. Schmising-Kerssenbrock * Breslau 3.5.1933 dau. of Benedikt Graf v. Praschma, and has issue:

XIII   1a.   **Marie Agnes Monika Freiin. v. Twickel** * Seveen, Kr. Geldern 21.1.1966

XII   (e)   **Nikolaus Frhr. v. Twickel** * Vogelsang 28.11.1937

            (f)   **Peter Hubertus Maria Frhr. v. Twickel** * Vogelsang 7.7.1943

            (g)   **Karl Hubertus Maria Frhr. v. Twickel** * Vogelsang 16.8.1945

XI   d)   **Maria Theresia Josepha Adolphina Agnes Irmgardis Margaretha Donata Felicitas Mamerta Bonifacia Cyriakus Freiin. v. Twickel** * Stovern 11.5.1901 + Königsberg i. Pr. 3.8.1941 = Havixbeck 8.7.1926 Hermann Frhr. v. Fürstenberg * Siedlinghausen 10.5.1900 — div. and had issue:

XII   (a)   **Pia Maria Huberta Margarethe Freiin. v. Fürstenberg** * Siedlinghausen 10.9.1927 = Körtlinghausen 14.6.1956 Elmar Graf v. Plettenberg * Lenhausen 1.6.1928, and has issue:

XIII   1a.   **Maria Theresia Anna Pia Ida Huberta Josefa Gräfin v. Plettenberg** * Hovestadt 2.4.1960

            2a.   **Friedrich August Maximilian Josef Ida Hubertus Maria Graf v. Plettenberg** * Hovestadt 16.11.1961

            3a.   **Ida Paula Johanna Monika Huberta Maria Gräfin v. Plettenberg** * Hovestadt 23.2.1966

VIII   3)   **Johann Maximilian Friedrich Graf zu Nesselrode-Reichenstein** * 28.2.1783 ⚔ Dresden ... 1813

        4)   **Maria Sophie Philippine Gräfin zu Nesselrode-Reichenstein** * 9.9.1784 + ...

        5)   **Johann Franz Josef Graf zu Nesselrode-Reichenstein** * 10.9.1786 + ... 10.1787

7 The Descendants of Marie Elisabeth Prinzessin zu Salm-Salm 1729-1775 and Eugen Erwein Graf zu Schönborn-Heussenstamm 1727-1801.

VI   **Marie Elisabeth Josepha Prinzessin zu Salm-Salm** * Hoogstraeten 4.4.1729 + Schloss Schönborn 4.3.1775 = Anholt 1.8.1751 Eugen Erwein Graf zu Schönborn-Heussenstamm * Mainz 17.1.1727 + Wien 25.7.1801 and had issue:

VII   1.   **Maria Christina Gabriella Elisabeth Gräfin zu Schönborn-Heussenstamm** * Wien 20.9.1754 + Wien 25.8.1797 = Wien 30.1.1772 Franz Stephan Graf v. Silva-Tarouca * Wien 30.1.1750 + Wien 5.3.1797 and had issue:

VIII   1)   **Franz Joseph Lothar Graf v. Silva-Tarouca** * Wien 27.4.1773 + Čech 2.12.1835 = Zasmuk 23.10.1811 **Marie Leopoldine Gräfin v. Sternberg-Manderscheid** * Prag 10.7.1791 + Čech 15.12.1870 dau. of Franz Josef Graf v. Sternberg-Manderscheid and had issue:

IX   (1)   **Erwein Wilhelm Graf v. Silva-Tarouca** * 17.4.1815 + Čech 22.9.1846

(2)   **Friedrich Graf v. Silva-Tarouca** * 11.12.1816 + Brünn 23.6.1881

(3)   **Augustinus Alexander Graf v. Silva-Tarouca** * Čech 14.4.1818 + Čech 24.10.1872 = (1) Nordkirchen 24.8.1847 Gisela Gräfin zu Stolberg-Stolberg * Visk Hungary 7.5.1824 + Čech 19.2.1864 dau. of Christian Ernst Graf zu Stolberg-Stolberg; = (2) Prödlitz 24.8.1865 Helene Gräfin Kálnoky v. Köröspatak * Lettowitz 2.6.1835 + Čech 10.8.1931 dau. of Gustav Graf Kálnoky v. Köröspatak and had issue:

by 1st marriage:

X   a.   **Marie Henriette Gräfin v. Silva-Tarouca** * 27.3.1856 + Brixen 17.12.1920

b.   **Franz Joseph Maria Augustin Graf v. Silva-Tarouca** * Čech 13.3.1858 + Brünn 4.8.1936 = Prag 23.5.1882 Gabriele Prinzessin zu Schwarzenberg * Prag 9.10.1856 + Čech 4.12.1934 dau. of Karl 3rd Fürst zu Schwarzenberg and had issue:

XI   a)   **Karl Borromäus Augustin Franz Joseph Maria Günther Patrick Graf v. Silva-Tarouca** * Čech 18.3.1883 + Soutello, near Braga 3.9.1958

b)   **Egbert Maria Stanislaus Joseph Antonius Graf v. Silva-Tarouca** * Čech 14.11.1887 = Prag 19.7.1919 Eleonore Gräfin Hoyos * Kulm 20.8.1894 dau. of Alfred Graf Hoyos and has issue:

XII   (a)   **Theresia Josepha Barbara Eleonore Helene Gräfin v. Silva-Tarouca** * Čech 13.5.1920 = Emmering 25.1.1947 Anton Kraus * Flaschenhütte b. Marienbad 3.1.1916 and has issue:

XIII   1a.   **Marie Elisabeth Kraus** * Übersee 16.4.1948

2a.   **Maria Beatrix Kraus** * Übersee 30.6.1950

3a.   **Johannes Kraus** * Übersee 16.8.1952

XII   (b)   **Maria Kunigunde Gräfin v. Silva-Tarouca** * Čech 15.5.1921 = Ölkofen 12.9.1947 Georg Paul * 20.4.1922 + Übersee 20.5.1960 and has issue:

XIII   1a.   **Christoph Paul** * Regensburg 8.4.1949

2a.   **Brigitte Paul** * Regensburg 5.8.1950

XII   (c)   **Gabriele Wilhelmine Maria Barbara Gräfin v. Silva-Tarouca** * Čech 11.11.1922 = New York 19.10.1957 Eduard Baron Neuman de Végvár * Arád, Roumania 12.6.1904 and has issue:

XIII   1a.   **Beatrix Baronin Neuman de Végvár** * New York 14.2.1959

XII   (d)   **Franz Maria Friedrich Graf v. Silva-Tarouca** * Luschitz 13.7.1925 X Königshofen 2.4.1945

XII		(e)	**Maria Beatrix Helene Theresia Gräfin v. Silva-Tarouca** * Luschwitz 3.9.1930 = Horn 13.9.1956 Fritz Berg * Wien 20.2.1930 and has issue:

XIII

        1a.   **Heinrich Berg** * Horn 11.2.1958

        2a.   **Hans-Martin Berg** * Horn 19.5.1960

        3a.   **Albrecht Berg** * Horn 8.8.1961

        4a.   **Elisabeth Berg** * Horn 29.7.1963

        5a.   **Nikolaus Berg** * Horn 27.10.1964

XI   c)   **Friedrich Augustin Maria Stanislaus Graf v. Silva-Tarouca** * Čech 12.11.1888 = Ércsi 18.8.1920 Maria Gräfin v. Wimpffen * Wien 14.2.1894 dau. of Siegfried Graf v. Wimpffen and has issue:

XII   (a)   **Karl Graf v. Silva-Tarouca** * Kainberg 25.5.1921 ✗ Wien 13.3.1945

        (b)   **Helene Gräfin v. Silva-Tarouca** * Kainberg 17.2.1923

XI   d)   **Franz Ernst Ignaz Alfons Graf v. Silva-Tarouca** * Čech 18.7.1890 + Čech 7.12.1943

        e)   **Aloysius Maria Georg Hubert Graf v. Silva-Tarouca** * Čech 12.3.1892 ✗ Breaza 30.7.1917

        f)   **Wilhelm August Maria Joseph Thomas Graf v. Silva-Tarouca** * Čech 28.7.1894 + Čech 2.1.1895

X   c.   **Ernst Emanuel Graf v. Silva-Tarouca** * Čech 3.1.1860 + Schwaigern 15.8.1936 = Smichow/ Prag 16.6.1885 Maria Antonia Gräfin v. Nostitz-Rieneck * Prag 31.1.1863 + Pruhonitz 23.7.1934 dau. of Albrecht Graf v. Nostitz-Rieneck and had issue:

XI   a)   **Marie-Adelheid Gräfin v. Silva-Tarouca** * Türmitz 26.6.1886 + Petschau 12.7.1945 = Wien 3.2.1910 **Heinrich Herzog v. Beaufort-Spontin** * Paris 11.3.1880 + Gallmansegg 25.4.1966 and had issue see elsewhere

        b)   **Gisela-Helene Gräfin v. Silva-Tarouca** * Türmitz 14.6.1887 + Prag 21.2.1958 = (1) Pruhonitz 21.10.1913 Maria Joseph Prinz v. Lobkowicz * Unterbeřkowicz 4.9.1885 ✗ Jaroslau, Galicia 25.10.1914; = (2) Unterbeřkowicz 27.1.1917 Moritz Prinz v. Lobkowicz * Unterbeřkowicz 3.5.1890 + Teleč 8.8.1944 and had issue:

by 1st marriage:

XII   (a)   **Maria Antonia Josepha Ignatia Kaspara Prinzessin v. Lobkowicz** * Pruhonitz 8.8.1914 = Prag 26.1.1937 Friedrich Graf Strachwitz v. Gross-Zauche u. Camminetz * Zdounek 2.6.1904 and has issue:

XIII

        1a.   **Maria Gisela Caroline Antonie Friederike Theresia Gräfin Strachwitz v. Gross-Zauche u. Camminetz** * Prag 14.12.1937

        2a.   **Maria Joseph Hugo Friedrich Anton Hyazinth Wenzel Graf Strachwitz v. Gross-Zauche u. Camminetz** * Bad Königswart 24.1.1940

        3a.   **Moritz Anton Graf Strachwitz v. Gross-Zauche u. Camminetz** * Prag 14.6.1943

        4a.   **Ernst Leopold Graf Strachwitz v. Gross-Zauche u. Camminetz** * Wien 31.8.1948

234

by 2nd marriage:

XII   (b)   **Maria Ida Josefa Maurizia Melchiora Princessin v. Lobkowicz** * Unterbeřkowicz 15.10.1917 = (1) Prag 3.5.1939 Humprecht Graf Czernin v.u. zu Chudenitz * Dymokur 9.2.1909 + Plesch b. Prag 19.9.1944 = (2) Prag 27.12.1946 Fabrizio Conte Franco * Verona 13.1.1903 s.p.

    (c)   **Josef Ferdinand Maria Mauritius Leonhard Christian Petrus Canisius Balthasar Prinz v. Lobkowicz** * Unterbeřkowicz 20.12.1918 + Melnik 24.4.1946 = Prag 29.8.1940 Gabriele Gräfin Czernin v.u. zu Chudenitz * Dymokur 18.1.1913 dau. of Theobold Graf Czernin v.u. zu Chudenitz and has issue:

XIII   1a.   **Maria Ferdinand Josef Leopold Judas Thaddäus Wenzel Hubert Melchior Linhart Prinz v. Lobkowicz** * Prag 3.11.1942

    2a.   **Prokop Wenzel Josef Linhart Judas Thaddäus Humprecht Remigius Theresia Jesu Balthasar Maria Prinz v. Lobkowicz** * Citow 1.10.1944

XII   (d)   **Maria Franz de Paula Moritz Josef Leonhard Wolfgang Franz v. Assisi Romanus Laurentius Pius Caspar Prinz v. Lobkowicz** * Prag 9.8.1927 = Prag 1.7.1952 Hanna Novák * Prag 17.1.1928 dau. of Bohumil Novák and has issue:

XIII   1a.   **Maria Jeanne d'Arc Zdenka Gisela Kaspara Prinzessin v. Lobkowicz** * Prag 20.10.1953

    2a.   **Marie Leopoldine Gabriele Melchioria Prinzessin v. Lobkowicz** * Prag 26.4.1959

    3a.   **Maria Michael Amadeo Ferdinand Balthasar Prinz v. Lobkowicz** * Prag 20.7.1964

XI   c)   **Anna Gräfin v. Silva-Tarouca** * Türmitz Böh. 28.9.1888 = Pruhonitz 19.10.1911 Anton Graf v. Neipperg * Hirschberg, in Böh. 18.12.1883 + Schwaigern 28.12.1947 and had issue:

XII   (a)   **Eleonore Maria Antonia Anna Ernestine Huberta Beatrix Gabrielle Benedikta Josefine Felicitas Gräfin v. Neipperg** * Schwaigern 26.8.1912 = Schwaigern 26.8.1912 = Schwaigern 27.8.1936 Richard Graf v. Matuschka-Greifenclau * Wiesbaden 11.5.1893 and has issue:

XIII   1a.   **Karl Philipp Maria Paul Urban Guido Kyrill Amadeus Graf v. Matuschka-Greifenclau** * Vollrads 7.7.1937

    2a.   **Erwein Maria Eberhard Joseph Benedikt Martin Graf v. Matuschka-Greifenclau** * Würzburg 14.11.1938

    3a.   **Ernst Egon Markus Graf v. Matuschka-Greifenclau** * Vollrads 25.4.1943

XII   (b)   **Maria Karl Reinhard Antonius Ernst Amadeus Georg Benediktus Hubertus Franziskus Christophorus Josef Erwin Faustinus Erbgraf v. Neipperg** * Schwaigern 15.2.1915 ✕ Propoisk, Russia 28.7.1941

    (c)   **Maria Joseph Hubert Ernst Vincenz Amadeus Anton Benediktus Konrad Apollinarius Graf v. Neipperg** * Schwaigern 22.7.1918 = München 3.2.1951 **Marie Franziska Gräfin v. Ledebur-Wicheln** * Krzemusch 5.11.1920 dau. of Eugen Graf. v. Ledebur-Wicheln and has issue:

XIII   1a.   **Maria Karl Eugen Johannes Nepomuk Erwin Michael Erbgraf v. Neipperg** * Schwaigern 20.10.1951

XIII   2a.   **Maria Reinhard Franz v. Assisi Ferdinand Benedikt Graf v. Neipperg** * Schwaigern 5.2.1953

         3a.   **Maria Anna Gabrielle Eleonore Gräfin v. Neipperg** * Schwaigern 14.2.1955

         4a.   **Maria Franziska Eleonore Katharina Gräfin v. Neipperg** * Schwaigern 7.4.1956

         5a.   **Maria Stephan-Christoph Heinrich Alfred Emmeran Graf v. Neipperg** * Schwaigern 28.6.1957

         6a.   **Maria Christoph Bernhard Amadeo Antonius Graf v. Neipperg** * Schwaigern 30.7.1958

         7a.   **Maria Barbara Sofie Michaela Elisabeth Eleonore Gräfin v. Neipperg** * Schwaigern 4.1.1960

XII   (d)   **Marie Gabrielle Anna Antonia Beatrix Pia Benedicta Felicitas Huberta Hedwig Wilhelmine Walburga Gräfin v. Neipperg** * Schwaigern 25.2.1920

XI   d)   **Joseph Graf v. Silva-Tarouca** * Pruhonitz 20.10.1889 ⚔ 24.5.1917

         e)   **Franz Xaver Graf v. Silva-Tarouca** * Pruhonitz 24.10.1895

         f)   **Amadeus Graf v. Silva-Tarouca** * Pruhonitz 14.7.1898 = Innsbruck 31.1.1941 Bertha Rabl * Innsbruck 24.2.1902 + Graz 25.6.1964 s.p.

         g)   **Eleonore Gräfin v. Silva-Tarouca** * Pruhonitz 8.3.1901

IX   (4)   **Christine Gräfin v. Silva-Tarouca** * 6.6.1819 + Tillysburg 26.5.1872 = 15.10.1849 Carl Graf O'Hergerty * Dublin 18.3.1801 + Tillysburg 4.12.1882 s.p.

VIII   2)   **Georg Graf v. Silva-Tarouca** * Wien 8.7.1775 + Prag 15.5.1839 = 1810 Maria Christine Gräfin v. Unwerth * 1788 + 16.4.1841 dau. of Johann v. Nepomuk Graf v. Unwerth and had issue:

IX   (1)   **Eugen Graf v. Silva-Tarouca-Unwerth** * 1.9.1813 + Troppau 20.5.1877 = (1) ... Julie v. Kaufmann * 10.8.1819 + 14.6.1859; = (2) 31.5.1864 Henriette Freiin. v. Skrbensky v. Hřistie * 14.3.1824 + 22.9.1890 dau. of Anton Frhr. v. Skrbensky v. Hřistie and had issue:

X   a.   **Eugen Graf v. Silva-Tarouca-Unwerth** * 10.6.1844 + Penzing 25.2.1889

IX   (2)   **Servatius Karl Graf v. Silva-Tarouca-Unwerth** * 14.12.1821 + 17.10.1876 = 4.10.1865 Mathilde Freiin. v. Bartenstein * 31.3.1836 + Troppau 30.6.1894 dau. of Joseph Frhr. v. Bartenstein s.p.

VIII   3)   **Eugen Graf v. Silva-Tarouca** * 17.12.1778 + 18.1.1842

         4)   **Elisabeth Gräfin v. Silva-Tarouca** * 17.2.1782 + 30.6.1842

         5)   **Emanuel Graf v. Silva-Tarouca** * 19.3.1783 + ...

         6)   **Amelia Gräfin v. Silva-Tarouca** * 2.9.1784 + 2.12.1852

VII   2.   **Maria Amalia Gräfin zu Schönborn-Heussenstamm** * 31.1.1756 + 31.12.1802

      3.   **Marquand Wilhelm Erwin Graf zu Schönborn-Heussenstamm** * & + 1756

      4.   **Maria Theresia Gräfin zu Schönborn-Heussenstamm** * Wien 7.6.1758 + Wien 23.2.1838 = Wien 22.10.1781 Johann Rudolf Graf Czernin v.u. zu Chudenitz * Wien 9.6.1757 + Wien 23.4.1845 and had issue:

VIII   1)   **Gabrielle Maria Gräfin Czernin v.u. zu Chudenitz** * 15.12.1782 + 12.11.1787

         2)   **Maria Theresia Gräfin Czernin v.u. zu Chudenitz** * 2.12.1783 + 23.11.1787

VIII   3)   **Eugen Karl Graf Czernin v.u. zu Chudenitz** * Wien 4.11.1796 + Petersburg i. Böh. 11.6.1868 = Wien 27.5.1817 Maria Therese Gräfin v. Orsini u. Rosenberg * Wien 25.9.1798 + Wien 18.4.1866 dau. of Franz 2nd Fürst v. Orsini u. Rosenberg and had issue:

IX   (1)   **Jaromir Graf Czernin v.u. zu Chudenitz** * Wien 13.3.1818 + Petersburg i. Böh. 26.11.1908 = (1) Brünn 26.2.1843 Karoline Gräfin Schaffgotsch gen Semperfrei v.u. zu Kynast u. Greiffenstein * Brünn 13.9.1820 + Petersburg i. Böh. 9.10.1876 dau. of Franz Graf Schaffgotsch gen Semperfrei v.u. zu Kynast u. Greiffenstein; = (2) Wien 19.3.1879 Josephine Gräfin Paar * Wien 1.1.1839 + Wien 6.2.1916 dau. of Karl 4th Fürst Paar, and had issue:

by 1st marriage:

X   a.   **Marie Therese Gräfin Czernin v.u. zu Chudenitz** * 19.12.1843 + Wien 26.4.1910 = Wien 30.1.1869 **Friedrich Erwein Graf v. Schönborn** * Dlažkovic 11.9.1841 + Wien 21.12.1907 s.p.

   b.   **Marie Rudolfine Gräfin Czernin v.u. zu Chudenitz** * Wien 6.3.1845 + Salzburg 17.4.1922 = Wien 10.5.1864 Siegfried Altgraf zu Salm-Reifferscheid-Raitz * Prag 10.6.1835 + Salzburg 14.8.1898, and had issue:

XI   a)   **Rudolf Hugo Leopold Maria Theodor Karl Altgraf zu Salm-Reifferscheidt-Raitz** * Raitz 9.11.1866 + Aigen b. Salzburg 2.3.1919 = Wien 30.6.1898 Marie Gräfin v. Wallis * Niederleis 25.5.1869 + Mährisch-Budwitz 23.4.1936 dau. of Maximilian Graf v. Wallis, and had issue:

XII   (a)   **Anna Maria Rudolfine Karoline Maximiliane Altgräfin zu Salm-Reifferscheidt-Raitz** * Mährisch-Budwitz 19.1.1901 = Büdischkowitz 20.4.1921 Guido Graf Schaffgotsch gen.Semperfrei v.u. zu Kynast u. Greiffenstein + Lienz 16.12.1894 + Salzburg 15.10.1958, and has issue:

XIII   1a.   **Rudolf Gotthard Josef Ignatius Graf Schaffgotsch gen.Semperfrei v.u. zu Kynast u. Greiffenstein** * Mährisch-Budwitz 13.2.1922–missing Stalingrad 1942

   2a.   **Marie Elisabeth Hedwig Rosa Anna Josefine Gräfin Schaffgotsch gen. Semperfrei v.u. zu Kynast u. Greiffenstein** * Mährisch-Budwitz 10.12.1925

   3a.   **Ernestine Hedwig Maria Anna Josefine Gräfin Schaffgotsch gen.Semperfrei v.u. zu Kynast u. Greiffenstein** * Mährisch-Budwitz 9.2.1929

   4a.   **Ulrich Gotthard Karl Borramäus Graf Schaffgotsch gen.Semperfrei v.u. zu Kynast Greiffenstein** * Mährisch-Budwitz 1.11.1932 = Herbstein 18.9.1961 **Lioba Gräfin v. Westerholt u. Gysenberg** * Fulda 17.11.1938 dau. of Paul Graf v. Westerholt u. Gysenberg, and has issue:

XIV   1b.   **Monika Hedwig Maria Magdalena Agnes Gräfin Schaffgotsch gen. Semperfrei v.u. zu Kynast u. Greiffenstein** * Passau 23.7.1963

   2b.   **Angela Hedwig Maria Irene Gräfin Schaffgotsch gen. Semperfrei v.u. zu Kynast u. Greiffenstein** * Passau 3.9.1964

   3b.   **Gertrud Hedwig Anna Gräfin Schaffgotsch gen.Semperfrei v.u. zu Kynast u. Greiffenstein** * Passau 27.6.1966

XIII   5a.   **Irene Hedwig Rosa Maria Anna Gräfin Schaffgotsch gen.Semperfrei v.u. zu Kynast u. Greiffenstein** * Mährisch-Budwitz 31.1.1935

   6a.   **Hubert Gotthard Friedrich Leopold Graf Schaffgotsch gen.Semperfrei v.u. zu Kynast u. Greiffenstein** * Büdischkowitz 12.4.1937 = Padberg 3.8.1963 **Maria Cornelia Gräfin Droste zu Vischering** * Padberg 27.3.1933 dau. of Joseph Graf Droste zu Vischering, and has issue:

237

XIV

        1b.   **Christin Hedwig Monika Maria Gräfin Schaffgotsch gen. Semperfrei v. u.
zu Kynast u. Greiffenstein** * Niedlerleis 6.9.1964

        2b.   **Maximilian Gotthard Alexander Albert Graf Schaffgotsch gen. Semperfrei
v. u. zu Kynast u. Greiffenstein** * Niederleis 22.11.1966

XI

    b)   **Erich Marie Jaromir Hieronymus Emilien Altgraf zu Salm-Reifferscheidt-Raitz**
* Hohentrebetitsch 20.7.1868 + 7.4.1945

    c)   **Robert Marie Clestin Hugo Carl Altgraf zu Salm-Reifferscheidt-Raitz** * Hohentrebetitsch
19.5.1870 + Aigen b. Salzburg 28.11.1918

    d)   **Leopoldine Marie Caroline Philippine Altgräfin zu Salm-Reifferscheidt-Raitz**
* Hohentrebetitsch 23.8.1873 + 20.6.1943

    e)   **Augustine Marie Caroline Lucienne Altgräfin zu Salm-Reifferscheidt-Raitz**
* Hohentrebetitsch 7.1.1877 + Berchtoldstein 28.9.1919

X   c.   **Karoline Gräfin Czernin v. u. zu Chudenitz** * Wien 15.2.1847 + Prag 14.4.1907 = Wien
7.1.1868 Johann Graf v. Ledebur-Wicheln * Krzemusch 30.5.1842 + Prag 14.5.1903, and
had issue:

XI

    a)   **Johanna Gräfin v. Ledebur-Wicheln** * Prag 18.12.1868 + Teplitz-Schönau 9.4.1940
= Prag 7.6.1887 Franz Graf v. Hartig * Wien 15.8.1859 + Niemes 21.8.1903, and had
issue:

XII

    (a)   **Johanna Friedrich Franz Maria Josef Graf v. Hartig** * Niemes 30.5.1891 + Niemes
5.10.1935 = Prag 28.7.1919 Eleonore Prinzessin zu Schwarzenberg * Wossow
15.8.1899 dau. of Karl 4th Fürst zu Schwarzenburg, and had issue:

XIII

        1a.   **Maria Johanna Ida Caroline Josefa Gräfin v. Hartig** * Niemes 9.11.1920
= St-Georgen i. Attergau 23.10.1948 Oswald Kostrba * ... and has issue:

XIV

        1b.   **Alexandra Kostrba** * 15.4.1955

XIII

        2a.   **Franz Karl Johann v. Nepomuk Maria Josef Graf v. Hartig** * Niemes
16.11.1921 = Niemes 9.5.1945 Sophie Gräfin v. Waldstein * Waldschloss b.
Stiahlau, Böh. 28.7.1921 dau. of Carl Graf v. Waldstein, and has issue:

XIV

        1b.   **Ferdinand-Carl Maria Lapidata Johannes v. Nepomuk Judas Thaddäus
Franz v. Assisi Georg Leopold Eleutherius Graf v. Hartig** * Litschau
2.2.1949

        2b.   **Johannes v. Nepomuk Maria Lapidata Emilia Bonifatius Georginius
Agapitus Wenzeslaus Georg Juadas Thaddäus Graf v. Hartig** * Wien
4.9.1950

        3b.   **Jakob Graf v. Hartig** * Waidhofen 12.6.1954

XIII

        3a.   **Karl Friedrich Johannes v. Nepomuk Maria Josef Graf v. Hartig** * Niemes
24.5.1923 ✗ Nikolajew 7.2.1944

        4a.   **Ida Eleonore Antonia Maria Josepha Gräfin v Hartig** * Niemes 13.6.1926

        5a.   **Johannes Eugen Maria Josef Graf v. Hartig** * Niemes 20.1.1929

        6a.   **Hubertus Karl Maria Josef Graf v. Hartig** * Niemes 13.1.1932

XII

    (b)   **Maria Karoline Amelie Franziska Josepha Gräfin v. Hartig** * Niemes 4.12.1893
= Niemes 2.8.1921 Rudolf Graf Hoyos-Sprinzenstein * Gutenstein 4.7.1884, and
has issue:

238

XIII   1a.   **Ernst Rudolf Franz Maria Josef Desiderius Thaddäus Graf Hoyos** * Horn 23.5.1922 ✗ Arnhem 5.9.1944

     2a.   **Johannes Nepomuk Felix Franz Maria Rudolf Pius Gregor Graf Hoyos** * Horn 5.5.1923

     3a.   **Heinrich Johannes Maria Josef Rudolf Georg Leopold Leonhard Graf Hoyos** * Horn 6.11.1924 = Glanegg 12.5.1949 **Maria Theresia Freiin. Mayr v. Melnhoff** * Glanegg 20.9.1926 dau. of Friedrich Frhr. Mayr v. Melnhoff, and has issue:

XIV   1b.   **Ernst Maria Johann Gregor Graf Hoyos** * Glanegg 10.5.1950

     2b.   **Alfred Maria Heinrich Graf Hoyos** * Salzburg 17.7.1951

     3b.   **Teresitta Gräfin Hoyos** * Salvador, Brazil 17.1.1953

     4b.   **Veronika Gräfin Hoyos** * Petropolis, Brazil 10.7.1955

     5b.   **Heinrich Graf Hoyos** * Petropolis 15.7.1956

     6b.   **Ladilsaja Gräfin Hoyos** * Petropolis 26.6.1957

     7b.   **Markus Graf Hoyos** * Wien 30.9.1960

     8b.   **Hemma Gräfin Hoyos** * Wien 29.6.1965

XIII   4a.   **Eleonore Maria Johanna Rudolfine Therese Inez Gräfin Hoyos** * Horn 26.11.1926 = Horn 18.9.1954 Matthias Graf v. Thun-Hohenstein-Salm-Reifferscheid * Wien 18.4.1914, and had issue:

XIV   1b.   **Marie Eleonore Agnes Christiane Gräfin v. Thun-Hohenstein** * Wien 23.3.1956

     2b.   **Johanna Gabrielle Gräfin v. Thun-Hohenstein** * Wien 2.4.1958

     3b.   **Paula Christiane Gräfin v. Thun-Hohenstein** * Wien 29.6.1959

     4b.   **Lukas Michael Ladislaus Graf v. Thun-Hohenstein** * Wien 8.10.1960

XIII   5a.   **Bernhard Heinrich Rudolf Maria Anton Ignaz Graf Hoyos** * Horn 30.7.1931 = Bleiburg 24.5.1961 Alexandra Gräfin v. Herberstein * Budapest 8.4.1933 dau. of Johann Graf v. Herberstein and has issue:

XIV   1b.   **Caroline Marie Elisabeth Antonia Gabrielle Gräfin Hoyos** * Wien 10.3.1962

     2b.   **Sophie Eleonore Marie Hemma Christiane Gräfin Hoyos** * Wien 11.6.1963

     3b.   **Alexandra Maria Anna Amelie Friederike Gräfin Hoyos** * Wien 10.7.1964

     4b.   **Elisabeth Marie Clara Bernadette Josefa Gräfin Hoyos** * Wien 7.2.1966

XII   (c)   **Franz Leopold Maria Joseph Anton Graf v. Hartig** * Niemes 1.8.1896 = Alfter b. Bonn 12.7.1933 Christina Altgräfin zu Salm-Reifferscheid-Krautheim u. Dyck * Dyck 29.4.1901 dau. of Alfred 5th Fürst u. Altgraf zu Salm-Reifferscheid Krautheim u. Dyck, and has issue:

XIII   1a.   **Franz Alfred Johannes Rudolf Maria Antonius Kletus Graf v. Hartig** * Wien 26.4.1934 = Salzburg 1.9.1963 Albertina v. Mihalovic * ... dau. of Karl v. Mihalovic

XIII			2a.	**Peter Eugen Maria Josef Antonius Rafael Graf v. Hartig** * Wien 23.9.1935 = Wien 24.4.1965 Camilla Edle von Hackens * Gmunden 2.3.1945 dau. of Herbert Edler v. Hackens and has issue:

XIV   1b.   **Natalie Elisabeth Stephanie Anna Maria Thaddea Gräfin v. Hartig** * Johannesburg 26.2.1966

XIII   3a.   **Paul Rudolf Maria Josef Antonius Michael Graf v. Hartig** * Wien 23.9.1935 = Wien 24.4.1965 Elisabeth Riedl von Riedenstein * Wien 10.10.1940 dau. of Gottfried Riedl v. Riedenstein and has issue:

XIV   1b.   **Isabella Christiane Elisabeth Paula Maria Alice Thaddaea Gräfin v. Hartig** * Rio de Janeiro 11.1.1966

XII   (d)   **Josepha Maria Franziska Antonia Gräfin v. Hartig** * Niemes 12.7.1899 = Mariaschein 22.10.1935 Theobald Graf v. Westphalen zu Fürstenberg * Kulm 19.7.1901, and has issue:

XIII   1a.   **Maria Thaddaea Gräfin v. Westphalen zu Fürstenberg** * Teplitz 8.10.1936 = Laar 14.5.1960 Jhr. Eduard Beelaerts van Blokland * Arnhem 30.12.1926 and has issue:

XIV   1b.   **Jhr. Henri Thaddeus Johannes Beelaerts van Blokland** * Bonn 13.4.1961

         2b.   **Jhr. Frederik Eduard Thaddeus Josef Beelaerts van Blokland** * Bonn 16.3.1962

XIII   2a.   **Johannes Ottakar Graf v. Westphalen zu Fürstenberg** * Teplitz 29.12.1937

XI   b)   **Adolf Maria Graf v. Ledebur-Wicheln** * Prag 2.1.1870 + Alkoven 20.2.1949 = Nisko 13.6.1896 Marie Gräfin Rességuier de Miremont * Nisko 14.7.1872 + Wien 28.3.1941 dau. of Olivier Graf Rességuier de Miremont, and had issue:

XII   (a)   **Johann Maria Graf v. Ledebur-Wicheln** * Wien 18.3.1897 + Wiener-Neustadt 3.10.1918

         (b)   **Karl Borramäus Josef Hubert Maria Graf v. Ledebur-Wicheln** * Wien 15.1.1898 = St. Moritz 18.6.1930 Beatrice v. Riedemann * Hamburg 26.4.1910 dau. of Heinrich v. Riedemann, and has issue:

XIII   1a.   **Mario Heinrich Graf v. Ledebur-Wicheln** * St. Moritz 28.7.1931 = Unternach 20.7.1959 **Marie Prinzessin v. Altenburg** * Wien 16.5.1931 dau. of Clemens Salvator Archduke of Austria, Pr. v. Altenburg and has issue:

XIV   1b.   **Maria Josepha Gräfin v. Ledebur-Wicheln** * München 25.1.1962

         2b.   **Clementine Gräfin v. Ledebur-Wicheln** * München 25.1.1963

         3b.   **Heinrich Johannes Maria Graf v. Ledebur-Wicheln** * München 27.7.1964

         4b.   **Anna Maria Mercedes Gräfin v. Ledebur-Wicheln** * München 29.9.1965

XIII   2a.   **Marie Elisabeth Gräfin v. Ledebur-Wicheln** * Alkoven 7.10.1932 = 15.10.1956 Robert Henggeler * Horw, Suisse 20.1.1931, and has issue:

XIV   1b.   **Christoph Henggeler** * Salisbury, Rhodesia 17.9.1957

XIV

        2b.   **Maria Theresa Henggeler** * Linz 11.3.1959

        3b.   **Karl Henggeler** * Marandellas, Southern Rhodesia 25.6.1960

        4b.   **Katherina Henggeler** * Wels 17.12.1961

        5b.   **Margarete Henggeler** * Marandellas, Southern Rhodesia 21.3.1963

        6b.   **Bernadette Henggeler** * Marandellas 24.3.1964

XIII

    3a.   **Christoph Graf v. Ledebur-Wicheln** * Alkoven 23.12.1933 = 21.6.1959
Vendeline Gräfin v. Bismark-Schönhausen * Berlin 7.12.1937 dau. of
Gottfried Graf v. Bismark-Schönhausen, and has issue:

XIV

        1b.   **Franziska Gräfin v. Ledebur-Wicheln** * München 19.3.1960

        2b.   **Stephan Graf v. Ledebur-Wicheln** * München 14.3.1962

        3b.   **Benedikt Graf v. Ledebur-Wicheln** * München 20.8.1964

XII

    (c)   **Josef Maria Graf v. Ledebur-Wicheln** * Wien 13.2.1899 + Buenos Aires 8.12.1963
= (1) Sage, Nevada 21.11.1932 Gladys Olcott-Waddington * New York 29.12.1904
— div; = (2) in Argentina 13.4.1954 Dagmar Freiin. v. Berg * Marienbad
28.7.1919 dau. of Tassilo Frhr. v. Berg, and had issue:

by 2nd marriage:

XIII

    1a.   **Jean Carlos Graf v. Ledebur-Wicheln** * 29.11.1954

    2a.   **Huberto Guillermo Graf v. Ledebur-Wicheln** * Buenos Aires November 1956

XII

    (d)   **Friedrich Maria Graf v. Ledebur-Wicheln** * Nisko 3.6.1900 = New York 1927
Iris Tree * London 27.1.1901 dau. of Sir Henry Beerbohm Tree, and has issue:

XIII

    1a.   **Christian Dion Graf v. Ledebur-Wicheln** * London 5.2.1928 = (1) Oslo
13.6.1950 Henriette Amundsen * 19.5.1932 dau. of Olaf Amundsen — div;
= (2) Genève 5.11.1960 Ilona Jagiello * Konopka, Poland 2.1.1937 dau. of
Josef Jagiello, and has issue:

by 1st marriage:

XIV

        1b.   **Marius Erik Graf v. Ledebur-Wicheln** * Santa Monica, California
            11.5.1951

by 2nd marriage:

        2b.   **Mayanne Aurelia Francesca Xenia Gräfin v. Ledebur-Wicheln** * Genève
            7.11.1962

XII

    (e)   **Hubertus Maria Graf v. Ledebur-Wicheln** * Ledény 2.9.1901 X Oplonica,
Slovakia 5.2.1945 = Budapest 5.5.1938 **Olga Prinzessin zu Windisch-Graetz**
* Gonobitz 5.3.1893 dau. of Hugo Fürst zu Windisch-Graetz s.p.

    (f)   **Elisabeth Antonia Maria Gräfin v. Ledebur-Wicheln** * Ledény 6.7.1905 = Wien
10.9.1930 Mario v. Riedemann * Hamburg 9.9.1908, and has issue:

XIII

    1a.   **Karl Anton v. Riedemann** * Samaden 3.10.1931 = Trieste 16.5.1961
Olga Prinzessin zu Windisch-Graetz * Graz 26.10.1934 dau. of Eduard Prinz
zu Windisch-Graetz, and has issue:

XIV

        1b.   **Mario v. Riedemann** * Vancouver, B.C. 7.4.1962

        2b.   **Peter Edward v. Riedemann** * Vancouver, B.C. 20.10.1963

XIV

      3b. **Mark v. Riedemann** * Victoria, B.C. 20.10.1964

      4b. **Cecilia v. Riedemann** * Victoria, B.C. 4.11.1965

XIII

      2a. **Sophie Beatrice v. Riedemann** * Wien 6.9.1932

      3a. **Myra Franziska v. Riedemann** * Siebersdorf 2.4.1934

      4a. **Martin v. Riedemann** * Siebersdorf 19.8.1936

XII

(g) **Eugen Kaspar Maria Graf v. Ledebur-Wicheln** * Ob-Siebenbrünn 7.9.1909 = Wien 29.2.1944 Maria Czizek * Wien 2.4.1917 dau. of August Czizek, — div.

XI

c) **Eugen Rudolf Maria Graf v. Ledebur-Wicheln** * Petersburg i. Böh. 14.11.1873 + Leitmeritz 12.11.1945 = Wien 8.1.1910 Eleonore Gräfin Larisch v. Moennich * Solza 9.6.1888 dau. of Heinrich Graf Larisch v. Moennich, and has issue:

XII

(a) **Henriette Karoline Rosalie Maria Gräfin v. Ledebur-Wicheln** * Krzemusch 19.12.1910 = Milleschau 29.6.1933 Ferdinand Graf Kinsky v. Wchinitz u. Tettau * Wien 30.1.1907, and has issue:

XIII

      1a. **Ferdinand Eugen Franz v. Assisi Bonaventura Maria Theresia Graf Kinsky v. Wchinitz u. Tettau** * Prag 25.10.1934 = Straubing 28.4.1962 Hedwig Gräfin v. Ballestrem * Plawniowitz 17.6.1933 dau. of Nikolaus Graf v. Ballestrem, and has issue:

XIV

          1b. **Maria Theresia Anna Henriette Gräfin Kinsky v. Wchinitz u. Tettau** * Regensburg 22.5.1963

          2b. **Johannes Ferdinand Nikolaus Maria Graf Kinsky v. Wchinitz u. Tettau** * Regensburg 7.8.1964

          3b. **Marie Valerie Elisabeth Hedwig Gräfin Kinsky v. Wchinitz u. Tettau** * Nice 2.3.1966

XIII

      2a. **Eleonore Aglaé Bonaventura Maria Theresia Gräfin Kinsky v. Wchinitz u. Tettau** * Prag 1.1.1936 = München 3.12.1966 Thomas Cornides v. Krempach * Berlin 11.9.1938

      3a. **Johannes Karl Augustinus Bonaventura Maria Theresia Graf Kinsky v. Wchinitz u. Tettau** * Prag 22.3.1937 = Wien 5.9.1964 Eleonore Gräfin v.u. zu Trauttmansdorff-Weinsberg * Pottenbrunn 8.2.1938 dau. of Josef Graf v.u. zu Trauttmansdorff-Weinsberg, and has issue:

XIV

          1b. **Henriette Eleonore Maria Elena Gräfin Kinsky v. Wchinitz u. Tettau** * Wien 18.10.1965

XIII

      4a. **Maria Aglaé Bonaventura Theresia Gräfin Kinsky v. Wchinitz u. Tettau** * Prag 14.4.1940

      5a. **Aglaé Ernestine Bonaventura Maria Theresia Gräfin Kinsky v. Wchinitz u. Tettau** * Prag 26.4.1941 = München 11.12.1965 Konrad Graf v. Ballestrem * Plawniowitz 6.10.1935

      6a. **Elisabeth Karoline Bonaventura Maria Theresia Gräfin Kinsky v. Wchinitz u. Tettau** * Prag 4.1.1944

      7a. **Carl Christian Wigbert Bonaventura Maria Theresia Graf Kinsky v. Wchinitz u. Tettau** * München 20.10.1954

XII   (b)   **Karoline Johanna Franziska Maria Gräfin v. Ledebur-Wicheln** * Krzemusch
23.3.1912 = Mariaschein, Böh. 16.11.1936 Johannes Prinz v.u. zu Liechtenstein
* Wien 18.5.1910, and has issue:

XIII   1a.   **Marie Eleonore Elisabeth Johanna Prinzessin v.u. zu Liechtenstein** * Mähr-
Sternberg 23.9.1937

                 2a.   **Eugen Hartmann Johannes Franz Prinz v.u. zu Liechtenstein** * Mähr-Sternberg
20.3.1939

                 3a.   **Albrecht Johannes Geza Augustinus Wilhelm Maria Prinz v.u. zu Liechtenstein**
* Mähr-Sternberg 28.5.1940

                 4a.   **Barbara Prinzessin v.u. zu Liechtenstein** * Mähr-Sternberg 9.7.1942

XII   (c)   **Franziska Marie Hedwig Eleonore Gräfin v. Ledebur-Wicheln** * Milleschau
18.6.1913 = Milleschau 19.9.1938 **Johannes Graf v. Waldburg zu Wolfegg u. Waldsee**
* Waldsee 10.8.1944, and has issue see elsewhere

       (d)   **Heinrich-Wigbert Johann Maria Michael Eugen Benedikt Graf v. Ledebur-Wicheln**
* Solza 19.10.1915—missing in Russia since December 1943

       (e)   **Franz-Eugen Jaromir Maria Gabriel Heinrich Benedikt Graf v. Ledebur-Wicheln**
* Krzemusch 13.4.1919 ✕ Stefanowska, Russia 11.1.1944

       (f)   **Marie Franziska Rudolfine Eleonore Gräfin v. Ledebur-Wicheln** * Krzemusch
5.11.1920 = München 3.2.1951 **Josef Graf v. Neipperg** * Schwaigern 22.7.1918,
and has issue see elsewhere

       (g)   **Gerhard Heinrich Maria Wenzel Benno Paulus Rafael Graf v. Ledebur-Wicheln**
* Krzemusch 25.1.1927 = München 19.11.1951 Gertrud Sailer * Regensburg
14.12.1929

XI   d)   **Karoline Maria Gräfin v. Ledebur-Wicheln** * Petersburg i. Böh. 1.7.1875 + Balaton-
Györök 4.1.1956 = Wien 26.4.1897 Viktor Graf Széchényi v. Sárvár-Felsövidék
* Pressburg 10.7.1871 + Budapest 19.4.1945, and had issue:

XII   (a)   **Zsigmond Graf Széchényi v. Sárvár-Felsövidék** * Nagy-Várad,Kom. Bihar
23.1.1898 = (1) Budapest 2.6.1936 Stella Crowther * Wimbledon 24.7.1913
— div.; = (2) Keszthely 5.5.1959 Margit Hertelendy de Hertelend et Vindornyalak
* Pasca, Kom Zla 2.6.1925 dau. of Josef Hertelendy de Hertelend et Vindornyalak,
and has issue:

            by 1st marriage:

XIII   1a.   **Péter Graf Széchényi v. Sárvár-Felsövidék** * London 4.2.1939

XII   (b)   **Sarlota Gräfin Széchényi v. Sárvár-Felsövidék** * Budapest 14.6.1900 = Sárpentele
27.6.1920 Ladislas Graf Esterházy v. Galántha * Sárosd 3.3.1891, and has issue:

XIII   1a.   **Ilona Maria Antonia Elisabeth Gabrielle Katherina Karoline Gräfin Esterházy
v. Galántha** * Sárosd 17.5.1921 = ... 8.1943 Nikolaus Graf Cziráky v. Czirák
u. Dénesfalva * Budapest 6.3.1918 ✕ b. Arad ... 9.1944 s.p.

                 2a.   **Maria Emerica Gabriella Gräfin Esterházy v. Galántha** * Sárosd 26.6.1922
= Budapest 26.2.1942 Franz Graf Batthyány v. Német-Ujvár * Kittsee
4.10.1915, and has issue:

XIV   1b.   **Bálint Graf Batthyány v. Német-Ujvár** * Budapest 22.11.1942

                      2b.   **Béla Graf Batthyány v. Német-Ujvár** * Budapest 18.4.1944 + 1.9.1945

XIII		3a.	**Béla Hubertus Graf Esterházy v. Galántha** * Sárosd 14.6.1926 = Budapest ... 7.1950 Ilona Gräfin Teleki v. Szék * Budapest 30.6.1924 dau. of Michael Graf Teleki v. Szék, and has issue:
XIV		1b.	**Ladislaus Graf Esterházy v. Galántha** * Budapest 29.9.1951
XII	(c)		**Irma Gräfin Széchényi v. Sávár-Felsövidék** * Sárpentele 18.4.1902 + Wien 18.1.1960
	(d)		**Marta Gräfin Széchényi v. Sárvár-Felsövidék** * Sárpentele 15.12.1905 = Budapest 23.2.1929 **Jaromir Graf Czernin v.u. zu Chudenitz** * Prag 30.1.1908 — div. and has issue see elsewhere
	(e)		**Antal Graf Széchényi v. Sávár-Felsövidék** * Budapest 24.3.1919 + Sarpentele 29.5.1921

XI   e)   **Franz Maria Graf v. Ledebur-Wicheln** * Petersburg i. Böh. 6.9.1877 + Wallerstein 24.5.1954 = Wien 5.9.1909 **Marie Felicitas Prinzessin v. Montenuovo** * Margarathen am Moos 20.10.1881 + Tegernsee 10.8.1954 dau. of Alfred 2nd Fürst v. Montenuovo, and had issue:

XII   (a)   **Franziska Xaveria Maria Carola Borromäa Bonifazia Gräfin v. Ledebur-Wicheln** * Wien 5.6.1912 = Wallerstein 28.4.1950 Henning Frhr. v. Stralenheim * Grossenhain 5.5.1912 s.p.

    (b)   **Charlotte Franziska de Paula Josefa Maria Anna Gräfin v. Ledebur-Wicheln** * Hermann-Mestetz 26.7.1913 = Karlsbad 24.3.1940 Ferdinand de Longueval Graf v. Buquoy * Wien 25.4.1915, and has issue:

XIII   1a.   **Michael Carl Maria de Longueval Graf v. Buquoy** * Prag 12.1.1941

    2a.   **Maria Charlotte Theresia de Longueval Gräfin v. Buquoy** * Prag 13.10.1942 = Bad Wiessee 7.5 1966 Benedikt Graf v.u. zu Hoensbroech * Köln 2.7.1939

    3a.   **Franz Hubertus Maria de Longueval Graf v. Buquoy** * Prag 12.10.1944

XII   (c)   **Johann Adam Alfred Franziskus de Paula Maria Thaddäus Flavian Graf v. Ledebur-Wicheln** * Wien 18.2.1916 ✘ in Partisan Raid, Korsör, Denmark 21.5.1945 = Gratzen 28.4.1941 Henriette de Longueval Gräfin v. Buquoy * Gratzen 4.8.1917 dau. of Karl de Longueval Graf v. Buquoy s.p.

X   d.   **Ernestine Gräfin Czernin v.u. zu Chudenitz** * Petersburg i. Böh. 13.11.1848 + Wien 22.6.1908 = Prag 19.8.1867 Karl 4th Fürst zu Oettingen-Oettingen u. Oettingen-Wallerstein * Wallerstein 16.9.1840 + Petersburg i. Böh. 22.12.1905, and had issue:

XI   a)   **Friedrich Karl Wolfgang Kraft Ernst Notger Prinz zu Oettingen-Oettingen u. Oettingen-Wallerstein** * 15.5.1869 + Schloss Hlubosch 11.6.1882

    b)   **Marie Anne Caroline Ernestine Friederike Notgere Prinzessin zu Oettingen-Oettingen u. Oettingen-Wallerstein** * 9.11.1870 + 24.12.1883

    c)   **Caroline Maria Aloisia Ernestine Notgere Prinzessin zu Oettingen-Oettingen u. Oettingen-Wallerstein** * Prag 22.2.1873 + Wien 15.3.1959 = Wien 14.1.1902 Otto Johann Graf v. Harrach zu Rohrau u. Thannhausen * Prag 10.2.1863 + Schloss Hradek b. Königgrätz, Böh. 10.9.1935, and had issue:

XII   (a)   **Ernestine Antonia Karoline Pia Marie Susanna Gräfin v. Harrach zu Rohrau u. Thannhausen** * Rohrau 11.8.1903 = Wien 7.11.1932 **Johann Graf Lexa v. Aehrenthal** * Tsarskoie Selo 9.8.1905, and has issue see elsewhere

XII

(b) **Johann Nepomuk Anton Karl Leonhard Otto Bonaventura Maria Kleophas Graf v. Harrach zu Rohrau u. Thannhausen** * Prugg 25.9.1904 + Bad Kreuznach 12.5.1945 = Alt-Aussee 16.10.1940 Stephanie Gräfin v.u. zu Eltz gen. Faust v. Stromberg * Alt-Aussee 30.9.1917 dau. of Erwein Graf v.u. zu Eltz gen. Faust v. Stromberg, and had issue:

XIII

    1a. **Ferdinand Bonaventura Ernst Otto Erwein Johann Nepomuk Leonhard Franz Roman Graf v. Harrach zu Rohrau u. Thannhausen** * Wien 18.11.1941 + Wien 25.8.1961

    2a. **Johanna Alexandra Georgine Amalie Gräfin v. Harrach zu Rohrau u. Thannhausen** * Könnigrätz 10.7.1944 = Wien 10.9.1966 Eberhard Graf v. Waldburg zu Zeil u. Trauchburg * Schloss Zeil 30.4.1940

XI

d) **Marie Karoline Ernestine Judith Notgere Prinzessin zu Oettingen-Oettingen u. Oettingen-Wallerstein** * Prag 10.12.1874 + Wallerstein 19.2.1960 = Wien 27.4.1897 August Graf v. Bellegarde * Hacking 26.5.1858 + Gr.-Herrlitz 24.2.1929 and had issue:

XII

(a) **Ernestine Maria Emanuela Gräfin v. Bellegarde** * Wien 23.2.1898

(b) **Rudolfine Gräfin v. Bellegarde** * Wien 30.11.1899

(c) **Marie Caroline Emanuela Gräfin v. Bellegarde** * Gr.-Herrlitz 20.8.1902

(d) **Elisabeth Maria Magdalena Gräfin v. Bellegarde** * Wien 19.12.1907

(e) **Sophie Maria Emanuela Gräfin v. Bellegarde** * Wien 21.2.1914 = Wien 13.5.1942 Gustav Graf v. Wedel * Hannover 16.12.1912, and has issue:

XIII

    1a. **Maria-Elisabeth Pauline Barbara Emanuela Theobalda Gräfin v. Wedel** * Troppau 18.6.1943

    2a. **Clemens-August Eugen Maria Emanuel Graf v. Wedel** * Troppau 22.7.1944

XI

e) **Karl Friedrich Wolfgang Kraft Notger Petrus 5th Fürst zu Oettingen-Oettingen u. Oettingen-Wallerstein** * Königsaal i. Böh. 27.4.1877 + München 24.5.1930 = Bruck a.d. Leitha 3.2.1914 **Julia Prinzessin v. Montenuovo** * Margarthen am Moos 15.11.1880 + Schloss Berg 27.6.1961 dau. of Alfred 2nd Fürst v. Montenuovo s.p.

f) **Sophie Marie Caroline Ernestine Notgera Prinzessin zu Oettingen-Oettingen u. Oettingen-Wallerstein** * Hlubosh 4.10.1878 + Wien 10.9.1944 = Wien 27.4.1897 Johannes Prinz v. Schönburg-Hartenstein * Enzesfeld 12.9.1864 + Wien 30.3.1937, and had issue:

XII

(a) **Karoline Ernestine Franziska Marie Prinzessin v. Schönburg-Hartenstein** * Wien 23.12.1898 = Wien 1.12.1925 **Georg Frhr. v.u. zu Franckenstein** * Nördlingen 20.8.1898, + 28.3.1965 and has issue see elsewhere

(b) **Ernestine Maria Sophia Johanna Prinzessin v. Schönburg-Hartenstein** * Rothen-Lhotta 12.7.1900 = Wien 10.12.1930 Ludwig Graf Marenzi v. Tagliano u. Talgate * Wien 16.10.1894, and has issue:

XIII

    1a. **Johannes Ludwig Ernst Josef Thaddäus Franz Maria Graf Marenzi v. Tagliano u. Talgate** * Wien 30.10.1931

    2a. **Ludwig Gabriel Ernst Maria Graf Marenzi v. Tagliano u. Talgate** * Wien 23.6.1933

    3a. **Friedrich Carl Franz Josef Otto Graf Marenzi v. Tagliano u. Talgate** * Wien 22.9.1935

    4a. **Franz Josef Ludwig Ernst Maria Graf Marenzi v. Tagliano u. Talgate** * Wien 21.11.1936

XIII		5a.	**Andreas Otto Ernst Georg Graf Marenzi v. Tagliano u. Talgate** * Wien 16.2.1943
XII	(c)		**Carl Maria Johann Alexander Anton Prinz v. Schönburg-Hartenstein** * Bukarest 23.12.1901
	(d)		**Marie Ernestine Karoline Sophie Prinzessin v. Schönburg-Hartenstein** * Roma 25.9.1903 + Bayreuth 21.1.1952 = Üllstadt 29.11.1938 Otto Frhr. Gross v. Trockau * Würzburg 10.11.1890 + Trockau 21.2.1957, and has issue:
XIII		1a.	**Benedikta Sophia Marie Eleonore Freiin. Gross v. Trockau** * Würzburg 1.2.1940
		2a.	**Johannes Eugen Otto Philipp Frhr. Gross v. Trockau** * Würzburg 19.5.1941
XII	(e)		**Aloys Alexander Prinz v. Schönburg-Hartenstein** * London 24.3.1906 = (1) London 20.9.1935 Dilys Marten * Glamorgan 7.3.1912 + Tenby 3.11.1943 dau. of E ... Marten; = (2) Salzburg 21.7.1949 Christine Strohschneider * Steeg 9.11.1924 dau. of Wolfgang Strohschneider, and has issue:

by 1st marriage:

XIII		1a.	**Johannes Carl Prinz v. Schönburg-Hartenstein** * Linz 13.2.1938
		2a.	**Nikolaus Alexander Prinz v. Schönburg-Hartenstein** * Tenby 6.4.1940

by 2nd marriage:

		3a.	**Michael Alexander Prinz v. Schönburg-Hartenstein** * Steeg 26.6.1950 + Steeg 10.5.1965
		4a.	**Alexander Prinz v. Schönburg-Hartenstein** * Bad Goisern 1.10.1955
XII	(f)		**Aloysia Alexandra Prinzessin v. Schönburg-Hartenstein** * London 24.3.1906 = Salzburg 31.10.1936 Otto v. Simson * Berlin-Dahlem 17.7.1912, and has issue:
XIII		1a.	**Ernest Martin v. Simson** * München 17.3.1938 = 29.8.1963 Kate Burke * Providence, Rhode Island 14.3.1941 dau. of Charles F. Burke, and has issue:
XIV		1b.	**Charles v. Simson** * Providence, Rhode Island 16.6.1964
XIII		2a.	**John v. Simson** * South Bend, Indiana 3.3.1944
XII	(g)		**Peter Karl Maria Anton Pius Benediktus Markus Johannes Prinz v. Schönburg-Hartenstein** * Roma 25.4.1913 = Tena, Columbia 8.9.1945 Lyna de Rodriguez Maldonado * Bruxelles 3.6.1914 − div., and has issue:
XIII		1a.	**Alexandra Carlotta Sophy Prinzessin v. Schönburg-Hartenstein** * Bogota 26.9.1946
XII	(h)		**Sophie Marie Karoline Johanna Ernestine Prinzessin v. Schönburg-Hartenstein** * Wien 19.4.1917 = Bogota 30.7.1948 Alberto de Carrillo Leisser * Barranquilla, Colombia 15.8.1920, and has issue:
XIII		1a.	**Juan Carlos Carrillo Schönburg-Hartenstein** * Bogota 13.6.1951
		2a.	**Luis Alberto Carrillo Schönburg-Hartenstein** * Bogota 26.8.1953
		3a.	**Marie Alicia Carrillo Schönburg-Hartenstein** * Bogota 13.4.1957
		4a.	**Laura Sophia Carrillo Schönburg-Hartenstein** * Bogota 7.9.1959

XI   g)   **Josephine Ernestine Marianne Karoline Notgere Prinzessin zu Oettingen-Oettingen u. Oettingen-Wallerstein** * Prag 22.3.1885 + Bad Reichenhall 11.10.1961

     h)   **Eugen Wolfgang Karl Friedrich Joseph Notger 6th Fürst zu Oettingen-Oettingen u. Oettingen-Wallerstein** * Prag 22.3.1885 = Schillingsfürst 3.8.1916 Marianne Prinzessin zu Hohenlohe-Waldenburg-Schillingsfürst * Alt-Aussee 19.8.1885 dau. of Moritz 9th Fürst zu Hohenlohe-Waldenburg-Schillingsfürst, and has issue:

XII   (a)   **Karl Friedrich Moritz Eugen Wolfgang Kraft Notger Alexander Maria Erbprinz zu Oettingen-Oettingen u. Oettingen-Wallerstein** * München 23.5.1917 = Greifenstein 26.7.1942 Delia Schenk Gräfin v. Stauffenberg * Stuttgart 4.3.1919 dau. of Markwart Schenk Graf v. Stauffenberg, and has issue:

XIII   1a.   **Ernestine Konstanze Olga Alexandra Maria Notgera Prinzessin zu Oettingen-Oettingen u. Oettingen-Wallerstein** * Wallerstein 18.10.1943

     2a.   **Moritz Eugen Carl Friedrich Anton Kraft Notger Maria Prinz zu Oettingen-Oettingen u. Oettingen-Wallerstein** * München 20.5.1946

     3a.   **Krafft Ernst Markwart Carl Friedrich Notger Maria Prinz zu Oettingen-Oettingen u. Oettingen-Wallerstein** * München 9.4.1951

XII   (b)   **Moritz Notger Karl Wolfgang Alexander Maria Prinz zu Oettingen-Oettingen u. Oettingen-Wallerstein** * München 18.2.1922 X bei Jassy, Roumania 3.5.1944

     (c)   **Rose-Marie Ernestine Elisabeth Notgera Prinzessin zu Oettingen-Oettingen u. Oettingen-Wallerstein** * München 12.3.1923 = Wallerstein 10.8.1949 Franz Karl Graf v. Strassoldo * München 22.2.1917, and has issue:

XIII   1a.   **Michael Leopold Eugen Vincenz Maria Graf v. Strassoldo** * Bonn 10.4.1950

     2a.   **Alexander Heinrich Vincenz Maria Graf v. Strassoldo** * Bonn 14.2.1955

     3a.   **Elisabeth Benedikta Rosa Maria Notgere Gräfin v. Strassoldo** * Bonn 22.9.1957

     4a.   **Christian-Gottfried Carl-Friedrich Heinrich Vincenz Maria Graf v. Strassoldo** * Burg Gudenau 26.6.1961

     5a.   **Franz-Peter Nikolaus Raimund Gabriel Graf v. Strassoldo** * Beuel am Rh. 12.10.1964

XII   (d)   **Wolfgang Kraft Notger Franz Joseph Alexander Maria Prinz zu Oettingen-Oettingen u. Oettingen-Wallerstein** * München 1.8.1924 = Wallerstein 18.6.1950 Henriette de Longueval Gräfin v. Buquoy * Gratzen 4.8.1917 dau. of Carl de Longueval Graf v. Buquoy, and has issue:

XIII   1a.   **Isabell Marie-Valerie Notgera Prinzessin zu Oettingen-Oettingen u. Oettingen-Wallerstein** * München 8.6.1952

     2a.   **Elisabeth-Marie Henriette Notgera Prinzessin zu Oettingen-Oettingen u. Oettingen-Wallerstein** * München 12.6.1953

     3a.   **Rose-Marie Sophie Notgera Prinzessin zu Oettingen-Oettingen u. Oettingen-Wallerstein** * München 26.10.1955

     4a.   **Karl Wolfgang Eugen Notger Maria Prinz zu Oettingen-Oettingen u. Oettingen-Wallerstein** * München 8.11.1956

X   e.   **Eugen Jaromir Franz Graf Czernin v.u. zu Chudenitz** * Wien 13.2.1851 + Petersburg i. Böh. 5.11.1925 = Wien 26.4.1876 Franziska Prinzessin v. Schönburg-Hartenstein * Karlsruhe 28.8.1857 + Petersburg i. Böh. 20.1.1926 dau. of Alexander 3rd Fürst v. Schönburg-Hartenstein s.p.

247

X   f.   **Franz Jaromir Eugen Graf Czernin v.u. zu Chudenitz** * Wien 3.3.1857 + Neuhaus 9.4.1932

IX   (2)   **Hermann Graf Czernin v.u. zu Chudenitz** * Wien 20.2.1819 + Dresden 2.8.1892 = Prag 13.11.1853 Aloysia Gräfin v. Morzin * Prag 6.5.1832 + Hohenelbe 26.7.1907 dau. of Rudolf Graf v. Morzin, and has issue:

X   a.   **Rudolf Graf Czernin v.u. zu Chudenitz u. Morzin** * Prag 8.1.1855 + Hohenelbe 5.9.1927 = (1) Prag 22.6.1878 Emma Gräfin v. Orsini u. Rosenberg * Graz 8.7.1858 + Marschendorf 6.7.1905 dau. of Joseph Graf v. Orsini u. Rosenberg; = (2) Černáhora 5.8.1907 Theresia Gräfin Fries v. Friesenberg * Černáhora 21.3.1874 + Černáhora 14.11.1946 dau. of August Graf Fries v. Friesenberg, and had issue:

by 1st marriage:

XI   a)   **Maria Aloysia Josefine Gräfin Czernin v.u. zu Chudenitz** * Bensen 10.5.1879 + Gauting 9.1.1963 = Prag 13.5.1899 Carl Fürst von Weikersheim * Weikersheim 25.1.1862 + Gräfeling b. München 28.9.1925, and had issue:

XII   (a)   **Carl Rudolf Maria Joseph Antonius Benedictus Graf v. Weikersheim** * Pardubitz 6.2.1900–missing since February 1945 = (1) Altberun 23.2.1925 Valérie Dlugay * Altberun 12.12.1905 + Brünn 27.9.1936; = (2) Mährisch-Schönberg 15.9.1940 Ludwiga Pospiech * Prachatitz 27.7.1916 s.p.

                (b)   **Maria Emma Josepha Antonia Benedicta Gräfin v. Weikersheim** * Przemsyl 3.4.1901 + Tunbridge Wells 18.3.1958

                (c)   **Franz Maria Joseph Antonius Benedictus Fürst v. Weikersheim** * Wien 26.2.1904 = Wien 25.4.1936 **Irma Prinzessin zu Windisch-Graetz** * Schloss Lána 22.9.1913 dau. of Hugo Fürst zu Windish-Graetz, and has issue:

XIII   1a.   **Cecile Leontine Mary Gräfin v. Weikersheim** * London 28.10.1937 = London 30.6.1960 Alexander McEwen * Marchmont, Berwickshire 16.5.1935 and has issue:

XIV   1b.   **Sophie Cristina McEwen** * Greenland, Berwickshire 8.4.1961

                     2b.   **Alexander Charles Francis McEwen** * Edinburgh 12.6.1962

                     3b.   **Hugo Gabriel McEwen** * Duns, Berwickshire 28.2.1965

XII   (d)   **Aloysia Maria Josepha Antonia Benedicta Gräfin v. Weikersheim** * Wien 19.4.1906 = Andechs 10.10.1938 Rudolf Hofmüller * Dresden-Niederlössnitz 12.2.1898, and has issue:

XIII   1a.   **Agnes Maria Hofmüller** * München 7.12.1941

                   2a.   **Lucinde Maria Bettina Josefa Hofmüller** * Gräfeling b. München 17.7.1945

                   3a.   **Sibylle Regina Alice Marion Hofmüller** * Gauting b. München 29.7.1948

XII   (e)   **Emma Philippine Maria Josepha Antonia Benedikta Gräfin v. Weikersheim** * Wien 4.9.1907

XI   b)   **Rudolf Hermann Maria Josef Graf Czernin v.u. zu Chudenitz u. Morzin** * Prag 15.2.1881 + Wien 24.3.1928 = Prag 7.6.1903 Vera Prinzessin zu Hohenlohe-Waldenburg-Schillingsfürst-Kaunitz * Görz 22.5.1882 + Prag 1.12.1940 dau. of Egon Karl Prinz zu Hohenlohe-Waldenburg-Schillingsfürst-Kaunitz, and had issue:

XII   (a)   **Vera Aloysia Emma Theresia Maria Josefine Gräfin Czernin v.u. zu Chudenitz**
   * München 4.6.1904 + Kirkwood, Missouri 18.9.1959 = (1) Wien 23.2.1924
   Leopold Graf Fugger v. Babenhausen * Ödenburg 18.7.1893 + Babenhausen
   8.7.1966 — div.; = (2) Wien 1.6.1938 Kurt Edler v. Schuschnigg * Riva a. Garasee
   14.12.1897, and had issue:

     by 1st marriage:

XIII   1a.   **Eleonore Vera Alexia Anna Maria Gräfin Fugger v. Babenhausen**
   * Babenhausen 31.1.1925 = (1) Walsertal 14.2.1946 Robert Bee * ...
   — div.; = (2) München 31.1.1961 **Burchard Prince of Prussia** * Potsdam
   8.1.1917, and has issue:

     by 1st marriage:

XIV   1b.   **Sylvia Rose Marie Elisabeth Bee** * New York 4.3.1947

   2b.   **Robert Joseph Leopold Rudolf Bee** * New York 3.4.1948

   3b.   **Victoria Anne Bee** * New York 6.3.1951

XIII   2a.   **Rudolf Karl Maria Graf Fugger v. Babenhausen** * Babenhausen 1.1.1927
   = (1) Milano 21.5.1949 Theresa Angela Crespi * Premeno 20.7.1922 dau. of
   Benigno Crespi, — div.; = (2) Genève 16.11.1959 Maria Leila Duarte
   * Karachi 8.9.1929 dau. of Adrian Duarte, and has issue:

     by 1st marriage:

XIV   1b.   **Maria Isabella Gräfin Fugger v. Babenhausen** * Milano 15.6.1950

     by 2nd marriage:

   2b.   **Christiane Vera Rani Gräfin Fugger v. Babenhausen** * Genève 18.1.1960

   3b.   **Patricia Elisabeth Sylvia Munira Gräfin Fugger v. Babenhausen**
   * Genève 3.8.1961

XIII   3a.   **Rose Marie Therese Gräfin Fugger v. Babenhausen** * Babenhausen 26.12.1927

   4a.   **Sylvia Theresia Karolina Maria Gräfin Fugger v. Babenhausen** * München
   19.5.1931 = 19.5.1961 Friedrich Kristinus * Wien 28.7.1913, and has
   issue:

XIV   1b.   **Georg Joachim Heinrich Leopold Kristinus** * Hamburg 18.6.1962

   2b.   **Andreas Burchard Rudolf Kristinus** * Hamburg 9.10.1964

     by 2nd marriage:

XIII   5a.   **Maria Dolores Edle v. Schuschnigg** * München 23.3.1941 = Paris 17.9.1966
   Vicomte Aubrey de Kergariou * Biarritz 3.9.1935

XII   (b)   **Alexia Emma Egona Theresia Antonia Maria Gräfin Czernin v.u. zu Chudenitz**
   * Griesshübel 6.7.1906 = (1) Wien 11.7.1927 Erwein Graf v. Thun u. Hohenstein
   * Wien-Hietzing 4.4.1896 + Ödenburg 12.2.1946 as Russian Prisoner of War
   — div.; = (2) Mähr-Budwitz 29.12.1943 Eduard Graf Larisch v. Moennich * Solza
   4.1.1916, and has issue:

     by 1st marriage:

XIII   1a.   **Erwein Graf v. Thun u. Hohenstein** * Wien 21.7.1928 + Rain b. Klagenfurt
   14.3.1947

XIII		2a. **Isabella Gräfin v. Thun u. Hohenstein** * Gross-Kuntschitz 29.3.1931 = Maria Saal 2.7.1954 **Franz Graf Czernin v.u. zu Chudenitz** * Marschendorf 30.3.1927 and has issue see elsewhere

by 2nd marriage:

	3a.	**Heinrich Graf Larisch v. Moennich** * Wien 29.6.1945
	4a.	**Alexandra Gräfin Larisch v. Moennich** * Unterach 29.9.1947

XII	(c)	**Jaromir Egon Rudolf Graf Czernin v.u. zu Chudenitz u. Morzin** * Prag 30.1.1908 + München 1.2.1966 = (1) Budapest 23.2.1929 **Marta Gräfin Széchényi v. Sárvár-Felsövidék** * Sárpentele 15.12.1905 dau. of Viktor Graf Széchényi v. Sárvár-Felsövidék, − div.; = (2) Starnberg 7.4.1938 Alix v. Frankenberg u. Ludwigsdorf * München 20.9.1907 dau. of Alexander v. Frankenberg u. Ludwigsdorf, − div.; = (3) Zurich ... 1951 Gertrud Marianne Liebl * ... − div.; = (4) Salzburg 5.5.1960 Margaritha Seyffert * ... dau. of Paul Seyffert, and had issue:

by 1st marriage:

XIII	1a.	**Alexander Rudolf Christophorus Franziskus de Paula Wolfgang Maria Graf Czernin v.u. zu Chudenitz u. Morzin** * Hohenelbe 24.3.1930 = Vancouver B.C. 9.6.1951 Aleida Koelewijn * Baarn, Holland 20.12.1925 dau. of Gerhard Koelewijn, and has issue:

XIV	1b.	**Victor Krisha Alexander Graf Czernin v.u. zu Chudenitz** * Vancouver 16.12.1952 + Vancouver 20.6.1953
	2b.	**Jacqueline Valerie Caroline Gräfin Czernin v.u. zu Chudenitz** * Vancouver 8.5.1956
	3b.	**Lukia Alexis Georgine Gräfin Czernin v.u. zu Chudenitz** * Vancouver 28.1.1958
	4b.	**Astrid Angela Alexandra Gräfin Czernin v.u. zu Chudenitz** * Vancouver 3.12.1963 + North Vancouver 18.2.1964

XIII	2a.	**Johannes Ladislas Franz de Paula Wolfgang Maria Graf Czernin v.u. zu Chudenitz** * Hohenelbe 2.5.1932 = Wien 3.8.1957 Marie Christine Freiin. v. Sacken * Wien 12.2.1935 dau. of Carl Frhr. v. Sacken, and has issue:

XIV	1b.	**Michael Graf Czernin v.u. zu Chudenitz** * Wien 31.3.1958
	2b.	**Christoph Graf Czernin v.u. zu Chudenitz** * Salzburg 28.5.1960

XIII	3a.	**Franz Rudolf Hermann Graf Czernin v.u. zu Chudenitz** * Trautenau 12.9.1935 = (1) Wien 17.2.1962 Ingrid Weirich * Wien 14.12.1934 dau. of Rudolf Weirich − div.; = (2) Wien 30.12.1963 Hermine Schlögl * Wien 27.10.1939 dau. of Leopold Schlögl, and has issue:

by 2nd marriage:

XIV	1b.	**Alexandra Gräfin Czernin v.u. zu Chudenitz** * Wien 29.12.1964
	2b.	**Thomas Graf Czernin v.u. zu Chudenitz** * Wien 16.6.1966

by 2nd marriage:

XIII	4a.	**Peter Otmar Rudolf Alexander Wolfgang Maria Graf Czernin v.u. zu Chudenitz** * Trautenau 6.9.1938 + 26.8.1962
	5a.	**Sofie Gräfin Czernin v.u. zu Chudenitz** * Graz 7.8.1945

XII

(d) **Emma Philippine Vera Theresia Josefa Antonia Maria Gräfin Czernin v.u. zu Chudenitz** * Prag 27.4.1909 = Schloss Hohenelbe 23.5.1935 Gerhard Honenmeyer * ... – div. s.p.

(e) **Egon Alexander Rudolf Josef Antonius Maria Graf Czernin v.u. zu Chudenitz** * Siessbühel 31.8.1911 + Jacun 4.8.1929

(f) **Eleonore Vera Ida Josefa Antonia Theresia Maria Gräfin Czernin v.u. zu Chudenitz** * Prag 31.1.1913 = Spindelmühle i. Riesengeb 30.4.1938 Wilhelm Möhwald * Hackelsdorf, Sudetengau 1.9.1908, and has issue:

XIII

1a. **Vera Möhwald** * Hohenelbe 27.4.1939

2a. **Sylvia Möhwald** * Schirgiswalde, Krs. Bautzen 21.7.1945

3a. **Sonja Möhwald** * Gauting 16.11.1948

XII

(g) **Sylvia Franziska Vera Theresia Antonia Josefa Maria Gräfin Czernin v.u. zu Chudenitz** * Prag 15.1.1916 = Schloss Hohenelbe 23.5.1935 Othmar Frhr. Nádherný v. Borutin * Nied-Adersbach 21.5.1910, and has issue:

XIII

1a. **Johannes Georg Constantin Frhr. Nádherný v. Borutin** * Nied-Adersbach 10.9.1936

2a. **Christian Jaromir Constantin Othmar Frhr. Nádherný v. Borutin** * Nied-Adersbach 22.7.1939

XII

(h) **Maria del Rosario Vera Josefa Antonia Theresia Gräfin Czernin v.u. zu Chudenitz** * Prag 22.7.1918 + Prag 25.2.1944 = (1) Windischgarten 14.8.1937 Otto Prexl * ... – div.; = (2) ... Roland Penka * ... – div., and had issue:

by 1st marriage:

XIII

1a. **Egon Prexl** * ...

by 2nd marriage:

2a. **Sonja Penka** * ...

XI

c) **Franz de Sales Maria Joseph Graf Czernin v.u. zu Chudenitz** * Marschendorf 24.5.1885 + Uberaba, Brasil 22.10.1954

d) **Carl Maria Joseph Graf Czernin v.u. zu Chudenitz** * Prag 24.12.1886 = Lissa 2.7.1912 Wilhelmine Gräfin Kinsky v. Wchinitz u. Tettau * Chotzen 6.7.1891 dau. of Rudolf 9th Fürst Kinsky v. Wchinitz u. Tettau, and has issue:

XII

(a) **Emma Maria Josefa Anna Ignatia Gertrud Elisabeth Ludmilla Gräfin Czernin v.u. zu Chudenitz** * Turnau 17.11.1913

(b) **Hermann Maria Rudolf Josef Karl Johann Ferdinand Theodor Julius Graf Czernin v.u. zu Chudenitz** * Lissa 12.4.1915 X Kertsch, Crimea 28.2.1942

(c) **Marie-Elisabeth Josefa Emma Ignatia Caroline Thaddäa Gregor Clemens Heribert Gräfin Czernin v.u. zu Chudenitz** * Marschendorf 13.3.1919

(d) **Josef Maria Rudolf Ferdinand Johann Nepomuk Thaddäus Ignatius Benno Gervasius Graf Czernin v.u. zu Chudenitz** * Marschendorf 16.6.1920 = 's-Gravenhage 16.2.1957 Jkvr. Maria Theresia Beelaerts van Blokland * 's-Gravenhage 23.1.1931 dau. of Jhr. Henri Beelaerts van Blokland, and has issue:

XIII

1a. **Johanna Maria Emma Abrosia Justine Gräfin Czernin v.u. zu Chudenitz** * Linz a.d. D. 7.12.1957

XIII		2a.	**Wilhelmine Theresia Maria Henriette Martina Ignatia Gräfin Czernin v.u. zu Chudenitz** * Linz 30.1.1959
		3a.	**Stanislaus Carl Maria Josef Agapit Romanus Franziskus Graf Czernin v.u. zu Chudenitz** * Linz 6.8.1961
		4a.	**Philippine Gräfin Czernin v.u. zu Chudenitz** * Linz 3.4.1964
XII	(e)		**Stanislaus Johann v. Nepomuk Maria Josef Ignatius Thaddäus Wolfgang Graf Czernin v.u. zu Chudenitz** * Marschendorf 31.10.1921 ⚔ Woronesh 25.7.1942
	(f)		**Benedikta Theresia Maria Josefa Ignatia Thaddäa Sigismunda Monica Gräfin Czernin v.u. zu Chudenitz** * Marschendorf 2.5.1923 = Grafenstein 11.10.1950 Otto Graf v. Manzano * Graz 22.12.1907, and has issue:
XIII		1a.	**Carl Benedikt Maria Josef Graf v. Manzano** * Wien 26.10.1953
		2a.	**Johannes Baptist Wilhelm Benedikt Maria Josef Otto Wolfgang Graf v. Manzano** * Salzburg 24.5.1955
		3a.	**Maria Wilhelmine Benedikta Josefa Gräfin v. Manzano** * Salzburg 20.5.1956
		4a.	**Benedikta Emma Maria Josefa Elisabeth Caecilia Gräfin v. Manzano** * Salzburg 9.11.1959
		5a.	**Marianne Josefa Ottilie Gabriele Gräfin v. Manzano** * Salzburg 19.2.1964
XII	(g)		**Aloysia Philippine Maria Josefa Thaddäa Ludovica Emma Theresia Gräfin Czernin v.u. zu Chudenitz** * Marschendorf 23.8.1924 = Grafenstein 14.8.1946 August Lovrek * Liesing b. Wien 20.5.1911, and has issue:
XIII		1a.	**Maria Theresia Lovrek** * Schloss Rain 8.7.1947
		2a.	**Elisabeth Lovrek** * Klagenfurt 29.12.1948
		3a.	**Peter Lovrek** * Salzburg 27.12.1952
		4a.	**Paul Lovrek** * Salzburg 11.1.1954
		5a.	**Michael Lovrek** * Salzburg 22.2.1955
		6a.	**Andreas Lovrek** * Salzburg 6.3.1958
XII	(h)		**Franz Carl Maria Josef Graf Czernin v.u. zu Chudenitz** * Marschendorf 30.3.1927 = Maria-Saal 2.7.1954 **Isabella Gräfin v. Thun u. Hohenstein** * Gr-Kuntschitz 29.3.1931 dau. of Erwein Graf v. Thun u. Hohenstein and has issue:
XIII		1a.	**Erwein Carl Maria Joseph Benedikt Alexius Graf Czernin v.u. zu Chudenitz** * Wien 17.7.1955
		2a.	**Hemma Maria Josepha Theresia Benedikta Alexia Gräfin Czernin v.u. zu Chudenitz** * Wien 3.10.1957
		3a.	**Elisabeth Wilhelmine Maria Joseph Benedikta Theresia Gräfin Czernin v.u. zu Chudenitz** * Wien 5.10.1959
XII	(i)		**Anna Maria Josefa Ignatia Thaddäa Theresa Hedwig Gräfin Czernin v.u. zu Chudenitz** * Klagenfurt 16.10.1928
	(j)		**Carl Wilhelm Rudolf Eugen Maria Josef Ignatius Thaddäus Graf Czernin v.u. zu Chudenitz** * Klagenfurt 28.5.1930 = Maria-Saal 19.7.1962 Erna Weinzierl * Vellach 3.9.1932 dau. of Wenzel Weinzierl, and has issue:
XIII		1a.	**Hermann Christian Paul Erich Maria Graf Czernin v.u. zu Chudenitz** * Salzburg 1.1.1963

XIII · 2a. **Christiane Emma Angela Maria Gräfin Czernin v.u. zu Chudenitz**
* Salzburg 2.10.1964

XII · (k) **Vincenz Maria Josef Franziskus Ignatius Thaddäus Gervasius Aloysius Modestus Graf Czernin v.u. zu Chudenitz** * Klagenfurt 19.6.1932 = Schloss Karneid 14.9.1963 Veronika v. Miller * München 13.4.1938 dau. of Rudolf v. Miller, and has issue:

XIII · 1a. **Monika Gräfin Czernin v.u. zu Chudenitz** * Klagenfurt 18.2.1965

· 2a. **Sophia Gräfin Czernin v.u. zu Chudenitz** * Klagenfurt 22.4.1966

XI · e) **Ida Alfonsa Maria Josefine Gräfin Czernin v.u. zu Chudenitz** * Marschendorf 30.8.1888 + Wien 16.5.1965 = Wien 26.2.1916 Matthäus Graf Thunn v. Castel-Thunn * Arezzo 17.6.1882 + as Russian P.O.W., Breslau 23.11.1945, and had issue:

XII · (a) **Leopold Graf v. Thun u. Hohenstein u. Castel-Thunn** * Wien-Hietzing 31.12.1916 = Wien-Dobling 24.12.1942 Margarethe Fiedler * Wien 21.12.1914 dau. of Gottfried Fiedler, and has issue:

XIII · 1a. **Berthold Matthäus Graf v. Thun u. Hohenstein v. Castel-Thunn** * Wien 5.1.1944

· 2a. **Edith Gräfin v. Thun u. Hohenstein v. Castel-Thunn** * Wien 6.3.1947

XII · (b) **Rudolf Maria Josef Benediktus Markus Graf v. Thun u. Hohenstein v. Castel-Thunn** * Wien-Hietzing 25.4.1918 + b. Bursa, Turkey 24.7.1959 = Lindau i. Bodensee 7.5.1942 Elisabeth Oettle * Lindau i. Bodensee 21.8.1921 dau. of Franz Xaver Oettle, and has issue:

XIII · 1a. **Marie Luise Christiane Gräfin v. Thun u. Hohenstein v. Castel-Thunn** * Lindau 15.2.1943

· 2a. **Eleonore Maria-Giulia Josefa Gräfin v. Thun u. Hohenstein v. Castel-Thunn** * Lindau 8.7.1947

· 3a. **Christiane Elisabeth Beatrix Maria Josepha Gräfin v. Thun u. Hohenstein v. Castel-Thunn** * Krumbach 6.8.1956

XII · (c) **Karl Max Maria-Josef, Josef v. Casalanz Graf v. Thun u. Hohenstein v. Castel-Thunn** * Oyenhausen b. Wien 27.8.1920 = Wien 21.12.1946 Gisela Pisarovic * Wien 23.5.1925 dau. of Ferdinand Pisarovic s.p.

· (d) **August Felix Maria-Josef Petrus Coelestinus Graf v. Thun u. Hohenstein v. Castel-Thunn** * Oyenhausen b. Wien 19.5.1922 ✕ Zerbst 6.12.1942

· (e) **Oswald Maria Josef Leopold Graf v. Thun u. Hohenstein v. Castel-Thunn** * Oyenhausen 10.11.1923 ✕ Comacchio See 2.4.1945

· (f) **Maria-Giulia Alexia Emma Josefine Daria Gräfin v. Thun u. Hohenstein v. Castel-Thunn** * Hohenelbe 25.10.1925 = Heiligenkreuz 22.5.1954 Walter Kiss * Kitzbühel 8.7.1924, and has issue:

XIII · 1a. **Alexander Maximilian Matthäus Josef Maria Aloisius Stefan Kiss** * Wien 20.6.1955

· 2a. **Wilhelmine Maria Therese Ida Margarethe Kiss** * Wien 2.5.1960

XII	(g)	**Therese Ida Maria-Josefine Daria Gräfin v. Thun u. Hohenstein v. Castel-Thunn** * Hohenelbe 25.10.1925 = (1) Bockstein 2.8.1951 Franz Euringer * München 3.3.1912 — div.; = (2) Wien 23.9.1964 Michel Hollande * Douai (Nord) 31.12.1919 s.p.
	(h)	**Christiane Maria-Josefine Angela Graf v. Thun u. Hohenstein v. Castel-Thunn** * Baden b. Wien 31.5.1927 = Salzburg-Morzg 18.6.1948 Wolfgang Frhr. v. Dürfeld * Morg b. Salzburg 25.4.1917, and has issue:

XIII

1a. **Mathilde Marie Ida Christiane Freiin. v. Dürfeld** * Salzburg 11.7.1949

2a. **Rudolf Matheus August Josef Maria Frhr. v. Dürfeld** * Williams Lake, B.C. Canada 6.7.1950

3a. **Elisabeth Marcella Christiane Maria Freiin. v. Dürfeld** * Williams Lake 16.4.1952

4a. **Matheo-Josef Heinrich Wolfgang Gerhard Maria Frhr. v. Dürfeld** * Williams Lake 1.11.1954

5a. **Heinrich-Caius Johannes Josef Maria Frhr. v. Dürfeld** * Williams Lake 21.9.1956

6a. **Rupert-Jost Wolfgang Maria Frhr. v. Dürfeld** * Williams Lake 12.2.1959

7a. **Wolfgang-Benjamin Bryan Oswald Maria Frhr. v. Dürfeld** * Williams Lake 1.6.1960

XII   (i) **Wolfgang Eugen Lukas Maria-Josef Graf v. Thun u. Hohenstein v. Castel-Thunn** * Baden b. Wien 18.10.1929 = Volkermarkt 5.11.1950 Gerda Klein * Klagenfurt 18.6.1929 dau. of Otto Klein, and has issue:

XIII

1a. **Matthäus Leopold Otto Maria Petrus Graf v. Thun u. Hohenstein v. Castel-Thunn** * Wien 22.2.1963

XII   (j) **Maria Philippine Josefine Dorothea Gräfin v. Thun u. Hohenstein v. Castel-Thunn** * Wels 2.2.1932 = Basle 21.1.1957 Wolfgang Luitlen * Koblenz 25.8.1931, and has issue:

XIII

1a. **Wolfgang Andreas Hermann Matheo Luitlen** * 12.7.1957

2a. **Verena Antoinette Johanna Viktoria Luitlen** * 20.10.1959

XI   f) **Eugen Alfonsus Maria Josef Graf Czernin v.u. zu Chudenitz** * Prag 3.1.1892 + Wien 16.6.1955 = Frauenberg 23.10.1919 Josefine Prinzessin zu Schwarzenberg * Protiwin 3.10.1895 + Wien 14.10.1965 dau. of Johann 9th Fürst zu Schwarzenberg, and has issue:

XII   (a) **Karl Eugen Rudolf Johann v. Nepomuk Wolfgang Cosmas Damian Wenzel Michael Maria Josef Graf Czernin v.u. zu Chudenitz** * Gestütthof 27.9.1920 ✗ Le Chèsne-en-Ardennes 18.5.1940

(b) **Therese Emma Ida Aloysia Josefine Ludmilla Maria Pelagia Irene Gräfin Czernin v.u. zu Chudenitz** * Wittingau 19.10.1921 = Wien 10.4.1947 Emil Graf Spannocchi * Aigen b. Salzburg 1.9.1916, and has issue:

XIII

1a. **Eugen Maria Anton Karl Thomas Graf Spannocchi** * Salzburg 29.12.1952

2a. **Elisabeth Maria Gabriele Josephine Pia Gräfin Spannocchi** * Salzburg 19.1.1949

XIII   3a.   **Silvia Maria Josefine Therese Lea Gräfin Spannocchi** * Milano 22.3.1952

                         4a.   **Huberta Maria Magdalena Benedikta Gabriele Gräfin Spannocchi** * Wien 22.7.1955

                         5a.   **Paul Maria Rudolf Gabriel Friedrich Graf Spannocchi** * Wien 18.7.1960

XII   (c)   **Rudolf Gabriel Adolf Johann v. Nepomuk Karl Wolfgang Simeon Nikophorus Maria Josef Graf Czernin v.u. zu Chudenitz** * Prag 18.2.1924 = Wien 3.11.1955 Lucia Hauser * Wien 27.2.1929 and had issue:

XIII   1a.   **Karl Eugen Maria Josef Graf Czernin v.u. zu Chudenitz** * Wien 25.7.1956

                         2a.   **Caroline Eleonore Maria Gräfin Czernin v.u. zu Chudenitz** * Wien 25.10.1959

X   b.   **Philippine Theresia Gräfin Czernin v.u. zu Chudenitz** * Prag 8.1.1855 + Rosenberg a.d. Moldau 6.8.1937 = Prag 1.5.1878 Carl de Longueval Graf v. Buquoy * Wien 24.9.1854 + Wien 9.8.1911 and had issue:

XI   a)   **Sophie Therese Marie Philippine Aloysia de Longueval Gräfin v. Buquoy** * Gratzen 28.4.1879 + Laër 31.1.1945 = Gratzen 28.7.1897 Clemens Graf v. Westphalen zu Fürstenberg * Kulm 4.3.1864 + Laër 31.10.1938, and had issue:

XII   (a)   **Friedrich Carl Graf v. Westphalen zu Fürstenberg** * Laër 22.4.1898 = (1) Herdringen 20.6.1923 Maria Felicitas Freiin. v. Fürstenberg * Dahlhausen 27.9.1898 + Köln 24.12.1939 dau. of Engelbert Graf v. Fürstenberg-Herdringen; = (2) Burg Vischering 2.9.1943 Maria Zdenka Freiin. v. Twickel * München 8.12.1901 dau. of Ferdinand Frhr. v. Twickel, and has issue:

by 1st marriage:

XIII   1a.   **Rosa Maria Gräfin v. Westphalen zu Fürstenberg** * Fürstenberg 31.3.1924 = Fürstenberg 28.7.1948 Philipp Leopold Frhr. v. Boeselager * Heimerzheim b. Bonn 6.9.1917, and has issue:

XIV   1b.   **Albrecht Frhr. v. Boeselager** * Kreuzberg-Ahr 4.10.1949

                         2b.   **Georg Frhr. v. Boeselager** * Kreuzberg-Ahr 28.4.1951

                         3b.   **Maria Felicitas Freiin. v Boeselager** * Kreuzberg-Ahr 28.3.1953

                         4b.   **Monica Freiin. v. Boeselager** * Frankfurt-am-Main 22.10.1957

XIII   2a.   **Brigitta Pia Gräfin v. Westphalen zu Fürstenberg** * Fürstenberg 26.9.1925 = Fürstenberg 3.7.1956 **Wilderich Graf v. Spee-Mirbach** * Schleiden 1.11.1926 s.p.

                         3a.   **Clemens August Graf v. Westphalen zu Fürstenberg** * Fürstenberg 23.3.1927 = Haus Assen 8.9.1956 **Johanna Gräfin v. Galen** * Haus Assen 24.9.1936 dau. of Christoph Graf v. Galen, and has issue:

XIV   1b.   **Friedrich Wilhelm Antonius Alexis Maria Graf v. Westphalen zu Fürstenberg** * Münster i. W. 5.7.1957

                         2b.   **Johannes Bernhard Maria Elisabeth Peter Paul Graf v. Westphalen zu Fürstenberg** * Münster i. W. 18.11.1958

                         3b.   **Matthias Wilderich Maria Johannes Eudes Lüdgerus Graf v. Westphalen zu Fürstenberg** * Münster i. W. 19.8.1960

                         4b.   **Marie Sophie Gräfin v. Westphalen zu Fürstenberg** * Münster i. W. 26.6.1962

XIV		5b.	**Marie Elisabeth Gräfin v. Westphalen zu Fürstenberg** * Münster i. W. 7.8.1963
		6b.	**Ferdinand Clemens Graf v. Westphalen zu Fürstenberg** * Münster i. W. 4.3.1965

XIII   4a.   **Elisabeth Sophie Gräfin v. Westphalen zu Fürstenberg** * Fürstenberg 9.4.1930 = 28.7.1958 Valentin Graf v. Ballestrem * Plawniowitz 1.11.1928, and has issue:

XIV   1b.   **Carl Ludwig Graf v. Ballestrem** * Nürnberg 3.6.1959

                   2b.   **Monica Gräfin v. Ballestrem** * Nürnberg 12.9.1960

                   3b.   **Pia Gräfin v. Ballestrem** * Nürnberg 17.4.1963

                   4b.   **Nikolaus Graf v. Ballestrem** * Regensburg 2.5.1966

XIII   5a.   **Monika Josepha Graf v. Westphalen zu Fürstenberg** * Fürstenberg 11.5.1932 = Fürstenberg 12.5.1955 Maximilian Dietrich Graf v. Landsberg-Velen * Wocklum 17.12.1925, and has issue:

XIV   1b.   **Maria Barbara Consuelo Roswitha Pia Gräfin v. Landsberg-Velen** * Münster i. W. 26.8.1960

                   2b.   **Maria Rosalia Elisabeth Franziska Romana Gräfin v. Landsberg-Velen** * Münster i. W. 5.3.1962

                   3b.   **Maria Veronika Brigitta Bernadette Gräfin v. Landsberg-Velen** * Münster i. W. 11.1.1964

XII   (b)   **Carl Philipp Graf v. Westphalen zu Fürstenberg** * Rixdorf 29.7.1907 ✕ Duchowtschina, Russia 23.8.1941

IX   (3)   **Rudolf Graf Czernin v.u. zu Chudenitz** * 13.4.1821 + Teplitz 31.7.1873

          (4)   **Humbert Graf Czernin v.u. zu Chudenitz** * Wien 15.1.1827 + Graz 30.11.1910 = Wien 19.11.1864 Therese Gräfin v. Grünne * Saaz 1.8.1840 + Graz 17.3.1911 dau. of Karl Graf v. Grünne, and had issue:

X   a.   **Eugen Graf Czernin v.u. zu Chudenitz** * Graz 11.10.1865 + Graz 12.6.1926

          b.   **Caroline Gräfin Czernin v.u. zu Chudenitz** * 25.6.1868 + Wien 6.6.1889

          c.   **Rudolf Graf Czernin v.u. zu Chudenitz** * Graz 21.10.1874 + Graz 12.5.1949 = Graz 20.11.1901 Anna Freiin. Kopfinger v. Trebbienau * Prag 8.8.1880 + Graz 4.4.1947 dau. of Eugen Frhr. v. Kopfinger v. Trebbienau, and had issue:

XI   a)   **Therese Gräfin Czernin v.u. zu Chudenitz** * Graz 21.12.1902 = (1) Graz 15.1.1927 Bruno Frhr. v. Albori * Trieste 10.8.1891 ✕ during the War, ... − div.; = (2) Stockholm 4.12.1937 Martin Linderoth * 25.12.1901 − div.; = (3) 5.6.1966 Kurt Englich * 28.2.1907 s.p.

          b)   **Humbert Graf Czernin v.u. zu Chudenitz** * Graz 24.12.1903

          c)   **Maria Anna Gräfin Czernin v.u. zu Chudenitz** * Leipnitz 19.8.1906 = Graz 24.7.1938 Max Frhr. v. Rüling * Brixen 25.5.1906, s.p.

IX   (5)   **Maria Therese Gräfin Czernin v.u. zu Chudenitz** * Wien 27.3.1829 + Hadersdorf b. Wien 29.11.1916 = Wien 20.6.1857 Ladislas Graf Pejacsevich von Veröcze * Ofen 14.11.1828 + Wien 30.1.1916, and had issue:

X   a.   **Franziska Romana Maria Theresia Gräfin Pejacsevich v. Veröcze** * Petersburg, Böh. 5.6.1859 + Salzburg 14.2.1938 = Wien 26.4.1884 **Manfred Graf v. Clary u. Aldringen** * Wien 14.11.1828 + Hernau b. Salzburg 12.2.1928, and has issue see elsewhere

      b   **Karoline Maria Theresia Gräfin Pejacsevich v. Veröcze** * Wien 18.1.1861 + Bad Ischl 15.5.1927 = Wien 21.9.1891 **Rudolf Graf v. Bellegarde** * Gr-Herrlitz 28.2.1862 + Bad Ischl 30.10.1937, and had issue:

XI   a)   **Marie Rudolfine Karoline Dominika Emanuela Gräfin v. Bellegarde** * Přilep 4.8.1892 + Brixen 17.1.1946 = Bad Ischl 21.9.1920 **Georg Graf Marzani v. Stainhof u. Neuhaus** * Bochnia 31.5.1896 + Genoa 5.2.1954, and has issue:

XII   (a)   **Marie Eleonore Caroline Georgine Rudolfine Franziska de Paula Elisabeth Gräfin Marzani v. Stainhof u. Neuhaus** * Reiterndorf 28.7.1921 = Trieste 7.4.1951 **Ghiani Giacomello** * ... s.p.

      (b)   **Marie Therese Rudolfine Leocadie Caroline Ladislaja Laurentia Stefanie Gräfin Marzani v. Stainhof u. Neuhaus** * Innsbruck 3.8.1922 = Villa Lagarina 5.7.1958 **Luigi Graf Ceschi a Santa Croce** * Haasberg 1.10.1912 and has issue see elsewhere

      (c)   **Maximilian Guido Georg Rudolf Julius Josef Maria Michael Graf Marzani v. Stainhof u. Neuhaus** * Innsbruck 26.9.1923 = Athens 21.11.1957 **Annunziata Theodora Christomannos** * Athens 22.1.1910 dau. of Anton Christomannos s.p.

XI   b)   **Wilhelmine Rudolfine Maria Theresia Franziska Josepha Gräfin v. Bellegarde** * Prerau 12.1.1894

      c)   **Ladislaja Maria Karolina Rudolfina Theresia Franziska Xaveria Gräfin v. Bellegarde** * Prerau 24.11.1895 = Bad Ischl 20.6.1923 **Joseph Graf v. Walterskirchen** * Pressburg 10.5.1879 s.p.

X   c.   **Maria Anne Agathe Eugenie Gräfin Pejacsevich v. Veröcze** * 19.9.1863 + Öber-Dobling 25.7.1901

      d.   **Maria Theresia Aloysia Gräfin Pejacsevich v. Veröcze** * Petersburg i. Böh. 30.5.1867 + Baumkirchen 29.6.1953 = Wien 3.6.1885 **Julius Graf v. Seilern u. Aspang** * Wien 17.8.1858 + Wien 21.2.1932, and had issue:

XI   a)   **Ladislaus Peter Julius Karl Maria Joseph Johann v. Nepomuk Graf v. Seilern u. Aspang** * Setteldorf 8.3.1886 = Bistritz 16.8.1916 **Antoinette Freiin. v. Loudon** * Bistritz 12.8.1883 + Svatobořice 6.6.1946 dau. of Olivier Frhr. v. Loudon, and has issue:

XII   (a)   **Marie Henriette Therese Alice Antoinette Gräfin v. Seilern u. Aspang** * Wien 25.1.1918

      (b)   **Elisabeth Alice Franziska de Paula Ladislaja Maria Vincenzia Gräfin v. Seilern u. Aspang** * Millotitz 15.1.1920

      (c)   **Therese Maria Anna Johanna Nepomucena Gräfin v. Seilern u. Aspang** * Millotitz 4.8.1921 = Rieden b. Reutte 4.5.1948 **Carl Graf v. Clary u. Aldringen** * Rétfalu 15.10.1919 s.p.

      (d)   **Karl Maximilian Julius Olivier Johann Nepomuk Mauritius Maria Graf v. Seilern u. Aspang** * Millotitz 22.9.1923 = Schloss Schönach b. Straubing 21.5.1952 **Gabriele Freiin. v. Moreau** * Schönach 3.8.1925 dau. of Ferdinand Frhr. v. Moreau, and has issue:

XIII   1a.   **Ladislaus Graf v. Seilern u. Aspang** * 9.3.1960

      2a.   **Peter Graf v. Seilern u. Aspang** * 29.10.1962

XI   b)   **Maria Theresia Margarete Karoline Lidwina Gräfin v. Seilern u. Aspang** * Prilep
13.7.1895 = Millotitz 25.7.1920 Christoph Graf v. Galen * Baumkirchen 28.7.1885
and has issue:

XII   (a)   **Paul Mathias Thaddäus Maria Theodor Josef Franz v. Sales Graf v. Galen**
* München 20.7.1922 X (missing) Russia 15.4.1944

                      (b)   **Johannes v. Nepomuk Julius Maria Wilhelm Bernard Thaddäus Graf v. Galen**
* München 27.11.1923 X (missing) Russia 15.1.1945

                      (c)   **Karl Ladislaus Bernard Maria Thaddäus Graf v. Galen** * München 11.10.1927
= Brixen 3.8.1950 Theresia Schumacher * Innsbruck 5.1.1929 dau. of Joseph
Schumacher, and has issue:

XIII   1a.   **Marie Elisabeth Josefa Antonia Gräfin v. Galen** * Innsbruck 4.2.1951

IX   (6)   **Caroline Gräfin Czernin v.u. zu Chudenitz** * 31.12.1830 + 15.7.1852

VII   5.   **Marie Elisabeth Gräfin zu Schönborn-Heussenstamm** * 7.6.1759 + 18.2.1813

     6.   **Maria Franziska Sophie Charlotte Caroline Gräfin zu Schönborn-Heussenstamm** * Wien 23.8.1763 + Prag
20.10.1825 = Göllersdorf 23.9.1787 **Franz Joseph Graf v. Sternberg-Manderscheid** * Prag 4.9.1763 + Prag
8.4.1830, and had issue see elsewhere

     7.   **Wilhelm Eugen Joseph Graf zu Schönborn-Heussenstamm** * 23.10.1765 + 26.5.1770

8 The Descendants of Marie Franziska Prinzessin zu
   Salm-Salm 1731-1806 and Georg Adam 1st Fürst v.
   Starhemberg 1724-1807.

VI   **Franziska Prinzessin zu Salm-Salm** * 28.10.1731 + Wien 5.9.1806 = Antwerp 1.7.1761 Georg Adam 1st Fürst von Starhemberg * London 10.8.1724 + Wien 19.4.1807 and had issue:

VII   1.   **Ludwig Joseph Maximilian 2nd Fürst von Starhemberg** * Paris 12.3.1762 + Schloss Durnstein 2.9.1833
= Héverlé, près Louvain 24.9.1781 Marie Louise Princesse d'Arenberg * Bruxelles 29.1.1764 + Wien 1.3.1835
dau. of Charles 5th Duc d'Arenberg, and had issue:

VIII   1)   **Ernestine Marguerite Gräfin von Starhemberg** * Bruxelles 8.10.1782 + Château de Florennes, Prov. de Namur 31.8.1852 = Wien 1.10.1807 Frédéric Auguste 1st Duc de Beaufort-Spontin * Namur 14.9.1751 + Bruxelles 22.4.1817 and had issue:

IX   (1)   **Frédéric Louis Ladislaus 2nd Duc de Beaufort-Spontin** * Château de Freyr 13.8.1809 + Bruxelles 10.11.1834

               (2)   **Valérie Georgine Marie Louise Comtesse de Beaufort-Spontin** * Bruxelles 11.10.1811 + Bruxelles 8.1.1887 = (1) 17.10.1828 **Georg Graf von Starhemberg** * London 22.1.1802 + Igal, Hungary 24.3.1834, = (2) Schloss Seftenegg 20.10.1835 Théodore Comte van der Straten-Ponthoz * 18.5.1809 + Bruxelles 5.7.1889, and had issue by 1st marriage see elsewhere;

               by 2nd marriage:

X   a.   **Bertha Ernestine Valeriane Hyacinthe Maria Comtesse van der Straten-Ponthoz** * Bruxelles 13.6.1841 + Bruxelles 31.1.1869 = Bruxelles 4.5.1864 Albert Comte de Robiano * Rumillies 27.10.1836 + Rumillies 25.8.1904, and had issue:

XI   a)   **Maria Josefine Himelda Gabriele Comtesse de Robiano** * Rumillies 4.5.1865 + Alsbach 5.5.1936 = Rumillies 4.4.1891 Johann Ignatz Graf von Westerholt u. Gysenberg * Westerholt 7.4.1856 + Lüdinghausen 19.11.1927, and had issue:

XII   (a)   **Marie Sophie Gräfin von Westerholt u. Gysenberg** * Schellenstein 10.5.1892 + Bielefeld 30.8.1945

                         (b)   **Otto Albrecht Graf von Westerholt u. Gysenberg** * Schellenstein 27.11.1893 ⚔ Russia 6.7.1917

                         (c)   **Albrecht Karl Graf v. Westerholt u. Gysenberg** * Schellenstein 5.7.1895 + Schellenstein 27.1.1896

                         (d)   **Ferdinande Bertha Gräfin v. Westerholt u. Gysenberg** * Oelde 7.1.1897 + Alsbach 10.5.1945 = Lüdinghausen 9.6.1925 Hermann Frhr. von Lünick * Ostwig 3.5.1893, and had issue:

XIII   1a.   **Maria Pauline Anna Therese Mathilde Pia Freiin. von Lünick** * Bonn 14.10.1926 = Engelskirchen 7.1.1954 Hermann Joseph Graf von Spee * Borken 1.9.1918, and has issue:

XIV   1b.   **Anna Ignatia Pia Maria Huberta Gräfin von Spee** * Neuenhof b. Lüdenscheid 3.11.1954

                                    2b.   **Ignatius Hermann Joseph Maria Hubertus Graf von Spee** * Allagen 15.4.1956

                                    3b.   **Gertrud Adelheid Maria Huberta Josepha Gräfin von Spee** * Allagen 19.3.1958

                                    4b.   **Meinolf Maria Hubertus Graf von Spee** * Allagen 25.7.1959

                                    5b.   **Pius Josef Hubertus Maria Graf von Spee** * Allagen 23.5.1961

                                    6b.   **Hedwig Anna Maria Huberta Gräfin von Spee** * Allagen 1.1.1963

XIV	7b.	**Agnes Huberta Maria Leopoldine Gräfin von Spee** * Allagen 6.6.1964
	8b.	**Ida Maria Mathilde Huberta Gräfin von Spee** * Neheim-Hüsten 26.4.1966
	9b.	**Hildegard Maria Agnes Huberta Gräfin von Spee** * Neheim-Hüsten 26.4.1966
XIII	2a.	**Elisabeth Anna Pia Pauline Maria Theresia Freiin. v. Lünick** * Bonn 2.1.1928 = 7.8.1957 Josef Graf von Plettenberg * Berlin 14.6.1929, and has issue:
XIV	1b.	**Hermann Joseph August Pius Michael Thadeus Maria Graf von Plettenberg** * Hannoversch-Münden 20.3.1958 + Göttingen 23.3.1958
	2b.	**Bertha Mathilde Luitgard Ida Maria Gräfin von Plettenberg** * Bubenheim 28.8.1959
	3b.	**Maria Bernadette Isabella Ida Gräfin von Plettenberg** * Bubenheim 10.10.1960
	4b.	**Franz Hermann-Josef Ludger Maria Graf von Plettenberg** * Rübenach b. Koblenz 15.1.1962
	5b.	**Ludger Hunold Hermann-Josef Maria Graf von Plettenberg** * Rübenach b. Koblenz 13.2.1963
	6b.	**Ulrich Hermann-Josef Maria Graf von Plettenberg** * Birkenfeld 6.8.1964
	7b.	**Rudolf Johannes Michael Maria Graf von Plettenberg** * Birkenfeld 10.9.1965
XIII	3a.	**Ignatius Pius Karl Maria Joseph Hermann Frhr. von Lünick** * Bonn 9.2.1929 + Arnsberg 9.6.1943
	4a.	**Mathilde Maria Theresia Pauline Pia Hedwige Freiin. von Lünick** * Bonn 25.10.1930
	5a.	**Adelheid Mathilde Maria Elisabeth Pauline Freiin. von Lünick** * Bonn 30.12.1931 = 7.10.1964 Oswald Frhr. von Fürstenberg * Ehreshoven 7.1.1908, and has issue:
XIV	1b.	**Gregor Tassilo Guido Hermann Michael Frhr. von Fürstenberg** * Münster i. W. 2.11.1965
	2b.	**Angela Marik Luise Bertha Adelheid Freiin. von Fürstenberg** * Münster i. W. 25.10.1966
XIII	6a.	**Therese Pia Pauline Maria Franziska Ida Freiin. von Lünick** * Koblenz 15.4.1934 = 3.5.1959 Hunold Graf von Plettenberg * Lenhausen 21.3.1934, and had issue:
XIV	1b.	· **Rabold Christophorus Aloys Hermann-Josef Pius Widukind Heidenreich Ida Hubertus Mariano Graf von Plettenberg-Lenhausen** * Lenhausen 3.4.1960
	2b.	**Rudger Hermann Karl Pius Widukind Heidenreich Ida Hubertus Mariano Graf von Plettenberg-Lenhausen** * Lenhausen 2.5.1961
	3b.	**Gudila Sophia Bertha Hedwig Pia Ida Maria Huberta Gräfin von Plettenberg-Lenhausen** * Lenhausen 14.10.1962

XIV   4b.   **Irmtrud Mathilde Sophia Bertha Theresia Paula Ida Maria Gräfin von Plettenberg-Lenhausen** * Lenhausen 30.9.1963

          5b.   **Gundolf Gottfried Liborius Benedict Widukind Michael Ida Mariano Graf von Plettenberg-Lenhausen** * Lenhausen 28.10.1964

          6b.   **Odilo Elmar Pius Aloys Hermann-Josef Widukind Ida Mariano Graf von Plettenberg-Lenhausen** * Lenhausen 4.4.1966

XIII   7a.   **Gertrud Freiin. von Lünick** * Alsbach 18.9.1940 + Alsbach 3.11.1946

XII   (e)   **Paul Graf von Westerholt u. Gysenberg** * Oelde 19.6.1898, missing in Poland since January 1945 = Schloss Plawniowitz 14.9.1926 Maria Therese Gräfin v. Ballestrem * Ob-Gläserdorf 14.3.1902 dau. of Valentin Graf v. Ballestrem, and had issue:

XIII   1a.   **Marie Agnes Monika Mathilde Therese Gräfin v. Westerholt u. Gysenberg** * Düsseldorf 22.9.1928 = 14.11.1957 Siguard Frhr. v. Ow-Wachendorf * Tübingen 4.7.1925, and has issue:

XIV   1b.   **Marie-Veronika Lioba Therese Freiin. von Ow-Wachendorf** * Ebingen 2.9.1958

          2b.   **Rosina Monika Gabriele Freiin. von Ow-Wachendorf** * Ebingen 24.3.1960

          3b.   **Friedrich Hans Rudolf Frhr. von Ow-Wachendorf** * Ebingen 20.11.1962

XIII   2a.   **Friedrich Leopold Johannes Ignatius Aloysius Graf v. Westerholt u.Gysenberg** * Düsseldorf 28.5.1930 + Fulda 3.9.1949

          3a.   **Monika Gräfin v. Westerholt u. Gysenberg** * Föhren 17.1.1932 + Föhren 28.1.1932

          4a.   **Johannes Ignaz Petrus Siegfried Maria Graf v. Westerholt u. Gysenberg** * Föhren 4.2.1935

          5a.   **Lioba Magdalena Angela Elisabeth Maria Gräfin v. Westerholt u. Gysenberg** * Fulda 17.11.1938 = Herbstein 18.9.1961 **Ulrich Graf Schaffgotsch gen. Semperfrei v.u. zu Kynast u. Greiffenstein** * Mährisch-Budwitz 1.11.1932, and has issue see elsewhere

XII   (f)   **Emanuel Maria Joseph Graf v. Westerholt u. Gysenberg** * Lüdinghausen 19.4.1900 = Freckenhorst 10.12.1943 Marie Luise Gräfin v. Merveldt * Freckenhorst 24.6.1913 dau. of Friedrich Graf v. Merveldt, and has issue:

XIII   1a.   **Johannes Maria Ignaz Everard Graf v. Westerholt u. Gysenberg** * Freckenhorst 11.1.1948

          2a.   **Friedrich August Johannes Maria Paul Otto Joseph Graf v. Westerholt u. Gysenberg** * Freckenhorst 8.6.1949

          3a.   **Marie Elisabeth Therese Luise Tiatilid Gräfin v. Westerholt u. Gysenberg** * Freckenhorst 10.10.1950

          4a.   **Johannes Maria Joseph Sarto Graf v. Westerholt u. Gysenberg** * Freckenhorst 18.3.1952

XI   b)   **Charles Théodore Georges Joseph Maria Comte de Robiano** * Rumillies 9.8.1866 + Rumillies 2.9.1873

XI		c)	**Mathilde Victorine Marie Alphonsine Comtesse de Robiano** * Rumillies 6.2.1868 + Rumillies 19.9.1946 = Rumillies 15.4.1896 **Charles Prince de Croy** * Roeulx 14.5.1869 + Rumillies 29.5.1943, and had issue see elsewhere

X   b.   **Rudolph Georges Gabriel Charles Fortuné Comte van der Straten Ponthoz** * Bruxelles 7.10.1851 + Weinern 1.3.1926 = Wien 29.4.1876 Maria Markgräfin v. Pallavicini * Wien 12.6.1856 + Weinern 23.7.1919 dau. of Alfons Markgraf v. Pallavicini, and had issue:

XI   a)   **Rudolf Roman Thedor Alfons Maria Fortuné Graf v. der Straten Ponthoz** * Weinern 28.2.1877 + Wien 15.5.1961 = Prag 1.9.1915 Isabella Gräfin v. Almeida * Prag 15.11.1887 dau. of Paul Graf v. Almeida, and had issue:

XII   (a)   **Maria Margarethe Gräfin v. der Straten Ponthoz** * Wien 10.6.1916 = Wien 28.4.1936 Friedrich Graf Bossi-Fedrigotti * Wien 18.3.1906, and has issue:

XIII
- 1a. **Gianpaolo Graf Bossi-Fedrigotti** * Sacco 4.2.1943
- 2a. **Maurizio Graf Bossi-Fedrigotti** * Sacco 22.4.1946
- 3a. **Isabella Gräfin Bossi-Fedrigotti** * Rovereto 3.3.1948
- 4a. **Maria José Gräfin Bossi-Fedrigotti** * Sacco 19.6.1951

XII   (b)   **Josephine Marie Gräfin v. der Straten Ponthoz** * Wien 28.5.1921 = 5.7.1956 Christian Graf Kinsky v. Wchinitz u. Tettau * Neutitschein 14.2.1924, and has issue:

XIII
- 1a. **Henriette Gräfin Kinsky v. Wchinitz u. Tettau** * Wien 13.1.1955
- 2a. **Peter Friedrich Graf Kinsky v. Wchinitz u. Tettau** * Wien 12.2.1961
- 3a. **Johannes Leopold Graf Kinsky v. Wchinitz u. Tettau** * Wien 10.7.1963

XII   (c)   **Sophie Rudolfine Maria Fortunata Gabriella Gräfin v. der Straten-Ponthoz** * Wien 15.4.1926 = Wien 1.8.1953 Gerhard Scholten * Trautenau, Böh. 16.8.1923 and has issue:

XIII
- 1a. **Rudolf Gerhard Hubertus Maria Scholten** * Wien 3.11.1955
- 2a. **Maria Isabella Margarete Sophie Scholten** * Wien 13.4.1960

XI   b)   **Valerie Maria Chrysostoma Gräfin v. der Straten-Ponthoz** * Wien 27.1.1879 + 22.4.1962

    c)   **Alexander Johann Maria Graf v. der Straten-Ponthoz** * Weinern 29.8.1882 + Wien 23.2.1949 = Wien 10.10.1907 Eleonore Gräfin v. Sternberg * Phořelic 8.1.1873 + Wien 3.10.1960 dau. of Leopold Graf v. Sternberg s.p.

    d)   **Friedrich Alfred Graf v. der Straten-Ponthoz** * Weinern 23.6.1886 + Leoben 24.11.1959 = Leoben 23.4.1920 Friederike v. Gasteiger zu Rabenstein u. Kobach * Leoben 30.3.1886 dau. of Friedrich Ernst v. Gasteiger zu Rabenstein u. Kobach, and had issue:

XII   (a)   **Karl Rudolf Fortuné Alexander Friedrich Graf v. der Straten-Ponthoz** * Leoben 23.2.1922 = Milano 4.6.1952 Donna Valerie, Baronessa Caccia Dominioni * Milano 26.8.1925 dau. of Don Federico Conte Caccia Dominioni, and has issue:

XIII
- 1a. **Elisabeth Maria Antonia Ippolita Agnes Valerie Gräfin v. der Straten-Ponthoz** * Milano 24.10.1953
- 2a. **Christiane Antonia Josefine Maria Gräfin v. der Straten-Ponthoz** * Milano 16.2.1955

264

XI   e)   **Gabrielle Marie Leopoldine Gräfin v. der Straten-Ponthoz** * Weinern 2.7.1896 = Wien 10.4.1920 Robert Frhr. Klinger von Klingerstorff * Neustadt 1.3.1884 s.p.

IX   (3)   **Marie Hermengilde Comtesse de Beaufort-Spontin** * Bruxelles 28.8.1813 + Vichy 24.9.1880 = Bruxelles 5.7.1836 Camille Mouchet de Battefort Comte de Laubespin * Clermont-Ferrard 10.5.1812 + Château de Freyr-sur-Meuse 3.3.1876, and had issue:

X   a.   **Camille Marie Josèphe Mouchet de Battefort de Laubespin** * Paris 11.6.1837 + Paris July 1925 = Bruxelles 27.3.1856 Wladimir Graf von Daun * Vettau 11.7.1812 * Wien 18.3.1896 s.p.

         b.   **Ernestine Mouchet de Battefort de Laubespin** * 1839 + 1840

         c.   **Georgine Marie Joséphine Mouchet de Battefort de Laubespin** * Paris 7.10.1840 + Château de Freyr-sur-Meuse 21.4.1871 = 10.11.1859 Gaspard Comte de Contades * Angers 15.9.1827 + Château de Sablé 8.10.1882, and has issue:

XI   a)   **Georges de Contades** * Paris 7.8.1860 + Paris 1862

         b)   **Marie Adèle Hermengilde de Contades** * Château de Dampierre 6.11.1861 + 1.9.1953 = Cannes 12.1.1882 Comte Arthur de Vogüé * 6.11.1858 + Paris 5.12.1924, and had issue:

XII   (a)   **Comte Charles de Vogüé** * Paris 17.12.1882 + Paris 5.12.1914 = 4.7.1906 Diane Pastré * 1.1.1888 dau. of Comte Andre Pastré, and has issue:

XIII   1a.   **Comte Charles-Louis de Vogüé** * Paris 10.1.1914 X 14.5.1940 = Château d'Ormesson 30.7.1934 Anne Lefevre d'Ormesson * Paris 30.7.1915 dau. of Comte Wladimir Lefevre d'Ormesson s.p.

XII   (b)   **Comte Georges de Vogüé** * Paris 24.10.1898 = (1) Paris 16.11.1920 Mathilde Pillet-Will * Paris 16.12.1900 + 1.3.1927 dau. of Comte Frédéric Pillet-Will, = (2) 20.10.1928 Simone Quemin * 24.3.1896 dau. of Jules Quemin, and has issue:

             by 2nd marriage:

XIII   1a.   **Elisabeth de Vogüé** * Paris 28.8.1929 = 25.6.1952 Baron Bertrand de Ladoucette * Rouxmesnil (S.M.) 14.7.1919, and has issue:

XIV   1b.   **Claire de Ladoucette** * Buenos Aires 1.6.1955

                   2b.   **Marie de Ladoucette** * Buenos Aires 24.7.1960

XI   c)   **Gaston Camille Marie Joseph Comte de Contades** * Paris 25.2.1866 + Cannes 4.2.1953 = Château de Blet 25.10.1899 Marie de Nicolay * Paris 22.11.1873 + Paris 9.2.1944 dau. of Aymard Comte de Nicolay, and has issue:

XII   (a)   **André Marie Artur Aymard Comte de Contades** * Paris 21.10.1900 + Paris 18.5.1958 = 15.5.1926 Daisy Thome * Sonchamp près Rambouillet 6.7.1907 dau. of André Thome, and has issue:

XIII   1a.   **Gilda de Contades** * Paris 7.4.1935 = Lausanne 18.7.1959 Pierre Chamorel * Lausanne 25.2.1920, and has issue:

XIV   1b.   **Arnaud Chamorel** * Genève 6.10.1960

                   2b.   **Gilone Chamorel** * Genève 25.1.1963

XIV			3b. **Diane Chamorel** * Genève 10.9.1965

XIII   2a.   **Jacqueline de Contades** * Paris 17.4.1940 = La Celle-les-Bordes 31.5.1958 François de Cossé Marquis de Brissac * Le Creusot 19.2.1929, and has issue:

XIV   1b.   **Agnes de Cossé-Brissac** * Paris 5.3.1960

      2b.   **Charles-André de Cossé-Brissac** * Paris 3.11.1962

      3b.   **Angélique de Cossé-Brissac** * Paris 6.9.1965

XII   (b)   **Aymardine de Contades** * Paris 7.2.1902 = Paris 9.2.1926 Roland Comte de Maillé * Tours 15.11.1898 + 6.4.1953, and has issue:

XIII   1a.   **Comte Artus Marie Gilles de Maillé** * Paris 29.11.1926 = Paris 22.3.1952 Nadine de Metz * 8.6.1929 dau. of Victor de Metz, and has issue:

XIV   1b.   **Carmen de Maillé** * Doula (Cameroons) 27.1.1953

      2b.   **Charles Armand de Maillé** * Bourges (Cher) 1.6.1955

      3b.   **Natalie de Maillé** * Bourges (Cher) 22.8.1959

XIII   2a.   **Marie Osmonde Consuelo de Maillé** * Paris 22.5.1928 = 3.6.1953 Claude Hersent * 27.11.1929 and had issue:

XIV   1b.   **Diane Hersent** * Paris 26.7.1954

      2b.   **Isabelle Hersent** * Paris 25.8.1955

      3b.   **Laurence Hersent** * Paris 27.3.1957

      4b.   **Marc Hersent** * Paris 12.5.1961

      5b.   **Antoine Hersent** * Paris 23.7.1965

X   d.   **Marie Joséphine Mouchet de Battefort de Laubespin** * Paris 8.4.1842 + Château d'Evry 31.3.1882 = Paris 26.1.1864 Georges Brunet Marquis d'Evry * Paris 28.5.1834 + Evry-les-Châteaux 30.5.1922, and has issue:

XI   a)   **Gilles Marie Raymonde Paul Brunet Marquis d'Evry** * Evry-les-Châteaux 8.12.1864 + Evry-les-Châteaux 4.9.1933 = Evry-les-Châteaux 8.2.1908 **Georgine de Fumel** * Château de Lamarque 14.9.1873 + Château de Lamarque 5.7.1963 dau. of Jacques Comte de Fumel, and had issue:

XII   (a)   **Gilles Henri Marie Georges Brunet Marquis d'Evry** * Evry-les-Châteaux 23.3.1909 + Lausanne 7.3.1940

    (b)   **Marie Louise Humberte Brunet d'Evry** * Paris 9.4.1918 = (1) 24.5.1939 Hervé Comte de Fleuriau de Morville * January 1909 – div. = (2) 1.7.1942 Roger Gromand * Paris 13.10.1905, and has issue:

by 1st marriage:

XIII   1a.   **Comte Eric de Fleuriau** * Lamarque 6.2.1940

by 2nd marriage:

      2a.   **Marie Béatrice Gromand** * Alger 11.4.1943

      3a.   **Pierre-Gilles Gromand** * Neuilly-sur-Seine 13.12.1948

XI · b) **Ernestine Camille Henriette Brunet d'Evry** * Evry-les-Châteaux 3.3.1871 + Paris
22.11.1921 = Paris 10.10.1891 Simon Comte de Wignacourt * Bruxelles 9.12.1852
+ Paris 17.5.1931, and had issue:

XII (a) **Comte Alof Georges Marie Ghislain de Wignacourt** * Paris 9.8.1892 + Cambo
(B.P.) 12.8.1920

(b) **Simone Marie Camille Ghislaine de Wignacourt** * Paris 22.4.1896 + Paris
25.4.1919

X e. **Marie Joseph Alfred Mouchet de Battefort Comte de Laubespin** * Paris 21.12.1844 + Paris
26.7.1920 = Bruxelles 10.2.1872 Marie d'Ennetières Comtesse d'Hulst * La Hulpe 2.2.1849
+ 2.10.1935 dau. of Victor Marquis d'Ennetières, and had issue:

XI a) **Camille Marie Joseph Mouchet de Battefort Comte de Laubespin** * Bruxelles 15.12.1872
+ Paris 14.1.1939 = Paris 12.7.1897 Simone de Marescot * St.-Leger-sur-Sarthe
26.1.1876 dau. of Georges Marquis de Marescot, and had issue:

XII (a) **Albert Antoine Lionel Victor Mouchet de Battefort Comte de Laubespin** * Paris
10.5.1899 = 16.7.1931 Alix de Kergorlay * Paris 14.12.1908 dau. of Thibaut
Comte de Kergorlay s.p.

(b) **Bernard Lionel Marie Georges Mouchet de Battefort Comte de Laubespin** * Paris
1.1.1901 = 24.4.1936 **Alix Dadvisard** * Paris 2.7.1909 dau. of Louis Marquis
Dadvisard, and has issue:

XIII 1a. **Anne Mouchet de Battefort de Laubespin** * Boulogne-Billancourt 28.7.1937
= 6.6.1959 **François de Rochechouart 14th Duc de Mortemart** * Entrains-
sur-Nohain 24.3.1930, and has issue see elsewhere

X f. **Hildegard Marie Joséphine Mouchet de Battefort de Laubespin** * Paris 17.5.1847 + Château
de Lamarque 14.4.1880 = Paris 13.6.1872 Jacques Comte de Fumel * Bordeaux 28.12.1831
+ Château de Lamarque 4.7.1901, and has issue:

XI a) **Marie Elisabeth Georgine de Fumel** * Château de Lamarque 14.9.1873 + Château de
Lamarque 5.7.1963 = Evry-les-Châteaux 8.2.1908 **Paul Brunet Marquis d'Evry** * Evry-les-
Châteaux 9.12.1864 + Evry-les-Châteaux 4.9.1933, and had issue, see elsewhere

X g. **Théodule Marie Joseph François Mouchet de Battefort Comte de Laubespin** * Bruxelles
7.9.1848 + Paris 20.11.1935 = Paris 19.7.1876 Louise d'Avesgo de Coulonges * Coulonges
11.8.1855 + Château de Freyr-sur-Meuse 25.1.1952 dau. of Ludovic d'Avesgo de Coulonges,
and has issue:

XI a) **Humbert Louis Camille Marie Joseph Mouchet de Battefort Comte de Laubespin** * Paris
16.5.1881 + Paris 9.6.1928 = Paris 21.4.1913 Odette Lagarde * Paris 31.7.1889 dau. of
Eugène Lagarde, and had issue:

XII (a) **Marie Ghislaine Jeanne Théodule Mouchet de Battefort de Laubespin** * Paris
18.1.1914 + 13.5.1917

(b) **Hermengilde Louise Mouchet de Battefort de Laubespin** * Paris 8.6.1919
= Château de Freyr 21.4.1941 François Baron Bonaert * Coutrai 7.9.1914, and
has issue:

XIII 1a. **Axele Philippe Marie Ghislain Baron Bonaert** * Etterbeek 24.1.1942

2a. **Baudry François Odette Marie Ghislain Baron Bonaert** * Etterbeek 20.4.1945

XIII			3a. **Aude Marie Hélène Ghislaine Baronne Bonaert** * Etterbeek 6.3.1951

XI   b)   **Léonie Mouchet de Battefort de Laubespin** * Château de Coulonges 1884, died young

           c)   **Marie Josèphe Françoise Charlotte Mouchet de Battefort de Laubespin** * Paris 13.4.1889 = Paris 19.6.1912 Comte Armand de Kergorlay * Paris 3.10.1883 + Paris 11.11.1949, and has issue:

XII   (a)   **Louise Pierette Marie Josèphe Ghislaine de Kergorlay** * Paris 6.9.1913 = Paris 30.1.1935 Comte René Chandon Moët * 13.12.1907 s.p.

           (b)   **Joëlle Thérèse Théodoline Renee Marie Josèphe Ghislaine de Kergorlay** * Biarritz 22.9.1918 = Paris 9.10.1945 François Millon de La Verteville * Tours 3.8.1917, and has issue:

XIII		1a.	**Danielle Mireille Millon de La Verteville** * Paris 13.7.1946
		2a.	**Jean-Eric Dominque Millon de La Verteville** * Paris 30.11.1947
		3a.	**Christian Armand Marie Millon de La Verteville** * Paris 3.12.1949
		4a.	**Elisabeth Josèphe Millon de La Verteville** * Paris 25.7.1952

XII   (c)   **Floriane Bernardine Camille Marie Josèphe Ghislaine de Kergorlay** * Paris 3.3.1920 = Paris 12.7.1950 Comte Gilles de Couëssin du Boisriou * St-Julien (C.-du-N.) 15.8.1921, and has issue:

XIII		1a.	**Michel Couëssin du Boisriou** * Paris 6.5.1951 + Paris 7.7.1951
		2a.	**Hubert de Couëssin du Boisriou** * Paris 20.8.1952
		3a.	**Charles de Couëssin du Boisriou** * Paris 1.12.1953
		4a.	**Marie Christine de Couëssin du Boisriou** * Paris 13.9.1955
		5a.	**Florence de Couëssin du Boisriou** * Paris 1.11.1956
		6a.	**Bertrand de Couëssin du Boisriou** * 5.7.1962

XII   (d)   **Christine Marguerite Humberte Marie Josèphe Ghislaine de Kergorlay** * Paris 7.7.1924 = Paris 11.10.1949 Guy Comte Artur de La Villarmois * 12.2.1923, and has issue:

XIII		1a.	**Henri Artur de La Villarmois** * Paris 9.11.1950
		2a.	**Jean Artur de La Villarmois** * Paris 1.5.1953
		3a.	**Bruno Artur de La Villarmois** * Paris 10.5.1955
		4a.	**Marie Gabrielle Artur de La Villarmois** * 29.7.1961

IX   (4)   **Alfred Charles August 3rd Duc de Beaufort-Spontin** * Bruxelles 16.6.1816 + Bruxelles 20.7.1888 = (1) Paris 26.7.1839 Pauline de Forbin-Janson * 22.7.1817 + Pau 29.5.1846 dau. of Charles Marquis de Forbin-Janson, = (2) Regensberg 27.7.1852 Therese Prinzessin v. Thurn u. Taxis * 31.8.1830 + 10.9.1883 dau. of Maximilian Karl 6th Fürst v. Thurn u. Taxis, and had issue:

by 1st marriage:

X   a.   **Frédéric Ernest Palamede Marie Maur Comte de Beaufort-Spontin** * Bruxelles 29.9.1840 + Wien 14.3.1842

         b.   **Frédéric Georges Marie Antoine Michel 4th Duc de Beaufort-Spontin** * Bruxelles 8.6.1843 + Petschau 26.12.1916 = Paris 2.6.1875 **Marie Melanie Princesse de Ligne** * Paris 25.11.1855 + Roma 2.4.1931 dau. of Henri Prince de Ligne, and has issue:

XI a) **Pauline Marie Marguerite Gräfin v. Beaufort-Spontin** * Paris 8.11.1876 + Langenselbold 11.12.1955 = Petschau 1.12.1900 **Alfons Prinz v. Isenburg-Birstein** * Offenbach-am-Main 29.2.1872 + Langenselbold 22.4.1951 and had issue, see elsewhere

b) **Henrich Marie Eugen 5th Herzog v. Beaufort-Spontin** * Paris 11.3.1880 + Gallmansegg 25.4.1966 = Wien 3.2.1910 **Marie Gräfin von Silva-Tarouca** * Türmitz 26.6.1886 + Petschau 12.7.1945 dau. of Ernst Graf v. Silva-Tarouca, and had issue:

XII (a) **Marie Elisabeth Melanie Ernestine Gräfin v. Beaufort-Spontin** * Wien 15.11.1911 = Petschau 7.10.1931 **Alexis Prinz von Croy** * Slabetz 24.2.1910, and has issue, see elsewhere

(b) **Friedrich Joseph Karl Maria Dominik 6th Herzog v. Beaufort-Spontin** * Smichow, Böh. 9.4.1916 = Berlin 19.8.1943 Christiane Steinheuer * Hanau 10.10.1920 dau. of Richard Steinheuer, and has issue:

XIII 1a. **Friedrich Christian Albert Graf v. Beaufort-Spontin** * Petschau 5.12.1944

2a. **Christian Friedrich Walter Graf v. Beaufort-Spontin** * Graz 13.10.1947

XII (c) **Carl Albrecht Amadeo Maria Emanuel Franz Graf v. Beaufort-Spontin** * Petschau 3.12.1918 ✗ in Russia 14.1.1942

(d) **Marie Guillemete Eleonore Gräfin v. Beaufort-Spontin** * Petschau 21.10.1924

XI c) **Marie Therese Ernestine Gräfin v. Beaufort-Spontin** * Château de Breuilpont (Eure) 6.8.1885 + Křimic 22.2.1942 = Petschau, Böh. 11.5.1905 Jaroslav 11th Fürst v. Lobkowicz * Konopischt, Böh. 26.3.1877 + Křimic, Böh. 24.10.1953, and had issue:

XII (a) **Marie Kunigunde Melanie Margarete Franziska Friederike Antonia Prinzessin v. Lobkowicz** * Křimic 11.9.1906 = Křimic 13.6.1932 Charles Comte de Limburg-Stirum * Huldenberg 15.9.1906, and has issue:

XIV 1a. **Marie Charlotte Jeanne Louise Françoise Xavière Melanie Gaëtane Thérèse de l'E. Josèphe Ghislaine Antonia Comtesse de Limburg-Stirum** * Huldenberg 6.5.1935 = Bois St—Jean Samree 8.8.1956 Gobert Léopold Comte d'Aspremont Lynden * Etterbeek 5.8.1931, and has issue:

XIV 1b. **Jean Charles Marie Gobert Comte d'Aspremont Lynden** * Uccle 5.5.1957

2b. **Elisabeth Marie Charlotte Comtesse d'Aspremont Lynden** * Uccle 21.6.1958

3b. **Philippe Léopold Marie Comte d'Aspremont Lynden** * Dar-es-Salam 1.8.1959

4b. **Geoffroy Jacques Eugène Comte d'Aspremont Lynden** * Dar-es-Salam 2.11.1962

5b. **Sophie Clotilde Marie Comtesse d'Aspremont Lynden** * Uccle 8.6.1964

XIII 2a. **Gabrielle Marie Eléonore Françoise Xavière Gaëtane Josèphe Ghislaine Comtesse de Limburg-Stirum** * Huldenberg 22.8.1936 = Bois St-Jean Samrée 12.8.1958 Didier Comte Cornet d'Elzius du Chenoy * Bruxelles 5.8.1929, and has issue:

XIV 1b. **Etienne Charles François Xavier Comte Cornet d'Elzius du Chenoy** * Uccle 9.7.1959

XIV		2b.	**François Xavier Frédéric Comte Cornet d'Elzius du Chenoy** * Uccle 29.6.1961
		3b.	**Béatrice Comtesse Cornet d'Elzius du Chenoy** * Uccle 4.10.1965

XIII   3a.   **Bernard Adolphe Evrard Marie Frédéric Louis François Xavier Gaëtan Joseph Ghislain Comte de Limburg-Stirum** * Huldenberg 12.8.1938

         4a.   **Emmanuel Thierry Jean Bosco François Xavier Marie Joseph Gaëtan Mathieu Ghislain Comte de Limburg-Stirum** * Huldenberg 19.9.1940

         5a.   **Sibylle Marie Philippine Béatrice Françoise Xavière Joséphine Gaëtane Ghislaine Comtesse de Limburg-Stirum** * Bois St-Jean Samrée 27.5.1942 = Bruxelles 27.8.1964 Pietro del Vaglio Rosati * Napoli 1.8.1934, and has issue:

XIV   1b.   **Christiana del Vaglio Rosati** * Uccle 22.5.1966

XIII   6a.   **Jacqueline Marie Elisabeth Jeanne Françoise Xavière Gaëtane Ignacia Ghislaine Comtesse de Limburg-Stirum** * Bois St-Jean Samrée 31.7.1943

         7a.   **Jean Charles Evrard Marie Raymond Xavier Gaëtan Ghislain Comte de Limburg-Stirum** * Etterbeek 20.10.1946

         8a.   **Louise Marie Mélanie Renée Françoise Xavière Joséphine Gaëtane Ghislaine Comtesse de Limburg-Stirum** * Louvain 7.1.1949

XII   (b)   **Friedrich Franz Jaroslav Aloys Heinrich Marie Andreas 12th Fürst v. Lobkowicz** * Křimic 28.11.1907 + Pacy-sur-Eure 25.12.1954

         (c)   **Jaroslav Claude Friedrich Aloys 13th Fürst v. Lobkowicz** * Zameček-Pilsen 18.6.1910 = Prag 11.7.1940 Gabriele Gräfin Korff gen. Schmising-Kersenbrock * Klattau, Boh. 29.11.1917 dau. of Klemens Graf Korff gen. Schmising-Kersenbrock, and has issue:

XIII   1a.   **Maria Lapidata Polyxena Prinzessin v. Lobkowicz** * Prag 28.4.1941 = Vejprnice b. Pilsen 22.4.1961 Theobold Graf Czernin v.u. zu Chudenitz * Prag 7.7.1936 and has issue:

XIV   1b.   **Thomas Aquinus Maria Rudolf Theobold Kazimir Polyxenos Graf Czernin v.u. zu Chudenitz** * Pilsen 4.3.1962

                     2b.   **Therese v. Kinde Jesu Marie Gabrielle Friederike Jaroslav Rudolf Johanna Pius Stephania Franziska Polyxena Theobold Gräfin Czernin v.u. zu Chudenitz** * Pilsen 1.12.1964

XIII   2a.   **Jaroslav Franz Erbprinz v. Lobkowicz** * Pilsen 16.8.1942

         3a.   **Marie Leopoldine Prinzessin v. Lobkowicz** * Pilsen 8.12.1943 = Vejprnice 4.7.1964 Bosco Graf von Sternberg * Prag 25.11.1936

         4a.   **Franz Karl Prinz v. Lobkowicz** * Pilsen 5.1.1948

         5a.   **Zdenko Adalbert Prinz v. Lobkowicz** * Pilsen 8.4.1954

XII   (d)   **Beatrice Marie Melanie Henriette Josepha Prinzessin v. Lobkowicz** * Zameček-Pilsen 20.1.1909

         (e)   **Margareta Marie Desideria Aloisia Josefa Johanna Prinzessin v. Lobkowicz** * Zameček-Pilsen 4.7.1913 = Křimic 16.5.1934 Zdenko Frhr. von Hoenning O'Carroll * Sünching 6.8.1906, and has issue:

XIII   1a.   **Marie Melanie Johanna v. Nepomucek Gabrielle Jaroslawa Pia Georgine**
Desiderie Theresia vom Kinde Jesu Karl Freiin. v. Hoenning O'Carroll
* Sünching 4.11.1935

         2a.   **Agnes Gabrielle Marie Jaroslawa Johanna v. Nepomucek Pia Georgine**
Desideria Theresia vom Kinde Jesu Kordula Freiin. von Hoenning O'Carroll
* Sünching 22.10.1936 = Sünching 20.7.1959 Serafim Miloradovich
* 24.8.1929, and has issue:

XIV   1b.   **Alexandra Maria Margit Olga Miloradovich** * Sünching 7.7.1960

              2b.   **Margarita Marina Maria Olga Miloradovich** * München 9.2.1962

              3b.   **Tatiana Maria Margit Olga Miloradovich** * München 7.10.1963

XIII   3a.   **Maria Kunigunde Jaroslawa Johanna v. Nepomucek Pia Desideria Theresia v.**
Kinde Jesu Josef v. Kopertino Freiin von Hoenning O'Carroll * Sünching
18.9.1937 = Sünching 17.7.1965 Jan Frhr. Raitz v. Frentz * Bonn
28.8.1928, and has issue:

XIV   1b.   **Christian Frhr. Raitz v. Frentz** * Pfalzel b. Trier 18.5.1966

XIII   4a.   **Sophie Gabrielle Stephanie Jaroslawa Johanna v. Nepomucek Pia Georgine**
Desideria Theresia v. Kinde Jesu Sidonia Freiin. v. Hoenning O'Carroll
* Sünching 24.8.1938 = 12.4.1961 Johannes Graf v. Walderdorff
* Salzburg 28.3.1936, and has issue:

XIV   1b.   **Stefan Graf v. Walderdorff** * 19.2.1963

XIII   5a.   **Johann v. Nepomucek Carl Erkinger Berthold Maria Jaroslaw Georg Pius**
Johann Don Bosco Konrad v. P. Ailred Frhr. v. Hoenning O'Carroll
* Sünching 12.1.1940 = München 23.7.1966 Katalin Gräfin Zichy zu Zich u.
Vásonykeö * Rötjök-Muzzaj 3.9.1946 dau. of Hubert Graf Zichy zu Zich u.
Vásonykeö

         6a.   **Christian Ehrenfried Daniel Maria Pius Konrad v. P. Johannes Don Bosco**
Sebastian Maurus Frhr. v. Hoenning O'Carroll * Sünching 15.1.1941
= Gut Holthausen 1.8.1964 Ilona Freiin. v. Fürstenberg * Potsdam-
Bablesberg 14.6.1941 dau. of Leopold Frhr. v. Fürstenberg, and has issue:

XIV   1b.   **Margit Maria Theresia Ilona Paula Gabrielle Elisabeth Freiin. v.**
Hoenning O'Carroll * Murnau 15.6.1965

XIII   7a.   **Maria Eleonore Pia Theresia Gabriella Bonaventura Freiin. v. Hoenning**
O'Carroll * Sünching 14.7.1942

         8a.   **Zdenko Leopold Maria Emil Petrus Pius Johannes Don Bosco Amatus Frhr. v.**
Hoenning O'Carroll * Sünching 13.9.1943

         9a.   **Maria Theresia Gabrielle Elisabeth Radegundis Desideria Pia Amata Freiin. v.**
Hoenning O'Carroll * Sünching 13.9.1943

      10a.   **Zdenko Leopold Maria Frhr. v. Hoenning O'Carroll** * Sünching 14.1.1945

      11a.   **Albert Maria Frhr. v. Hoenning O'Carroll** * & + Sünching 13.2.1946

XII   (f)   **Eleonore Klementine Epiphania Pia Johanna Kunigunde Melanie Marie Prinzessin v.**
Lobkowicz * Křimic 6.1.1916 = Křimic 20.5.1943 Franz Xaver Graf Basselet de la
Rosée * Neuburg 6.10.1906, and has issue:

XIII	1a.	**Maria Franziska Berta Antonia Jakoba Gräfin Basselet de la Rosée** * Landshut 12.5.1944
	2a.	**Monika Ludovika Ida Polyxena Antonie Marguerite Maria Franziska Gräfin Basselet de la Rosée** * Isareck 20.7.1945
	3a.	**Isabella Gabriele Sophie Eleonore Johanna Matilde Elisabeth Antonie Maria Franziska Gräfin Basselet de la Rosée** * Isareck 30.1.1947
	4a.	**Gabrielle Agnes Eleonore Aloisia Theodora Josepha Antonia Maria Franziska Gräfin Basselet de la Rosée** * Isareck 11.3.1949
	5a.	**Felix v. Cantalice Theodor Jaroslav Rudolf Pius Antonius Kastulus Maria Franziska Graf Basselet de la Rosée** * Isareck 29.5.1951
	6a.	**Franz-Anton Xaver Alexis Korbinian Konrad v. Paryham Maria Franziska Graf Basselet de la Rosée** * Isareck 25.6.1953
XII	(g)	**Gabrielle Therese Karoline Friederike Pia Johanna Maria Prinzessin v. Lobkowicz** * Křimic 8.1.1919
	(h)	**Johann Nepomuk Emanuel Maria Josef Prinz v. Lobkowicz** * Křimic 25.12.1920 = Paris 29.6.1949 Marie Therese Gräfin von Belcredi * Losch 23.4.1922 dau. of Karl Graf v. Belcredi and has issue:
XIII	1a.	**Wenzel Eusebius Karl Jaroslav Friedrich Johann Ludwig Maria et omnes Sancti Patroni Bohemiae Prinz v. Lobkowicz** * Paris 14.3.1953
	2a.	**Therese Eleonore Marie Kunigunde Melanie et omnes Sancti Patroni Bohemiae Prinzessin v. Lobkowicz** * Paris 20.10.1954
	3a.	**Marguerite Melanie Therese Marie Jaroslava Franziska Anna et omnes Sancti Patroni Bohemiae Prinzessin v. Lobkowicz** * Paris 9.9.1957
XII	(i)	**Karl Zdenko Maria Aloys Friedrich Franz Pius Johann Prinz v. Lobkowicz** * Křimic 22.9.1922
	(j)	**Christian Friedrich Karl Jaroslav Aloys Anton Johann Pius Maria Prinz v. Lobkowicz** * Křimic 12.6.1924 = Kremsmünster 26.6.1954 Maria Theresia Gräfin v.u. zu Trauttmansdorff-Weinsberg * Prag 1.8.1922 dau. of Ferdinand Graf v.u. zu Trauttmansdorff-Weinsberg, and has issue:
XIII	1a.	**Ferdinand Johannes Jaroslav Eleonore Karl Anton Pius Maria Prinz v. Lobkowicz** * Ipamu, Belgian Congo 17.12.1955
	2a.	**Ladislav Friedrich Joseph Karl Camille Christian Pius Maria Prinz v. Lobkowicz** * Ipamu 11.6.1957
	3a.	**Marie Isabelle Christine Wilhelmine Jaroslava Andrea Pia Bartolomea Prinzessin v. Lobkowicz** * Knokke-sur-Mer 24.8.1960
XII	(k)	**Ladislas Otto Karl Friedrich Raffael Alois Johann Nepomuk Pius Maria Prince de Lobkowicz** * Křimic 24.10.1925 = Maleves, Belgium 28.8.1954 Thérèse Comtesse Cornet d'Elzius du Chenoy * Bruxelles 23.1.1932 dau. of Etienne Comte Cornet d'Elzius du Chenoy, and has issue:
XIII	1a.	**Stephan-Ladislas Pie Marie Ghislain Prince de Lobkowicz** * Louvain 29.7.1957
	2a.	**Nathalie Pie Charlotte Marie de Lorette Ghislaine Princesse de Lobkowicz** * Louvain 17.12.1958
	3a.	**Bernard-Ladislas Philippe Pie Marie Prince de Lobkowicz** * Louvain 14.5.1960

XII   (l)   **Marie Melanie Johanna Therese vom Kinde Jesu Friederika Anna-Agnes Pia Prinzessin v. Lobkowicz** * Křimic 28.1.1928 = Breuilpont 4.11.1961 Pierre Bazinet * Angoulême 13.12.1925, and has issue:

XIII   1a.   **Emmanuel Marie Joseph Pierre Bazinet** * Boulogne (Seine) 11.8.1962

                               2a.   **Marie Gabrielle Thérèse Françoise Bazinet** * Boulogne (Seine) 4.11.1963

                               3a.   **Michel Marie Xavier Vincent Bazinet** * Boulogne (Seine) 18.12.1964

                               4a.   **Paul Marie Noël Charles Bazinet** * Boulogne (Seine) 20.12.1965

XI   d)   **Eleonore Camille Marie Henriette Gräfin v. Beaufort-Spontin** * Paris 2.3.1891

VIII   2)   **Georg Adam 3rd Fürst v. Starhemberg** * Bruxelles 1.8.1785 + Wien 7.4.1860 = 23.5.1842 Aloisia Prinzessin v. Auersperg * 17.4.1812 + Salzburg 16.11.1891 dau. of Karl Prinz v. Auersperg s.p.

        3)   **Franziska Marie Gräfin v. Starhemberg** * Wien 6.1.1787 + Wien 21.12.1864 = Twickenham 26.7.1803 Stephan Graf Zichy v. Zich u. Vásonykeö * 13.4.1780 + Wien 8.6.1853, and had issue:

IX   (1)   **Eduard Graf Zichy v. Zich u. Vásonykeö** * 11.7.1808 + 31.7.1839

           (2)   **Wilhelm Graf Zichy v. Zich u. Vásonykeö** * 12.7.1811 + Wien 17.6.1838

           (3)   **Therese Gräfin Zichy v. Zich u. Vásonykeö** * 31.5.1813 + 8.10.1868 = 17.2.1844 Johann Graf v. Waldstein-Wartenberg * 21.8.1809 + Wien 3.6.1876 s.p.

           (4)   **Anne Marie Gräfin Zichy v. Zich u. Vásonykeö** * 21.7.1824 + Wien 29.1.1902 = 3.8.1846 Anton Graf Kinsky v. Wchinitz u. Tettau * 12.3.1817 + 20.11.1846 s.p.

VIII   4)   **Leopoldine Georgine Marie Louise Gräfin v. Starhemberg** * London 29.12.1793 + Linz 15.11.1859 = Lausanne 5.6.1816 Joseph Graf v. Thürheim * Hut, Près Liège 15.5.1794 + Linz 8.9.1832, and had issue:

IX   (1)   **Marie Leopoldine Gräfin v. Thürheim** * 4.4.1817 + Weinberg 12.3.1886 = Schwertberg 28.8.1838 Camillo Fürst v. Starhemberg * Pressburg 8.9.1804 + Wien 9.6.1892 s.p.

           (2)   **Ludwig Josef Egbert Graf v. Thürheim** * Wien 27.5.1818 + Schwertberg 19.7.1894

           (3)   **Josef Andreas Goswin Aribo Georg Maria Graf v. Thürheim** * Efferding 17.5.1827 + Weinberg 23.12.1904 = (1) Prag 26.4.1886 Klothilde Freiin. v. Hennet * Prag 26.9.1834 + Teplitz 12.12.1871 dau. of Leopold Frhr. v. Hennet; = (2) Dobritschan 8.7.1873 Sophie Freiin. Zessner v. Spitzenberg, * Prag 24.1.1844 + Weinberg 3.1.1915 dau. of Vincenz Frhr. Zessner v. Spitzenberg and had issue:

X   a.   **Maria Leopoldine Therese Karoline Klothilde Gräfin v. Thürheim** * Linz 11.9.1868 + Weinberg 22.2.1954 = Linz 3.10.1899 Richard Frhr. v. Gablenz * Wien 29.11.1872 + Weinberg 28.4.1925, and had issue:

XI   a)   **Hans Ludwig Carl Maria Richard Alfred Frhr. v. Gablenz** * Weinberg 12.8.1900 + Wien 16.12.1954 = (1) Schloss Zeist 30.8.1921 Jkvr. Henriette Schuurbeque-Boeye * Zeist 27.12.1900 dau. of Leendert Jhr. Schuurbeque-Boeye – div. = (2) Weinberg 23.2.1938 Maria Freiin. v. Seckendorff * Dresden 7.8.1897 dau. of Friedrich Frhr. v. Seckendorff, and has issue:

                 by 1st marriage:

XII   (a)   **Renatus Richard Alfred Maria Hans Frhr. v. Gablenz** * Schloss Weinberg 3.6.1922 ✕ Oberrampach, Luxemburg 17.1.1945

XII		(b)	**Mariette Irene Agnes Pauline Freiin. v. Gablenz** * Schloss Weinberg 7.7.1923 = Benkendorf 25.10.1942 Ralf Frhr. v. Gregory * Düren 26.6.1913 s.p.
		(c)	**Verena Maria Olga Freiin. v. Gablenz** * Schloss Weinberg 13.8.1925 = Warwick 20.5.1949 John Reginald Ryecart * London 2.3.1907, and has issue:

XII — (b) **Mariette Irene Agnes Pauline Freiin. v. Gablenz** * Schloss Weinberg 7.7.1923 = Benkendorf 25.10.1942 Ralf Frhr. v. Gregory * Düren 26.6.1913 s.p.

(c) **Verena Maria Olga Freiin. v. Gablenz** * Schloss Weinberg 13.8.1925 = Warwick 20.5.1949 John Reginald Ryecart * London 2.3.1907, and has issue:

XIII

1a. **Christopher John Ryecart** * Leamington Spa 8.12.1949

2a. **Patrick Geoffrey Ryecart** * Leamington Spa 9.5.1952

XI — b) **Maria Margarete Johanna Philippine Freiin. v. Gablenz** * Schloss Weinberg 17.7.1903 + Linz 16.4.1962 = (1) Schloss Weinberg 9.7.1925 Achim Frhr. v. Haebler * Lodz 12.5.1899 – div. = (2) Innsbruck 16.2.1950 Jules Fabritius * Hermannstadt 1897, and had issue:

by 1st marriage:

XII — (a) **Alexander Frhr. v. Haebler** * Wien 1.4.1926

(b) **Beatrice Freiin. v. Haebler** * Wien 8.6.1927 = Salzburg 25.7.1963 Peter Pr. v. Odescalchi * Vatta 15.9.1922 – div.

XI — c) **Ernst Rüdiger Frhr. v. Gablenz** * Weinberg 17.7.1905 + Mährisch-Weidkirchen 19.1.1906

X — b. **Therese Leopoldine Josephine Klothilde Gräfin v. Thürheim** * Teplitz 2.12.1871 + Salzburg 2.6.1902 = Weinberg 3.10.1895 Joseph Graf v. Plaz * Freudenau 5.2.1857 + Schloss Hoch b. Radstadt, Salzburg 7.1.1939, and had issue:

XI — a) **Maria Felicitas Walburga Gräfin v. Plaz** * Salzburg 12.5.1902 = Wien 30.11.1940 Ludwig Frhr. v. Cornaro * Wien 1.6.1895 X (missing since) May 1945, and has issue:

XII — (a) **Johannes Maria Leopold Frhr. v. Cornaro** * Wien 31.10.1941

X — c. **Ludwig Goswin Sebastian Vincenz Maria Graf v. Thürheim** * Salzburg 3.6.1874 + Wien 15.1.1960 = Wien 15.5.1922 Elisabeth Edle v. Pilat * Wien 28.8.1875 + Wien 21.12.1961 s.p.

IX — (4) **Therese Marie Leopoldine Josefa Antonia Katherine Gräfin v. Thürheim** * Linz 30.4.1831 + Schwertberg 5.11.1909 = Eferding 1.2.1865 Ludwig August Baron v. Schwiter * Weinberg 1.2.1805 + Salzburg 20.8.1889, and had issue:

X — a. **Henry Leopold Louis Marie Baron v. Schwiter** * Paris 24.5.1866 + Karlsbad 6.8.1915 = Craiova, Roumania 7.11.1904 Marie Gräfin Talevitch-Coman * Craiova 27.8.1863 + Craiova 7.1.1908 s.p.

b. **Louise Leopoldine Marie Therese Johanna v. Schwiter** * Paris 13.3.1869 + Bad Ischl 20.5.1943

c. **Leopoldine Marie Felicie v. Schwiter** * Salzburg 26.9.1873 + Bad Ischl 5.1.1952 = Linz 3.10.1899 Philipp Frhr. v. Blittersdorff * Frankfurt-am-Main 16.11.1869 + Bad Ischl 5.11.1944, and had issue:

XI — a) **Ludwig Maximilian Heinrich Maria Frhr. v. Blittersdorff** * Innsbruck 10.4.1901

b) **Ranier-Ferdinand Maria Anton Frhr. v. Blittersdorff** * Linz 13.2.1902 + Wien 13.2.1965 = Linz 17.9.1932 Hildegarde Weingartner * Linz 6.10.1900 + Linz 22.7.1966 dau. of Robert Weingartner – div. s.p.

XI   c) **Zdenka-Marie Henriette Gabrielle Therese Freiin. v. Blittersdorff** * Linz 28.2.1905
+ Schwertberg 24.8.1905

     d) **Franz-Heinrich Leopold Blithar Maria Frhr. v. Blittersdorff** * Linz 8.4.1907 = Bad Ischl
31.7.1940 Lucia Aemillia Barta * Reszow 1915 dau. of Emil Barta and has issue:

XII   (a) **Tassilo Maria Philipp Emil Hubert Wilhelm Frhr. v. Blittersdorff** * Bad Ischl
13.10.1946

XI   e) **Maria-Immaculata Therese Camilla Gabriele Freiin. v. Blittersdorff** * Linz 9.12.1909

     f) **Paul Leo Eugen Maria Philipp Felix Frhr. v. Blittersdorff** * Linz 2.8.1914 = Chistkindl
b. Steyr 7.9.1959 Heidemarie Lehner * ... and has issue:

XII   (a) **Andrea Freiin. v. Blittersdorff** * Steyr ... 1960

      (b) **Barbara Freiin. v. Blittersdorff** * Steyr ... 1961

VIII 5) **Georg Friedrich Ludwig Graf v. Starhemberg** * London 22.1.1802 + Igal, Hungary 24.3.1834
= 17.10.1828 **Valérie Comtesse de Beaufort-Spontin** * Bruxelles 11.10.1811 + Bruxelles 8.1.1887 dau.
of Frédéric August 1st Duc de Beaufort-Spontin, and had issue:

IX   (1) **Louise Gräfin v. Beaufort-Spontin** * 1830 + 1834

    (2) **Marie Gräfin v. Beaufort-Spontin** * Eferding 27.10.1832 + Schloss Hebattendorff 15.11.1838

VII 2. **Joseph Graf v. Starhemberg** * 1.3.1767 + 17.2.1768

9 The Descendants of Maria Anna Prinzessin zu Salm-Salm 1740-1816 and Don Pedro de Alcántara de Toledo y Silva Pimental Enriquez Hurtado de Mendoza 12 Duque del Infantado e Lerma 1729-1790.

VI   **Maria Anna Viktoria Wilhelmine Princess zu Salm-Salm** * Anholt 17.2.1740 + Heussenstamm 4.7.1816 = by Proxy,
Malines 6.11.1758 Don Pedro de Alcántara de Toledo y Silva Pimentel Enriquez Hurtado de Mendoza 12 Duque del
Infantado e Lerma, Grandee of Spain * Madrid 27.12.1729 + bei Frankfurt-am-Main 1.6.1790, and had issue:

VII   1.   **Doña Maria do los Dolores Leopolda Cristina Ana Manuela Joquina Josefa Teresa Petronila Antonia Vincenta
Buenaventura Francisca Sinforosa Diéga Sebastiana Rafaela Barbara Camila Isidora Andrea Cayetana Bibiana de
Toledo y Salm-Salm** * ... 1760 + Bruxelles 4.7.1792 = (1) ... Don Francisco de Asis Silva Bazán y Fernandez
de la Cueva Marqués del Viso * 8.10.1756 + Valencia 4.1.1779; = (2) Paris 7.1.1782 Frédéric Auguste Duc de
Beaufort-Spontin * Namur 14.9.1751 + Bruxelles 22.4.1817, and had issue:

by 2nd marriage:

VIII   1)   **Pierre Marie Ignaz Frédéric Comte de Beaufort-Spontin** * Paris 2.2.1784 + Wien 13.12.1796

    2)   **Françoise Philippine Thomasine Comtesse de Beaufort-Spontin** * Paris 7.3.1785 + Madrid 28.1.1830
= Madrid 19.3.1802 Don Francisco de Borja Téllez-Giron y Alfonso-Pimental 10 Duque de Osuna, and a
Grandee of Spain * Madrid 6.10.1785 + Pozuelo de Alaracón, near Madrid 21.5.1820, and had issue:

IX   (1)   **Don Pedro de Alcántara Maria Tomás Téllez-Girón y Beaufort 11 Duque de Osuna 14 Duque del
Infantado, and a Grandee of Spain** * Cádiz 10.9.1810 + Madrid 29.9.1844

        (2)   **Don Mariano Francisco de Borja José Justo Téllez-Girón y Beaufort 12 Duque de Osuna 15 Duque
del Infantado, and a Grandee of Spain** * Madrid 19.7.1814 + Château de Beauraing, près Namur
2.6.1882 = Wiesbaden 4.4.1866 **Eleonore Prinzessin zu Salm** * Frankfurt-am-Main 21.1.1842
+ Dülmen 18.6.1891 dau. of Franz Prinz zu Salm-Salm s.p.

VIII   3)   **Maria Emmanuele Josephine Comtesse de Beaufort-Spontin** * Issy, près Paris 17.6.1786 + Bologna
24.10.1824 = Wien 25.2.1807 Don Clemente Spada-Veralli, Principe di Castelviscardo * Roma 3.7.1778
+ Bologna 24.10.1824, and had issue:

IX   (1)   **Donna Maria Spada-Veralli** * Roma 22.12.1811 + 19.8.1841 = Bologna 13.2.1831 Marchese
Girolamo Sacchetti Marchese di Castelromano * Roma 22.3.1806 + Roma 13.6.1864, and had
issue:

X   a.   **Donna Eleonora dei Marchesi Sacchetti** * Roma 5.9.1834 + 10.11.1872

            b.   **Marchese Don Urbano Sacchetti Marchese di Castelromano** * Roma 25.5.1835 + Roma
3.2.1912 = Roma 22.2.1857 Donna Beatrice Orsini * Roma 27.7.1837 + Roma 28.1.1902
dau: of Don Domenico Principe Orsini, Duca di Gravina, and had issue:

XI   a)   **Don Giulio dei Marchesi Sacchetti** * Roma 28.12.1857 + Santa Marinella 27.5.1908
= Firenze 28.10.1888 Donna Teresa Gerini * Firenze 11.2.1868 + Roma 23.1.1948
dau. of Marchese Antonio Gerini, and had issue:

XII   (a)   **Marchese Don Giovanni Battista Sacchetti, Marchese di Castelromano** * Firenze
18.7.1893 = 5.6.1919 Donna Matilde Lante della Rovere * Napoli 4.8.1891
+ Roma 16.2.1954 dau. of Don Pietro Duca Lante della Rovere, and had issue:

XIII   1a.   **Donna Beatrice dei Marchesi Sacchetti** * Roma 28.6.1920 = 29.4.1946
Marchese Antonio Malvezzi Campeggi * Roma 2.1.1905, and has issue:

XIV   1b.   **Marchese Gherardo Malvezzi Campeggi** * Roma 9.3.1947

                            2b.   **Matilde dei Marchesi Malvezzi Campeggi** * Roma 18.7.1949 + Roma
1.12.1952

                            3b.   **Marchese Luigi Malvezzi Campeggi** * Bologna 20.9.1950

                            4b.   **Anna Maria dei Marchesi Malvezzi Campeggi** * Roma 13.11.1952

XIV		5b.	**Maria Giulia dei Marchesi Malvezzi Campeggi** * Roma 26.7.1954
		6b.	**Marchese Francesco Malvezzi Campeggi** * Roma 31.12.1956

XIII 2a. **Donna Teresa dei Marchesi Sacchetti** * Roma 18.9.1921

    3a. **Donna Oretta Anna Maria dei Marchesi Sacchetti** * Roma 10.6.1923
= Roma 29.10.1947 **Don Paolo Enrico Principe Massimo Lancellotti**
* Merode 9.6.1911, and had issue see elsewhere

    4a. **Don Giulio dei Marchesi Sacchetti** * Roma 21.1.1926 = Padova 15.4.1953
Giovanella Contessa Emo-Capodilista * Padova 1.11.1928 dau. of Conte
Alvise Emo-Capodilista, and had issue:

XIV   1b. **Don Urbano dei Marchesi Sacchetti** * Roma 17.1.1954

      2b. **Don Giovanni Battista dei Marchesi Sacchetti** * Roma 9.12.1955

      3b. **Donna Enrica dei Marchesi Sacchetti** * Roma 20.12.1959

      4b. **Donna Matilde dei Marchesi Sacchetti** * Roma 5.6.1962

XIII 5a **Donna Camilla dei Marchesi Sacchetti** * Roma 4.9.1928 = Roma 2.10.1952
Marchese Don Alfonso Theodoli Marchese di San Vito e Pisoniano and had
issue:

XIV   1b. **Don Guglielmo dei Marchesi Theodoli** * Roma 3.7.1953

      2b. **Donna Maria Alberica dei Marchesi Theodoli** * Roma 26.9.1954

      3b. **Don Giacomo dei Marchesi Theodoli** * Roma 24.12.1955

      4b. **Don Giovanni dei Marchesi Theodoli** * Roma 16.10.1960

      5b. **Donna Diana dei Marchesi Theodoli** * Roma 12.6.1962

      6b. **Don Luca dei Marchesi Theodoli** * 29.1.1964

XIII 6a. **Don Marcello dei Marchesi Sacchetti** * Roma 9.12.1931 = Roma 29.4.1957
Baronne Beatrice van der Elst * Wien 24.1.1934 dau. of Baron Joseph van
der Elst.

XI b) **Don Clemente dei Marchesi Sacchetti** * Roma 4.3.1860 + Roma 3.12.1919

  c) **Don Luigi Tomasso Calcedonio Paolo Giuseppe Gaspare Baldassare Melchiorre dei
Marchesi Sacchetti** * Roma 20.12.1863 + Roma 20.1.1936 = Roma 21.11.1891
Donna Maria Barberini-Colonna 8 Principessa di Palestrina * Castel-Gandolfo 6.4.1872
+ Roma 17.6.1955 dau. of Don Enrico Barberini-Colonna Principe di Palestrina, and had
issue:

XII (a) **Don Enrico-Urbano Barberini-Sacchetti 9 Principe di Palestrina** * Roma
24.10.1892 + Roma 23.4.1958 = Roma 11.6.1921 Contessa Anna Henriette
Franckenstein * Roma 7.6.1895 dau. of Conte Enrico Franckenstein, and had
issue:

XIII   1a. **Don Urbano Maria Barberini-Sacchetti** * Castel Gandolfo 23.9.1923
+ Roma 4.4.1927

XII (b) **Don Urbano Nazareno Barberini-Sacchetti 10 Principe di Palestrina** * Roma
21.10.1895 = Brixen 5.9.1953 **Maria Concetta dei Marchesi Fossi** * Firenze
11.2.1896 dau. of Federico Marchesi Fossi s.p.

XII   (c)   **Don Maffeo Nazareno Barberini-Sacchetti** * Roma 14.8.1897 = 12.6.1948 Maria Rosario Tracagni * Roma 3.2.1901 dau. of Conte Andrea Tracagni s.p.

   (d)   **Don Francesco Agapito Barberini-Sacchetti** * Palestrina 5.11.1898 + Roma 27.10.1959 = Roma 10.12.1922 Donna Ippolita Imperia Cattaneo della Volta Paleologo Principessa e Duchessa di Termoli * Napoli 28.2.1897 dau. of Don Mariano Augusto Cattaneo Principe di San Nicandro and had issue:

XIII   1a.   **Don Augusto Ippolito Clemente Barberini-Sacchetti** * Roma 3.12.1923 = Roma 4.10.1960 Giovanna dei Marchesi della Chiesa * Roma 20.4.1932 dau. of Marchese Giuseppe della Chiesa, and has issue:

XIV   1b.   **Don Benedetto Barberini-Sacchetti** * Roma 12.8.1961

     2b.   **Don Urbano Barberini-Sacchetti** * Roma 11.10.1962

     3b.   **Donna Francesca Barberini-Sacchetti** * Roma 23.8.1965

XII   (e)   **Don Giulio Maria Barberini-Sacchetti** * Palestrina 10.9.1900 = Osimo 20.6.1927 Constanza Briganti Bellini * Osimo 15.1.1902 dau. of Nob. Fabrizio Briganti Bellini, and has issue:

XIII   1a.   **Don Antonio Giuseppe Barberini-Sacchetti** * Osimo 27.5.1928 = Roma 6.6.1957 Maria Fiamma Bosio * 11.12.1931 dau. of Giovanni Bosio, and has issue:

XIV   1b.   **Donna Antonella Barberini-Sacchetti** * Roma 12.6.1958

     2b.   **Don Francesco Barberini-Sacchetti** * Osimo 19.11.1960

     3b.   **Donna Paola Barberini-Sacchetti** * Osimo 8.6.1962

XIII   2a.   **Donna Teresa Giuseppina Barberini-Sacchetti** * Osimo 11.12.1932 = Roma 4.12.1961 Emilio Taliani de Marchio * 6.8.1922, and has issue:

XIV   1b.   **Enrico Taliani de Marchio** * 21.10.1962

     2b.   **Giulio Taliani de Marchio** * 15.1.1963

     3b.   **Irene Taliani de Marchio** * 6.9.1965

XIII   3a.   **Donna Luisa Marina Barberini-Sacchetti** * Roma 13.3.1939 = Roma 1.6.1960 Virgilio dei Conti Lucangeli * Porto Recanati 1.1.1929, and has issue:

XIV   1b.   **Eleonore dei Conti Lucanageli** * Roma 4.3.1961

     2b.   **Antonio dei Conti Lucangeli** * Roma 15.2.1962

     3b.   **Clemente dei Conti Lucangeli** * Roma 21.10.1963

XII   (f)   **Don Carlo Maria Barberini-Sacchetti** * Roma 13.2.1905 + Roma 28.6.1959, = Roma 14.4.1937 Giacinta Guglielmi dei Marchesi di Vulci * Roma 14.4.1915 dau. of Benedetto Guglielmi Marchese di Vulci, and had issue:

XIV   1a.   **Don Luigi Barberini-Sacchetti** * Roma 7.4.1939

     2a.   **Donna Enrica Barberini-Sacchetti** * Roma 29.11.1942

     3a.   **Donna Maria Giulia Barberini-Sacchetti** * Roma 9.3.1948

XII		(g)	**Donna Beatrice Barberini-Sacchetti** * Roma 13.4.1906 = 29.4.1939 Conte Carlo Mopelli Mozzi * Torino 18.2.1889 + 12.5.1966 s.p.

XI   d)   **Donna Maria dei Marchesi Sacchetti** * Roma 10.8.1867 + Roma 2.3.1927 = 28.2.1886 Carlo Marchese Serlupi Crescenzi * Roma 5.10.1861 + Roma 19.10.1903, and had issue:

XII   (a)   **Marchese Giacomo Serlupi Crescenzi** * Roma 24.3.1893 = Roma 20.1.1916 **Donna Clothilde Antici-Mattei** * Recanati 25.9.1886 dau. of Don Tomasso Principe Antici Mattei and has issue:

XIII   1a.   **Crescenzio dei Marchesi Serlupi Crescenzi** * Roma 13.5.1917 = Palermo 24.1.1946 Silvia dei Marchesi di Paternó * Palermo 24.1.1926 dau. of Don Achille Paternò Marchese di Regiovanni, and had issue:

XIV   1b.   **Maria Giulia dei Marchesi Serlupi Crescenzi** * Roma 12.2.1947

XIV   2b.   **Gregorio dei Marchesi Serlupi Crescenzi** * Roma 8.5.1951

XIII   2a.   **Carlo dei Marchesi Serlupi Crescenzi** * Roma 9.9.1918 = Genova 4.6.1952 Donna Alberta Nob. Manzi Fè de Riseis * Napoli 29.8.1931 dau. of Nob. Don Gian Galeazzo Manzi Fè de Riseis, and has issue:

XIV   1b.   **Francesco dei Marchesi Serlupi Crescenzi** * Roma 10.7.1953

XIV   2b.   **Maria dei Marchesi Serlupi Crescenzi** * Roma 25.6.1956

XIV   3b.   **Marino dei Marchesi Serlupi Crescenzi** * Roma 12.11.1960

XIII   3a.   **Uberto dei Marchesi Serlupi Crescenzi** * Roma 19.2.1922 + 10.4.1952

XIII   4a.   **Giovanni dei Marchesi Serlupi Crescenzi** * Roma 14.2.1925 = Torino 29.10.1951 Luisa Bellardo * Torino 3.6.1930 dau. of Armando Bellardo, and has issue:

XIV   1b.   **Uberto dei Marchesi Serlupi Crescenzi** * Roma 30.8.1952

XIV   2b.   **Ottaviano dei Marchesi Serlupi Crescenzi** * Roma 16.9.1953

XIV   3b.   **Stefania dei Marchesi Serlupi Crescenzi** * Roma 30.4.1955

XIV   4b.   **Alessandro dei Marchesi Serlupi Crescenzi** * Roma 8.3.1960

XIV   5b.   **Livia dei Marchesi Serlupi Crescenzi** * Roma 22.5.1963

XI   e)   **Don Franco dei Marchesi Sacchetti** * 14.11.1870 + 21.12.1953 = 30.4.1900 Francesco dei Marchesi Guglielmi * 2.12.1873 + 18.8.1956 dau. of Giulio Guglielmi Marchese di Vulci, and had issue:

XII   (a)   **Donna Maria Immaculata dei Marchesi Sacchetti** * Roma 30.3.1901 = 10.1.1927 Marchese Giovanni Malvezzi Campeggi * Firenze 27.5.1889 + Roma 24.6.1955, and had issue:

XIII   1a.   **Giovanella dei Marchesi Malvezzi Campeggi** * Roma 27.8.1931 = Roma 27.12.1951 Don Paolo Cecni Bolognetti Principe di Vicovaro * Roma 28.11.1929 and has issue:

XIV   1b.   **Donna Fabiola Cenci Bolognetti** * Roma 7.4.1954

XIV   2b.   **Donna Domitilla Cenci Bolognetti** * Roma 25.11.1958

XIV		3b. **Donna Livia Cenci Bolognetti** * Roma 30.11.1963

XIII   2a. **Donna Beatrice dei Marchesi Sacchetti** * Roma 5.12.1903 = 11.1.1932 Marchese Angelo Pagani Planca Icoronati * 18.7.1902, and has issue:

XIV

         1b. **Anna Maria dei Marchesi Pagani Planca Icoronati** * 29.4.1933 = 30.4.1960 Oreste Ruggeri * 26.4.1917

         2b. **Conte Francesco Pagani Planca Icoronati** * 5.7.1934

         3b. **Conte Giulio Pagani Planca Icoronati** * 16.9.1936 = 3.6.1964 Paola Latini Macioti * 27.1.1942 dau. of Conte Wladimiro Latini Macioti, and has issue:

XV

            1c. **Benedetto Pagani Planca Icoronati** * 15.3.1965

XI   f) **Donna Eleonore dei Marchesi Sacchetti** * 1.7.1875 + Firenze 4.10.1949 = 3.2.1895 Marchese Federico Fossi * Firenze 25.5.1871, and has issue:

XII   (a) **Maria Concetta dei Marchesi Fossi** * Firenze 11.2.1896 = Brixen 5.9.1953 **Don Urbano Barberini Sacchetti Principe di Palestrina** * Roma 21.10.1895

       (b) **Nob. Pier Filippo dei Marchesi Fossi** * Firenze 19.7.1898 = Firenze 30.4.1924 Nannina dei Conti Rucellai 5.8.1896 dau. of Conte Cosimo Rucellai, and has issue:

XIII   1a. **Maria Gabriella dei Marchesi Fossi** * Firenze 27.10.1926 = Firenze 15.6.1958 Giorgio Todorow di San Giorgio * Firenze 30.8.1925, and has issue:

XIV   1b. **Andrea Todorow di San Giorgio** * Firenze 9.12.1963

XIII   2a. **Nob. Giulio dei Marchesi Fossi** * Firenze 20.12.1933 = Parigi 9.11.1961 Aliki Yatrakos * Sparta 25.12.1932 dau. of George Yatrakos, and has issue:

XIV   1b. **Giorgio Piero dei Marchesi Fossi** * Firenze 8.10.1962

           2b. **Alexi-Carlo dei Marchesi Fossi** * Boulogne-sur-Seine 9.11.1964

XII   (c) **Nob. Camillo dei Marchesi Fossi** * Firenze 23.7.1900 + Firenze 11.1.1953

       (d) **Nob. Luigi dei Marchesi Fossi** * Firenze 23.7.1900 = Roma 27.4.1958 Constanza Straneo * Vicenza 9.5.1897 dau. of Ottavio Straneo s.p.

XI   g) **Donna Anna dei Marchesi Sacchetti** * Roma 30.4.1879 = Roma 27.6.1897 Conte Francesco Bezzi Scali * Roma 30.8.1869 + Roma 16.3.1949, and had issue:

XII   (a) **Conte Antonio Domenico Nazzareno Bezzi Scali** * Roma 15.5.1898 = Roma 22.4.1925 Maria Luisa Dotti * ... marriage annulled s.p.

       (b) **Maria Cristina dei Conti Bezzi Scali** * Roma 1.4.1900 = Roma 15.6.1927 Guglielmo Marchese Marconi * Bologna 25.4.1874 + Roma 20.7.1937, and has issue:

XIII   1a. **Maria Elettra dei Marchesi Marconi** * Roma 30.7.1930

XII   (c) **Don Camillo dei Marchesi Sacchetti** * Roma 2.8.1836 + Roma 26.2.1909

       (d) **Don Luigi dei Marchesi Sacchetti** * Roma 26.7.1837 + 2.8.1837

IX	(2)		**Donna Teresa Spada-Veralli** * Bologna 15.10.1815 + 23.1.1874
	(3)		**Don Vincenzo Spada-Veralli, Principe di Castelviscardo** * Bologna 16.8.1821 + Napoli 22.11.1855 = Napoli 7.10.1846 Donna Lucrezia Fieschi Ravaschieri * Napoli 5.2.1822 + Napoli 14.1.1899 dau. of Don Antonio Fieschi Ravaschieri Duca di Roccapiomonte, and had issue:

X   a.   **Don Federico Spada-Veralli, Principe di Castelviscardo** * 1847 + 21.3.1921

        b.   **Donna Maria Spada-Veralli** * Bologna 25.1.1853 + Roma 2.2.1902 = ... 1872 Don Giovanni Grabinski, Principe Potenziani, Principe di San Mauro * Bologna 8.11.1850 + Roma 19.3.1899 and had issue:

XI   a)   **Donna Beatrice Spada-Veralli-Potenziani** * Bologna 10.7.1873 + Roma 16.10.1959 = San Mauro di Umbria 2.12.1899 Don Vincenzo Fieschi Ravaschieri, Duca di Roccapiomonte * Napoli 16.8.1870 + Roma 31.7.1929, and had issue:

XII   (a)   **Donna Ornella Fieschi Ravaschieri** * Roma 14.6.1908 = Roma 6.6.1928 **Carl Prinz v. Schönburg Waldenburg** * Gavernitz 2.6.1902–marriage annulled s.p.

XI   b)   **Donna Angelica Spada-Veralli-Potenziani** * Bologna 7.10.1874 + Roma 18.10.1919 = Roma 4.3.1894 **Don Ferdinando del Drago** * Roma 21.2.1857 + Roma 2.5.1906 and had issue see elsewhere.

        c)   **Don Ludovico Spada-Veralli-Potenziani, Principe di, Castelviscardo** * Rieti 19.9.1880 = (1) Venezia 21.2.1903 Contessa Maria Papadopoli * 6.11.1883 + Roma 17.11.1965 dau. of Nicolò Conte Papadopoli-Aldobrandino (marriage annulled); = (2) 21.2.1948 Sita Halenke * ... and has issue:

by 1st marriage:

XII   (a)   **Donna Myriam Spada-Veralli-Potenziani Principessa di Castelviscardo** * Rieti 29.11.1903 + Roma 12.9.1961 = 18.1.1937 Gaetano Parente * Aversa 10.6.1909 s.p.

X   c.   **Donna Olga Spada-Veralli** * Bologna ... + Roma 23.7.1934 = 16.8.1882 Conte Don Astrore Montevecchio Martinozzi Benedetti, Duca di Ferentillo * Fano 19.7.1853 + Fano 1.5.1928, and had issue:

XI   a)   **Donna Luisa Montevecchio Martinozzi Benedetti** * Bologna 25.7.1883 + Roma 14.7.1952 = 27.4.1908 Conte Giulio Ricci Paracciani * Roma 4.10.1881 + Roma 4.2.1961, and has issue:

XII   (a)   **Conte Francesco Ricci Paraccini** * Roma 22.7.1911

        (b)   **Dionora Ricci Paracciani** * Montesicuro 31.10.1913

XI   b)   **Conte Don Ermanno Montevecchio Martinozzi Benedetti, Duca di Ferentillo** * Bologna 2.6.1885 + Roma 5.11.1948 = 16.5.1920 Matilde Saladini dei Conti di Rovetino * Fano 22.11.1900 dau. of Mariano Saladini Conte di Rovetino, and had issue:

XII   (a)   **Donna Maria Olga Montevecchio Martinozzi Benedetti** * Roma 12.4.1921 = 12.4.1947 Thomas Storer * North Shields 4.2.1915 s.p.

        (b)   **Donna Maria Adelaide Monteveccio Martinozzi Benedetti** * Fano 11.10.1922 = 15.1.1948 Conte Paolo Violante Falzacappa * Roma 17.6.1915, and has issue:

XIII   1a.   **Gianluca dei Conti Violante Falzacappa** * Roma 24.10.1948

        2a.   **Massimo dei Conti Violante Falzacappa** * Roma 29.9.1951

XIII   3a.   **Pier Marco dei Conti Violante Falzacappa** * Bibbiena 23.6.1955

         4a.   **Enrico dei Conti Violante Falzacappa** * Fano 7.10.1959

XII   (c)   **Donna Laura Monteveccio Martinozzi Benedetti** * Fano 15.11.1923 = 29.10.1949 Conte Luciano Aventi di Sorivoli * Roma 25.5.1919, and has issue:

XIII   1a.   **Conte Carlo Aventi di Sorivoli** * Roma 4.8.1951

         2a.   **Conte Francesco Aventi di Sorivoli** * Roma 3.1.1954

         3a.   **Maria Chiara dei Conti Aventi di Sorivoli** * Fano 27.7.1955

XII   (d)   **Conte Don Cante Montevecchio Martinozzi Benedetti, Duca di Ferentillo** * Fano 17.2.1925 = 27.4.1957 Francesca Ambrosi Rosati Sacconi Natali dei Marchesi di Cavaceppo * Ascoli Aceno 25.12.1932 dau. of Marchese Piero Ambrosi Rosati Sacconi Natali, and has issue:

XIII   1a.   **Donna Luisa Monteveccio Martinozzi Benedetti** * Roma 14.7.1958

         2a.   **Donna Giulia Montevecchio Martinozzi Benedetti** * Roma 24.8.1963

XI   c)   **Conte Don Gualfredo Montevecchio Martinozzi Benedetti** * Fano 29.6.1892 = 9.9.1936 Nilde Stefani * ... and has issue:

XII   (a)   **Conte Don Astorre Montevecchio Martinozzi Benedetti** * 4.6.1938 + Cesenatico (Forli) 19.3.1956

XI   d)   **Conte Don Cante Montevecchio Martinozzi Benedetti** * Fano 16.10.1897 ✕ Monte Grappa 20.1.1918

VIII   4)   **Thérèse Charlotte Comtesse de Beaufort-Spontin** * Issy, near Paris 19.7.1789 + 9.1.1857 = Don Ferdinando Strozzi Majorca Renzi Principe di Forano, Duca di Bagnolo * 20.10.1774 + 15.8.1835, and had issue:

IX   (1)   **Ferdinando Strozzi Majorca Renzi Duca di Bagnolo, Principe di Forano** * 31.7.1821 + 23.2.1878 = Firenze 29.4.1851 Donna Antoinetta Centurione Scotto * Genova 25.5.1830 + 31.7.1919 dau. of Don Giulio Marchese Centurione Scotto, Principe di S.R.I., and had issue:

X   a.   **Don Piero Strozzi Majorca Renzi Principe di Forano, Duca di Bagnolo** * Firenze 20.9.1855 + Firenze 3.11.1907 = Paris 29.7.1897 Sophie Countess Branicka * Nice 15.2.1871 + February 1935 dau. of Michael Count Branicki (div.) s.p.

         b.   **Don Leone Strozzi Majorca Renzi Principe di Forano, Duca di Bagnolo** * Firenze 10.10.1856 + Pozzuolo 2.11.1929 = Firenze 14.4.1890 Donna Clementina Corsini * Firenze 23.8.1869 + Firenze 4.10.1928 dau. of Don Andrea Corsini, Marchese di Giovagallo dei Principi di Sismano, and had issue:

XI   a)   **Donna Antoinetta Strozzi Majorca Renzi** * Firenze 22.5.1891 + Pozzuoli 16.4.1932

         b)   **Donna Beatrice Strozzi Majorca Renzi** * Firenze 5.4.1894 + Gioiella (Perugia) 25.1.1932 = Firenze 18.4.1918 Conte Paolo Paolozzi * Chiusi 7.5.1896, and had issue:

XII   (a)   **Piero dei Conti Paolozzi** * Firenze 2.5.1920 + 30.6.1944

         (b)   **Giuseppe dei Conti Paolozzi** * Gioiella 30.7.1921 + Gioiella 6.6.1922

         (c)   **Leone dei Conti Paolozzi** * Gioiella 24.4.1923 = 3.4.1948 Leda Franchesi * Montepulciano 13.12.1923 and has issue:

XIII		1a.	**Beatrice dei Conti Paolozzi** * Cortona 26.8.1949
		2a.	**Piero die Conti Paolozzi** * Cortona 30.1.1951
		3a.	**Giovanna dei Conti Paolozzi** * Cortona 30.9.1952

X   c.   **Dona Luisa Strozzi Majorca Renzi** * Firenze 23.2.1859 + Firenze 22.12.1933 = Firenze 15.1.1880 Conte Francesco Guicciardini * Firenze 5.10.1851 + Firenze 1.9.1916, and had issue:

XI   a)   **Conte Paolo Guicciardini** * Firenze 27.11.1880 + Firenze 8.2.1955 = Firenze 10.9.1908 Augusta dei Conti Orlandini del Beccuto * 7.12.1875 + Firenze 31.10.1952 dau. of Conte Fabio Orlandini del Beccuto s.p.

     b)   **Conte Piero Guicciardini** * Firenze 14.7.1882 + Firenze 31.10.1961 = Firenze 9.6.1932 Maria Luisa dei Conti Bombicci Pontelli * Firenze 25.3.1895 dau. of Conte Cesare Enrico Bombicci Pontelli, and had issue:

XII   (a)   **Conte Roberto Guicciardini** * Firenze 20.5.1933 = Firenze 11.10.1961 Marghereta Pecol * Torino 25.2.1938 dau. of Agostino Pecol, and has issue:

XIII		1a.	**Conte Piero Paolo Guicciardini** * Torino 24.5.1962
		2a.	**Conte Tuccio Francesco Guicciardini** * Firenze 2.1.1966

XII   (b)   **Maria Antoinetta dei Conti Guicciardini** * Firenze 14.1.1936 = 3.10.1960 Francesco dei Conti Pamparto * 4.7.1925, and has issue:

XIII		1a.	**Carlo Ottavio dei Conti Pamparto** * Firenze 23.8.1961
		2a.	**Alessandro dei Conti Pamparto** * Firenze 3.10.1962
		3a.	**Enrico Giovanni dei Conti Pamparto** * Firenze 11.8.1966

XII   (c)   **Don Girolamo Strozzi Majorca Renzi, Principe di Forano, Duca di Bagnolo, Conte Guicciardini** * Firenze 26.9.1938

XI   c)   **Conte Niccolò Guicciardini** * 4.12.1883 + Firenze 9.1.1956 = 15.2.1915 Ameriga dei Conti Cadida Gonzaga Filangieri * Ferrara 23.2.1896 dau. of Conte Diego Candida Gonzaga Filangieri, and had issue:

XII   (a)   **Conte Francesco Guicciardini** * 26.1.1917

XI   d)   **Antoinetta dei Conti Guicciardini** * 1886 + 22.7.1906

     e)   **Dianora dei Conti Guicciardini** * Firenze 23.1.1889 + Poggiosecco (Firenze) 25.7.1965 = Firenze 8.5.1912 Conte Don Emanuele Giuseppe Canevaro Duca di Zoagli * Lima 28.3.1872 + Forte dei Marmi 21.8.1946, and had issue:

XII   (a)   **Conte Don Raffaele Canevaro di Zoagli Duca di Castelvaro** * Firenze 17.8.1913 + San Rocco al Porto 15.9.1960 = Villa Santa, Milano 5.7.1941 Terry Camperio * 1.4.1918 and has issue:

XIII		1a.	**Conte Don Emanuel Canevaro di Zoagli, Duca di Castelvari e di Zoagli** * Wien 27.3.1942
		2a.	**Donna Dafne Dianora Canevaro di Zoagli** * Wien 4.9.1943
		3a.	**Donna Rosita Canevaro di Zoagli** * Firenze 26.9.1945
		4a.	**Don Carlos Canevaro di Zoagli** * Lima, Peru 14.1.1954

16　Don Girolamo Strozzi Majorca Renzi, Principe di Forano,
Duca di Bagnolo, Conte Guicciardini

XIII   5a.   **Donna Roberta Canevaro di Zoagli** * Baltimore, U.S.A. 29.7.1955

                         6a.   **Don Ottaviano Canevaro di Zoagli** * Baltimore 27.3.1957

XI   f)   **Maria Marcella dei Conti di Guicciardini** * Firenze 25.11.1890 = Firenze 7.9.1922 Marchese Don Massimiliano Majnoni d'Intignano di Poggio Boldavinetti * Milano 25.1.1894 + Roma 16.12.1957, and has issue:

XII   (a)   **Marchese Don Stefano Majnoni d'Intignano di Poggio Boldavinetti** * Villa 'Incino 3.8.1923 = Frassanelle 1.6.1953 **Contessa Benedicta Papafava Antonini dei Carraresi** * Roma 1.12.1926 dau. of Conte Novello Papafava Antonini dei Carraresi

             (b)   **Don Francesco dei Marchesi Majnoni d'Intignano di Poggio Baldovinetti** * Villa 'Incino 13.7.1924 = Roma 14.2.1953 Margherita Carandini * Roma 17.5.1928 dau. of Conte Nicolò Carandini, and has issue:

XIII   1a.   **Don Giovanni dei Marchesi Majnoni d'Intignano di Poggio Baldovinetti** * Roma 18.1.1954

                         2a.   **Don Pietro dei Marchesi Majnoni d'Intignano di Poggio Baldovinetti** * Roma 14.3.1955

                         3a.   **Donna Elena dei Marchesi Majnoni d'Intignano di Poggio Baldovinetti** * Roma 22.6.1958

                         4a.   **Don Lorenzo dei Marchesi Majnoni d'Intignano di Poggio Baldovinetti** * Roma 18.2.1962

                         5a.   **Donna Maria Marcella dei Marchesi Majnoni d'Intignano di Poggio Baldovinetti** * Roma 11.11.1965

XI   g)   **Conte Leone Guicciardini** * Firenze 8.6.1895 = Firenze 20.12.1944 Lola Perissi * 29.5.1913, and has issue:

XII   (a)   **Conte Iacopo Guicciardini** * Castelfiorentino 15.6.1945

             (b)   **Elisabetta dei Conti Guicciardini** * Firenze 11.3.1948

X   d.   **Don Roberto Strozzi Majorca Renzi Principe di Forano, Duca di Bagnolo** * Firenze 20.2.1861 + Firenze 9.9.1951 = 28.7.1919 Uberta dei Marchesi Niccolini Sirigatti * Firenze 3.10.1883 + Firenze 24.12.1963 dau. of Marchese Eugenio Niccolini Sirigatti s.p.

IX   (2)   **Donna Ottavia Strozzi Majorca Renzi** * Firenze 22.5.1825 + Firenze 20.8.1903 = Firenze 7.2.1847 Marchese Lorenzo Ginori Lisci * Firenze 23.5.1823 + 13.2.1878, and had issue:

X   a.   **Marchesa Giulia Ginori Lisci** * Firenze 16.12.1847 + Firenze 6.4.1926 = 17.9.1867 Marchese Pietro Torrigiani * Firenze 1.6.1846 + Firenze 12.6.1920, and had issue:

XI   a)   **Vittoria dei Marchesi Torrigiani** * 4.9.1868 + Imola 28.12.1945 = ... Conte Francesco Tozzoni * ... + ... February 1928 s.p.

        b)   **Maria Elisabetta dei Marchesi Torrigiani** * Firenze 8.9.1870 + Filetto (Ravenna) 31.10.1959 = 5.2.1894 Amerigo Amerighi * Firenze 21.11.1857 + Viareggio 6.2.1927, and had issue:

XII   (a)   **Fabio Amerighi** * Firenze 11.1.1895

            (b)   **Maria Luisa Amerighi** * Villa Torrigiani, Quinto (Firenze) 24.7.1898 = Firenze 11.5.1921 Conte Giuseppe Cini de Pianzano * Settimello (Firenze) 4.9.1897 + Filetto (Ravenna) 19.11.1965, and has issue:

XIII		1a.	**Paola dei Conti Cini di Pianzano** * Settimello 15.2.1928
		2a.	**Anna Camilla dei Conti Cini di Pianzano** * Settimello 29.10.1929
		3a.	**Mario dei Conti Cini di Pianzano** * 21.5.1938 + 12.12.1938

XI c) **Marchese Luigi Torrigiani** * Livorno 14.7.1872 = Firenze 12.5.1908 Clarissa Fiaschi * Sydney, Australia 4.11.1885 dau. of Tomasso Fiaschi, and has issue:

XII (a) **Giulia dei Marchesi Torrigiani** * Firenze 27.2.1909

(b) **Waltha dei Marchesi Torrigiani** * Firenze 11.10.1910 = (1) Pieteccio 22.4.1937 Nob. Paolo dei Baroni Ricci Lotteringi * Roma 11.8.1896; = (2) Lurano (Bergamo) 15.7.1950 Conte Suardino Secco Suardo * Milano 6.11.1916, and has issue:

by 2nd marriage:

XIII 1a. **Conte Lanfranco Secco Suardo** * Roma 18.12.1953

X b. **Marchesa Mariana Ginori Lisci** * 29.3.1850 + 25.3.1913 = 21.9.1874 Conte Andrea Digerini Nutti * 1848 + 27.9.1915, and has issue:

XI a) **Giulia dei Conti Digerini Nutti** * Firenze 19.11.1876 + Marina di Pietrasanta 23.10.1953 = ... Dandolo Mattoli * 26.7.1882, and has issue:

XII (a) **Attilio Mattoli** * Perugia 5.6.1913

XI b) **Margherita dei Conti Digerini Nutti** * Callenzano 17.1.1877 + Firenze 11.1.1956 = Callenzano 16.6.1904 Conte Goretto Goretti dei Flamini * Firenze 1.12.1873 + Firenze 3.10.1943, and had issue:

XII (a) **Flaminia dei Conti Digerini Nutti** * Romena 17.10.1905 = 3.7.1946 George Specht * Springfield, Minnesota 29.3.1899, and has issue:

XIII 1a. **Marta Specht** * Firenze 3.11.1950

XII (b) **Conte Luca Goretti dei Flamini** * Firenze 3.12.1907 = Vittorio Veneto 5.8.1936 Nora Bernadis * 27.8.1908 dau. of Curio Bernadis, and has issue:

XIII		1a.	**Niccolò dei Conti Goretti dei Flamini** * Roma 7.5.1937
		2a.	**Fiamma dei Conti Goretti dei Flamini** * Firenze 21.8.1938
		3a.	**Marco dei Conti Goretti dei Flamini** * Firenze 25.8.1942
		4a.	**Gregorio dei Conti Goretti dei Flamini** * Venezia 7.1.1948

XI c) **Beatrice dei Conti Digerini Nutti** * 5.9.1882 = (1) 21.2.1906 Davide Gerra * 29.12.1857 + 12.5.1918; = (2) 24.4.1922 Conte Giuseppe Catucci * Roma 31.12.1871 + Piestrasanta 25.7.1962 s.p.

X c. **Marchese Carlo Ginori Lisci** * Firenze 29.11.1851 + München 23.8.1905 = Paris 6.10.1875 Maria Luisa dei Conti Alvarez Calderon * Lima, Peru 21.6.1857 + Sesto Fiorentino 2.1.1886 dau. of Conte Andrea Alvarez Calderon, and had issue:

XI a) **Marchese Lorenzo Ginori Lisci** * Firenze 3.1.1877 + Firenze 4.1.1960 = 9.11.1896 Paolina Civelli * Milano 12.6.1877 + Firenze 3.10.1964 dau. of Antonio Civelli, and had issue:

XII   ·(a)   **Marchese Carlo Antonio Ginori Lisci** * Firenze 16.1.1898 + Firenze 5.7.1964 = 22.4.1953 Maria Monnari Rocca * 12.6.1900 dau. of Paolo Monnari Rocca s.p.

      (b)   **Marchese Leonardo Ginori Lisci** * Sesto Fiorentino 30.11.1908 = Firenze 18.4.1934 Maria Cristina dei Marchesi Torrigiani Malaspina * Firenze 16.8.1906 dau. of Marchese Alessandro Torrigiani Malaspina, and has issue:

XIII   1a.   **Marchesa Maria Teresa Ginori Lisci** * Sesto Fiorentino 26.9.1935 = Firenze 9.3.1964 Nob. Alessandro dei Baroni Rubin de Cervin Albrizzi * Venezia 1934

           2a.   **Marchesa Paola Ginori Lisci** * Firenze 4.3.1937 = Firenze 28.4.1962 Uberto dei Conti Sannazzaro Natta * Milano 10.10.1925, and has issue:

XIV   1b.   **Alessandra dei Conti Sannazzaro Nattà** * Firenze 24.9.1963

              2b.   **Iacopo dei Conti Sannazzaro Natta** * Firenze 23.10.1965

XIII   3a.   **Marchesa Francesca Ginori Lisci** * Firenze 2.2.1938 = Doccia di Sesto Fiorentino 10.10.1960 Andrea dei Marchesi Malenchini * Firenze 5.7.1930, and has issue:

XIV   1b.   **Pietro Gioacchino dei Marchesi Malenchini** * Firenze 12.3.1962 + Firenze 20.3.1963

              2b.   **Luigi dei Marchesi Malenchini** * Firenze 18.9.1964

              3b.   **Maria Smeralda dei Marchesi Malenchini** * Firenze 19.1.1966

XIII   4a.   **Marchese Lionardo-Lorenzo Ginori Lisci** * Firenze 26.8.1945

XI   b)   **Marchesa Isabella Ginori Lisci** * Firenze 25.12.1881 = Villa Ginori, Massarosa 4.7.1903 Guido Gondi * Monteriggioni 22.11.1871 + Pontassieve 30.9.1953, and had issue:

XII   (a)   **Amerigo Gondi** * Firenze 8.1.1909 = Firenze 29.12.1954 **Donna Andreola Corsini** * Firenze 5.3.1913 dau. of Don Emanuele Corsini dei Principi di Sismano — marriage annulled s.p.

XI   c)   **Marchesa Bianca Ginori Lisci** * La Piagetta 29.3.1897 = Quiesa 18.11.1929 Conte Antonio Gaddi Pepoli * Forli 11.10.1900 + Forli 25.6.1940, and has issue:

XII   (a)   **Francesca dei Conti Gaddi Pepoli** * Firenze 27.10.1930 = Piagetta 24.4.1961 Mario Pancaccini * ..., and has issue:

XIII   1a.   **Gian Francesco Pancaccini** * Lucca 15.2.1962

XII   (b)   **Conte Gaddo Gaddi Pepoli** * Firenze 26.12.1936 = Firenze 5.2.1966 Maria Villa * ... and has issue:

XIII   1a.   **Claudia dei Conti Gaddi Pepoli** * Lucca 21.12.1966

X   d.   **Marchese Ippolito Venturi Ginori Lisci** * 12.12.1858 + Firenze 11.7.1947 = 1882 Tecla dei Conti Rucellai * 7.5.1860 + 13.10.1927 dau. of Conte Giovanni Rucellai, and had issue:

XI   a)   **Marchese Roberto Venturi Ginori Lisci** * 2.4.1883 + Firenze 24.2.1965 = 15.4.1910 Margherita dei Principi Abro Pagratide * 18.3.1885 dau. of Tigran Pasha, and had issue:

XII		(a)	**Marchesa Simonetta Venturi Ginori Lisci** * 24.4.1911 = 7.1.1932 Conte Alberto Guidi * 26.2.1896 s.p.
		(b)	**Marchesa Laura Venturi Ginori Lisci** * Vallambrosa 8.8.1913 = Firenze 25.3.1938 Conte Don Neri Corsini dei Principi di Sismano * Firenze 22.3.1909, and has issue:

XII   (a)   **Marchesa Simonetta Venturi Ginori Lisci** * 24.4.1911 = 7.1.1932 Conte Alberto Guidi * 26.2.1896 s.p.

           (b)   **Marchesa Laura Venturi Ginori Lisci** * Vallambrosa 8.8.1913 = Firenze 25.3.1938 Conte Don Neri Corsini dei Principi di Sismano * Firenze 22.3.1909, and has issue:

XIII   1a.   **Donna Paola Corsini dei Principi di Sismano** * Bergamo 4.3.1939

           2a.   **Conte Don Andrea Corsini dei Principi di Sismano** * Firenze 11.1.1943

           3a.   **Conte Don Lorenzo Corsini dei Principi di Sismano** * San Piero a Sieve 8.7.1946

           4a.   **Conte Don Roberto Corsini dei Principi di Sismano** * Firenze 4.10.1950

           5a.   **Conte Don Clemente Corsini dei Principi di Sismano** * Firenze 18.12.1953

XII   (c)   **Marchese Paolo Venturi Ginori Lisci** * Firenze 2.4.1915 = Roma 27.11.1940 **Doña Laetitia de Borbón y Bosch-Labrus** * Madrid 22.6.1915 dau. of Don Fernando de Borbón y Madran, Duque de Durcal, and has issue:

XIII   1a.   **Marchese Gabriel Venturi Ginori Lisci** * 27.9.1941

XII   (d)   **Marchesa Oretta Venturi Ginori Lisci** * 3.11.1921

XI   b)   **Marchese Nello Venturi Ginori Lisci** * 16.9.1884 + 25.9.1943

           c)   **Marchesa Anna Venturi Ginori Lisci** * Firenze 19.3.1892 = Firenze 16.11.1911 Marchese Migliore Torrigiani * Firenze 19.10.1878 + Firenze 26.6.1955, and has issue:

XII   (a)   **Valeria dei Marchesi Torrigiani** * Treviso 10.3.1913 + 26.12.1962 = Firenze 20.7.1940 Nardo Nob. Nardi Dei * Firenze 22.8.1910 s.p.

           (b)   **Marchese Marcello Torrigiani** * Padova 25.4.1914 X 21.7.1941

           (c)   **Donella dei Marchesi Torrigiani** * Firenze 17.6.1924 = Firenze 26.7.1958 Giorgio Torelli * Livorno 16.12.1931 s.p.

IX   (3)   **Donna Leopolda Strozzi Majorca Renzi** * 2.10.1826 + Pisa 26.3.1868 = Firenze 17.2.1851 Guido Guintini * Firenze 8.6.1822 + 14.10.1870, and had issue:

X   a.   **Michele Guintini** * Firenze 7.12.1851 + 20.2.1870

           b.   **Maria Anna Guintini** * ... 1853 + 1.7.1871

           c.   **Matilde Guintini** * 1854 + 13.9.1881

           d.   **Giulia Guintini** * Firenze 26.1.1856 + 13.10.1858

           e.   **Rudolfo Guintini** * Firenze 16.4.1858 + 16.6.1858

           f.   **Maria Guintini** * 19.9.1859 + 10.4.1868

           g.   **Emilia Guintini** * 31.3.1861 + Firenze 11.3.1938 = Firenze 2.6.1883 Roberto Antinori * 2.12.1854 + 15.3.1910 s.p.

           h.   **Giuseppe Guintini** * Firenze 19.3.1863 + Selvapiana Rufina (Firenze) 1.5.1936 = Cremona 24.11.1887 Contessa Maria Concetta Mocenigo Soranzo * 18.4.1861 + Firenze 8.7.1938 dau. of Conte Tommaso Mocenigo Soranzo, and had issue:

XI   a)   **Maria Carolina Guintini** * Firenze 24 ?.1890 = Firenze 26.11.1911 Conte Don Emanuele Corsini Marchese di Lajatico dei Principi di Sismano * Firenze 10.8.1876 + Firenze 5.2.1958, and had issue:

XII   (a)   **Donna Andreola Corsini dei Principi di Sismano** * Firenze 5.3.1913 = Firenze 29.12.1954 Amerigo Gondi * Firenze 8.1.1909—marriage annulled s.p.

       (b)   **Donna Simonetta Corsini dei Principi di Sismano** * Firenze 4.12.1914 = Firenze 25.4.1946 Don Giovanni Montaperto Duca di Montaperto e di Santa Elisabetta dei Principi di Raffadali * Torino 5.2.1912, and has issue:

XIII   1a.   **Don Gerlando Emanuele Montaperto** * Firenze 28.1.1948

          2a.   **Donna Elisabetta Begonia Montaperto** * Lausanne 5.7.1950

XII   (c)   **Conte Don Cino Tommaso Corsini dei Principi di Sismano, Marchese di Lajatico** * Firenze 28.3.1917 = Firenze 26.11.1945 Aimée Gaillard Russell * Nahant, Mass 28.7.1921 dau. of William Russell, and has issue:

XIII   1a.   **Donna Desideria Corsini dei Principi di Sismano** * Firenze 28.3.1950

          2a.   **Donna Immacolata Corsini dei Principi di Sismano** * Islip, N.Y. 24.1.1954

          3a.   **Conte Don Alessandro Emanuele Corsini dei Principi di Sismano** * Islip, N.Y. 1.12.1957

          4a.   **Donna Allegra Corsini dei Principi di Sismano** * 17.9.1962

XII   (d)   **Conte Don Niccolò Corsini dei Principi di Sismano** * Firenze 4.12.1920

       (e)   **Donna Giuliana Corsini dei Principi di Sismano** * Firenze 31.5.1928 = Firenze 27.4.1961 Nob. Clemente dei Baroni della Noce * Bologna 28.6.1922

XI   b)   **Guido Guintini** * Firenze 13.3.1892 + Firenze 19.9.1939 = Firenze 29.11.1918 Anna Antinori * Firenze 29.3.1892 dau. of Marchese Lodovico Antinori, and has issue:

XII   (a)   **Maria Concetta Guintini** * Firenze 12.11.1921 = Firenze 16.1.1943 **Gian Luca dei Marchesi Spinola** * Roma 23.11.1919 + 14.6.1945, and has issue see elsewhere

       (b)   **Francesco Guintini** * Firenze 14.9.1932

XI   c)   **Maria Luisa Guintini** * Pelago (Firenze) 21.10.1895 = 19.6.1919 Andrea Stucchi Prinetti * Merate 4.9.1883 + Milano 9.5.1963, and has issue:

XII   (a)   **Gian Carlo Stucchi Prinetti** * Firenze 21.12.1921 + 1.6.1949

       (b)   **Piero Stucchi Prinetti** * Firenze 23.4.1923 = 18.4.1953 Donna Lorenza de 'Medici dei Principi di Ottaiano * Milano 17.7.1926 dau. of Don Paolo de 'Medici dei Principi di Ottaiano, and has issue:

XIII   1a.   **Emanuela Stucchi Prinetti** * Milano 22.10.1954

          2a.   **Paolo Stucchi Prinetti** * Milano 20.10.1956

          3a.   **Roberto Stucchi Prinetti** * Milano 10.10.1958

XII   (c)   **Francesco Stucchi Prinetti** * Firenze 28.12.1924 + 14.6.1944

IX   (4)   **Donna Mariana Strozzi Majorca Renzi** * 7.8.1829 + 21.1.1854

VII   2.   **Don Pedro de Alcántara Manuel de Toledo y Salm-Salm Hurtado de Mendoza 13 Duque del Infantado e Lerma, Grandee of Spain** * Madrid 20.7.1768 + Madrid 27.11.1841

     3.   **Don Manuel Maria do los Dolores de Toledo y Salm-Salm** * Madrid 28.9.1772 + ... unmarried after 1797

10 The Descendants of Elisabeth Prinzessin zu Salm
    1704-1739 and Claude Lamoral II Prince de Ligne
    1685-1766.

V   **Elisabeth Alexandrine Felicité Charlotte Gotfriede Prinzessin zu Salm** * Anholt 21.7.1704 + Bruxelles 27.12.1739 = Anholt 18.3.1721 Claude Lamoral II 6th Prince de Ligne, Prince d'Amblise et d'Epinoy, and a Grandee of Spain 1st Class * 7.8.1685 + Boloeil, près Mons 7.4.1766, and had issue:

VI   1.   **Henri Ernest Prince de Ligne** * December 1721 + August 1722

     2.   **Charles Joseph Lamoral François Alexis 7th Prince de Ligne** * Bruxelles 23.5.1735 + Wien 13.12.1814 = Feldsberg 6.8.1755 Marie Franziska Prinzessin v.u. zu Liechtenstein * Wien 27.11.1739 + Wien 17.5.1821 dau. of Emanuel Prinz v.u. zu Liechtenstein, and had issue:

VII   1)   **Marie Christine Léopoldine Philippine Princesse de Ligne** * Bruxelles 25.5.1757 + Teplitz 13.9.1830 = Bruxelles 31.1.1775 Johann 2nd Fürst v. Clary u. Aldringen * Wien 17.12.1753 + Wien 3.1.1826 and had issue:

VIII   (1)   **Carl Joseph 3rd Fürst v. Clary u. Aldringen** * Wien 12.12.1777 + Wien 31.5.1831 = Neuhof 26.10.1802 Luise Gräfin Chotek v. Chotkowa u. Wognin * Neuhof 21.6.1777 + Teplitz 8.3.1864 dau. of Johann Rudolf Graf Chotek v. Chotkowa u. Wognin and had issue:

IX   a.   **Mathilde Christine Gräfin v. Clary u. Aldringen** * Wien 13.1.1806 + Berlin 11.11.1896 = Teplitz 4.5.1832 **Fryderyk Wilhelm Prince Radziwill, Duke of Nieswiez** * 19.3.1797 + Berlin 15.8.1870 and had issue see elsewhere

     b.   **Euphemie Flore Gräfin v. Clary u. Aldringen** * 30.4.1808 + Berlin 17.12.1867

     c.   **Léontine Gabrielle Gräfin v. Clary u. Aldringen** * Teplitz 26.9.1811 + Teplitz 10.6.1890 = Ruhberg 17.10.1832 **Boguslaw Prince Radziwill, Duke of Olyka** * 9.1.1809 + Berlin 2.1.1873 and had issue see elsewhere

     d.   **Edmund Moritz 4th Fürst v. Clary u. Aldringen** * Wien 3.2.1813 + Teplitz 21.6.1894 = Wien 5.12.1841 Elisabeth Alexandra Comtesse de Ficquelmont * Napoli 10.11.1825 + Venezia 14.2.1878 dau. of Charles Louis Comte de Ficquelmont, and had issue:

X   a)   **Edmée Caroline Luise Dorothée Therese Marie Gräfin v. Clary u. Aldringen** * Wien 13.10.1842 + Torino 14.2.1927 = Venezia 26.8.1867 Carlo Felice Nicolis Conte di Robilant e Cereaglio * Torino 8.8.1826 + London 17.10.1888 and had issue:

XI   (a)   **Marie Nicolis dei Conti di Robilant e Cereaglio** * Torino 24.3.1870 + Roma 5.10.1960 = Torino 25.5.1891 Eduardo Conte Rignon * Torino 27.10.1861 + Torino 6.2.1932 and had issue:

XII   1a.   **Felice dei Conti Rignon** * Torino 4.5.1892 + Padova 15.12.1892 + Padova 15.12.1892

     2a.   **Enrico dei Conti Rignon** * Padova 24.7.1893 + Milano 25.2.1894

     3a.   **Paolo Conte Rignon** * Milano 17.6.1895 + Torino 16.5.1964 = Torino 30.9.1931 Francesca dei Conti Claretta Assandri * Torino 29.1.1910 dau. of Conte Carlo Claretta Assandri and has issue:

XIII   1b.   **Eduardo Conte Rignon** * Torino 13.5.1934

     2b.   **Carlo Alberto dei Conti Rignon** * Torino 11.6.1935

     3b.   **Ornelia Consolata dei Conti Rignon** * Torino 4.10.1940

XII   4a.   **Luisa dei Conti Rignon** * Milano 11.3.1897 = Torino 27.10.1927 Don Lelio Principe Orsini dei Duchi di Gravina * Roma 5.12.1877 + Roma 12.2.1952 and had issue:

XIII	1b.	**Donna Sveva Principessa Orsini** * Roma 19.3.1930 = Roma 24.10.1953 Francesco Mancini * ... (marriage annulled)
	2b.	**Don Raimondo Umberto Maria Principe Orsini** * Roma 18.11.1931

XII **5a.** **Maria Cristina dei Conti Rignon** * Milano 27.3.1899 = Torino 29.4.1920 Don Fabrizio Aragona Pignatelli Cortes, Principe Pignatelli dei Duchi di Terranova * Napoli 17.6.1897 + Roma 4.4.1953 and has issue:

XIII 1b. **Don Carlo Ettore Principe Pignatelli** * Napoli 25.2.1921 + Napoli 13.2.1933

2b. **Don Nicola Maria Principe Pignatelli** * Napoli 22.5.1923 = Roma 30.6.1954 Luciana Malgheri * Roma 13.1.1935 dau. of Francesco Malgheri and has issue:

XIV 1c. **Donna Fabrizia Principessa Pignatelli** * Roma 30.1.1956

2c. **Don Diego Principe Pignatelli** * Roma 21.5.1958

XIII 3b. **Donna Giovanna Alfonsa Principessa Pignatelli** * Napoli 23.11.1933 = Roma 24.6.1954 Georges Roulet * L'isle de Brehat 14.10.1923 and has issue:

XIV 1c. **Fabrizio Roulet Doria di Angri** * Roma 24.2.1956

2c. **Olivier Roulet Doria di Angri** * Roma 7.12.1957

XII **6a.** **Carolina dei Conti Rignon** * Torino 17.2.1904 = Roma 7.1.1935 Karl 8th Fürst zu Löwenstein-Wertheim-Rosenberg * Kleinheubach 8.2.1904 and has issue:

XIII 1b. **Maria Aloisia Josephine Consolata Immaculata Benedicta Theresia Antonia Johanna Carla Conrada Leonharda Prinzessin zu Löwenstein-Werthein-Rosenberg** * München 6.11.1935 = Bronnbach 12.9.1956 **Joseph Arpád Archduke of Austria** * Budapest 8.2.1933 and had issue see elsewhere

2b. **Josephine Aloisia Edoarda Maria Immaculata Consolata Theresia Antonia Johanna Benedicta Carla Conrada Prinzessin zu Löwenstein-Werthein-Rosenberg** * Bronnbach 17.5.1937 = Bronnbach 7.1.1961 **Alexander Prinz v.u. zu Liechtenstein** * Wien 14.5.1929 and has issue see elsewhere

3b. **Monika Maria Immaculata Consolata Bendikta Aloisia Josephine Theresia Antonia Johanna Carla Conrada Paula Vitalis Prinzessin zu Löwenstein-Wertheim-Rosenberg** * Bronnbach 28.4.1939

4b. **Christiana Maria Josephine Aloisia Consolata Immaculata Theresia Antonia Johanna Carla Conrada Rita Prinzessin zu Löwenstein-Wertheim-Rosenberg** * Würzburg 18.9.1940 = Bronnbach 13.4.1966 **Michael Archduke of Austria** * Budapest 5.5.1942

5b. **Aloys-Konstantin Karl Eduard Joseph Johann Konrad Antonius Gerhard Georg Benediktus Pius Eusebius Maria Erbprinz zu Löwenstein-Wertheim-Rosenberg** * Würzburg 16.12.1941 = Erbach 7.11.1965 **Anastasia Princess of Prussia** * Brieg 14.2.1944 dau. of Hubertus Prince of Prussia, and has issue:

A. C. L. Bruxelles

17   Charles Joseph Lamoral, Prince de Ligne, 1735–1814

XIV

        1c.   **Carl Friedrich Prinz zu Löwenstein-Wertheim-Rosenberg**
            * Frankfurt-am-Main 30.9.1966

XIII

      6b.   **Elisabeth Alexandra Ninfa Paula Nicoletta Franziska Anastasia Carla
Johanna Benedicta Conrada Rita Consolata Maria Prinzessin zu
Löwenstein-Wertheim-Rosenberg** * Würzburg 2.5.1944

      7b.   **Lioba Ernestina Paola Aloisia Josephine Edoarda Benedicta Consolata
Immaculata Rita Conrada Maria Prinzessin zu Löwenstein-Wertheim-
Rosenberg** * Bronnbach 2.10.1946

XI

    (b)   **Edmondo Nicolis Conte de Robilant e Cereaglio** * Wien 4.8.1871 + Roma
14.3.1941 = Venezia 3.11.1896 **Valentina Contessa Mocenigo** * Salzburg 5.7.1878
+ Sintra 1.5.1950 dau. of Andrea Conte Mocenigo and had issue:

XII

    1a.   **Carlo Nicolis Conte di Robilant e Cereaglio** * Kalksburg 3.7.1897 = Venezia
1.10.1929 Caroline Kent * Ashville, North Carolina 15.7.1905 dau. of
Frederick Kent, and has issue:

XIII

      1b.   **Federico Carlo Nicolis dei Conti di Robilant e Cereaglio** * Roma
29.8.1930 = Roma 21.4.1958 Giovanna Stringher * Roma 24.9.1934
dau. of Donaldo Stringher and has issue:

XIV

        1c.   **Alberto Carlo Nicolis dei Conti di Robilant e Cereaglio** * Roma
21.9.1958

        2c.   **Massimiliano Nicolis dei Conti di Robilant e Cereglio** * Roma
8.9.1960

        3c.   **Luigi Nicolis dei Conti de Robilant e Cereaglio** * Udine 9.9.1962

XIII

      2b.   **Olga Alessandra Nicolis dei Conti di Robilant e Cereaglio** * Venezia
3.11.1934

XII

    2a.   **Andrea Nicolis dei Conti di Robilant e Cereaglio** * Venezia 13.1.1899 = (1)
Bologna 10.7.1920 Gabriella dei Conti di Bosdari * Bologna 1.3.1900 dau. of
Conte Felix di Bosdari, = (2) London 22.7.1937 Alice Allen * Riga
11.7.1901 dau. of Henry Allen and has issue:

by 1st marriage:

XIII

      1b.   **Alvise Nicolis dei Conti di Robilant e Cereaglio** * Venezia 19.2.1925
= Roma 30.4.1956 Elisabeth Stokes * Lynchburg, Virginia U.S.A.
21.8.1931 dau. of William Miles Stokes, and has issue:

XIV

        1c.   **Andrea Nicolis dei Conti di Robilant e Cereaglio** * Roma
3.2.1957

        2c.   **Filippo Nicolis dei Conti di Robilant e Cereaglio** * Roma
3.4.1959

        3c.   **Tristano Nicolis dei Conti di Robilant e Cereaglio** * London
11.9.1964

XIII

      2b.   **Carlo Felice Nicolis dei Conti di Robilant e Cereaglio** * Venezia
11.7.1927 = Lausanne 19.12.1949 **Marie Amelie v. Heller** * Aubonne
9.8.1926 dau. of Edouard v. Heller, and has issue:

XIV

        1c.   **Maurizio Nicolis dei Conti di Robilant e Cereaglio** * Roma
2.4.1951

XIV		2c.	**Alessandro Nicolis dei Conti di Robilant e Cereaglio** * Milano 23.10.1953
		3c.	**Edmondo Nicolis dei Conti di Robilant e Cereaglio** * Milano 30.4.1958
XII		3a.	**Olga Nicolis dei Conti di Robilant e Cereaglio** * Torino 17.1.1900 = Venezia 5.7.1926 **Dom António Alvares Pereira de Mello Marquis de Cadaval** * St-Jean-de-Luz 26.9.1894 + Leysin 17.2.1939 and has issue see elsewhere
		4a.	**Edmondo Nicolis dei Conti di Robilant e Cereaglio** * Torino 13.1.1901 = New York 28.9.1931 Helen Tompkins-Westerveld * Salt Lake City ... 1900 + Lisboa 11.8.1964 s.p.
		5a.	**Gian Francesco Nicolis dei Conti di Robilant e Cereaglio** * Torino 7.3.1905 = 3.8.1946 Lina Biondi * Firenze 24.11.1907 dau. of Biondo Biondi s.p.
XI	(c)		**Elisabetta Nicolis dei Conti di Robilant e Cereaglio** * Wien 14.10.1873 + Roma 11.6.1951 = Lingotto 30.7.1903 Luigi Nob. Heukensfeldt-Slaghek-Fabbri * Livorno 15.11.1873 + Roma 2.12.1957 and has issue:
XII		1a.	**Ida Nob. Heukensfeldt-Slaghek-Fabbri** * La Spezia 24.8.1906
		2a.	**Carlo Nob. Heukensfeldt-Slaghek-Fabbri** * La Spezia 23.4.1908 = Roma 27.10.1937 Carla Capannelli * Nice 29.1.1917 dau. of Giorgio Capannelli, and has issue:
XIII		1b.	**Monica Nob. Heukensfeldt-Slaghek-Fabbri** * Roma 20.11.1938 = = Roma 28.1.1956 Carlo Nob. Alvarez de Castro * Roma 15.2.1907, and has issue:
XIV		1c.	**Paolo Emilio Nob. Alvarez de Castro** * Roma 19.10.1956
		2c.	**Marco Nob. Alvarez de Castro** * Roma 25.4.1960
XIII		2b.	**Solagne Nob. Heukensfeldt-Slaghek-Fabbri** * Roma 18.11.1943
		3b.	**Diderico Nob. Heukensfeldt-Slaghek-Fabbro** * Roma 30.10.1945
		4b.	**Chantal Nob. Heukensfeldt-Slaghek-Fabbri** * Roma 15.5.1948
XII		3a.	**Luigi Nob. Heukensfeldt-Slaghek-Fabbri** * La Spezia 30.10.1909 + Venezia 10.4.1920
XI	(d)		**Luigi Nicolis dei Conti di Robilant e Cereaglio** * Wien 9.2.1876 + Firenze 6.2.1944 = Venezia 16.6.1913 Morosina Contessa Morosini * Vittorio Veneto 4.8.1886 dau. of Conte Michel Morosini, and has issue:
XII		1a.	**Anna Edmée Nicolis dei Conti di Robilant e Cereaglio** * Venezia 11.9.1914 = Rapallo 22.9.1941 Emanuele Conte Asinari dei Marchesi di San Marzano * Pino Torinese 5.7.1915 and has issue:
XIII		1b.	**Metella dei Conti Asinari di San Marzano** * Firenze 1.7.1942
		2b.	**Averardo dei Conti Asinari di San Marzano** * Firenze 3.3.1944
		3b.	**Christna dei Conti Asinari di San Marzano** * Rapallo 21.6.1946
XII		2a.	**Francesco Nicolis dei Conti di Robilant e Cereaglio** * Torino 10.1.1917

XII   3a.   **Paolo Nicolis dei Conti di Robilant e Cereaglio** * Rapallo 1.4.1920

XI   (e)   **Carlo Nicolis dei Conti di Robilant e Cereaglio** * Wien 4.6.1878 + Torino 9.1.1955 = Torino 5.11.1917 Anna Engelfred * Torino 19.1.1891 dau. of Giuseppe Engelfred and has issue:

XII   1a.   **Maurizio Nicolis dei Conti di Robilant e Cereaglio** * Torino 26.9.1918 ✗ North Africa 14.2.1942

        2a.   **Enrico Nicolis dei Conti di Robilant e Cereaglio** * Torino 30.1.1924

XI   (f)   **Teresa Nicolis dei Conti di Robilant e Cereaglio** * Wien 8.2.1883 = Lingotto 27.8.1903 Luigi Balbo Bertone Conte di Sambuy * Torino 14.3.1873 + San Salvà 14.8.1945 and has issue:

XII   1a.   **Bonna Edmée Balbo Bertone dei Conti di Sambuy** * Genova 18.7.1904 + Milano 16.3.1932 = La Spezia 4.1.1925 Don Alfonso Orombelli * Cantù 17.8.1898 and had issue:

XIII   1b.   **Don Carlo Orombelli** * Milano 1.11.1925 = Merate 11.5.1950 Donna Margherita Brivio Sforza dei Marchesi di Santa Maria * Milano 7.8.1930 dau. of Marchese Annibale Brivio di Santa Maria and has issue:

XIV   1c.   **Donna Edmée Orombelli** * Milano 8.11.1951

            2c.   **Don Martino Orombelli** * Milano 2.6.1954

            3c.   **Donna Elisabetta Alessandra Orombelli** * Milano 4.1.1962

XIII   2b.   **Donna Lina Orombelli** * Milano 29.8.1927 = Milano 6.3.1954 Edoardo Conte Amman * Milano 29.6.1922 and has issue:

XIV   1c.   **Mario Emanuele Cesare dei Conti Amman** * Milano 18.12.1954

            2c.   **Francesco Saverio Agostino dei Conti Amman** * Milano 25.4.1957

            3c.   **Sebastiano Antonio Luigi dei Conti Amman** * Milano 1.7.1958

            4c.   **Bona Luisa dei Conti Amman** * Milano 25.11.1959

XIII   3b.   **Donna Teresa Orombelli** * Milano 18.6.1929 = Fecchio di Cantù 24.9.1956 Luigi Longhini * Brescia 12.12.1917 and has issue:

XIV   1c.   **Stefano Longhini** * Milano 4.8.1957

            2c.   **Carla Longhini** * Milano 22.1.1959

XIII   4b.   **Don Luigi Orombelli** * Milano 10.10.1930 = Milano 16.9.1961 Nicoletta de Fernex * Milano 3.9.1934 dau. of Robert Fernex and has issue:

XIV   1c.   **Don Alfonso Orombelli** * Milano 10.1.1963

            2c.   **Donna Giulia Orombelli** * Milano 28.2.1965

XII   2a.   **Ernesto Balbo Bertone dei Conti di Sambuy** * 11.11.1905 + Messina 16.8.1907

XII		3a.	**Carlo Balbo Bertone dei Conti di Sambuy** * 1.11.1908 + Torino 12.11.1959 = San Salvà 25.9.1930 Bernardo Conte Vasallo di Castiglione * Altiniano 22.3.1893 and has issue:

XIII		1b.	**Ignacio dei Conti Vasallo di Castiglione** * Torino 21.7.1931
		2b.	**Luigi dei Conti Vasallo di Castiglione** * Torino 17.6.1933
		3b.	**Maria dei Conti Vasallo di Castiglione** * Torino 15.12.1936
		4b.	**Vittorio dei Conti Vasallo di Castiglione** * Saluzzo 26.8.1943
		5b.	**Alfonsine dei Conti Vasallo di Castiglione** * Saluzzo 31.8.1945

XII		4a.	**Elisa Balbo Bertone dei Conti di Sambuy** * Lingotto 5.8.1910
		5a.	**Anna Balbo Bertone dei Conti di Sambuy** * ·Venezia 24.4.1914 = São Paulo 16.9.1939 Angelo Carrara * Genova 27.9.1902 and has issue:

XIII		1b.	**Carla Carrara** * São Paulo 21.10.1940 = Genova 28.1.1962 Dario Ceragioli * Firenze 12.12.1933 and has issue:

XIV		1c.	**Vittorio Cereagioli** * São Paulo 16.2.1963
		2c.	**Alessandra Cereagioli** * São Paulo 3.10.1965

XIII		2b.	**Luigi Carrara** * São Paulo 21.11.1941 = São Paulo 16.10.1965 Ilse Ellen Eben * Mainz 26.1.1942 dau. of Gert Eben, and has issue:

XIV		1c.	**Anne-Edmée Carrara** * São Paulo 19.9.1966

XIII		3b.	**Andrea Carrara** * São Paulo 1.3.1943 = São Paulo 20.2.1965 Ludovica Nurra * Bologna 4.7.1946 dau. of Antonio Nurra and has issue:

XIV		1c.	**Manuella Carrara** * São Paulo 8.12.1965

XIII		4b.	**Pio Carrara** * São Paulo 29.5.1945
		5b.	**Fabrizio Carrara** * Genova 19.12.1946
		6b.	**Massimo Carrara** * São Paulo 29.3.1948
		7b.	**Anna Maria da Gloria Carrara** * São Paulo 4.4.1952
		8b.	**Bona Carrara** * São Paulo 10.5.1953

XII		6a.	**Manfredo Balbo Bertone dei Conti di Sambuy** * 8.8.1917 + Torino 14.8.1917
		7a.	**Emanuele Balbo Bertone dei Conti di Sambuy** * Venezia 21.8.1921 + Torino 31.1.1948 = Genova 18.2.1946 Giuseppina Carena * Genova 31.1.1922 dau. of Mario Carena, and had issue:

XIII		1b.	**Maria Edmée Balbo Bertone di Sambuy** * Torino 2.2.1947

X	b)		**Marie Carl Richard 5th Fürst v. Clary u. Aldringen** * Wien 3.4.1844 + Teplitz 25.3.1920 = Antonin 5.6.1873 **Felicie Princess Radziwill** * Teplitz 25.12.1849 + Teplitz 7.12.1930 dau. of Boguslav Prince Radziwill and had issue:

XI	(a)		**Marie Léontine Elisabeth Felicie Gräfin v. Clary u. Aldringen** * Teplitz 19.9.1874 + Brixen 11.4.1929

XI   (b)   **Johannes Baptist Maria Edmund Alexander Laurenzius Graf v. Clary u. Aldringen**
           * Teplitz 11.8.1878 + Reichenhall 5.3.1930 = London 16.7.1910 Eugenie
           Hospodář * Smichow 24.10.1882 + Hemmingen 30.3.1959 s.p.

X   c)   **Siegfried Franz Johann 6th Fürst v. Clary u. Aldringen** * Teplitz 14.10.1848 + Teplitz
           11.2.1929 = Wien 12.2.1885 Therese Gräfin Kinsky v. Wchinitz u. Tettau * Wien
           10.12.1867 + Teplitz 22.2.1943 dau. of Friedrich Karl Graf v. Kinsky v. Wchinitz u.
           Tettau and has issue:

XI   (a)   **Elisalex Alexandrine Marie Edmée Sophie Felicie Gräfin v. Clary u. Aldringen**
           * München 14.12.1885 + Bruxelles 3.8.1955 = Bruxelles 14.7.1904 Henri Comte
           de Baillet Latour * Bruxelles 1.3.1875 + Bruxelles 2.1.1942 and had issue:

XII   1a.   **Guy Comte de Baillet Latour** * Bruxelles 30.5.1905 ✗ in an accident whilst
           on active service, Isle of Arran 1.9.1941 Washington 30.4.1936 Marianna Dunn
           * New York 30.11.1915, dau. of James Clement Dunn and had issue:

XIII   1b.   **Anne Comtesse de Baillet Latour** * Bruxelles 4.2.1937 = Washington
           28.5.1960 Fergus Reid III * Cambridge, Mass. 12.8.1932 and has issue:

XIV   1c.   **Mary Armour Reid** * New York 26.6.1961

           2c.   **Fergus Reid** * New York 4.5.1963

XIII   2b.   **Elisalex Comtesse de Baillet Latour** * Washington 20.11.1939 = Roma
           3.7.1964 Antoine d'Albis * Limoges 14.2.1940 and has issue:

XIV   1c.   **Mary Antonia Alexandra d'Albis** * Limoges 31.12.1965

XII   2a.   **Thérèse Comtesse de Baillet Latour** * Bruxelles 8.2.1908 = Teplitz
           31.10.1933 Harold Peake * Bawtry 28.10.1899 − div. and has issue:

XIII   1b.   **David Peake** * Sheffield 27.9.1934 = London 22.11.1962 Susanna
           Kleinwort * Haywards Heath 3.1.1942 dau. of Cyril Kleinwort and
           has issue:

XIV   1c.   **Edward Peake** * London 19.2.1964

           2c.   **Catherine Peake** * Holland Park, London 27.11.1965

XI   (b)   **Alfons Maria Edmund Friedrich Karl Joseph Aloisius Gregor 7th Fürst v. Clary u.
           Aldringen** * Dresden 12.3.1887 = Eltville 5.1.1916 Ludwine Gräfin v.u. zu.
           Eltz gen. Faust v. Stromberg * Eltville 15.8.1894 dau. of Jakob Graf v.u. zu Eltz
           gen. Faust v. Stromberg and has issue:

XII   1a.   **Hieronymus Siegfried Marie Jakob Antonius Joseph Karl Augustinus Graf v.
           Clary u. Aldringen** * Teplitz 27.8.1917 ✗ Sokolowka, Ukraine 28.7.1941

           2a.   **Johann Georg Markus Erwein Maria Ägidius Augustinus Graf v. Clary u.
           Aldringen** * Teplitz 1.9.1919 = Koppitz 12.10.1942 Paula Gräfin
           Schaffgotsch gen. Semperfrei v.u. zu Kynast u. Greiffenstein * Koppitz
           10.2.1920 dau. of Hans Ulrich Graf v. Schaffgotsch gen. Semperfrei v.u. zu.
           Kynast u. Greiffenstein, and has issue:

XIII   1b.   **Hieronymus Graf v. Clary u. Aldringen** * Teplitz 25.3.1944

           2b.   **Therese Gräfin v. Clary u. Aldringen** * Teplitz 21.4.1945

301

XIII		3b. **Christian Graf v. Clary u. Aldringen** * Göppingen 2.6.1949

XII   3a.   **Maria Carl Georg Friedrich Longin Josef Graf v. Clary u. Aldringen** * Teplitz 14.3.1921 ✗ Koprivnica, Croatia 14.12.1944

               4a.   **Elisalex Winifred Therese Maria Anna Sophie Veronika Gräfin v. Clary u. Aldringen** * Teplitz 4.2.1923 = Venezia 5.6.1950 Michaelangelo Gaspari * Latisana 24.11.1925 and has issue:

XIII   1b.   **Camilla Gaspari** * Venezia 15.3.1951

                        2b.   **Lidvine Gaspari** * Venezia 13.4.1956

                        3b.   **Lorenzo Gaspari** * Latisana 17.7.1962

XI   (c)   **Sophie Marie Therese Gräfin v. Clary u. Aldringen** * Adlerkosteletz 2.9.1891 + London 31.12.1961

X   d)   **Manfred Alexander Robert Johann Adalbert Graf v. Clary u. Aldringen** * Wien 30.5.1852 + Salzburg 12.2.1928 = Wien 26.4.1884 **Franziska Gräfin Pejacsevich v. Veröcze** * Petersburg,Böh. 5.6.1859 + Salzburg 14.2.1938 dau. of Ladislaus Graf Pejacsevich v. Veröcze and had issue:

XI   (a)   **Edmund Maria Ladislaus Alexander Athanasius Peter Pius Sigismund Graf v. Clary u. Aldringen** * Wien 2.5.1885 + Salzburg 10.7.1953 = Graz 27.2.1911 Margarita Gräfin zu Lodron-Laterano u. Castelromano * Himmelberg 26.8.1889 dau. of Albert Graf zu Lodron-Laterano u. Castelromano and has issue:

XII   1a.   **Marie Margarethe Edmée Franziska Angelika Gräfin v. Clary u. Aldringen** * Trieste 11.11.1911 = Salzburg 2.3.1942 Hans Erich Mühlenburg * Berlin 23.9.1908 and has issue:

XIII   1b.   **Johann Mühlenburg** * Salzburg 29.5.1944

                        2b.   **Margarethe Mühlenburg** * Traunstein 12.2.1948

XII   2a.   **Ladislaus Marie Edmund Manfred Albert Graf v. Clary u. Aldringen** * Trieste 31.10.1912 + Rétfalu 16.10.1919

               3a.   **Manfred Marie Edmund Nikolaus Albert Graf v. Clary u. Aldringen** * Pola 12.9.1913 + Salzburg 31.3.1934

               4a.   **Elisabeth-Alexandrine Angelika Maria vom Siege Franziska Margarethe Gräfin v. Clary u. Aldringen** * Graz 9.6.1916 = Salzburg 23.8.1945 Peter Frhr. Forstner v. Billau * Trento 22.9.1903 and has issue:

XIII   1b.   **Marian Freiin. v. Forstner v. Billau** * München 16.5.1946

                        2b.   **Manfred Frhr. v. Forstner v. Billau** * München 23.6.1948

                        3b.   **Ferdinand Frhr. v. Forstner v. Billau** * München 18.2.1958

XII   5a.   **Edmund Maria Alois Karl Anton Roman Zeno Graf v. Clary u. Aldringen** * Graz 9.8.1918 = Hochburg/Ach 21.4.1948 Marie-Agnes Freiin. v. Ledebur * Obernfelde 21.11.1920 dau. of Albrecht Frhr. v. Ledebur and has issue:

XIII   1b.   **Felix Maria Hieronymus Michael Graf v. Clary u. Aldringen** * Rif 18.11.1948

                        2b.   **Hieronymus Manfred Karl Markus Graf v. Clary u. Aldringen** * Rif 6.6.1950

Österreichische Nationalbibliothek

Above: 18   Edmond Fürst *v.* Clary u. Aldringen,
1813–1894

Right: 19   Alfons Fürst *v.* Clary u. Aldringen

XIII   3b.   **Alberich Maria Nikolaus Michael Graf v. Clary u. Aldringen** * Rif 13.7.1952

           4b.   **Elisabeth Alexandrine Dorothea Marie Gräfin v. Clary u. Aldringen** * Salzburg 25.9.1954

           5b.   **Ludwine Johanna Marie Gräfin v. Clary u. Aldringen** * Salzburg 6.6.1957

XII   6a.   **Karl Anton Maria Markus Edmund Nikodemus Graf v. Clary u. Aldringen** * Rétfalu 15.10.1919 = Rieden 4.5.1948 **Theresia Gräfin v. Seilern u. Aspang** * Millotitz 4.8.1921 dau. of Ladislaus Graf v. Seilern u. Aspang s.p.

           7a.   **Franziska Romana Maria Margarita Gräfin v. Clary u. Aldringen** * Rétfalu 15.10.1919, = Buenos Aires 10.3.1949 Alfred Frhr. Rukavina v. Vidovgrad * Belec 1.1.1907 and has issue:

XIII   1b.   **Hubertus Marie Gustav Thaddäus Frhr. Rukavina v. Vidovgrad** * Buenos Aires 17.12.1949

                    2b.   **Margarita Elisabeth Maria Franziska Thaddäa Freiin. Rukavina v. Vidovgrad** * Buenos Aires 17.5.1951

                    3b.   **Georg Karl Maria Edmund Thaddäus Frhr. Rukavina v. Vidovgrad** * Buenos Aires 9.11.1952

XI   (b)   **Marie Karoline Cölestine Felice Gräfin v. Clary u. Aldringen** * Hütteldorf 19.5.1886 = Graz 26.1.1918 Joseph Graf zu Hardegg auf Glatz im Machlande * Wien 17.12.1876 + Wien 18.2.1945 and has issue:

XII   1a.   **Johanna Maria Franziska Romana Dorothea Leopoldine Josefa Gräfin zu Hardegg auf Glatz u. im Machlande** * Wien 28.10.1919

           2a.   **Johann Maria Franz de Paula Julius Josef Nikolaus Philipp Neri Graf zu Hardegg auf Glatz u. im Machlande** * Schmida 26.5.1921 + Ybbs 24.11.1948

           3a.   **Johanna Maria Theresia Leopoldine Gräfin zu Hardegg auf Glatz u. im Machlande** * Wien 15.9.1931

XI   (c)   **Ladislas Graf v. Clary u. Aldringen** * Sebestein 11.7.1888 + Klagenfurt 12.2.1895

           (d)   **Dorothea Maria Pia Gräfin v. Clary u. Aldringen** * Wien 30.10.1892

IX   e.   **Felicie Sidonie Gräfin v. Clary u. Aldringen** * Wien 9.10.1815 + Wien 17.2.1902 = 7.6.1845 Robert Altgraf zu Salm-Reifferscheidt-Raitz * 19.12.1804 + 25.3.1875 s.p.

VIII   (2)   **Moritz Franz Graf v. Clary u. Aldringen** * 21.9.1782 + 17.1.1829

VII   2)   **Charles Joseph Emmanuel Prince de Ligne** * Bruxelles 25.9.1759 X at Roux (Champagne) 14.9.1792 = 20.7.1779 Helene Princess Massalska * 9.2.1763 + 10.10.1814 dau. of Joseph Prince Massalski and had issue:

VIII   (1)   **Sidonie Françoise Charlotte Princesse de Ligne** * 9.12.1786 + Wien 14.5.1828 = Mariaschen b. Teplitz 8.9.1807 François Count Potocki * Niemiròw 2.7.1788 + Warsaw 15.1.1853 s.p.

VII   3)   **Louis Eugène Marie Lamoral Leopold Prince de Ligne** * Bruxelles 7.5.1766 + Bruxelles 10.5.1813 = Bruxelles 27.4.1803 Josèphe Louise Comtesse van der Noote et Duras * Bruxelles 15.9.1785 + Paris 4.3.1863 dau. of Joseph Comte van der Noot et Duras, and had issue:

VIII	(1)		**Eugène François Charles Lamoral 8th Prince de Ligne** * Bruxelles 24.1.1804 + Bruxelles 20.5.1880 = (1) Roeulx 12.5.1823 Amélie de Conflans d'Armentières * Bruxelles 18.6.1802 + Firenze 31.1.1833 dau. of Louis de Conflans, Marquis d'Armentières; = (2) Bruxelles 28.7.1834 Nathalie de Trazégnies * Bruxelles 7.9.1811 + Beleoil 4.6.1835 dau. of Georges Philippe Marquis de Trazégnies; = (3) Wien 28.10.1836 Hedwige Princess Lubomirska * 29.6.1815 + Bruxelles 14.2.1895 dau. of Heinrich Fürst Lubomirski, and had issue:

by 1st marriage:

IX	a.		**Henri Maximilian Joseph Charles Louis Lamoral Prince de Ligne** * Paris 16.10.1824 + Beloeil 27.11.1871 = Paris 30.9.1851 Marguerite de Talleyrand-Pérogord * Paris 29.3.1832 + Paris 3.7.1917 dau. of Comte Ernest de Talleyrand-Périgord, and had issue:
X		a)	**Louis Eugène Henri Marie Lamoral 9th Prince de Ligne** * Paris 18.7.1854 + Beloeil 27.8.1918 = Paris 26.7.1884 **Elisabeth de La Rochefoucauld** * La Vallée-aux-Loups 4.8.1865 + Paris 9.11.1946 — div. dau. of Sosthènes de La Rochefoucauld 4th Duc de Doudeauville, and had issue:
XI		(a)	**Marie Suzanne Marguerite Louise Princesse de Ligne** * Mauny 22.7.1885 = Paris 27.1.1906 Alexander Prinz v. Thurn u. Taxis, 1st Duca di Castel Duino * Schloss Mcell, Böh. 8.7.1881 + Château de Duino 11.3.1937 — div. and had issue:

XII		1a.	**Raymond Alexander Louis Lamoral Principe della Torre e Tasso, 2 Duca di Castel Duino** * Duino 16.3.1907 = Athens 28.11.1949 **Eugenie Princess of Greece and Denmark** * Paris 10.2.1910 dau. of George Prince of Greece and Denmark and has issue:
XIII		1b.	**Karl-Alexander George Peter Lucius Maria Raimand Lucian Lamoral Principe della Torre e Tasso** * Paris 10.1.1952
XII		2a.	**Ludwig Almerich Lamoral Alexander Konstantin Maximilian Lucian Principe della Torre e Tasso** * Duino 5.10.1908 = Buffalo, N.Y. 18.6.1939 Frances Goodyear * Buffalo N.Y. 18.6.1914 and has issue:
XIII		1b.	**Alexander Principe della Torre e Tasso** * Prag 1.3.1940
XII		3a.	**Marguerite Marie Therese Elisabeth Friedrike Alexandrine Louise Prinzessin v. Thurn u. Taxis** * Beloeil 8.11.1909 = Paris 29.4.1931 **Gaetano Prince of Bourbon-Parma** * Pianore 11.6.1905 + Cannes 9.3.1958 — div. and had issue see elsewhere

X		b)	**Marie Mélanie Ernestine Hedwige Princesse de Ligne** * Paris 25.11.1855 + Roma 2.4.1931 = Paris 2.6.1875 **Frédéric 4th Duc de Beaufort-Spontin** * Bruxelles 8.6.1843 + Petschau 26.12.1916 and had issue see elsewhere
		c)	**Ernest Louis Henri Lamoral 10th Prince de Ligne** * Paris 12.1.1857 + Bruxelles 23.6.1937 = Paris 4.1.1887 Diane de Cossé-Brissac * Paris 19.12.1869 + Beloeil 10.4.1950 dau. of Roland Marquis de Cossé-Brissac, and had issue:
XI		(a)	**Jeanne Marie Louise Princesse de Ligne** * Bruxelles 2.10.1887 = Bruxelles 5.6.1906 Léonel Marquis de Moustier * Paris 5.4.1882 + in the deportation, Hamburg-Neuegamme March 1945, and had issue:
XII		1a.	**Renée de Moustier** * Paris 25.10.1907 = Paris 18.1.1928 Comte Jean Armand * Paris 1.4.1900 + in the deportation Bremen-Farge 8.11.1944, and has issue:

304

XIII	1b.	**Comte Philippe Armand** * Ville d'Avray (S.-et-O) 26.8.1929 = Paris 25.10.1962 Jeanne Marie Burin des Roziers * 28.5.1938 dau. of Jacques Burin des Roziers, and has issue:
XIV	1c.	**Jean François Armand** * Paris 2.2.1964
	2c.	**Stanislas Armand** * Paris 4.4.1965
XIII	2b.	**Ghislaine Armand** * Ville d'Avray 2.11.1930 = Noyen-sur-Sarthe 9.10.1954 Comte Pierre de Viry * Mulhouse (Haut-Rhin) 8.11.1926 and has issue:
XIV	1c.	**Anne de Viry** * Chicoutini, Quebec 10.11.1956
	2c.	**Françoise de Viry** * Mandeville, Jamaica 13.8.1957
	3c.	**Etienne de Viry** * Noyen-sur-Sarthe 6.9.1960
XIII	3b.	**Hélène Armand** * Ville d'Avray 11.12.1931
	4b.	**Comte Etienne Armand** * Matran, Canton de Fridbourg 7.11.1934 ✕ Tizin Bechar, Algeria 1.2.1959
	5b.	**Inès Armand** * Noyen-sur-Sarthe 31.8.1944
XII	2a.	**Louise de Moustier** * Château de Bournel, Cubry (Doubs) 8.10.1908 = Paris 4.12.1929 Comte Louis Jousseaume de La Bretesche * Château de Couboureau 14.12.1901 and has issue:
XIII	1b.	**Comte René Jousseaume de La Bretesche** * Château de Bournel 25.9.1930
	2b.	**Odile Jousseaume de La Bretesche** * Bitche 25.10.1931 = Plestan 26.10.1957 Gilles Comte Le Pays du Teilleul * Romagné (I.-et-V.) 27.12.1929 and has issue:
XIV	1c.	**Sabine Le Pays du Teilleul** * Château de la Chasse-Beauvais, Romagné 11.8.1958
	2c.	**Brigitte Le Pays du Teilleul** * Château de la Chasse-Beauvais 5.10.1959
	3c.	**Hervé Le Pays du Teilleul** * Château de la Chasse-Beauvais 4.2.1962
	4c.	**Philippe Le Pays du Teilleul** * Château de la Chasse-Beauvais 24.1.1964
XIII	3b.	**Thérèse Jousseaume de La Bretesche** * Bitche 25.10.1932 = Plestan 28.5.1955 Comte Bernard de Lambilly * Paris 16.6.1927 and has issue:
XIV	1c.	**Anne de Lambilly** * Château de Lambilly, Taupont (Morbihan) 11.7.1956
	2c.	**Antoinette de Lambilly** * Château de Lambilly 11.9.1957
	3c.	**Marie Charlotte de Lambilly** * Château de Lambilly 11.9.1957
	4c.	**Marie Pierre de Lambilly** * Château de Lambilly 26.5.1959
	5c.	**Catherine de Lambilly** * Château de Lambilly 30.5.1961
	6c.	**Christian de Lambilly** * Château de Lambilly 8.10.1963

XIII		4b.	**Comte Michel Jousseaume de La Bretesche** * Bitche 8.1.1934 = Paris 14.12.1961 Magdeleine d'Andigné * Beville-le-Comte 23.7.1935 dau. of Comte Gilles d'Andigné, and has issue:

XIV
- 1c. **Louis Jousseaume de La Bretesche** * Château de Baronville 14.9.1962
- 2c. **Baudouin Jousseaume de La Bretesche** * Château de Baronville 3.10.1964

XIII
- 5b. **Comte Emmanuel Jousseaume de La Bretesche** * Caen 15.3.1935 = Saint-Alban (C.-du-N) 18.11.1961 Marie France Fraval de Coatparquet * Angoulême 24.2.1935 dau. of Alain Fraval de Coatparquet, and has issue:

XIV
- 1c. **Eric Marie Bertrand Jousseaume de La Bretesche** * St-Briene 18.2.1963
- 2c. **Marie Lys Odile Louise Jousseaume de La Bretesche** * St-Briene 30.4.1964
- 3c. **Elisabeth Marie Marguerite Jousseaume de La Bretesche** * St-Briene 15.12.1965

XIII
- 6b. **Comte Christian Jousseaume de La Bretesche** * Caen 15.7.1936
- 7b. **Marguerite Jousseaume de La Bretesche** * Caen 14.12.1938 = Plestan 14.11.1959 Vicomte Bruno de Ponton d'Amécourt * Paris 18.5.1930, and has issue:

XIV
- 1c. **Guillemette de Ponton d'Amécourt** * Angers 25.8.1960
- 2c. **Aude de Ponton d'Amécourt** * Angers 10.8.1962
- 3c. **Antoine de Ponton d'Amécourt** * Avoise (Sarthe) 21.9.1964

XIII
- 8b. **Henriette Jousseaume de La Bretesche** * Caen 12.3.1940 = Plestan 8.5.1965 Jean Thibaut Marquis de La Rochethulon * 2.9.1934 and has issue:

XIV
- 1c. **Beatrice de La Rochethulon** * 30.5.1966

XIII
- 9b. **Comte Alain Jousseaume de La Bretesche** * Le Mans 24.7.1947
- 10b. **Comte Bertrand Jousseaume de La Bretesche** * Le Mans 19.10.1949

XII
- 3a. **Roland Marquis de Moustier** * Paris 30.10.1909 = Paris 18.4.1940 Anne Normant * Romorantin (L.-et-C.) 4.3.1918 dau. of Hippolyte Normant, and has issue:

XIII
- 1b. **Lorraine de Moustier** * Paris 21.11.1941
- 2b. **Arielle de Moustier** * Paris 14.3.1943
- 3b. **Léonel de Moustier** * Paris 24.3.1947
- 4b. **Georges de Moustier** * Paris 13.12.1948
- 5b. **Anne de Moustier** * Paris 7.4.1950
- 6b. **Hubert de Moustier** * Château de Bournel 13.8.1953
- 7b. **Laurence de Moustier** * Paris 8.6.1961

306

XII   4a.   **Diane de Moustier** * Château de Bournel 27.9.1910 = Paris 27.10.1933 Hubert Marquis Guilhem de Pothau * Fossé (L.-et-C.) 16.8.1902, and has issue:

XIII

1b.   **Abbe Aymar Guilhem de Pothau** * Chitenay (L.-et-C.) 13.7.1934

2b.   **Monique Guilhem de Pothau** * Chitenay 23.8.1935 + Paris 15.1.1960 = Chitenay 28.8.1959 Comte Louis Law de Lauriston * 6.7.1929 s.p.

3b.   **Bernadette Guilhem de Pothau** * Bruxelles 4.1.1937 = Paris 6.7.1965 Theodose Coutsoumaris * Athens 11.11.1934

4b.   **Comte Charles Guilhem de Pothau** * Paris 28.12.1937 = Villeherviers (L.-et-C.) 14.5.1966 Anne Barluet de Beauchesne * Château des Roches, Villeherviers 1.11.1945 dau. of Bernard Barluet de Beauchesne

5b.   **Béatrice Guilhem de Pothau** * Chitenay 27.8.1939 = Chitenay 4.7.1964 Comte Michel Leclerc de Hauteclocque * St-Cyr École 17.3.1933, and has issue:

XIV

1c.   **Isabelle Leclerc de Hauteclocque** * St-Mande 3.6.1965

XIII

6b.   **Marie Guilhem de Pothau** * Chitenay 26.8.1940

7b.   **Dominique Guilhem de Pothau** * Tours 8.6.1947

8b.   **Henri Armand Guilhem de Pothau** * Tours 5.8.1952

XII   5a.   **Gabrielle de Moustier** * Paris 24.4.1913 = Paris 4.2.1939 Vicomte Roger Le Sellier de Chézelles * Paris 7.10.1910, and has issue:

XIII

1b.   **Vicomte Georges Le Sellier de Chézelles** * Paris 7.3.1940 = Issac (Dordogne) 5.8.1964 Ghislaine de Montferrard * Paris 30.3.1941 dau. of Bertrand Marquis de Montferrard, and has issue:

XIV

1c.   **Anne Le Sellier de Chézelles** * Dieppe 11.2.1966

XIII

2b.   **Gilles Le Sellier de Chézelles** * Paris 22.12.1953

XII   6a.   **Comte Baudouin de Moustier** * Paris 26.1.1915 = Solignac 25.9.1951 Annie Lemaigre Dubreuil * Paris 26.10.1928 dau. of Jacques Lemaigre Dubreuil, and has issue:

XIII

1b.   **Jean Charles de Moustier** * Paris 31.7.1952

2b.   **Sybille de Moustier** * Paris 10.10.1953

3b.   **Luc de Moustier** * Paris 2.5.1957

XII   7a.   **Comte Georges de Moustier** * Paris 1.9.1916 ✗ Lorraine 7.10.1939

8a.   **Françoise de Moustier** * Cubry 26.8.1917 = Paris 27.5.1942 Jacques Delcassé d'Huc de Monségou * Lescar 25.1.1905, and has issue:

XIII

1b.   **Elisabeth Delcassé d'Huc de Monségou** * Paris 8.3.1946

2b.   **Henri Delcassé d'Huc de Monségou** * Buenos Aires 16.3.1948

3b.   **Tristan Delcassé d'Huc de Monségou** * Paris 15.2.1949

4b.   **Jean Charles Delcassé d'Huc de Monségou** * Buenos Aires 9.8.1955

XII		9a.	**Comte Guy de Moustier** * Paris 19.3.1920 = 15.12.1947 May de La Poëze d'Harambure * Paris 12.6.1925 dau. of Raoul Marquis de La Poëze d'Harambure, and has issue:

XIII

  1b. **Patrick de Moustier** * Paris 2.2.1949

  2b. **Sonia de Moustier** * Paris 20.1.1951

  3b. **Diane de Moustier** * Paris 27.11.1952

  4b. **Philibert de Moustier** * Boran-sur-Oise 3.11.1956

  5b. **Pierre Etienne de Moustier** * Boran-sur-Oise 21.10.1959

XII 10a. **Comte Philibert de Moustier** * Cubry 7.4.1922

  11a. **Claude Moustier** * Cubry 23.1.1924 = Paris 21.1.1948 Comte Aymard du Buisson de Courson * Paris 16.4.1914, and has issue:

XIII

  1b. **Roselyne du Buisson de Courson** * Paris 20.3.1949

  2b. **Richard du Buisson de Courson** * Paris 3.6.1950

  3b. **Charles du Buisson de Courson** * Paris 2.4.1952

  4b. **Yolaine du Buisson de Courson** * Paris 10.4.1953

  5b. **Béatrice du Buisson de Courson** * Varrault-les-Dames (Marne) 16.9.1958

  6b. **Isabelle du Buisson de Courson** * Paris 19.4.1961

XII 12a. **Comte Henri de Moustier** * Hornu, Belgium 15.8.1926 = Chaumont-d'Anjou 24.9.1955 Françoise Grimaudet de Rochebouët * Paris 27.4.1930 dau. of Vicomte Jean de Grimaudet de Rochebouët, and has issue:

XIII

  1b. **Christian de Moustier** * Neuilly-sur-Seine 4.7.1956

  2b. **Segolène de Moustier** * Neuilly-sur-Seine 18.10.1959

  3b. **Laetitia de Moustier** * Boulogne–Billancourt 11.9.1965

XI (b) **Marguerite Françoise Marie Princesse de Ligne** * Bruxelles 15.10.1888 + Bruxelles 19.2.1889

  (c) **Isabelle Mélanie Marie Princesse de Ligne** * Bruxelles 23.9.1889 = Bruxelles 25.10.1920 **Reginald Prince de Croy** * London 26.9.1878 + Bruxelles 13.4.1961, and had issue see elsewhere

  (d) **Claude Maurice René Lamoral Prince de Ligne** * Bruxelles 19.10.1890 + Bruxelles 4.3.1900

  (e) **Henriette Marie Juliette Princesse de Ligne** * Bruxelles 31.12.1891 = Paris 13.8.1919 Robert Vicomte de Chabot-Tramecourt * Mouchamps 13.2.1890 + in the Deportation 14.7.1944, and had issue:

XII 1a. **Victor Vicomte de Chabot-Tramecourt** * Beloeil 27.5.1920 + in the Deportation Hamburg-Neuengamme 22.1.1945

  2a. **Renaud Vicomte de Chabot-Tramecourt** * Tramecourt (P.-de-C.) 11.5.1921 = Paris 22.3.1945 Clotilde de Chabot * Mouchamps-en-Vendee 23.4.1923 dau. of Pierre Comte de Chabot, and has issue:

XIII

  1b. **Chantal de Chabot-Tramecourt** * Paris 15.5.1946

  2b. **Elisabeth de Chabot-Tramecourt** * Paris 19.11.1947

XIII		3b. **Véronique de Chabot-Tramecourt** * Paris 15.4.1949
		4b. **Marguerite de Chabot-Tramecourt** * Château de Lignereuil (P.-de-C.) 9.6.1950
		5b. **Christian de Chabot-Tramecourt** * Château de Lignereuil 15.5.1952
		6b. **Pierre de Chabot-Tramecourt** * Château de Lignereuil 11.9.1953
		7b. **Henriette de Chabot-Tramecourt** * Château de Lignereuil 25.8.1955
		8b. **Philippine de Chabot-Tramecourt** * Château de Lignereuil 20.9.1956
		9b. **Odile de Chabot-Tramecourt** * Château de Lignereuil * 13.10.1958
		10b. **Paule de Chabot-Tramecourt** * Château de Lignereuil 23.2.1962
		11b. **Marie Charlotte de Chabot-Tramecourt** * Château de Lignereuil 22.12.1963

XII   3a. **Vicomte Antoine de Chabot-Tramecourt** * Tramecourt 10.11.1922 = Paris 17.7.1948 Marie Yolande Camus de La Giubourgère * Monbrun 7.2.1926 dau. of Gaston Camus Comte de La Guibourgère and has issue:

XIII   1b. **Isabelle de Chabot-Tramecourt** * Paris 25.4.1949

2b. **Robert de Chabot-Tramecourt** * Tramecourt 9.8.1950

3b. **Amicie de Chabot-Tramecourt** * Tramecourt 23.4.1953

4b. **Béatrice de Chabot-Tramecourt** * Tramecourt 5.6.1955

XII   4a. **Vicomte Raymond de Chabot-Tramecourt** * Tramecourt 28.3.1924 = Rixensart 14.10.1947 Marie Cécile Princesse de Merode * Rixensart 14.8.1923 dau. of Felix Prince of Merode, and has issue:

XIII   1b. **Christine de Chabot-Tramecourt** * Rixensart 2.9.1948

2b. **Amélie de Chabot-Tramecourt** * Rixensart 16.8.1949

3b. **Alexandra de Chabot-Tramecourt** * Rixensart 16.11.1950

4b. **Irène de Chabot-Tramecourt** * Brailly (Somme) 28.9.1954

XII   5a. **Christian de Chabot-Tramecourt** * Bruxelles 3.9.1925 + in the Deportation Hamburg-Neuengamme 10.4.1945

6a. **Vicomte François de Chabot-Tramecourt** * Tramecourt 14.6.1927 = Lille 21.11.1951 Elisabeth Vandenbush * 1.9.1917, and has issue:

XIII   1b. **Anne de Chabot-Tramecourt** * 24.12.1953

2b. **Luc de Chabot-Tramecourt** * 15.12.1955

3b. **Diane de Chabot-Tramecourt** * 9.1.1958

XII   7a. **Thierry de Chabot-Tramecourt** * Tramecourt 26.10.1928 + Bournel 16.10.1945

8a. **Vicomte Stanislas de Chabot-Tramecourt** * Tramecourt 25.7.1930 = Wailly (Somme) 7.7.1955 Solange van Cappel de Premont * Wailly 23.9.1934 and has issue:

XIII   1b. **Anita de Chabot-Tramecourt** * Wailly 16.8.1956

2b. **Thierry de Chabot-Tramecourt** * Wailly 2.2.1959

3b. **Ludovic de Chabot-Tramecourt** * Wailly 26.5.1962

XII	9a.	**Vicomte Bernard de Chabot-Tramecourt** * 28.2.1932 = Paris 3.7.1956 Solange de Vigneral * 16.4.1936, and has issue:

XIII
    1b. **Sophie de Chabot-Tramecourt** * Abbeville (Somme) 10.4.1957

    2b. **Eric de Chabot-Tramecourt** * Herdin (P.-de-C.) 6.7.1961

    3b. **Olivier de Chabot-Tramecourt** * Herdin (P.-de-C.) 3.11.1966

XII
    10a. **Geneviève de Chabot-Tramecourt** * Tramecourt 8.1.1934 = Tramecourt 7.7.1955 Comte Charles Leclerc de Hauteclocque * Versailles 20.6.1929, and has issue:

XIII
    1b. **Henri Leclerc de Hauteclocque** * Amiens 26.8.1956

    2b. **Florence Leclerc de Hauteclocque** * Lisieux 25.9.1957

    3b. **Catherine Leclerc de Hauteclocque** * Caen 17.6.1960

    4b. **Yolaine Leclerc de Hauteclocque** * Caen 23.9.1961

    5b. **Gauthier Leclerc de Hauteclocque** * Caen 27.1.1963

XI   (f) **Eugène II Marie Fréderic Lamoral 11th Prince de Ligne** * Château de Breuilpont 10.8.1893 + Beloeil 26.6.1960 = Paris 31.3.1917 Philippine de Noailles * Paris 23.8.1898 dau. of François de Noailles Prince et Duc de Poix, and had issue:

XII
    1a. **Baudouin Marie Lamoral 12th Prince de Ligne** * Paris 27.11.1918 = Bruxelles 19.1.1946 Monique Comtesse de Bousies * St-Gilles, près Bruxelles 11.12.1922 dau. of Jean Comte de Bousies; − div. s.p.

    2a. **Isabelle Marie Diane Françoise Princess de Ligne** * Bucarest 14.2.1921 = Beloeil 13.12.1941 Don Carlos Saavedra y Ozores, Marqués de Villalobar * Madrid 18.8.1912, and has issue:

XIII
    1b. **Don José de Saavedra y Ligne** * Paris 16.10.1942

    2b. **Don Santiago de Saavedra y Ligne** * Paris 27.6.1945

    3b. **Doña Carla de Saavedra y Ligne** * Genève 17.1.1948

    4b. **Don Alfonso de Saavedra y Ligne** * Genève 15.12.1949

XII
    3a. **Jolande Marie Johanne Charlotte Princesse de Ligne** * Madrid 6.5.1923 = Beloeil 19.1.1950 **Carl Archduke of Austria** * Baden b. Wien 10.3.1918, and has issue see elsewhere

    4a. **Antoine Joachim Lamoral Prince de Ligne** * Bruxelles 8.3.1925 = ·Luxembourg 17.8.1950 **Alix Marie Princess of Luxembourg and Nassau, Princess of Bourbon-Parma** * Schloss Colmar-Berg 24.8.1929 dau. of Charlotte Grand Duchess of Luxembourg, and has issue:

XIII
    1b. **Michael Charles Eugène Marie Lamoral Prince de Ligne** * Beloeil 26.5.1951

    2b. **Wauthier Philippe Félix Marie Lamoral Prince de Ligne** * Beloeil 10.7.1952

    3b. **Anna Isabelle Jeanne Marie Princesse de Ligne** * Beloeil 3.4.1954

    4b. **Christine Marie Elisabeth Princesse de Ligne** * Beloeil 11.8.1955

    5b. **Sophie Charlotte Léontine Gabrielle Marie Princesse de Ligne** * Beloeil 24.3.1957

XIII

6b.   **Antoine Lamoral Prince de Ligne** * Schloss Colmar-Berg 28.12.1959

7b.   **Yolande Marie Gabrielle Princess de Ligne** * Beloeil 16.6.1964

XI

(g)   **Baudouin Henri Lamoral Prince de Ligne** * Bruxelles 28.1.1896 ✕ (died of wounds) Herenthals 8.9.1914

(h)   **Marie Charlotte Béatrice Princesse de Ligne** * Moulbaix 23.8.1898 = Beloeil 19.7.1921 **Paul Comte de Lannoy** * Bruxelles 19.7.1898, and has issue see elsewhere

(i)   **Thérèse Marie Eugénie Princesse de Ligne** * Bruxelles 27.12.1905 = Bruxelles 22.11.1927 **Bernard Comte d'Ursel** * Paris 11.11.1904 + Bruxelles 4.10.1965 and has issue see elsewhere

X

d)   **Eugène Charles Lamoral Prince de Ligne** * Paris 15.12.1858 + París 17.6.1882

IX

b.   **Louis Marie Charles Gabriel Lamoral Prince de Ligne** * 2.3.1827 + Köln 12.4.1845

by 2nd marriage:

c.   **Nathalie Flore Georgine Eugénie Princesse de Ligne** * Beloeil 31.5.1835 + Trazégnies 23.7.1863 = Beloeil 15.9.1853 **Rudolf Herzog v. Croy** * Dülmen 13.3.1823 + Cannes 8.2.1902 and has issue see elsewhere

by 3rd marriage:

d.   **Charles Joseph Eugène Henri Georges Lamoral Prince de Ligne** * Bruxelles 17.11.1837 + Bruxelles 10.5.1914 = Paris 1.6.1876 Charlotte de Gontaut-Biron * Paris 19.7.1854 + Bruxelles 27.6.1933 dau. of Charles Comte de Gontaut-Biron and had issue:

X

a)   **Hedwige Marie Gabrielle Princesse de Ligne** * Paris 4.5.1877 + Neuilly-sur-Seine 22.9.1938 = Bruxelles 14.10.1897 Engelbert 9th Duc d'Arenburg * Salzburg 10.8.1872 + Lausanne 15.1.1949 and had issue:

XI

(a)   **Engelbert Charles Marie Henri Antoine François Gaspard 10th Duc d'Arenberg** * Château de Héverlé 20.4.1899 = (1) Münster 9.10.1940 Valerie zu Schleswig-Holstein * Liptovsky Sväti Mikulas, Hung. 3.4.1900 + Mont Boron, France 14.8.1953, = (2) Berchem, Prov. d'Anvers 23.5.1955 Mathilde Callay * Hemiksem 28.2.1913 dau. of Henri Callay s.p.

(b)   **Erik Engelbert Prince et Duc d'Arenberg** * Château de Héverlé 17.10.1901 = Lausanne 20.8.1949 Marie Thérèse de La Poëze d'Harambure * Dijon 5.6.1911 dau. of Jean Marquis de La Poëze d'Harambure s.p.

(c)   **Lydia Princesse et Duchesse d'Arenberg** * Bruxelles 1.4.1905 = Torino 30.4.1928 **Filiberto, Duke of Genova, Prince of Savoy** * Torino 10.3.1895 s.p.

X

b)   **Henri François Eugène Florent Lamoral Prince de Ligne** * Paris 29.12.1881 = Paris 13.4.1910 Charlotte Princesse de La Trémoïlle * Paris 20.11.1892 dau. of Louis 11th Prince et Duc de La Tremoïlle et Thouars, and has issue:

XI

(a)   **Jean Charles Lamoral Prince de Ligne** * Bruxelles 16.6.1911 = Paris 11.3.1942 Maria del Rosario de Lambertye-Gerbevillers * Paris 14.10.1922 dau. of Charles Marquis de Lambertye-Gerbevillers, and has issue:

XII

1a.   **Hedwige Princesse de Ligne** * Madrid 18.2.1943

2a.   **Charles Antoine Marie Lamoral Prince de Ligne** * Paris 30.9.1946

3a.   **Nathalie Princesse de Ligne** * Paris 22.9.1948

IX   e.   **Edouard Henri Auguste Lamoral Prince de Ligne** * Bruxelles 8.2.1839 + La Neuville-sous-Hay 17.10.1911 = (1) London 11.9.1866 Augusta Cunynghame * ... + London 27.10.1872 dau. of Sir David Cunynghame 6th Bart; (2) Baden 12.3.1874 Eulalie Prinzessin zu Solms-Braunfels * Kleinheubach 2.2.1851 + Amay 21.8.1922 dau. of Karl Prinz zu Solms-Braunfels and had issue:

by 2nd marriage:

X   a)   **Albert Edouard Eugène Lamoral Prince de Ligne** * Bruxelles 12.12.1874 + Bruxelles 4.7.1957 = Angleur, Belgium 9.8.1906 Marie Louise Calley de Saint-Paul de Sinçay * Angleur 22.3.1885 dau. of Gaston Calley de Saint-Paul de Sinçay and had issue:

XI   (a)   **Elisabeth Marie Eulalie Adrienne Hélène Princess de Ligne** * Bruxelles 1.6.1908 = Beloeil 19.9.1932 Guillaume Comte de Limburg-Stirum * Bruxelles 5.1.1908 and has issue:

XII   1a.   **Guillemette Anne Marie Louise Henriette Ghislaine Comtesse de Limburg-Stirum** * Bruxelles 26.7.1933 = Bruxelles 19.8.1961 Pierre Mouriau de Meulenacker * Uccle 6.8.1932 and has issue:

XIII   1b.   **Jean Marc Mouriau de Meulenacker** * Düren 25.7.1962

     2b.   **Alexandra Mouriau de Meulenacker** * Düren 19.2.1964

XII   2a.   **Henri Albert Antoine Bernard Comte de Limburg-Stirum** * Bruxelles 22.4.1936

     3a.   **Antoinette Philippine Emmanuelle Jeanne Marie Comtesse de Limburg-Stirum** * Bruxelles 9.5.1937

     4a.   **Edouard Louis François Marie Marc Anselm Comte de Limburg-Stirum** * 25.4.1941

XI   (b)   **Marie Antoinette Anne Princesse de Ligne** * Bruxelles 28.10.1910

     (c)   **Albert-Edouard Philippe Marie Lamoral Prince de Ligne** * 's-Gravenhage 29.8.1912 + Natoye, Belgium 27.4.1963 = Gerbevillers 26.3.1949 Leontine de Lambertye-Gerbevillers * Paris 24.6.1925 dau. of Charles Marquis de Lambertye-Gerbevillers, and has issue:

XII   1a.   **Wanda Marie Rita Alix Princesse de Ligne** * Bruxelles 13.5.1950

XI   (d)   **Hélène Henriette Anne Marie Princesse de Ligne** * 's-Gravenhage 9.6.1917 = Bruxelles 9.9.1948 Peter Whitwell * Nany Brow Rydal and Boughrigg, Ambleside 30.6.1911, and has issue:

XII   1a.   **Alexandra Marie Louise Rita Whitwell** * London 18.4.1952

X   b)   **Eleonore Marie Princesse de Ligne** * Bruxelles 25.1.1877 * Hohenberg 13.8.1959 = La Neuville-sous-Huy 30.11.1907 Friedrich Prinz v. Thurn u. Taxis * Raab 23.12.1871 + Biskupitz 10.5.1945 and had issue:

XI   (a)   **Eulalia Maria Antonie Eleonore Prinzessin v. Thurn u. Taxis** * Schloss Biskupitz 21.12.1908 = Schloss Taxis 8.9.1929 **Philipp Ernst Prinz v. Thurn u. Taxis** * Schloss Prüfening b. Regensburg 7.5.1908 + Schloss Hohenberg 23.7.1964 and has issue see elsewhere

     (b)   **Georg Lamoral Alexander Anton Joseph Maria Prinz v. Thurn u. Taxis** * Schloss Biskupitz 26.4.1910 = Berlin-Steglitz 7.1.1943 Editha Scheer * Königsberg i. Pr. 9.8.1921 dau. of Max Scheer, − div., and has issue:

XII   1a.   **Maria Katherina Eleonore Prinzessin v. Thurn u. Taxis** * Brünn 22.4.1944

XI   (c)   **Hugo Lamoral Nikolaus Prinz v. Thurn u. Taxis** * Schloss Biskupitz 21.9.1916 = (1) Wien 16.12.1940 Ingeborg Sponer * Wien 9.8.1921 dau. of Karl Sponer − div; = (2) München 31.7.1953 Beatrice Gräfin v. Bethusy-Huc * Bankau 17.4.1925 + Perlach b. München 13.12.1954 dau. of Otto Graf v. Bethusy-Huc, = (3) München 29.12.1961 Dorothea van der Elst * Dessau 29.10.1931 dau. of Wolfgang van der Elst, and has issue:

by 1st marriage:

XII   1a.   **Carl Friedrich Lamoral Hugo Prinz v. Thurn u. Taxis** * Pähl, Obayern 20.7.1941

     2a.   **Friedrich Lamoral Prinz v. Thurn u. Taxis** * Kornitz 8.9.1943

by 3rd marriage:

     3a.   **Marie Louise Prinzessin v. Thurn u. Taxis** * München 30.7.1963

X   c)   **Georges Alexandre Lamoral Prince de Ligne** * La Neuville-sous-Huy 7.12.1879 ✗ died of wounds Wynyhe-St.-Georges, near Louvain 18.8.1914

     d)   **Hélène Marie Princesse de Ligne** * La Neuville-sous-Huy 14.8.1887 + Etterbeek 21.11.1963 = La Neuville-sous-Huy 28.9.1912 Hadelin Comte d'Oultremont de Wegimont et Warfusée * Ixelles 5.3.1877 + Warfusée 10.12.1943 and had issue:

XI   (a)   **Angelique Marie Eulalie Comtesse d'Oultremont de Wegimont et Warfusée** * Bruxelles 13.2.1914

     ⸱(b)   **Charles-Emile Albert Antoine Comte d'Oultremont de Wegimont et Warfusée** * London 12.6.1915 = Waillet 10.4.1947 Beatrice Baronne van der Straten-Waillet * Waillet 9.5.1920 dau. of Joseph Baron van der Straten-Waillet, and has issue:

XII   1a.   **Baudouin Comte d'Oultremont de Wegimont et Warfusée** * St-Georges-sur-Meuse 25.2.1948

     2a.   **Antoine Comte d'Oultremont de Wegimont et Warfusée** * Etterbeek 28.11.1952

     3a.   **Anne Louise Comtesse d'Oultremont de Wegimont et Warfusée** * Liège 24.10.1956

XI   (c)   **Edouard Charles Antoine Comte d'Oultremont de Wegimont et Warfusée** * Paris 27.9.1916

IX   f.   **Isabelle Hedwige Mathilde Eugènie Princess de Ligne** * 15.4.1840 + 11.3.1858

     g.   **Marie Georgine Sophie Hedwige Eugénie Princesse de Ligne** * Bruxelles 19.4.1843 + Paris 3.3.1898 = Beloeil 8.7.1862 Sosthènes de La Rochefoucauld 4th Duc de Doudeauville * Paris 1.9.1825 + Château de Bonnetable (Sarthe) 27.8.1908 and had issue:

X   a)   **Charles Marie François Vicomte de La Rochefoucauld, Duque d'Estrées** * Paris 7.5.1863 + Château de Bonnetable 25.2.1907 = Paris 19.10.1885 Charlotte Princesse de La Trémoïlle * Château de Chantilly 19.10.1864 + La Ville-au-Maire 20.8.1944 dau. of Louis Charles Prince et 10th Duc de La Trémoïlle et Thouars and had issue:

XI	(a)		**Marguerite Françoise Marie de La Rochefoucauld** * Paris 9.8.1886 + Versailles 14.3.1929 = (1) Paris 2.7.1907 François de Rochechouart Prince de Tonnay-Charente * Paris 22.3.1881 + Verdun 16.3.1918 = (2) Paris 1.10.1919 Comte Alain de Kergariou * Bonaban 20.9.1882 + Fontainbleau 29.5.1920; = (3) Goeusinière 24.8.1922 Henri Vicomte Dufrense de Saint-Léon * Morigny (S.-et-O.) 23.8.1886 + Nice 25.4.1952 and had issue:

by 1st marriage:

XII		1a.	**Charles Marie Louis Arthur Victurnien de Rochechouart 13th Duc de Mortemart** * Paris 8.4.1908 + Amenas (Saraha) 10.5.1961 = Paris 16.5.1929 Simone Brossaud de Juigné * St-Herblon 15.7.1909 dau. of Henri Brossaud de Juigné, and had issue:
XIII		1b.	**François Marie Charles Arthur Georges Victurnien de Rochechouart 14th Duc de Mortemart** * Entrains-sur-Nohain (Nièvre) 24.3.1930 = 6.6.1959 **Anne Mouchet de Battefort de Laubespin** * Boulogne-Billancourt 28.7.1937 dau. of Bernard Comte de Laubespin, and has issue:
XIV		1c.	**Isabelle Marguerite Marie Victurnienne de Rochechouart** * Paris 15.4.1960
		2c.	**Diane Marie Gabrielle Sybille Victurnienne de Rochechouart** * Paris 1.4.1962
		3c.	**Sylvie Anne Marie Victurnienne de Rochechouart** * Paris 10.4.1963
XIII		2b.	**Marguerite Marie Hélène Armande Victurnienne de Rochechouart** * Paris 18.12.1931 = Paris 11.6.1952 Comte Bruno Gaillard de Lavaldène * Verna (Isère) 2.10.1927
		3b.	**Charles Arthur Gabriel Henri Victurnien de Rochechouart Marquis de Mortemart** * Paris 20.3.1934 + Amenas (Saraha) 10.5.1961 = Paris 3.7.1958 Hélène de Pierre de Bernis-Calvière * Paris 27.12.1937 dau. of Comte Adolphe de Pierre de Bernis-Calvière, and had issue:
XIV		1c.	**Patricia Aude Gabrielle Marie Victurnienne de Rochechouart** * Paris 17.5.1959
XIII		4b.	**Gabrielle Marie Jeanne Solange Victurnienne de Rochechouart** * Paris 15.2.1936 = Paris 25.2.1961 **Humbert Marquis de La Tour du Pin Chambly de La Charce** * Paris 19.10.1934, and has issue see elsewhere
		5b.	**Sylviane Marie Neige Françoise Victurnienne de Rochechouart** * Entrains-sur-Nohain 21.1.1940 = Paris 8.9.1962 **Comte Charles Edouard de Bruce** * Paris 4.7.1933, and has issue see elsewhere
XII		2a.	**Louis Victor Marie François Victurnien de Rochechouart Comte de Mortemart, Duc de Vivonne** * Paris 13.3.1909 + Paris 28.5.1938 = Paris 21.10.1932 **Solange d'Harcourt** * Paris 19.5.1913 dau. of Comte Guillaume d'Harcourt, and had issue:
XIII		1b.	**Comte Charles Louis de Rochechouart de Mortemart** * Pau 1.11.1933 = Paris 4.10.1960 Hélène Paultre de Lamotte * Paris 28.9.1930 dau. of Vicomte Robert Paultre de Lamotte and has issue:
XIV		1c.	**Alexandre-Victurnien de Rochechouart** * Boulogne-sur-Seine 19.7.1961

314

XIV

    2c.   **Athénaïs Victurnienne de Rochechouart** * Boulogne-sur-Seine 14.6.1963

XIII

    2b.   **Athénaïs de Rochechouart** * Paris 17.4.1935 = London 3.8.1955 Anthony St. Clair-Erskine 6th Earl of Rosslyn * London 18.5.1917 — div. and has issue:

XIV

        1c.   **Peter St. Clair-Erskine, Lord Loughborough** * London 31.3.1958

        2c.   **Lady Caroline St. Clair-Erskine** * London 7.6.1956

X

b)   **Elisabeth Françoise Marie de La Rochefoucauld** * La Vallée-aux-Loups 4.8.1865 + Paris 9.11.1946 = Paris 26.7.1884 **Louis 9th Prince de Ligne** * Paris 18.7.1854 + Beloeil 27.8.1918 — div. and had issue see elsewhere

c)   **Armand François Jules Marie de La Rochefoucauld 5th Duc de Doudeauville** * Paris 27.2.1870 + Paris 15.11.1963 = Paris 19.6.1894 Louise Princess Radziwill * Monte Carlo 9.1.1877 + Paris 2.3.1942 dau. of Constantine Prince Radziwill, and had issue:

XI

    (a)   **Hedwige de La Rochefoucauld** * Paris 15.2.1896 = Paris 12.11.1919 **Sixte Prince of Bourbon-Parma** * Schloss Wartegg 1.8.1886 + Paris 14.3.1934 and has issue see elsewhere

    (b)   **Sosthènes de La Rochefoucauld 6th Duc de Doudeauville** * Paris 20.6.1897 = (1) Madrid 16.1.1924 Doña Leonora de Saavedra y Collado 8th Condessa de Torrehermosa * Madrid 6.7.1900 + Malaga 14.3.1955 — div. = (2) 28.10.1963 Elisabeth Heymann v. Dreyhausen * Wien 9.2.1906, and has issue:

        by 1st marriage:

XII

        1a.   **Sylvie de La Rochefoucauld** * Paris 12.10.1925

XI

    (c)   **Marie de La Rochefoucauld** * Paris 6.7.1901 = Paris 22.7.1920 Henri de Noailles 7th Duc de Mouchy * Paris 9.4.1890 + Paris 1.11.1947, and has issue:

XII

        1a.   **Philippe François Armand Maria de Noailles 8th Duc de Mouchy** * Paris 17.4.1922 = Paris 20.4.1948 Diane de Castellane * Paris 19.2.1937 dau. of Comte Georges de Castellane, and has issue:

XIII

            1b.   **Natalie de Noailles** * Paris 11.2.1949

            2b.   **Antoine Georges Marie de Noailles** * Paris 7.9.1950

            3b.   **Alexis de Noailles** * Paris 5.9.1952

XII

        2a.   **Philippine Louise Charlotte Marie de Noailles** * Paris 4.9.1925 = Paris 30.7.1946 Jean-Louis Comte de Ganay * Paris 6.2.1922 and has issue:

XIII

            1b.   **Anne Marie de Ganay** * Paris 29.6.1947

            2b.   **Martine de Ganay** * Paris 9.10.1948

            3b.   **Lauraine de Ganay** * Paris 23.3.1951

            4b.   **Valentine de Ganay** * Paris 3.9.1962

XII

        3a.   **Sabine Marie de Noailles** * Paris 11.10.1931 = Paris 7.12.1953 Nicolas Wyrouboff * 7.12.1915

XI

    (d)   **Comte Armand Charles François Marie de La Rochefoucauld** * Paris 22.9.1902 = Gstaad 5.2.1957 Millicent Clarke * Yokohama 2.9.1921 dau. of Richard Clarke, and has issue:

XII		1a. **Lise de La Rochefoucauld** * Paris 13.4.1958

X d) **Marie Henriette Françoise Amélie de La Rochefoucauld** * Versailles 27.4.1871 + Paris 28.3.1952 = Paris 27.7.1892 Henri d'Harcourt 9th Duc d'Harcourt * Argenteau 1.8.1864 + Paris 17.5.1908, and had issue:

XI (a) **Lydie Marie Françoise d'Harcourt** * Paris 25.10.1898 = Paris 30.4.1919 **Armand Marquis de Pomereu d'Aligre** * Paris 17.8.1895, and had issue see elsewhere

(b) **Elisabeth Charlotte Gabrielle Marie d'Harcourt** * Paris 12.3.1901 = Paris 1.8.1927 Comte Christian de Jumilhac * Tracy-le-Mont 14.9.1900 + 25.1.1963 s.p.

(c) **François Charles Jean Marie d'Harcourt 10th Duc d'Harcourt et de Beuvron** * Thury-Harcourt 12.7.1902 = (1) Paris 17.12.1927 Antoinette Gérard * Paris 23.1.1909 + Antibes 16.9.1958 dau. of François Baron Gérard, = (2) Paris 17.1.1961 Thyra de Zayas * Palma de Mallorca 31.8.1930 dau. of Alphonse Marquis de Zayas, and has issue:

by 1st marriage:

XII 1a. **François Henri Michel d'Harcourt** * Paris 10.12.1928

2a. **Jean Louis Maurice Michel d'Harcourt** * Paris 15.3.1930

X e) **Edouard François Marie Comte de La Rochefoucauld, Duca di Bisaccia** * Paris 4.2.1874 = Paris 19.6.1901 Camille de Colbert-Chabanais * Nantes 5.3.1883 dau. of Edward Marquis de Chabanay, and has issue:

XI (a) **Marie Carmen Elisabeth Françoise Gabrielle de La Rochefoucauld** * Paris 21.5.1902 = Paris 5.12.1928 Comte Louis de Mailly Nesle * Paris 19.8.1892 + Paris 27.11.1958, and has issue:

XII 1a. **Comte Gilles Edouard Louis Marie de Mailly Nesle** * Paris 6.9.1929

2a. **Comte Arnould Augustin Marie de Mailly Nesle** * Paris 27.6.1931

3a. **Laure Suzanne Marie de Mailly Nesle** * Requeil (Sarthe) 4.3.1942 = 14.6.1963 Comte Josselin Maingard * Paris 28.2.1938, and has issue:

XIII 1b. **Diane Maingard** * Paris 8.5.1964

2b. **Gaël Maingard** * Buenos Aires 9.6.1965

XI (b) **Comte Stanislas Edouard François Marie de La Rochefoucauld** * Paris 2.5.1903 + 26.1.1965 = (1) Paris 2.1.1926 Alice Cocea * Sinaia, Roumania 28.7.1899 – div. = (2) Paris 19.7.1947 Donna Ivonne San Felice di Viaggiano * Paris 21.10.1895 dau. of Don Ludovico Felice Principe di Viggiano s.p.

(c) **Elisabeth de La Rochefoucauld** * Château d'Esclimont 3.7.1909 = (1) Paris 14.3.1929 Comte Robert-Elliot Le Gras de Luart de Montsaulnin * 21.6.1903 + 21.11.1952; = (2) Roma 26.6.1958 Mario Conte Pinci * Roma 29.9.1896, and has issue:

by 1st marriage:

XII 1a. **Yolande Le Gras du Luart de Montsaulnin** * Paris 6.9.1930

2a. **Irène Le Gras du Luart de Montsaulnin** * Paris 13.1.1934 = Antibes 6.6.1964 Harold Brooks-Baker * Washington D.C. 16.11.1933, and has issue:

XIII 1b. **Nadia Brooks-Baker** * 24.4.1965

XII   3a.   **Comte Roland Le Gras du Luart de Montsaulnin** * Paris 12.3.1940 = Luynes (I.-et-L) 23.7.1962 Elisabeth d'Albert de Luynes * Buenos Aires 29.5.1942 dau. of Philippe d'Albert 11th Duc de Luynes, and has issue:

XIII   1b.   **Isabelle Le Gras du Luart de Montsaulnin** * Neuilly-sur-Seine 21.5.1963

                     2b.   **Florence Le Gras du Luart de Montsaulnin** * Neuilly-sur-Seine 19.5.1964

                     3b.   **Constance Le Gras du Luart de Montsaulnin** * Neuilly-sur-Seine 21.8.1965

           4a.   **Diane Le Gras du Luart de Montsaulnin** * 9.5.1946 = Paris 4.5.1965 Guy Allard * ... 1938

VIII   (2)   **Jules Louis Paulin Prince de Ligne** * 24.1.1806 + Bruxelles 28.11.1810

           (3)   **Octavie Louise Philippine Princesse de Ligne** * 29.5.1808 + Beloeil 7.11.1810

VII   4)   **Euphemie Christine Philippe Thérèse Princesse de Ligne** * Bruxelles 18.7.1773 + Wien 30.3.1834 = 11.9.1798 Johann Baptist Graf Pálffy v. Erdöd * 6.4.1775 + 15.3.1811 s.p.

           5)   **Flore Princesse de Ligne** * Bruxelles 8.11.1775 + Wien 9.12.1851 = 1812 Raban Frhr. v. Spiegel u. Pickelsheim * Bayreuth 6.11.1772 + 9.1.1836 s.p.

VI   3.   **Louise Marie Elisabeth Christine Princesse de Ligne** * Bruxelles 17.2.1728 + Mons 26.1.1784

     4.   **Marie Josèphe Princesse de Ligne** * 23.5.1730 + Mons 2.1.1783

11 The Descendants of Eleonore Christine Prinzessin zu Salm 1678-1757 and Conrard Albert 1st Duc d'Ursel 1665-1738.

IV   **Eleonore Christine Elisabeth Prinzessin zu Salm** * 14.3.1678 + Bruxelles 23.3.1757 = by Proclamation 17.8.1713 Conrard Albert Charles I Duc d'Ursel * 10.2.1665 + Namur 3.5.1738 and had issue:

V   1.   **Charles Elisabeth Conrard Albert Philippe François de Paule Norbert 2 Duc d'Ursel** * 26.6.1717 + Bruxelles 11.1.1775 = 15.8.1740 Marie Eleonore Prinzessin v. Lobkowicz * 17.10.1721 + 9.5.1756 dau. of Georg Christian Fürst v. Lobkowicz, and had issue:

VI   1)   **Charlotte Philippine Elisabeth Leonarde Comtesse d'Ursel** * 20.11.1741 + Wien 17.4.1776 = Hingen 4.12.1773 Leopold Carl Graf von Stain * Bruxelles 27.12.1729 + Nieder-Stotzingen 5.3.1809, and had issue:

VII   (1)   **Leopold Frhr. v. Stain** * Wien 5.3.1775 + Wien 12.5.1776

VI   2)   **Marie Henriette Christine Eleonore Comtesse d'Ursel** * 20.1.1743 + Wien 4.9.1810 = Bruxelles 25.11.1776 Joseph Graf v. Ferraris * Lunéville 20.4.1726 + Wien 1.4.1814, and had issue:

VII   (1)   **Marie Wilhelmine Gräfin Ferraris** * Wien 3.9.1780 + Wien 25.1.1866 = Wien 6.5.1799 Franz Graf Zichy zu Zich u. Vásonykeö since 1811 styled Graf Zichy-Ferraris * 25.6.1777 + 6.10.1839, and had issue:

VIII   a.   **Henriette Gräfin Zichy-Ferraris zu Zich u. Vásonykeö** * 10.2.1800 + 12.12.1852 Wien = 13.3.1831 Innocenz Prinz Odescalchi * 22.7.1778 + Obermeidling 24.9.1833, and had issue:

IX   a)   **Viktor Innocenz Carl Franz Maria Peter Prinz Odescalchi** * 27.7.1833 + Reichenau 20.7.1880 = Graz 21.1.1864 **Johanna Gräfin Grimaud d'Orsay** * Graz 14.3.1846 + Wien 31.12.1936 dau. of Oscar Graf Grimaud d'Orsay s.p.

VIII   b.   **Josef Graf Zichy-Ferraris zu Zich u. Vásonykeö** * 21.1.1801 + 17.12.1825

                c.   **Emilie Gräfin Zichy-Ferraris zu Zich u. Vásonykeö** * 13.11.1803 + 13.9.1836 = 15.12.1823 Pál Graf Széchényi v. Sárvár-Felsövidék * 10.11.1789 + 30.3.1871, and had issue:

IX   a)   **Kálmán Graf Széchényi v. Sárvár-Felsövidék** * Ödenburg 6.10.1824 + Ödenburg 17.1.1914 = 27.4.1852 Karoline Gräfin v. Grünne * Wien 5.7.1832 + Graz 21.3.1911 dau. of Carl Ludwig Graf v. Grünne, and had issue:

X   (a)   **Károly Philipp Maria Graf Széchényi v. Sárvár-Felsövidék** * 8.5.1853 + ... 193 ...

                     (b)   **Paula Karolina Maria Emilia Gräfin Széchényi v. Sárvár-Felsövidék** * 23.3.1854 + Högyész 20.2.1928 = Wien 24.4.1876 Géza Graf Apponyi v. Nagy-Appony * Wien 13.2.1853 + Högyész 19.2.1927, and had issue:

XI   1a.   **Maria Gräfin Apponyi v. Nagy-Appony** * Wien 24.5.1877 + Rosegg 24.11.1956 = Wien 14.10.1897 Friedrich Aloys Prinz v.u. zu Liechtenstein * Arad 12.9.1871 + Rosegg 10.10.1959, and had issue:

XII   1b.   **Aloys Géza Georg Hubert Maria Prinz v.u. zu Liechtenstein** * Wien 18.6.1898 X Burzowka, Russia 19.2.1943 = Würzburg 20.10.1938 Hertha-Marie Gräfin Wolffskeel v. Reichenberg * Würzburg 31.8.1919 dau. of Luitpold Graf Wolffskeel v. Reichenberg, and had issue:

XIII   1c.   **Luitpold Rudolf Georg Hubertus Prinz v.u. zu Liechtenstein** * Würzburg 11.4.1940

                          2c.   **Maria-Gabrielle Prinzessin v.u. zu Liechtenstein** * Würzburg 7.9.1942

XII	2b.	**Andrea Maria Anna Prinzessin v.u. zu Liechtenstein** * Wien 18.6.1898 + Salzburg 6.4.1944 = Högyész 14.4.1921 Peter Graf v. Ueberacker * Aigen 21.10.1895 + Weyregg 22.6.1961, and had issue:

XIII — 1c. **Wolf Maria Friedrich Othmar Pius Graf v. Ueberacker** * Rosegg 4.2.1922 X France 6.12.1942

XII — 3b. **Alfred Joseph Karl Maria Prinz v.u. zu Liechtenstein** * Pressburg 6.6.1900 = Ungarschitz 24.6.1928 Polixena Gräfin v. Collato u. San Salvatore * Teschendorf 16.10.1905 dau. of Manfred 5 Fürst v. Collato u. San Salvatore, and has issue:

XIII — 1c. **Alexander Friedrich Manfred Maria Prinz v.u. zu Liechtenstein** * Wien 14.5.1929 = Bronnbach 7.1.1961 **Josephine Prinzessin zu Löwenstein-Wertheim-Rosenberg** * Bronnbach 17.5.1937 dau. of Karl 8 Fürst zu Löwenstein-Wertheim-Rosenberg, and has issue:

XIV — 1d. **Christian Prinz v.u. zu Liechtenstein** * Klagenfurt 14.11.1961

XIV — 2d. **Stephan Prinz v.u. zu Liechtenstein** * Klagenfurt 14.11.1961

XIV — 3d. **Emanuel Prinz v.u. zu Liechtenstein** * Klagenfurt 5.5.1964

XIII — 2c. **Elisabeth Franziska Anna Thekla Maria Therese Manfreda Leopoldine Juliane Antonia Prinzessin v.u. zu Liechtenstein** * Wien 17.1.1932

XIII — 3c. **Franz de Paula Alfred Johannes Manfred Maria Theodor Omnes Sancti Prinz v.u. zu Liechtenstein** * Wien 1.11.1935

XII — 4b. **Aloysia Emanuela Maria Prinzessin v.u. zu Liechtenstein** * Wien 23.1.1904 = Rosegg 17.8.1929 Joseph Ritter v. Miller zu Aichholz * Triest 23.5.1897, and has issue:

XIII — 1c. **Alexandra v. Miller zu Aichholz** * Schloss Rosegg 18.5.1930 = 8.4.1961 Siegfried v. Schuckmann * Berlin 25.2.1929, and has issue:

XIV — 1d. **Friedrich Cyril Godfrey v. Schuckmann** * Caracas 4.2.1961

XIV — 2d. **Georg Heinrich Alfred v. Schuckmann** * Bad Aussee 26.7.1963

XIII — 2c. **Godfrey Ritter v. Miller zu Aichholz** * Bronxville, New York 13.3.1933 = Philadelphia, Pa. 31.10.1964 **Maria Countess Plater-Zyberk** * Wilno 9.7.1939 dau. of Count Joseph Plater-Zyberk, and has issue:

XIV — 1d. **Alexander Valerian Arthur Maria Ritter v. Miller zu Aichholz** * 1.8.1965

XIII — 3c. **Alfred Ritter v. Miller zu Aichholz** * New York 26.10.1940

XIII — 4c. **Andrew Ritter v. Miller zu Aichholz** * New York 27.10.1940

2a. **Károly Graf Apponyi v. Nagy-Appony** * Högyész 28.8.1878 + Pálfa, Hung.
3.4.1959 = Wien 25.1.1908 Maria Aglaë Prinzessin zu Windisch-Graetz
* Tachau 11.1.1887 + Wien 2.5.1961 dau. of Alfred 3 Fürst zu Windisch-
Graetz, and had issue:

    1b. **Géza Graf Apponyi v. Nagy-Appony** * Pressburg 27.11.1908
    + Siberia as Prisoner of War 5.5.1946 = Budapest 16.2.1937
    Elisabeth Májó * Pitvaros 9.9.1908 s.p.

    2b. **Gabriella Gräfin Apponyi v. Nagy-Appony** * Lieszko b. Jablonicz
    25.4.1910 = (1) Budapest 22.10.1935 Anton Prinz Eszterházy v.
    Galántha * Lockenhaus 22.7.1903 ✗ Komárom ... 1944; = (2)
    8.1.1948 Iván Graf Draskovich v. Trakostján * Selle 2.4.1916 − div.;
    = (3) Wien 15.11.1948 Wladimir Graf Mittrowsky v. Mittrowitz
    * Sokolnitz 18.2.1901 − div., and has issue:

    by 1st marriage:

        1c. **Anton Rudolf Marie Georg Christoph Hubertus Johannes Karl
        Aglaë Prinz Eszterházy v. Galántha** * Wien 27.12.1936

    3b. **Alfred Graf Apponyi v. Nagy-Appony** * Högyész 17.10.1911
    = Budapest 28.2.1938 Zenaide Gräfin Majláth v. Székhely * Budapest
    29.3.1914 dau. of Georg Graf Majláth v. Székhely, and has issue:

        1c. **Rudolf Graf Apponyi v. Nagy-Appony** * Karlsbad 24.8.1940

        2c. **Alfred Graf Apponyi v. Nagy-Appony** * Prag 25.11.1941

    4b. **Sándor Graf Apponyi v. Nagy-Appony** * Tachau 30.9.1919
    ✗ Russia 3.10.1944

    5b. **Marie-Paula Gräfin Apponyi v. Nagy-Appony** * Tachau 11.1.1921
    = ... Ladislas Béry * 19.10.1898, and has issue:

        1c. **Bálint Béry** * Budapest 11.1.1944

        2c. **Balázs Béry** * Budapest 25.5.1945

        3c. **Bea Béry** * Budapest 21.2.1947

3a. **Alice Gräfin Apponyi v. Nagy-Appony** * Högyész 8.8.1879 = Högyész
15.12.1901 Paul Graf Forni * Modena 5.9.1849 + Bozen 19.3.1925, and
has issue:

    1b. **Maria Josefa Paula Cajetana Aloisia Vincentia Gräfin Forni** * Bozen
    2.4.1903 = Bozen 9.9.1930 Karl Frhr. Plappart v. Leenheer * Wien
    3.6.1877 + Schloss Neuhaus 6.9.1941, and has issue:

        1c. **Karl Maria August Paul Franz Josef Frhr. Plappart v. Leenheer**
        * Neuhaus 10.9.1931 = Wien 21.2.1957 Ingrid Huckel * Wien
        12.5.1933, and has issue:

            1d. **Alexander Frhr. Plappart v. Leenheer** * Wien 30.5.1958

            2d. **Otto Frhr. Plappart v. Leenheer** * Wien 8.2.1960

            3d. **Paul Frhr. Plappart v. Leenheer** * 16.4.1966

XIII		**2c.** **Elisabeth Julie Caroline Marie Freiin. Plappart v. Leenheer** * Neuhaus 18.12.1932 = Neuhaus 3.6.1956 Sigmund Graf v. Spiegelfeld-Schneeburg * Schärding 19.3.1920,and has issue:

XIV

    1d. **Georg Graf v. Spiegelfeld-Schneeburg** * Greiskirchen 1.6.1957

    2d. **Marie-Eleonore Gräfin v. Spiegelfeld-Schneeburg** * Greiskirchen 21.9.1958

    3d. **Josefa-Theresia Gräfin v. Spiegelfeld-Schneeburg** * Greiskirchen 16.9.1963

XIII

3c. **Aglaë Franziska Edouardine Marie Freiin. Plappart v. Leenheer** * Neuhaus 18.12.1932 = Neuhaus 9.5.1964 Hansgeorg v. Löw-Baselli * Braunau 19.9.1937, and has issue:

XIV

    1d. **Martina v. Löw-Baselli** * 27.2.1965

    2d. **Alexandra v. Löw-Baselli** * 6.9.1966

XII

2b. **Franz Josef Géza Maria Alois Heinrich Graf Forni** * Schwarz 9.6.1904 = Meran 25.6.1941 Clementine Gräfin v. Waldstein * Mitterbrabern 14.10.1957 + Kreuzlingen 13.12.1957 dau. of Eugen Graf v. Waldstein s.p.

3b. **Carolina Josefa Alberta Maria Aloisia Angela Gräfin Forni** * Bozen 2.9.1905

4b. **Josefa Agalë Blanca Maria Aloisia Elisabeth Gräfin Forni** * Bozen 14.12.1909

XI

4a. **Rudolf Graf Apponyi v. Nagy-Appony** * Högyész 12.3.1882 + 19.7.1939 = Wien 16.6.1915 Franziska Freiin. v. Holtz * Wien 11.9.1884 + Budapest 29.3.1936 dau. of Georg Frhr. v. Holtz; − div. = (2) Budapest 21.9.1931 Ida Freiin. v. Sammaruga * Wien 25.9.1906 dau. of Guido Frhr. v. Sammaruga s.p.

5a. **Gisella Gräfin Apponyi v. Nagy-Appony** * Ausee 15.7.1886 + Budapest 15.10.1918 = Högyész 25.11.1916 Iván Baron Rubido-Zichy de Zágorja Nich et Zajk * Graz 17.6.1874 + Graz 16.5.1964, and had issue:

XII

1b. **Paula Baronesse Rubido-Zichy de Zágorja Nich et Zajk** * Pressburg 2.9.1917 = 12.2.1940 Pál Graf Erdödy v. Monyorókerék u. Monoszló * Vép 2.2.1904, and has issue:

XIII

    1c. **Gisella Gräfin Erdödy v. Monyorókerék u. Monoszló** * Szombathely 26.7.1941

    2c. **Iván Graf Erdödy v. Monyorókerék u. Monoszló** * Szombathely 23.9.1942

X

(c) **Maria Karolina Felix Gräfin Széchényi v. Sárvár-Felsövidék** * Odenburg 28.6.1855 + Jamnitz 7.10.1932 = Wien 20.6.1876 Alexander Markgraf v. Pallavicini * Wien 6.5.1853 + Wien 14.4.1933, and has issue:

XI

1a. **Karl Maria Alfons Markgraf v. Pallavicini** * 21.3.1877 + Melton Mowbray, England 15.1.1900

2a. **Alfons Maria Markgraf v. Pallavicini** * Wien 10.11.1883 + 18.1.1958
= Gr-Schützen 30.5.1922 Maria Gräfin v. Wenckheim * Gr-Schützen
2.6.1898 dau. of István Graf v. Wenckheim, and had issue:

XII

1b. **Karl Alexander Maria Markgraf v. Pallavicini** * Budapest 12.4.1923
= Lanzago 25.5.1963 Contessa Avogara degli Azzoni Avogardo
* Venezia 23.3.1926 dau. of Conte Alteniero degli Azzoni Avogardo,
and has issue:

XIII

1c. **Alfonso Markgraf v. Pallavicini** * Treviso 5.7.1964

2c. **Edoardo Markgraf v. Pallavicini** * Treviso 7.11.1965

XII

2b. **Friedrich Maria Markgraf v. Pallavicini** * Budapest 23.12.1924 = (1)
Meran 25.5.1945 Maria Gräfin Kinsky v. Wchinitz u. Tettau * Mähr-
Kromau 5.6.1924 + Buenos Aires 14.2.1960 dau. of Ulrich Fürst
Kinsky v. Wchinitz u. Tettau; = (2) Friedrichshafen 23.8.1961
Helene Duchess of Württemberg * Stuttgart 29.6.1929 dau. of Philipp
Duke of Württemberg, and has issue:

by 1st marriage:

XIII

1c. **Alexander Markgraf v. Pallavicini** * Milano 14.5.1946

by 2nd marriage:

2c. **Maria Christina Markgräfin v. Pallavicini** * Salzburg 4.1.1963

3c. **Maria Antoinetta Markgräfin v. Pallavicini** * Ravensburg
9.1.1964

4c. **Gabriella Markgräfin v. Pallavicini** * Ravensburg 23.4.1965

XII

3b. **Alexander Maria Alfons Markgraf v. Pallavicini** * Budapest 8.4.1929

4b. **Elisabeth Maria Markgräfin v. Pallavicini** * Szilvásvárad 19.12.1933
= 16.6.1959 David Harth * East Greenwich, U.S.A. 25.4.1927, and
has issue:

XIII

1c. **Stephan Harth** * Gmunden 26.4.1960

2c. **Nikolaus Harth** * Wien 28.9.1961

XI

3a. **Sándor Koloman Maria Markgraf v. Pallavicini** * Jamnitz 15.11.1890
+ Budapest 26.12.1941

X

(d) **Melanie Karoline Ludovika Maria Gräfin Széchényi v. Sárvár-Felsövidék**
* 5.3.1857 + Sopron 25.11.1927

(e) **Manó Graf Széchényi v. Sárvár-Felsövidék** * 30.7.1858 + Senyefa 29.12.1926
= Raab 11.11.1907 Maria Theresia Gräfin Revertera v. Salandra * St. Petersburg
15.10.1864 + Sopron 27.5.1933 dau. of Friedrich Graf Revertera v. Salandra s.p.

IX

b) **Maria Gräfin Széchényi v. Sárvár-Felsövidék** * 2.10.1825 + 11.3.1849

c) **Elise Gräfin Széchényi v. Sárvár-Felsövidék** * 17.3.1827 + Madrid 28.11.1910
= 8.5.1848 Don Pedro Caro y Alvarez de Toledo 5 Marqués de la Romana * 9.7.1827
+ ... 1890, and had issue:

X	(a)	**Don Pedro Caro y Széchényi 6 Marqués de la Romana** and a Grandee of Spain * 3.7.1849 + 11.4.1916 = 3.4.1880 Doña Maria-de-la-Piedad Martinez de Irujo y del Alcázar * 25.4.1851 + 26.9.1898 dau. of Don Carlos Martinez de Irujo y MacKean, Marqués of Casa Irujo, and Doña Gabriela del Alcázar y Vera de Aragon, in her own right 7 Duchess of Sotomayor, and had issue:	

XI	1a.	**Don Pedro Caro y Martinez de Irujo 7 Marqués de la Romana** and a Grandee of Spain * 20.12.1882 + 26.4.1935 = 2.12.1916 Doña Maria-de-la-Asunción Falcó y de la Gándara, in her own right Marquesa de Almonacid de los Oteros * 17.8.1883, dau. of Don Juan Falcó y Trivulzio, Prince Pio de Saboya 15 Marqués de Castel-Rodrigo and a Grandee of Spain s.p.	
	2a.	**Doña Maria-de-la-Piedad Caro y Martinez de Irujo**, in her own right **8 Marquésa de la Romana** and a Grandee of Spain * 20.1.1884 + 27.3.1965 = 15.6.1922 Don Diego del Alcázar y Roca de Togores, Marqués de Peñafuente * 18.9.1882 + 31.7.1964, and has issue:	

XII	1b.	**Don Diego del Alcázar y Caro 9 Marqués de la Romana, Marqués de Peñafuente** and a Grandee of Spain * 8.10.1925 = 26.11.1949 Doña Maria Teresa Silvela y Arenas * 11.7.1925 dau. of Don Mariano Silvela, and has issue:	

XIII	1c.	**Don Diego del Alcázar y Silvela** * 30.8.1950
	2c.	**Don Mariano del Alcázar y Silvela** * 24.9.1951
	3c.	**Don José del Alcázar y Silvela** * 15.6.1953
	4c.	**Don Jaime del Alcázar y Silvela** * 4.7.1954
	5c.	**Don César del Alcázar y Silvela** * 4.7.1954
	6c.	**Don Isidro del Alcázar y Silvela** * 16.8.1955
	7c.	**Doña Ana Teresa del Alcázar y Silvela** * 5.7.1958

XII	2b.	**Doña Maria-de-la-Piedad del Alcázar y Caro** * 7.10. ... + ...
	3b.	**Don Pedro del Alcázar y Caro, Vizconde de Tuy** * 12.8.1928 = 12.12.1951 Doña Maria-de-la-Piedad Gómez-Acebo y Silvela * 14.6.1930 dau. of Don Juan Gómez-Acebo y Cavmen, and has issue:

XIII	1c.	**Don Juan Pedro del Alcázar y Gómez-Acebo** * 16.2.1956

X	(b)	**Doña Maria Caro y Széchényi** * 28.9.1853 + 7.9.1897 = 28.5.1875 Don Carlos Martinez de Irujo y del Alcázar 8 Duque de Sotomayor and a Grandee of Spain * 3.4.1846 + 14.9.1909, and had issue:	

XI	1a.	**Don Carlos Martinez de Irujo y Caro, Marqués de Casa Irujo** * 28.7.1877 + 3.2.1906
	2a.	**Doña Asunción Isabel Martinez de Irujo y Caro** * Madrid 25.4.1879 + Madrid 12.6.1964 = Madrid 26.11.1902 Don Cristóbal Garcia-Loygorri y Murrieta 3 Duque and 9 Conde de Vistahermosa and a Grandee of Spain * Biarritz 21.7.1873 + Navas de Riofrio (Pr. Sergovia) 9.10.1959 and had issue:

XII	1b.	**Doña Maria Cristina Garcia-Loygorri y Martinez de Irujo** * Madrid 12.12.1903
	2b.	**Doña Teresa Garcia-Loygorri y Martinez de Irujo** * Madrid 20.10.1905

3b. **Doña Victoria Eugenia Garcia-Loygorri y Martinez de Irujo** * Madrid
8.1.1907 = Madrid 26.11.1930 Don Luis de Zulueta * 10.8.1897 s.p.

4b. **Don Mariano Garcia-Loygorri y Martinez de Irujo 4 Duque and 10 Conde
of Vistahermosa** and a Grandee of Spain * Madrid 9.1.1909
= 9.11.1937 Doña Mercedes Urzáiz y Guzmán * Madrid 12.3.1911
dau. of Don Leon Urzáiz y Cuesta, and has issue:

1c. **Don Cristóbal Garcia-Loygorri y Urzáiz** * Madrid 31.5.1940

2c. **Don Carlos Garcia-Loygorri y Urzáiz** * Madrid 2.12.1941

3c. **Doña Mercedes Garcia-Loygorri y Urráiz** * Madrid 9.9.1943

4c. **Don Alvaro Garcia-Loygorri y Urráiz** * Madrid 17.12.1945

5c. **Doña Maria Cristina Garcia-Loygorri y Urráiz** * Madrid
21.9.1950

6c. **Doña Maria del Rosario Garcia-Loygorri y Urráiz** * Madrid
11.10.1955

7c. **Doña Ana Maria Garcia-Loygorri y Urráiz** * Madrid 29.8.1957

5b. **Don Gabriel Garcia-Loygorri y Martinez de Irujo** * Madrid 30.12.1910
= Madrid 10.12.1940 Doña Teresa Escudero y Rivaflecha * Algorta
(Vizcaya) 20.9.1911 dau. of Don José Escudero y Toledo, and has issue:

1c. **Doña Paloma Garcia-Loygorri y Escudero** * Madrid 16.10.1941
= Madrid 18.6.1964 Don Alfredo Illera * Madrid 15.5.1940

2c. **Don Gonzalo Garcia-Loygorri y Escudero** * Madrid 11.5.1943

3c. **Don Juan Garcia-Loygorri y Escudero** * Madrid 25.4.1945

4c. **Don Alfonso Garcia-Loygorri y Escudero** * Madrid 20.5.1948

5c. **Doña Maria Garcia-Loygorri y Escudero** * Navas de Riofrio 10.7.1950

6c. **Don Iñigo Garcia-Loygorri y Escudero** * Madrid 3.3.1952

7c. **Doña Gabriela Garcia-Loygorri y Escudero** * Madrid 20.11.1953

8c. **Doña Carmen Garcia-Loygorri y Escudero** * Madrid 20.10.1957

6b. **Don Pedro Garcia-Loygorri y Martinez de Irujo** * Madrid 29.12.1913
= Madrid 9.4.1942 Doña Concepción Garcia * 2.12.1918 dau. of
Don Diego Garcia y Concha, and has issue:

1c. **Don Diego Garcia-Loygorri y Garcia** * 28.2.1943

2c. **Doña Isabel Garcia-Loygorri y Garcia** * 13.2.1944

3c. **Don Pedro Garcia-Loygorri y Garcia** * 14.1.1945

4c. **Don Luis Garcia-Loygorri y Garcia** * 18.6.1946

5c. **Don Santiago Garcia-Loygorri y Garcia** * 21.8.1947

6c. **Don José Garcia-Loygorri y Garcia** * 18.8.1948

7c. **Don Miguel Garcia-Loygorri y Garcia** * 15.7.1950

8c. **Don Javier Garcia-Loygorri y Garcia** * 3.11.1951

9c. **Doña Concepción Garcia-Loygorri y Garcia** * 24.11.1952

10c. **Don Rafael Garcia-Loygorri y Garcia** * 16.6.1957

11c. **Doña Marta Garcia-Loygorri y Garcia** * 12.9.1959

12c. **Don Angela Garcia-Loygorri y Garcia** * 9.3.1962

XII		7b.	**Doña Isabel Garcia-Loygorri y Martinez de Irujo** * Madrid 4.10.1916 = Madrid 17.11.1951 Don Luis Zavala y Igartúra * 29.8.1915, and has issue:

XIII

    1c.   **Don Martin Zavala y Garcia-Loygorri** * Madrid 17.9.1952

    2c.   **Don Luis Zavala y Garcia-Loygorri** * Madrid 29.12.1953

    3c.   **Don Jaime Zavala y Garcia-Loygorri** * Madrid 16.3.1955

    4c.   **Doña Mercedes Zavala y Garcia-Loygorri** * Madrid 29.11.1959

XI   3a.   **Doña Maria-de-la-Piedad Martinez de Irujo y Caro** * 10.8.1880 + Madrid 20.5.1954

            4a.   **Doña Maria-del-Rosario Martinez de Irujo y Caro** * 2.10.1881 + Madrid 24.1.1951 = ... 1916 Don Manuel de Mendivil y Elio * 4.11.1874 + San Sebastian 5.4.1942, and had issue:

XII   1b.   **Don Manuel Mendivil y Martinez de Irujo** * 19.4.1917 + San Sebastian 31.1.1938

XI   5a.   **Don Pedro Martinez de Irujo y Caro 9 Duque de Sotomayor** and a Grandee of Spain * 3.10.1882 + San Sebastian 5.9.1957 = 26.10.1910 Doña Ana-Maria de Artázcoz y Labayen * 20.9.1892 + Torres Lodornes 9.1.1930 dau. of Don Francisco-Javier de Artázcoz, and had issue:

XII   1b.   **Don Carlos Martinez de Irujo y Artázcoz** * 18.8.1911 ✗ in Civil War 13.6.1937

            2b.   **Doña Maria Victoria Martinez de Irujo y Artázcoz** * 18.8.1912 = San Sebastian 3.6.1937 Don Alfonso de Hoyos y Sanchez Duque de Almodóvar del Rio and a Grandee of Spain * 5.5.1906, and has issue:

XIII   1c.   **Doña Ana-Maria Hoyos y Martinez de Irujo** * 2.4.1938 + 16.1.1941

            2c.   **Doña Isabel Hoyos y Martinez de Irujo** * 15.6.1939 = 6.9.1962 Don Jaime Carvajal y Urquijo Marqués de Isasi * 7.6.1939, and has issue:

XIV   1d.   **Doña Ana-Maria Carvajal y Hoyos** * 22.7.1963

            2d.   **Don Jaime Carvajal y Hoyos** * 3.8.1964

            3d.   **Doña Victoria Carvajal y Hoyos** * 19.3.1966

XIII   3c.   **Don Isidoro Hoyos y Martinez de Irujo** * 19.10.1940

            4c.   **Doña Teresa Hoyos y Martinez de Irujo** * 15.11.1942 = 27.6.1966 Don Lucas Oriol y López Montenegro * 7.11.1944

            5c.   **Doña Mercedes Hoyos y Martinez de Irujo** * 27.2.1944

            6c.   **Doña Genoveva Hoyos y Martinez de Irujo** * 13.5.1945 = 27.10.1966 Don Rámon Serrano Suner * 17.2.1946

            7c.   **Doña Maria Luisa Hoyos y Martinez de Irujo** * 27.9.1946

            8c.   **Doña Victoria Hoyos y Martinez de Irujo** * 11.9.1949

            9c.   **Don Juan Manuel Hoyos y Martinez de Irujo** * 7.1.1953

3b. **Don Ignacio Martinez de Irujo y Artázcoz 10 Duque de Sotomayor**
and a Grandee of Spain * 24.12.1913 = Madrid 8.4.1947 Doña
Antonia Crespo y Rayband * 24.1.1922, dau. of Don Antonio Crespo
y Vivot, and has issue:

    1c.   **Don Carlos Martinez de Irujo y Crespo** * 29.3.1948

    2c.   **Doña Maria Martinez de Irujo y Crespo** * 27.6.1949

    3c.   **Doña Mercedes Martinez de Irujo y Crespo** * 11.8.1950

    4c.   **Don Ignacio Martinez de Irujo y Crespo** * 21.3.1954

    5c.   **Doña Maria Luisa Martinez de Irujo y Crespo** * 11.3.1955

    6c.   **Don José Martinez de Irujo y Crespo** * 30.10.1962

4b. **Don Francisco-Javier Martinez de Irujo y Artázcoz** * 27.6.1916
= Madrid 25.11.1943 Doña Teresa Garnica y Mansi * 3.2.1919 dau.
of Don Pablo Garnica y Rosario, and has issue:

    1c.   **Doña Ana-Maria Martinez de Irujo y Garnica** * 16.8.1945

    2c.   **Don Francisco-Javier Martinez de Irujo y Garnica** * 27.12.1946

    3c.   **Don Pedro Martinez de Irujo y Garnica** * 1.8.1948 + 5.7.1965

    4c.   **Doña Maria José Martinez de Irujo y Garnica** * 19.3.1950

    5c.   **Don Jaime Martinez de Irujo y Garnica** * 4.6.1951

    6c.   **Doña Maria Teresa Martinez de Irujo y Garnica** * 21.9.1956

    7c.   **Doña Mónica Martinez de Irujo y Garnica** * 4.4.1958

5b. **Don Pedro Martinez de Irujo y Artázcoz** * 17.8.1917 X in Civil War
22.9.1938

6b. **Don Luis Martinez de Irujo y Artázcoz** * Madrid 17.11.1919
= Seville 12.10.1948 Doña Maria del Rosario Cayetana Fitz-James
Stuart y Silva, 18 Duquesa de Alba and a Grandee of Spain * Madrid
28.3.1926 dau. of Don Jacobo Fitz-James Stuart y Falcó
17 Duque de Alba and has issue:

    1c.   **Don Carlos Martinez de Irujo y Fitz-James Stuart, Duque de
Heuscar** and a Grandee of Spain * Madrid 2.10.1948

    2c.   **Don Alfonso Martinez de Irujo y Fitz-James Stuart, Duque de
Hijar** and a Grandee of Spain * Madrid 22.10.1950

    3c.   **Don Jacobo Martinez de Irujo y Fitz-James Stuart** * Madrid
15.7.1954

    4c.   **Don Fernando José Martinez de Irujo y Fitz-James Stuart**
* Madrid 11.7.1959

    5c.   **Don Cayetano Luis Martinez de Irujo y Fitz-James Stuart**
* Madrid 4.4.1963

7b. **Doña Ana-Maria Martinez de Irujo y Artázcoz** * 20.4.1921 = Madrid
8.3.1943 Don Manuel Loring y Gilhou, Conde de Mieres * 17.3.1917,
and has issue:

    1c.   **Doña Ana-Maria Loring y Martinez de Irujo** * 12.12.1943

           Doña Cristina Loring y Martinez de Irujo * 11.3.1945

XIII		3c.	**Don Manuel Loring y Martinez de Irujo** * 8.5.1946
		4c.	**Don Carlos Loring y Martinez de Irujo** * 11.8.1947
		5c.	**Doña Enriqueta Loring y Martinez de Irujo** * 5.9.1948
		6c.	**Doña Maria Julia Loring y Martinez de Irujo** * 21.12.1949
		7c.	**Don Pedro Loring y Martinez de Irujo** * 30.1.1951
		8c.	**Doña Mónica Loring y Martinez de Irujo** * 19.3.1952
		9c.	**Don Jaime Loring y Martinez de Irujo** * 24.7.1953
		10c.	**Don José Loring y Martinez de Irujo** * 7.7.1954
		11c.	**Doña Marta Loring y Martinez de Irujo** * 2.8.1958

XII 8b. **Doña Maria Cristina Martinez de Irujo y Artázcoz** * 16.1.1923 = Madrid 28.8.1952 Don Maurico Obregón y Andreu * 22.9.1921, and has issue:

XIII 1c. **Don Sancho Obregón y Martinez de Irujo** * 14.7.1953

2c. **Don Javier Obregón y Martinez de Irujo** * 3.12.1954

3c. **Don Santiago Obregón y Martinez de Irujo** * 1.12.1955

4c. **Doña Inés Obregón y Martinez de Irujo** * 1.4.1957

5c. **Doña Ana-Maria Obregón y Martinez de Irujo** * 10.8.1960

6c. **Don Beltran Obregón y Martinez de Irujo** * 3.10.1964

XII 9b. **Don Jaime Martinez de Irujo y Artázcoz** * 23.5.1925 = Madrid 2.7.1961 **Doña Blanca Figueroa y Borbon** * 8.8.1932 dau. of Don Luis de Figueroa y Alfonso Martinez, Conde de Romanones, and a Grandee of Spain, and has issue:

XIII 1c. **Don Jaime Martinez de Irujo y Figueroa** * 13.4.1962

2c. **Don Luis Martinez de Irujo y Figueroa** * 21.3.1964

XII 10b. **Don José Maria Martinez de Irujo y Artázcoz** * 7.7.1928

XI 6a. **Don Juan Gualberto Martinez de Irujo y Caro** * 10.12.1883 + 6.2.1892

7a. **Don Luis Martinez de Irujo y Caro, Marqués de los Arcos** * 15.1.1886 + Madrid 11.10.1962 = 8.5.1922 Doña Guadalupe Aspe y Suinaga * 4.5.1899 + Madrid 14.9.1960, and had issue:

XII 1b. **Doña Maria Luisa Martinez de Irujo y Aspe, Marquesa de los Arcos** * 4.3.1923 = 9.5.1955 Don Javier Chapa y Galindez * 11.4.1918, and has issue:

XIII 1c. **Doña Cristina Chapa y Martinez de Irujo** * 16.12.1955

2c. **Don Luis Chapa y Martinez de Irujo** * 17.1.1957

XII 2b. **Doña Ana Teresa Martinez de Irujo y Aspe** * 10.2.1925 = 28.6.1963 Don Hernán Calero y Charles * 5.2.1923, and has issue:

XIII 1c. **Doña Maria Luisa Calero y Aspe** * 18.6.1964

XI 8a. **Doña Teresa Martinez de Irujo y Caro** * 25.2.1888 + 22.2.1892

Photo "Amer"

20   Don Carlos Martinez de Irujo y FitzJames Stuart,
Duque de Huescar

9a. **Doña Gabriela Martinez de Irujo y Caro** * 25.4.1890 + 21.2.1892

10a. **Doña Fernanda Martinez de Irujo y Caro** * 30.5.1895 + 22.2.1901

11a. **Doña Cristina Martinez de Irujo y Caro** * 2.7.1892 = Madrid 31.5.1929
Don Emilio Aznar y Puente, Marqués de Zuya * 11.7.1898 + 14.3.1950 s.p.

X

(c) **Don José Caro y Széchényi** * 21.10.1863 X during the Spanish Civil War

(d) **Doña Maria-del-Pilar Caro y Széchényi** * 26.2.1864 + 28.12.1931 = 1.3.1886
Don José-Maria Guillamas y Piñeyro 10 Marqués of San Felices, and a Grandee of
Spain * ... 1857 + 21.4.1895; = (2) 11.3.1899 Don Carlos Martinez y Irujo del
Alcázar, 8 Duque de Sotomayor, and a Grandee of Spain * 3.4.1846 + 14.9.1909;
= (3) ... Don Pedro Alvarez de Toledo y Samaniego, 11 Marqués de Martorell
* 27.10.1867 + ... and had issue:

by 1st marriage:

XI

1a. **Doña Isabel Guillamas y Caro Marquesa de San Felices** * Madrid 10.3.1887
= Madrid 11.6.1906 Don José Azlor de Aragón y Hurtado de Zaldivar 17 Duque
de Villahermosa e Luna and a Grandee of Spain * Biarritz 14.1.1873
+ San Sebastian 18.7.1960

XII

1b. **Doña Maria-del-Pilar Azlor de Aragón y Guillamas** * Saint-Sebastian
1.10.1908, in her own right 18 Duquesa de Villahermosa e Luna,
= Madrid 12.6.1935 Don Mariano Urzáiz y Silva, Conde del Puerto
* 23.4.1904, and has issue:

XIII

1c. **Doña Pilar Urzáiz y Azlor de Aragón** * 4.6.1936 = 7.10.1959
Don Santiago Muguiro y Liniers * 30.6.1932, and has issue:

XIV

1d. **Doña Marcelina Muguiro y Urzáiz** * 22.4.1962

XIII

2c. **Don Alvaro Urzáiz y Azlor de Aragón** * 14.6.1937

3c. **Don Javier Urzáiz y Azlor de Aragón** * 10.8.1940

4c. **Don Luis Urząiz y Azlor de Aragón** * 16.9.1943

5c. **Don Alfonso Urząiz y Azlor de Aragón** * 19.12.1944

XII

2b. **Doña Maria-del-Carmen Azlor de Aragón y Guillamas** * Saint-Sebastian
20.10.1912 8 Duquesa de Granada de Ega = 16.6.1941 Don Alfonso
Martos y Zabálburu Marqués de Casa Tilly * 23.6.1907, and has issue:

XIII

1c. **Don Juan Alfonso Martos y Azlor de Aragón** * 28.8.1942

2c. **Don Marcelino Martos y Azlor de Aragón** * 19.9.1943

3c. **Doña Carmen Martos y Azlor de Aragón** * 20.9.1944

4c. **Don José Martos y Azlor de Aragón** * 13.1.1948

5c. **Don Javier Martos y Azlor de Aragón** * 23.2.1950

6c. **Doña Isabel Martos y Azlor de Aragón** * 18.6.1953

XII

3b. **Doña Isabel Azlor de Aragón y Guillamas, Marquésa de Narros**
* Madrid 9.4.1919

4b. **Doña Maria de la Concepción Azlor de Aragón y Guillamas, Marquesa
de San Felices** * Madrid 31.5.1924 = 2.9.1952 Don Pablo de Churruca
y de la Plaza * 3.4.1924, and has issue:

XIII	1c.	**Don Ignacio Churruca y Azlor de Aragón** * 26.7.1953
	2c.	**Don Pablo Churruca y Azlor de Aragón** * 6.5.1955
	3c.	**Doña Maria Isabel Churruca y Azlor de Aragón** * 13.11.1957
	4c.	**Don Jaime Churruca y Azlor de Aragón** * 9.7.1960
	5c.	**Doña Elena Churruca y Azlor de Aragón** * 11.4.1963

XI   2a. **Doña Maria-de-los-Dolores Guillamas y Caro, Condessa de Alcolea del Torote** * 22.3.1888 = 28.6.1911 Don Pedro Diez de Rivera y Figueroa 4 Conde de Almodóvar, and a Grandee of Spain * 25.6.1886, and has issue:

XII   1b. **Doña Dolores Diez de Rivera y Guillamas** * 19.8.1912 = 11.5.1940 Don Camilo Juliá y Bacardi Marqués de Juliá * 15.5.1907, and has issue:

XIII	1c.	**Don Javier Juliá y Diez de Rivera** * 24.7.1941
	2c.	**Doña Belén Juliá y Diez de Rivera** * 23.12.1942
	3c.	**Don Miguel Juliá y Diez de Rivera** * 27.2.1946 + 19.10.1959
	4c.	**Doña Josefa Juliá y Diez de Rivera** * 1.11.1944
	5c.	**Doña Dolores Juliá y Diez de Rivera** * 9.12.1947
	6c.	**Doña Ana Maria Juliá y Diez de Rivera** * 29.9.1949
	7c.	**Doña Isabel Juliá y Diez de Rivera** * 9.8.1951
	8c.	**Don Jorge Juliá y Diez de Rivera** * 16.3.1955

XII   2b. **Doña Cristina Diez de Rivera y Guillamas** * 9.8.1913 = 4.5.1944 Don Fernando Merry del Val y Zapata * 22.2.1902, and has issue:

XIII	1c.	**Don Pedro Merry del Val y Diez de Rivera** * 24.4.1945
	2c.	**Don Fernando Merry del Val y Diez de Rivera** * 16.5.1947

XII   3b. **Doña Victoria Diez de Rivera y Guillamas** * 31.3.1918 = 27.12.1940 Don Joaquin Fernández de Córdoba * 11.1.1905 s.p.

         4b. **Doña Maria Francisca Diez de Rivera y Guillamas** * 7.8.1924 = 5.7.1944 Don Alfonso Armada y Comyn * 12.2.1920, and has issue:

XIII	1c.	**Don Juan Armada y Diez de Rivera** * 18.4.1945
	2c.	**Doña Rosario Armada y Diez de Rivera** * 28.9.1946
	3c.	**Don Pedro Armada y Diez de Rivera** * 25.6.1948
	4c.	**Doña Victoria Armada y Diez de Rivera** * 21.6.1950
	5c.	**Doña Maria Armada y Diez de Rivera** * 27.1.1952
	6c.	**Don Alfonso Armada y Diez de Rivera** * 10.7.1954
	7c.	**Don Ignacio Armada y Diez de Rivera** * 1.8.1957
	8c.	**Doña Isabel Armada y Diez de Rivera** * 22.1.1961
	9c.	**Doña Paz Armada y Diez de Rivera** * 5.7.1962
	10c.	**Don Luis Armada y Diez de Rivera** * 11.1.1964

XI   3a. **Doña Maria-del-Pilar Guillamas y Caro, Marquesa de Campofértil** * 19.3.1890 = 10.2.1914 Don José Beneyto y Rostoll * Altea (Alicante) 1882 + 22.11.1936, and has issue:

XII

    1b.   **Doña Teresa Beneyto y Guillamas** * 15.10.1914 + 5.3.1937

    2b.   **Doña Ana-Maria Beneyto y Guillamas** * 23.11.1917

    3b.   **Doña Josefa Beneyto y Guillamas** * 18.3.1920 = 12.10.1949 Don José Antonio Sopranis y Salto * 7.7.1917, and has issue:

XIII

        1c.   **Doña Maria Sopranis y Beneyto** * 14.7.1950

        2c.   **Doña Teresa Sopranis y Beneyto** * 1.6.1953

        3c.   **Doña Isabel Sopranis y Beneyto** * 23.9.1954

        4c.   **Don José Sopranis y Beneyto** * 14.10.1959

XII

    4b.   **Don Alvaro Beneyto y Guillamas** * 3.5.1923 = 30.3.1950 Doña Nieves Sanz y Martinez * Madrid 3.8.1925 dau. of Emilio Sanz, and has issue:

XIII

        1c.   **Don Alvaro Beneyto y Sanz** * Madrid 9.2.1951

        2c.   **Don José Santiago Beneyto y Sanz** * Palma de Mallorca 15.10.1956

XI

    4a.   **Doña Josefa Guillamas y Caro, Condessa de Buenavista de la Victoria** * 28.6.1892 = 15.1.1920 Don Mariano Cabeza de Vaca y Santos-Suárez 11 Conde de Catres * 1.5.1895, and has issue:

XII

    1b.   **Doña Josefa Cabeza de Vaca y Guillamas** * 12.3.1921 = 7.7.1944 Don Manuel Aguilar y Hardisson * 27.3.1919 s.p.

    2b.   **Don Joaquin Cabeza de Vaca y Guillamas 12 Conde de Catres** * 25.3.1922 = 13.10.1955 Doña Carmen Torroja y Cavanillas * 8.3.1930 dau. of Don Eduardo Torroja, and has issue:

XIII

        1c.   **Don Joaquin Cabeza de Vaca y Torroja** * 16.4.1957

        2c.   **Don Alvar Cabeza de Vaca y Torroja** * 27.9.1958

        3c.   **Doña Isabel Cabeza de Vaca y Torroja** * 11.3.1960

        4c.   **Don Ignacio Cabeza de Vaca y Torroja** * 14.4.1961

        5c.   **Doña Myriam Cabeza de Vaca y Torroja** * 3.9.1963

XII

    3b.   **Doña Pilar Cabeza de Vaca y Guillamas** * 18.5.1923 = 14.10.1949 Don Juan Torroba y Gómez Acebo * 21.3.1915, and has issue:

XIII

        1c.   **Doña Marta Torroba y Cabeza de Vaca** * 30.7.1950

        2c.   **Don Juan Torroba y Cabeza de Vaca** * 15.8.1951

        3c.   **Don Manuel Torroba y Cabeza de Vaca** * 9.5.1953

        4c.   **Doña Maria Torroba y Cabeza de Vaca** * 25.5.1958

XI

    5a.   **Doña Maria Guillamas y Caro** * 16.6.1893 = 17.5.1917 Don Miguel Angel de Muguiro * 3.7.1880 + 4.10.1954 s.p.

Issue by 2nd marriage:

    6a.   **Doña Maria-del-Carmen Martinez de Irujo y Caro** * 12.10.1899 = 22.2.1922 Don Alejandro Pidal y Guilhou * 20.5.1899 + 26.6.1962, and has issue:

XII	1b.	**Doña Maria Pidal y Martinez de Irujo** * 3.12.1922 = 14.7.1949 Don Juan Figaredo y Sela * 9.4.1924, and has issue:

XIII

1c. **Doña Maria Figaredo y Pidal** * 16.4.1950

2c. **Don Juan Figaredo y Pidal** * 24.12.1952

3c. **Don Alejandro Figaredo y Pidal** * 16.12.1954

4c. **Doña Covadogna Figaredo y Pidal** * 15.3.1956

5c. **Don Luis Figaredo y Pidal** * 15.3.1957

6c. **Don Pedro Figaredo y Pidal** * 3.4.1959

7c. **Doña Teresa Figaredo y Pidal** * 11.6.1960

XII   2b. **Doña Jacoba Pidal y Martinez de Irujo** * 25.7.1924 = 1.7.1944 Don Mariano Suarez y Pola * 15.10.1913, and has issue:

XIII

1c. **Don Mariano Suarez y Pidal** * 20.5.1945

2c. **Doña Carmen Suarez y Pidal** * 18.6.1946

3c. **Doña Cristina Suarez y Pidal** * 15.9.1947

4c. **Don Luis Suarez y Pidal** * 31.3.1952

5c. **Doña Maria Suarez y Pidal** * 7.12.1953

6c. **Doña Jacoba Suarez y Pidal** * 22.6.1961

XII   3b. **Doña Carlota Pidal y Martinez de Irujo** * 27.1.1927 = 1.7.1948 Don José Tartierre y Diaz * 1.4.1926, and has issue:

XIII

1c. **Don José Tartierre y Pidal** * 2.5.1949

2c. **Doña Carlota Tartierre y Pidal** * 19.8.1950

3c. **Doña Carmen Tartierre y Pidal** * 25.2.1952

4c. **Doña Maria Dolores Tartierre y Pidal** * 18.7.1953

5c. **Doña Pilar Tartierre y Pidal** * 20.8.1956

6c. **Doña Ana Tartierre y Pidal** * 23.1.1959

7c. **Don Alejandro Tartierre y Pidal** * 14.10.1960

8c. **Don Ramón Tartierre y Pidal** * 12.6.1962

9c. **Don Manuel Tartierre y Pidal** * 30.3.1964

XII   4b. **Doña Pilar Pidal y Martinez de Irujo** * 3.4.1928 = 9.9.1957 Don Cándido Figar y Alvarez * 5.5.1923, and has issue:

XIII

1c. **Don Santiago Figar y Pidal** * 25.8.1958

2c. **Doña Gabriela Figar y Pidal** * 16.3.1960

XII   5b. **Doña Marta Pidal y Martinez de Irujo** * 23.1.1929 = 22.7.1958 Don Juan Uhagón y Fernández * 26.8.1924, and has issue:

XIII

1c. **Don Juan Uhagón y Pidal** * 5.7.1959

2c. **Doña Marta Uhagón y Pidal** * 30.12.1961

XII   6b. **Don Alejandro Pidal y Martinez de Irujo** * 15.4.1931 + 24.5.1947

334

XII	7b.	**Don Ignacio Pidal y Martinez de Irujo** * 13.5.1935 + 2.2.1963
	8b.	**Don Manuel Pidal y Martinez de Irujo** * 1.1.1939 + 25.2.1963
	9b.	**Doña Carmen Pidal y Martinez de Irujo** * 25.5.1941
	10b.	**Don Enrique Pidal y Martinez de Irujo** * 16.12.1944

XI   7a.   **Don Ignacio Martinez de Irujo y Caro** * 20.11.1901 + 8.11.1924

     8a.   **Doña Carlota Martinez de Irujo y Caro** * 13.9.1904 + 25.9.1946
= 3.3.1927 Don Gonzalo Taboada y Sangro * 10.9.1900 + 10.8.1956,
and had issue:

XII   1b.   **Don Ignacio Taboada y Martinez de Irujo** * Madrid 5.1.1928
= 8.4.1957 Doña Maria Rosa Arechabala y Rodrigo * 6.10.1934
Don José Nicolas Arechabala y Teresa, and has issue:

XIII   1c.   **Don Ignacio Taboada y Arechabala** * Valencia 29.10.1958

         2c.   **Don Javier Taboada y Arechabala** * Madrid 27.1.1960

         3c.   **Don Gonzalo Taboada y Arechabala** * Madrid 24.10.1962

         4c.   **Doña Teresa Taboada y Arechabala** * Madrid 12.4.1965

XII   2b.   **Don Gonzalo Taboada y Martinez de Irujo** * Madrid 6.11.1928
= 7.6.1966 Doña Isabel Marichalar y Silva * San Sebastian 25.12.1939

     3b.   **Don Jaime Taboada y Martinez de Irujo** * Madrid 11.6.1931

     4b.   **Doña Victoria Taboada y Martinez de Irujo** * Zarauz 30.3.1939

X   (e)   **Don Alvaro Caro y Széchényi** * Palma de Mallorca 12.10.1856 + San Sebastian
29.9.1923 = 14.2.1885 Doña Isabel Guillamas y Piñeyro * Madrid 21.5.1864
+ San Sebastian 27.6.1932, Marquesa de Villamayor and Condessa de Torrubia,
dau. of Don Fernando Guillamas y Castañón 9 Marqués de San Felices, and a
Grandee of Spain, and had issue:

XI   1a.   **Don Alvaro Caro y Guillamas Conde de Torrubia** * 24.9.1887 + 16.12.1962
= 29.9.1913 Doña Maria Francisca Diaz de Tuesta y Garcia * 21.4.1891
dau. of Don Miguel Diaz de Tuesta, and has issue:

XII   1b.   **Don Alvaro Caro y Diaz de Tuesta Marqués de Villamayor** * 18.1.1915

     2b.   **Doña Maria Isabel Caro y Diaz de Tuesta** * 12.4.1919 + 20.1.1957

     3b.   **Doña Maria Francisca Caro y Diaz de Tuesta** * 17.5.1920 + 26.8.1947

     4b.   **Doña Ana Maria Caro y Diaz de Tuesta** * 11.5.1921

     5b.   **Don Luis Caro y Diaz de Tuesta** * 12.6.1925 = 20.9.1950 Regine
Franck * Bayonne 14.5.1927 dau. of Guy Franck, and has issue:

XIII   1c.   **Doña Cristina Caro y Franck** * Paris 20.7.1951

         2c.   **Doña Paloma Caro y Franck** * Paris 23.2.1961

XII   6b.   **Don Juan Caro y Diaz de Tuesta** * 17.10.1926

     7b.   **Don Fernando Caro y Diaz de Tuesta** * 16.8.1931

XI   2a.   **Don Juan Caro y Guillamas** * Madrid 31.12.1891 + Madrid 6.5.1963
= 12.8.1926 Doña Mercedes Aznar y Gonzalez * 10.11.1894 dau. of
Don Edouardo Aznar, and has issue:

335

XII	1b.	**Don Rafael Caro y Aznar** * Bérriz (Vizcaya) 24.10.1927 = 7.10.1952 Doña Maria-del-Carmen Aguirre y Laiseca * Las Arenas (Vizcaya) 18.7.1930 dau. of Don Jaime Aguirre, and has issue:

<blockquote>

XIII   1c. **Don Alfonso Caro y Aguirre** * Bilbao 11.11.1953

2c. **Don Gonzalo Caro y Aguirre** * Bilbao 7.1.1955

3c. **Don Jaime Caro y Aguirre** * Bilbao 5.5.1956

4c. **Don Juan Caro y Aguirre** * Bilbao 4.4.1957

5c. **Doña Victoria Caro y Aguirre** * Bilbao 2.4.1959

6c. **Don Rafael Caro y Aguirre** * Bilbao 24.10.1961

</blockquote>

XII   2b. **Don Ignacio Caro y Aznar** * Bérriz 30.7.1929 = 11.2.1957 Doña Elisa Echevarria y Wakonigg * Bilbao 13.2.1933 dau. of Don Arturo Echevarria, and has issue:

<blockquote>

XIII   1c. **Doña Cristina Caro y Echevarria** * Bilbao 25.5.1958

2c. **Don Diego Caro y Echevarria** * Bilbao 11.8.1962

</blockquote>

XII   3b. **Don José Maria Caro y Aznar** * Las Arenas 14.2.1931 = 24.9.1955 Doña Lourdes Olávarri y Sota * Bilbao 8.8.1931 dau. of Don Luis Olávarri, and has issue:

<blockquote>

XIII   1c. **Doña Mercedes Caro y Olávarri** * Bilbao 12.7.1956

2c. **Doña Catalina Caro y Olávarri** * Bilbao 24.6.1957

3c. **Doña Lourdes Caro y Olávarri** * Bilbao 12.12.1958

4c. **Doña Guadalupe Caro y Olávarri** * Bilbao 23.6.1960

5c. **Doña Pilar Caro y Olávarri** * Bilbao 12.10.1961

6c. **Don Luis Caro y Olávarri** * Bilbao 22.11.1962

</blockquote>

XII   4b. **Doña Isabel Caro y Aznar** * Las Arenas 22.10.1932

5b. **Don Eduardo Caro y Aznar** * Las Arenas 18.7.1934

XI   3a. **Don José Caro y Guillamas** * 7.11.1894 = 12.9.1927 Doña Maria Carvajal y Xifrré * 7.3.1907, dau. of Don Francisco Carvajal y Hurtado de Mendoza Conde de Fontanar, and has issue:

XII   1b. **Don Alvaro Caro y Carvajal** * 10.7.1928 = 19.11.1958 Donna Suzanna Zezza * 24.7.1935 dau. of Francesco Barone Zezza, and has issue:

<blockquote>

XIII   1c. **Don Alvaro Caro y Zezza** * 9.9.1959

2c. **Doña Marina Caro y Zezza** * 27.12.1960

</blockquote>

XI   4a. **Doña Isabel Caro y Guillamas** * San Sebastian 5.9.1897 + Barcelona 26.1.1929 = 3.11.1919 Don Carlos de Salamanca y Hurtado de Zaldivar Visconde de Bahia Honda * Bayonne 23.8.1887, and has issue:

XII   1b. **Doña Maria Salamanca y Caro** * San Sebastian 2.8.1920 = (1) Paris 28.12.1938 Don Alberto Monteiro de Carvalho * Santos, Brazil 10.12.1912 + Rio de Janeiro 18.7.1946; = (2) Madrid 11.9.1952 Hans Graf Larisch v. Moennich * 15.11.1917, and has issue:

by 1st marriage:

XIII

1c.   **Doña Beatrix Monteiro de Carvalho y Salamanca** * 24.9.1939
= Rio de Janeiro 28.5.19 ... Don Manuel Bayard Lucas de Lima
* Uruguayana, Brazil 6.10.1936, and has issue:

XIV

1d.   **Don Manoel Bayard Monteiro Lucas de Lima** * Rio de
Janeiro 18.11.1961

2d.   **Doña Maria de Graca Betina. Monteiro Lucas de Lima**
* Rio de Janeiro * 25.6.1963

XIII

2c.   **Don Olavo Egidio Monteiro de Carvalho y Salamanca** * Rio de
Janiero 24.2.1941

by 2nd marriage:

3c.   **Heinrich Graf Larisch v. Moennich** * Rio de Janeiro 7.7.1953

4c.   **Johann Graf Larisch v. Moennich** * Rio de Janeiro 6.8.1955

5c.   **Alexander Graf Larisch v. Moennich** * Rio de Janeiro 26.5.1957

6c.   **Ludwig Graf Larisch v. Moennich** * Rio de Janeiro 3.8.1959

XII

2b.   **Doña Maria Cristina Salamanca y Caro** * 6.1.1922 = 27.6.1959
Don Iñigo de Arteaga y Falguera, Duque del Infantado, and a Grandee
of Spain * 14.11.1905 s.p.

3b.   **Doña Isabel Salamanca y Caro** * 27.1.1923 = 15.12.1952 Don Antonio
Menchaca y Careaga * 15.7.1921, and has issue:

XIII

1c.   **Doña Maria Menchaca y Salamanca** * 22.1.1957

XII

4b.   **Doña Teresa Salamanca y Caro** * 11.2.1926 = 17.12.1954 Don José
Moreno y Benjumea * 7.5.1929, and has issue:

XIII

1c.   **Doña Isabel Moreno y Salamanca** * 13.11.1955

2c.   **Doña Maria Moreno y Salamanca** * 27.2.1958

3c.   **Doña Cristina Moreno y Salamanca** * 13.10.1959

4c.   **Don José Carlos Moreno y Salamanca** * 10.12.1963

XI

5a.   **Don Fernando Caro y Guillamas** * 19.1.1900 + 1.7.1931

6a.   **Doña Maria-del-Carmen Caro y Guillamas** * 27.1.1902 = 19.11.1926
Don Eduardo Brunet y Isasi * 9.1.1902 + 27.7.1949, and has issue:

XII

1b.   **Don Alvaro Brunet y Caro** * 15.12.1927 = 5.5.1962 Doña Maria
Victoria Alvarez de Sotomayor y Zircola * 13.11.1936 dau. of Don
German Alvarez de Sotomayor, and has issue:

XIII

1c.   **Doña Maria Brunet y Alvarez de Sotomayor** * 27.2.1963

2c.   **Don Eduardo Brunet y Alvarez de Sotomayor** * 13.9.1964

XII

2b.   **Doña Teresa Brunet y Caro** * 18.12.1929 = 28.4.1949 Don Dario
Crespo y Medina * 13.11.1915, and has issue:

XIII

1c.   **Don Eduardo Crespo y Brunet** * 23.8.1950

337

XIII	2c.	**Don Juan Ignacio Crespo y Brunet** * 27.12.1951
	3c.	**Doña Maria Teresa Crespo y Brunet** * 23.4.1954
	4c.	**Doña Isabel Crespo y Brunet** * 12.6.1957
	5c.	**Doña Silvia Crespo y Brunet** * 12.1.1960
	6c.	**Don Diego Crespo y Brunet** * 2.6.1962
XII	3b.	**Don Alfonso Brunet y Caro** * 28.3.1934
	4b.	**Doña Isabel Brunet y Caro** * 8.8.1938 = 14.10.1959 Don Ignacio Colmenares y Gómez Acebo, Conde de las Posadas * 10.9.1932, and has issue:
XIII	1c.	**Don Ignacio Colmenares y Brunet** * 7.2.1961
	2c.	**Doña Maria Colmenares y Brunet** * 28.6.1962
XI	7a.	**Don Pedro Caro y Guillamas** * 13.1.1905 = 25.7.1932 Doña Maria Rosa Vázquez y Silva, Marquesa de Sobroso * 15.5.1907 dau. of Don Luis-Carlos Vázquez y Chavarri, and has issue:
XII	1b.	**Don Pedro Caro y Vázquez, Marqués de Orani** * 24.1.1936 = 17.4.1963 Doña Carmen Carvajal y Salas, Marquesa de Cenete, and a Grandee of Spain * 29.8.1941
	2b.	**Doña Maria Rosa Caro y Vázquez** * 25.6.1933 = 10.6.1960 Don Gonzalo Chávarri y Santiago Concha * 12.6.1922 and has issue:
XIII	1c.	**Doña Maria Teresa Chávarri y Caro** * 13.9.1961
	2c.	**Don Francisco de Borje Chávarri y Caro** * 11.4.1964
XII	3b.	**Doña Isabel Caro y Vázquez** * 13.10.1934 = 11.2.1960 Don Julio González Valerio y Saenz de Heredia * 14.1.1929 and has issue:
XIII	1c.	**Don Julio González Valerio y Caro** * 16.11.1960
XII	4b.	**Doña Ana Teresa Caro y Vázquez** * 16.8.1937 + 7.12.1966
	5b.	**Don Carlos Caro y Vázquez** * 17.3.1939
	6b.	**Doña Maria Caro y Vázquez** * 9.3.1943 = 15.2.1964 Don Ramón Rodriguez Escanet * 31.8.1927
XI	8a.	**Don Tomás Caro y Guillamas** * 16.9.1905 + 3.11.1959 = 10.8.19 ... Doña Antonia Arcos y Perez del Pulgar Condessa de Calvijo * ... 1907 dau. of Don Antonio Arcos y Sarasin
X	(f)	**Doña Joaquina Caro y Széchényi** * Palma de Mallorca 11.11.1867 + 14.6.1961 = 30.6.1891 Don Francisco Fernández del Valle y Martinez * Guadalajara Jalisco 30.6.1861 + 20.3.1930 and has issue:
XI	1a.	**Doña Joaquina Fernández del Valle y Caro** * Guadalajara ... 1892 + 7.11.1920 = ... 1918 Don Enrique Palomar y Vizcarra * Guadalajara 14.1.1885 + 30.3.1953, and had issue:
XII	1b.	**Doña Carmen Palomar y Fernández del Valle** * Guadalajara 20.5.1919 = 2.10.1948 Don Carlos Robles Leon y Martin del Campo * 25.3.1919, and has issue:

1c. **Don Carlos Robles Leon y Palomar** * 22.8.1949

2c. **Don Pablo Robles Leon y Palomar** * 22.8.1950

3c. **Don Joaquin Robles Leon y Palomar** * 5.5.1953

4c. **Don Ignacio Robles Leon y Palomar** * 10.2.1955

5c. **Doña Carmen Robles Leon y Palomar** * 1.1.1959

6c. **Doña Maria Robles Leon y Palomar** * 24.11.1962

XII

2b. **Don Javier Palomar y Fernández del Valle** * Guadalajara 11.10.1920
= 31.10.1953 Dona Berta Lever Baumann * 20.1.1925 and has issue:

XIII

1c. **Don Javier Palomar y Lever** * Guadalajara 5.8.1955

2c. **Don Eduardo Palomar y Lever** * Guadalajara 28.7.1956

3c. **Don José Palomar y Lever** * Guadalajara 26.1.1958

4c. **Don Andres Palomar y Lever** * Guadalajara 29.8.1961

5c. **Doña Berta Palomar y Lever** * Guadalajara 20.10.1963

6c. **Doña Joaquina Palomar y Lever** * Guadalajara 3.3.1965

XI

2a. **Doña Maria Fernández del Valle y Caro** * Guadalajara 1.1.1894 = 26.1.1918
Don José Saldivar y de Goribar * Mexico D.F. 28.6.1893 + 17.9.1963, and
has issue:

XII

1b. **Doña Isabel Saldivar y Fernández del Valle** * Mexico City 16.12.1918
= 9.7.1943 Don Carlos Ludlow Landero * 25.6.1918, and has issue:

XIII

1c. **Doña Maria Joaquina Ludlow y Saldivar** * 8.5.1944

2c. **Doña Margarita Ludlow y Saldivar** * 10.8.1945 + 13.6.1947

3c. **Don Carlos Ludlow y Saldivar** * 4.3.1947

4c. **Doña Isabel Ludlow y Saldivar** * 15.10.1948

5c. **Doña Teresa Ludlow y Saldivar** * 10.3.1950

6c. **Don Juan Ludlow y Saldivar** * 28.10.1951

7c. **Don Francisco Ludlow y Saldivar** * 30.10.1956

8c. **Doña Pilar Ludlow y Saldivar** * 16.6.1959

XII

2b. **Don José Saldivar y Fernández del Valle** * Mexico D.F. 21.9.1921

3b. **Don Jaime Saldivar y Fernández del Valle** * Mexico D.F. 26.12.1922
= 21.3.1960 Doña Paz González de León y Miranda * Mexico D.F.
1.9.1932, and has issue:

XIII

1c. **Doña Joaquina Saldivar y González de León** * 7.1.1961

2c. **Don Santiago Saldivar y González de León** * 17.11.1961

3c. **Don Sebastian Saldivar y González de León** * 18.7.1963

XII

4b. **Doña Pilar Saldivar y Fernández del Valle** * Mexico D.F. 3.3.1926

5b. **Doña Maria Josefa Saldivar y Fernández del Valle** * Mexico D.F.·
21.3.1927 = 8.5.1947 Alberto Charles Sierra * Mexico D.F.
4.2.1920, and has issue:

XIII		1c.	**Sofia Charles y Saldivar** * Mexico D.F. 20.2.1948
		2c.	**Alberto Charles y Saldivar** * 15.1.1949
		3c.	**José Charles y Saldivar** * 28.5.1953

XII 6b. **Doña Ana Saldivar y Fernández del Valle** * Mexico D.F. 4.4.1928 + 3.1.1961 = 30.6.1954 Hernán Calero y Charles * 23.2.1923, and has issue:

XIII 1c. **Don Juan Calero y Saldivar** * 29.8.1955

2c. **Doña Ana Calero y Saldivar** * 17.1.1958

XII 7b. **Doña Teresa Saldivar y Fernández del Valle** * Mexico D.F. 28.11.1931 = 17.9.1952 Antonio Souza y Souza * Mexico D.F. 27.5.1928, and has issue:

XIII 1c. **Don Valente Souza y Saldivar** * 9.7.1953

2c. **Don Antonio Souza y Saldivar** * 9.7.1954

3c. **Doña Valeria Souza y Saldivar** * 28.4.1958

XII 8b. **Don Antonio Saldivar y Fernández del Valle** * Mexico D.F. 4.10.1933 = 19.1.1963 **Francesca von Wuthenau** * Taxco (Mexico) 10.9.1940, and has issue:

XIII 1c. **Don Alejandro Francisco Saldivar v. Wuthenau** * 12.5.1965

2c. **Don Juan Saldivar v. Wuthenau** * 11.4.1966

XI 2a. **Don Pedro Fernández del Valle y Caro** * Madrid 25.1.1896 + Mexico City 3.6.1960 = 20.5.1928 Doña Luz Cuesta y Moreno * Guadalajara Jalisco 13.7.1903, and had issue:

XII 1b. **Doña Maria de la Luz Joaquina Fernández del Valle y Cuesta** * Guadalajara 6.3.1929 = 25.11.1950 Don Jaime Sahagún Acuna * 22.9.1919, and has issue:

XIII 1c. **Don Jaime Sahagún y Fernández del Valle** * Guadalajara 3.9.1951

2c. **Don Jorge Sahagún y Fernández del Valle** * Guadalajara 28.1.1953

XII 2b. **Don Pedro Fernández del Valle y Cuesta** * Guadalajara 14.12.1932 = 27.1.1962 Doña Luz Ochoa y Castiello * Guadalajara 26.12.1935 dau. of Eduardo Ochoa Montes de Oca, and has issue:

XIII 1c. **Don Pedro Fernández del Valle y Ochoa** * Guadalajara 3.1.1963

2c. **Doña Luz Fernández del Valle y Ochoa** * Guadalajara 22.12.1965

XI 3a. **Don Carlos Fernández del Valle y Caro** * Guadalajara Jalisco 27.1.1898 + Guadalajara 25.11.1964 = ... 1935 Nancy Faneuf y Medrano * Guadalajara 27.10.1912, and had issue:

XII 1b. **Doña Nancy Fernández del Valle y Faneuf** * Guadalajara 31.8.1937

XII

2b.   **Don Carlos Fernández del Valle y Faneuf** * Guadalajara 22.2.1944

3b.   **Doña Patricia Fernández del Valle y Faneuf** * Guadalajara 10.9.1945
= 1964 Luis Garibay Bagnis * ... and has issue:

XIII

1c.   **Patricia Garibay y Fernández del Valle** * Guadalajara 16.12.1964

2c.   **Mónica Garibay y Fernández del Valle** * Guadalajara 6.12.1965

XII

4b.   **Doña Maria de la Palma Fernández del Valle** * Guadalajara 11.5.1948

IX

d)   **Gábor Graf Széchényi v. Sárvár-Felsövidék** * 1.3.1828 + Hegyfalu 2.4.1921
= 26.4.1859 Felice von Szent György Horváth * 10.11.1837 + Hegyfalu 5.8.1920, and
had issue:

X

(a)   **Eugenia Gräfin Széchényi v. Sárvár-Felsövidék** * 12.12.1873 + 30.4.1893

IX

e)   **Gyula Graf Széchényi v. Sárvár-Felsövidék** * Wien 11.11.1829 + Budapest 13.1.1921
= (1) Oroszvár 6.7.1863 **Karoline Gräfin Zichy-Ferraris zu Zich u. Vásonykeö** * Güns
13.10.1845 + Wien 25.12.1871 dau. of Felix Graf Zichy-Ferraris zu Zich u. Vásonykeö;
= (2) Wien 3.2.1875 Paula v. Klinkosch * Wien 18.2.1851 + Abbazia 3.1.1901 dau. of
Josef Carl v. Klinkosch, and had issue:

by 1st marriage:

X

(a)   **Andor Pál Graf Széchényi v. Sárvár-Felsövidék** * Oroszvár 13.6.1864 + Marczali
13.4.1943 = (1) Zsombolya 13.10.1894 Andrea Gräfin Csekonics v. Zsombolya
u. Janova * Budapest 27.12.1870 + Wien 20.6.1913 dau. of Andreas Graf
Csekonics v. Zsombolya u. Janova; = (2) Marczali 25.3.1925 Maria Freiin.
Szegedy-Ensch v. Mezö-Szeged * Inke, Kom. Somogy 21.4.1897 dau. of Alexander
Frhr. Szegedy-Ensch v. Mezö-Szeged, and has issue:

by 1st marriage:

XI

1a.   **Joseph Maria Andreas Graf Széchényi v. Sárvár-Felsövidék** * Marczali
26.2.1897 = Lublin 2.6.1945 Hedwig Mórgo-Mórgowska * Zdoldónow
17.2.1919 dau. of Florian Mórgo-Mórgowski, and has issue:

XII

1b.   **Maria Andrea Karolina Emilia Julia Gräfin Széchényi v. Sárvár-
Felsövidék** * Lublin 20.7.1946

2b.   **Beata Andrea Constancia Leonida Julia Gräfin Széchényi v. Sárvár-
Felsövidék** * Lublin 14.3.1948

3b.   **Joseph Andreas Maria Julius Florian Graf Széchényi v. Sárvár-
Felsövidék** * Innsbruck 15.2.1958

XI

2a.   **Juliana Maria Margarethe Eugenie Gräfin Széchényi v. Sárvár-Felsövidék**
* Marczali 6.12.1900 = Budapest 15.1.1931 János Graf Széchényi v.
Sárvár-Felsövidék * Linz a.d. Donau 7.8.1897, and has issue:

XII

1b.   **Andrea Marie Johanna Emilie Julia Huberta Gräfin Széchényi v.
Sárvár-Felsövidék** * Wien 3.11.1931 = Austin, Texas 23.12.1955
Michael Somerville-Withers * Shanghai 17.6.1926, and has issue:

XIII

1c.   **Anne Somerville-Withers** * Port Arthur,Texas 20.2.1957

2c.   **Elizabeth Somerville-Withers** * Port Arthur, Texas 17.4.1958

3c.   **Adrienne Somerville-Withers** * Port Arthur, Texas 6.11.1959

XIII		4c.	**Andrew Somerville-Withers** * Parkersburg, West Virginia 6.4.1961
		5c.	**Brian Somerville-Withers** * Wilmington, Delaware 4.9.1963

XII   2b. **Susanna Marie Bernadette Denise Gabrielle Ursula Gräfin Széchényi v. Sárvár-Felsövidék** * Wien 10.12.1932 = Grundlsee 7.10.1954 Ottokar Fürst v. Lobkowicz * Prag 28.1.1922, and has issue:

XIII   1c. **Georg Prinz v. Lobkowicz** * Zürich 23.4.1956

         2c. **Anton Prinz v. Lobkowicz** * Zürich 23.4.1956

         3c. **Elisabeth Prinzessin v. Lobkowicz** * Bad Aussee 3.4.1959

XII   3b. **János-Peter Maria Joseph Alexander Dénes Ignaz Christof Graf Széchényi v. Sárvár-Felsövidék** * Wien 31.7.1934 = Absam, Tirol 10.10.1959 Adrienne Anders * Budapest 7.10.1941, dau. of Karl Anders, and has issue:

XIII   1c. **Judith Gräfin Széchényi v. Sárvár-Felsövidék** * Zürich 27.11.1961

         2c. **Ferdinand Graf Széchényi v. Sárvár-Felsövidék** * Wien 20.1.1962

         3c. **Dénes-Philipp Graf Széchényi v. Sárvár-Felsövidék** * Baden b. Wien 7.5.1963

XII   4b. **Maria-Alice Julia Margit Huberta Maria Piroska Gräfin Széchényi v. Sárvár-Felsövidék** * Budapest 29.7.1938

         5b. **István Maria Dénes János Imre Hubertus Eustachius András-Gellért Graf Széchényi v. Sárvár-Felsövidék** * Szombathely 25.9.1941 = St. Gallen 6.4.1966 Ursula Kneght * St. Gallen 23.7.1937 dau. of Johann Jakob Kneght

XI   3a. **Endre Maria Paul Julius Graf Széchényi v. Sárvár-Felsövidék** * Marczali 29.4.1902 = Budapest 2.6.1932 Ella Gräfin Somssich de Sáard * Ormánd, Kom. Zala 12.1.1907 dau. of Anton Graf Somssich de Sáard, and has issue:

XII   1b. **Gabrielle Gräfin Széchényi v. Sárvár-Felsövidék** * Budapest 18.7.1936 = Buenos Aires 31.7.1957 Tomas Graf Semsey de Semse * Roma 28.11.1926, and has issue:

XIII   1c. **Julia Gabriela Andrea Clara Gräfin Semsey de Semse** * Buenos Aires 19.4.1964

         2c. **András Graf Semsey de Semse** * Buenos Aires 10.12.1966

X   (b) **Margareta Gräfin Széchényi v. Sárvár-Felsövidék** * Marczali 27.5.1866 + Kesselstatt 17.2.1915 = Abbazia 20.4.1892 Eugen Graf v. Kesselstatt * Gleichenberg 10.6.1870 + Grundlsee 10.11.1933, and had issue:

XI   1a. **Caroline Ida Maria Marguerite Gräfin v. Kesselstatt** * Grundlsee 17.7.1893 = Heckenmünster 14.1.1920 Joseph Graf v. Spee * Düsseldorf 18.4.1876 + Bonn 10.11.1941, and has issue:

XII   1b.   **Joseph Eugen Wilderich Ferdinand Hubertus Maria Gerhard Graf v. Spee**
        * Schleiden 19.10.1920 ✗ Leeuwarden, Holland 17.2.1945
        = Klagenfurt 16.9.1943 Edith v. Kleinmayr * Klagenfurt 28.2.1925
        dau. of Walter v. Kleinmayr

     2b.   **Antonia Margaretha Maria Wilhelmine Elisabeth Julia Gräfin v. Spee**
        * Schleiden 14.2.1922 = Bingen a. Rh. 20.5.1943 Egon Frhr. v. Wendt
        * Hermeskeil 16.10.1917, and has issue:

XIII   1c.   **Franz Egon Ferdinand Hermann Joseph Maria Frhr. v. Wendt**
        * Burg Maubach 6.3.1944

     2c.   **Max Hubertus Wilderich Frhr. v. Wendt** * Schellenstein
        17.3.1945

     3c.   **Clemens August Sturmius Hubertus Maria Frhr. v. Wendt**
        * Schellenstein 14.8.1946

     4c.   **Marie-Agnes Georgina Antonia Elisabeth Freiin. v. Wendt**
        * Schellenstein 25.9.1948

     5c.   **Karl Michael Klemens Ferdinand Bonifatius Maria Frhr. v. Wendt**
        * Wuppertal-Elberfeld 10.5.1951

XII   3b.   **Franz Wilhelm Joseph Hubertus Gerhard Maria Graf v. Spee**
        * Schleiden 14.3.1923 = (1) Stepperg 6.8.1953 **Anna Maria Gräfin
        Henckel v. Donnersmarck** * Grambschütz 14.12.1928 + Burg
        Maubach 12.11.1954 dau. of Georg Graf Henckel v. Donnersmarck;
        = (2) Kirchberg 4.6.1956 Marie Charlotte Freiin. v. Mylius * Kaphof
        9.2.1929 dau. of Joseph Frhr. v. Mylius, and has issue:

        by 1st marriage:

XIII   1c.   **Pia Theresia Huberta Maria Anna Ursula Gräfin v. Spee**
        * Burg Maubach 17.7.1954

        by 2nd marriage:

     2c.   **Brigida Monika Maximiliana Anna Maria Huberta Gräfin v. Spee**
        * Burg Maubach 28.5.1957

     3c.   **Mariano Antonius Peter Hubertus Pius Apollinarius Graf v. Spee**
        * Burg Maubach 23.7.1958

     4c.   **Johannes Maria Georg Ruppert Hubertus Graf v. Spee**
        * Burg Maubach 4.1.1960

     5c.   **Wilderich Rochus Paul Hermann-Joseph Hubertus Maria Graf v.
        Spee** * Burg Maubach 16.4.1964

     6c.   **Peter Pius Franz Martin Hubertus Maria Graf v. Spee**
        * Burg Maubach 13.11.1966

XII   4b.   **Maximilian Friedrich Augustinius Hubertus Maria Graf v. Spee**
        * Schleiden 28.8.1924 = Düren 28.12.1955 Marie-Elisabeth Gräfin v.
        Ballestrem * Breslau 17.3.1933 dau. of Franz Georg Graf v. Ballestrem,
        and has issue:

XIII   1c.   **Jan Seger Graf v. Spee** * Bremen 15.12.1956

     2c.   **Per-Degenhardt Graf v. Spee** * Emden 24.10.1958

     3c.   **Juliane-Hedwig Gräfin v. Spee** * Emden 11.3.1960

     4c.   **Monika Antonia Gräfin v. Spee** * Emden 28.8.1963

XIII	5c.	**Franz-Hilarius Graf v. Spee** * Emden 15.1.1965

XII

5b. **Degenhardt-Wilderich Carl Gerhardt Maria Hubertus Luitpold Graf v. Spee-Mirbach** * Schleiden 1.11.1926 = Fürstenberg 3.7.1956 **Brigitta Gräfin v. Westphalen zu Fürstenberg** * Fürstenberg 26.9.1925 dau. of Friedrich Graf v. Westphalen zu Fürstenberg s.p.

6b. **Georg Seger Jakob Gerhard Maria Hubertus Graf v. Spee** * Schleiden 10.3.1929 = Düsseldorf-Oberkassel 11.2.1966 Maria Zita Freiin. v. Pereira-Arnstein * Rotterdam 12.11.1928 dau. of Ferdinand Frhr. v. Pereira-Arnstein

XI

2a. **Franz de Paula Georg Eugen Klemens Graf v. Kesselstatt** * Grundlsee 17.7.1894 + Darmstadt 2.9.1938 = Wien 23.6.1925 Gabrielle Prinzessin v.u. zu Liechtenstein * Wien 2.5.1905 dau. of Eduard Prinz v.u. zu Liechtenstein, and has issue:

XII

1b. **Franz Eugen Eduard Clemens Maria Graf v. Kesselstatt** * Kesselstatt 1.5.1926 = St-Peter-Freienstein 27.10.1953 Louisette v. Laveran-Stiebar v. Hinzberg * St-Peter-Freienstein 12.1.1926 dau. of Rudolf v. Laveran-Stiebar v. Hinzberg, and has issue:

XIII

1c. **Gabrielle Antoinette Maria Gräfin v. Kesselstatt** * Trier 1.11.1954

2c. **Rudolf Georg Maria Graf v. Kesselstatt** * Trier 31.1.1956

3c. **Georg Johannes Maria Graf v. Kesselstatt** * Trier 26.9.1957

4c. **Clemens Friedrich Maria Graf v. Kesselstatt** * Trier 7.6.1959

5c. **Franz Degenhardt Maria Graf v. Kesselstatt** * Trier 26.5.1961

6c. **Theresa Maria Bernadette Gräfin v. Kesselstatt** * Trier 28.2.1964

XII

2b. **Johannes Gabriel Franz Georg Maria Graf v. Kesselstatt** * Kesselstatt 21.5.1927

XI

3a. **Elisabeth Bianka Maria Marguerite Gräfin v. Kesselstatt** * Kesselstatt 1.6.1896

4a. **Franziska Bianka Maria Theresia Gräfin v. Kesselstatt** * Grundlsee 3.10.1898 + Königswinter 21.8.1949 = Nürnberg 15.11.1935 Hanns Günther v. Obernitz * Düsseldorf 5.5.1899 + Bromberg 14.1.1944 s.p.

5a. **Marguerite Andrea Maria Eugenia Gräfin v. Kesselstatt** * Kesselstatt 24.3.1900

6a. **Johannes Georg Julius Eugen Maria Graf v. Kesselstatt** * Grundlsee 16.4.1902 + Berenbach, Eifel 9.1.1963 = (1) Kesselstatt 3.1.1929 Ferdinande-Johanna Gräfin v. Hahn * Arenfels 1.7.1902 + Logenburg b. Königswinter 22.4.1944 dau. of Ferdinand Graf v. Hahn; = (2) Logenburg 28.6.1945 Alexandra Elisabeth Gräfin v. Schmettow * Potsdam 28.6.1914 dau. of Lazarus Graf v. Schmettow, and had issue:

by 1st marriage:

XII

1b. **Ferdinand Hans Stephan Mulich Eugen Josef Maria Graf v. Kesselstatt** * Bonn 16.12.1930 = Kiedrich 2.8.1958 Hella Witte * Eltville 22.8.1937 dau. of Rudolf Witte, and has issue:

344

1c. **Aiga Alice Eugenie Johanna Hedwig Maria Gräfin v. Kesselstatt**
* Wiesbaden 7.3.1959

2c. **Maximilian Franz Edmund Mulich Maria Graf v. Kesselstatt**
* Wiesbaden 14.7.1961

3c. **Johannes Baptist Ferdinand Rudolf Helmut Maria Graf v.
Kesselstatt** * Wiesbaden 9.2.1964

4c. **Isabella Alexandra Agnes Maria Gräfin v. Kesselstatt** * Eltville
2.8.1965

2b. **Alice-Eugenie Johanna Margarete Paula Franziska Maria Gräfin v.
Kesselstatt** * Bad Godesberg 4.5.1932 = Mettlach 25.4.1966
Rolf Alfred Wirtz * Köln 25.4.1939

3b. **Eugen Georg Nikolaus Peter Franziskus Theresia Maria Graf v.
Kesselstatt** * Bad Godesberg 23.2.1935 + Logenburg 22.4.1944

4b. **Franz Edmund Ekhard Johannes Theresia Graf v. Kesselstatt**
* Bad Godesberg 6.4.1936 + Longenburg 22.4.1944

7a. **Georg Alois Franz Joseph Balduin Maria Graf v. Kesselstatt** * Kesselstatt
9.6.1905 = Buenos Aires 5.11.1955 Adelma Baronesse Vay de Vaja
* Debreczen 11.5.1932 dau. of Ladislaus Baron Vay de Vaja

(c) **Karoline Gräfin Széchényi v. Sárvár-Felsövidék** * 8.3.1869 + Pechtoldsdorf b.
Wien 27.4.1932 = 30.5.1890 Simon Graf v. Wimpffen * Böslau b. Wien 21.8.1867
+ Wien 11.4.1925 s.p.

(d) **Pauline Gräfin Széchényi v. Sárvár-Felsövidék** * Wien 25.11.1871 + Doxan,Böh.
14.8.1945 = Wien 22.7.1902 Aloys Graf Lexa v. Aehrenthal * Gross-Skal 27.9.1854
+ Wien 17.2.1912, and had issue:

1a. **Caroline Marie Antoinette Henriette Luise Gräfin Lexa v. Aehrenthal**
* St. Petersburg 13.9.1904

2a. **Johann Maria Felix Anton Carl Graf Lexa v. Aehrenthal** * Tsarskoie Selo
9.8.1905 = Wien 7.11.1932 **Ernestine Gräfin v. Harrach zu Rohrau u.
Thannhausen** * Rohrau 11.8.1903 dau. of Otto Graf v. Harrach, and has issue:

1b. **Johann Aloys Otto Paul Ernst Carl Maria Stephan Graf Lexa v.
Aehrenthal** * Prag 28.11.1933 = Pörtschach 4.8.1963 Alice Freiin.v.
Warsberg * Zagreb 7.7.1936 dau. of Oskar Frhr. v. Warsberg

2b. **Marie Caroline Gräfin Lexa v. Aehrenthal** * Prag 24.12.1935
= 26.4.1960 Guy Debièvre * Lille 21.7.1931, and has issue:

1c. **Françoise Ernestine Debièvre** * Chatoux (S.-et-O.) 16.11.1960

2c. **Jean-Luc Debièvre** * Haubourdin 23.1.1962 (Nord)

3b. **Marie Pauline Gräfin Lexa v. Aehrenthal** * Prag 17.2.1941

3a. **Elisabeth Maria Josefa Antoinette Aloysia Gräfin Lexa v. Aehrenthal**
* Hietzing b. Wien 9.8.1909 = Prag 3.1.1943 Josef Graf v. Thun u.
Hohenstein * Prag 31.12.1907 s.p.

by 2nd marriage:

(e) **Gyula Joseph Pál Graf Széchényi v. Sárvár-Felsövidék** * Wien 10.12.1878
+ Budapest 21.4.1956 = Abbazia 8.2.1908 Gisela Freiin. Haas v. Teichen
* Wien 18.12.1890 + Wien 15.4.1945 dau. of Philipp Frhr. Haas v. Teichen, and
had issue:

XI   1a.   **Béla Graf Széchényi v. Sárvár-Felsövidék**   * Achau 27.2.1909

        2a.   **Gyula Graf Széchényi v. Sárvár-Felsövidék**   * Achau 11.10.1910
= Budapest 26.6.1937 Bernadette Prinzessin Eszterházy v. Galántha
* Eszterháza 17.7.1910 dau. of Miklós Fürst Eszterházy v. Galántha, and
has issue:

XII   1b.   **Margit Maria Bernadette Magdalena Gräfin Széchényi v. Sárvár-Felsövidék**   * Budapest 22.7.1938

        2b.   **Erzsébet Marie Bernadette Gräfin Széchényi v. Sárvár-Felsövidék**
* Budapest 13.4.1940

        3b.   **Alice Maria Bernadette Hanna Gabriella Gräfin Széchényi v. Sárvár-Felsövidék**   * Budapest 29.11.1941

        4b.   **Gyula Gabriel Nikolaus Christof Hubertus Georg Graf Széchényi v. Sárvár-Felsövidék**   * Budapest 4.2.1943

        5b.   **Béla Gyula Anton Kristof Hubertus Georg Graf Széchényi v. Sárvár-Felsövidék**   * Budapest 12.9.1944

XI   3a.   **Hanna Gräfin Széchényi v. Sárvár-Felsövidék**   * Abbazia 8.10.1911
= Köröshegy, Kom. Somogy 24.10.1953 Károly Dusoczky   * Budapest
14.11.1898 + 31.10.1963 s.p.

        4a.   **Gábor Graf Széchényi v. Sárvár-Felsövidék**   * Abbazia 12.3.1914
= Budapest 10.6.1942 Hanna Baronesse Rubido-Zichy de Zágorja Nich et
Zajk   * Nágocs 26.1.1922 dau. of Iván Baron Rubido-Zichy de Zágorja Nich
et Zajk, and has issue:

XII   1b.   **Gábor Graf Széchényi v. Sárvár-Felsövidék**   * Pécs 12.4.1943

        2b.   **Andrea Gräfin Széchényi v. Sárvár-Felsövidék**   * Pécs 20.6.1944

IX   f)   **Géza Graf Széchényi v. Sárvár-Felsövidék**   * 15.12.1830 + 15.12.1832

        g)   **Kálmán Graf Széchényi v. Sárvár-Felsövidék**   * 3.4.1833 + 24.3.1839

        h)   **Ferenc Graf Széchényi v. Sárvár-Felsövidék**   * 4.3.1835 + Tarnócza, Kom. Somogy
... 9.1908 = 20.9.1861 Franziska Gräfin Erdödy v. Monyorókerék u. Monoszló
* 16.4.1841 + Tarnócza 4.10.1906 dau. of István Graf Erdödy v. Monyorókerék u.
Monoszló, and has issue:

X   (a)   **Rudolf Graf Széchényi v. Sárvár-Felsövidék**   * 11.10.1862 + Graz 6.11.1928
= Eggenberg 30.4.1888 Marie Gräfin v. Herberstein   * Herberstein 2.7.1867
+ Budapest 9 or 11.6.1945 dau. of Sigmund Graf v. Herberstein, and had issue:

XI   1a.   **Rudolf Graf Széchényi v. Sárvár-Felsövidék**   * Schloss Eggenberg b. Graz
4.1.1891 + Szombathely 4.4.1931 = Gyöngyösapáti 17.9.1913 Sophie
Baronesse Lipthay v. Lubelle u. Kisfalud   * Lovrin 25.7.1893 dau. of
Friedrich Baron Lipthay v. Lubelle u. Kisfalud, and has issue:

XII   1b.   **Judith Maria Sophia Rudolfina Margarete Gräfin Széchényi v. Sárvár-Felsövidék**   * Graz 29.7.1915 = (1) Budapest 27.2.1935 Márton Graf
Széchényi v. Sárvár-Felsövidék   * Segesd 17.9.1909 − div.; = (2)
Graz 29.7.1949 Lajos Dezsö Gobi   * Budapest ... 1911, and has issue:
by 1st marriage:

XIII   1c.   **Agathe Maria Gobertina Alexandra Nathalie Josephine Gräfin Széchényi v. Sárvár-Felsövidék**   * Budapest 5.2.1936

XIII

    2c.   **Bertalan Alexander Rudolf Maria Gobert Graf Széchényi v.
Sárvár-Felsövidék** * Budapest 22.5.1937

    3c.   **Alexandra Frederica Martina Maria Gobertina Gräfin Széchényi
v. Sárvár-Felsövidék** * Budapest 27.2.1940

    4c.   **Domonkos Márton Alexander Bertalan Rudolf Maria Gobert Graf
Széchényi v. Sárvár-Felsövidék** * Budapest 8.8.1944

XII

  2b. **Maria Gräfin Széchényi v. Sárvár-Felsövidék** * Gyöngyösapáti
15.6.1917 = Budapest 19.8.1941 Georg Graf v. Wenckheim
* Budapest 24.4.1917, and has issue:

XIII

    1c.   **László Graf v. Wenckheim** * Gyula, Kom. Békés 2.11.1942

    2c.   **Sylvia Gräfin v. Wenckheim** * Gyula,24.3.1944

    3c.   **Thomas Graf v. Wenckheim** * Graz 8.9.1945

XII

  3b. **Friederike Gräfin Széchényi v. Sárvár-Felsövidék** * Gyöngyösapáti
18.12.1918 = (1) Budapest 30.1.1940 Jenö Döry de Jobaháza * ...
+ Salta, Argentina 21.8.1965; = (2) ... László Balogh-Kovács
* ... + ... s.p.

X

(b) **Ernö Graf Széchényi-Wolkenstein** * Rothenthurm 15.7.1864 + Bodrogkereztúr
30.10.1935 = Budapest 19.5.1904 Marie Baronesse Senney de Kis-'Sennye
* Budapest 26.2.1867 + Bodrogkereztúr 30.10.1935 dau. of Pál Baron Senney de
Kis-'Sennye s.p.

(c) **Antal Graf Széchényi v. Sárvár-Felsövidék** * Rothenthurm 22.9.1867 + Bad Nauhein
17.10.1924 = Budapest 22.1.1895 Christine Gräfin v. Wenckheim * Ó-Kigyós
21.10.1874 dau. of Friedrich Graf v. Wenckheim, and had issue:

XI

  1a. **Antonia Friederika Franziska Maria Gräfin Széchényi v. Sárvár-Felsövidék**
Ó-Kigyós 22.1.1896 = Póstelek 15.9.1920 Emmerich Graf Almásy v.
Zsadány u. Törökszentmiklós * Szent-Tamás 29.1.1896, and has issue:

XII

  1b. **Ursula Marie Krisztina Kornelie Gräfin Almásy v. Zsadány u.
Törökszentmiklós** * Póstelek 23.7.1921 = Budapest 6.7.1947
Georg Benesch * ... and has issue:

XIII

    1c.   **Stephan Benesch** * 13.2.1955

    2c.   **Georg Benesch** * 25.4.1956

XII

  2b. **Miklós Emmerich Anton Maria Graf Almásy v. Zsadány u.
Törökszentmiklós** * Felsöpetény 5.1.1923 = (1) Budapest 1947
Sári Déry * Nyitra 2.8.1911 + Mád, Kom. Zemplén 25.8.1952;
= (2) Bruxelles 26.5.1962 Maria Erzsébet Baronesse Szentkereszty de
Zágon * Budapest 14.8.1933 dau. of Pál Zsigmond Baron
Szentkereszty de Zágon, and has issue:

XIII

    1c.   **Dénes Antal Graf Almásy v. Zsadány u. Törökszentmiklós**
* Bruxelles 8.4.1963

    2c.   **Antal István Graf Almásy v. Zsadány u. Törökszentmiklós**
* Bruxelles 4.3.1965

    3c.   **Christine Elisabeth Gräfin Almásy v. Zsadány u. Törökszentmiklós**
* Bruxelles 19.5.1966

XII		3b.	**István Emmerich Anton Franz Maria Graf Almásy v. Zsadány u. Törökszentmiklós** * Felsöpetény 6.4.1929 = Würzburg 15.10.1949 Emöke Rettegi de Kisbudak et Retteg * Marosvásárhely 28.5.1929 dau. of Stefan Rettegi de Kisbudak et Retteg, and has issue:
XIII		1c.	**Emmerich Stefan Anton Franz Maria Graf Almásy v. Zsadány u. Törökszentmiklós** * Würzburg 4.8.1950

XI   2a.   **Ilona Christine Franziska Maria Gräfin Széchényi v. Sárvár-Felsövidék** * Ö-Kigyós 2.6.1898 = Póstelek 16.6.1923 Viktor Graf Károlyi v. Nagy-Károly * Nagy-Mágocs 25.4.1902, and has issue:

XII   1b.   **Lajos Georg Viktor Emmerich Anton Graf Károlyi v. Nagy-Károly** * Nagy-Mágocs 10.5.1924 = Lindau-am-Bodensee 1946 Helen Tellér de Litér * Budapest 31.10.1926 dau. of Gyula Tellér de Litér, and has issue:

XIII   1c.   **Imre Antonius Julius Graf Károlyi v. Nagy-Károly** * Lindau 8.6.1947

                               2c.   **Franziska Georgina Caroline Maria Gräfin Károlyi v. Nagy-Károly** * São Paulo 20.6.1950

XII   2b.   **Christine Viktoria Maria Franziska Helene Sophie Gräfin Károlyi v. Nagy-Károly** * Póstelek 1.3.1926 = London 7.5.1949 Willian Hugh Edwards * Taihirion, Llangaffo 13.11.1910, and has issue:

XIII   1c.   **Helen Mary Judith Károlyi Edwards** * Kampala, East Africa 21.6.1950

                               2c.   **Victor Hugh Llewellyn Károlyi Edwards** * Kampala 15.1.1952

                               3c.   **Sheila Eleanor Christine Károlyi Edwards** * Kampala 18.3.1955

                               4c.   **Richard John Anthony Károlyi Edwards** * 26.4.1957

XII   3b.   **Antal Julius Viktor Emmerich Graf Károlyi v. Nagy-Károly** * Budapest 26.2.1929 = São Paulo 13.8.1953 Josette Ladron de Guevara Gore O'Daly * Caracas 29.9.1923, and has issue:

XIII   1c.   **Antal Viktor Emmerich Graf Károlyi v. Nagy-Károly** * São Paulo 2.7.1954

                               2c.   **István Ferenc Sándor Graf Károlyi v. Nagy-Károly** * São Paulo 16.12.1956

                               3c.   **Josita Gräfin Károlyi v. Nagy-Károly** * São Paulo 26.6.1959

XI   3a.   **Ferenc Joseph Friedrich Maria Graf Széchényi v. Sárvár-Felsövidék** * Budapest 9.2.1901 = Puszta-Nagy-Szent-Tamás 8.8.1924 Maria Gräfin Almásy v. Zsadány u. Törökszentmiklós * Szent-Tamás 1.2.1902 dau. of Emmerich Graf Almásy v. Zsadány u. Törökszentmiklós, and has issue:

XII   1b.   **Marie Antoinette Dénes Gräfin Széchényi v. Sárvár-Felsövidék** * Nagy-Szent-Tamás 18.7.1925 = Hohenems 2.9.1948 Thomas Graf Zichy zu Zich u. Vásonykeö * Zákány 17.10.1923, and has issue:

1c. **Andrew Karl Maria Graf Zichy zu Zich u. Vásonykeö** * Hohenems 22.5.1949

2c. **Bernadette Maria Countess Zichy zu Zich u. Vásonykeö** * Asheville, North Carolina 16.1.1951

3c. **Charles Thomas Count Zichy zu Zich u. Vásonykeö** * Asheville 17.2.1953

4c. **Doris Christina Countess Zichy zu Zich u. Vásonykeö** * Asheville 12.8.1955

XII

2b. **Ferenc Imre Károly Maria Graf Széchényi v. Sárvár-Felsövidék** * Aranyos-Puszta 2.10.1926 = (1) Asheville 27.6.1956 Anita Brickner * ... − div.; = (2) Norton, Conn. 14.10.1962 Daphne Christina Stavies * London 31.8.1936 dau. of Reginald Stavies, and has issue:

by 1st marriage:

XIII

1c. **Christóf Antal Count Széchényi v. Sárvár-Felsövidék** * New York 14.5.1957

XII

3b. **Kornelie Ilona Maria Gräfin Széchényi v. Sárvár-Felsövidék** * Aranyos-Puszta 9.3.1929 = Asheville 28.12.1957 Georg Szele * Szolnok 27.6.1928, and has issue:

XIII

1c. **Beatrix Szele** * Washington, D.C. 27.4.1959

2c. **Monika Szele** * Washington, D.C. 12.7.1960

3c. **Cornelia Szele** * Washington, D.C. 9.5.1962

4c. **Francis Szele** * Washington, D.C. 6.8.1963

XII

4b. **László Anton Emmerich Maria Graf Széchényi v. Sárvár-Felsövidék** * Aranyos-Puszta 14.11.1931 = New York 6.9.1958 Therese Freiin. Schell v. Bauschlott * Nagyida 26.8.1930 dau. of Péter Frhr. Schell v. Bauschlott, and has issue:

XIII

1c. **Andrea Countess Széchényi v. Sárvár-Felsövidék** * New York 9.3.1960

2c. **Alexandra Charlotte Countess Széchényi v. Sárvár-Felsövidék** * New York 9.3.1960

3c. **Péter Count Széchényi v. Sárvár-Felsövidék** * New York 30.12.1961

XII

5b. **Susanne Ilona Maria Gräfin Széchényi v. Sárvár-Felsövidék** * Aranyos-Puszta 16.12.1938 = Asheville, North Carolina 2.10.1965 Aloysius Kramers * Vught, Holland 31.5.1925, and has issue:

XIII

1c. **Dominic Aloysius Kramers** * Asheville 8.6.1966

XII

6b. **Barbara Ilona Maria Gräfin Széchényi v. Sárvár-Felsövidék** * Aranyos-Puszta 15.2.1940 = 17.6.1961 Paul Kandó * Budapest 20.6.1936, and has issue:

XIII

1c. **Michael Francis Kandó** * Asheville, North Carolina 1.7.1962

2c. **Dominic Aloysius Kandó** * 8.6.1966

XII	7b.	**Mátyás Karl Anton Maria Graf Széchényi v. Sárvár-Felsövidék** * Aranyos-Puszta 4.1.1944 = Holy Hill, Winsconsin 18.6.1966 Ilona Márton * Leva, Hungary 9.10.1943 dau. of László Márton
XI	4a.	**Károly Friedrich Balathasar Rudolf Maria Graf Széchényi v. Sárvár-Felsövidék** * Ö-Kigyós 13.3.1906 = Budapest 19.3.1936 Gabrielle Maria Vágvölgyi * Esztergom 4.8.1902 dau. of Béla Vágvölgyi s.p.
X	(d)	**Ferenc Graf Széchényi v. Sárvár-Felsövidék** * 18.11.1869 + 3.12.1874
	(e)	**György Graf Széchényi v. Sárvár-Felsövidék** * 3.4.1871 + 24.3.1874
	(f)	**Frigyes Graf Széchényi v. Sárvár-Felsövidék** * Somogy-Tarnócza 29.10.1875 + Budapest 27.9.1937 = Wien 10.10.1910 Karoline Freiin. v. Schloissnigg * Wien 12.3.1884 dau. of Franz Frhr. v. Schloissnigg, and had issue:
XI	1a.	**Sophia Maria Rudolfine Franziska Gräfin Széchényi v. Sárvár-Felsövidék** * Somogy-Tarnócza 9.1.1911 = Somogy-Tarnócza 12.3.1934 **Zeno Graf Welser v. Welsersheimb** * Pola 21.9.1902, and has issue see elsewhere
	2a.	**Frigyes Maria Ernst Franz Graf Széchényi v. Sárvár-Felsövidék** * Wien 22.4.1912
	3a.	**Ernö Nikolaus Gobert Graf Széchényi v. Sárvár-Felsövidék** * Wien 19.10.1913 = Budapest 16.3.1944 Gabrielle Gräfin Szirmay v. Szirma-Bessenyö, Csernek u. Tarkö * Facset 3.8.1907 dau. of Otto Graf Szirma-Bessenyö, Csernek u. Tarkö, and has issue:
XII	1b.	**Otto Maria Jenö Friedrich Gobert Graf Széchényi v. Sárvár-Felsövidék** * Budapest 3.8.1945
	2b.	**Ernst Gobert Friedrich Maria Graf Széchényi v. Sárvár-Felsövidék** * Salzburg 21.3.1948
XI	4a.	**Franziska Maria Antonia Christine Gräfin Széchényi v. Sárvár-Felsövidék** * Wien 31.12.1915
	5a.	**Irma Maria Therese Elisabeth Gräfin Széchényi v. Sárvár-Felsövidék** * Fünfkirchen 15.9.1917 = Fünfkirchen 15.10.1946 Tibor Dehény * Sümeg, Kom. Zala 9.1.1915, and has issue:
XII	1b.	**Andrea Dehény** * Pécs 20.8.1947
	2b.	**Tibor Dehény** * Budapest 22.12.1951
XI	6a.	**Sándor Maria Rudolf Ignatius Graf Széchényi v. Sárvár-Felsövidék** * Fünfkirchen 27.6.1919 + Budapest 1.8.1955
	7a.	**Jenö Maria Adalbert Thomas Graf Széchényi v. Sárvár-Felsövidék** * Wien 15.7.1921 ✕ Kápolnásnyék 16.12.1944
	8a.	**Antal Maria Friedrich Franz Graf Széchényi v. Sárvár-Felsövidék** * Wien 31.3.1924 = Buenos Aires 15.11.1952 Christine Prinzessin v. Auersperg * Goldegg 16.9.1920 dau. of Adolf Erbprinz v. Auersperg, and has issue:
XII	1b.	**Jenö Maria Karl Franz Gobertus Graf Széchényi v. Sárvár-Felsövidék** * Montevideo 4.12.1953
	2b.	**Sándor Maria Adolf Anton Gobertus Graf Széchényi v. Sárvár-Felsövidék** * Montevideo 31.5.1957

3b.   **Agathe Marie Caroline Gobertine Gräfin Széchényi v. Sárvár-Felsövidék**
* Lisboa 7.6.1962

IX   i)   **Jenö Graf Széchényi v. Sárvár-Felsövidék** * Wien 7.2.1836 + Vörösvár 12.3.1911
= July 1864 Henriette Gräfin Erdödy v. Monyorókerék u. Monoszló * Wien 22.5.1838
+ Szány b. Ödenburg 8.9.1905 dau. of Stephan Graf Erdödy v. Monyorókerék u. Monoszló
and had issue:

X   (a)   **Helene Gräfin Széchényi v. Sárvár-Felsövidék** * Vörösvár 9.7.1865 + Szombathely
12.6.1931

(b)   **Emilie Gräfin Széchényi v. Sárvár-Felsövidék** * Vörösvár 17.9.1866 + Vörösvar
17.6.1928 = Tarnócza 24.2.1885 Gyula Graf Erdödy v. Monyorókerék u. Monoszló
* Vörösvár 24.2.1845 + Vörösvár 15.1.1917, and had issue:

XI   1a.   **Tomás Stephan Gobert Maria Graf Erdödy v. Monyorókerék u. Monoszló**
* Vörösvár 1.7.1886 + Köszeg 20.4.1931 = ... 192 ... Antonia Albrecht
* ... s.p.

2a.   **Lajos Franz Gobert Maria Graf Erdödy v. Monyorókerék u. Monoszló**
* Vörösvár 12.5.1890 + Vörösvár 17.5.1926

X   (c)   **Miklós Graf Széchényi v. Sárvár-Felsövidék** * 6.1.1868 + Budapest 1.12.1923
Bishop of Nagyvárad

(d)   **Jenö Graf Széchényi v. Sárvár-Felsövidék** * Vörösvár 30.11.1872 + Mailáthgárdony
23.11.1935 = Budapest 16.4.1903 Huberta Gräfin Almásy v. Zsadány u.
Törökszentmiklós, * Graz 19.5.1880 + Budapest 5.2.1946 dau. of Tassilo Graf
Almásy v. Zsadány u. Törökszentmiklós, and had issue:

XI   1a.   **Anna Marie Gobertine Gräfin Széchényi v. Sárvár-Felsövidék** * Révfalu
17.1.1904 = Szent-Lörincz 23.2.1922 Géza Graf Majláth v. Székhely
* Gárdony 25.1.1896, and has issue:

XII   1b.   **Maria Rozaria Anna Ferdinanda Gobertina Gräfin Majláth v. Székhely**
* Gárdony 5.5.1923 = 20.5.1944 Anton Graf Zichy zu Zich u.
Vásonykeö * Budapest 30.1.1921, and has issue:

XIII   1c.   **Antoinette Elisabeth Maria Gräfin Zichy zu Zich u. Vásonykeö**
* Toronto 5.9.1964

XII   2b.   **Maria Anna Georgine Gobertina Gräfin Majláth v. Székhely** * Gárdony
3.3.1926 = (1) 25.5.1948 Béla Hosszufalussy de Hosszufalu * Miskolc
6.9.1920 − div.; = (2) Santiago de Chile ... 5.1961 Franz Karl Graf v.
Podstatzky-Lichtenstein * Brünn 26.10.1933, and has issue:

by 1st marriage:

XIII   1c.   **Margarete Hosszufalussy de Hosszufalu** * Miskolc 3.2.1949

XII   3b.   **Maria Victoria Gobertina Gräfin Majláth v. Székhely** * Cserhátsurány
28.11.1928 = 25.7.1952 Andreas Geyger * 20.6.1916, and has issue:

XIII   1c.   **Steven Geyger** * Santiago de Chile 28.4.1953

2c.   **Ladislaus Geyger** * Santiago de Chile 16.10.1954

3c.   **Michael Geyger** * Santiago de Chile 11.4.1956

4c.   **Kristof Geyger** * Santiago de Chile 27.10.1959

XIII	5c.	**Andrea Geyger** * Toronto 16.10.1964

XII   4b.   **Péter Maria Gobert Graf Majláth v. Székhely** * Cserhátsurány 29.10.1929 = Toronto 22.9.1956 Alice Princess Sulkowska * Wien 15.6.1933 dau. of Edgar Prince Sulkowski, and has issue:

XIII

1c.   **Teresa Maria Victoria Antoinette Gobertina Gräfin Majláth v. Székhely** * Santiago de Chile 27.8.1957

2c.   **Sándor Karolus Maria Gustav Gobert Graf Majláth v. Székhely** * Toronto 18.7.1959

3c.   **Victor Edgar Peter Maria Gobert Graf Majláth v. Székhely** * Toronto 30.5.1964

XII   5b.   **Pál Maria Gobert Graf Majláth v. Székhely** * Cserhátsurány 29.10.1929

XII   6b.   **Steven Maria Gobert Graf Majláth v. Székhely** * Cserhátsurány 30.9.1930 = Montreal 10.5.1955 Helene Walsh * ... — div., and has issue:

XIII

1c.   **Steven Graf Majláth v. Székhely** * Montreal 5.7.1957

XI   2a.   **Henriette Marie Gobertine Gräfin Széchényi v. Sárvár-Felsövidék** * Sebes 28.10.1905 = (1) Felsö-Szemeréd 27.12.1930 Moritz Frhr. v. Hoeller-Bertram * Töre 7.5.1878 + Hallstatt 22.5.1956; = (2) Hollywood, Calif. 24.11.1960 Raymond Weller * Albany, New York 13.5.1895, and has issue:

by 1st marriage:

XII   1b.   **Stephan Frhr. v. Hoeller-Bertram** * Budapest 27.11.1931

XI   3a.   **Miklós Josef Marie Gobert Graf Széchényi v. Sárvár-Felsövidék, Graf Széchényi-Erdödy** * Sebes 15.11.1906 + Budapest December 1944 = (1) Budapest 17.10.1928 Eva Maria Baronesse Gutmann v. Gelse u. Beliscse * Budapest 2.3.1908 dau. of Artur Baron Gutmann v. Gelse u. Beliscse — div.; = (2) Ujpest 11.9.1939 Gabrielle Gräfin Keglevich v. Buzin * Egreskáta 21.1.1914 dau. of Nikolaus Graf Keglevich v. Buzin, and had issue:

by 1st marriage:

XII   1b.   **Stefanie Maria Gobertine Gräfin Széchényi v. Sárvár-Felsövidék** * Budapest 14.1.1930

XI   4a.   **Huberta Marie Gobertine Gräfin Széchényi v. Sárvár-Felsövidék** * Sebes 18.12.1908 = (1) Semmering 22.2.1927 Ferdinand Graf Majláth v. Székhely * Zavar 13.3.1891 + Wien 22.2.1929; = (2) Varna 18.8.1939 János Graf Révay v. Réva * Tajna 27.5.1900 + Budapest 12.7.1953 and has issue:

by 1st marriage:

XII   1b.   **Ferdinanda Huberta Carolina Georgina Anna Maria Gobertina Gräfin Majláth v. Székhely** * Gbelany 26.11.1927 = 18.11.1947 Rudolf Kubinec * ... + Prag 6.4.1965, and has issue:

XIII

1c.   **Tatiana Kubinec** * Žilina 6.5.1948

2c. **Anna Maria Kubinec** * Žilina 3.7.1949

3c. **Katarina Kubinec** * Bratislava 14.5.1953

4c. **Rudolf Ferdinand Kubinec** * Bratislava 21.4.1953

5c. **József Kubinec** * Bratislava 31.10.1956

6c. **Mihály Kubinec** * Bratislava 24.9.1960

2b. **Karolina Maria Gobertina Gräfin Májlath v. Székhely** * Gbelany 16.12.1928 = 6.8.1951 Tibor Fluck v. Ragamb * Nyiregyháza 20.8.1923, and has issue:

1c. **Ferdinand Fluck v. Ragamb** * Budapest 8.8.1953

2c. **Hubertus Fluck v. Ragamb** * Stockholm, Sweden 2.11.1964

by 2nd marriage:

3b. **Ferenc Graf Révay v. Réva** * Budapest 31.12.1941

4b. **Zsuzsanna Gräfin Révay v. Réva** * Budapest 16.3.1943 = (1) 30.4.1961 Gyözö Döme * ... — div.; = (2) Göteborg 7.2.1963 Levente Edler v. Erdeös * Budapest 23.8.1935, and has issue:

by 1st marriage:

1c. **Tünde Döme** * Göteborg 15.8.1962

by 2nd marriage:

2c. **Paula Charlotte Marietta Edle v. Erdeös** * Göteborg 16.7.1964

3c. **Edward Péter János Edler v. Erdeös** * Mölndal, Sweden 27.10.1966

5b. **Péter Graf Révay v. Réva** * Budapest 15.11.1945

5a. **Marie-Agnes Gobertine Gräfin Széchényi v. Sárvár-Felsövidék** * Sebes 20.9.1910 = Bodrog-Keresztúr 12.2.1929 Johannes Graf Sennyey de Kis-Sennye * Bély 18.11.1902, and has issue:

1b. **Maria Johanna Wolfganga Gobertine Therese Gräfin Sennyey de Kis-Sennye** * Budapest 1.6.1930 = Santiago de Chile 9.7.1955 Peter Frhr. v. Hahn * Karlsberg, Kurland 13.2.1928, and has issue:

1c. **Alexandra Freiin. v. Hahn** * Santiago de Chile 9.1.1957

2c. **Anatol Frhr. v. Hahn** * Santiago de Chile 11.2.1959

3c. **Antoinette Freiin. v. Hahn** * Santiago de Chile 12.8.1964

2b. **Pál-Imre Graf Sennyey de Kis-Sennye** * Kassa 25.9.1932 = São Paulo 15.9.1963 Maritta de Purgly de Joszás * Budapest 1941 dau. of Lajos de Purgly de Joszás, and has issue:

1c. **Pongrácz Gobert Graf Sennyey de Kis-Sennye** * São Paulo 25.7.1965

6a. **Tassilo Emanuel Marie Gobert Graf Széchényi v. Sárvár-Felsövidék** * Sebes 19.6.1912 = Budapest 9.5.1940 Sarlota Gräfin v. Wenckheim * Wien 17.7.1916 dau. of Carl Graf v. Wenckheim, — div. and has issue:

XII		1b.	**Elisabeth Gräfin Széchényi v. Sárvár-Felsövidék** * Budapest 9.3.1941 = Budapest 10.12.1960 Attila Ágh * Balatonszemes 23.6.1939, and has issue:
XIII		1c.	**Zoltán Ágh** * Siófok 23.4.1964
XII		2b.	**Irma Gräfin Széchényi v. Sárvár-Felsövidék** * Budapest 9.3.1941 = Budapest 12.5.1962 Andreas Prékopa * Nyiregyháza 11.9.1929, and has issue:
XIII		1c.	**Monika Prékopa** * Budapest 3.2.1963
XI		7a.	**Eugenie Marie Gobertine Gräfin Széchényi v. Sárvár-Felsövidék** * Sebes 31.3.1914 = 10.2.1945 Anders Haakon Lilliestierna * 6.9.1910, and has issue:
XII		1b.	**Hedvig Erzsébet Lilliestierna** * Mariestad, Sweden 23.9.1945
		2b.	**Carl Hubert Andreas Lilliestierna** * Mariestad, Sweden 15.3.1950
		3b.	**Anders Gerhard Lilliestierna** * Mariestad, Sweden 15.5.1951
		4b.	**Christer Gábor Lilliestierna** * Mariestad, Sweden 8.7.1952
XI		8a.	**Béla Graf Széchényi v. Sárvár-Felsövidék** * Sebes 28.8.1917 + Szent Lörincz 22.3.1920
X	(e)		**Mariette Gräfin Széchényi v. Sárvár-Felsövidék** * Gyöngyösapáti 19.9.1878 + Varpalota 4.2.1938 = Szent-Lörincz 18.10.1899 Fridos Graf Zichy zu Zich u. Vásonykeö * Szent-Péter 2.2.1860 + Budapest 7.12.1927, and has issue:
XI		1a.	**Ludviga Fanny Gräfin Zichy zu Zich u. Vásonykeö** * Varpalota 15.9.1900 = Balázstag 15.5.1920 Eugen de Kiss * ... + Sid b. Gömör 4.6.1937, and had issue:
XII		1b.	**Irma Kiss** * Budapest 13.12.1922 = Deurne-Anvers 8.3.1944 Leopold Agie de Selsaeten * La Haye 30.9.1916, and has issue:
XIII		1c.	**Cedric Ghislain Jacques Desire Joseph Marie Agie de Selsaeten** * Etterbeek 10.4.1945
		2c.	**Anne Henriette Marie Ghislaine Josephine Agie de Selsaeten** * Anvers 22.9.1946
		3c.	**Olivier Ghislain Jean Marie Joseph Agie de Selsaeten** * Anvers 1.8.1950
		4c.	**Martine Genevieve Josephine Marie Ghislaine Agie de Selsaeten** * Anvers 6.7.1953
		5c.	**Bernard Marie Marc Joseph Ghislain Agie de Selsaeten** * Anvers 7.12.1954
XII		2b.	**Mariette Kiss** * Sid 26.4.1926
XI		2a.	**Miklós Gyula Graf Zichy zu Zich u. Vásonykeö** * Várpalota 2.9.1902
		3a.	**Imre Graf Zichy zu Zich u. Vásonykeö** * Sopron-Rákos 14.9.1904 = (1) Budapest ... 1935 Wilhelmine v. Ferentheil u. Gruppenberg * Marosvásárhely 6.8.1901 − div.; = (2) ... Maria de Zekany * ..., and has issue:

354

by 1st marriage:

XII

    1b.   **Frigyes Graf Zichy zu Zich u. Vásonykeö** * 6.8.1938

by 2nd marriage:

    2b.   **Stephan Graf Zichy zu Zich u. Vásonykeö** * Klagenfurt 16.11.1946

XI

4a.   **Henriette Gabrielle Gräfin Zichy zu Zich u. Vásonykeö** * Komárom-Szemere
25.4.1906 = Senyefa 29.11.1924 Alexander de Varasdy von Izdenc
* Szombathely 11.2.1896, and has issue:

XII

    1b.   **Emmi de Varasdy** * Szombathely 29.7.1925 = (1) Budapest 25.11.1946
Kornél Zempléni * Debrecen 4.9.1921 = (2) ... 1964 György Frigyesi
* Budapest 22.9.1923, and has issue:

by 1st marriage:

XIII

    1c.   **László Zempléni** * Budapest 21.8.1947

    2c.   **Maria Luiza Zempléni** * Budapest 21.2.1949

    3c.   **Tamás Zempléni** * Budapest 19.2.1952

XII

    2b.   **Ernö de Varasdy** * Szombathely 24.3.1927 = Budapest 1953
Margit Kaposy * Debrecen 6.12.1927, and has issue:

XIII

    1c.   **Zsuzsanna de Varasdy** * Budapest 14.7.1955

XII

    3b.   **Frigyes de Varasdy** * Szombathely 22.6.1930 = Budapest 1958
Bella Jasper * Budapest ...

XI

5a.   **Therese Gräfin Zichy zu Zich u. Vásonykeö** * Komárom-Szemere 5.1.1908
+ Budapest ... 5.1966 = Budapest 7.2.1932 György Horváth * ... and has
issue:

XII

    1b.   **György Horváth** * Budapest 3.11.1933 = Budapest ... Anna Buday
* ..., and has issue:

XIII

    1c.   **Gyöngyi Horváth** * 2.6.1963

XII

    2b.   **Miklós Horváth** * Budapest 20.7.1938

XI

6a.   **Elisabeth Gräfin Zichy zu Zich u. Vásonykeö** * Budapest 11.4.1913
+ Klagenfurt 15.2.1953 = Varpalota 20.4.1933 Alexander Posch * ...
— div. s.p.

X

(f)   **Pál Graf Széchényi v. Sárvár-Felsövidék** * Apáti 24.9.1880 + Vörösvár
21.11.1918 = Acsád 22.7.1908 Elisabeth Szegedy de Mezö-Szeged * Ascád
6.7.1881 dau. of György Szegedy de Mezö-Szeged, and had issue:

XI

1a.   **Irma Elisabeth Gobertine Gräfin Széchényi v. Sárvár-Felsövidék** * Ascád
31.5.1909 = Ötvös 1.6.1932 Nicolaus Döry de Jobaháza * ... — div., and
has issue:

XII

    1b.   **Maria Döry de Jobaháza** * Szombathely 1932

XI   2a.   **György Maria Gobert Graf Széchényi v. Sárvár-Felsövidék** * Acsád 14.7.1910 = Budapest 9.4.1954 Rose Marie Zalán de Alsódomboru * Budapest 24.3.1908 dau. of Julius Zalán de Alsódomboru s.p.

IX   j)   **Tivadar Graf Széchényi v. Sárvár-Felsövidék** * 12.3.1837 + Pistyan 18.6.1912 = ... Johanna Gräfin Erdödy v. Monyorókerék u. Monoszló * 24.11.1835 + Felsölendva 3.12.1915 dau. of István Graf Erdödy v. Monyorókerék u. Monoszló, and had issue:

X   (a)   **Tivadar Graf Széchényi v. Sárvár-Felsövidék** * ... + 21.10.1915

IX   k)   **Pál Klemens Graf Széchényi v. Sárvár-Felsövidék** * Sopron 6.11.1838 + Budapest 28.10.1901 = Wien 27.4.1861 Elisabeth Gräfin Andrássy v. Csik-Szent-Király u. Krasza-Horka * Wien 26.1.1840 + Budapest 2.10.1926 dau. of Georg Graf Andrássy v. Csik-Szent-Király u. Krasza-Horka, and had issue:

X   (a)   **Aladár Pál Georg Julian Maria Graf Széchényi v. Sárvár-Felsövidék** * Wien 15.2.1862 + Budapest 11.5.1936 = (1) Budapest 5.7.1884 Natalie Gräfin Andrássy v. Csik-Szent-Király u. Krasza-Horka * Parnó 16.1.1864 + Budapest 6.4.1951 dau. of Emanuel Graf Andrássy v. Csik-Szent-Király u. Krasza-Horka – div.; = (2) Kaposvár 5.12.1918 Flora Viszay * Marczali Somogy 29.7.1897, and had issue:

XI   1a.   **Gabrielle Marie Pauline Gräfin Széchényi v. Sárvár-Felsövidék** * Lábod 15.8.1885 + Basel 4.9.1924 = Budapest 1.6.1904 Heinrich Graf v. Haugwitz * Namiesto 5.10.1870 + Brünn 26.3.1927 s.p.

                                2a.   **Marie Elisabeth Natalie Gräfin Széchényi v. Sárvár-Felsövidék** * Lábod 8.9.1887 = Budapest 18.11.1907 Ludwig 4 Fürst zu Windisch-Graetz * Krakau 20.10.1882, and has issue:

XII   1b.   **Ludwig Aladár 5 Fürst zu Windisch-Graetz** * Sárospatak 4.12.1908 = Wien 29.7.1936 Christine Ebert * Wien 21.10.1905 dau. of Alfred Ebert, and has issue:

XIII   1c.   **Alfred Erbprinz zu Windisch-Graetz** * Wien 1.6.1939

                                    2c.   **Ludwig Anton Prinz zu Windisch-Graetz** * Wien 12.1.1942

XII   2b.   **Gabriele Maria Dionysia Karolina Paula Emilia Prinzessin zu Windisch-Graetz** * Sárospatak 14.12.1909 = Sárospatak 20.11.1934 Wolfgang Frhr. Reichlin v. Meldegg * München 29.7.1906 + Sárospatak 2.5.1939, and has issue:

XIII   1c.   **Maria Gabrielle Freiin. Reichlin v. Meldegg** * Sárospatak 22.8.1935

                                  2c.   **Stephan Ludwig Anton Maria Frhr. Reichlin v. Meldegg** * Sárospatak 21.2.1937 = Paris 5.10.1962 Nicole de Surmont * St. Claude, Guadalupe 29.9.1937 dau. of Alain de Surmont, and has issue:

XIV   1d.   **Tomás Frhr. Reichlin v. Meldegg** * Paris 28.6.1964

XII   3b.   **Maria Magdalena Valerie Paula Georgine Justine Karolina Prinzessin zu Windisch-Graetz** * Sárospatak 26.9.1911 = Sárospatak 8.7.1930 István Graf Károlyi v. Nagy-Károly * Fóth 9.12.1898, and has issue:

356

      1c.   **Maria Ladislaus Vincenz Peter Paul Graf Károlyi v. Nagy-Károly** * Fóth 29.6.1931

      2c.   **Maria Barbara Gabriele Gräfin Károlyi v. Nagy-Károly** * Fóth 6.8.1932

      3c.   **Eduard Kristof Maria Graf Károlyi v. Nagy-Károly** * Budapest 15.12.1937

      4c.   **Alexander Maria Aurel Graf Károlyi v. Nagy-Károly** * Budapest 26.5.1941

    4b.   **Vincenz Alfred Karl Ludwig Valerian Maria Gabriel Prinz zu Windisch-Graetz** * Sárospatak 14.9.1913 = Salzburg 8.10.1945 Martha de Becsky * Delhi 10.11.1915 dau. of Emil de Becsky s.p.

    5b.   **Natalie Juliane Sofie Maria Viktoria Prinzessin zu Windisch-Graetz** * Sárospatak 21.8.1917

    6b.   **Elisabeth Mathilda Zita Carola Rosalia Maria Prinzessin zu Windisch-Graetz** * Sárospatak 4.9.1923 = (1) Budapest 12.1.1944 Joseph Graf Eszterházy zu Galántha * Salgócska 8.9.1917 − div.; = (2) Genève 30.12.1949 Fredy Dusendschön * London 6.8.1911, and has issue:

    by 1st marriage:

      1c.   **Marie Elisabeth Helene Anna Josefa Walpurga Gräfin Eszterházy zu Galántha** * Budapest 12.11.1944

  3a.   **György Marie Graf Széchényi v. Sárvár-Felsövidék** * Lábod 28.5.1889 + Monok 26.8.1938 = Budapest 10.12.1917 Anastasia Gräfin Zichy zu Zich u. Vásonykeö * Bellatincz 16.7.1891 dau. of August Graf Zichy zu Zich u. Vásonykeö, and had issue:

    1b.   **Pál August Maria Aladár Franz Graf Széchényi v. Sárvár-Felsövidék** * Budapest 8.9.1918 ✘ Budapest 23.11.1944

    2b.   **Ferenc Maria August Georg Thaddäus Graf Széchényi v. Sárvár-Felsövidék** * Káloz 15.8.1919

    3b.   **August Emanuel Maria Theodor Aloysius Graf Széchényi v. Sárvár-Felsövidék** * Káloz 23.1.1921

    4b.   **György Gabriel Maria Emanuel Eugen Graf Széchényi v. Sárvár-Felsövidék** * Káloz 30.6.1923

    5b.   **Benedikt Maria Josef Aloysius István Graf Széchényi v. Sárvár-Felsövidék** * Káloz 23.12.1926

  4a.   **Mihály Maria Pál Graf Széchényi v. Sárvár-Felsövidék** * Unt-Schmeks 16.7.1895 + Budapest 1959 = (1) Budapest 8.6.1923 Sarlota de Cséry de Csér * Budapest 17.1.1895 − div.; = (2) ... and had issue:

  by 1st marriage:

    1b.   **Mihály Graf Széchényi v. Sárvár-Felsövidék** * Budapest 25.5.1924 ✘ 27.10.1944

  by 2nd marriage:

    2b.   **Mihály Graf Széchényi v. Sárvár-Felsövidék** * ...

by 2nd marriage:

XII

XI

5a. **Emilie Maria Franziska Gräfin Széchényi v. Sárvár-Felsövidék** * Budapest 31.1.1921 = (1) ... 1940 Tivadar Baron Bornemisza de Kászony * ... + Ebreichsdorf b. Wien ... = (2) 17.1.1953 Joseph Muszay * ... − div., and has issue:

by 1st marriage:

XII

1b. **Miklós Baron Bornemisza de Kászony** * 5.9.1942

2b. **Emily-Beryl Baronesse Bornemisza de Kászony** * 29.11.1944

X   (b) **Maria Franziska Georgine Gräfin Széchényi v. Sárvár-Felsövidék** * Románfalva 19.9.1863 + Budapest 30.4.1932 = Budapest 10.6.1886 Joseph Graf Majláth v. Székhely * Pécs 11.4.1858 + Ófehertó 2.4.1940, and had issue:

XI

1a. **Elisabeth Gräfin Majláth v. Székhely** * Perbenyik 7.12.1889

2a. **Stephanie Gräfin Majláth v. Székhely** * Perbenyik 23.2.1891 + 2.5.1952 = Budapest 7.5.1925 Pál Sztankovánszky de Sztankován * Kajdacs 22.5.1890 + Mocsolád 5.3.1945, and had issue:

XII

1b. **Imre Sztankovánszky de Sztankován** * Budapest 25.2.1925 = Kárász 18.11.1948 Katalin Zag * Magyaregregy 15.10.1930, and has issue:

XIII

1c. **Klara Sztankovánszky de Sztankován** * Magyaregregy 2.1.1950

2c. **Agnes Sztankovánszky de Sztankován** * Magyaregregy 10.10.1954

XII

2b. **Pál Sztankovánszky de Sztankován** * Budapest 30.5.1932 = Macsekjánosi 26.5.1955 Maria Fisli * Galambok 2.12.1929, and has issue:

XIII

1c. **Maria Magdalena Sztankovánszky de Sztankován** * Komló 17.9.1957

XI

3a. **Joseph Graf Majláth v. Székhely** * Perbenyik 24.7.1895 + Budapest 23.1.1939 = Nagy-Ida 8.1.1920 Luise-Anne Freiin. Schell v. Bauschlott * Nagyida 17.3.1895 dau. of Julius Frhr. Schell v. Bauschlott, and has issue:

XII

1b. **Marie-Rosalie Stephanie Georgine Gräfin Majláth v. Székhely** * Ó-Fehertó 14.11.1920 = Budapest 4.11.1944 Marton Solymossy * Zagreb 3.9.1918, and has issue:

XIII

1c. **Joseph-Martin Solymossy** * Wegscheid 11.10.1945

2c. **László Solymossy** * Ascholding 9.1.1947

3c. **Imre Solymossy** * Wolfratshausen 1.12.1948

4c. **István Solymossy** * Milwaukee, U.S.A. 12.7.1957

XII

2b. **Luise Anne Gräfin Majláth v. Székhely** * Perbenyik 15.11.1922 = 23.3.1953 René David Escalante Orozco * ..., and has issue:

XIII

1c. **Carmen Luise Escalante Majláth** * Caracas, Venezuela 20.1.1954

XIII	2c.	**David Salvador Escalante Majláth** * Caracas 11.3.1955
	3c.	**Isabel Elena Escalante Majláth** * Caracas 11.3.1955

XII	3b.	**Joseph Graf Majláth v. Székhely** * Perbenyik 29.3.1924 = 9.1.1957 Eva Maria Mohay * Törökszentmiklós 25.9.1937 dau. of Martin Mohay, and has issue:

XIII	1c.	**Georg Joseph Martin Graf Majláth v. Székhely** * Perth, Western Australia 23.11.1957
	2c.	**Louise Anne Maria Gräfin Majláth v. Székhely** * Medina, Western Australia 20.6.1959
	3c.	**Vivienne Catherine Gräfin Majláth v. Székhely** * Canberra, Australia 15.2.1964

XII	4b.	**Elisabeth Gräfin Majláth v. Székhely** * Budapest 29.11.1926
	5b.	**Imre Graf Majláth v. Székhely** * Nyiregyhaza 15.8.1930 = (1) Broken Hill, N.S.W. 13.4.1950 Eva Laurel Deslandes * ... = (2) Adelaide, S.A. 15.10.1962 Bertha Lipps ... and has issue:

by 1st marriage:

XIII	1c.	**Marie Louise Gräfin Majláth v. Székhely** * Broken Hill, New South Wales, Australia 12.5.1951 + February 1957
	2c.	**Paul Joseph Graf Majláth v. Székhely** * Broken Hill, N.S.W. 12.3.1954

XII	6b.	**Margarete Gräfin Majláth v. Székhely** * Nyiregyháza 8.5.1934 = Budapest 18.8.1957 Elemér v. Horváth * Cinkota 23.11.1921
	7b.	**Helena Gräfin Majláth v. Székhely** * Nyiregyháza 21.4.1936 = Budapest 6.12.1959 Kálmán Somogyi * Balatonfüred 26.7.1935

XI	4a.	**Marie Gräfin Majláth v. Székhely** * Perbenyik 3.9.1897 + Asunción 5.5.1963 = Perbenyik 29.8.1921 Béla Graf Teleki v. Szék * Gyömrö 2.10.1896, and had issue:

XII	1b.	**Alice Maria Johanna Ilona Elisabeth Gräfin Teleki v. Szék** * Gyömrö 25.5.1922 = Clorinda, Argentina 15.9.1951 Gerhard Rönnebeck * Berlin 24.7.1904, and has issue:

XIII	1c.	**Béla Rönnebeck** * Asunción 21.7.1952
	2c.	**Ermö Rönnebeck** * Asunción 25.11.1954

XII	2b.	**Maria Gräfin Teleki v. Szék** * Budapest 2.7.1925
	3b.	**Tibor Graf Teleki v. Szék** * Budapest 15.5.1928 = (1) Buenos Aires 18.8.1953 Maria Freiin. Kast v. Ebelsberg * Alttitschein 14.11.1929 dau. of Karl Frhr. Kast v. Ebelsberg — div. = (2) Montevideo 16.3.1961 Esther Gonzales Correa-Bustos * Buenos Aires 5.11.1936 dau. of Victor Gonzales, and has issue:

by 2nd marriage:

XIII	1c.	**Tibor Graf Teleki v. Szék** * Buenos Aires 13.2.1963
	2c.	**Caroline Gräfin Teleki v. Szék** * Buenos Aires 15.10.1964

XII   4b.   **István Graf Teleki v. Szék** * Nagykanizsa 7.4.1934 = Lafayette, U.S.A. 8.12.1962 Beatrix Eggers Lan * Buenos Aires 30.5.1934 dau. of Conrado Esteban de Eggers, and has issue:

XIII   1c.   **Marianne Gräfin Teleki v. Szék** * Lafayette, Indiana U.S.A. 15.7.1963

                         2c.   **Annabelle Gräfin Teleki v. Szék** * Walnut Creek, U.S.A. 7.6.1965

XI   5a.   **Pál Graf Majláth v. Székhely** * Perbenyik 23.11.1899

X   (c)   **Emil Joseph Karl Maria Graf Széchényi v. Sárvár-Felsövidék** * Wien 9.1.1865 + Pusztazámor 30.6.1932 = Budapest 23.1.1892 Marie Gräfin Hunyady v. Kéthely * Ürmény 15.7.1870 + ... 1945 dau. of Emmerich Graf Hunyady v. Kéthely, and had issue:

XI   1a.   **Aloys Paul Maria Graf Széchényi v. Sárvár-Felsövidék** * 11.12.1892 ✕ b. Dobronoutz 25.6.1915

                2a.   **Elisabeth Henriette Maria Gräfin Széchényi v. Sárvár-Felsövidék** * Vajszka 2.8.1895 + Erzsébet-Tanya 14.1.1957 = (1) Budapest 19.2.1916 Ernst Prinz zu Schwarzenberg * Wossow 11.10.1892 − div.; = (2) Budapest 11.2.1935 Tibor Baron Collas de Ramaille et Lincour * ... s.p.

                3a.   **Henriette Marie Pauline Gräfin Széchényi v. Sárvár-Felsövidék** * Budapest 22.2.1900 = Balaton-Földvár 13.6.1925 Emmerich Barcza de Nagyalásony * Budapest 30.3.1896, and has issue:

XII   1b.   **Emmerich-Alois Barcza de Nagyalásony** * Budapest 11.5.1926

XI   4a.   **Pál Imre Graf Széchényi v. Sárvár-Felsövidék** * Sopron 14.3.1904 = Balaton-Földvár 4.9.1935 Gabrielle Weimess * Budapest 27.3.1907 s.p.

                5a.   **Magdalene Gräfin Széchényi v. Sárvár-Felsövidék** * Vajszka 18.2.1907

IX   1)   **Dorothée Gräfin Széchényi v. Sárvár-Felsövidék** * 29.11.1841 + Wien 22.2.1892 = Ödenburg 15.10.1860 Heinrich Frhr. Pereira-Arnstein * Reindorf b. Wien 17.6.1836 + Feldorf b. Graz 10.7.1903, and had issue:

X   (a)   **Dorothée Paula Marie Henriette Eva Freiin. v. Pereira-Arnstein** * Wien 29.11.1866 + Wien 1.6.1957

            (b)   **Heinrich Maria Franz Johann Frhr. v. Pereira-Arnstein** * Wien 7.5.1868 + Purfersdorf 17.1.1912 = Ebergassing 2.6.1896 Marie Freiin. v. Schloissnigg * Ebergassing 23.6.1876 + Allentstieg 1.10.1916 dau. of Franz Frhr. v. Schloissnigg s.p.

            (c)   **Victor Franz Seraphim Maria Frhr. v. Pereira-Arnstein** * Wien 21.1.1870 + Wien 9.1.1933 = Wien 18.2.1918 Elisabeth Prinzessin zu Sayn-Wittgenstein * Kassel 16.12.1883 dau. of Friedrich Prinz zu Sayn-Wittgenstein s.p.

VIII   d.   **Melanie Gräfin Zichy-Ferraris zu Zich u. Vásonykeö** * Wien 28.1.1805 + Wien 3.3.1854 = Wien 30.1.1831 Clemens Wenzel 2 Fürst v. Metternich-Winneburg,Duca della Porta,Grandee 1st Class of Spain * Koblenz 15.5.1773 + Wien 11.6.1859, and had issue:

IX   a)   **Melanie Marie Pauline Alexandrine Prinzessin v. Metternich-Winneburg** * Wien 27.3.1832 + Wien 16.9.1919 = Wien 20.11.1853 Joseph Graf Zichy zu Zich u. Vásonykeö * 9.7.1814 + Wien 14.1.1897 s.p.

360

IX   b)   **Clemens Prinz v. Metternich-Winneburg** * 21.4.1833 + 10.6.1833

         c)   **Paul Clemens Lothar 4 Fürst v. Metternich-Winneburg** * Wien 14.10.1834 + Wien 6.2.1906 = Carlburg 9.5.1868 **Melanie Gräfin Zichy-Ferraris zu Zich u. Vásonykeö** * Carlburg 16.8.1843 + Schloss Johannisberg 3.8.1925 dau. of Franz Graf Zichy-Ferraris zu Zich u. Vásonykeö, and had issue:

X   (a)   **Klemens-Wenzel Lothar Richard Felix 5 Fürst v. Metternich-Winneburg** * Wien 9.2.1869 + München 13.5.1930 = Madrid 4.10.1905 Doña Isabel de Silva y Carvajal * 3.5.1880 dau. of Alvaro de Silva 12 Marqués de Santa Cruz, and had issue:

XI   1a.   **Paul Alfons Maria Clemens Lothar Philippus Neri Felix Nikomedes 6 Fürst v. Metternich-Winneburg** * Wien 26.5.1917 = Berlin 6.9.1941 Tatiana Princess Wassiltschikow * St. Petersburg 1.1.1915 dau. of Illarion Prince Wassiltschikow s.p.

X   (b)   **Emilie Marie Felicitas Prinzessin v. Metternich-Winneburg** * 24.2.1873 + 20.1.1884

               (c)   **Pauline Felix Maria Prinzessin v. Metternich-Winneburg** * Pressburg 6.1.1880 + Bullachberg b. Füssen 19.5.1960 = Wien 5.2.1906 Maximilian Theodor Prinz v. Thurn u. Taxis * Mentone 8.3.1876 + Schloss Plass b. Pilsen 3.10.1939, and has issue:

XI   1a.   **Margarete Charlotte Klementine Maria Alexandra Melanie Prinzessin v. Thurn u. Taxis** * Berlin 19.10.1913 = Regensburg 24.5.1932 **Raphael Prinz v. Thurn u. Taxis** * Regensburg 30.5.1906, and has issue see elsewhere

IX   d)   **Lothar Stephan August Clemens Marie Prinz v. Metternich-Winneburg** * Wien 12.9.1837 + Wien 2.10.1904 = (1) Wien 21.4.1868 Caroline Reittner * ... + 21.9.1899; = (2) Wien 5.6.1900 Franziska Gräfin Mittrowsky v. Mittrowitz * Prag 10.11.1846 + Wien 19.3.1918 dau. of Anton Graf Mittrowsky v. Mittrowitz s.p.

VIII   e.   **Viktor Graf Zichy-Ferraris zu Zich u. Vásonykeö** * 11.6.1806 + 29.12.1846

         f.   **Emanuel Graf Zichy-Ferraris zu Zich u. Vásonykeö** * 26.12.1808 + Budapest 5.4.1877 = 2.4.1837 Charlotte Strachan * ... + November 1851 s.p.

         g.   **Felix Graf Zichy-Ferraris zu Zich u. Vásonykeö** * 20.11.1810 + 8.9.1885 = 10.3.1839 **Emilie Gräfin v. Reichenbach-Lessonitz** * 8.6.1826 + Budapest 30.1.1891 dau. of Wilhelm II Elector of Hesse-Kassel by his morganatic wife Emilie Ortlöpp, and had issue:

IX   a)   **Viktor Graf Zichy-Ferraris zu Zich u. Vásonykeö** * 1.7.1842 + Budapest 28.5.1880

         b)   **Melanie Gräfin Zichy-Ferraris zu Zich u. Vásonykeö** * Carlburg 16.8.1843 + Schloss Johannisberg 3.8.1925 = Carlburg 9.5.1868 **Paul Clemens Lothar 4 Fürst v. Metternich-Winneburg** * Wien 14.10.1834 + Wien 6.2.1906 and had issue see elsewhere

         c)   **Ludwig Graf Zichy-Ferraris zu Zich u. Vásonykeö** * 11.8.1844 + Wien 29.5.1899

         d)   **Caroline Gräfin Zichy-Ferraris zu Zich u. Vásonykeö** * Guns 13.10.1845 + Wien 25.12.1871 = Oroszvar 6.7.1863 **Gyula Graf Széchényi v. Sárvár-Felsövidék** * Wien 11.11.1829 + Budapest 13.1.1921, and had issue see elsewhere

         e)   **Emilie Gräfin Zichy-Ferraris zu Zich u. Vásonykeö** * Guns 1.7.1847 + Somlószöllös 6.7.1935 = Carlburg 12.1.1870 **Konrad Frhr. v. Watzdorff** * Dresden 22.8.1844 + Somlószöllös 28.5.1922, and had issue see elsewhere

IX   f)   **Emanuel Graf Zichy-Ferraris zu Zich u. Vásonykeö** * 19.2.1852 + 2.6.1914

VIII   h.   **Ludwig Graf Zichy-Ferraris zu Zich u. Vásonykeö** * 1.8.1814 + 30.12.1859 = 3.6.1845 Auguste Gräfin Bleszinska * 24.5.1819 + ... dau. of Hippolyte Graf Bleszinski s.p.

            i.   **Karl Graf Zichy-Ferraris zu Zich u. Vásonykeö** * 16.11.1817 + 1.4.1832

VI   3)   **Wolfgang Guillaume Joseph Léopold Vital 3 Duc d'Ursel** * Bruxelles 28.4.1750 + Bruxelles 17.5.1804 = Château de Héverlé 18.4.1771 Marie Flore Princesse d'Arenberg * Bruxelles 25.6.1752 + Bruxelles 15.4.1832 dau. of Charles Duc d'Arenberg, and had issue:

VII   (1)   **Louise Marie Caroline Comtesse d'Ursel** * Bruxelles 4.1.1775 + Anvaing 30.6.1834 = Bruxelles 20.2.1797 Jacques Comte de Lannoy * Tournai 10.1.1769 + Bruxelles 1.1.1835, and had issue:

VIII   a.   **François de Lannoy** * Breda 1797 + ...

            b.   **Augustin Guillaume de Lannoy** * Bruxelles 28.12.1798 + 11.1.1799

            c.   **Gustave Ferdinand Guillaume Comte de Lannoy** * Bruxelles 5.8.1800 + Anvaing 6.11.1892 = Bruxelles 11.7.1827 Marie Joséphine Comtesse van der Noot d'Assche * Bruxelles 19.4.1805 + Bruxelles 1.3.1861 dau. of Maximilian Louis Comte van der Noot d'Assche, and had issue:

IX   a)   **Charles Maximilien Marie Joseph Comte de Lannoy** * Bruxelles 12.9.1828 + Bruxelles 13.5.1901 = Bruxelles 31.5.1862 Emma du Parc * Ypres 26.7.1843 + Bruxelles 27.4.1902 dau. of Charles Vicomte du Parc, and had issue:

X   (a)   **Charlotte Marie Josèphe Zénaide Comtesse de Lannoy** * Bruxelles 27.9.1863 + Pulle 12.8.1930 = Bruxelles 5.5.1887 Ludovic Vicomte van de Werve d'Immerseel * Anvers 4.6.1859 + Anvers 16.12.1942, and had issue:

XI   1a.   **Marguerite Gaétane Florence Augustine Ghislaine Marie Josèphe van de Werve d'Immerseel** * Anvers 5.6.1891 = St-Gervais, près Blois 10.10.1916 Albert Comte d'Oultremont * Bruxelles 27.1.1887 + Heylissem 6.8.1946, and has issue:

XII   1b.   **Gaétane Clotilde Louise Marie Ghislaine Comtesse d'Oultremont** * Guines, Pas-de-Calais 15.10.1917 = Heylissem 26.10.1944 **Michel Comte de Brouchoven de Bergeyck** * Braine-le-Château 22.1.1920, and has issue see elsewhere

             2b.   **Adrien Hermann Edmond Charles Marie Ghislain Marie Joseph Comte d'Oultremont** * Guines 10.12.1918 = Bruxelles 14.6.1948 **Marie Blanche Comtesse du Chastel de la Howarderie** * Paris 24.8.1921 dau. of Ferdinand Comte du Chastel de la Howarderie, and has issue:

XIII   1c.   **Sophie Marie Georgine Marguerite Ghislaine Blanche Comtesse d'Oultremont** * Heylissem 16.6.1949

             2c.   **Clotilde Blanche Charlotte Georgine Marie Ghislaine Comtesse d'Oultremont** * Heylissem 9.11.1952

XII   3b.   **Thierry Jean Marie Ghislain Comte d'Oultremont** * Bruxelles 9.2.1920 = Bousval 3.8.1948 Thérèse van der Linden d'Hooghvorst * Bousval 17.3.1927 dau. of Victor Baron van der Linden d'Hooghvorst, and has issue:

XIII   1c.   **Rodolphe Adrien Victor Emile Marie Ghislain Comte d'Oultremont** * Bousval 13.10.1949

By kind permission of le Duc d'Ursel

21 Flore d'Arenberg, Duchesse d'Ursel and her children

Left to right: Charles Joseph, 4th Duc d'Ursel; Flore d'Arenberg, Duchesse d'Ursel; Emilie, Marquise de Mun; Louise, Comtesse de Lannoy

By kind permission of le Duc d'Ursel

22 Charles, 2nd Duc d'Ursel with his family

Left to right: Benoite Charlotte, Duchesse de Bournonville; Charlotte Gräfin *v.* Stain; Henriette Gräfin *v.* Ferraris; Wolfgang Guillaume, later 3rd Duc d'Ursel; Flore d'Arenberg, Duchesse d'Ursel; Charles, 2nd Duc d'Ursel

XIII

2c.   **Dominique Emmanuelle Marguerite Thérèse Marie Ghislaine Comtesse d'Oultremont** * Bousval 26.1.1951

3c.   **Catherine Charlotte Marguerite Comtesse d'Oultremont** * Centellas, Spain 12.4.1955

4c.   **Emilie Jeanne Dominique Comtesse d'Oultremont** * Centellas, Spain 19.4.1959

5c.   **Frédéric Rudolphe Comte d'Oultremont** * Vich, Spain 12.1.1962

XII

4b.   **Gaëtan Yves Marie Ghislain Comte d'Oultremont** * Heylissem 21.5.1921 = Lillois-Witterzée 31.8.1948 Nadine de Meeûs d'Argenteuil * Lillois-Witterzée 26.7.1926 dau. of Jean Comte de Meeûs d'Argenteuil, and has issue:

XIII

1c.   **Christine Miquelina Marie Marguerite Jeanne Ghislaine Comtesse d'Oultremont** * Schaerbeek 21.12.1949

2c.   **Marie Clotilde Ghislaine Comtesse d'Oultremont** * Lillois-Witterzée 6.1.1951

3c.   **Cécile Geneviève Marie Ghislaine Comtesse d'Oultremont** * Uccle 23.5.1952

4c.   **Charlotte Jacqueline Michèle Marie Ghislaine Comtesse d'Oultremont** * Uccle 16.7.1953

5c.   **Anne Françoise Roberte Danielle Marie Ghislaine Comtesse d'Oultremont** * Uccle 2.10.1954

6c.   **Albert Humbert Marie Ghislain Comte d'Oultremont** * Uccle 21.1.1956

7c.   **Pascale Christiane Marie Ghislaine Comtesse d'Oultremont** * Bruxelles 10.2.1962

XII

5b.   **Danielle Marie Ghislaine Comtesse d'Oultremont** * Heylissem 5.1.1923

6b.   **André Etienne Marie Ghislain Comte d'Oultremont** * Heylissem 17.6.1924 = Tirlemont 31.7.1952 Diane Konincz * 23.12.1931 dau. of Julien Konincz, and has issue:

XIII

1c.   **Carole Marguerite Julienne Marie Ghislaine Comtesse d'Oultremont** * Tirlemont 20.10.1953

2c.   **Régine Marie Reginald Ghislaine Comtesse d'Oultremont** * Tirlemont 10.10.1954

3c.   **Gautier André Joseph Marie Ghislain Comte d'Oultremont** * Tirlemont 8.2.1962

XII

7b.   **Humbert Pierre Gaëtan Marie Ghislain Comte d'Oultremont** * Heylissem 23.12.1928 = Woluwe-St-Pierre 25.10.1955 Odette Comtesse de Briey * Bruxelles 16.5.1932 dau. of Albert Comte de Briey, and has issue:

XIII

1c.   **Jean-Michel Camille Albert Marie Ghislain Comte d'Oultremont** * Bruxelles 29.10.1956

2c.   **Bernard Réginald Marie Ghislain Comte d'Oultremont** * Bruxelles 11.1.1958

XIII		3c. **Martine Danielle Marie Ghislaine Comtesse d'Oultremont** * Louvain 6.2.1959
XII		8b. **Réginald Jean Adrien Marie Ghislain Comte d'Oultremont** * Heylissem 12.9.1930

XI 2a. **Elisabeth Gaëtane Emma Marie Josèphe Ghislaine van de Werve d'Immerseel** * Anvers 23.5.1892 = Anvers 7.5.1913 Jean Baron de Villenfagne de Vogelsanck * Zolder 27.11.1888, and has issue:

XII 1b. **Alphonse Marie Joseph Charles Benoît Ghislain Léon Baron de Villenfagne de Vogelsanck** * Ostende 1.10.1914

2b. **Henri Louis Marie Joseph Benoît Ghislain Baron de Villenfagne de Vogelsanck** * St-Gervais-la-Forêt 17.9.1916 = Bruxelles 20.2.1941 Louise Marie Comtesse de Lichtervelde * Bruxelles 5.12.1919 dau. of Louis Hermann Comte de Lichtervelde, and has issue:

XIII 1c. **Gaëtane Baronne de Villenfagne de Vogelsanck** * Zolder 17.11.1941 = Zolder 16.5.1964 Claude Baron de Vinck * Kerkom 24.2.1933, and has issue:

XIV 1d. **Emmanuel Baron de Vinck** * Bruxelles 6.11.1965

2d. **Juan Baron de Vinck** * Bruxelles 16.11.1966

XIII 2c. **Claude Louis Baron de Villenfagne de Vogelsanck** * Zolder 16.11.1942 = 15.9.1966 Isabelle Baronne t'Kint de Roodenbeke * Uccle 6.4.1946 dau. of Henri Comte t'Kint de Roodenbeke

3c. **Marie Noëlle Baronne de Villenfagne de Vogelsanck** * Zolder 24.12.1943

4c. **Patrick Baron de Villenfagne de Vogelsanck** * Zolder 2.12.1945

5c. **Bénédicte Baronne de Villenfagne de Vogelsanck** * Zolder 23.3.1948

6c. **Jean Ignace Baron de Villenfagne de Vogelsanck** * Zolder 7.7.1949

7c. **Anne Muriel Baronne de Villenfagne de Vogelsanck** * Zolder 16.5.1953

8c. **Tangui Baron de Villenfagne de Vogelsanck** * Hasselt 21.9.1955

XII 3b. **Gaëtane Hélène Marie Josèphe Benoîte Ghislaine Baronne de Villenfagne de Vogelsanck** * Guines, Pas-de-Calais 2.9.1917

4b. **Robert Marie Joseph Benoît Ghislain Baron de Villenfagne de Vogelsanck** * Anvers 13.5.1920 = Ixelles 12.1.1949 Nicole de Meeûs d'Argenteuil * Bruxelles 16.6.1925 dau. of Ludovic Comte de Meeûs d'Argenteuil, and has issue:

XIII 1c. **Baudouin Antoine Baron de Villenfagne de Vogelsanck** * Uccle 20.7.1951

2c. **Sabine Hélène Baronne de Villenfagne de Vogelsanck** * Uccle 26.8.1952

3c. **Marc Louis Baron de Villenfagne de Vogelsanck** * Uccle 18.2.1956

364

XIII   4c.   **Michel Baron de Villenfagne de Vogelsanck** * Uccle 14.5.1962

XII   5b.   **Léon Marie Joseph Yves Ghislain Benoît Baron de Villenfagne de Vogelsanck** * Anvers 26.7.1921 = Hermalle-sous-Huy 16.5.1947 Hélène de Potesta * Hermalle-sous-Huy 29.8.1922 dau. of René Baron de Potesta, and has issue:

XIII

       1c.   **Elisabeth Renée Baronne de Villenfagne de Vogelsanck** * Etterbeek 31.1.1949

       2c.   **Françoise Baronne de Villenfagne de Vogelsanck** * Liège 1.2.1950

       3c.   **Christine Baronne de Villenfagne de Vogelsanck** * Annevoie 29.3.1952

       4c.   **Marie Pauline Baronne de Villenfagne de Vogelsanck** * Schaerbeek 27.12.1953

XII   6b.   **Françoise Baronne de Villenfagne de Vogelsanck** * Anvers 14.6.1922

       7b.   **Guy Marie Alain Benoît Baron de Villenfagne de Vogelsanck** * Anvers 3.8.1927 = Bruxelles 1.4.1953 Marina de Crombrugghe de Lorringhe * Bruxelles 2.4.1933 dau. of Roger Baron de Crombrugghe de Lorringhe, and has issue:

XIII   1c.   **Marie Hélène Baronne de Villenfagne de Vogelsanck** * Schaerbeek 24.3.1954

       2c.   **Annaic Elisabeth Baronne de Villenfagne de Vogelsanck** * Bruxelles 30.5.1955

       3c.   **Yolande Marie Baronne de Villenfagne de Vogelsanck** * Bruxelles 30.5.1955

       4c.   **Eric Louis Lambert Baron de Villenfagne de Vogelsanck** * Gand 13.10.1959

       5c.   **Sybille Marie Thérèse Baronne de Villenfagne de Vogelsanck** * Turhout 19.12.1961

       6c.   **François Léon Marie Job Baron de Villenfagne de Vogelsanck** * Bruxelles 3.4.1966

XI   3a.   **Gaëtane Hélène Antoinette Marie Josèphe Ghislaine van de Werve d'Immerseel** * Pulle 21.6.1895 + Guines 28.7.1917 = Saint-Gervais 26.6.1916 **Georges Comte d'Ursel** * Ormeignies 20.7.1890, and had issue see elsewhere

       4a.   **Gaëtan Antoine Philippe Marie Joseph Vicomte van de Werve d'Immerseel** * Anvers 14.4.1897 = Anvers 12.4.1920 Yvonne Geelhand de la Bistrate * Anvers 12.1.1896 dau. of Raoul Geelhand de la Bistrate, and has issue:

XII   1b.   **Hervé Marie Ludovic Valentine van de Werve d'Immerseel** * Anvers 29.1.1921 = Woluwe-St-Pierre 22.10.1945 **Suzanne Comtesse de Lannoy** * Woluwe-St-Pierre 11.5.1925 dau. of Maurice Comte de Lannoy, and has issue:

XIII   1c.   **Anne Rose Isabelle van de Werve d'Immerseel** * Woluwe-St-Pierre 29.7.1946

       2c.   **Olivier Alain van de Werve d'Immerseel** * Woluwe-St-Pierre 26.6.1947

XIII	3c.	Gaëtan Charles Yves van de Werve d'Immerseel * Woluwe-St-Pierre 15.9.1948
	4c.	Chantal Edmée van de Werve d'Immerseel * Etterbeek 30.11.1951 + Pulle 6.1.1954
	5c.	Patricia Madeleine Gaëtane van de Werve d'Immerseel * Etterbeek 13.5.1955
	6c.	Alain Paul van de Werve d'Immerseel * Etterbeek 26.6.1958
XII	2b.	Nadine Charlotte Marie van de Werve d'Immerseel * Anvers 18.4.1923 = Pulle 27.12.1945 André Comte d'Oultremont * Polleur 4.9.1922, and has issue:
XIII	1c.	Emmanuel Gaëtan Jean Comte d'Oultremont * Woulwe-St-Pierre 4.12.1942
	2c.	Patrick Philippe Marie Ghislain Comte d'Oultremont * Elisabethville 21.8.1949
	3c.	Alexis Stanislas Marie Ghislain Comte d'Oultremont * Elisabethville 8.3.1951
	4c.	Marie Isabelle Yvonne Comtesse d'Oultremont * Elisabethville 8.6.1954
	5c.	Hervé Alain Marie François Ghislain Comte d'Oultremont * Elisabethville 30.12.1956
	6c.	Véronique Fernanda Vinciane Marie Comtesse d'Oultremont * Elisabethville 6.1.1959
	7c.	Nathalie Béatrice Marie Comtesse d'Oultremont * Elisabethville 9.12.1961
XII	3b.	Alain Albert van de Werve d'Immerseel * Pulle 30.8.1924 + Berry-au-Bac, France 5.5.1955
XI	5a.	Marie Mercédès Joséphine Barbe Ghislaine van de Werve d'Immerseel * Anvers 5.2.1907 = Pulle 29.11.1928 Charles Baron de Montpellier de Vedrin * Namur 31.5.1896, and has issue:
XII	1b.	Béatrice Marie Mercédès Charlotte Emilie Colette Ghislaine de Montpellier de Vedrin * Anvers 14.1.1930
	2b.	Charlotte Mercédès Ludovic Yvonne Emille Ghislaine de Montpellier de Vedrin * Anvers 15.2.1931 = Erpent 18.10.1955 Philippe Comte de Meeûs d'Argenteuil * Bruxelles 6.7.1927, and has issue:
XIII	1c.	Anne Mercédès Cécile Charlotte Ghislaine de Meeûs d'Argenteuil * Etterbeek 3.4.1957
	2c.	Géry Charles Stanislas Eusébian Ghislain Comte de Meeûs d'Argenteuil * Etterbeek 25.8.1959
	3c.	Christian Guy Marie Eusébian Ghislain Comte de Meeûs d'Argenteuil * Ixelles 12.2.1961
XII	3b.	Lambert Charles Bernard Emile Théodore Ghislain Baron Montpellier de Vedrin * Anvers 15.4.1932 = Onoz 17.8.1957 Claudine Comtesse de Beauffort * Etterbeek 13.9.1928 dau. of Albert Comte de Beauffort, and has issue:

XIII

       1c. **Isabelle Albertine Béatrice Claudine Marie Ghislaine de Montpellier de Vedrin** * Ixelles 18.6.1958

       2c. **Louis Lambert Charles Adrien Marie Ghislain de Montpellier de Vedrin** * Ixelles 24.8.1961

       3c. **François Philippe Marie Lambert Ghislain de Montpellier de Vedrin** * Ixelles 14.11.1963

XII

      4b. **Bernadette Mercédès Gabrielle Ghislaine de Montpellier de Vedrin** * Anvers 5.2.1935 = Erpent 25.8.1958 Comte Michel Pelletier de Chambure * 12.12.1927, and has issue:

XIII

       1c. **Christophe Pelletier de Chambure** * Dompierre-sur-Helpe (Nord) 6.6.1959

       2c. **Olivier Pelletier de Chambure** * Dompierre-sur-Helpe 3.6.1960

       3c. **Marie Pelletier de Chambure** * Dompierre-sur-Helpe 8.12.1961

       4c. **Guillaume Pelletier de Chambure** * Namur 28.6.1964

X

(b) **Philippe Marie Joseph François Alain Comte de Lannoy** * Bruxelles 23.4.1866 + Anvaing 9.3.1937 = Bruxelles 22.6.1897 Rosalie de Beeckman * Bruxelles 13.9.1877 + Bruxelles 1.4.1963 dau. of Albert Baron de Beeckman, and had issue:

XI

      1a. **Paul Charles Albert Louis Marie Emmanuel Ghislain Comte de Lannoy** * Bruxelles 17.7.1898 = Beloeil 19.7.1921 **Béatrice Princesse de Ligne** * Château de Moulbaix 23.8.1898 dau. of Ernest Prince de Ligne, and has issue:

XII

      1b. **Philippe Marie Ernest Albert Comte de Lannoy** * Bruxelles 14.8.1922 = 17.7.1965 Alix della Faille de Leverghem * Louvain 20.9.1941 dau. of Harold della Faille de Leverghem, and has issue:

XIII

       1c. **Jehan Comte de Lannoy** * 23.12.1966

XII

      2b. **Guillebert Ernest Marie Ghislain Comte de Lannoy** * Bruxelles 10.12.1923 = Overijssche 14.5.1959 Anne Comtesse de Marnix de Sainte-Adelgonde * Overijssche 26.5.1938 dau. of Jacques Comte de Marnix de Sainte-Adelgonde, and has issue:

XIII

       1c. **Eléonore Adelgonde Louise Marie Comtesse de Lannoy** * Ixelles 4.3.1960

       2c. **Amélie Béatrice Marie Comtesse de Lannoy** * Ixelles 1.6.1962

XII

      3b. **Albert Eugène Marie Ghislain Comte de Lannoy** * Bruxelles 10.1.1925 = Sorinnes-la-Longue 29.7.1952 Chantal t'Serstevens * Etterbeek 5.1.1929 dau. of Jean Chevalier t'Sertstevens, and has issue:

XIII

       1c. **Béatrice Marie Louise Chantal Ghislaine Comtesse de Lannoy** * Etterbeek 18.8.1953

       2c. **Clotilde Béatrice Jeanne-de-Chantal Marie Ghislaine Comtesse de Lannoy** * Etterbeek 26.11.1954

       3c. **Didrik Philippe Marie Ghislain René Comte de Lannoy** * Renaix 8.8.1956

       4c. **Marina Ghislaine Diane Comtesse de Lannoy** * Renaix 3.3.1958

XIII	5c.	**Régine Isabelle Bernadette Chantal Marie Ghislaine Comtesse de Lannoy** * Renaix 30.6.1960
	6c.	**Emmanuel Guillebert Marie Ghislain Comte de Lannoy** * Renaix 4.7.1963
XII	4b.	**Myriam Jeanne Rosalie Ghislaine Comtesse de Lannoy** * Etterbeek 24.11.1926 = Elisabethville 5.4.1958 Charles Coppieters de Gibson * Saint-Josse ten Noode 10.10.1926, and has issue:
XIII	1c.	**Eric Béatrice Philippe Marie Coppieters de Gibson** * Bukavu, Congo 31.12.1959
	2c.	**Joëlle Wilhelmine Pauline Marie Coppieters de Gibson** * Léopoldville 12.6.1961
	3c.	**Philippe Coppieters de Gibson** * 12.8.1964
XII	5b.	**Diane Régine Aline Marie Ghislaine Comtesse de Lannoy** * Etterbeek 13.7.1928
	6b.	**Isabelle Marie Yvonne Comtesse de Lannoy** * Etterbeek 16.5.1930
	7b.	**Claude Emmanuel Marie Léonel Comte de Lannoy** * Etterbeek 7.5.1932 = Maizeret 7.7.1962 **Claudine Comtesse d'Ursel** * Namur 11.5.1940 dau. of Antoine Comte d'Ursel, and has issue:
XIII	1c.	**Alain Emmanuel Marie Paul Ghislain Comte de Lannoy** * Namur 6.9.1963
	2c.	**Tanguy Pascal Marie Baudouin Ghislain Comte de Lannoy** * Namur 9.4.1965
XI	2a.	**Marie Marthe Albertine Charlotte Emma Ghislaine Comtesse de Lannoy** * Annevoie 23.6.1899 = Bruxelles 27.10.1925 Yves Mériadec le Gentil Comte de Rosmorduc * Versailles 18.8.1891 + Bruxelles 9.1.1949, and has issue:
XII	1b.	**Yves Alain le Gentil Comte de Rosmorduc** * Bruxelles 20.9.1926 = Warnant 6.10.1956 Nadine de Meester de Betzenbroeck * Woluwe-Saint-Lambert 22.7.1935 dau. of Raymond Baron de Meester de Betzenbroeck, and has issue:
XIII	1c.	**Geoffrey le Gentil Vicomte de Rosmorduc** * Bruxelles 15.4.1960
	2c.	**Gaëlle le Gentil de Rosmorduc** * Bruxelles 13.8.1963
XII	2b.	**Philippine le Gentil de Rosmorduc** * Bruxelles 19.5.1930
	3b.	**Gwennolée le Gentil de Rosmorduc** * Bruxelles 12.12.1933 = Bruxelles 23.6.1956 Michel Terlinden * Hever 15.8.1929, and has issue:
XIII	1c.	**Joëlle Terlinden** * Bruxelles 7.12.1957
	2c.	**Eric-Alain Terlinden** * Bruxelles 17.2.1960

| XII | 4b. | **Alain Marie le Gentil Vicomte de Rosmorduc** * Bruxelles 17.6.1935 = Woluwe-St-Lambert 21.9.1963 Mireille de Meester de Betzenbroeck * Woluwe-Saint-Lambert 5.4.1937 dau. of Raymond Baron de Meester de Betzenbroeck |

| XI | 3a. | **Henriette Marie Ghislaine Françoise Augustine Comtesse de Lannoy** * Anvaing 31.8.1901 + 12.7.1966 = Anvaing 12.4.1926 Tanguy le Gentil Vicomte de Rosmorduc * Tremel 23.11.1892, and had issue: |

| XII | 1b. | **Tanguy le Gentil Vicomte de Rosmorduc** * Bruxelles 12.11.1927 = Bruxelles 9.11.1957 **Sophie Princesse de Croÿ** * Paderborn 28.3.1932 dau. of Anton Prinz v. Croÿ, and has issue: |

XIII	1c.	**Olivier Tanguy Antoine Marie Ghislain le Gentil Vicomte de Rosmorduc** * Bruxelles 11.3.1959
	2c.	**Marie Gabrielle Marguerite Ghislaine le Gentil de Rosmorduc** * Bruxelles 6.6.1961
	3c.	**Michel Hervé Emmanuel Marie Ghislain le Gentil Vicomte de Rosmorduc** * 10.3.1965

| XII | 2b. | **Hervé le Gentil Vicomte de Rosmorduc** * Anvaing 8.10.1929 |
| | 3b. | **Yvonne le Gentil de Rosmorduc** * Bruxelles 22.9.1932 = Bruxelles 25.8.1956 Joseph Comte du Parc-Locmaria * Hamal 19.8.1925, and has issue: |

XIII	1c.	**Anne Henriette Alain Marie Ghislaine du Parc-Locmaria** * Etterbeek 10.6.1957
	2c.	**Alain Tanguy Yves Marie Ghislain Comte du Parc-Locmaria** * Etterbeek 10.5.1959
	3c.	**Gwennolée Françoise Anne Marie Ghislaine du Parc-Locmaria** * Etterbeek 5.4.1961

| XII | 4b. | **Anne le Gentil de Rosmorduc** * Brest 29.9.1934 = Bruxelles 28.9.1963 Louis Terlinden * Schaerbeek 4.6.1931, and has issue: |

| XIII | 1c. | **Antoine Mériadec Terlinden** * 14.10.1964 |
| | 2c. | **Aliénor Terlinden** * ... 9.1966 |

| XI | 4a. | **Baudouin Ferdinand Charles Marie Ghislain Comte de Lannoy** * Anvaing 25.6.1905 = Overijssche 14.11.1941 Odette Comtesse de Marnix de Sainte-Adelgonde * Overijssche 24.4.1906 dau. of Comte John de Marnix de Sainte-Adelgonde, and has issue: |

XII	1b.	**Marie Gabrielle Jeanne Rosalie Ghislaine Comtesse de Lannoy** * Louvain 31.8.1943
	2b.	**Hugues Joseph Paul Marie Ghislain Comte de Lannoy** * Overijssche 18.11.1944
	3b.	**Thérèse Marthe Adrienne Emilie Marie Ghislaine Comtesse de Lannoy** * Louvain 30.11.1946
	4b.	**Anne Jeanne Gwennolée Marie Ghislaine Comtesse de Lannoy** * Bruxelles 21.6.1951

XI	5a.	**Jacqueline Caroline Antoinette Marie Ghislaine Comtesse de Lannoy** * Anvaing 24.1.1908 = Bruxelles 18.1.1939 Guillaume Comte du Parc-Locmaria * Moestroff-Bettendorf 2.7.1901, and has issue:

<table>
<tr><td>XII</td><td>1b.</td><td>Marie Thérèse Rosalie Antoinette Pauline Ghislaine du Parc-Locmaria * Etterbeek 27.1.1940 = Bruxelles 22.5.1965 Charles d'Udekem de Guertechin * Héverlée 28.10.1937</td></tr>
<tr><td></td><td>2b.</td><td>Alice Rosalie Thérèse Ghislaine du Parc-Locmaria * Anvaing 15.5.1942</td></tr>
<tr><td></td><td>3b.</td><td>Jean Raphaël François Paul Ghislain Vicomte du Parc-Locmaria * Anvaing 23.9.1943</td></tr>
<tr><td></td><td>4b.</td><td>Hadelin Gustave Marie Joseph Ghislain Vicomte du Parc-Locmaria * Ixelles 14.4.1948</td></tr>
</table>

X	(c)	**Aline Marie Josèphe Adrienne Françoise Comtesse de Lannoy** * Bruxelles 7.9.1867 + Bruxelles 22.1.1936
	(d)	**Anna Louise Marie Josèphe Françoise Antoinette Comtesse de Lannoy** * Bruxelles 28.3.1870 + Ixelles 27.3.1942 = Ixelles 22.6.1906 Auguste Burnell * Alost 28.3.1845 + Folkstone 16.1.1918, and had issue:

XI	1a.	**Marie Josèphe Louise Alexandrine Caroline Henriette Ghislaine Burnell** * Ixelles 19.3.1907 = Ixelles 14.4.1928 Guy Baron de Lhoneux * Namur 3.3.1898 + Woluwe-Saint-Pierre 17.12.1956, and has issue:

XII	1b.	**Colette Joséphine Ghislaine Anne Thérèse de Lhoneux** * Etterbeek 19.7.1930 = Kurukwatha 5.3.1952 Wladimir Aksakow * Wilna, Poland 10.1.1923, and has issue:

XIII	1c.	**Michel Aksakow** * Kurukwatha (Congo) 8.11.1953
	2c.	**Marc Aksakow** * Kurukwatha 13.7.1956
	3c.	**Stéphane Aksakow** * Cannes 1.2.1965

XII	2b.	**Danièle Marie Joséphine Ghislaine Colette de Lhoneux** * Ixelles 29.5.1936 = Woluwe-Saint-Pierre 12.9.1957 Camille Comte de Briey * Bruxelles 9.1.1936, and has issue:

XIII	1c.	**Brigitte Comtesse de Briey** * Bruxelles 8.5.1958
	2c.	**Patricia Comtesse de Briey** * Bruxelles 14.10.1959
	3c.	**Muriel Comtesse de Briey** * Bruxelles 9.3.1961
	4c.	**Florence Comtesse de Briey** * Bruxelles 13.6.1965

XII	3b.	**Dominique Jacques Maria Joseph Ghislain Baron de Lhoneux** * Bruxelles 28.5.1938 = Melle 8.6.1961 Anne Comtesse de Marchant d'Ansembourg * Gand 2.3.1940 dau. of Raymond Comte de Marchant d'Ansembourg, and has issue:

XIII	1c.	**Pascale de Lhoneux** * Dallas, Texas 15.7.1962
	2c.	**Guy Joël de Lhoneux** * Bruxelles 28.8.1965

XI	2a.	**Pierre Armand Charles Ghislain Marie Joseph Burnell** * Middelkerke 8.8.1908 = 30.3.1937 Clotilde Reyntiens * 11.7.1909 dau. of Jean-Marie Reyntiens, and has issue:

XII — 1b. **Myriam Burnell** * Bruxelles 12.2.1938 = 16.1.1958 Carl-Eric de Sivers * 15.2.1933, and has issue:

XIII — 1c. **Valérie de Sivers** * 20.4.1960

2c. **Yves de Sivers** * 27.1.1962

XII — 2b. **Priscilla Burnell** * Bruxelles 21.6.1939

3b. **Beatrice Burnell** * Bruxelles 22.2.1943

4b. **Michèle Burnell** * Bruxelles 4.4.1944 = 26.9.1963 Christian Sepulchre * 22.5.1933, and has issue:

XIII — 1c. **Jerôme Sepulchre** * 11.9.1965

XII — 5b. **Régine Burnell** * Bruxelles 8.7.1945

XI — 3a. **Marthe Anne Marie Josèphe Ghislaine Burnell** * Ixelles 7.11.1910 = Ixelles 30.10.1930 Guy Comte de Meeûs d'Argenteuil * Ixelles 2.3.1906, and has issue:

XII — 1b. **Béatrice Anne Marie Denyse Ghislaine Françoise de Meeûs d'Argenteuil** * Ixelles 2.9.1934 = Etterbeek 12.5.1958 **Antoine Vicomte d'Hennezel** * Ixelles 20.10.1927, and has issue see elsewhere

2b. **Bertrand Roger Marie Joseph Ghislain Francis Comte de Meeûs d'Argenteuil** * Ixelles 9.6.1936

3b. **Chantal Marie Gabriele Ghislaine Françoise de Meeûs d'Argenteuil** * Ixelles 13.6.1942

4b. **Anita Marie Joséphine Colette Ghislaine Françoise de Meeûs d'Argenteuil** * Overyssche 11.3.1945

5b. **Marie Axelle Marguerite Adeline Françoise de Meeûs d'Argenteuil** * Ixelles 12.11.1946

X — (e) **Marie Anne Josèphe Françoise Antoinette Comtesse de Lannoy** * Ixelles 29.4.1873 + Yercaud, India 7.6.1961

(f) **Gustave Adhémar Marie Joseph François Antoine Comte de Lannoy** * Bruxelles 18.3.1875 + Uccle 22.3.1925 = Ixelles 31.7.1905 Marthe van Praet * Bruxelles 16.1.1884 + Uccle 26.5.1954 dau. of Chevalier Werner van Praet, and had issue:

XI — 1a. **Hedwige Jeanne Emma Marie Josèphe Comtesse de Lannoy** * Rhode-Saint-Genèse 17.6.1906

2a. **Antoinette Aline Valérie Marie Josèphe Comtesse de Lannoy** * Schoten 5.8.1907 = Schoten 14.6.1927 Charles Baron van Havre * Anvers 14.11.1881 + Wilrijk 10.11.1952, and has issue:

XII — 1b. **Camille Marthe Hedwige Henriette Marie van Havre** * Etterbeek 28.6.1929 = Schoten 7.6.1949 Michel Baron della Faille d'Huysee van den Hecke de Lembeke * Ixelles 14.9.1924, and has issue:

XIII		1c. **Catherine Stéphanie Antoinette Joséphine Marie Ghislaine Baronne della Faille d'Huysee van den Hecke de Lembeke** * Wilrijk 18.5.1950
		2c. **Vincent Charles Anne Marie Joseph Ghislain Baron della Faille d'Huysee van den Hecke de Lembeke** * Courtrai 7.5.1952
		3c. **Fabienne Monique Marie Joséphine Ghislaine Baronne della Faille d'Huysee van den Hecke de Lembeke** * Anvers 4.12.1956
XII	2b.	**Monique Eva Gabrielle Marie Juliette van Havre** * Schoten 28.5.1932 = 17.2.1952 Jean Grutering * Anvers 14.12.1927, and has issue:
XIII		1c. **Bernard Grutering** * Anvers 7.8.1954
		2c. **Marc Grutering** * Anvers 17.2.1957
		3c. **Nathalie Grutering** * Anvers 1.10.1958
		4c. **Ariane Grutering** * Anvers 22.12.1960
		5c. **Dominique Grutering** * Anvers 24.2.1962
XII	3b.	**Jacques Gustave Henri Gabriel Baron van Havre** * Schoten 24.8.1933 = Anvers 7.9.1959 Vivianne de Cock de Rameyen, * Anvers 16.4.1937 dau. of Roger de Cock de Remayen, and has issue:
XIII		1c. **Charles Marie Roger Antoine Chevalier van Havre** * Wilrijk 22.2.1961
		2c. **Caroline Marie Alain Christiane Ghislaine van Havre** * Wilrijk 15.5.1962
		3c. **Stéphane van Havre** * Wilrijk 15.4.1965
XII	4b.	**Nadine Jeanne Marie Antoinette van Havre** * Schoten 4.12.1936 = Eckeren 10.7.1958 Didier de Cock de Rameyen * Anvers 7.3.1934, and has issue:
XIII		1c. **Anne-Marie Alexandrine Antoinette Ghislaine de Cock de Rameyen** * Anvers 18.10.1959
		2c. **Marie Sophie Baudouin Vivienne Ghislaine de Cock de Rameyen** * Anvers 18.12.1960
		3c. **Philippe de Cock de Rameyen** * Anvers 23.2.1962
		4c. **Géraldine de Cock de Rameyen** * Anvers 10.3.1965
XII	5b.	**Anne Marie Louise Claude Antoinette van Havre** * Anvers 5.7.1940 = Wilrijk 27.9.1962 Michel Comte Cornet d'Elzius du Chennoy * Heyst-sur-Mer 19.6.1935, and has issue:
XIII		1c. **Sylvie Comtesse Cornet d'Elzius du Chennoy** * Bruxelles 7.1.1964
		2c. **Frédéric Comte Cornet d'Elzius du Chennoy** * Konkke 20.6.1965
XI	3a.	**Gabriele Marie Valérie Comtesse de Lannoy** * Schoten 7.10.1909

(g) **Antoinette Marie Josèphe Françoise Comtesse de Lannoy** * Bruxelles 24.2.1876
+ Bruxelles 30.1.1941 = Bruxelles 4.11.1902 Jean Vicomte de Chérisy * Lille
1.1.1867 + Berchem-Sainte-Agathe 27.3.1937 s.p.

(h) **Baudouin Gustave Louis Marie Joseph Antoine François Comte de Lannoy**
* Bruxelles 10.12.1878 + Anvaing 15.10.1901

(i) **Maurice Marie Joseph Antoine François Comte de Lannoy** * Anvaing 7.6.1884
+ Woluwe-Saint-Pierre 27.4.1942 = Doiceau 11.8.1910 Louise Vicomtesse de
Spoelberch * Cortil-Wodon 12.7.1888 + Woluwe-Saint-Pierre 6.1.1953 dau. of
Louis Vicomte de Spoelberch, and had issue:

XI

1a. **Ghislaine Marie Françoise Emma Comtesse de Lannoy** * Bruxelles 30.8.1911
= Woluwe-Saint-Pierre 19.11.1935 Comte Henri Moretus Plantin de Bouchout
* Hoboken 23.9.1905, and has issue:

XII

1b. **Jean Marie Louis Ghislain Moretus Plantin de Bouchout** * Woluwe-
Saint-Pierre 13.1.1940 = Anzegem 11.9.1965 Charlotte Comtesse de
Limburg-Stirum * Louvain 31.5.1941 dau. of Philippe-Evrard Comte
de Limburg-Stirum

2b. **Reynald Marie Maurice Ghislain Moretus Plantin de Bouchout**
* Wiljrik 28.10.1941

3b. **Geoffroy Marie Charles Ghislain Moretus Plantin de Bouchout**
* Wiljrik 22.6.1945

4b. **Danièle Marie Thérèse Philippine Ghislaine Moretus Plantin de Bouchout**
* Wiljrik 17.7.1947

XI

2a. **Antoine Maurice Marie Ghislain Comte de Lannoy** * Bruxelles 29.5.1913

3a. **Marie Ghislaine Michelle Aline Andrée Comtesse de Lannoy** * Bruxelles
1.10.1914 = Woluwe-St-Pierre 16.7.1935 Philippe Baron d'Huart
* Vonêche 4.6.1908 + Crainhem 24.1.1962, and has issue:

XII

1b. **Alain Marie Ghislain Frédéric Louis Baron d'Huart** * Bruxelles
19.5.1936

2b. **Nicole Marie Ghislaine Baronne d'Huart** * Crainhem 2.6.1939

3b. **Guy Marie Ghislain Baron d'Huart** * Ixelles 11.5.1943

4b. **Anita Marie Ghislaine Baronne d'Huart** * Ixelles 20.7.1954

XI

4a. **Monique Hélène Marie Ghislaine Comtesse de Lannoy** * Hampstead,
London 11.11.1915 = Bruxelles 17.6.1937 **Elie Comte d'Ursel** * Paris
9.3.1915, and has issue see elsewhere

5a. **Gérard Antoine Gabriel Marie Joseph Ghislain Comte de Lannoy** * Neuilly-
sur-Seine 6.7.1917 = Woluwe-Saint-Pierre 13.3.1948 Isabelle de Menten de
Horne * Bruxelles 19.6.1926 dau. of Chevalier Henry de Menten de Horne,
and has issue:

XII

1b. **Thierry Maurice Louis Henri Marie Ghislain Comte de Lannoy**
* Etterbeek 9.1.1949

2b. **Michel Henry Charles Marie Ghislain Comte de Lannoy** * Vieux
Waleffe 24.7.1951

3b. **Myriam Thérèse Jacqueline Ghislaine Renelde Comtesse de Lannoy**
* Vieux Waleffe 20.9.1954

XI	6a.	**Gabrielle Christiane Madeleine Josèphe Marie Ghislaine Comtesse de Lannoy** * Bruxelles 9.10.1919 = Woluwe-Saint-Pierre 22.10.1945 Jacques Baron van der Straten-Waillet * Anvers 30.4.1914, and has issue:

XII

1b. **Béatrice Baronne van der Straten-Waillet** * 6.10.1947

2b. **Sabine Baronne van der Straten-Waillet** * 5.10.1948

3b. **Georges Baron van der Straten-Waillet** * 28.7.1950

4b. **Bernard Baron van der Straten-Waillet** * 4.10.1952

XI

7a. **Madelaine Gabrielle Marie Ghislaine Comtesse de Lannoy** * Bruxelles 15.10.1921 = Woluwe-Saint-Pierre 4.4.1942 Charles Albert Comte de Lichtervelde * Ecaussinnes-d'Enghien 28.9.1915, and has issue:

XII

1b. **Emmanuel Pierre Christian Marie Joseph Ghislain Comte de Lichtervelde** * Ixelles 9.12.1943

2b. **Nathalie Elisabeth Gérardine Marie Ghislaine Comtesse de Lichtervelde** * Etterbeek 5.8.1946

3b. **Hedwige Louise Suzanne Marie Ghislaine Comtesse de Lichtervelde** * Etterbeek 14.5.1951

4b. **Pierre Léopold Yves Marie Joseph Ghislain Comte de Lichtervelde** * Etterbeek 19.8.1955

XI

8a. **Suzanne Antoinette Ghislaine Marie Josèphe Comtesse de Lannoy** * Woluwe-Saint-Pierre 11.5.1925 = Woluwe-Saint-Pierre 22.10.1945 **Hervé van de Werve d'Immerseel** * Anvers 29.1.1921, and has issue see elsewhere

9a. **Léopold Ignace Ghislain Marie Joseph Comte de Lannoy** * Woluwe-Saint-Pierre 10.11.1926 = St-Benin-d'Azy 23.7.1955 **Florence Princesse de Croÿ** * Château de St-Benin-d'Azy 14.12.1927 dau. of Léopold Prince de Croÿ, and has issue:

XII

1b. **Dorothée Catherine Jacqueline Léopoldine Comtesse de Lannoy** * Etterbeek 16.4.1956 + Etterbeek 18.4.1956

2b. **Hermine Marie Jacqueline Léopoldine Comtesse de Lannoy** * Lausanne 1.3.1959

3b. **Claire Constance Emmanuela Léopoldine Comtesse de Lannoy** * Lausanne 22.11.1961

XI

10a. **Charles Albert Ignace Ghislain Marie Joseph Comte de Lannoy** * Woluwe-Saint-Pierre 10.11.1926 = Ixelles 6.4.1953 Bernadette Cruysmans * Ixelles 15.2.1932 dau. of Jean Cruysmans, and has issue:

XII

1b. **Dominique Marie Ghislaine Solange Léopoldine Comtesse de Lannoy** * Etterbeek 19.2.1954

2b. **Patrick Marie François Philippe Ghislain Comte de Lannoy** * Etterbeek 1.5.1955

3b. **Brigitte Anne Marie Hervé Ghislaine Comtesse de Lannoy** * Ixelles 21.11.1956

4b. **Marc Marie Joseph Ghislain Comte de Lannoy** * Ixelles 18.4.1959

5b. **François Xavier Jacques Roland Marie Comte de Lannoy** * Brasschaet 6.10.1962

374

11a. **Françoise Marie Joséphine Comtesse de Lannoy** * Woluwe-Saint-Pierre 20.3.1929 = Woluwe-Saint-Pierre 29.6.1963 Xavier Coppieters de Gibson * St-Josse-ten-Noode 11.10.1928, and has issue:

XII

   1b. **Clothilde Wilhelmine Marie Josèphe Coppieters de Gibson** * Soest 30.4.1964

   2b. **Arnold Gabriel Marie Joseph Ghislain Coppieters de Gibson** * Bruxelles 8.10.1966

IX

b) **Blanche Marie Jeanne Adèle Françoise Comtesse de Lannoy** * Bruxelles 10.2.1831 + Bruxelles 15.8.1852

c) **Marie Jeanne Philippine Comtesse de Lannoy** * Bruxelles 3.2.1832 + Bruxelles 27.4.1873

d) **Ferdinand Charles Marie Joseph Comte de Lannoy** * Bruxelles 8.6.1833 + Bruxelles 15.7.1881 = Bruxelles 25.11.1858 Marie Joséphine de la Pierre de Fremeur * Tournai 4.6.1840 + Bruxelles 25.6.1920 dau. of Aimé Vicomte de la Pierre de Fremeur, and had issue:

X

(a) **Blanche Ernestine Charlotte Marie Josèphe Comtesse de Lannoy** * Bruxelles 20.11.1859 + Eysden 19.4.1936 = Bruxelles 1.7.1880 René Comte de Geloes d'Eysden * Liège 1.6.1856 + Eysden 25.8.1930, and had issue:

XI

   1a. **Marie Ferdinande Augustine Catherine Josèphe Ghislaine Comtesse de Geloes d'Eysden** * Eysden 25.11.1881 + Uccle 6.1.1956 = Eysden 25.6.1902 Marcel Comte de Liedekerke de Pailhe * St-Gilles 26.2.1875 + Bruxelles 15.4.1931, and had issue:

XII

   1b. **Rasse Raphaël Emilie Marie Joseph Ghislain Comte de Liedekerke de Pailhe** * Bruxelles 15.4.1903 ✗ près Utrecht 3.10.1943 = Bruxelles 6.5.1929 Elisabeth Comtesse de Lichtervelde * Ixelles 23.1.1908 dau. of William Comte de Lichtervelde, and had issue:

XIII

      1c. **Renée Blanche Marcelle Marie Louise Ghislaine Comtesse de Liedekerke de Pailhe** * Bruxelles 27.4.1931 = Woluwe-Saint-Lambert 24.8.1957 Paul Roberti de Winghe * Louvain 17.1.1927

      2c. **Solange Augustine Marie Josèphe Ghislaine Comtesse de Liedekerke de Pailhe** * Eysden 28.8.1932

      3c. **Jeanne-de-Chantal Renée Madeleine Marie Josèphe Ghislaine Comtesse de Liedekerke de Pailhe** * Eysden 26.11.1933

      4c. **Marcel Rasse Frédéric Maur Marie Joseph Ghislain Comte de Liedekerke de Pailhe** * Eysden 4.4.1935 = La Cazerie-Celles 14.9.1960 Béatrice Christyn Comtesse de Ribeaucourt * Celles 3.11.1936 dau. of Adolphe Christyn Comte de Ribeaucourt, and has issue:

XIV

         1d. **Raphaël Rasse Alfred Marie Ghislain Comte de Liedekerke de Pailhe** * Etterbeek 20.6.1961

         2d. **Clotilde Marie Geneviève Ghislaine Comtesse de Liedekerke de Pailhe** * Etterbeek 22.10.1962

         3d. **Françoise Comtesse de Liedekerke de Pailhe** * Eysden 3.6.1966

XIII	5c.	**Christian Rasse Jacques Claude Marie Joseph Ghislain Comte de Liedekerke de Pailhe** * Eysden 1.8.1937 = La-Cazerie-Celles 11.7.1964 Jacqueline Christyn Comtesse de Ribeaucourt * Uccle 2.8.1937 dau. of Adolphe Christyn Comte de Ribeaucourt, and has issue:

XIV   1d.   **Benoît Comte de Liedekerke de Pailhe** * Ixelles 9.8.1965

XII   2b.   **Rasse René Antoine Marie Joseph Ghislain Comte de Liedekerke de Pailhe** * Eysden 21.8.1906 = Duras 12.4.1934 **Henriette Comtesse d'Oultremont** * Bruxelles 20.5.1910 dau. of Emmanuel Comte d'Oultremont s.p.

3b.   **Hélène Philippine Blanche Marie Josèphe Ghislaine Comtesse de Liedekerke de Pailhe** * Bruxelles 14.12.1910 = Eysden 23.8.1933 Jacques Comte de Beauffort * Bruxelles 18.5.1902 s.p.

XI   2a.   **Isabelle Alice Lucienne Marie Josèphe Ghislaine Comtesse de Geloes d'Eysden** * Château d'Eysden 31.5.1884 + Tavier 9.11.1960 = Breust-Eysden 7.7.1904 Joseph Comte d'Oultremont de Wégimont de Warfusée * Amay 15.8.1877 + Tavier 7.10.1942, and had issue:

XII   1b.   **Etienne Antoine Gaston Marie Joseph Ghislain Comte d'Oultremont de Wégimont et de Warfusée** * Château de Beusdael, Sippenaeken 16.4.1905 = Bruxelles 16.5.1935 Jacqueline Comtesse de Lalaing * Oostcamp 16.12.1910 dau. of Max Comte de Lalaing, and has issue:

XIII   1c.   **Antoinette Marie Ghislaine Comtesse d'Oultremont de Wégimont et de Warfusée** * Uccle 13.10.1936 = Tavier 6.9.1958 Baudouin Vicomte de Ghellinck d'Elseghem Vaernewyck * Bruxelles 9.5.1928, and has issue:

XIV   1d.   **Marc Jacques Charles Ghislain Chevalier de Ghellinck d'Elseghem Vaernewyck** * Etterbeek 16.9.1959

2d.   **Brigitte Marguerite Marie Colette Ghislaine de Ghellinck d'Elseghem Vaernewyck** * Uccle 5.10.1960

3d.   **Chantal Colette Ghislaine de Ghellinck d'Elseghem Vaernewyck** * Uccle 21.9.1964

XIII   2c.   **Claire Isabelle Marie Ghislaine Comtesse d'Oultremont de Wégimont et de Warfusée** * Uccle 23.9.1938 = Tavier 12.10.1960 Gérald Baron Snoy * Bruxelles 27.12.1928, and has issue:

XIV   1d.   **Charles Henry Baron Snoy** * Karachi 18.7.1961

2d.   **Stéphanie Snoy** * San Francisco 12.1.1965

XIII   3c.   **Régine Diane Marie Ghislaine Comtesse d'Oultremont de Wégimont et de Warfusée** * 30.5.1940

4c.   **Viviane Marie Ghislaine Comtesse d'Oultremont de Wégimont et de Warfusée** * Tavier 26.6.1948

5c.   **Isabelle Marie Madeleine Ghislaine Comtesse d'Oultremont de Wégimont et de Warfusée** * Tavier 23.9.1951

2b. **Marc Eugène Antoine René Marie Joseph Ghislain Comte d'Oultremont de Wégimont et de Warfusée** * Château de Beusdael 28.10.1909

3b. **Antoine Albert Marie Joseph Ghislain Comte d'Oultremont de Wégimont et de Warfusée** * Château de Beusdael 27.10.1911 X Wervicq 26.5.1940

4b. **Alix Adrienne-Adolphine Marie Josèphe Ghislaine Comtesse d'Oultremont de Wégimont et de Warfusée** * Eysden 17.8.1915 = Tavier 24.6.1943 Edouard Ullens de Schooten * Anvers 21.11.1898, and has issue:

1c. **Béatrice Ullens de Schooten** * Tavier 5.6.1944

2c. **Myriam Ullens de Schooten** * Tavier 5.4.1946

3c. **Jean Ullens de Schooten** * Tavier 8.7.1948

4c. **Antoine Ullens de Schooten** * Etterbeek 21.4.1950

3a. **Marguerite Marie Gabrielle Philippine Ghislaine Josèphe Comtesse de Geloes d'Eysden** * Château d'Eysden 23.4.1889 + Château d'Eysden 1.3.1890

(b) **Charlotte Rose Marie Josèphe Comtesse de Lannoy** * Bruxelles 24.1.1862 + Bruxelles 28.3.1862

(c) **Elisabeth Rose Marie Josèphe Comtesse de Lannoy** * Bruxelles 23.4.1863 + Bruxelles 23.6.1869

(d) **Adrienne Jeanne Marie Josèphe Comtesse de Lannoy** * Bruxelles 27.2.1864 + Château de la Martinière (Solesmes) 16.2.1922 = Bruxelles 24.11.1887 Diederik Jhr. van den Berch van Heemstede * Leyde 16.4.1860 + 's-Gravenhage 24.10.1917, and had issue:

1a. **Ferdinand Gustave Diederik Marie Joseph Jhr. van den Berch van Heemstede** * Bruxelles 10.10.1888 + 's-Gravenhage 4.10.1963 = Katwijk 11.11.1911 Alida van Santen * 's-Gravenhage 24.4.1888 dau. of Wilhelmus van Santen, and had issue:

XII

1b. **Elisabeth Wilhelmine Jeanne Anna Marie Josèphe Jkvr. van den Berch van Heemstede** * Harfleur 21.1.1912

2b. **Etienne Jhr. van den Berch van Heemstede** * Middleburgh 15.1.1916 + Vlissingen 16.11.1916

3b. **Etienne Jhr. van den Berch van Heemstede** * Vlissingen 8.12.1917 = Eindhoven 31.10.1941 Hazina Jeanette van Eedenburg * St. Petersburg 7.6.1917 dau. of Daam Carel van Eedenburg — div.; = (2) Waterloo, Belgium 4.5.1960 Marie Plétinckx * Hennuyères, Belgium 12.9.1933 dau. of Pierre Joseph Plétinckx, and has issue:

by 1st marriage:

1c. **Barbara Jeannette Jkvr. van den Berch van Heemstede** * 's-Gravenhage 5.4.1945

by 2nd marriage:

2c. **Pierre Marie François Jhr. van den Berch van Heemstede** * Malo-les-Bains (Nord) 29.1.1956

3c. **Alexandre Etienne Jhr. van den Berch van Heemstede** * Bilthoven 23.2.1961

XIII		4c. **Karen Ann Jkvr. van den Berch van Heemstede** * Bilthoven 16.6.1962

XII   4b. **Solange Valentine Hubertine Jkvr. van den Berch van Heemstede** * Nogent-sur-Marne 5.7.1920 = Loosduinen 28.5.1940 Petrus Trompert * 's-Gravenhage 18.10.1906, and has issue:

XIII

        1c. **Diederik Marie Joseph Trompert** * 30.6.1942

        2c. **Bernadette Maria Theresia Trompert** * 29.1.1944

        3c. **Ewald Ferdinand Trompert** * 23.12.1946

        4c. **Rheinhart Etienne Maria Trompert** * 15.3.1948

        5c. **Stephen Franciscus Trompert** * 23.1.1952

        6c. **Michel Nicolas Trompert** * 14.5.1956

XII   5b. **Odette Jkvr. van den Berch van Heemstede** * Berck-Plage 17.3.1924 = Alexandria, Egypt 24.2.1938 Michel Christoph Démétriadis * Mansourah, Egypt 13.2.1909 + Alexandria 4.2.1962, and has issue:

XIII

        1c. **Christophe Michel Démétriadis** * Lausanne 21.1.1940

        2c. **Nicolas Alexander Démétriadis** * Lausanne 26.7.1943

XI   2a. **Louise Blanche Elisabeth Adrienne Marie Josèphe Jkvr. van den Berch van Heemstede** * 's-Gravenhage 6.10.1897 = Bruxelles 24.4.1922 Gilbert Lamothe * Solesmes (Sarthe) 21.4.1896, and has issue:

XII

     1b. **Louis Lamothe** * 22.12.1927 + 6.3.1957

     2b. **Marie Christine Lamothe** * Paris 8.4.1929 = 3.6.1953 Comte Jacques de la Tullaye * St-Martin-les-Boulogne (P.-de-C.) 5.10.1925, and has issue:

XIII

        1c. **Michel de la Tullaye** * Neuilly-sur-Seine 6.1.1962

XII   3b. **Françoise Lamothe** * Neuilly-sur-Seine 11.8.1933

XI   3a. **Antoine Godefroy René Marie Joseph Jhr. van den Berch van Heemstede** * Bruxelles 1.1.1895 + Neuilly-sur-Seine 30.4.1954 = Breda 24.8.1920 Hortense van Mierlo * Breda 10.1.1896 dau. of Johannes Wilhelmus van Mierlo, and had issue:

XII   1b. **Hélène Marie Josèphe Jkvr. van den Berch van Heemstede** * Vught 13.8.1921 = Breda 29.9.1945 Johannes van Schaik * Arnhem 27.7.1917, and has issue:

XIII

        1c. **Josephus Robertus Hendricus van Schaik** * 's-Gravenhage 7.7.1946

        2c. **Stephanus Hendricus Bernardus van Schaik** * Batavia 10.10.1949

        3c. **Michiel Jerome van Schaik** * 's-Gravenhage 20.4.1951

        4c. **Hélène Christine van Schaik** * Breda 26.9.1957

XII   2b. **Diederik Marie Joseph Jhr. van den Berch van Heemstede** * Vught 22.4.1923 = Paris 17.10.1959 Claude Chasseloup de Chatillon * 27.12.1935 dau. of Jacques Chasseloup de Chatillon, and has issue:

378

XIII   1c.   **Christine Marie Edith Jkvr. van den Berch van Heemstede**
      * Rotterdam 28.7.1960

    2c.   **Florence Marie Thérèse Jkvr. van den Berch van Heemstede**
      * Rotterdam 31.10.1961

    3c.   **Véronique Marie Hortense Jkvr. van den Berch van Heemstede**
      * Paris 19.1.1964

    4c.   **Frédéric Marie Joseph Jhr. van den Berch van Heemstede**
      * Paris 27.4.1965

XII   3b.   **William Marie Joseph Jhr. van den Berch van Heemstede** * Vught
19.5.1924 = São Paulo 12.2.1953 Felicita von Fock * Sagad,
Estonia 23.8.1930 dau. of Axel von Fock, and has issue:

XIII   1c.   **Tatjana Jkvr. van den Berch van Heemstede** * São Paulo
18.4.1954

    2c.   **Maurice Marie Joseph Jhr. van den Berch van Heemstede**
      * Itajuba, Brasil 10.7.1957

XII   4b.   **Gilbert Marie Joseph Jhr. van den Berch van Heemstede** * Neuilly-
sur-Seine 5.3.1930

    5b.   **Edith Louise Marie Josèphe Jkvr. van den Berch van Heemstede**
* Neuilly-sur-Seine 22.9.1931 = Bussum 22.1.1965 Udo Joseph
Oidtmann * Amsterdam 26.7.1919

X   (e)   **François Paul Joseph Marie Ferdinand Comte de Lannoy** * Bruxelles 13.10.1867
+ Etterbeek 11.3.1945 = Paris 28.4.1914 Marie Loïsa Boyer de Cadusch * Paris
3.3.1869 + Woluwe-Saint-Pierre 16.6.1946 dau. of Victor Boyer de Cadusch s.p.

    (f)   **Jean Ferdinand Louis Armand Marie Joseph Comte de Lannoy** * Bruxelles
18.4.1869 + Schaerbeek 26.3.1942 = Schaerbeek 10.4.1913 Jeanne Paindeville
* Limal 9.2.1884 + Schaerbeek 4.11.1963 dau. of Victor Paindeville and had
issue:

XI   1a.   **Julie Elise Gertrude Comtesse de Lannoy** * Etterbeek 15.3.1902 = (1)
Saint-Josse-ten-Noode 20.11.1940 René Jacob * Verviers 24.6.1895
− div. = (2) Schaerbeek 17.12.1952 Georges Flies * La Hupe 17.7.1926
+ Bruxelles 22.5.1957

X   (g)   **Charles Antoine Marie Joseph Comte de Lannoy** * Velaines (Hainaut) 24.7.1870
+ Tours 14.6.1930 = 1.5.1897 Suzanne Comtesse de Baillet-Latour * Bruxelles
30.1.1877 + Knokke 2.7.1966 dau. of Ferdinand Comte de Baillet-Latour, and
had issue:

XI   1a.   **Yvonne Ferdinande Caroline Gabrielle Marie Josèphe Ghislaine Comtesse de
Lannoy** * Bruxelles 29.5.1898 = Brasschaet 3.6.1922 Adrien Barbanson
* Ixelles 6.12.1880 + St. Gilles 21.10.1953, and has issue:

XII   1b.   **Nicole Barbanson** * Bruxelles 8.5.1923 = St. Gilles 23.12.1949
Christian Tibbaut * Bruxelles 20.4.1928, and has issue:

XIII   1c.   **Brigitte-Pierrette Tibbaut** * Le Caire 26.2.1951

    2c.   **Roland-Claude Tibbaut** * Bruxelles 21.8.1952

    3c.   **Thierry-Claude Tibbaut** * Bruxelles 6.7.1955

XIII		4c. **Olivier-Roland Tibbaut** * Le Caire 17.3.1960
XII		2b. **Claude Barbanson** * Bruxelles 25.5.1925

XI 2a. **Elisabeth Caroline Françoise Marie Josèphe Ghislaine Comtesse de Lannoy** * Velaines 20.10.1900 + Ixelles 27.5.1956 = Brasschaet 11.8.1921 Jean Baron Buffin de Chosal * Bruxelles 3.12.1896 + Cannes 12.8.1953, and had issue:

XII 1b. **Henry Léopold Victor Charles Marie Joseph Ghislain Baron Buffin de Chosal** * Bruxelles 8.7.1924 = Dumfries, Scotland 13.8.1957 Lucienne Tasiaux * Dinant 12.7.1933 dau. of Pierre-Nicolas Tasiaux, and has issue:

XIII 1c. **Yves Marie Lucien Henri Charles Ghislain Baron Buffin de Chosal** * Namur 31.7.1958

2c. **Elisabeth Marie Louise Yvonne Ghislaine Baronne Buffin de Chosal** * Namur 26.8.1959

3c. **Didier Baron Buffin de Chosal** * Ixelles 31.8.1962

4c. **Thierry Baron Buffin de Chosal** * Ixelles 23.1.1965

XII 2b. **Charles Jean Victor Léopold Marie Joseph Ghislain Baron Buffin de Chosal** * Bruxelles 13.5.1926 = Anvers 3.1.1953 Antoinette Geelhand de la Bistrate * Anvers 19.1.1930 dau. of Robert Geelhand de la Bistrate, and has issue:

XIII 1c. **Jean Marie Ghislain Baron Buffin de Chosal** * Léopoldville 9.9.1953

2c. **Frédéric Léopold Ghislain Baron Buffin de Chosal** * Etterbeek 9.10.1954

3c. **Caroline Marie Thérèse Baronne Buffin de Chosal** * Ottignies 26.3.1956

4c. **Nathalie Christine Ghislaine Baronne Buffin de Chosal** * Etterbeek 20.2.1958

5c. **Isabelle Thérèse Ghislaine Baronne Buffin de Chosal** * Etterbeek 26.2.1960

6c. **Christoph Nicolas Ghislain Baron Buffin de Chosal** * Etterbeek 6.8.1963

XII 3b. **Christiane Solange Félicie Elisabeth Marie Joséphine Ghislaine Baronne Buffin de Chosal** * Bruxelles 2.5.1958 = 14.12.1957 Pierre Tasiaux * Dinant 28.3.1930, and has issue:

XIII 1c. **Baudouin Tasiaux** * 23.7.1958

2c. **Chantal Tasiaux** * 16.11.1959

3c. **Miguel Tasiaux** * 13.4.1961

4c. **Philippe Tasiaux** * 30.8.1965

XI 3a. **Solange Gabrielle Ferdinande Marie Josèphe Ghislaine Comtesse de Lannoy** * Brasschaet 2.6.1902 = Celles-sur-Semois 12.2.1944 Victor Doret * 23.8.1897 s.p.

X   (h)   **Gustave Adrien Marie Joseph Philippe Ferdinand Comte de Lannoy** * Bruxelles 5.12.1873 + Bruxelles 28.7.1929

IX   e)   **Philippe Marie Joseph Adrien Comte de Lannoy** * Bruxelles 24.3.1836 + Anvaing 29.8.1841

       f)   **Louise Marie Joséphine Henriette Comtesse de Lannoy** * Anvaing 15.7.1845 + Lombise 18.12.1923 = Bruxelles 18.5.1869 Gaëtan Marquis de La Boëssière-Thiennes * Bruxelles 25.1.1843 + Lombise 4.9.1931, and had issue:

X   (a)   **Françoise Charlotte Thérèse Barbe Anne Marie Ghislaine de La Boëssière-Thiennes** * Lombise 13.9.1872 + Anvers 22.9.1951 = Lombise 10.7.1890 Gaston Baron van de Werve et Schilde * Paris 22.3.1867 + Anvers 18.8.1923 s.p.

       (b)   **Marc Antoine Adrien Gaëtan Gustave Adolphe Marie Ghislain Comte de La Boëssière-Thiennes** * Lombise 23.10.1873 + Lombise 18.6.1920 = Paris 20.10.1908 Amicie Anne de La Grange * Paris 3.8.1887 + Paris 16.12.1937 dau. of Baron Louis de La Grange, and had issue:

XI   1a.   **Marc Antoine Philippe Gaëtan Marie Ghislain Marquis de La Boëssière-Thiennes** * Bruxelles 7.10.1911 + 15.9.1963 = Lives 17.8.1938 Comtesse Renée Victoire Carton de Wiart * London 28.10.1918 dau. of Edouard Comte Carton de Wiart, and had issue:

XII   1b.   **Elisabeth Amicie Foy Marie Ghislaine Comtesse de La Boëssière-Thiennes** * Lives 20.8.1939 = 15.12.1962 Christian Ritter Mencik v. Zebinsky * Zagreb 13.12.1940

         2b.   **Prisca Louise Françoise Marie Ghislaine Comtesse de La Boëssière-Thiennes** * Lombise 16.11.1941

         3b.   **Michèle Charlotte Marie Ghislaine Comtesse de La Boëssière-Thiennes** * Woluwe-Saint-Pierre 18.5.1944 = 12.12.1965 Emmanuel Janssen * 6.1.1933, and has issue:

XIII   1c.   **Marc Eric Janssen** * 21.9.1966

XII   4b.   **Françoise Nathalie Edmée Comtesse de La Boëssière-Thiennes** * Lombise 19.9.1947

XI   2a.   **Jean Albert Louis Drogo Marie Ghislain Comte de La Boëssière-Thiennes** * Bruxelles 26.11.1912 + Montana, Valais 11.3.1931

X   (c)   **Charlotte Marie Pauline Gaëtane Anne Ghislaine de La Boëssière-Thiennes** * 19.7.1875 + Bruges 3.10.1959

       (d)   **Gaëtan Emmanuel Adolphe Joseph Marie Ghislain Comte de La Boëssière-Thiennes** * Lombise 19.5.1881 + Montana, Valais 24.12.1930

       (e)   **Jacques Hilaire Eugène Marie Ghislain Joseph Venant Comte de La Boëssière-Thiennes** * Lombise 18.5.1883 X Mont-sur-Marne 31.12.1916

       (f)   **Elisabeth Catherine Charlotte Josèphe Marie Ghislaine de La Boëssière-Thiennes** * Bruxelles 16.3.1885 = Bruxelles 31.7.1907 Victor Marquis de La Bourdonnaye * Château de La Bourdonnaye, Carentoir (Morbihan) 29.9.1883 + Château de La Bourdonnaye 11.12.1943, and has issue:

XI   1a.   **Marie Antoinette Louise Gaëtane Elisabeth de La Bourdonnaye** * Château de La Bourdonnaye 24.7.1909 = Carentoir 19.8.1934 Jean Chevalier de Ghellinck d'Elseghem * St-Denis-Westrem 26.11.1898, and has issue:

381

XII	1b.	**Jean Baptiste Antoine Elisabeth Marie Alfred Chevalier de Ghellinck d'Elseghem** * Anvers 12.1.1936 + Gand 20.2.1959
	2b.	**Gaëtan Louis Esprit Chevalier de Ghellinck d'Elseghem** * Wannegem-Lede 8.6.1938
	3b.	**François Emmanuel Joseph Louis Rita Marie Ghislain Chevalier de Ghellinck d'Elseghem** * Gand 10.1.1941
	4b.	**Henri Arthur Marie Joseph Jean Ghislain Chevalier de Ghellinck d'Elseghem** * Gand 2.1.1942
	5b.	**Marie Elisabeth Thérèse Louise Josèphe de Ghellinck d'Elseghem** * Wilrijk-Anvers 11.3.1946

XI	2a.	**Louise Marie Elisabeth Charlotte Françoise de La Bourdonnaye** * Château de La Bourdonnaye 30.4.1911 = Carentoir 20.8.1934 Comte Louis de Lambilly * 24.5.1908 ✗ Limal (Belgium) 16.5.1940, and has issue:
XII	1b.	**Comte Hubert Esprit Marie Yves de Lambilly** * Carentoir 15.6.1935 = 3.3.1962 Yseult Le Mintier de Léhélec * 1.2.1939 dau. of Vicomte Gonzague Le Mintier de Léhélec, and has issue:
XIII	1c.	**Louis Ghislain de Lambilly** * Pont-Audemar 2.6.1963
	2c.	**Olivier de Lambilly** * 23.5.1966
XII	2b.	**Comte Gilles Marie Françoise de Lambilly** * Carentoir 14.10.1937 = Rennes 4.7.1964 Odile de Marcellus * 28.12.1944 dau. of Comte Bernard de Marcellus
	3b.	**Comte Michel-Henri Marie François de Lambilly** * Carentoir 27.2.1939 = 29.5.1965 Chantal de Launay * 4.7.1943 dau. of Pierre de Launay, and has issue:
XIII	1c.	**Frédéric de Lambilly** * Suresnes (H.-S.) 1.4.1966
XII	4b.	**Comte Jacques-Louis Henri Marie Antoine de Lambilly** * Carentoir 7.9.1940

XI	3a.	**Françoise de La Bourdonnaye** * Château de La Bourdonnaye 3.9.1914 = Château de La Bourdonnaye 29.5.1939 Vicomte Henri de Kerautem * Vitre 17.12.1912, and has issue:
XII	1b.	**Vicomte Louis de Kerautem** * Carentoir 2.1.1941
	2b.	**Vicomte Philippe de Kerautem** * Carentoir 16.10.1942
	3b.	**Vicomte Yves de Kerautem** * Angrie (M.-et-L.) 17.7.1946
	4b.	**Arthur de Kerautem** * Angrie 21.5.1948
	5b.	**Elisabeth de Kerautem** * Angers 3.1.1956
	6b.	**Olivier de Kerautem** * Malestroit (Morbihan) 25.8.1958

XI	4a.	**Arthur Marquis de La Bourdonnaye** * Carentoir 7.5.1919
	5a.	**Gaëtane de La Bourdonnaye** * Carentoir 18.3.1922 = Carentoir 5.7.1944 Geoffroy Marquis de Lambilly * Nantes 24.1.1921, and has issue:
XII	1b.	**Humbert Comte de Lambilly** * Carentoir 27.7.1945

XII

    2b. **Comte Antoine de Lambilly** * Ploërmel (Morbihan) 23.11.1946

    3b. **Denys de Lambilly** * Ploërmel 28.11.1947

    4b. **Anne de Lambilly** * Fougeré (Vendée) 15.9.1950

    5b. **Marc de Lambilly** * La-Roche-sur-Yon (Vendée) 27.5.1955

    6b. **Françoise-Charlotte de Lambilly** * La-Roche-sur-Yon 19.12.1959

    7b. **Isabelle de Lambilly** * Fougères (Ille-et-Vilaine) 29.1.1966

XI

    6a. **Jacqueline de La Bourdonnaye** * Lombise (Belgium) 4.1.1924 = 11.8.1953
Vicomte François de Poulpiquet du Halgouët * 20.3.1920 + Neuilly-sur-
Seine 19.11.1963 s.p.

    7a. **Ghislaine de La Bourdonnaye** * Carentoir 17.9.1927 = 25.8.1959
Comte Gilles du Plessis d'Argentré * Louvigné (Mayenne) 17.6.1922, and
has issue:

XII

    1b. **Alain du Plessis d'Argentré** * Fougères (Ille-et-Vilaine) 13.7.1960

    2b. **Eliane du Plessis d'Argentré** * Fougères 14.7.1961

    3b. **Jean-Luc du Plessis d'Argentré** * Fougères 28.6.1963

VIII

    d. **Emilie Blanche Ferdinande de Lannoy** * Bruxelles 3.2.1802 + Amiens 9.5.1883

    e. **Charles François de Lannoy** * 10.11.1803 + 9.12.1803

    f. **Pauline Joséphine Philippine de Lannoy** * 22.12.1804 + 24.12.1804

    g. **Adrien Marie Faustin Comte de Lannoy** * Hingene 15.2.1806 + Bruxelles 15.5.1880
= Anvaing 14.1.1834 Alix de Lannoy * Tournai 21.6.1814 + Bruxelles 21.2.1886 dau. of
Ferdinand Joseph Comte de Lannoy s.p.

    h. **Paul Marie Henri Comte de Lannoy** * Hingene 15.7.1809 + Bruxelles 2.6.1877

VII

    (2) **Charles Joseph 4 Duc d'Ursel** * Bruxelles 9.8.1777 + Hingene 27.9.1860 = Paris 10.12.1804
Joséphine Ferrero-Fieschi de Crèvecoeur dei Principi di Masserano * Madrid 23.12.1779
+ Bruxelles 18.1.1847 dau. of Antonio Ferrero-Fieschi de Crèvecoeur Principe di Masserano, and
had issue:

VIII

    a. **Jean Charles Marie Léon 5 Duc d'Ursel** * Hingene 4.10.1805 + Bruxelles 7.3.1878 = (1)
Paris 31.7.1832 Sophie d'Harcourt * Paris 4.2.1812 + Bruxelles 31.3.1842 dau. of
Eugène Duc d'Harcourt; = (2) Paris 6.10.1847 Henriette Marie d'Harcourt * Paris 8.10.1828
+ Château de Gissey (Côte-du-Nord) 16.5.1904 dau. of Eugène Duc d'Harcourt, and had issue:

    by 1st marriage:

IX

    a) **Marie Joséphine Madeleine Comtesse d'Ursel** * Bruxelles 17.9.1833 + Bruxelles
18.4.1885 = Bruxelles 28.9.1854 Juste Prince de Croÿ * Paris 19.2.1824 + Bruxelles
7.12.1908, and had issue:

X

    (a) **Marie Josèphe Constance Caroline Princesse de Croÿ** * Bruxelles 8.3.1856
+ Wez-Velvain 1.10.1914 = Bruxelles 10.10.1882 Adolphe Comte du Chastel de
la Howarderie * Wez-Velvain 5.6.1851 + Cappelle (Nord) 7.11.1918, and had
issue:

XI

    1a. **Henriette Marie Ghislaine Françoise Joachime Comtesse du Chastel de
la Howarderie** * Wez-Velvain 20.8.1883 = Bruxelles 12.4.1920 Gaspard
Comte du Bourbon-Châlus * Neuvy-les-Moulins 9.4.1876 + Châlus
13.6.1936 s.p.

XI	2a.	**Jacques Emmanuel Juste Marie Octave Comte du Chastel de la Howarderie** * Hingene 11.8.1885 = Paris 5.2.1919 Françoise de Cossé-Brissac * Prusly-sur-Ource (Côte d'Or) 26.5.1887 dau. of Comte Emmanuel de Cossé-Brissac, and has issue:

XII

1b. **Emmanuel Henry Marie Charles Raymond Adolphe Christian Juste Timoléon Ghislain Comte du Chastel de la Howarderie** * Bruxelles 5.2.1920 + Freetown, Sierre Leone 8.11.1945

2b. **Christian Marie Germain François Gérard Joseph Ghislain Comte du Chastel de la Howarderie** * Prusly-sur-Ource (Côte d'Or) 14.2.1921 = Grez-Doiceau 9.10.1947 Régine Vicomtesse de Spoelberch * Grez-Doiceau 10.7.1926 dau. of Thierry Vicomte de Spoelberch, and has issue:

XIII

1c. **Philippe Jacques Thierry Marie Ghislain Comte du Chastel de la Howarderie** * Grez-Doiceau 10.7.1948

2c. **Laurence Marie Françoise Isabelle Ghislaine Comtesse du Chastel de la Howarderie** * Wez-Velvain 30.11.1950

3c. **Isabelle Henriette Bernadette Marie Ghislaine Comtesse du Chastel de la Howarderie** * Grez-Doiceau 13.7.1957

4c. **Arnould Pierre Germain Marie Ghislain Comte du Chastel de la Howarderie** * Etterbeek 8.8.1958

XII

3b. **Pierre Marie Fernand François Ghislain Comte du Chastel de la Howarderie** * Bruxelles 22.4.1922 = Bruxelles 16.10.1946 Yolande Vermeersch * Ixelles 6.9.1925 dau. of Pierre Vermeersch, and has issue:

XIII

1c. **Anne Charlotte Marie Laurence Yvonne Françoise Rhingarde Ghislaine Comtesse du Chastel de la Howarderie** * Wez-Velvain 24.9.1947

2c. **Rodolphe Marie Hadelin Fernand André Pierre Ghislain Yves Comte du Chastel de la Howarderie** * Etterbeek 7.10.1956

XII

4b. **Henri Marie Théodore Louis Fernand Ghislain François Comte du Chastel de la Howarderie** * Wez-Velvain 25.10.1924 = Paris 12.12.1957 Doña Victoria-Elena López de Carrizosa y Patiño Marquesa del Merito * Paris 26.11.1932 dau. of Don José López de Carrizosa y Martel Marqués del Merito, and has issue:

XIII

1c. **Marie Hélène Françoise Gabrielle Ghislaine Comtesse du Chastel de la Howarderie** * Tournai 14.9.1958

2c. **Jacques André Nicolas Joseph Comte du Chastel de la Howarderie** * Tournai 16.1.1961

3c. **Constance Comtesse du Chastel de la Howarderie** * Deauville (Calvados) 30.7.1963

4c. **Nicolas Comte du Chastel de la Howarderie** * Bruxelles 13.11.1964

5c. **Sophie Comtesse du Chastel de la Howarderie** * Bruxelles 21.9.1966

XII

5b. **Louis Georges Germain Adolphe Ghislain Mutien Marie Comte du Chastel de l⸗ Howarderie** * Prusly-sur-Ource 15.8.1928

384

3a. **Emmanuel Marie Edouard François Ghislain Comte du Chastel de la Howarderie**
* Bruxelles 18.10.1888 ✗ Boesinghe 23.6.1915

4a. **François Jean Gérard Auguste Marie Comte du Chastel de la Howarderie**
* Berlin 2.6.1890 + Wez-Velvain 23.4.1912

5a. **Ferdinand Marie Antoine Jean Gérard Léonard Ghislain Comte du Chastel de
la Howarderie** * Wez-Velvain 31.8.1892 = Paris 2.7.1919 Blanche de
Coëtnempren de Kersaint * Paris 10.2.1891 dau. of Raoul de Coëtnempren
Comte de Kersaint, and has issue:

1b. **Marie Blanche Françoise Ferdinande Henriette Ghislaine Comtesse du
Chastel de la Howarderie** * Paris 24.8.1921 = 14.6.1948 **Adrien
Comte d'Oultremont** * Guines (Pas-de-Clais) 10.12.1918, and has
issue see elsewhere

2b. **François Marie Ghislain Michel Adolphe Joseph Comte du Chastel de
la Howarderie** * Bruxelles 10.10.1924 = (1) Woluwe-Saint-Pierre
27.6.1951 Michelle du Roy de Blicquy * Bruxelles 2.3.1931 dau. of
Jacques du Roy de Blicquy, marriage annulled; = (2) Bruxelles
17.1.1959 Régine Comtesse de Liedekerke de Pailhe * Bruxelles
4.1.1936 dau. of Guillaume Comte de Liedekerke de Pailhe, and has
issue:

by 1st marriage:

1c. **Dominique Marie Laure Ferdinande Comtesse du Chastel de
la Howarderie** * Uccle 17.4.1952

by 2nd marriage:

2c. **Edouard Ferdinand Guillaume Eric Marie Ghislain Comte du
Chastel de la Howarderie** * Namur 22.10.1959

3c. **Sibylle Madeleine Marie Hélène Ghislaine Comtesse du Chastel
de la Howarderie** * Namur 16.12.1960

4c. **Françoise Anne Blanche Henriette Marie Ghislaine Comtesse du
Chastel de la Howarderie** * Namur 8.1.1962

5c. **Béatrice Charlotte Marie Ghislaine Comtesse du Chastel de la
Howarderie** * Bruxelles 8.9.1964

3b. **Eliane Marie Suzanne Ghislaine Comtesse du Chastel de la Howarderie**
* Bruxelles 19.1.1927 = Wien 25.6.1955 Georg-Christian Prinz v.
Auersperg * Salzburg 11.9.1922, and has issue:

1c. **Zdenka Maria Bianca Hedwig Franziska Ferdinanda Prinzessin v.
Auersperg** * Wien 7.10.1956

2c. **Elisabeth Maria Josefa Ghislaine Prinzessin v. Auersperg**
* Wien 27.2.1960

(b) **Sophie Marie Ferdinande Princesse de Croÿ** * Bruxelles 15.2.1858 + Château de
Wez (Hainaut) 26.5.1933

(c) **Henri François Ghislain Louis Marie Prince de Croÿ** * Bruxelles 8.3.1860
+ Rumillies 6.2.1946 = London 26.11.1936 Cornelia Paumier * Jersey City, N.J.
4.10.1877 + Ghlin (Belgium) 17.12.1943 dau. of Jesse Paunier s.p.

(d) **Alfred Henri Joseph Marie Rodolphe Prince de Croÿ** * Roeulx 17.2.1862
+ Zoug 28.11.1934

X	(e)	**Ferdinand Charles Joseph Léon Marie Prince de Croÿ** * Roeulx 4.5.1867 + Louvain 8.5.1958
	(f)	**Charles Joseph Henri Marie Prince de Croÿ** * Roeulx 14.5.1869 + Rumillies 29.5.1943 = Rumillies 15.4.1896 **Mathilde Comtesse de Robiano** * Rumillies 6.2.1868 + Rumillies 19.9.1946 dau. of Albert Comte de Robiano, and had issue:

XI

1a. **Marie Madeleine Mathilde Gérardine Princesse de Croÿ** * Rumillies 10.6.1897 + Köln 3.8.1957

2a. **Albert Marie Henri Gérard Prince de Croÿ** * Rumillies 24.2.1900

3a. **Mathilde Marie Gérardine Sébastienne Princesse de Croÿ** * Rumillies 20.1.1902 = Rumillies 1.7.1926 Charles Marquis d'Yve de Bavay * Bois de Lessines 8.5.1885, and has issue:

XII

1b. **Marie Mathilde Anne Comtesse d'Yve** * Bruxelles 2.6.1927 = Bruxelles 27.3.1951 Emmanuel Comte Marnix de Sainte-Adelgonde * Egzer 24.10.1923, and has issue:

XIII

1c. **Marguerite Marie Ghislaine Thérèse Comtesse Marnix de Sainte-Adelgonde** * Kisantu (Congo) 29.2.1952

2c. **Charles Jean Marie Ghislain Comte Marnix de Sainte-Adelgonde** * Kisantu (Congo) 5.7.1953

3c. **Christian Adrien François Ghislain Marie Comte Marnix de Sainte-Adelgonde** * Léopoldville 26.12.1956

4c. **Baudouin Jean Emmanuel Marie Ghislain Comte Marnix de Sainte-Adelgonde** * Léopoldville 2.3.1960

5c. **Guy Jean Emmanuel Marie Ghislain Comte Marnix de Sainte-Adelgonde** * Etterbeek 14.11.1961

XII

2b. **Henri Félix Alphonse Comte d'Yve** * Bruxelles 2.8.1928 = 27.5.1961 Dominique Comtesse de Borchgrave d'Altena * Etterbeek 22.4.1942 dau. of Bernard Comte Borchgrave d'Altena s.p.

3b. **Félix Marie Joseph Comte d'Yve** * Bruxelles 5.1.1930 = Ansembourg 10.10.1959 Diane Comtesse Marchant d'Ansembourg * Bruxelles 11.10.1935 dau. of Gaston Comte Marchant d'Ansembourg, and has issue:

XIII

1c. **Antoine Comte d'Yve** * Gwaka (Congo) 26.8.1960

2c. **Michel Comte d'Yve** * Mons 3.7.1962

3c. **Yolande Comtesse d'Yve** * Bruxelles 21.9.1965

XII

4b. **Bernard Marie Ghislain Comte d'Yve** * Bruxelles 5.1.1932

5b. **Agnès Marie Hélène Comtesse d'Yve** * Bruxelles 23.1.1936 = 17.7.1962 Alexander Jhr. v. Loudon * 13.8.1935, and has issue:

XIII

1c. **Diane Jkvr. v. Loudon** * Bruxelles 8.11.1963

2c. **Gregory Jhr. v. Loudon** * Bruxelles 5.4.1965

XII

6b. **Jean Marie Joseph Ghislain Comte d'Yve** * Bruxelles 23.1.1936

4a. **Maria Immaculée Claire Elisabeth Gérardine Marguerite Princesse de Croÿ**
* Rumillies 16.10.1905 = Rumillies 7.9.1926 Thierry Comte de Limburg-
Stirum * Bruxelles 28.12.1904, and has issue:

    1b. **Evrard Louis François Xavier Marie Joseph Ghislain Comte de
Limburg-Stirum** * Huldenberg 31.10.1927 = Dreux 16.1.1957
Hélène Princesse d'Orleans * Woluwe-Saint-Pierre 17.9.1934 dau. of
Mgr. Henri Comte de Paris, and has issue:

        1c. **Catherine Isabelle Marie Françoise Xavière Comtesse de Limburg-
Stirum** * Salisbury, Rhodesia 21.10.1957

        2c. **Thierry Henri François Xavier Christian Comte de Limburg-
Stirum** * Lisboa 24.7.1959

        3c. **Louis Léopold François Xavier Ghislain Comte de Limburg-
Stirum** * Etterbeek 10.6.1962

        4c. **Bruno François Xavier Guillaume Comte de Limburg-Stirum**
* Sallanches (Haute-Savoie) 20.2.1966

    2b. **Elisabeth Louise Charlotte Marie Josèphe Ghislaine Comtesse de
Limburg-Stirum** * Huldenberg 11.11.1928 = Huldenberg 10.7.1954
Guy Comte de Renesse * Bruxelles 26.11.1926, and has issue:

        1c. **Marguerite Régine Marie Françoise Xavière Ghislaine Comtesse
de Renesse** * Louvain 6.6.1955

        2c. **Catherine Anne Gérardine Françoise Xavière Charlotte Amicie
Comtesse de Renesse** * Louvain 26.1.1958

        3c. **Jean François Xavier Gérard Thérèse Comte de Renesse**
* Louvain 3.10.1959

    3b. **Albert Louis Gabriel Ghislain Marie Joseph François Xavier Ludger
Comte de Limburg-Stirum** * Huldenberg 26.3.1930 = Schoten
27.2.1965 Marianne Bracht * Schoten 19.7.1945 dau. of Charles
Victor Baron Bracht, and has issue:

        1c. **Geneviève Marie Ghislaine Françoise Xavière Comtesse de
Limburg-Stirum** * Ixelles 14.1.1966

    4b. **Frédéric Albert Gaëtan Joseph François Xavier Marie Ghislain
Gabriel Comte de Limburg-Stirum** * Huldenberg 23.3.1931

    5b. **Marguerite Madeleine Philippine Maria Josèphe Ghislaine Gaëtane
Comtesse de Limburg-Stirum** * Huldenberg 21.5.1932

    6b. **Christian Charles Elie Marie Joseph François Xavier Ghislain
Gaëtan Comte de Limburg-Stirum** * Huldenberg 23.10.1934

5a. **Emmanuel Marie Joseph Pierre Gérard Prince de Croÿ** * Rumillies
24.4.1908 = Overyssche 12.8.1944 Nicole Comtesse Marnix de Sainte-
Adelgonde * Eyzer 25.6.1919 dau. of Jean Comte Marnix de Sainte-
Adelgonde, and has issue:

    1b. **Isabelle Gabrielle Marie Emmanuelle Mathilde Jeanne Gaëtane
Ghislaine Princesse de Croÿ** * Bruxelles 4.7.1945

XII			2b.	**Marie Gabrielle Gaëtane Thérèse Nicole Ghislaine Princesse de Croÿ** * Rumillies 4.12.1946
			3b.	**Guillaume Gabriel Joseph Juste Pierre Gaëtan Marie Ghislain Prince de Croÿ** * Rumillies 10.4.1950
			4b.	**Charles Louis Gabriel Joseph Gaëtan Marie Ghislain Prince de Croÿ** * Rumillies 17.6.1951
XI			6a.	**Jean Marie Joseph Ghislain Gérard Prince de Croÿ** * Rumillies 8.10.1910
X		(g)		**Joseph Emmanuel Marie Sophie Ignace Prince de Croÿ** * Bruxelles 20.2.1873 = Paris 9.2.1904 Geneviève Collinet de La Salle * Tarbes 22.11.1883 + Spa 18.10.1937 dau. of Adolphe Collinet de La Salle, and had issue:
XI			1a.	**Marie Elisabeth Madeleine Princesse de Croÿ** * Bruxelles 30.10.1904
			2a.	**Marguerite Geneviève Marie Françoise Ghislaine Princesse de Croÿ** * Spa 11.7.1912
			3a.	**Hélène Elisabeth Marie Princesse de Croÿ** * Bruxelles 20.2.1916
IX	b)			**Charles Marie Henri Comte d'Ursel** * Bruxelles 12.12.1839 + Funchal 9.9.1875 = Paris 16.6.1873 Isabelle de Clermont-Tonnere * Glisolles (Eure) 6.3.1849 + Sceaux 3.7.1921 dau. of Vicomte Gaspard de Clermont-Tonnere, and had issue:
X		(a)		**Caroline Chantal Léonie Marie Noël Comtesse d'Ursel** * Bruxelles 25.12.1874 + Château de Virieu (Isère) 6.12.1933 = Bruxelles 21.5.1896 Henri Marquis de Virieu * Paris 21.10.1861 + Paris 22.7.1929, and had issue:
XI			1a.	**Marie Charles François Geoffroy Xavier Marquis de Virieu** * Paris 14.5.1898 + Paris 22.1.1953 = Paris 4.10.1929 Marie-Françoise Brugière de Barante * Paris 17.5.1906 dau. of Baron Edouard Brugière de Barante, and had issue:
XII			1b.	**François Henri Michel Marie Marquis de Virieu** * Paris 18.12.1931 = Paris 11.7.1959 Claude Marie Emy * Paris 17.2.1934 dau. of Jean Emy, and has issue:
XIII			1c.	**Isabelle Marie Françoise Marguerite de Virieu** * Paris 14.12.1960
			2c.	**Stéphanie Chantal Antoinette Marie de Virieu** * Paris 11.12.1962
			3c.	**Guillaume Aymon Xavier Marie de Virieu** * Paris 10.12.1964
XII			2b.	**Comte Antoine Geoffroy Léopold Marie de Virieu** * Paris 16.7.1933 = Paris 31.12.1966 Isabelle de Vitton de Peyrius * Paris 5.10.1942
			3b.	**Comte Wilfrid Charles Marie de Virieu** * 28.1.1936 = 30.4.1964 Elisabeth de La Rochefoucauld * 6.8.1944 dau. of Comte Jean de La Rochefoucauld, and has issue:
XIII			1c.	**Jean Ghislain Xavier Marie de Virieu** * Neuilly-sur-Seine 29.10.1965
XII			4b.	**Isabelle Chantal Raymonde Marie de Virieu** * 1.7.1938 = 27.5.1961 Comte Louis-Olivier Frotier de la Coste Messelière * Paris 11.6.1927, and has issue:
XIII			1c.	**Pierre-Edouard Benjamin Antoine Marie Frotier de la Coste Messelière** * 18.4.1962

XIII		2c. **Béatrice Odile Yvonne Geneviève Marie Frotier de la Coste Messelière** * Les Ousches-Melle 29.8.1963
		3c. **Chantal Frotier de la Coste Messelière** * Les Ousches-Melle August 1966
XII		5b. **Odile Geneviève Jeanne Marie de Virieu** * Virieu-sur-Bourbre (Isère) 28.7.1946 = Paris 18.2.1966 Comte Artus de Montalembert * 22.3.1941, and has issue:
XIII		1c. **Aimery de Montalembert** * Paris 26.11.1966
XI		2a. **Marie Aimée Gabriel Josèphe Chantal de Virieu** * Paris 11.8.1900 + Paris 8.4.1910

by 2nd marriage:

IX	c)	**Marie Charles Joseph 6 Duc d'Ursel** * Bruxelles 3.7.1848 + Strombeek-Bever 15.11.1903 = Paris 16.3.1872 **Antonine de Mun** * Paris 14.11.1849 + Bruxelles 11.5.1931 dau. of Adrien Marquis de Mun, and had issue:
X	(a)	**Robert Marie Léon 7 Duc d'Ursel** * Bruxelles 7.1.1873 + Bruxelles 16.4.1955 = Paris 14.4.1898 Sabine de Francqueville * Paris 15.8.1877 + Boussu 16.12.1941 dau. of Amabale Charles Comte de Francqueville, and had issue:
XI		1a. **Henri Charles François Joseph Marie 8 Duc d'Ursel** * Bruxelles 18.11.1900 = (1) Paris 3.3.1923 Antoinette Princesse de La Trémoïlle * Paris 12.12.1904 — div., dau. of Louis Charles Duc de La Trémoïlle; = (2) Bruxelles 26.9.1940 Madeleine André * Dieppe 29.11.1919 + Fuentenovilla (Prov. Guadalajara, Spain) 13.8.1956 dau. of François André, and has issue:

by 1st marriage:

XII		1b. **Thérèse Antonine Hélène Marie Sabine Comtesse d'Ursel** * Brasschaet 27.1.1924 = Neuilly-sur-Seine 21.3.1946 Comte Jacques d'Oilliamson * Paris 4.2.1914, and has issue:
XIII		1c. **Pierre-Apollinaire d'Oilliamson** * Neuilly-sur-Seine 13.1.1947
		2c. **Sabine d'Oilliamson** * Rouen 14.11.1954
XII		2b. **Antonin Louis Jean Marie Robert Comte d'Ursel** * Bruxelles 28.4.1925
		3b. **Roland Charles Gérard Comte d'Ursel** * Bruxelles 1.10.1926 = Auderghem 3.6.1947 Rose de Meeûs d'Argenteuil * Etterbeek 15.3.1926 dau. of Antoine Comte de Meeûs d'Argenteuil, and has issue:
XIII		1c. **Jan Antoine Henri Marie Robert Comte d'Ursel** * Uccle 8.6.1950
		2c. **Isabelle Sabine Rose Antoinette Comtesse d'Ursel** * Bruxelles 21.11.1951
		3c. **Cécile Comtesse d'Ursel** * Bruxelles 5.8.1953
		4c. **Dominique Comte d'Ursel** * Bruxelles 15.6.1955
		5c. **Antoinette Comtesse d'Ursel** * Bruxelles 24.8.1957

by 2nd marriage:

XII   4b. **Marie Madeleine Thérèse Arnold Irène Comtesse d'Ursel**
           * Meise 28.6.1941 + Fuentenovilla, Spain 12.8.1956

           5b. **Léopold Antonin Chantal François Julien Marie Robert Comte d'Ursel**
           * Bruxelles 21.8.1942

           6b. **Pascal Richard Roland Marie Comte d'Ursel** * Bruxelles 3.4.1944

           7b. **Jacques Quentin Marie Comte d'Ursel** * Bruxelles 31.10.1946

XI   2a. **Chantal Josèphe Hedwige Marie Sabine Comtesse d'Ursel** * Middelkerke
           18.6.1902 = Bruxelles 24.4.1929 Gaston Marquis de Maupeou Monbail
           * Nantes 16.11.1896, and has issue:

XII   1b. **Aurian Noël Comte de Maupeou Monbail** * Bruxelles 26.2.1930
           = Paris 21.5.1958 Anne de Simard de Pitray * Paris 13.1.1935 dau.
           of Vicomte Louis de Simard de Pitray, and has issue:

XIII   1c. **Claire Sabine de Maupeou-Monbail** * Paris 20.5.1959

XII   2b. **Comte Daniel Ange de Maupeou Monbail** * Bruxelles 17.10.1932

           3b. **Comte Pascal Dominique de Maupeou Monbail** * Bruxelles 19.1.1934
           = Chamonix 25.7.1959 Bernadette Genoud-Prachet * Valencienne
           25.6.1937 dau. of Georges Genoud-Prachet, and has issue:

XIII   1c. **Godefroy de Maupeou Monbail** * Paris 24.6.1960

           2c. **Segolene de Maupeou Monbail** * Paris 18.7.1964

XII   4b. **Comte Raphaël François de Maupeou Monbail** * Bruxelles 4.10.1937

XI   3a. **Antonine Gabrielle Marie Comtesse d'Ursel** * Bruxelles 1.5.1905

X   (b) **Adrienne Carola Claire Henriette Marie Comtesse d'Ursel** * Paris 2.3.1875 + Paris
           13.6.1934 = Bruxelles 30.11.1904 Henri Comte de Boissieu * Varambon Par
           ⸱Pont-d'Ain 25.2.1871 + Varambon 23.5.1912 s.p.

           (c) **Marie Louise Pauline Comtesse d'Ursel** * Bruxelles 17.2.1880 + Casablanca
           4.5.1915

           (d) **Wolfgang Pie Benoît Marie Joseph Gabriel Comte d'Ursel** * Hingene 7.9.1882
           ✗ Budingen, par Saint-Trond 18.8.1914 = Paris 7.12.1905 Jacqueline de Néverlée
           * Paris 23.3.1884 dau. of Comte Philippe de Néverlée, and has issue:

XI   1a. **Gérard Philippe François Marie Joseph Comte d'Ursel** * Bruxelles 5.6.1907
           + Werl, Westfalen 6.4.1945 = Villers-lez-Heest 4.5.1933 Anne Marie de
           Pitteurs de Budingen * Lüttich 16.11.1908 + Villers-lez-Heest 24.9.1964
           dau. of Hermann Baron de Pitteurs de Budingen, and had issue:

XII   1b. **Colette Jacqueline Marie Ghislaine Comtesse d'Ursel** * Villers-lez-Heest
           3.10.1934 = Villers-lez-Heest 9.1.1960 Comte Louis Espiennes Cornet
           d'Elzius du Chennoy * Pailhe 2.1.1928, and has issue:

XIII   1c. **Jean Gérard Marie Ghislain Comte Cornet d'Elzius du Chennoy**
           * Louvain 6.2.1961

           2c. **Anne Emilie Marie Ghislaine Comtesse Cornet d'Elzius du Chennoy**
           * Louvain 18.11.1962

P. A. de Laszlo   *By kind permission of le Duc d'Ursel*

Above: 23   Robert, 7th Duc d'Ursel, 1873–1955

P. A. de Laszlo

Right: 24   Hedwige d'Ursel,
Marquise de Maupeou

XII

2b. **Wolfgang Guillaume Laurent Marie Joseph Ghislain Comte d'Ursel**
* Grez-Doiceau 1.3.1936

3b. **Christian Simon Henri Marie Ghislain Comte d'Ursel** * Villers-lez-
Heest 2.8.1937

4b. **Baudouin François Marie Ghislain Comte d'Ursel** * Villers-lez-Heest
7.12.1940

5b. **Evrard Nicolas Bernard Marie Ghislain Comte d'Ursel** * Villers-lez-
Heest 29.6.1942

XI

2a. **Antonine Jeanne Marie Simone Comtesse d'Ursel** * Watermael-Boitsfort
10.9.1908 = Bruxelles 30.6.1930 Comte Albert du Pouget de Nadaillac
* Paris 17.6.1906, and has issue:

XII

1b. **Comte Sigismond du Pouget de Nadaillac** * Le Mans (Sarthe)
22.7.1931

2b. **Jacqueline du Pouget de Nadaillac** * Le Mans 20.10.1932 = La Ferrière
(I.-et-L.) 4.9.1965 André de Montgazon * 31.10.1932

3b. **Chantal du Pouget de Nadaillac** * Le Mans 14.4.1934 = St-Etienne du
Gres (B.-du-Rh.) 25.7.1964 Philippe de Greling 21.1.1941, and has issue:

XIII

1c. **Jacques de Greling** * Avignon (B.-du-Rh.) 30.4.1965

XII

4b. **Eliane du Pouget de Nadaillac** * Le Mans 10.7.1936 = La Ferrière
20.8.1960 Comte François de Colbert-Cannet * 12.5.1932, and has
issue:

XIII

1c. **Stéphane de Colbert-Cannet** * Douala, Cameroons 2.8.1961

2c. **Caroline de Colbert-Cannet** * Tours (I.-et-L.) 10.1.1963

3c. **Bénédicte de Colbert-Cannet** * Libreville (Gabon) 3.2.1966

XII

5b. **Nicole du Pouget de Nadaillac** * Le Mans 8.11.1938 = La Ferrière
24.4.1962 Comte Jean de Boisgrollier de Ruolz * 10.12.1939, and
has issue:

XIII

1c. **Christophe de Boisgrollier du Ruolz** * Tours 20.2.1963
+ Abidjan (Côte d'Ivoire) 6.10.1964

2c. **Sophie de Boisgrollier de Ruolz** * Abidjan 21.9.1965

XII

6b. **Françoise du Pouget de Nadaillac** * St-Honorine-des-Pertes (Calvados)
18.1.1942 = La Ferrière 26.10.1963 Philippe-Henri de la Porte des
Vaux * 13.11.1934, and has issue:

XIII

1c. **Jacqueline de la Porte des Vaux** * Paris 23.12.1964

XII

7b. **Anne Marie du Pouget de Nadaillac** * La Ferrière 2.8.1944

XI

3a. **Henriette Gabrielle Marie Nicole Comtesse d'Ursel** * Bruxelles 20.3.1911
+ 2.4.1961 = Bruxelles 4.9.1935 Comte Paul de Maupeou d'Ableiges
* Pontivy (Morbihan) 2.10.1906 + La Flèche 31.3.1963, and had issue:

XII		1b.	**Comte Philippe de Maupeou d'Ableiges** * La Flèche (Sarthe) 23.10.1936
		2b.	**Comte Alain de Maupeou d'Ableiges** * La Flèche 22.1.1938
		3b.	**Jacqueline de Maupeou d'Ableiges** * La Flèche 6.5.1939 = La Flèche 23.12.1965 Comte Jean de Montesson * 10.12.1935
		4b.	**Elisabeth de Maupeou d'Ableiges** * Le Mans 18.4.1946
		5b.	**Guy de Maupeou d'Ableiges** * Le Mans 19.2.1948

XI   4a.   **Elie Wolfgang Comte d'Ursel** * Paris 9.3.1915 = Bruxelles 17.6.1937 **Monique Comtesse de Lannoy** * Hampstead 11.11.1915 dau. of Maurice Comte de Lannoy, and has issue:

XII   1b.   **Robert Marie Ghislain Comte d'Ursel** * Bruxelles 13.3.1939 = Château d'Ecaussins 5.9.1964 Adriene Cartuyvels * 28.10.1941 dau. of Freddy Cartuyvels, and has issue:

XIII   1c.   **Geoffroy Comte d'Ursel** * Uccle 16.7.1965

XII   2b.   **Geneviève Marie Josèphe Comtesse d'Ursel** * Anvaing 16.5.1940 = Etterbeek 8.6.1963 Philippe Comte d'Oultremont * 12.3.1938, and has issue:

XIII   1c.   **Gilles Théodore Elie Marie Ghislain Comte d'Oultremont** * St. Quentin 25.3.1964

           2c.   **Marie Sophie Monique Ghislaine Comtesse d'Oultremont** * St. Quentin 2.7.1965

XII   3b.   **Odette Marie Louise Jacqueline Comtesse d'Ursel** * Bruxelles 20.5.1942

           4b.   **Eric Henri Marie Ghislain Comte d'Ursel** * Louvain 1.12.1943

           5b.   **Nadine Bernadette Marie Henriette Ghislaine Comtesse d'Ursel** * Louvain 24.4.1946

           6b.   **Yolande Johanna Nicole Marie Ghislaine Comtesse d'Ursel** * Louvain 24.4.1946

           7b.   **Thérèse Marie Francisca Comtesse d'Ursel** * Louvain 16.8.1947

           8b.   **Bruno Charles Marie Ghislain Comte d'Ursel** * Louvain 15.2.1949

           9b.   **Anne Christiane Marie Ghislaine Comtesse d'Ursel** * Etterbeek 8.9.1952

          10b.   **Hélène Geneviève Marie Ghislaine Comtesse d'Ursel** * Louvain 2.10.1953

          11b.   **Jacques Dominique Marie Ghislain Comte d'Ursel** * Louvain 16.2.1955

IX   d)   **Marie Eugénie Léonarde Sophie Comtesse d'Ursel** * Bruxelles 29.6.1851 + Wechselburg 29.2.1932 = Bruxelles 19.3.1879 Carl Graf v. Schönburg-Glauchau * Wechselburg 13.5.1832 + Genève 27.11.1898 s.p.

     e)   **Juliette Louise Marie Comtesse d'Ursel** * Bruxelles 25.4.1853 + Moulins 31.1.1936 = Paris 1.7.1882 Robert Comte de Bourbon-Busset * Paris 26.2.1848 + Moulins (Allier) 3.2.1918, and had issue:

X   (a)   **Henri Charles Louis Marie de Bourbon-Busset** * 5.9.1883 + 22.8.1884

X   (b)   **Comte Antoine de Bourbon-Busset** * Paris 28.7.1885 + Moulins 25.10.1913

       (c)   **Sophie de Bourbon-Busset** * Paris 1.11.1887 = Paris 22.7.1919 Comte Urbain de Rougé * Paris 7.1.1882 + Château de Busset 2.10.1933, and has issue:

XI   1a.   **Marie Magdeleine de Rougé** * Paris 6.6.1920 = 9.10.1946 Comte Jacques de la Tour du Pin * St-Germains-Lespinasse 28.12.1911, and has issue:

XII   1b.   **Philippe de la Tour du Pin** * Moulins 19.9.1947

          2b.   **Claire de la Tour du Pin** * Moulins 21.5.1950

          3b.   **Xavier de la Tour du Pin** * Moulins 11.12.1951

          4b.   **Arnaud de la Tour du Pin** * Moulins 31.10.1954

          5b.   **Michel de la Tour du Pin** * Moulins 9.2.1958

XI   2a.   **Hélène de Rougé** * Paris 27.7.1921

       3a.   **Pierre Marquis de Rougé** * Paris 17.12.1922

       4a.   **Comte Hervé de Rougé** * Paris 30.5.1929

       5a.   **Elisabeth de Rougé** * Paris 30.5.1929

X   (d)   **Comte Jean de Bourbon-Busset** * 25.10.1889 ✗ 26.8.1914

       (e)   **Jacques de Bourbon-Busset** * 23.7.1892 + Louvain 16.12.1911

IX   f)   **Augustine Caroline Marie Comtesse d'Ursel** * Bruxelles 9.8.1860 + Bruxelles 4.4.1874

       g)   **Henriette Madeleine Marguerite Marie Comtesse d'Ursel** * Bruxelles 11.4.1863 + Nice 25.11.1877

       h)   **Léon Léopold Marie Comte d'Ursel** * Bruxelles 7.8.1867 Bettignies 26.6.1934 = Bruxelles 26.4.1900 **Jeanne de Francqueville** * Paris 8.1.1881 + Paris 28.1.1931 dau. of Comte Roger de Francqueville, and had issue:

X   (a)   **Hélène Henriette Louise Marie Comtesse d'Ursel** * Berlin 27.5.1901 + Kain, près Tournai 31.5.1919

       (b)   **Xavier Adrien Louis Marie Comte d'Ursel** * Berlin 11.6.1902

       (c)   **Bernard Robert Joseph Marie Comte d'Ursel** * Bruxelles 11.11.1904 + Bruxelles 4.10.1965 = Bruxelles 22.11.1927 **Thérèse Princesse de Ligne** * Bruxelles 27.12.1905 dau. of Ernest Prince de Ligne, and has issue:

XI   1a.   **Guy Marie Ernest Léon Comte d'Ursel** * Bruxelles 1.10.1928 = Bruxelles 17.9.1953 Jeannine de la Croix d'Oigimont * Bruxelles 9.4.1928 dau. of Pierre de la Croix d'Oigimont, and has issue:

XII   1b.   **Bernard Marie Ghislain Comte d'Ursel** * Bruxelles 15.8.1961

          2b.   **Eliane Thérèse Marie Comtesse d'Ursel** * Bruxelles 17.11.1962

XI   2a.   **Alain Comte d'Ursel** * 26.9.1929 + 15.12.1929

       3a.   **Hervé Marie Xavier Comte d'Ursel** * Bruxelles 24.11.1930 = 1.6.1959 Marie Cécile Bonvoisin * Etterbeek 18.7.1934 dau. of Baron Pierre Bonvoisin, and has issue:

XII   1b.   **Elisabeth Comtesse d'Ursel** * Ixelles 26.2.1961

          2b.   **Alexandre Comte d'Ursel** * Uccle 11.3.1964

XI			4a.	**Emmanuel Bernard Marie Joseph Comte d'Ursel** * Bruxelles 12.6.1932 = Uccle 5.5.1959 Marie Chantal de Meester de Heyndock * Bruxelles 28.4.1938 dau. of Paul de Meester de Heyndock, and has issue:

XII

        1b. **Prisca Comtesse d'Ursel** * Ixelles 4.10.1960

        2b. **Sylviane Comtesse d'Ursel** * Ixelles 24.5.1962

        3b. **Béatrice Comtesse d'Ursel** * Ixelles 13.3.1965

XI

        5a. **Viviane Marie Renée Comtesse d'Ursel** * Bruxelles 5.2.1940 = Bruxelles 9.2.1963 Eric de la Serna * Bruxelles 10.6.1923, and has issue:

XII

        1b. **Charles Antoine de la Serna** * Bruxelles 15.9.1965

XI

        6a. **Anita Marie Louise Comtesse d'Ursel** * Bruxelles 4.7.1942 = Etterbeek 6.6.1964 Marc-Antoine de Halloy de Waulsort * Anthée 18.8.1936, and has issue:

XII

        1b. **Philippe de Halloy de Waulsort** * Bruxelles 2.9.1965

X

    (d) **Guillaume Thibaut Eugène Marie Comte d'Ursel** * Paris 8.2.1906

    (e) **Marc Jules Robert Louis Marie Comte d'Ursel** * Bruxelles 22.8.1910 + Bruxelles 4.3.1935

    (f) **Bertrand Henri Gérard Marie Comte d'Ursel** * Bruxelles 3.11.1912

VIII   b. **Marie Augustine Caroline Comtesse d'Ursel** * Hingene 21.6.1807 + Bruxelles 5.12.1868

    c. **Ludovic Marie Comte d'Ursel** * Hingene 27.2.1809 + Watermael-Boitsfort 13.10.1886 = Bruxelles 5.10.1842 Louise Gueulluy de Rumigny * Stockholm 19.3.1820 + Bruxelles 5.3.1872 dau. of Hippolyte Gueulluy Marquis de Rumigny, and had issue:

IX   a) **Marie Caroline Eve Comtesse d'Ursel** * Bruxelles 22.2.1844 + Versailles 9.11.1904 = Bruxelles 21.10.1872 Victor Baron Nau de Champlouis * Essonnes (S.-et-O.) 30.5.1833 + Paris 3.9.1878, and had issue:

X   (a) **Marie Henriette Louise Amélie Claude Françoise Nau de Champlouis** * Paris 5.12.1873 + Versailles 20.10.1929 = Paris 26.4.1894 Ferdinand Mercier Marquis du Paty de Clam * Versailles 21.2.1853 + Versailles ... 9.1917, and had issue:

XI   1a. **Charles Claude Marie Victor Mercier Marquis du Paty de Clam** * Paris 16.2.1895 + Versailles 8.4.1948 = Gonfreville L'Orcher 27.9.1928 Jeanne d'Harcourt * Le Harve 8.8.1897 dau. of Comte Amedée d'Harcourt, and had issue:

XII

    1b. **Arlette du Paty de Clam** * Paris 9.3.1930

    2b. **Sylvie du Paty de Clam** * Gonfreville L'Orcher (Seine-Marit.) 3.12.1931 = 7.11.1953 Vicomte Alfred de La Barre de Nanteuil * Arçonnay (Sarthe), 24.4.1928, and has issue:

XIII

    1c. **Harold de La Barre de Nanteuil** * Versailles 21.8.1954

    2c. **Mathilde de La Barre de Nanteuil** * Versailles 22.5.1956

    3c. **Thibaut de La Barre de Nanteuil** * Versailles 8.8.1957

    4c. **Laurent de La Barre de Nanteuil** * Versailles 10.12.1958

XIII   5c.   **Mathieu de La Barre de Nanteuil** * Versailles 6.9.1965

XII   3b.   **Amedée du Paty de Clam** * Tripoli 1.12.1937

XI   2a.   **Françoise Jacqueline Marie du Paty de Clam** * Paris 9.12.1895 + Paris 12.12.1895

     3a.   **Claude Françoise Marie-Pierre du Paty de Clam** * Versailles 29.4.1903

X   (b)   **Claude Elisabeth Françoise Gabrielle Marie Nau de Champlouis** * Paris 26.5.1875 + Paris 31.1.1880

   (c)   **François Jacques Joseph Léon Marie Baron Nau de Champlouis** * Paris 10.6.1876 + ... 1941 = Luxémont 10.8.1910 Marie de Klopstein * Luxémont (Marne) 23.1.1885 + Paris 14.11.1921, and had issue:

XI   1a.   **Clotilde Marie Henriette Nau de Champlouis** * Luxémont 16.8.1913 = ... 1938 Jacques Lorber * ... 1911, and has issue:

XII   1b.   **François Lorber** * ... 1942 + ... 1942

       2b.   **Paul Lorber** * ... 1952

XI   2a.   **Albert Ferdinand Marie Victor Baron Nau de Champlouis** * Vitry-le-François (Marne) 20.5.1917

     3a.   **Claude Elisabeth Marie Nau de Champlouis** * Vitry-le-François 4.12.1920

IX   b)   **Marie Josèphe Caroline Gabrielle Comtesse d'Ursel** * Bruxelles 20.9.1845 + San Remo 24.3.1885 = Bruxelles 26.8.1873 Alfred Comte Dadvisard de Talairan * Toulouse 16.4.1836 + Boitsfort 31.8.1881, and had issue:

X   (a)   **François Marie Pons Louis Marquis Dadvisard de Talairan** * Toulouse 29.1.1875 + Paris 14.6.1962 = Paris 4.7.1904 Elisabeth Haincque de Saint-Senoch * Paris 8.6.1877 + Paris 16.6.1938 dau. of Edouard Haincque de Saint-Senoch, and had issue:

XI   1a.   **Marie Marguerite Gabrielle Claude Dadvisard de Talairan** * Paris 19.5.1907 = Paris 9.1.1934 René Comte de La Tour du Pin Chambly La Charce * 27.6.1896 + Paris 13.6.1948, and had issue:

XII   1b.   **Humbert Marquis de La Tour du Pin Chambly La Charce** * Paris 19.10.1934 = Paris 25.2.1961 **Gabrielle de Rochechouart de Mortemart** * 15.2.1936 dau. of Charles 12 Duc de Mortemart, and has issue:

XIII   1c.   **Charles René de La Tour du Pin Chambly La Charce** * Paris 9.12.1961

         2c.   **Phylis de La Tour du Pin Chambly La Charce** * Paris 28.11.1962

         3c.   **Louis de La Tour du Pin Chambly La Charce** * Paris 17.3.1966

XII   2b.   **Sibyl de La Tour du Pin Chambly La Charce** * Toulouse 11.5.1944

XI   2a.   **Agnès Marie Alexandrine Dadvisard de Talairan** * Paris 2.7.1909 = 24.4.1936 **Comte Bernard Mouchet Battefort de Laubespin** * Paris 1.1.1901, and has issue see elsewhere

X	(b)		**Comte Marie François Claude Henri Dadvisard de Talairan** * Mondouzil (Haute-Garonne) 4.7.1877 ✗ Langemarck Flandre Occ. 27.4.1915
	(c)		**Charles Marie François Gustave Marquis Dadvisard de Talairan** * Mondouzil 27.8.1879 = Paris 27.9.1913 Jeanne Marie Daru * Angoulême 27.4.1889 dau. of Bruno Comte Daru, and has issue:

XI   1a.   **Comte Emmanuel Dadvisard de Talairan** * Tours (I.-et-L.) 27.1.1915 ✗ Jusciro, near Napoli 27.3.1942

        2a.   **Henri Comte Dadvisard de Talairan** * Rochecorbon (I.-et-L.) 30.8.1917 = Noironte (Doubs) 8.4.1944 Colette de Chateaubrun * Paris 6.10.1922 dau. of René Marquis Le Roy Lisa de Chateaubrun, and has issue:

XII   1b.   **Béatrice Dadvisard de Talairan** * Besancon 6.7.1945

        2b.   **Ghislaine Dadvisard de Talairan** * Besancon 28.6.1946

        3b.   **Geneviève Dadvisard de Talairan** * Besancon 16.8.1947

        4b.   **Bertrand Dadvisard de Talairan** * Besancon 14.2.1949

        5b.   **Gabrielle Dadvisard de Talairan** * Besancon 12.7.1950

        6b.   **François Dadvisard de Talairan** * Paris 2.3.1952

        7b.   **Marie Elisabeth Dadvisard de Talairan** * Besancon 12.9.1954

        8b.   **Agnes Dadvisard de Talairan** * Besancon 23.8.1958

        9b.   **Natalie Dadvisard de Talairan** * Paris 29.5.1964

XI   3a.   **Comte Bruno Dadvisard de Talairan** * Tours 25.12.1919 = Presle (Belgium) 6.12.1944 **Nathalie Comtesse d'Oultremont** * Presles 19.9.1920 dau. of Jacques Comte d'Oultremont, and has issue:

XII   1b.   **Anne Chantal Dadvisard de Talairan** * Presles 3.10.1945

        2b.   **Priscilla Dadvisard de Talairan** * Presles 12.3.1947

        3b.   **Emmanuel Dadvisard de Talairan** * Shanghai 7.11.1948

        4b.   **Claude Dadvisard de Talairan** * Shanghai 14.7.1950

        5b.   **Louis Dadvisard de Talairan** * Tangier 24.6.1955

XI   4a.   **Comte Christian Dadvisard de Talairan** * St-Germain-en-Laye 21.2.1921 = Paris 16.6.1950 Yolande Vieljeaux * 1926 dau. of Pierre Vieljeaux, and has issue:

XII   1b.   **Jean Philippe Dadvisard de Talairan** * St-Germain-en-Laye 6.8.1953

        2b.   **Frédéric Dadvisard de Talairan** * St-Germain-en-Laye 14.5.1955

        3b.   **Marie Caroline Dadvisard de Talairan** * Brest 19.12.1956

        4b.   **Antoine Dadvisard de Talairan** * Paris 3.2.1963

XI   5a.   **Gabrielle Dadvisard de Talairan** * St-Germain-en-Laye 19.12.1922 = 2.7.1946 Humbert du Hays * 6.1.1914, and has issue:

XII   1b.   **Charles du Hays** * St-Germain-en-Laye 9.5.1947

        2b.   **Elisabeth du Hays** * St-Germain-en-Laye 10.7.1948

        3b.   **Emmanuel du Hays** * St-Germain-en-Laye 2.6.1949

        4b.   **Laurent du Hays** * St-Germain-en-Laye 12.10.1951

XII   5b.   **Xavier du Hays** * St-Germain-en-Laye 8.6.1953

XI   6a.   **Marie Dadvisard de Talairan** * St-Germain-en-Laye 8.12.1923 = St-Germain-en-Laye 27.6.1957 Baron Bernard Féral * Rochecorbon (I.-et-L.) 11.1.1918 and has issue:

XII   1b.   **Laurent-Bernard Marie Artus Féral** * Neuilly-sur-Seine 24.7.1958

                                   2b.   **Marie-Laure Johanne Aïcha Féral** * Neuilly-sur-Seine 22.6.1961

XI   7a.   **Lucie Dadvisard de Talairan** * St-Germain-en-Laye 2.4.1925

                         8a.   **Comte Paul Dadvisard de Talairan** * St-Germain-en-Laye 27.7.1927 = Abidjan (Ivory Coast) 22.12.1955 Denise Cardinale * Vinh (Indo-China) 13.7.1932 and has issue:

XII   1b.   **Alix Dadvisard de Talairan** * Libreville (Gambon) 7.10.1956

                                   2b.   **Christophe Dadvisard de Talairan** * Libreville 6.4.1958

                                   3b.   **Valérie Dadvisard de Talairan** * Libreville 7.7.1960

                                   4b.   **Charles-Eric Dadvisard de Talairan** * Le Havre 27.2.1965

XI   9a.   **Comte Jean Dadvisard de Talairan** * St-Germain-en-Laye 9.11.1929 = Paris 12.1.1963 Marie Claude Seguin de la Salle * Paris 6.1.1935 dau. of Comte Bertrand Seguin de la Salle, and has issue:

XII   1b.   **Christine Dadvisard de Talairan** * Paris 27.9.1963

                                   2b.   **Véronique Dadvisard de Talairan** * Strasbourg 19.8.1964

IX   c)   **Charles Marie Léon Comte d'Ursel** * Bruxelles 20.1.1848 + Oostkamp 28.6.1903 = Paris 18.4.1885 Anne Caroline Le Roux * Paris 20.8.1862 + Paris 6.11.1945 dau. of Ernest Le Roux, and had issue:

X   (a)   **Louis Marie Alexandre Comte d'Ursel** * Berlin 1.5.1886 = Paris 19.5.1919 Geneviève Le Peletier de Rosanbo * Angers 14.10.1893 dau. of Raymond Marquis Le Peletier de Rosanbo, and has issue:

XI   1a.   **Philippe Marie Eugène Comte d'Ursel** * Bern 28.6.1920 = Paris 9.7.1956 Marie Roche de La Rigodière * Lyon 4.3.1933 Jean Camille de La Rigodière, and has issue:

XII   1b.   **Etienne Comte d'Ursel** * Bruxelles 16.4.1957

                                   2b.   **Nicolas Comte d'Ursel** * Bruges 1.7.1958

                                   3b.   **Christophe Comte d'Ursel** * Bruxelles 28.7.1960

                                   4b.   **Valentine Comtesse d'Ursel** * Bruxelles 21.7.1963

XI   2a.   **Charles Marie Robert Comte d'Ursel** * Oostkamp 27.8.1921 = Bruxelles 21.1.1950 Marguerite Baronne Guillaume * Napoli 9.2.1928 dau. of Gustave Baron Guillaume, and has issue:

XII   1b.   **Marie-Christine Agathe Comtesse d'Ursel** * Bruxelles 17.3.1951

                                   2b.   **Alain Marie Louis Philippe Comte d'Ursel** * Bruxelles 25.3.1952

                                   3b.   **Ludovic Comte d'Ursel** * Bruxelles 21.12.1953

                                   4b.   **Jeanne Comtesse d'Ursel** * Bruxelles 4.10.1956

XII		5b.	**Laurent Comte d'Ursel** * Bruxelles 4.5.1959
		6b.	**Damien Comte d'Ursel** * Bruxelles 2.5.1964

XI   3a.   **Lucie Marie Madeleine Comtesse d'Ursel** * Bruxelles 20.7.1924 = Oostkamp 18.7.1951 Comte Lionel de Warren * La Rochelle (Manche) 28.7.1920, and has issue:

XII   1b.   **Laurence de Warren** * Paris 25.1.1957

          2b.   **Richard de Warren** * Paris 16.2.1958

          3b.   **Patrice de Warren** * Roma 18.12.1959

XI   4a.   **Pauline Marie Jeanne Comtesse d'Ursel** * Berlin 7.4.1926

       5a.   **Anne Louise Geneviève Marie Comtesse d'Ursel** * Oostkamp 24.6.1929 = Bruxelles 24.11.1956 Comte Jean de Madre * London 8.12.1926, and has issue:

XII   1b.   **Wallerand de Madre** * Paris 5.4.1958

          2b.   **Patrick de Madre** * Bruges 31.7.1959

          3b.   **Brenda de Madre** * Paris 8.4.1962

X   (b)   **Anne Marie Gabrielle Comtesse d'Ursel** * Berlin 13.4.1887 = Ixelles 30.4.1908 Renaud Comte de Briey * Bruxelles 6.2.1880 + Bruxelles 8.2.1960, and has issue:

XI   1a.   **Anne Marie Louise Geneviève Charlotte Comtesse de Briey** * Bruxelles 10.3.1909 + Buissière-Galant 31.10.1942 = Woluwe-Saint-Pierre 14.5.1929 Comte Bernard de Lambertye * Cons-la-Grandville 28.3.1906 + Couture-sur-Loir 13.7.1951, and has issue:

XII   1b.   **Comte Philippe de Lambertye** * Etterbeek 19.4.1930 = St. Didier de la Tour (Isère) 24.4.1954 Chantal du Parc-Locmaria * Luxembourg 1.4.1933 dau. of Yann Comte du Parc-Locmaria and has issue:

XIII   1c.   **Anne de Lambertye** * Villerupt (M.-et-Moselle) 18.2.1955

          2c.   **Pascal de Lambertye** * Villerupt 21.4.1956

          3c.   **Bénédicte de Lambertye** * Versailles 6.10.1957

          4c.   **Jean-François de Lambertye** * Versailles 13.2.1960

          5c.   **Marie Christine de Lambertye** * Boulogne-Billancourt 14.1.1962

          6c.   **Odile de Lambertye** * Boulogne-Billancourt 3.10.1963

XII   2b.   **Comte Thibaut de Lambertye** * Bruxelles 16.4.1931 = Vern d'Anjou 29.8.1959 Elisabeth d'Aviau de Ternay * Vern d'Anjou (M.-et-L.) 23.1.1937 dau. of Comte Guy d'Aviau de Ternay, and has issue:

XIII   1c.   **Caroline de Lambertye** * Angers 16.8.1960

          2c.   **Florence de Lambertye** * Longwy 23.2.1961

XII   3b.   **Comte Bertrand de Lambertye** * Sementilon (Yonne) 1.10.1932 = Muzillac 9.6.1962 Geneviève d'Andigné * Muzillac (Morbihan) 28.1.1935 dau. of Comte Guy d'Andigné, and has issue:

XIII   1c.   **Erwan Marie Hugues Bernard de Lambertye** * Paris 30.4.1963

                   2c.   **Ghislain de Lambertye** * Paris 26.5.1966

XII   4b.   **Françoise de Lambertye** * Caen (Calvados) 12.1.1937 = Couture-sur-Loir 3.9.1960 Jean-François Marès * Saint-Ferdinand, Algeria 3.4.1945, and has issue:

XIII   1c.   **Anne-France Marès** * 19.7.1961

                   2c.   **Hugues Marès** * 25.9.1962 + 23.3.1965

                   3c.   **Loic Marès** * 11.11.1963

XI   2a.   **Elisabeth Marie Charlotte Augustine Louise Comtesse de Briey** * Bruxelles 17.4.1910

       3a.   **Charles Marie Louis Comte de Briey** * Bruxelles 19.5.1911 = Vedrin 1.9.1938 Anne de Montpellier de Vedrin * 27.4.1917 dau. of Baron Adrien de Montpellier de Vedrin, and has issue:

XII   1b.   **Geoffroy Anne Adrien Ghislain Thérèse Constant Comte de Briey** * Bruxelles 26.7.1939

                   2b.   **Aynard Charles Marie Aimery Ghislain Thérèse Comte de Briey** * Uccle 5.8.1940

                   3b.   **Eric René Constant Marie Anne Charles Thérèse Ghislain Comte de Briey** * Uccle 14.7.1946

XI   4a.   **Aimery Marie Charles Jean Paul Comte de Briey** * Woluwe-Saint-Pierre 31.10.1913 = Corbeek-Loo 26.9.1935 Marie-Antoinette de Dieudonné de Corbeek-over-Loo * Louvain 16.5.1912, dau. of Pierre Baron de Dieudonné de Corbeek-over-Loo, and had issue:

XII   1b.   **Yolande Marie Mathilde Renaudine Comtesse de Briey** * Corbeek-Loo 23.7.1936 = Bruxelles 9.10.1957 Alain de Thomaz de Bossierre * Limal 21.7.1932, and has issue:

XIII   1c.   **Raynald de Thomaz de Bossierre** * Ottignies 12.6.1958

                   2c.   **Guy de Thomaz de Bossierre** * Ottignies 12.7.1959

                   3c.   **Anne de Thomaz de Bossierre** * Ottignies 17.7.1960

                   4c.   **Gilles de Thomaz de Bossierre** * Ottignies 20.2.1963

                   5c.   **Gaëtane de Thomaz de Bossierre** * Ottignies 20.9.1964

XII   2b.   **Arnaud Marie Pierre Edouard Comte de Briey** * Corbeek-Loo 26.5.1938 = 31.5.1963 Mireille Goeyens * Anvers 16.9.1941, and has issue:

XIII   1c.   **Tanguy Comte de Briey** * Anvers 4.3.1964

                   2c.   **Patrick Comte de Briey** * Anvers 21.11.1965

XII		3b. **Geneviève Marie Mathilde Charlotte Comtesse de Briey** * Uccle 24.4.1941
		4b. **Anne-Astrid Marie Elisabeth Comtesse de Briey** * Uccle 28.9.1945
		5b. **Béatrice Marie Françoise Emmanuelle Comtesse de Briey** * Uccle 21.1.1949
		6b. **Dominique Marie Yolande Claude Comtesse de Briey** * Uccle 13.5.1955

XI 5a. **Claude Marie Charles Jean Joseph Comte de Briey** * Versailles 3.4.1917 = Thuin 26.9.1939 Marie-Elisabeth Gendebien 2.1.1919 dau. of Paul Baron Gendebien, and has issue:

XII

1b. **Bernard Marie Anne Paul François Ghislain Comte de Briey** * Etterbeek 11.9.1940

2b. **Chantal Marie Ghislaine Charlotte Françoise Comtesse de Briey** * Uccle 2.12.1941

3b. **Nathalie Marie Suzanne Guillelmine Pascale Ghislaine Françoise Comtesse de Briey** * Ixelles 8.4.1944

4b. **Baudouin Marie Edouard Renaud François Ghislain Comte de Briey** * Etterbeek 28.1.1946

5b. **Emmanuel Marie Hubert Christian François Ghislain Comte de Briey** * Etterbeek 5.5.1948

6b. **Etienne Marie Nicolas Aimery François Ghislain Joseph Comte de Briey** * Etterbeek 13.6.1950

7b. **Edouard Marie Bernard Marguerite François Ghislain Comte de Briey** * Etterbeek 11.8.1955

XI 6a. **Arnoul Marie Charles Jules Camille Comte de Briey** * Bruxelles 26.4.1925 = Watermael-Boitsfort 5.8.1947 Marie Louise van Zeeland * Saint-Josse-ten-Noode 27.10.1927 dau. of Paul van Zeeland, and has issue:

XII

1b. **Mathilde Comtesse de Briey** * Manhattan, N.Y. 21.5.1948

2b. **Marie-Renée Pauline Anne Françoise Georgette Comtesse de Briey** * Etterbeek 9.1.1950

3b. **Renaud Charles Michel Marie Georges François Ermesinde Comte de Briey** * Bascharage 16.8.1952

4b. **Paul Arnold Edouard Marie François Georges Etienne Comte de Briey** * Petange 21.1.1955

5b. **François Guillaume Marie Georges Simon Comte de Briey** * Etterbeek 27.4.1956

6b. **Hélène Anne Françoise Marie Roberte Georgette Comtesse de Briey** * Etterbeek 11.8.1957

7b. **Thérèse Mathilde Oscar Marie Françoise Georgette Comtesse de Briey** * Uccle 22.4.1959

X (c) **Edouard Marie Ernest Comte d'Ursel** * Bruxelles 13.8.1888 X Dixemund 8.7.1917

(d) **Jeanne Marie Emilie Waudru Comtesse d'Ursel** * Mons (Hainaut) 6.10.1889 + Angers 4.12.1926 = Oostkamp 4.8.1910 Palamède Pierre Vicomte de la Grandière * Paris 1.1.1881 + 14.3.1947 s.p.

X   (e)   **Juliette Marie Françoise Comtesse d'Ursel** * Mons 21.11.1890 + Couterne (Orne)
18.10.1965 = Ixelles 24.4.1911 Robert Marquis de Frotté * Falaise (Calvados)
28.12.1873 + Paris 28.7.1953, and has issue:

XI   1a.   **Geneviève Etienette Marie de Frotté** * Paris 8.5.1917 = 7.7.1942
Baron François de Ladoucette * Rouxmesnil-Bouteilles (S.-M.) 7.9.1913
+ Offranville 17.11.1964, and had issue:

XII   1b.   **Laure de Ladoucette** * Offranville (S.-M.) 28.7.1943

                  2b.   **Baron Charles Louis de Ladoucette** * Offranville 10.11.1945

                  3b.   **Baron Maurice de Ladoucette** * Offranville 12.3.1947

                  4b.   **Anne de Ladoucette** * Offranville 1.3.1949

                  5b.   **Catherine de Ladoucette** * Offranville 28.11.1952

XI   2a.   **Jean Charles Henri Marie Comte de Frotté** * Paris 29.8.1919 + in the
Deportation in Germany 7.4.1945

          3a.   **Comte Charles-Louis Arthur de Frotté** * Paris 6.7.1921 + in the Deportation
in Austria 8.7.1944

          4a.   **Suzanne Marie Anne de Frotté** * Paris 1.11.1923 = Couterne 17.12.1946
Baron Michel du Boisberranger * Orleans 1.1.1915, and has issue:

XII   1b.   **Gabriel du Boisberranger** * Montenay (Mayenne) 8.10.1947
+ Paris 27.5.1957

                  2b.   **Arnaud du Boisberranger** * Montenay 20.6.1949

                  3b.   **Nicole du Boisberranger** * Montenay 30.3.1951

                  4b.   **Béatrice du Boisberranger** * Montenay 15.3.1952

                  5b.   **Jean du Boisberranger** * Paris 12.8.1954

                  6b.   **Véronique du Boisberranger** * Hiesville (Manche) 22.3.1959

XI   5a.   **Edouard Joseph Marie Marquis de Frotté** * Couterne 18.5.1928 = Paris
26.4.1958 Nadege de Laugier-Villars * Paris 9.7.1939 dau. of Comte Jean de
Laugier-Villars, and has issue:

XII   1b.   **Oriane de Frotté** * Paris 28.11.1962

                  2b.   **Thierry de Frotté** * Paris 30.1.1965

                  3b.   **Cordelia de Frotté** * Paris 12.10.1966

X   (f)   **Emilie Marie-Geneviève Comtesse d'Ursel** * Nice 22.12.1891 = Bruxelles
7.5.1914 Comte Charles de Montalembert * Montiny (Morbihan) 12.4.1885
+ Troyes 3.10.1918, and had issue:

XI   1a.   **Comte Bertrand de Montalembert** * Paris 13.8.1916 = Paris 14.11.1955
Natalie de Manneville * Paris 4.8.1930 dau. of Comte Charles de Manneville

          2a.   **Comte Charles Edouard de Montalembert** * Paris 26.11.1917 = Paris
5.5.1951 Geneviève de Vasselot de Régné * 1920 dau. of Comte Gaston de
Vasselot de Régné, and has issue:

XII   1b.   **Marie-Odile de Montalembert** * Neuilly-sur-Seine 4.6.1952

                  2b.   **Nathalie de Montalembert** * Neuilly-sur-Seine 23.10.1953

XII		3b.	**Béatrice de Montalembert** * Metz 17.9.1954
		4b.	**Hélène de Montalembert** * Neuilly-sur-Seine 29.2.1956
		5b.	**Laurence de Montalembert** * Paris 18.2.1959
		6b.	**Charles-Henri de Montalembert** * Paris 19.5.1961
		7b.	**Ghislain de Montalembert** * Paris 31.5.1966

X   (g)   **Septima Gabrielle Marie Comtesse d'Ursel** * Oostkamp, Flandre Occ. 2.6.1893 = Paris 26.1.1920 Edouard Antoine * Alais (Gard) 10.4.1889, and has issue:

XI   1a.   **Jean-Claude Antoine** * Paris 2.11.1922 = 12.12.1959 Alix Michet de Varine-Bohan * 7.9.1928 dau. of Baron Bernard Michet de Varine-Bohan, and has issue:

XII		1b.	**Jerôme Antoine** * Neuilly-sur-Seine 17.9.1960
		2b.	**Thierry Antoine** * Boulogne-sur-Seine 21.9.1961
		3b.	**Isabelle Antoine** * Neuilly-sur-Seine 2.2.1963

XI   2a.   **Bernard Antoine** * 24.2.1926 = 13.6.1952 Geneviève Virot * 19.8.1928 dau. of Louis Virot, and has issue:

XII		1b.	**Dominique Antoine** * Paris 13.7.1953
		2b.	**Charles Antoine** * Paris 9.7.1958
		3b.	**Agnes Antoine** * Boulogne-sur-Seine ... + 20.6.1961
		4b.	**François Antoine** * Paris ... + 7.2.1963

X   (h)   **Françoise Octavie Marie Comtesse d'Ursel** * Oostkamp 28.8.1897 = Bruxelles 1.6.1920 Comte Bertrand de Sartiges * Saint-Chamant, Corrèze 1.5.1884, and has issue:

XI   1a.   **Marie de Sartiges** * Paris 7.7.1922 = Paris 3.2.1948 Augustin Jordan * Paris 10.12.1910, and has issue:

XII		1b.	**Françoise Jordan** * Paris 18.11.1948
		2b.	**Louis Jordan** * Paris 22.1.1950
		3b.	**Bernard Jordan** * Montargis 10.8.1956
		4b.	**Charles-Etienne Jordan** * Paris 26.10.1959

XI   2a.   **Comte Eugène de Sartiges** * Paris 2.7.1923 = Paris 22.9.1949 Reine Merlin d'Estreux de Beaugrenier * Paris 7.6.1927 dau. of Baron Hubert Merlin d'Estreux de Beaugrenier, and has issue:

XII		1b.	**Amaury de Sartiges** * Neuilly-sur-Seine 14.12.1950
		2b.	**Delphine de Sartiges** * Neuilly-sur-Seine 5.1.1953
		3b.	**Yolande de Sartiges** * Paris 26.7.1956
		4b.	**Isabelle de Sartiges** * Paris 1.3.1962

XI   3a.   **Comte Emmanuel de Sartiges** * Conflans-sur-Loing 4.11.1924 = Paris 8.7.1947 Huguette de Clermont-Tonnerre * Dieppe 8.12.1925 dau. of Comte Joseph de Clermont Tonnerre, Principe Romano, and has issue:

XII
    1b. **Sophie de Sartiges** * Paris 6.6.1948

    2b. **Marie-Pierre de Sartiges** * Paris 15.2.1950

    3b. **Grégoire de Sartiges** * Paris 8.2.1954

    4b. **Philibert de Sartiges** * Amilly (Loiret) 4.8.1960

XI   4a. **Jeanne de Sartiges** * Conflans-sur-Loing 10.8.1926 = Conflans 16.9.1950
Comte Maurice de Forton * Montpellier (Hérault) 23.3.1923, and has issue:

XII
    1b. **Antoine de Forton** * Neuilly-sur-Seine 11.7.1951

    2b. **Charles-Henri de Forton** * Paris 20.6.1953

    3b. **Jerôme de Forton** * Paris 23.12.1955

XI   5a. **Anne de Sartiges** * 8.7.1928 = 31.12.1954 Antoine Vicomte de
La Boussinière * 31.7.1925 and has issue:

XII
    1b. **Renaud de La Boussinière** * 7.11.1955

    2b. **Guénola de La Boussinière** * 16.5.1957

    3b. **Catherine de La Boussinière** * 13.12.1959

    4b. **Bertrand de La Boussinière** * 19.12.1963

    5b. **Louis de La Boussinière** * 27.4.1966.

IX d) **Marie Henri Adrien Aymard Comte d'Ursel** * Bruxelles 31.5.1849 + Bruxelles 9.2.1939
= (1) Bruxelles 22.1.1883 Mathilde Comtesse du Chastel de la Howarderie * Bruxelles
4.6.1854 + Bruxelles 1.3.1892 dau. of Camille Comte du Chastel de la Howarderie;
= (2) Bruxelles 22.8.1911 Jacqueline Comtesse Wassenaer-Starrenburg * Almelo 8.5.1853
+ Bruxelles 5.8.1930 dau. of William Comte Wassenaer-Starrenburg, and had issue:

by 1st marriage:

X (a) **Marie Louise Camille Barbe Ghislaine Comtesse d'Ursel** * Bruxelles 20.6.1884
+ Boitsfort 19.8.1884

  (b) **Marie Thérèse Aymardine Albertine Barbe Ghislaine Comtesse d'Ursel** * Braine-le-
Château 13.7.1885 = Bruxelles 12.7.1904 Philippe Comte de Brouchoven de
Bergeyck * Bevern-Waes 5.4.1877 + Braine-le-Château 21.10.1929, and has issue:

XI   1a. **Aymard Florimond Marie Joseph Maurice Ghislain Comte de Brouchoven
de Bergeyck** * Braine-le-Château 22.9.1905 + Bruxelles 13.3.1926

    2a. **Charles Marie Aymard Emmanuel Joseph Ghislain Comte de Brouchoven de
Bergeyck** * Bruxelles 20.1.1907 + Bruxelles 31.8.1930

    3a. **Ferdinand Marie Louis Joseph Adolphe Florimond Jean Ghislain Comte de
Brouchoven de Bergeyck** * Bruxelles 27.1.1908 = Woluwe-Saint-Lambert
4.2.1952 Marie Vandersype * Reningelst 18.3.1913 dau. of Henri Cornelius
Vandersype s.p.

    4a. **Emmanuel Marie Vincent Emile Conrard Claire Ghislain Comte de Brouchoven
de Bergeyck** * Château de Mouffrin, Natoye 12.8.1909 + St-Gilles
4.12.1958

    5a. **Jacques Marie Henri Joseph Albert Gérard Ghislain Comte de Brouchoven
de Bergeyck** * Braine-le-Château 29.11.1916 + Braine-le-Château 9.10.1922

    6a. **Michel Joseph Marie Vincent Anastase Ghislain Comte de Brouchoven de
Bergeyck** * Braine-le-Château 22.1.1920 = Opheylissem 26.10.1944
Gaëtane Comtesse d'Oultremont * Guines, Pas-de-Calais 15.10.1917 dau. of
Albert Comte d'Oultremont, and has issue:

403

XII		**1b.** **Marie Brigitte Anne Marguerite Gabrielle Gaëtane Rita Ghislaine Comtesse de Brouchoven de Bergeyck** * Bruxelles 11.8.1945
		2b. **Marie-Axelle Marguerite Fernande Gabrielle Rita Ghislaine Comtesse de Brouchoven de Bergeyck** * Heylissem 15.12.1947
		3b. **Danielle Marguerite Marie Emma Rita Ghislaine Comtesse de Brouchoven de Bergeyck** * Heylissem 23.12.1948
		4b. **Philippe-Albert Adrien Joseph Michael Rita Marie Ghislain Comte de Brouchoven de Bergeyck** * Watermael-Boitsfort 1.3.1951
		5b. **Marguerite Marie Georgine Bridget Andrée Rita Ghislaine Comtesse de Brouchoven de Bergeyck** * Uccle 9.5.1952
		6b. **Muriel Marie Axelle Christiane Marguerite Gaëtane Rita Ghislaine Comtesse de Brouchoven de Bergeyck** * Uccle 6.5.1954
		7b. **Emmanuel Pio Philippe Albert Daniel Michel Rita Marie Ghislain Comte de Brouchoven de Bergeyck** * Uccle 10.2.1959

XI — **7a.** **Marie Isabelle Thérèse Aymardine Georgine Caroline Comtesse de Brouchoven de Bergeyck** * Braine-le-Château 21.7.1926 + 27.5.1964

X — (c) **Berthe Marie Caroline Louise Camille Gabrielle Ghislaine Barbe Comtesse d'Ursel** * Braine-le-Château (Brabant) 25.8.1886

(d) **Gabrielle Ghislaine Marie Henriette Barbe Comtesse d'Ursel** * Bruxelles 9.2.1888 = Bruxelles 22.5.1912 Jacques Comte d'Oultremont * Ixelles 26.1.1879 + Presles 3.3.1946, and has issue:

XI — **1a.** **Marie Chantal Jacqueline Henriette Aymardine Ghislaine Colette Marguerite Marie Claire Catherine Comtesse d'Oultremont** * Château de Presles 1.5.1919

2a. **Nathalie Marie Jacqueline Edouardine Ghislaine Anne Josèphe Gabrielle Comtesse d'Oultremont** * Château de Presles 19.9.1920 = 6.12.1944 **Comte Bruno Dadvisard de Talairan** * Tours 25.12.1919, and has issue see elsewhere

3a. **Eugène Charles Paul Marie Ghislain Corneille Comte d'Oultremont** * Ixelles 30.4.1922 = Faulx-les-Tombes 27.7.1949 Madeleine Comtesse de Liedekerke de Pailhe * Bruxelles 24.4.1929 dau. of Guillaume Comte de Liedekerke de Pailhe, and has issue:

XII — **1b.** **Jacques-Guillaume Eric Antoine Marie Ghislain Comte d'Oultremont** * Charleroi 30.6.1950

2b. **Marie Hélène Gabrielle Anne Ghislaine Comtesse d'Oultremont** * Etterbeek 31.1.1952

3b. **Colienne Antoinette Marie Ghislaine Comtesse d'Oultremont** * Namur 13.8.1956

4b. **Elisabeth Antoinette Régine Bernadette Gabrielle Marie Ghislaine Comtesse d'Oultremont** * Namur 29.7.1957

XI — **4a.** **Antoinette Marie Thérèse Emilie Ghislaine Comtesse d'Oultremont** * Ixelles 7.2.1924

5a. **Anne-Elisabeth Pia Marie Thérèse Philippine Ghislaine Comtesse d'Oultremont** * Ixelles 9.4.1925

XI

6a. **Claude Marguerite Marie Thérèse Emma Ghislaine Comtesse d'Oultremont**
    * Ixelles 23.6.1927 = Presles 7.10.1951 Jean Baron Mosneron-Dupin
    * Nantes 1.9.1924, and has issue:

XII

    1b. **Charles-Edouard Mosneron-Dupin** * Nantes 27.4.1953

    2b. **Laurence Mosneron-Dupin** * Nantes 5.4.1955

    3b. **Aymard Mosneron-Dupin** * Lille 11.11.1961

X

(e) **Marguérite Marie Louise Barbe Ghislaine Comtesse d'Ursel** * Braine-le-Château
2.11.1889 = Braine-le-Château 11.2.1920 Ralph Morton Mansel-Pleydell
* Branston, Lincs 17.5.1895 + London 11.4.1932, and has issue:

XI

1a. **John Aymard Morton Mansel-Pleydell** * Bruxelles 22.11.1920 + 17.11.1940

2a. **Philip Morton Mansel-Pleydell** * Bruxelles 16.2.1922 = Antigua, British West
Indies 21.8.1961 Dagmar Rosalie Bowring * Hebden Bridge, Yorkshire
14.3.1932 dau. of Theodore Bowring, and has issue:

XII

    1b. **John Bowring Morton Mansel-Pleydell** * Poole, Dorset 2.11.1963

    2b. **Rosanna Vivien Mansel-Pleydell** * Poole, Dorset 19.2.1965

XI

3a. **David Gabriel Morton Mansel-Pleydell** * Bruxelles 26.3.1923 = London
5.12.1963 Elizabeth Luard * Hamadan, Persia 5.8.1939 dau. of John McVean
Luard, and has issue:

XII

    1b. **Toby Edmund Luard Morton Mansel-Pleydell** * Athens 30.9.1964

    2b. **Harry Rupert Delalynd Morton Mansel-Pleydell** * London 27.5.1966

X

(f) **Conrard Marie Joseph Gaspard Melchior Balthasar Ghislain Comte d'Ursel**
* Braine-le-Château 11.4.1891 = Bruxelles 20.1.1919 Yvonne Baronne Snoy
* Bruxelles 1.4.1891 dau. of Albert Baron Snoy, and has issue:

XI

1a. **Marie Caroline Yvonne Ghislaine Comtesse d'Ursel** * Bruxelles 4.3.1920

2a. **Claude Yvonne Guillemine Marie Ghislaine Comtesse d'Ursel** * Bruxelles
14.10.1921 = Moulbaix 27.8.1953 Jack Bruce Walker * Ussery, Arkansas,
U.S.A. 24.7.1897

3a. **Aymard Henri Jacques Conrard Marie Ghislain Comtesse d'Ursel** * Bruxelles
25.4.1923 = Grez-Doiceau 14.7.1949 Nadine Vicomtesse de Spoelberch
* Grez-Doiceau 19.10.1922 dau. of Thierry Vicomte de Spoelberch, and
has issue:

XII

    1b. **Diane Comtesse d'Ursel** * Grez-Doiceau 27.4.1950

    2b. **Yves Comte d'Ursel** * Grez-Doiceau 6.7.1951

    3b. **Eleonore Comtesse d'Ursel** * Grez-Doiceau 13.9.1952

    4b. **Collienne Comtesse d'Ursel** * Grez-Doiceau 16.3.1956

    5b. **Barbara Comtesse d'Ursel** * Ath 31.5.1957

    6b. **Rodolphe Comte d'Ursel** * Moulbaix 10.4.1961

    7b. **Régine Comtesse d'Ursel** * Ath 16.9.1963

XI

4a. **Béatrice Marie Thérèse Ferdinande Yvonne Ghislaine Comtesse d'Ursel**
    * Melsbroeck 19.7.1924 = Moulbaix 4.8.1952 Colin Broun-Lindsay
    * London 4.11.1924, and has issue:

XII		1b.	**Ludovic David Broun-Lindsay** * Edinburgh 12.1.1954
		2b.	**Christian Georgiana Broun-Lindsay** * Edinburgh 30.12.1956

XI   5a.   **Edouard Adrien Gabriel Conrard Charles Marie Ghislain Comte d'Ursel** * Bruxelles 14.12.1929 = Geetbets 16.5.1959 Françoise de Ryckman de Betz * 14.10.1929 dau. of André de Ryckman de Betz, and has issue:

XII   1b.   **Réginald Comte d'Ursel** * Uccle 5.1.1960

                2b.   **Nathalie Comtesse d'Ursel** * Uccle 27.2.1961

                3b.   **Anne Caroline Comtesse d'Ursel** * Hasselt 23.1.1963

                4b.   **Melanie Comtesse d'Ursel** * Huy 17.12.1965

IX   e)   **Marie Hippolyte Adrien Ludovic Comte d'Ursel** * Bruxelles 17.11.1850 + Bruxelles 9.12.1937 = St-Josse-ten-Noode 30.1.1878 Georgine de Rouillé * Bruxelles 13.3.1859 + Bruxelles 28.2.1926 dau. of Adhémar Comte de Rouillé, and had issue:

X   (a)   **Louis Marie Victor Edouard Jean Comte d'Ursel** * Ormeignies 15.5.1879 + Bruxelles 3.4.1880

     (b)   **Marie Gabrielle Raphaëlle Comtesse d'Ursel** * Bruxelles 11.2.1882 = Watermael-Boitsfort 20.1.1908 Jacques Comte de Lichtervelde * Wien 11.10.1878 + London 6.4.1916, and has issue:

XI   1a.   **Thierry Hippolyte Gontran Marie Ghislain Ludovic Comte de Lichtervelde** * Watermael-Boitsfort 4.11.1908

            2a.   **Ferdinand Gontran Louis Georges Marie Ghislain Comte de Lichtervelde** * Etterbeek 16.12.1910 + Baelegem 30.7.1934

            3a.   **Godelieve Marie Louise Gabrielle Isabelle Ghislaine Comtesse de Lichtervelde** * Etterbeek 5.2.1913 = Etterbeek 11.2.1942 Edouard Harmant * Bruxelles 11.3.1911, and has issue:

XII   1b.   **Jacques Eugène Marie Thierry Ghislain Harmant** * Liège 4.3.1943

                   2b.   **Antoine Marie Ghislain Thierry Pascal Harmant** * Liège 7.4.1944

                   3b.   **Ghislaine Marie de Fatima Lucie Emma Harmant** * Uccle 17.11.1946

                   4b.   **Marie Isabelle Ghislaine Harmant** * Uccle 9.10.1948

                   5b.   **Anne Marie Ghislaine Jacqueline Bernadette Harmant** * Uccle 21.10.1951

XI   4a.   **Roger Georges Marie Gontran Ghislain Comte de Lichtervelde** * Dickelvenne 26.8.1914 = Bruxelles 22.4.1942 Marie Cécile de Kerchove d'Exaerde * Bosluut Wuestwezel 30.9.1917 dau. of Robert Baron de Kerchove d'Exaerde and has issue:

XII   1b.   **Antoinette Jacqueline Marie Roberte Colette Ghislaine Comtesse de Lichtervelde** * Ixelles 11.4.1943 = Woluwe-Saint-Lambert 1.7.1964 Xavier de Brabandère * Anvers 16.1.1939

                   2b.   **Jacques Fernand Marie Ghislain Comte de Lichtervelde** * Wuestwezel 18.7.1944

                   3b.   **Chantal Marie Claire Colette Ghislaine Comtesse de Lichtervelde** * Aix-la-Chapelle 24.2.1948

4b.   **Ferdinand Thierry Antoine Marie Charles Ghislain Comte de Lichtervelde** * Watermael-Boitsfort 19.4.1951

X

(c) **Gabrielle Charlotte Josèphe Emma Marie Comtesse d'Ursel** * Bruxelles 27.1.1884 + München 29.3.1921 = Watermael-Boitsfort 21.11.1906 Carl Graf des Enffans d'Avernas * Freybühel 16.1.1877 + Freybühel 24.12.1966, and has issue:

XI

1a.   **Beatrice Marie Immaculata Gabrielle Louise Georgine Dominika Gräfin des Enffans d'Avernas** * Freybühel 21.11.1907 = Freybühel 29.6.1942 Gustav Petti * Hitzendorf 1.7.1906 s.p.

2a.   **Heinrich Marie Hippolyt Carl Graf des Enffans d'Avernas** * Freybühel 23.5.1910 = St. Martin am Grimming 27.8.1957 Hilde Sedlaček * Graz 31.7.1915 s.p.

3a.   **Monika Marie Pia Anna Johanna Emmanuelle Gräfin des Enffans d'Avernas** * Pitten 16.10.1911 = Maria Zell 14.10.1948 Franz Kopczyk * Nadole 2.11.1918, and has issue:

XII

1b.   **Aniela Kopczyk** * 7.2.1950

2b.   **Jadwiga Kopczyk** * 11.6.1951

3b.   **Christine Kopczyk** * 23.6.1952

4b.   **Franz Kopczyk** * 25.10.1954

5b.   **Benedikt Kopczyk** * 30.12.1955

XI

4a.   **Franz Marie Heinrich Ernst Graf des Enffans d'Avernas** * Graz 12.1.1913 X Sacharowo, Russia 11.2.1942

5a.   **Pia Maria Isabella Johanna Gräfin des Enffans d'Avernas** * Weduyne 28.5.1914 + Freybühel 5.2.1961

6a.   **Marie Theresia Isabelle Gaëtane Lucie Gräfin des Enffans d'Avernas** * Graz 13.12.1917 = Freybühel 7.11.1964 Paul Silbert * ...

7a.   **Johannes Marie Ferdinand Judas Thaddäus Ladislas Graf des Enffans d'Avernas** * Graz 27.6.1919 = 1.10.1946 Anita Comtesse de Bousies * 17.1.1925 dau. of Jean Comte de Bousies, and has issue:

XII

1b.   **Alain Marie Jean Charles François Comte des Enffans d'Avernas** * Havanna 23.12.1947

2b.   **Roland Marie Henri Comte des Enffans d'Avernas** * Havanna 21.2.1949

3b.   **Dominique Marie Baudouin Comte des Enffans d'Avernas** * Montevideo 8.11.1953

4b.   **Diane Marie Gabrielle Monique Comtesse des Enffans d'Avernas** * Washington 7.3.1957

X

(d) **Jean Marie Henri Ghislain Hubert Comte d'Ursel** * Bruxelles 21.1.1887 + Lausanne 23.6.1913

(e) **Georges Marie Joseph Louis Ghislain Comte d'Ursel** * Ormeignies 30.7.1890 + Bruxelles 16.12.1944 = (1) St-Gervais 26.6.1916 **Gaëtane van de Werve d'Immerseel** * Pulle 21.6.1895 + Guines 28.7.1917 dau. of Ludovic Vicomte van de Werve d'Immerseel; = (2) Gand 5.2.1920 Elisabeth Comtesse de Bousies * Gand 20.12.1892 + Bruxelles 1.7.1958 dau. of Baudouin Comte de Bousies, and had issue:

XI	1a.	**Jean Albert Hippolyte Charles Wolfgang Marie Ghislain Comte d'Ursel** * Guines 27.3.1917 = (1) Pepinster 5.5.1942 Jeanne Lejeune de Schierevel * Pepinster 28.8.1918 + Ravensbrück 4.3.1945 dau. of Charles Lejeune de Schierevel = (2) Linkebeek 19.7.1947 Arlette Comtesse d'Oultremont * Gand 28.8.1922 dau. of Pierre Comte d'Oultremont, and has issue:

by 1st marriage:

XII	1b.	**Gaëtane Charlotte Camille Marie Joséphine Ghislaine Comtesse d'Ursel** * Düsseldorf 7.3.1943

by 2nd marriage:

	2b.	**Lancelot Comte d'Ursel** * Louvain 6.7.1953
	3b.	**Aurian Comtesse d'Ursel** * Madrid 3.6.1955
	4b.	**Cedric Comte d'Ursel** * Madrid 13.2.1957
	5b.	**Gaël Comtesse d'Ursel** * Madrid 12.2.1959
	6b.	**Wauthier Comte d'Ursel** * Khartoum 18.11.1961

by 2nd marriage:

XI	2a.	**Bénédicte Georgine Baudouin Marie Ghislaine Comtesse d'Ursel** * Watermael-Boitsfort 8.2.1921 = Bruxelles 8.9.1942 Albert Baron Kervyn de Letenhove * Bruxelles 8.4.1917, and has issue:

XII	1b.	**Guy Bruno Adrien Baron Kervyn de Letenhove** * London 18.7.1946
	2b.	**Bruno Georges Hubert Jean Marie Baron Kervyn de Letenhove** * Genève 6.9.1947
	3b.	**Jeanne Elisabeth Juliette Marie Baronne Kervyn de Letenhove** * Genève 6.10.1948
	4b.	**Anne Noëlle Madeleine Marie Baronne Kervyn de Letenhove** * Genève 29.3.1950
	5b.	**Elisabeth Nicole Marie Baronne Kervyn de Letenhove** * Boston, Mass. 16.6.1952
	6b.	**Michel Bruno Pierre Marie Baron Kervyn de Letenhove** * Hodoumont 16.8.1955
	7b.	**Claude Marie Arlette Baronne Kervyn de Letenhove** * Hodoumont 28.8.1956
	8b.	**Pascale Nadine Marie Baronne Kervyn de Letenhove** * Bruxelles 24.4.1960

XI	3a.	**Hubert Pierre Luc Marie Ghislain Comte d'Ursel** * Boitsfort 22.1.1922 X Hulst 17.9.1944
	4a.	**Michel Alfred Isabelle Marie Ghislain Comte d'Ursel** * Hansbeke 6.9.1924 = Bruxelles 27.10.1951 Ferdinanda Diana * Roma 25.11.1928 dau. of Pasquale Marchese Diana, and has issue:

XII	1b.	**Ghislain Marie Pascal Comte d'Ursel** * Louvain 13.8.1952
	2b.	**Hubert Comte d'Ursel** * Louvain 26.8.1953
	3b.	**Amaury Comte d'Ursel** * 2.5.1955 + 27.8.1955
	4b.	**Augustin Comte d'Ursel** * Elisabethville 5.4.1957

XII   5b.   **Barbara Comtesse d'Ursel** * Elisabethville 8.8.1958

       6b.   **Bénédicte Comtesse d'Ursel** * Louvain 6.1.1962

       7b.   **François-Albert Comte d'Ursel** * Louvain 7.8.1963

XI   5a.   **Noëlle Anne Jeanne Marie Ghislaine Comtesse d'Ursel** * Watermael-Boitsfort 4.10.1927 = Ixelles 8.3.1956 Georges Nève de Mévergnies * Lekuni, Congo 7.8.1927, and has issue:

XII   1b.   **Paul Michel Jacques Marie Nève de Mévergnies** * Luena, Congo 22.4.1957

         2b.   **Jacques Jean Ghislain Marie Nève de Mévergnies** * Elisabethville 20.10.1958

         3b.   **Florence Bénédicte Marie Ghislaine Nève de Mévergnies** * Uccle 16.10.1961

         4b.   **Gabriel Albert Corneille Marie Nève de Mévergnies** * Uccle 30.5.1964

X   (f)   **Pierre Aymard Marie Ghislain Corneille Comte d'Ursel** * Watermael-Boitsfort 24.11.1892 + Bruxelles 18.10.1926 = Bruxelles 28.1.1920 Jacqueline de Néverlée * Paris 23.3.1884 dau. of Philippe Comte de Néverlée, and had issue:

XI   1a.   **Odette Marie Simone Comtesse d'Ursel** * Le Bercuit (Grez-Doiceau) 19.4.1921

X   (g)   **Isabelle Antoinette Caroline Ghislaine Henriette Marie Comtesse d'Ursel** * Watermael-Boitsfort 28.2.1897

IX   e)   **Marie Emilie Madeleine Comtesse d'Ursel** * Bruxelles 14.2.1853 + Wiesbaden 16.7.1902 = Bruxelles 26.2.1876 Charles Vicomte de Spoelberch dit de Lovenjoul * Bruxelles 30.4.1836 + Royat (Puy-de-Dôme) 4.7.1907 s.p.

   f)   **Marie Joachim Auguste Paul Comte d'Ursel** * Bruxelles 9.2.1857 + Bruxelles 26.8.1916 = Bruxelles 23.1.1883 Emma de Rouillé * Bruxelles 27.7.1860 + Bruxelles 7.10.1947 dau. of Adhémar Comte de Rouillé, and had issue:

X   (a)   **Albert Marie Joseph Louis Comte d'Ursel** * Bruxelles 8.8.1885 + Ormeignies 3.12.1885

   (b)   **Louise Marie Joséphine Juliette Anne Comtesse d'Ursel** * Dongelberg 10.9.1886 + St-Gilles 12.5.1966 = Bruxelles 2.2.1926 Joseph Vicomte d'Hennezel * Lyon 12.4.1879 + St-Gilles 28.2.1962, and had issue:

XI   1a.   **Antoine Marie Armand Désiré Joseph Vicomte d'Hennezel** * Ixelles 20.10.1927 = Etterbeek 29.5.1958 **Beatrice de Meeûs d'Argenteuil** * Ixelles 2.9.1934 dau. of Guy Comte de Meeûs d'Argenteuil, and has issue:

XII   1b.   **Bruno Marie Louis Bertrand Joseph d'Hennezel** * Uccle 12.5.1959

         2b.   **Pascal Philippe Marie Guy d'Hennezel** * Etterbeek 9.4.1960

         3b.   **Emmanuel Claude Guy Louis d'Hennezel** * Namur 25.12.1962

         4b.   **Nathalie Marie Marguerite Ghislaine d'Hennezel** * Ixelles 9.3.1964

X   (c)   **Hélène Comtesse d'Ursel** * & + Bruxelles 6.2.1888

X	(d)		**Elisabeth Marie Joséphine Louise Georgine Charlotte Comtesse d'Ursel** * Sempst 12.8.1889 = Bruxelles 4.2.1920 Richard du Pré de Saint Maur * Saint-Péreuse (Nièvre) 3.6.1891, and has issue:
XI		1a.	**Jacqueline du Pré de Saint-Maur** * Saint-Péreuse 1.10.1920 = 28.7.1948 Philippe Boyer de Bouillane * Montélimar 17.6.1921, and has issue:
XII			1b. **Bruno Boyer de Bouillane** * Bellevue (S.-et-O.) 10.6.1949
			2b. **Catherine Boyer de Bouillane** * Bellevue 26.5.1952
			3b. **Arnaud Boyer de Bouillane** * Boulogne (Seine) 21.5.1954
			4b. **Thibaut Boyer de Bouillane** * Montbéliard (Doubs) 10.7.1960
XI		2a.	**Nicole Marie Louise Emma du Pré de Saint Maur** * Bruxelles 12.12.1921 = Saint-Péreuse 30.1.1954 Comte Xavier de Galzain * Royan 17.1.1916, and has issue:
XII			1b. **Olivier de Galzain** * Alger 16.10.1954
			2b. **Hugues Frédéric de Galzain** * Paris 15.9.1955
			3b. **Loïc de Galzain** * Neuilly-sur-Seine 12.5.1957
			4b. **Ombline de Galzain** * Neuilly-sur-Seine 1.7.1961
XI		3a.	**Pierre du Pré Saint Maur** * 1.4.1923 = 6.5.1950 France de Roquefeuil * 26.4.1926 dau. of Comte Bertrand de Roquefeuil-Cahuzac, and has issue·
XII			1b. **Bernard du Pré de Saint Maur** * 27.4.1951
			2b. **Roselyne du Pré de Saint Maur** * 14.4.1952
			3b. **Olivier Richard du Pré de Saint Maur** * 15.7.1954
			4b. **Bénédicte du Pré de Saint Maur** * 24.3.1956
XI		4a.	**Anne du Pré de Saint Maur** * St-Péreuse 3.7.1924 = St-Péreuse 14.6.1949 Antoine de La Villéon * Hoechts 17.11.1919, and has issue:
XII			1b. **Jacques de La Villéon** * Château Chinon (Nièvre) 24.5.1950
			2b. **Hubert de La Villéon** * St-Briene (Côte-du-Nord) 15.8.1951
			3b. **Béatrice de La Villéon** * Bizerta, Tunisia 12.11.1952
			4b. **Alain de La Villéon** * St-Briene 30.8.1957
			5b. **Elisabeth de La Villéon** * Aix-en-Provence 22.6.1960
XI		5a.	**Christiane du Pré de Saint Maur** * St-Péreuse 21.3.1926
		6a.	**Alain du Pré de Saint Maur** * St-Péreuse 16.10.1928
		7a.	**Monique du Pré de Saint Maur** * Bellevue (S.-et-O.) 12.11.1935 = St-Péreuse 20.5.1961 Baron Gabriel Angleys * Les Abrets (Isère) 5.5.1928 and has issue:
XII			1b. **Philippe Angleys** * Paris 11.4.1962
			2b. **Gilles Angleys** * Paris 6.9.1963
			3b. **Aliette Angleys** * Paris 19.12.1966

X   (e)   **Marthe Marie Joséphine Louise Comtesse d'Ursel** * Bruxelles 20.3.1891 = Bruxelles 28.5.1921 Charles Comte Hennequin de Villermont * Anvers 9.6.1890 and has issue:

XI   1a.   **Jacqueline Caroline Emma Marie Benoîte Clémence Comtesse Hennequin de Villermont** * Bruxelles 29.6.1922 = Boussu-en-Fagne 25.5.1948 Gérard de Montpellier d'Annevoie * Denée 1.7.1906, and has issue:

XII   1b.   **Claude Marie Joseph Frédéric Ghislain de Montpellier d'Annevoie** * Louvain 19.3.1949

                                2b.   **Cécile Marie Jeanne Ghislaine de Montpellier d'Annevoie** * Louvain 28.5.1950

                                3b.   **Benoît Marie Charles Ghislain de Montpellier d'Annevoie** * Louvain 7.7.1951

                                4b.   **Claire Marie Françoise Ghislaine de Montpellier d'Annevoie** * Louvain 30.8.1953

                                5b.   **Marie Jeanne Viviane Ghislaine de Montpellier d'Annevoie** * Louvain 2.7.1955

XI   2a.   **Charles Claude Clement Edouard Martin Marie Benoît Comte Hennequin de Villermont** * Bruxelles 29.10.1923 ✗ Bure (Ardennes) 31.12.1944

                3a.   **Anne Marie Henriette Caroline Marthe Pauline Comtesse Hennequin de Villermont** * Bruxelles 8.6.1925

                4a.   **Viviane Renée Marthe Caroline Marie Comtesse Hennequin de Villermont** * Bruxelles 12.4.1927

                5a.   **Françoise Yolande Marie Martine Caroline Joséphine Comtesse Hennequin de Villermont** * Bruxelles 4.8.1928

                6a.   **Henri Jacques Marie Charles Ghislain Benoît Comte Hennequin de Villermont** * Bruxelles 2.5.1934

X   (f)   **Yvonne Marie Molly Louise Josèphe Comtesse d'Ursel** * Bruxelles 20.12.1892 + Bruxelles 24.4.1893

         (g)   **Antoine Aymard Louis Marie Joseph Adhémar Comte d'Ursel** * Bruxelles 23.1.1896 ✗ Biriatou (H.P.) 24.12.1943 = (1) Singapore 17.3.1920 Jeanne Thibault * Buzancy 12.4.1895 + Saigon 9.1.1924 dau. of Charles Thibault; = (2) Jurbise 8.4.1939 Marguerite de La Barre d'Erquelinnes * Buysingen 11.5.1895 dau. of Roger Comte de La Barre d'Erquelinnes and had issue:

                by 1st marriage:

XI   1a.   **Monique Marie Anne Emma Suzanne Comtesse d'Ursel** * Kwala Simpang, Sumatra 5.2.1921 = Parranquet 13.2.1950 Gaston Defrène * Godinne-sur-Meuse 19.3.1910, and has issue:

XII   1b.   **Antoine Defrène** * Villeneuve 22.3.1952

                                2b.   **Alain Defrène** * Parranquet 5.2.1954

                                3b.   **Guy Defrène** * Lalandusse 4.10.1956

XI   2a.   **Molly Elisabeth Marie Emma Comtesse d'Ursel** * Cannes 20.4.1922 = Fort Worth, Texas 31.12.1947 James Mitchell Sinex * Fort Worth, Texas 17.1.1921, and has issue:

XII		1b.	**Patrick Serge Sinex** * Paris 23.10.1948
		2b.	**Colette Marie Sinex** * Frankfurt-am-Main 14.2.1951
		3b.	**Michael Daniel Sinex** * Dallas, Texas 9.2.1952
		4b.	**Monique Emily Sinex** * Dallas, Texas 10.10.1954

XI 3a. **Serge Edouard Auguste Charles Antoine Comte d'Ursel** * Saigon 3.1.1924 = 23.12.1952 Michelle de Faestraets * Bardoux-Condroz 23.10.1929 dau. of Roger de Faestraets, and has issue:

XII		1b.	**Antoine Comte d'Ursel** * Bruxelles 23.11.1953
		2b.	**Renaud Comte d'Ursel** * Bruxelles 24.1.1955
		3b.	**Chantal Comtesse d'Ursel** * Bruxelles 22.1.1957

by 2nd marriage:

XI 4a. **Didier Marie Joseph Robert Ghislain Comte d'Ursel** * Bruxelles 4.4.1931 = Lourdes 15.2.1958 Geneviève Jacottet * Liesle 1.12.1933 dau. of Pierre Jacottet, and has issue:

XII		1b.	**Humbert Comte d'Ursel** * Luxembourg 20.11.1958
		2b.	**Ariane Comtesse d'Ursel** * Phom-Penh (Cambodia) 6.9.1959
		3b.	**Benoît Comte d'Ursel** * Phom-Penh 10.10.1961
		4b.	**Véronique Comtesse d'Ursel** * Phom-Penh 20.2.1964

XI 5a. **Géry Marie Joseph François Ghislain Comte d'Ursel** * Uccle 10.5.1933 = München 1.8.1959 Elisabeth Freiin. v. Steinling zu Boden u. Stainling * Sünching 11.2.1935 dau. of Friedrich Frhr. v. Steinling zu Boden u. Stainling, and has issue:

XII		1b.	**Olivier Comte d'Ursel** * Bruxelles 4.3.1960
		2b.	**Dominique Comtesse d'Ursel** * Namur 11.6.1961
		3b.	**Arnauld Comte d'Ursel** * Namur 25.7.1963

XI 6a. **Baudouin Marie Joseph Henri Ghislain Comte d'Ursel** * Uccle 18.11.1934 = Sorinnes 26.5.1962 Anne Baronne de Villenfagne de Sorinnes * Polleur 25.5.1938 dau. of Jacques Baron de Villenfagne de Sorinnes, and has issue:

XII		1b.	**Eric Comte d'Ursel** * Namur 23.3.1963

XI 7a. **Claudine Marie Joséphine Emilie Jacqueline Comtesse d'Ursel** * Namur 11.3.1940 = Maizeret 7.7.1962 **Claude Comte de Lannoy** * Bruxelles 9.3.1932, and has issue see elsewhere

X (h) **François Marie Joseph Hippolyte Louis Comte d'Ursel** * Sempst 2.2.1899

(i) **Madeleine Marie Joséphine Henriette Comtesse d'Ursel** * Sempst 17.8.1901 = Sempst 4.11.1933 Paul Comte d'Oultremont * Ixelles 27.5.1882 + St-Josse-ten-Noode 5.1.1939, and has issue:

XI 1a. **Eric Emmanuel Eugène Désiré Joseph Marie Ghislain Comte d'Oultremont** * Etterbeek 2.9.1934 = Saint-Trond 8.9.1964 Isabelle Imperiali dei Principi di Francavilla * Woluwe-St-Lambert 4.4.1943 dau. of Marchese Etienne Imperiali dei Principi di Francavilla, and has issue:

412

XII		1b.	**Stéphane Comtesse d'Oultremont** * Ixelles 26.12.1966

XI 2a. **Myriam Henriette Antoinette Thérèse Joséphine Ghislaine Comtesse d'Oultremont** * Etterbeek 14.1.1936

3a. **Jocelyne Monique Jacqueline Thérèse Joséphine Marie Ghislaine Comtesse d'Oultremont** * Etterbeek 14.7.1937

4a. **Diane Marthe Robertine Thérèse Marie Joséphine Ghislaine Fernande Comtesse d'Oultremont** * Uccle 24.12.1938 = Forest 28.5.1964 Damien de Radiguès de Chennevière * Ixelles 7.10.1936, and has issue:

XII 1b. **Quentin de Radigues de Chennevière** * Uccle 15.3.1965

XI 5a. **Noël Marie Thérèse Françoise Joséphine Ghislaine Fernande Comtesse d'Oultremont** * Uccle 24.12.1938 = Forest 5.9.1963 Charles van Ypersele de Strihou * Uccle 20.9.1933, and has issue:

XII 1b. **Patrick van Ypersele de Strihou** * Louvain 29.6.1964

2b. **Laurence van Ypersele de Strihou** * Louvain 4.5.1966

X (j) **Marie Henriette Joséphine Louise Comtesse d'Ursel** * Bruxelles 18.3.1904

(k) **Jacques Joseph Marie Adrien Comte d'Ursel** * Sempst 26.9.1905 ✗ Duisburg 6.8.1942

(l) **Etienne Marie Joseph Léon Comte d'Ursel** * Bruxelles 15.3.1909 + Sempst 1.7.1910

VIII b. **Marie Adrien Conrard Comte d'Ursel** * Hingene (Prov. d'Anvers) 10.8.1813 + Bruxelles 18.1.1854

c. **Marie Auguste Comte d'Ursel** * Bruxelles 8.2.1815 + Hingene 19.7.1878 = Paris 15.5.1860 Marie de Croix * Paris 17.3.1836 + Bruxelles 27.7.1910 dau. of Charles Comte de Croix and had issue:

IX a) **Marie Camille Caroline Amélie Comtesse d'Ursel** * Bruxelles 8.5.1861 + Bruxelles 6.4.1930

b) **Marie Joséphine Charlotte Comtesse d'Ursel** * Paris 16.5.1862 + Bruxelles 6.3.1866

c) **Marie Louis Conrard Comte d'Ursel** * Bruxelles 28.12.1863 + Bruxelles 5.3.1866

d) **Marie Henri Ernest Comte d'Ursel** * Bruxelles 26.5.1866 + Luluabourg, Congo 9.1.1892

e) **Joseph Marie Adrien Comte d'Ursel** * Bruxelles 17.1.1868 + Durbuy 5.8.1933 = Paris 2.5.1900 Henriette de Dreux * Paris 9.1.1880 dau. of Pierre Marquis de Dreux Brézé, and had issue:

X (a) **Ernest Marie Pierre Auguste Comte d'Ursel** * Bruxelles 25.5.1901 = Oostmalle 19.8.1924 Claire Comtesse de Renesse * Bruxelles 26.9.1899 dau. of Maximilian Comte de Renesse, and has issue:

XI 1a. **Adrien Marie Henri Maximilian Bernard François Ghislain Joseph Comte d'Ursel** * Etterbeek 10.7.1926 = Anvers 12.3.1955 Christiane della Faille de Leverghem d'Huysse * Ekeren 16.10.1930 dau. of Alexandre della Faille de Leverghem, and has issue:

XII 1b. **Marc Ernest Jean Ghislain Comte d'Ursel** * Léopoldville 30.5.1956

413

XII		2b.	**Ivan Marie Claire Alexandre Comte d'Ursel** * Léopoldville 14.7.1958
		3b.	**Tanguy Simon Marie Monique Comte d'Ursel** * Etterbeek 11.1.1962
		4b.	**Jean Michel Marie Elisabeth Adolphe Comte d'Ursel** * Bruxelles 2.11.1963

XI   2a.   **Daniel Bernard Auguste Adrien Godelive François Marie Ghislain Comte d'Ursel** * Bruxelles 1.10.1928 = Woluwe-St-Pierre 22.1.1949 Eliane Dedeynç * Paris 14.4.1927 dau. of Alfred Dedeynç, and has issue:

XII   1b.   **Patrick Ernest Simon Alfred Comte d'Ursel** * Bruxelles 2.10.1949

                 2b.   **Kathleen Comtesse d'Ursel** * Bruxelles 11.7.1953

                 3b.   **Olivier Comte d'Ursel** * Bruxelles 16.12.1956

                 4b.   **Anita Comtesse d'Ursel** * Bruxelles 19.4.1959

XI   3a.   **Isabelle Marie Aline Jeanne Josèphe Nicole Ghislaine Comtesse d'Ursel** * Etterbeek 6.12.1931 = Durbuy 31.8.1959 Adolphe Malevez * Namur 18.12.1931

         4a.   **Pierre Antoine Frédéric François Marie Joseph Ghislain Comte d'Ursel** * Bruxelles 13.8.1936

X   (b)   **Aline Maria Josèphe Comtesse d'Ursel** * Bruxelles 14.7.1902 = Bruxelles 27.8.1938 Roger Vicomte le Sergent d'Hendecourt * Rhines 24.8.1882 + Woluwe-St-Pierre 20.3.1962, and has issue:

XI   1a.   **Bernadette le Sergent d'Hendecourt** * Uccle 1.6.1939 = Woluwe-St-Pierre 2.9.1965 Arnold d'Oreye de Lantremange * Ixelles 23.10.1938, and has issue:

XII   1b.   **Maximilian Frédéric Louis Roger Arnold Marie d'Oreye de Lantremange** * Ixelles 24.7.1966

XI   2a.   **Marie Emmanuelle le Sergent d'Hendecourt** * Uccle 24.10.1942

X   (c)   **Charlotte Marie Henriette Comtesse d'Ursel** * Bruxelles 16.10.1903 = Durbuy 2.8.1927 Hervé Comte d'Oultremont * Bruxelles 13.7.1901, and has issue:

XI   1a.   **Jeanne Marie Henriette Comtesse d'Oultremont** * Durbuy 28.7.1928 = Marcinelle 19.6.1951 Francis Comte de Meeûs d'Argenteuil * Bruxelles 25.4.1926, and has issue:

XII   1b.   **Marie Christine Isabelle Ghislaine de Meeûs d'Argenteuil** * Waremme 6.4.1952

                 2b.   **Catherine Beatrix Marie Ghislaine de Meeûs d'Argenteuil** * Waremme 12.6.1953

                 3b.   **Claire Charlotte Fernande Marie Ghislaine de Meeûs d'Argenteuil** * Waremme 12.8.1954

                 4b.   **Yolande Marie Françoise Michel Ghislaine de Meeûs d'Argenteuil** * Waremme 23.7.1955

                 5b.   **Bruno Francis Didier Jacques Marie Ghislain Comte de Meeûs d'Argenteuil** * Waremme 7.7.1960

6b.   **Charlotte Marie Christine Françoise Ghislaine de Meeûs d'Argenteuil**
* Waremme 31.5.1964

2a.   **Ferdinand Adrien Yves Marie Comte d'Oultremont** * Marcinelle 21.1.1930
= Pailhe 3.8.1961 Olga Comtesse de Liedekerke de Pailhe * Pessoux
19.4.1936 dau. of Emmanuel Comte de Liedekerke de Pailhe

3a.   **Claude Emmanuel Alain Baudouin Comte d'Oultremont** * Marcinelle
9.5.1931 = 10.9.1960 Edith Christyn Comtesse de Ribeaucourt * Anthée
7.6.1939 dau. of Victor Christyn Comte de Ribeaucourt, and has issue:

1b.   **Elisabeth Charlotte Anne Marie Comtesse d'Oultremont** * Bruxelles
11.7.1961

2b.   **Véronique Charlotte Victor Marie Comtesse d'Oultremont** * Bruxelles
21.8.1965

4a.   **Michel Pierre Marie Comte d'Oultremont** * Marcinelle 29.1.1933

5a.   **Béatrice Aline Ernest Marie Comtesse d'Oultremont** * Marcinelle 30.6.1934
= Marcinelle 24.4.1958 Thierry Baron de Crombrugghe de Looringhe
* Gand 4.4.1927, and has issue:

1b.   **Reginald Gaëtan Charles Marie Baron de Crombrugghe de Looringhe**
* Etterbeek 27.12.1959

2b.   **Gaëtan Ferdinand Gérard Marie Baron de Crombrugghe de Looringhe**
* Etterbeek 9.1.1961

3b.   **Joëlle Baronne de Crombrugghe de Looringhe** * Etterbeek 19.3.1962

4b.   **Didier Baron de Crombrugghe de Looringhe** * Ixelles 3.10.1963

6a.   **Didier Paul Simon Marie Comte d'Oultremont** * Marcinelle 2.8.1937
= Liège 14.1.1966 Hélène de Hemptinne * Liège 7.8.1940 dau. of
Paul de Hemptinne

7a.   **Jacqueline Marie Elisabeth Comtesse d'Oultremont** * Marcinelle 28.10.1938

8a.   **Léopold Théodule Jean Marie Comte d'Oultremont** * Marcinelle 28.11.1940

(d)   **Emmanuel Marie Antoine Théodule François Ferdinand Comte d'Ursel**
* Bruxelles 20.11.1905 + Spa 7.7.1908

(e)   **Simon Marie Aymard Alexandre Emmanuel Comte d'Ursel** * Bruxelles 21.10.1908

(f)   **Claude Marie Antoinette Théodule Sophie Comtesse d'Ursel** * Bruxelles
18.1.1911 + Etterbeek 11.8.1939 = Durbuy 20.8.1935 Comte Eugène de
Bethune-Hesdigneul * Flostoy 12.8.1910 + Renaix 10.12.1965, and has issue:

1a.   **Alix Marie Adolphine Henriette Ghislaine Comtesse de Bethune-Hesdigneul**
* Etterbeek 30.11.1936 + Etterbeek 1.12.1936

2a.   **Françoise Henriette Adolphine Marie Louise Ghislaine Josephine Comtesse de
Bethune-Hesdigneul** * Bruxelles 5.8.1938 = Wattripont 25.5.1960
Chevalier Gaëtan de Ghellinck d'Elseghem Vaernewyck * Elseghem
23.7.1937, and has issue:

1b.   **Véronique Yves Monique Gabrielle Joséphine Ghislaine de Ghellinck
d'Elseghem Vaernewyck** * Etterbeek 24.3.1961

2b.   **Isabelle de Ghellinck d'Elseghem Vaernewyck** * Etterbeek 21.6.1963

X   (g)   **Ferdinand Marie Comte d'Ursel** * Bruxelles 23.5.1913 = Bruxelles 10.6.1942 Monique de Kerchove * Wuestwezel 24.9.1916 dau. of Robert Baron de Kerchove, and has issue:

          XI   1a.   **Claude Henri Robert Marie Ghislain Comte d'Ursel** * Louvain 26.9.1946 + Louvain 30.9.1946

                            2a.   **Henriette Marie Claire Erneste Colette Comtesse d'Ursel** * Louvain 26.10.1947

                            3a.   **Françoise Charlotte Fernande Comtesse d'Ursel** * Louvain 11.1.1949

                            4a.   **Thierry Simon Gwendoline Comte d'Ursel** * Louvain 18.12.1950

                            5a.   **Ghislain Marie Elie Thierry Comte d'Ursel** * Louvain 14.5.1952

                            6a.   **Michelle Comtesse d'Ursel** * 23.4.1954

X   (h)   **Anna Marie Josèphe Erneste Aline Françoise Comtesse d'Ursel** * Durbuy 19.3.1916 + Villars-de-Lans 10.5.1946

            (i)   **Marie Elisabeth Jeanne Charlotte Simone Françoise Comtesse d'Ursel** * Durbuy 8.9.1918

            (j)   **Théodule François Louis Marie Comte d'Ursel** * Durbuy 7.6.1922 = Boitsfort 24.10.1956 Marie Antoinette de Bus de Warnaffe * Etterbeck 20.11.1930 dau. of Paul de Bus de Warnaffe s.p.

IX   f)   **Marie Louise Antoinette Comtesse d'Ursel** * Bruxelles 4.9.1870 + Bruxelles ... 9.1939

           g)   **Eléonore Léonie Marie Thérèse Comtesse d'Ursel** * Bruxelles 9.10.1876 + Epoisses 31.1.1964 = Bruxelles 24.1.1906 Henri de Pechpeyrou-Comminges Comte de Guitaut, Marquis d'Epoisses * Changy-les-Bois (Loiret) 7.1.1876 + Epoisses (Côte-d'Or) 9.12.1946, and has issue:

X   (a)   **Marie de Pechpeyrou-Comminges de Guitaut** * Epoisses 29.12.1906 + Epoisses 29.12.1906

            (b)   **Charles Athanase Marie Antoine de Pechpeyrou-Comminges Comte de Guitaut, Marquis d'Epoisses** * Paris 16.7.1908 = 30.9.1935 Anne Gilormini * 11.3.1910 dau. of André Gilmorini, and has issue:

          XI   1a.   **Jacqueline de Pechpeyrou-Comminges de Guitaut** * Marseilles 20.12.1937

                            2a.   **Comte Christian de Pechpeyrou-Comminges de Guitaut** * Toulon 7.9.1939

X   (c)   **Comte Aymard Adrien Louis Marie de Pechpeyrou-Comminges de Guitaut** * Paris 4.1.1910

            (d)   **Jeanne Eliane Antoinette Marie de Pechpeyrou-Comminges de Guitaut** * Paris 12.6.1911

            (e)   **Comte Jean Robert Marie de Pechpeyrou-Comminges de Guitaut** * Paris 2.5.1913 = Paris 2.2.1946 Elisabeth Blanquet du Chayla * Havre 19.1.1913 dau. of Henri Blanquet du Chayla, and has issue:

          XI   1a.   **Bénigne Jean Marie Aymar de Pechpeyrou-Comminges de Guitaut** * Semur 5.1.1948

                            2a.   **Aleth Marie Elisabeth Jeanne Eliane de Pechpeyrou-Comminges de Guitaut** * Semur 4.5.1949

                            3a.   **Hedwige Marie Elisabeth Jacqueline de Pechpeyrou-Comminges de Guitaut** * Semur 14.10.1950